EYEWITNESS TO
AMERICA'S
WARS

VOLUME I

ALAN AXELROD

Facts On File
An Infobase Learning Company

Eyewitness to America's Wars

Copyright © 2011 by Alan Axelrod

Facts On File, Inc.
An imprint of Infobase Learning
132 West 31st Street
New York NY 10001

Library of Congress Cataloging-in-Publication Data

Axelrod, Alan, 1952–
    Eyewitness to America's wars / Alan Axelrod.
        p. cm.
    Includes bibliographical references and index.
    ISBN 978-0-8160-7414-3 (hc : alk. paper) 1. United States—History,
Military—Sources. I. Title.
    E181.A943 2011
    355.00973—dc22   2010007278

Facts On File books are available at special discounts when purchased in bulk quantities for businesses, associations, institutions, or sales promotions. Please call our Special Sales Department in New York at (212) 967-8800 or (800) 322-8755.

You can find Facts On File on the World Wide Web at
http://www.factsonfile.com

Text design by Kerry Casey
Composition by Hermitage Publishing Services
Cover printed by Sheridan Books, Ann Arbor, Mich.
Book printed and bound by Sheridan Books, Ann Arbor, Mich.
Date printed: March 2011

Printed in the United States of America

10 9 8 7 6 5 4 3 2 1

This book is printed on acid-free paper.

CONTENTS

★　★　★　★　★　★　★　★　★　★

VOLUME I

The Saratoga Campaign, September 19–October 7, 1777

The Paoli Massacre, September 20–21, 1777

The Capture of Philadelphia, September 26, 1777

The Battle of Germantown, October 4, 1777

Valley Forge, Winter 1777–1778

The Battle of Monmouth Courthouse, June 28, 1778

The Capture of Kaskaskia, July 4, 1778

Sullivan's Punitive Campaign on the Indian Frontier, Summer 1779

Bon Homme Richard v. HMS Serapis, September 23, 1779

The Siege of Charleston, April 11–May 12, 1780

VOLUME II

FOREWORD

★ ★ ★ ★ ★ ★ ★ ★ ★ ★

Eyewitness to America's Wars offers first-hand accounts of American warfare and the experience of combat from the 17th century to the 21st. As the title suggests, the emphasis is on documents supplied by the combatants themselves—accounts by commanders, junior officers, and soldiers—as well as, where appropriate, from civilian eyewitnesses and journalists. In the case of certain colonial wars, the work of early historians and chroniclers, whose texts were based on firsthand accounts, is also offered. Official reports, including after-action reports and, in some cases, testimony in courts-martial, tribunals, and congressional hearings, are included when these contain vivid eyewitness material. In every instance, the texts have been chosen for their value as primary documents that vividly convey the intellectual, emotional, and physical experience of America's armed conflicts so as to suggest the meaning of American warfare from the perspective of the front lines.

The two-volume book is arranged chronologically. Each chapter treats a single major war or two or more minor and closely related conflicts. The chapters include historical overviews of the conflicts and, as necessary, other material to provide the context of the eyewitness documents. The documents themselves are presented as they were written, including original spellings, misspellings, and idiosyncrasies of expression. A bibliography of eyewitness sources at the back of volume II identifies the sources from which the historical material has been taken.

The Colonial Wars

On October 12, 1492, the *Santa Maria's* lookout sighted land, bringing to an end the first voyage of Christopher Columbus. The natives called their island Guanahani, but Columbus christened it San Salvador. Most modern historians believe this was present-day Watling Island, although in 1986, a group of scholars suggested that landfall was actually made at another Bahamian island, Samana Cay, 65 miles south of Watling. Whatever the precise location of their landing, Columbus and his crew were greeted by friendly people of the Arawak tribe. Columbus, of course, believing that he had reached Asia—the "Indies"—called the native inhabitants Indians, and because he believed he was in the Indies, he sailed on to Cuba, in search of the court of the emperor of China, with whom he hoped to negotiate an agreement for trade in spices and gold. When he was disappointed in this, Columbus sailed next to an island he called Hispaniola (modern Santo Domingo), but, near Cap-Haïtien, a Christmas Day storm wrecked his flagship, the *Santa Maria*. He brought his crew to safety onshore and installed a 39-man garrison among the friendly "Indians" of a place he decided to call La Navidad. Columbus and the rest of his crew then left for Spain on January 16, 1493, sailing on the *Niña*.

The garrison Columbus left behind, among friendly natives, set about pillaging goods and ravaging women, apparently almost as soon as their commander had departed. That night, the Indians retaliated, murdering 10 Spaniards as they slept and then hunting down the rest of the garrison. When Columbus returned in November 1493, on his second New World voyage, not a single member of the garrison was left alive.

As the experience of Columbus's garrison demonstrated, a provocation for war was the very first of the Old World's exports to the new. Nor was colonial warfare restricted to the Spanish. Early English, French, and Dutch colonizers also fought, with Native Americans as well as among themselves. Because this book focuses on firsthand accounts and other primary documents of war, our concentration will be on those conflicts in which English colonists were involved and which, therefore, produced accounts and other primary documents in English. The sole exception is Kieft's War (1643–45), a Dutch-Indian conflict, which was nevertheless important to relations both between the Dutch and English colonists and between the English colonists and the Indians.

Although this chapter is selective in the wars it covers, it is important to understand the larger context in which these and the other colonial wars were fought. The Europeans who came to America harbored no doubts about their right to colonize the "New World"; nevertheless, colonists, colonial leaders, and European heads of states and administrators disagreed on and debated the issue of just how the Native Americans should be treated. Some advocated the peaceful acquisition of land and conduct of trade, whereas others called for the religious conversion of the Indians to Christianity, by force if need be. Still others advocated policies of outright conquest and even extermination, with or without the pretense of religious conversion. For their part, various Indian tribes, groups, alliances, and individual leaders espoused a variety of attitudes toward the colonists. These ranged from advocacy of peaceful coexistence—with profitable trade—to intractable hostility. Euro-American historians tend to portray the Indians as having been helplessly "caught up" in colonial wars between the colonists of various European countries. In some instances this was undoubtedly the case, but more often, Indian tribes and other groups consciously allied themselves with one colonial group or another, typically with the object of achieving trade advantages.

Although many colonial conflicts were fought between colonists and Indians or involved the participation of Native Americans, few European settlers came to America with the purpose of conquering territory by fighting with its native inhabitants. Most of the colonial wars were, in effect, extensions of European enmities. In the Old World, Spain, France, and England were the major powers vying for dominance. These nations saw in America an opportunity to extend their empires, and thus European conflicts were exported to the New World. Four major colonial conflicts may be considered the American theater of European wars. King William's War (1689–97) was the New World theater of the War of the League of Augsburg (1688–97), also known as the War of the Grand Alliance and the Nine Years' War, in which France opposed England, the Dutch

Republic, Spain, the Spanish Netherlands, Austria, the Holy Roman Empire, and various smaller principalities and electorates. Queen Anne's War (1702–13) was the New World phase of the European War of the Spanish Succession (1701–14), which pitted France, Bourbon Spain, and various smaller allies against a new Grand Alliance consisting of the Hapsburg Empire, England, the Netherlands, and many of the German-speaking states of Europe. King George's War (1744–48; not treated in this book) was the North American phase of the War of the Austrian Succession (1740–48), which aligned Prussia, France, Spain, and Bavaria against the so-called Quadruple Alliance, consisting of Austria, Saxony, Britain, and the Netherlands. Finally, the French and Indian War (1754–63) was the North American theater of what many historians denominate as the first "world war," the Seven Years' War (1756–63), in which Britain and its ally Prussia squared off against France, Russia, Saxony, Sweden, and—after 1762—Spain. Unlike the other North American extensions of European conflicts, the French and Indian War began prior to the Seven Years' War, which, indeed, it helped to spark. In North America, the French and Indian War was the culmination of colonial warfare for dominance of the continent. As for the Seven Years' War, it covered Germany and central Europe as well as British and French colonies in the Caribbean and India, while the so-called French and Indian War was "confined" to the English and French holdings on the North American mainland.

Why was North America an object of so much and such violent contention? The leaders of the European empires were, at bottom, hard-bitten economists who saw the wealth of the world as finite. The empire that came into possession of most of that finite commodity would perforce be the dominant power on earth. Moreover, the contest for wealth was a zero-sum game. An empire acquired wealth and control of wealth at the expense of the other empires. For this reason, no amount of force was perceived as excessive in acquiring and holding on to colonial territories and the wealth they represented. Moreover, the colonial players in North America continually provoked one another by countering the action of one imperial power with a move by another. If Dutch colonists built an Indian trading "fort" on the Connecticut River, the English defiantly built one of their own nearby. When the French expanded their holdings by entering the mouth of the Mississippi River at present-day New Orleans, the Spanish settled and fortified Pensacola on the Florida panhandle. As the French pressed into what are today western Louisiana and Missouri, Spain erected forts in the territory corresponding to modern east Texas and fortified various outposts in the Midwest. Then, when French missionaries and traders established both spiritual and commercial relations with Indians in the Mississippi Valley region, the English dispatched a small army of traders to compete with them. Each power waited and watched for the others to flinch or show the slightest sign of weakness. When Spain withdrew to a position north of the St. Johns River in Florida, the English were quick to establish forts in the vacated area and then to establish the colony Georgia, which was located in territory claimed by Spain but not occupied by the Spanish. Similarly, when the French faltered in supplying the Choctaw Indians (their allies), English traders "invaded," offering the Choctaw a variety of tempting goods. The result was a civil war within the tribe, between factions that remained loyal to the French and factions that saw a brighter future as allies of the English.

Although the European powers made the New World a battleground for the conflicts of the Old, not all American warfare stemmed directly from the imperial ambitions of the colonies' mother countries. The colonists themselves engaged in some very violent conflicts with their Indian neighbors. Of the wars covered in this chapter, these colonist–Native American conflicts include the Pequot War (1637), Kieft's War (1643–45), and King Philip's War (1675–76). The latter remains to this day the costliest war

on the North American continent in proportion to population. Approximately one of 16 male colonists of military age (roughly, ages 16–60) was killed in the war, and Indian casualties were so ruinously heavy that none of the tribes engaged ever recovered.

Two more wars involved extensive colonist-Indian conflict, although they were related to other matters as well. Bacon's Rebellion (1676) was a popular uprising against the established government of Virginia, but it also entailed combat with the Indians, and Pontiac's Rebellion (1763) may be seen as a direct outgrowth of the French and Indian War, despite the surrender of the French in 1763.

It is all too easy for us, from our 21st-century perspective, to condemn the colonists and imperial powers behind them as ruthless conquerors. To be sure, the forcible subjugation of Native Americans and fierce combat between colonial powers were very much part of the history of early Euro-America, yet warfare was less a part of a calculated program of conquest than it was an inevitable product of a struggle for survival and the push for early growth. No sooner were the immediate problems of survival successfully addressed by the earliest European settlers than the colonies had to cope with an influx of new immigrants and internal population increase, which meant that new land had to be acquired—typically at the expense of the Indians, although sometimes at the cost of encroaching on territory claimed by a rival colony. The result of this situation was that colonists living on the frontier—whether that meant the frontier with Indian territory or with colonies claimed by other nations—found themselves in a perpetual state of war, sometimes at a low level of violence, sometimes at a level more intense. Thus, warfare became a way of life in the North American colonies, culminating in the French and Indian War. English victory in this conflict, coupled with the resolution of Pontiac's Rebellion, which followed, reduced the frequency of the violence, but, as we will see in chapter 2, it also set up some of the conditions in which the American Revolution developed.

The Pequot War, 1637

By the mid-1630s, the Dutch and English settlements in the Connecticut Valley were expanding sufficiently to encroach on the territory of the Pequot, an Algonquian-speaking tribe related to the Mohegan (not to be confused with the Mahican). Like the Mohegan, the Pequot had long been settled along the Hudson River. Tensions between the Pequot and the colonists were running high in 1634, when the ship of Captain John Stone, a trader who also had a reputation for piracy, rode at anchor in the mouth of the Connecticut River. Indian raiders fell upon Stone, killing him and eight of his companions. The raiders were probably western Niantic, who, in the often complex politics of the Indians of the eastern seaboard, were members of a tribe that, although nominally independent, was economically subordinate to the Pequot—not so much allied with the Pequot as beholden to them. Just why the raiders attacked has never been established with certainty, but one Pequot version holds that Stone had previously kidnapped a party of Niantic and was therefore killed by the raiders, who sought to rescue the captives. Another, totally different Pequot explanation ascribes the raid to a case of mistaken identity. In this version, the Pequot admitted to having commissioned the raiders to hit Dutch traders who had killed a Pequot tribal sachem named Tatobam, but they attacked Stone by mistake. Whichever of these versions was true—if either of them was—the colonist John Mason, who would emerge as an English hero of the war, in effect acknowledged that Stone had taken certain Indians; however, he declared that the captain, who had been engaged in trade with the Dutch, had "procured" (Mason's own somewhat ambiguous word) some Indians to guide two of his men and himself to a Dutch trading outpost, and while en route, the party was ambushed.

Even though the stories conflicted, the Pequot did not attempt to evade responsibility for the death of Captain Stone. They disavowed having killed him, but they admitted that a tribe connected to them had. As the Pequot leaders had no wish to go to war with the English, they acted quickly to placate colonial authorities and, on November 7, signed the Massachusetts Bay–Pequot Treaty, by which the Pequot agreed to hand over those guilty of killing Stone; to pay a heavy indemnity; to relinquish rights to any Connecticut land that the English might wish to settle; and to trade exclusively with the English, renouncing all trade with the Dutch.

The treaty was ludicrously one-sided; nevertheless, the Pequot scraped together a portion of the promised indemnity and paid it, but the total amount demanded, wampum worth £250 sterling, remained in dispute, and the Pequot council declined to ratify the treaty their sachems had signed. Moreover, the tribe failed to produce Stone's killers. For their part, the English colonists bided their time, taking no action for a full two years. At last, on June 16, 1636, a Plymouth Colony trader reported having received a warning from Uncas, chief of the Mohegan. According to Uncas, the Pequot feared that the colonists were about to attack and, therefore, decided to make a preemptive strike. Acting on this information, Connecticut and Massachusetts Bay Colony officials convened a conference in July with representatives of the Western Niantic and Pequot at Fort Saybrook, on the Connecticut River. The colonists repeated the demands made in the treaty of 1634. This produced a pledge of compliance from the Indians, but a few days later, word arrived that another captain of a trading vessel, John Oldham, together with his crew, had been killed off Block Island.

This time, there was little doubt as to the identity of the perpetrators. They were Narragansett or members of a tribe subject to them. No one accused the Pequot or any tribe connected to them. Moreover, the Narragansett sachems Canonchet (whom the English called

Canonicus) and Miantonomo were quick to disavow and condemn the murders. They offered reparations, and they promised not to make any alliance with the Pequot in the ongoing dispute between the English and that tribe. To prove that he was in earnest, Miantonomo volunteered to personally lead 200 warriors to Block Island to execute a punitive raid on behalf of the Massachusetts Bay Colony.

The history of relations between whites and Indians is marked by much irrationality and intolerance, and here was a case in point. The colonists unilaterally rejected the contrite gestures of the Narragansett leaders and decided, quite simply, to start a war, targeting not only the Narragansett but, even more directly, the Pequot. Accordingly, on August 25, militiamen under Captains John Endecott (sometimes spelled Endicott), John Underhill, and William Turner were sent off to Block Island to find and apprehend the killers of Stone and Oldham and to secure "thousand fathoms" of wampum as reparation. Even if the Indians sincerely wanted to comply, this demand alone would have been virtually impossible to meet. *Wampum* refers to a string of white shell beads fashioned from the North Atlantic channeled whelk, a traditional Native American medium of value in trade and in ceremonial, legal, and diplomatic transactions. The English were demanding some 6,000 feet—more than a mile—of wampum, which, in labor alone would have represented many thousands of British pounds in value. It is therefore clear that the colonists had no realistic or even good-faith intention of avoiding a war and, in fact, had every intention of fomenting one.

Endecott landed on the island, swept aside the light resistance that met his force, and advanced inland, only to discover that most of the Indians had retreated deep into the forest. Foiled in his expedition against the Narragansett, he loaded his troops on boats and set off for Fort Saybrook, on the Connecticut mainland, with the purpose of punishing the Pequot, despite the fact (which everyone acknowledged) that these Indians had played no part in the killing of John

Oldham. En route to the fort, Endecott's men burned crops and razed Indian shelters as well as food stores. These acts of destruction were sufficient to provoke the Pequot to war.

From our remove in history, it is difficult to understand the motives for Endecott's attack. Naked racist hatred may well have played a role. On the face of it, the attack surely appears irrational, and wholly irrational it may well have been. Yet larger political considerations might also have come into play. At this time, control over much of the Connecticut Valley was disputed between the Massachusetts Bay Colony and a group of Connecticut settlers. Endecott was doubtless aware that whoever could successfully assert dominance over the Pequot, who occupied both sides of the Pequot River—territory in the very midst of the contested land—would have a strong legal claim to the region. It was a peculiarity of the colonial outlook, especially among the English and Dutch, that much importance was attached to the Indians' legal possession (by "primal right") of the lands they occupied. This did not discourage colonial powers from conducting wars of conquest against some Indian groups, but wherever possible, there was a general preference to purchase lands from Native Americans and thereby claim a legal right to them. It was important for a colony to be able to trace its claim to a given territory, whether it was acquired by conquest or by purchase from the "primal" owners, the Indians. This created a form of possession that was asserted to resolve conflicts between rival colonizing groups. Thus, in the case of the disputed portions of the Connecticut Valley, there would have been an advantage in seizing Pequot lands, not merely to take them from the Indians, but to affirm the Bay Colony's right to the territory over the claims of the Connecticut colonists. There was also one other important political advantage to fighting the Pequot. If Endecott could prevail over the Pequot, a dominant tribe in the region, tribes allied and associated with them would also fall into line.

If these were Endecott's motives, what happened next demonstrated the great gulf that often exists between strategy as planned and war as fought. Endecott's orgy of destruction around Fort Saybrook provoked Pequot warriors into laying siege to the fort and attacking the surrounding houses of settlers. This fighting would continue sporadically for months, and by spring 1637, approximately 30 English colonists had fallen victim to the Pequot. It was now apparent that the war was expanding beyond a mere local conflict. Lurid stories of Indian raids, depredations, and tortures spread throughout the colonies, so that authorities in the Plymouth Colony, the Massachusetts Bay Colony, and Connecticut decided to take the unprecedented step of uniting to fight the Pequot. Even among colonies of the same nationality, competition rather than cooperation was the rule, and this alliance was the first instance of formal union among the English colonies of North America.

Resolving on united action was one thing, but actually getting it under way proved quite another. As Massachusetts Bay and Plymouth struggled to get their parts of the joint retaliatory expedition on the march, Captain John Mason, commander of the Connecticut forces, marched out of Hartford on May 10, 1637, at the head of 90 colonists and 60 Mohegan (under Chief Uncas). They were headed for the principal Pequot stronghold, a "fort" built by the "grand sachem" Sassacus (also called Sassious) on Pequot Harbor. When Mason and his band reached Fort Saybrook on May 15, colonial authorities ordered him not to await the arrival of Plymouth and Massachusetts Bay Colony troops but to launch an immediate amphibious assault against Sassacus's fort. Feeling that he lacked sufficient strength, Mason instead sailed past that stronghold, entered Narragansett territory, and set about recruiting additional Indian allies. After lengthy negotiations, Mason, along with John Underhill, persuaded the Narragansett to join forces against the Pequot. This gave him a total of about 650 troops, about 500 Narragansett (under Miantonomo) and Eastern Niantic (under Ninigret) having joined him.

Surviving records fail to provide a complete picture of what happened next, on May 25, as Mason's large force approached Sassacus's fort. As best as can be determined, either at this time or somewhat earlier, a renegade Pequot named Wequash revealed to the English the existence of yet another Pequot stronghold, this one on the Mystic River. This fort was closer than the assigned objective in Pequot Harbor, and mindful that his men were "exceedingly spent in our March with extreme Heat and want of Necessaries," Mason—according to his own account—decided again to disobey his orders: Instead of attacking Sassacus's fort on Pequot Harbor, he would strike at the Mystic fort. At least one modern historian, Francis Jennings (in *The Ambiguous Iroquois Empire*), has speculated that Mason's decision to bypass Sassacus's fort to attack the Mystic stronghold was a deliberate decision to avoid a genuine battle against armed warriors and instead perpetrate a massacre of unarmed noncombatants. Jennings believes that Mason had intelligence revealing that the Mystic fort was occupied by women, children, and old men and was defended by no more than a handful of warriors. Whether or not Mason did actually know it, the Mystic fort was occupied mostly by nonwarriors, and the English assault amounted to a slaughter. At dawn on May 26, the troops fired a single volley and then stormed the fort via entrances at opposite ends. Mason led a group through the northeast entrance while Underhill attacked the southwest. Although the handful of Pequot warriors attached to the fort were vastly outnumbered and totally taken by surprise, they fought with so much ferocity that Mason abandoned his plan to loot the place. Instead of attempting to seize the spoils of war, he ordered the Indian fort put to the torch, touching off a blaze so intense that Underhill's men were compelled to run out of the fort almost as soon as they had entered it. Eighty huts housing some 800 men, women, and children were razed, and within the space of an hour, as many as 700 Pequot were dead, mostly victims of fire. Mason's losses were two killed and 20–40 wounded. According to Mason's own account, just seven Pequot were captured; another seven got away, and the rest in and around the Mystic fort died.

Mason had achieved a decisive and devastating victory, but he was keenly aware that he and his men were still deep in hostile territory. They were, furthermore, spent by battle, critically short on provisions, and entirely unsure as to when their boats would arrive to pick them up. Mason convened his commanders in order to deliberate their next action. Even as they met, Captain Daniel Patrick, with 40 fresh Massachusetts troops and a store of ammunition, was sighted in the distance. At this very moment, however, Mason's lookout also noted the approach of perhaps 300 Pequot warriors, who had arrived from Sassacus's fort. Captain Underhill, with a detachment of Narragansett and English troops, was sent to intercept them. It was a mere skirmish, but it seemed to have been sufficient to discourage the Pequot arrivals from attacking in full force. Mason and his men quickly commenced a march toward the harbor, where—fortunately for them—boats were waiting. In the course of the march, Mason paused to set fire to wigwams and to exchange gunfire with a few Indian snipers encountered.

Late in May or early in June, Mason's troops formally joined forces with the Massachusetts troops under Captain Patrick and, soon after, with a larger body of Massachusetts men commanded by Israel Stoughton. No sooner was this combined force organized than word arrived that a large number of Pequot had been discovered near the Connecticut River. Mason assigned his Narragansett allies to extend to the Pequot an offer of their protection. The Pequot accepted, and the Narragansett surrounded them—whereupon Mason and the others led the colonial troops in a general attack, taking many Pequot prisoner, only to slaughter them after they had surrendered. The Pequot who evaded capture scattered, most of them eventually finding their way to Manhattan Island.

On July 13, English forces turned their attention to the survivors of the Mystic fort massacre, running them to ground in a swamp near New Haven. Surrounded, about 200 Pequot surrendered and quickly signed a treaty by which they agreed that, henceforth, no Pequot would return to the tribe's former country and that, furthermore, the very name *Pequot* would be expunged. Survivors would become slaves of the tribes allied to the English and would take the name of their "host" tribe.

Effectively, the Pequot tribe ceased to exist in any meaningful way. The warrior chief Sassacus and a few other Pequot fugitives begged refuge from among neighboring tribes, but the utter cruelty of the English had thoroughly intimidated the tribes of the region. In any case, few of those peoples had been on friendly terms with the Pequot, an aggressive tribe. In the end, no tribe in the region gave Sassacus or any other prominent Pequot sanctuary, and by late summer, various representatives of other tribes called on colonial authorities, presenting to them the severed heads of Pequot warriors and sachems. The Mohawk sent the greatest prize of all: the head of Sassacus.

On September 21, 1638, English leaders concluded the Treaty of Hartford, which formally apportioned the survivors of the swamp siege as slaves among the English-allied tribes. As for the English colonists, they had ended what they believed was the Pequot menace—a menace their own hostile policies had created. Because the colonies united to oppose the Pequot, disputed hegemony in the Connecticut Valley remained unresolved.

Kieft's War, 1643–1645

In their relations with the Indians, the 17th-century Dutch colonists of New Netherland chronically vacillated among belligerence (typified by extreme cruelty), timid defensiveness, and an embrace of vigorous trade. This ambivalence increased throughout the 17th century, but, generally speaking, conflict between the Dutch colonists and the neighboring Indians was, in the earliest period of settlement, less frequent and less violent than was the case between the English and Indians and between the Spanish and Indians. This was probably because the Dutch had come to New Netherland principally as traders rather than farmers and were therefore less interested in acquiring large tracts of land than were the other European colonists. Content to stay within small settlements and trading posts, the Dutch did not encroach on Indian territory and thereby avoided a major source of conflict. As the years passed, however, Dutch-Indian relations steadily decayed in ratio to the developing desire among Dutch settlers for land. As the supply of the principal trade good, beaver pelts, in the vicinity of the main Dutch trading settlement, Fort Orange (modern Albany, New York), dwindled under pressure of overtrapping, more and more colonists turned from trade to farming. In this way, the Dutch settlements expanded, encroaching more and more into Indian country.

By 1639, when Willem Kieft replaced Wouter Van Twiller as governor of New Netherland, territorial acquisition had become a top priority for the Dutch colonists, even at the cost of sacrificing friendly relations with the Indians. Largely in an effort to drive them off their lands, Kieft imposed heavy taxes on the Algonquian-speaking tribes living in the vicinity of Manhattan and Long Island.

Kieft's policy of hostility was bound to create violent friction sooner or later; all that was required was a precipitating act. That came in 1641, when Dutch livestock, allowed to graze freely, ventured onto cornfields belonging to Raritan Indians living on Staten Island and ravaged them. Raritan representatives called on Governor Kieft to complain. When he refused to take action, the Indians took matters into their own hands and attacked some of the Staten Island farmers. In response, Kieft advertised a bounty on Raritan scalps.

During the following year, 1642, an Indian killed a wheelwright, Claes Swits, in revenge

for the murder of his uncle, whom a band of settlers—apparently not including Swits—had attacked and robbed of his beaver pelts. In response to the wheelwright's death, Governor Kieft led a small army through the villages near New Amsterdam (present-day New York City) with the object of intimidating the Indians. This force, however, seems hardly to have presented an intimidating spectacle. The men marched out by cover of night and, in the darkness, managed to get lost.

One of the chronic problems the colonial Dutch experienced was a shortage of military manpower. Kieft decided to address this issue by recruiting a band of Mohawk into the service of New Netherland. The Mohawk enjoyed a vigorous trading relationship with the Dutch and were especially eager to obtain guns and ammunition. They also relished the assertion of their dominance over other tribes, especially when these assertions were sanctioned by the colonists. In February 1643, at Kieft's behest, a party of Mohawk warriors went up the Hudson on a mission of extortion. Acting on behalf of themselves and the colony, they were to squeeze an exorbitant payment of tribute out of the Wappinger Indians. Terrorized by the Mohawk, and ignorant of Kieft's role in what amounted to a violent shakedown scheme, the Wappinger responded to the Mohawk by fleeing to Pavonia (the environs of present-day Jersey City, New Jersey) and across the Hudson to New Amsterdam, where they appealed to Kieft for protection. The governor responded by summarily turning the Mohawk loose upon them. In an orgy of violence, Mohawk warriors killed 70 Wappinger and enslaved others.

Yet there was even worse to come. During the night of February 25–26, Kieft dispatched bands of Dutch soldiers to Pavonia with orders to finish off any refugees from the Mohawk assault. The night of horror in that settlement would become infamous as the "Slaughter of the Innocents." The Dutch troops returned to New Amsterdam bearing the severed heads of some 80 Indians, which soldiers and citizens alike used as footballs on the streets of New Amsterdam. Thirty prisoners taken alive were tortured to death in the city for the public amusement.

Not surprisingly, the Pavonia Massacre—or "Slaughter of the Innocents"—touched off a major Indian uprising, so that New Amsterdam and its outlying dependencies soon found themselves at war with no fewer than 11 tribes. In March 1643, Kieft, in a panic, attempted to negotiate with tribal representatives, who did agree to a truce. But no one believed it would last, and it did not.

Once again, all it took to shatter the fragile peace was a single incident. On October 1, 1643, nine Indians called at a small Dutch fort in Pavonia where three or four soldiers were stationed to protect a local farmer. The Indians feigned friendliness, then turned on the soldiers and the farmer. They spared the farmer's stepson, whom they took as a captive to Tappan, up the Hudson. Before they left Pavonia, however, the war party razed the farmer's house, together with all the houses in the settlement.

Word of this act of vengeance spread rapidly throughout the region, emboldening tribes from the Delaware Bay to the Connecticut River to raid widely throughout New Netherland. Dutch settlers abandoned the hinterlands of their colony and fled to New Amsterdam, to which the pursuing Indians laid siege for more than a year.

Of the tribes inhabiting New Netherland, only the Mohawk, who still enjoyed a profitable trading alliance with the Dutch, refrained from taking the warpath. Kieft hired Captain John Underhill, who had distinguished himself alongside John Mason in the Pequot War, to lead a combined force of Dutch and English militiamen in a punitive sweep of the countryside. The force attacked whatever targets of opportunity presented themselves. Any Indians encountered were indiscriminately killed, and all Indian villages and food stores were burned. In contrast to the prevailing colonial tactic of striking with short, violent attacks in a brief war, the Dutch hunkered down for a protracted struggle. Having hired outside professional military help, they were committed to waging a war of attrition, concentrating on the destruction of food and shelter. This was the kind of warfare for which the Indians were ill equipped, and by 1644, the tribes had lifted their siege of New Amsterdam and sued for peace. The long truce prevailed for an entire decade, until a new outbreak of violence—incited by Indian pilferage of a Dutch orchard and thus dubbed the Peach War—erupted in 1655.

King Philip's War, 1675–1676

King Philip's War was catastrophic for New England, its colonial and Indian populations alike. During 1675–76, the war devastated nearly half of the towns in the region, destroying a dozen totally. The colonial economy, always fragile, suffered a severe blow, not only from the direct cost of the war—estimated at some £100,000 as valued during the period—but also because of the long disruption of the fur trade with the Indians and the almost complete cessation of coastal fishing as well as trade with the West Indies. The war drew off the manpower normally dedicated to these activities, and even when the war was over, many people never returned to their former places of residence and their former occupations. Fully one in 16 colonists of military age, roughly 16–60, was killed. Noncombatant casualties among men, women, and children were also high, as many civilians were killed in raids, captured, or starved. Historians estimate that, in proportion to New England's colonial population of 30,000 at the time, King Philip's War was the costliest armed conflict in American history—and that is in terms of colonial casualties alone. Because of a dearth of records, Indian losses are more difficult to estimate, but it is believed that at least 3,000 perished in combat or as a result of causes directly related to combat. Many Indians who were not killed were captured and shipped to the Caribbean islands as slaves.

Contemporary colonial chroniclers ascribed the cause of the war to the Wampanoag sachem Metacom (or Metacomet), whom they called King Philip. These chroniclers reported that King Philip betrayed the friendship that had existed between his tribe and the English when he waged war against the colonials with the objective of either driving them out of the country or simply annihilating them. But to the degree that it is possible to achieve objectivity at this remove in time, it is clear that the origins of King Philip's War, as with virtually all white-Indian conflicts, were at once more complex and yet more basic than what those early chroniclers had described. The pressure of a growing colonial population created an ever-increasing demand for land, which pushed the frontier of the settlement farther into Indian territory, inevitably creating friction. The conflicts over land were exacerbated by colonial racist attitudes that were reinforced by Puritan religious doctrine, which held that the New World was a New Jerusalem, which the settlers were not only entitled to but were predestined, by God, to possess. These combined forces collided head-on with King Philip's growing resentment of colonial affronts to his sovereignty, which contributed to the erosion of his power and authority.

Despite the problems created by the colonies, the major tribes profited from trade with the English, and they typically competed with one another for colonial favor. In New England at this time, the Wampanoag and the Narragansett were the two major competitors for trade with the English. They vied with one another even as they struggled with colonial authorities to maintain a degree of autonomy and to retain land. But as English pressure on the tribes to sell more land increased, along with demands for greater submission to colonial authority in matters of politics and religion, the rival tribes began to see a common cause and to unite with one another against what they increasingly perceived as their common enemy. In all dimensions—racially, culturally, politically, economically, and spiritually—the stage was set for a fierce conflict in New England.

The first Wampanoag chief the English colonists known as the Pilgrims encountered when they landed in the New World in 1620 was Massasoit, whose aid helped them survive their first terrible winter in New England. He remained a good friend of the English throughout his long life, and when he died in 1661 at the age of 81, his son Wamsutta, whom the English called Alexander, succeeded him. Wamsutta continued the tradition of friendship with the English, but during the time that he was sachem, the Wampanoag divided their political and economic allegiance between two competing English colonies, Plymouth and Rhode Island. Shortly after Wamsutta's succession, Plymouth Colony's major (later Governor) Josiah Winslow abducted the sachem at gunpoint and took him to Duxbury, ostensibly to answer charges of "conspiracy" against the colony. In fact, Winslow's motive was a bid to force the tribe to unify in their allegiance to Plymouth, and he wanted to compel Wamsutta to demonstrate his loyalty to the colony by selling certain tracts of land to Plymouth rather than to Rhode Island. During his captivity, Wamsutta contracted a fever and died. This made his 24-year-old brother, Metacom—King Philip—sachem. Like many other Wampanoag, King Philip believed that Wamsutta had not succumbed to illness, but that Winslow had tortured and poisoned him. Thus, Philip's "reign" as sachem began with relations between the colony and the Wampanoag at a low ebb and greatly strained.

The first flash point came early in 1671 when King Philip, outraged that the new Plymouth settlement of Swansea had encroached on his land, descended on the village with an armed display that was intended to intimidate the settlers. Although it was no more than a demonstration, and no one was hurt, Philip was summoned to Taunton on April 10, 1671, to admit to and apologize for what colonial authorities characterized as "plotting." Furthermore, he was compelled to sign the Taunton Agreement, in which, among other concessions, he agreed to surrender his people's arms. He signed, but by the end of September, he was hauled into a Plymouth court to stand trial for failure to abide by the Taunton Agreement. Found guilty, he was fined £100—a large amount of money—and was additionally humiliated by having to agree that, henceforth, he would obtain colonial permission in all matters involving the purchase or sale of land. Furthermore, he was forbidden to wage war against other Indians without authority from the colonial government. In effect, he had been deprived of all vestiges of genuine sovereignty and was thus rendered a sachem in name only.

King Philip returned to his people and spent the next three years stealthily forging anti-English alliances with the Nipmuck Indians as well as with his tribe's former rivals, the Narragansett. In January 1675, however, Plymouth authorities were alerted to Philip's scheming by a Praying Indian (an Indian who had converted to Christianity) known as John Sassamon, or Saussaman. For the English, he was the ultimate mole, having been the equivalent of King Philip's private secretary. On January 29, sometime after he delivered his information, Sassamon's body was found on the ice of a frozen pond, and the Plymouth court summoned King Philip, who was accused of complicity in the murder. Because there was no evidence against him, however, he was soon released. Plymouth authorities subsequently identified other Indians as the murderers; tried them; and, on June 8, hanged them. Three days later, on June 11, word that the Wampanoag were arming near Swansea and Plymouth Town reached authorities. At this time, they also received reports of cattle killing and house looting in frontier settlements. A panic was beginning as settlers started leaving certain towns. Swansea, which was directly adjacent to Wampanoag country, was soon partially abandoned, and Indians rushed in to appropriate vacated property. A determined settler who had remained in the town shot and killed a looter. This was the first blood drawn in King Philip's War.

During the 17th century, the English colonies of North America were highly competitive with one another and were by no means united. Nevertheless, menaced by King Philip and his coalition, the Massachusetts Bay Colony, Plymouth, and Rhode Island made an uneasy alliance, pooling their resources to mobilize an army that was mustered from June 21 through June 23 at Miles's Garrison, opposite what had been identified as King Philip's principal base of operations in Mount Hope Neck, Rhode Island. Before the force could be assembled, however, a Wampanoag raiding party struck Swansea on the Sabbath, falling upon the people of the settlement as they made their way to worship. On the next Sabbath, the Indians returned and burned down half the town, this time as worshippers returned from church. Four days after this attack, the Rhode Island militia captain Benjamin Church and his troops were ambushed near beleaguered Swansea.

On June 29, the Wampanoag made hit-and-run raids in the vicinity of Rehoboth and Taunton. On July 1, the Connecticut colony joined in the war effort, sending a contingent of militiamen to aid Massachusetts, Plymouth, and Rhode Island. At this time, King Philip was in the process of negotiating an alliance of his own with the powerful Pocasset "squaw-sachem" (as the English called her) Weetamoo.

Early in July, in Rhode Island, Benjamin Church seized the offensive, pursuing Philip and his men in the swamplands; however, in "Captain Almy's Pease Field," Church's 20-man party was suddenly counterattacked by some 300 Indians. Church and his badly outnumbered forces held off annihilation for six hours until they were finally rescued by an English river sloop, which evacuated them.

Up to this point, the colonial militia had proven ineffectual against King Philip and his Indian coalition, and by mid-July, much of New England was subject to raiding. Emboldened by the Wampanoag's success, the Narragansett and the Nipmuck of eastern and central Massachusetts joined forces with King Philip. For their part, colonial authorities, deeply discouraged by their army's performance against the Indians in close combat, broke off pursuit of Philip. Against Church's strident objections, they decided to relinquish the offensive and fight the war defensively, ordering the construction of a fort from which the militia would lay protracted siege to King Philip in his swamp stronghold. The intention was to starve him and his men out.

As Benjamin Church easily recognized, this approach was a strategic error, and it did nothing more than prolong the war. As the colonial militia busied itself in building the fort, Philip and his men slipped out of the Pocasset swamp on July 29 and headed into Nipmuck country to the northeast. Far from containing the war, the ill-chosen colonial strategy allowed it to expand, so that by the end of August, the theater had broadened into the upper Connecticut Valley and the Merrimac Valley and into the present states of New Hampshire and Maine. Having already endured months of bloodshed, the colonies proclaimed themselves the "United Colonies"—the first time this designation had ever been used—and, as such, officially declared war on September 9, levying on members of the union an army of 1,000.

As the new United Colonies assembled its forces, the Indians continued a drearily bloody pattern of raid after raid. Colonial officials made various attempts to negotiate peace or even a truce, but all failed. One conference, at Wickford, Rhode Island, looked hopeful. It sought to divide the Narragansett from the others, but when talks irretrievably broke down on September 22, hitherto friendly or neutral Indians now turned against the colonies with devastating results. Springfield, Massachusetts, which had enjoyed cordial trading relations with the Indians for more than 40 years, maintained no garrisons. Indians raided it on October 4–5, and 32 houses, about half the town, were destroyed. On October 18 or 19, approximately 700 Indians hit another frontier settlement, Hatfield, Massachusetts, but were driven off.

Despite Indian successes, the war was hard on them. Most tribes had come to depend on trade with the colonies, and they suffered severe economic hardship. The Narragansett, who had walked out of a peace conference on September 22, concluded a treaty in Boston at the end of October. However, on November 2, Connecticut's colonial council broke with the United Colonies and resolved unilaterally to make a peremptory strike against the Narragansett, deeming it (paradoxically enough) the most effective way of *preventing* war with them. Even more remarkably, when this was proposed to Plymouth and Massachusetts, the two colonies—treaty or no treaty—agreed, and the army of the United Colonies, finally having been mustered during November and early December, assembled at Wickford, Rhode Island, under the command of the Plymouth governor Josiah Winslow.

Winslow marched the 1,000-strong, together with a separate company under the always redoubtable Benjamin Church, through a blinding snowstorm on December 18 to attack the stronghold of the Narragansett sachem Canonchet (whom the English called Canonicus) in a frozen swamp at Kingston, Rhode Island. The colonial forces arrived at the Indian fort on the 19th. Despite having suffered miserably in the stormy cold, Winslow's men attacked ferociously. They killed about 600 Narragansett—half that number women and children—for a loss of 80 colonials, including 14 company commanders. Church, who had been seriously wounded in the attack, raised an urgent objection to Winslow's order to burn down the Indians' wigwams, pointing out that the battered English army had urgent need of these shelters. Winslow ignored him, however, put the wigwams to the torch, and then, to compound his poor judgment, ordered a withdrawal instead of pressing the pursuit of the surviving Narragansett, who escaped into Nipmuck country. In the end, the battle known as the Great Swamp Fight—the central engagement of King Philip's War—inflicted very heavy losses on the Narragansett, but it failed to be decisive and therefore served to strengthen a number of desperate anti-English alliances among the Wampanoag, Nipmuck, and Narragansett.

With the New Year, Philip, feeling far from defeated, began an effort to extend his alliances beyond New England, leading many of his people to Mohawk country near modern Albany, New York, in search of allies and ammunition. His efforts were effectively countered by New York's very able royal governor, Edmund Andros, who had gotten to the Mohawk first and managed to persuade them not only to reject the overtures of alliance but to attack Philip. Finding himself under assault, he was compelled to flee back to New England.

Warfare between Indians and colonists was never a simple matter of "them versus us," but typically involved multiple alliances and enmities, often subject to change. Andros's efforts to establish an alliance with the Mohawk served to foil Philip's ambitious efforts to assemble a grand Indian confederacy—the one thing the colonists feared about all else. Despite this achievement, the forces of New England's United Colonies were not prepared to take immediate advantage of Philip's predicament. Despite having achieved victory in the Great Swamp Fight, Winslow's army was crippled by its losses, especially because so many of those losses had been sustained at the command level. Also suffering an acute shortage of provisions, the army was effectively immobilized for more than a month. Thus, with the principal English force paralyzed and even in disarray, the Indians, despite their losses, were able to rally and renew their offensive.

Yet again, they commenced a string of hit-and-run raids throughout Massachusetts, Rhode Island, and Connecticut, so that the early spring of 1676 became the nadir of colonial fortunes. Connecticut soldiers operating in western Rhode Island captured the key Narragansett sachem and war leader Canonchet (Canonicus), whom they duly executed, but the area of English settlement throughout New England continued to

contract. In an effort to arrest the exodus of settlers, who yielded more and more ground to the Indians, authorities in all the colonies enacted emergency laws forbidding the evacuation of towns without official permission. Few obeyed, and by late spring 1676, the outlying settlements around Boston had been mostly abandoned.

With their backs against the wall, the colonial forces finally seized the initiative in late spring 1676 and took the offensive. By the end of April, Captain Daniel Henchman led a force in a violent sweep of eastern Massachusetts, forcing hostile Indians to negotiate ransom terms for English captives on May 1. But even as Henchman triumphed in eastern Massachusetts, King Philip's warriors attacked the Plymouth town of Bridgewater on May 6 in the start of a general offensive of their own against that colony. On May 11, they raided Plymouth Town.

On May 19, in western Massachusetts, Captain William Turner led 150 mounted troops against an Indian encampment at the Falls of the Connecticut above Deerfield, Massachusetts. Taking the encampment by surprise, the troops unleashed a full-out massacre, poking their muskets into the wigwams and opening fire on Indians, including many women and children, as they slept. Yet again, although the enemy had been routed, the English held back and declined to give chase, and though Turner had meted out a devastating blow, it failed to be decisive. The surviving Indians rallied, reversed their retreat, and made a counterattack in which some 40 men, including Captain Turner, were killed.

Despite continued tactical and strategic blunders, colonial forces became increasingly aggressive in attack and—finally—also in follow-up pursuit. Responding to reports of enemy Indians fishing in the Pawtucket River near Rehoboth, Captain Thomas Brattle led a combined force of colonists and Indian allies in an attack, killing a dozen or more of Philip's warriors for the loss of a single colonial militiaman. On June 2, Connecticut major John Talcott launched a combined Indian-English assault against Philip in western Massachusetts, and a little later in the same month, Benjamin Church began building a new army on behalf of the United Colonies—this one made up of white as well as Indian soldiers.

Nevertheless, King Philip continued to fight, launching an ambitious but ultimately unsuccessful assault against Hadley, Massachusetts. Then, at Nipsachuck, Rhode Island, on July 2–3, John Talcott dealt the Narragansett two crushing blows. First, he attacked a band consisting of 34 men and 137 women and children, killing all of the men and 92 of the women and children. On the following day, at Warwick, he killed 18 men and 22 women and children, taking 27 prisoners as well.

Talcott's victories coincided with the end of warfare against what were called the North Indians—the Abenaki, Sokoki, and Pennacook—when the Pennacook sachem Wannalancet signed a treaty with Major Richard Waldron, bringing peace to the territory corresponding to the modern state of Maine.

On July 11, Benjamin Church, leading his newly constituted United Colonies army, triumphed in skirmishes at Middleborough and Monponsett. A week later, his forces tangled with Philip's men in and around Taunton. Major William Bradford broke away in pursuit of King Philip himself, narrowly failing to run him to ground on July 16. On July 24, Church was commissioned to enlarge his second army to 200 men, of which a majority, 140 men, were to be friendly Indians. Quickly assembled, this force set out on July 30 in pursuit of Philip.

On July 31, as they closed in on their quarry, Church's soldiers killed King Philip's uncle, then captured the sachem's wife and son on August 1. Philip himself, however, continued to elude capture. Despite this, his followers were becoming increasingly demoralized, and later in August, a deserter from King Philip's camp approached Church with an offer to lead him and his men to Philip's camp. Church followed and carefully deployed his troops to surround the leader's encampment after midnight on August 12. At first light, they closed in. Taking

alarm, Philip rose to flee. An English soldier fired and missed, but the marksmanship of an English-allied Indian, known to history only as Alderman, proved better. King Philip was felled by a single shot, whereupon Benjamin Church ordered the sachem's body to be butchered, awarding the head and one hand to Alderman. The remainder of the corpse was quartered and hung on four trees—the customary old English practice when a traitor was executed.

For all practical purposes, the death of King Philip marked the end of the war named for him. The rest was essentially a mop-up operation, as, on September 11, Church captured and executed Annawon, Philip's "chief captain." There were sporadic skirmishes during October, but the last unified band of Indians surrendered to English authorities on August 28.

The war left many tribes demoralized and sent them in abject submission to the English colonies. Some, however, responded differently. Fleeing New England for Canada, New York, and the Delaware and Susquehanna valleys, they contemplated a vengeance that exploded periodically in the series of raids and outright wilderness wars culminating in the French and Indian War of 1754–63.

Bacon's Rebellion, 1676

An earlier generation of historians, mainly in the 19th century, tended both to romanticize and inflate the importance of Bacon's Rebellion, seeing in it a kind of foreshadow of—if not prelude to—the American Revolution. Short-lived and contained, the "rebellion" was, in fact, less important in and of itself than for its relationship to ongoing warfare between colonists and Indians.

By the 1670s, Maryland tobacco planters were becoming increasingly hungry for more land, which moved colonial leaders to make certain accommodations with the Iroquois tribes in violation of the colony's existing alliance with the Susquehannock. In 1674, Maryland concluded a treaty with the Seneca (an Iroquois tribe), giving them license to campaign militarily against the Susquehannock for the purpose of forcing them south to the Potomac River. This created the conditions for a war between Maryland and its betrayed ally, the Susquehannock tribe, and all that was required to touch off hostilities was a precipitating event. It happened during July and August 1675, when a group of Maryland Nanticoke Indians (also called Doeg) opened a dispute with a wealthy Virginia planter, Thomas Mathew, who (they claimed) had refused to pay them for some goods traded. When Mathew persisted in withholding payment, the Indians took the matter into their own hands by appropriating some of Mathew's hogs. Mathew responded by arming a band of his workers and sending them against the Indians. The men killed a number of Nanticoke and recovered the hogs.

In a pattern all too typical of white-Indian warfare, the Nanticoke now responded violently, killing three Virginians by way of revenge, including Mathew's chief herdsman. Mathew called upon local officials to muster the militia, and a patrol was dispatched to hunt down and kill a Nanticoke chief. This escalated the violence, launching a battle that involved not only the Nanticoke but an allied tribe, the far more powerful Susquehannock.

The battle was over quickly, but Maryland as well as parts of Virginia were swept by hit-and-run raids. Virginia's governor, William Berkeley, ordered the militia colonel John Washington (great-grandfather of the future president) and Major Isaac Allerton to muster all of the officers of the militia regiments between the Rappahannock and Potomac Rivers and order them to conduct an inquiry into the raids to determine what had caused them.

A reasonable and cautious man well aware of the difficulties of conducting any extensive military operation, Berkeley was determined to take action only if the investigation absolutely proved just cause. In the event that the evidence warranted it, he intended to conduct a punitive campaign against the Nanticoke

and Susquehannock. Unwilling to bide their time, however, Washington and Allerton twisted Berkeley's commission into full authority to raise a militia immediately, and they quickly organized 750 Virginians. Washington then wrote to the Maryland authorities, who furnished an additional 250 cavalrymen and dragoons (troops using horses as transportation, but who fought dismounted) under Major Thomas Trueman. Late in September 1675, this combined force of 1,000 converged on and surrounded the junction of the Piscataway Creek and the Potomac, which had been designated by the Maryland Assembly as the location for home village of the Susquehannock. At the time, approximately 100 warriors and their families lived there. Seeing the approach of the large army, the Indians hoisted a flag of truce, but it had no effect. The militia attacked, wreaking havoc on the village.

The attack escalated the prevailing violence, moving the Indians to raid with greater frequency as well as ferocity. But in the midst of this, Susquehannock chiefs sent a message to Governor Berkeley—not surrendering but, rather, simply declaring the war to be at an end. With (approximately) 10 common Englishmen having been killed for each of their chiefs slain, the Indians expressed their opinion that restitution had been made, and they were now willing to conclude a peace. Much as he wanted peace, however, Berkeley deemed the proposal insulting. He spurned the offer, and the war continued.

Berkeley laid out a hunker-down defensive strategy, calling for the construction of a chain of fortifications around the settled parts of the colony. Not only did many Virginians find the idea of fighting defensively unacceptable, they saw in Berkeley's strategy an abandonment of the frontier. The outlying regions were to be sacrificed, it seemed, to protect the settled areas. Outraged, frightened, feeling betrayed, and generally desperate, the people of the Maryland and Virginia frontier were ripe for rebellion.

Popular discontent is red meat for a demagogue, and Nathaniel Bacon was just such a figure. Cousin to Lord Bacon and to Lady Berkeley, he had been expelled from Cambridge University for unspecified "extravagances"; therefore, in 1673, he left England for Virginia, bringing with him a new bride and a patrimony of £1,800, which he used to purchase a pair of plantations on the James River. Governor Berkeley welcomed his in-law by presenting him with an appointment to the House of Burgesses, but he quickly discovered that the young man was as unscrupulous as he was incendiary. While carousing with friends, Bacon heard about a band of frontiersmen who had proclaimed themselves fed up with Berkeley's cautious policies and who were openly preparing to take Indian matters into their own hands. Seeing an opportunity, Bacon wasted no time in insinuating himself among these men as their leader. He led the malcontents early in May 1676 to the Occaneechi Indians, who lived along the Roanoke River, near the present Virginia–North Carolina state line. He announced to them his intention of going to war with the Susquehannock, knowing full well that the Occaneechi were their traditional rivals. The Occaneechi chief responded by offering to do the fighting for Bacon and his Virginians—as proof of his friendship with the English. Bacon accepted, and he sent the Occaneechi warriors on their way.

Soon, the war party returned victorious, bearing with them Susquehannock prisoners as well as a captured cache of fur pelts. Bacon expressed his gratitude to his allies by attempting to steal the pelts for himself and his men. Moreover, he attempted to seize as slaves a band of friendly Manikin Indians who, operating in concert with the Occaneechi as moles and insurgents within the Susquehannock camp, had been instrumental allies in the victory. Bacon's high-handed treachery stunned the Occaneechi, who flatly refused to relinquish either the fur or their allies. Bacon broke off negotiations and ordered his men to attack. Then he ordered a general withdrawal, he and his men carrying off as many pelts as they could gather.

Bacon and his "boys" returned to the English settlements and found themselves roundly hailed as heroes—not, however, by Governor Berkeley. He proclaimed Bacon to be a traitor on May 26, 1676, and ordered Bacon's arrest when he entered Jamestown to take his seat in the House of Burgesses. Professing contrition, Bacon admitted his transgression and threw himself on Berkeley's mercy. Unwilling to make a martyr of the man, Berkeley issued a pardon and ordered Bacon's release from custody on June 5.

At this time, seeing that Berkeley was distracted by his in-law's "rebellion," Sir Edmund Andros, governor of the duke of York's patent territories (which encompassed New York), decided that it was necessary to take action in order to prevent the kind of catastrophe that had befallen New England in King Philip's War. Accordingly, he offered the Susquehannock refuge within his colony, provided that they stop raiding Maryland and Virginia. Some eagerly accepted the offer and took refuge peacefully; others, however, continued to raid Maryland settlers but fled periodically to New York and the protection of the Iroquois. That raiders were using New York as a safe haven created outrage throughout Maryland. To Bacon and his followers in particular, the intervention of Governor Andros seemed yet another instance of the tyranny that habitually issued from leaders who were indifferent to the welfare of the frontier.

Spurred by the outrage created by Andros's actions, Bacon soon abrogated the gestures of atonement he had made to Berkeley. He returned to Henrico County, Virginia, where he raised an army of 500 men and then led them marching into Jamestown on June 23. Standing before the State House and backed by his troops, he demanded that the burgesses instantly commission him commander of all forces fighting the Indians. To drive home the demand, his men leveled their weapons at the burgesses, who were watching the proceedings from the windows of the State House. Thoroughly intimidated, the burgesses gave him a summary commission.

In this way legitimated, Nathaniel Bacon embarked on a new campaign, this time against the Pamunkey Indians of eastern Virginia, a tribe that was not only at peace with Virginia but had always professed friendship. At the same time, back in Jamestown, on July 29, Governor Berkeley repealed Bacon's commission and once again proclaimed him a traitor. Yet Bacon was now a popular figure, and the burgesses were so fearful of him that Berkeley found it impossible to muster an army to oppose him. Worse, within a week of Berkeley's recall of Bacon's commission and his posting him as a traitor, a group of Virginia's most substantial planters took an oath to support Bacon, who was, even then, leading his army in the indiscriminate murder of local Indians.

When word of Berkeley's latest edict against him caught up with Bacon on the frontier, he returned to Jamestown with his men on September 13. He and his troops rounded up the wives of the burgesses who had declared their loyalty to the governor. Holding them hostage, he employed them as human shields to protect his men as they built siege lines before the town. With these fortifications completed, Bacon drove Berkeley and his outnumbered supporters out of the capital and into exile on the Eastern Shore (the eastern side of Chesapeake Bay). As if that were not victory enough, on September 18, he and his rebels set fire to Jamestown, the hated center of the Tidewater establishment—the concentration of colonial economic and political power on the seaboard.

This was the height of Bacon's Rebellion, which put its leader in control of all of the settled Virginia colony, save the Eastern Shore. Yet, from his place of exile, Governor Berkeley finally rallied a large force to oppose the rebel. Leading his men to the capital, he easily retook Jamestown and then set out in pursuit of Bacon, most of whose followers melted away before his approach. Berkeley's army forced Bacon and a handful of diehards to a stand at Yorktown, but there would be no final battle. In October 1676, Bacon fell desperately ill and died. With

him died both the rebellion in his name and the unauthorized war he had led against the Indians of Virginia.

King William's War, 1689–1697

On May 12, 1689, shortly after ascending the throne, King William III of England joined the League of Augsburg and the Netherlands to form the Grand Alliance in opposition to France's Louis XIV, who had invaded the Rhenish Palatinate on September 24, 1688. This resulted in a European war known variously as the War of the League of Augsburg, the War of the Grand Alliance, and the Nine Years' War. Ongoing low-level hostilities in the North American colonies were exacerbated by the eruption of this war, and the result may be seen as the American phase, or American theater, of the European conflict. In North America, the war was called King William's War, and it pitted the French and Abenaki Indians on one side against the English and their Iroquois allies on the other.

The governor of New France (Canada), Louis de Buade, comte de Frontenac, favored a strong offensive approach, beginning with an invasion of New York. He was sufficiently realistic, however, to appreciate that he lacked the troop strength for such a large-scale conventional military operation and therefore proposed an alternative manner of warfare, which he called *la petite guerre*—a little war. In short time, the French phrase would evolve into the English expression *guerrilla war* to describe a set of tactics and combat doctrine that effectively exploited whatever military resources were available. *La petite guerre* employed small, stealthy bands of woodsmen and skilled Indian warriors, all "soldiers" prepared to fight a war consisting not so much of battles as of ruthless murders, committed without warning or mercy, often against targets of opportunity and without distinguishing between combatants and civilians. First and foremost, the French made use of their Abenaki allies, actively encouraging them to terrorize the English settlements throughout Maine and New Hampshire. Thus, King William's War represented an escalation in the Euro-American practice of employing Native American military auxiliaries as instruments of terror, agents able and willing to practice a style of combat repugnant to the European traditions on which conventional North American colonial military policy and doctrine were based.

Through the summer of 1689, French-instigated Indian raids became increasingly frequent, forcing the English to abandon all settlements northeast of Falmouth, Maine. Boston authorities acted to muster an army of 600, but the conventional militia force they sent to the frontier had little effect against Indian guerrilla fighters. Moreover, whereas conventional armies traditionally suspended combat in the winter, Frontenac used the winter as an ally. With the onset of cold weather, he put together a mixed force of 160 Canadians and about 100 Indians to make a three-pronged assault from Montreal into New York, New Hampshire, and Maine; however, after finally reaching the Hudson River following an epic frozen trek down Lake Champlain to the southern tip of Lake George, the commanders of the New York assault force decided to attack, in concert, Schenectady instead of their assigned objective, Albany. Schenectady was closer, and the leaders of the force did not want to risk losing men to the harsh elements on the longer trek.

On the afternoon of February 8, 1690, following a forced march over frozen swampland, the New York strike force approached the outskirts of Schenectady. Holding their positions in hiding, members of the force launched their attack after nightfall—and were surprised to find no resistance. The entire village was "guarded" by nothing more formidable than a pair of snowmen. For some two hours, the French and Indians raked over Schenectady, killing 60 men,

women, and children, most of them as they slept in their beds.

The next month, on March 27, the New Hampshire segment of Frontenac's invasion force attacked Salmon Falls, New Hampshire, killing 34 settlers there. In May, the Maine force hit its first major target: Fort Loyal (Falmouth), Maine; nearly 100 English colonists were killed.

In the midst of catastrophe, on May 1, 1690, delegates from Massachusetts, Plymouth Colony, Connecticut, and New York convened at Albany to plan a course of united action. Colonial leaders decided that the best defense was an ambitious offense and resolved to invade Canada with two land forces launched from New York and New England. These were to be coordinated with a naval force, which would sail up the St. Lawrence River.

Sir William Phips, governor of Massachusetts, was assigned command of the amphibious assault. He started out triumphantly, on May 11, 1690, with 14 vessels, capturing Port Royal, Acadia (present-day Annapolis Royal, Nova Scotia). On land, Phips was far less successful. Delayed and repeatedly evaded, he ran his army to exhaustion. By November, smallpox (an epidemic disease that dogged colonial armies in the 17th and 18th centuries) had ravaged and reduced Phips's forces, giving him no choice but to abort the overland portion of the offensive. This opened the way for further French conquest. During 1690, French forces pushed the English out of their important Hudson Bay outpost at the mouth of the Severn River, and the next year, the French retook Port Royal.

Although the combat of King William's War, which consisted mainly of hit-and-run raids rather than pitched or set battles, brought great misery to the settlements of the English frontier, the action produced no decisive victories for Frontenac either. His "little war" created significant terror, it is true, but achieved virtually nothing of enduring strategic value. Most significantly, the tribes of the powerful Iroquois Confederacy remained loyal to the English, even though they paid heavily for that loyalty. Of all the combatants, they suffered the greatest losses in the war.

In September 1691, desperate to take action to halt the monotonous and destructive pattern of raids, English colonial authorities called out of retirement the aged—and now quite infirm—hero of King Philip's War, Benjamin Church, and put in his charge a force of 300 militiamen, leading them to Saco, Maine, an English outpost that had been the target of repeated attacks. Church enjoyed a measure of success, especially against the Abenaki, who were sufficiently hurt by his assault to sue for peace. On November 29, 1691, the Abenaki signed a treaty by which they agreed to release their captives; to duly report to the English any French designs against them; and to abstain from making war until May 1, 1692.

No sooner did they sign the treaty, however, than the Abenaki resumed raiding, and the English answered with counterraids. On February 5, 1692, the Abenaki joined forces with Canadians in an assault on York, Maine. In June, the Indians hit Wells, Maine, and (on June 6) Deerfield, Massachusetts. In January 1693, a large French expedition ravaged Mohawk villages throughout New York. Three hundred Mohawks, most of them women, children, and old men, were captured, and many more fled to the Caughnawaga Mission in Canada, seeking asylum. This was significant because the so-called Caughnawaga, although Iroquois, had accepted Catholicism and allied themselves not with the Protestant English but with the Catholic French. Clearly, the colonial wars between Euro-American powers were starting to tear at the tissue of ancient Indian tribal solidarity and alliances.

No decisive or culminating battle or other event brought an end to King William's War. Rather, in September 1697, the Treaty of Ryswick ended the War of the League of Augsburg in Europe, and that treaty also stipulated an end to hostilities in North America as well. The war, then, was over—although spasmodic outbreaks of violence continued on the frontier.

Queen Anne's War, 1702–1713

As with the recently ended King William's War, Queen Anne's War was the North American phase or theater of a European conflict. With the commencement of Queen Anne's War, it had become clear that the imperial powers of Europe intended to fight their wars on a truly imperial scale and were no longer content to confine them to European battlegrounds.

To defend against an alliance concluded between France and Spain, England, Holland, and Austria formed a new anti-French Grand Alliance in 1701 after the Hapsburg king of Spain, Charles, died in 1700, having chosen a Bourbon as his successor. The French supported the man Charles had designated, Philip of Anjou, a grandson of Louis XIV, but the members of the Grand Alliance supported the second son of the Hapsburg emperor Leopold I, the obscure Bavarian archduke Charles. The result of this conflict was the War of the Spanish Succession, which was declared in Europe on May 4, 1702. On September 10 of that year, it spread to the colonies as Queen Anne's War when the South Carolina legislature authorized an expedition to seize the Spanish-held fort and town of St. Augustine, Florida. In the first phase of the assault, a British naval expedition landed and plundered the town; then, in a second phase in December, a mixed force of some 500 colonists and Chickasaw allies assaulted the fort. When they failed to breach it, they turned their wrath back on the town, putting the old settlement to the torch.

Following the usual pattern of white-Indian warfare, these acts brought Indian raids in retaliation, which, in turn, incited further colonial response. James Moore, the former governor of South Carolina, mustered a new force of militia and Chickasaw, whom he led through the territory of the Appalachee Indians of western Florida during most of July 1704. Moore and his men killed or captured the inhabitants of seven villages, virtually annihilating the small Appalachee tribe. For good measure, they also razed 13 of the 14 Spanish missions in the country.

Moore's march was so relentlessly devastating that it actually succeeded in breaking the typical pattern of raid and reprisal. The campaign proved to be strategic in its effect, throwing open a route directly into the heart of French Louisiana territory and the settlements along the Gulf of Mexico. But the French were not idle during this time: They busied themselves in vigorously recruiting allies among the southern tribes, using a combination of cajolery and bribery to court alliances with the Choctaw, Cherokee, Creek, and Chickasaw. The Chickasaw held fast, cleaving to their ongoing English alliance, and the Cherokee chose to maintain neutrality. The Creek, never very unified, divided their allegiance, some bands siding with the French, others with the English, and still others remaining neutral. But out of this effort, one very powerful Indian ally did emerge for the French: the Choctaw, who quickly organized an army that marched out to intercept Moore. He and his men found themselves thwarted in their advance into Louisiana. A quick and decisive English victory in Queen Anne's War was thereby prevented.

To the north, alliances between the French and the Indians were both more extensive and of longer standing than those in the south. In part, this was the fault of English colonial authorities, who typically treated the Indians with undisguised contempt. Whereas the French courted and recruited Indian allies, giving their religious and cultural practices a wide berth—even among those Indian groups that converted to Catholicism—the English abused their Indian neighbors and sought to coerce them out of their traditional practices. Moreover, French colonists freely intermarried with Indians, thereby cementing strong relationships with the tribes.

In the north, the French-allied Abenaki proved to be the English colonists' most determined and fiercest opponents. On August 10,

1703, a party of English settlers broke into and plundered the Maine house belonging to the son of Jean Vincent de l'Abadie, baron de St. Castin. Because his mother was the daughter of an Abenaki chief, St. Castin was likewise considered a chief, and the attack on his house therefore touched off retaliatory raids along 200 miles of the northern New England frontier.

In the far north, in Nova Scotia, Benjamin Church, hero of King Philip's War—now so infirm and advanced in age that he had to be carried over fallen logs in his path—led 550 men into Acadian French territory in July 1704 and brought down violent terror upon two settlements, Minas and Beaubassin. Farther north, in Newfoundland, between August 18 and 29, a mixed force of French and Indians operating out of Placentia destroyed the English settlement at Bonavista in a series of raids. The raids were in direct retaliation for the destruction of Minas and Beaubassin.

In both its northern and southern theaters, Queen Anne's War ground on in a dreary succession of murders, raids, and counterraids. There were terror and destruction, and trade was badly disrupted—a particularly crippling aspect of early colonial warfare—but nothing decisive emerged on either side. Desperate to break the ruinous cycle of raid and reprisal and achieve a breakthrough victory, the English colonies sent a contingent of English-allied Mohawk chiefs to England and the court of Queen Anne in 1710. Colonial leaders were at great pains to orchestrate the visit so as to extract sympathy and support from the monarch and her court. The chiefs were outfitted in magnificent "savage" attire, which had, in fact, been supplied by a prominent London theatrical costumer. Their audience with the queen produced the desired effect: They created a sensation at court, and Anne instantly authorized a large contingent of English regular troops to be sent to the colonies. These land forces were placed under the command of Colonel Francis Nicholson, and the naval transports and warships that supported the land operations were under Admiral Sir Francis Hobby.

In well-coordinated land-and-sea operations, the English reduced Port Royal, Nova Scotia, by October 16, 1710. By the following summer, all of French Acadia had fallen to the British. With ultimate victory in sight, Hobby's subordinate commander, Sir Hovendon Walker led another naval expedition, this time targeting Quebec. Then catastrophe struck. As his flotilla was entering the mouth of the St. Lawrence River, it was swept by storms and wrecked with the staggering loss of 1,600 men. The war continued.

In 1711, the English organized a fresh push against the French Canadian capital, but it was so poorly managed that it was aborted before it got under way properly. By this time, however, the failure hardly mattered. France's Louis XIV was weary of war and laboring under a crushing burden of debt. Undefeated, but seeing no prospect for achieving victory, he was ready to bring hostilities to an end, in the Old World and well as the New. Moreover, the ultimate source of the entire conflict, the issue of who would succeed to the Spanish throne, had become moot. During the course of the 11-year struggle, Archduke Charles, the Bavarian candidate supported by the Grand Alliance, had died, and Louis's grandson Philip of Anjou ascended the throne by default. Fate and nature, it seemed, had taken his side, and Louis XIV saw no percentage in continuing to fight against them. On July 13, 1713, his minister signed the Treaty of Utrecht, ceding Hudson Bay and Acadia to the English but retaining for France Cape Breton Island and other small islands in the St. Lawrence. On the issue of the boundaries separating the French from the English colonies in North America, however, the treaty was silent, and this would prove a fertile source of ongoing contention and war. As for the Abenaki and other French-allied Indians, they also signed treaties with the New Englanders, pledging to become loyal subjects of Queen Anne.

The French and Indian War, 1754–1763

King William's War (1689–97), Queen Anne's War (1702–13), and King George's War (1744–48; not included in this book) are often collectively referred to as the "French and Indian Wars." So far as determining whether the English or the French would gain hegemony in North America, none were decisive, but they led up to and culminated in a war that did prove decisive in determining which empire, France or England, would control the destiny of North America. This was *the* French and Indian War (1754–63).

Whereas the three wars that had preceded it each corresponded to a European war and were, in fact, the North American theater of the corresponding war—King William's War corresponded to the War of the League of Augsburg (War of the Grand Alliance), Queen Anne's War to the War of the Spanish Succession, and King George's War to the War of the Austrian Succession—the French and Indian War erupted *before* the European war with which it would become associated. The Seven Years' War began in Europe in 1756, but the French and Indian War had started in North America two years earlier, in 1754.

Fought over control of territory, the three French and Indian Wars settled nothing permanently, and the frontiers of the French and the English colonies remained both disputed and unstable. On March 16, 1749, King George II granted vast western tracts to the Ohio Company, a syndicate of British speculators, conditioning the grant on the stipulation that, within seven years, the company was obliged to plant a settlement of 100 families and build a fort for their protection. This grant and its stipulation revived enmity between the English on the one hand and the French and Indians on the other, who regarded the charter as a license to invade their lands; indeed, throughout 1749, British traders poured into territories over which the French had enjoyed a trading monopoly. Moreover, the English traders energetically recruited Indian support against the French in the region.

Responding to the English influx, Jacques-Pierre de Jonquière, marquis de la Jonquière, governor of New France, built Fort Rouillé (at the location of present-day Toronto), which was aimed at interdicting English trade between the northern Great Lakes and Oswego, the English stronghold on the south shore of Lake Ontario in New York. Additionally, Jonquière strengthened French fortifications at Detroit and launched a raid against the Shawnee, most powerful of the tribes who regularly traded with the English in the Ohio Country. This proved to be a strategic error, for while the raids were insufficient to hurt the Shawnee decisively, they did drive the tribe more fully into an English alliance.

While the French responded to the English, the English intensified their bellicose stance, as British colonial authorities encouraged English traders to act boldly and aggressively. The English colonies negotiated the purchase of new western lands from the Indians, and from May to July 1752, the British negotiated a treaty at Logstown (now Ambridge, Pennsylvania) between the powerful Iroquois Six Nations, Delaware, Shawnee, and Wyandot on the one side and Virginia and the Ohio Company on the other, thereby securing a quitclaim to all of the Ohio Country—roughly corresponding to much of the upper Midwest between the Appalachian Mountain chain and the Mississippi River. Never mind that this vast region was also claimed by France.

The great weakness of this diplomatic triumph was that the English were not prepared to back the territorial advances of their traders militarily. During the Logstown Treaty negotiations, news reached the Miami (also called Twightwee) delegates that Pickawillany (present-day Piqua, Ohio), their "capital" and the center of English trade in the Ohio Country, had been ravaged by French-led Indian forces on June 21, 1752. The Indian leaders present at Logstown asked the

Virginia delegates to persuade their government to build a fort at the Forks of the Ohio (site of present-day Pittsburgh) for the common defense against the French and their Indian allies. When no fort was built—and when Virginians failed to retaliate for the attack on Pickawillany—the Miami returned to their original French alliance, thereby largely undoing the Logstown Treaty, which ultimately resulted in reversing the trade advances the English had made. Seeing that an opportune moment had arrived, Ange Duquesne de Menneville, marquis Duquesne, who had replaced Jonquière as governor of New France on July 1, 1752, ordered construction of new forts to secure the Ohio Country and thereby to protect the narrow French corridor extending from Montreal down to New Orleans. This action so intimidated the Iroquois that this key English ally was effectively neutralized, as were other English-allied tribes throughout the Ohio Country. Worse, those tribes that now appealed to the English for help in resisting the French were generally turned away, and so the English colonies lost most of their Indian allies.

In London, uninformed or simply heedless of the deteriorating situation in North America, the president of the Board of Trade, Lord Halifax, prodded the government toward a declaration of war against France, arguing that the French, in trading throughout the Ohio Valley, had committed an act of war by invading Virginia. Accordingly, the cabinet and Crown authorized Virginia's lieutenant governor Robert Dinwiddie to take measures to evict the French from territory under his jurisdiction. Dinwiddie, in turn, commissioned 24-year-old George Washington, a Virginia planter and surveyor with virtually no military experience, to carry an ultimatum to Captain Jacques Legardeur de Saint-Pierre, commandant of Fort LeBoeuf (present-day Waterford, Pennsylvania). Washington set out from the Virginia capital of Williamsburg on October 31, 1753, with a small delegation. At Fort LeBoeuf, on December 12, 1753, Captain Legardeur politely rebuffed him, rejecting Virginia's order to vacate. Governor

Dinwiddie responded by ordering (albeit belatedly) the construction of a fort at the Forks of Ohio, and work began in January 1754. Once completed, the fort was garrisoned with a pitifully small party of troops, and on April 17, 1754, the French captured it and renamed the stronghold Fort Duquesne.

On the very day that the new Ohio fort fell, Dinwiddie (ignorant of the loss of the fort) sent Washington with 150 militiamen to reinforce it. En route, on May 28, Washington led 40 of his provincials and a dozen Indian warriors in a surprise assault on a 33-man French reconnaissance party, killing 10 Frenchmen and taking the remaining 23 prisoner. This engagement, near Great Meadows, Pennsylvania, may be considered the first battle of the French and Indian War.

Although he was victorious, Washington realized the French in the region would retaliate. After trying unsuccessfully to recruit more Delaware Indian warriors, he hastily constructed a fortification at Great Meadows but was forced to surrender on July 4 to Major Coulon de Villiers and a mixed French and Indian force of some 900 men. Nearly half of Washington's command had been killed, but he and the other survivors were paroled, save for two who were taken back to Fort Duquesne as hostages. Given free run of the fort, one of the hostages, Captain Robert Stobo, recorded careful observations of the fort's personnel and defenses and, via friendly Delaware, conveyed the intelligence to Philadelphia. He recommended an immediate attack on the stronghold, but he was ignored, and Fort Duquesne remained a key French position for a long time.

With the loss of the Ohio fort and the defeat of Washington, the English, not the French, were expelled from the Ohio Country. Leaders convened a colonial congress at Albany from June 19 to July 10, 1754, but they failed to produce a workable plan for unified colonial action; furthermore, the congress concluded an ill-advised treaty with the Iroquois, which sent the Delaware and other tribes running into the arms of the French. Despite the treaty, the Iroquois, for the most part—with the exception of the staunchly pro-English Mohawk—struggled to remain neutral, even as most of the other tribes sided in varying degrees with the French.

The French used the vast Ohio Country as a staging area for raids into the East. Many raids on Pennsylvania, Maryland, and Virginia involving Shawnee, Delaware, and even some French-allied Iroquois were launched from Fort Duquesne. The English colonial frontier reeled under these assaults, and it was not until December 1754 that the Crown authorized Massachusetts governor William Shirley to reactivate for service two colonial regiments, about 2,000 men, who were to be joined by two British regiments of regulars. The regulars set out for America in January 1755 from Cork, Ireland, under Major General Edward Braddock. The French responded the next month by sending to Canada 78 companies of the king's regulars, whereupon the British Crown added another five regiments to the two previously authorized, raising the American-bound British force to about 10,000 men.

As the French and Indian War rapidly escalated in North America, the Seven Years' War erupted in Europe when, in 1756, Prussia invaded Saxony and, the next year, the Holy Roman Empire declared war on Prussia, which responded by invading Bohemia. As would be the case at the outbreak of World War I two centuries later, a complex series of treaties and secret agreements rapidly drew the French, British, Spanish, and Russians into the war. Believing (correctly) that France's position as a world power was at stake, the French government officially sanctioned Indian hostility against the English colonies on February 17, 1755. Just days after this decree, on February 23, Braddock arrived in Williamsburg, Virginia, and on April 14, he laid out his war plan. He assigned Brigadier General Robert Monckton to invade Nova Scotia, while he himself would capture Forts Duquesne and Niagara. Governor William Shirley of Massachusetts was assigned to lead "provincial" (colonial) forces to reinforce Fort Oswego in New York and then proceed to Fort Niagara, to hold that position in case Braddock was delayed at Fort Duquesne. Another colonial leader, William Johnson, who had married into the Mohawk tribe and enjoyed close relations with them, was tasked with capturing Fort Saint Frédéric at Crown Point on Lake Champlain. In the meantime, at sea, Admiral Edward Boscawen sailed from England on April 23, 1755, on a mission to intercept an anticipated French troop-transport fleet. Bad weather caused Boscawen to miss most of that fleet, however, and the bulk of the French army was able to land, although he had managed to delay the arrival of reinforcements at Fort Beauséjour, the center of guerrilla resistance against the English in Nova Scotia. That territory, therefore, easily fell to the English by the end of June—all of it, that is, except for Louisbourg, a strategically positioned French naval base at Cape Breton, guarding the Saint Lawrence River.

Certainly the most celebrated casualties of the British invasion of Nova Scotia were the Acadians. When they refused to submit to the loyalty oath the victorious British demanded, Governor Charles Lawrence ordered their deportation on July 28, 1755, and nearly 7,000 Acadians were exiled throughout the French colonies, many fleeing to Louisiana, where the passage of years contracted their name to "Cajuns."

While victory was readily won in Nova Scotia, Braddock struggled even to get his centerpiece expedition to Fort Duquesne under way. He was hampered by a paucity of Indian allies—hardly surprising, given the English attitude toward Native Americans—and by his own contempt for the "provincials." When he failed even to consult the colonial governors on his plan of attack, colonial legislatures generally resisted war levies and even refused to render the most rudimentary cooperation. Despite these impediments, Braddock (with Virginia's George Washington serving as his aide-de-camp) finally led two regiments of British regulars and a provincial detachment out of Fort Cumberland, Maryland. The

unwieldy force of 2,500 men, laden with heavy equipment, made such agonizingly slow progress through the dense forest lands that Washington advised detaching a lightly equipped "flying column" of 1,500 men to make the initial attack on Fort Duquesne, which Braddock believed was defended by no more than 800 French and Indians. By July 7, the flying column had set up camp 10 miles from their objective. French-allied Potawatomi and Ottawa scouts observed Braddock's clumsy advance, and on the morning of July 9, Captain Liénard de Beaujeu led 72 regulars of the French Marine, 146 Canadian militiamen, and 637 assorted Indians out of Fort Duquesne in a preemptive attack on Braddock as he approached.

The attack fell swiftly and with total surprise, routing the British. Of 1,459 British regulars and provincials engaged, only 462 survived to return from the battle. Washington, although unhurt, had two horses shot from under him, and his coat was pierced by four bullets. Braddock was mortally wounded. French and Indian casualties amounted to no more than 60 men.

In their panic, the British troops flung away a fortune in arms and ammunition and abandoned their artillery. They also left behind Braddock's well-stocked money chest and, worst of all, his personal papers, which detailed the proceedings of his earlier council of war, including the campaigns proposed against Forts Niagara and Saint Frédéric. Acting on the information found in Braddock's abandoned papers, the French adjusted their war plans by reinforcing Forts Niagara and Saint Frédéric with the very cannon the British had abandoned.

While the Pennsylvania, Maryland, and Virginia frontiers were ravaged by Indian raids in the aftermath of Braddock's defeat, William Johnson was encamped at the southern tip of Lake George, preparing, as Braddock had ordered, to move against Fort Saint Frédéric, which had been reinforced by 3,000 French and Indian troops under the command of Jean Armand, baron de Dieskau. Acting contrary to Governor Vaudreuil's orders, which were simply to reinforce the fort, Dieskau sent 1,400 men out to make a preemptive strike on Johnson's camp. The inept attack on September 8, 1755, failed, and Dieskau was defeated; however, believing Fort Saint Frédéric to be still heavily reinforced (Johnson mistakenly thought some 8,000 French and Indians were there), Johnson did not attempt to capture the fort but instead began construction of an English fort, Fort William Henry, on the south end of Lake George. As it turned out, this inaugurated a change in English strategy generally, as George Washington and others persuaded authorities to build a chain of forts between the Potomac and James and Roanoke Rivers, down into South Carolina. Thus, the British switched from an offensive to a defensive strategy. No longer aiming at evicting the French from the western frontier, they hoped now to prevent them from pushing any farther east, into English territory.

New France's Governor Vaudreuil quickly adapted to this change. Let the English build forts. Instead of attacking them, he would increase the use of Indians to make hit-and-run raids; he would revert to guerrilla tactics rather than assault the forts. New York, Pennsylvania, Virginia, and the Carolinas were ravaged, whereas New England proved more effective in resisting the raids. In the meantime, early in 1756, having failed to take Forts Frontenac and Niagara as prescribed in Braddock's original battle plan, the Massachusetts governor William Shirley retreated to Albany to regroup and, on March 17, dispatched Lieutenant Colonel John Bradstreet to reinforce Fort Oswego, on the southeast shore of Lake Ontario, which was one of the most important English bases. It was, however, too late: The French were already well on their way to cutting the supply line to Oswego. On March 27, 1756, 360 Indians, Canadians, and French regulars under the command of Lieutenant Gaspard-Joseph Chaussegros de Léry attacked Fort Bull at the west end of the portage between the Mohawk River and Wood Creek, which feeds into Lake Oneida. Great quantities of munitions and stores, all intended

for Fort Oswego, were destroyed, and the massacre at Fort Bull was terrible. Bradstreet responded by rapidly building a hundred new bateaux (riverboats) and, with 1,000 men and a total of 350 bateaux, delivered food and supplies over 160 miles from Albany to Oswego by the end of May, thereby preventing the collapse of the now-isolated fort. On July 3, as Bradstreet and his men were returning from Oswego, a mixed force of about 700 Canadians and Indians ambushed his vanguard, but Bradstreet counterattacked and defeated the ambushers.

Such British victories were rare during the first three years of the war, and by June 1756, the English settlers of Virginia had withdrawn 150 miles from the prewar frontier. On May 11, 1756, a new French military commander arrived in Canada; Louis-Joseph de Montcalm-Gozon, marquis de Montcalm de Saint-Véran. On May 17, Britain officially declared war on France in the start of the Seven Years' War. On July 12, Bradstreet warned his commanders that Fort Oswego remained in grave danger, but by this time Governor Shirley, who respected Bradstreet, had been replaced as commander of the provincial forces by Major General James Abercromby, a British regular, who contemptuously excluded Bradstreet from a council of war he convened on July 16. Even worse, impatient with the lack of conventional military discipline shown by the "bateaumen" (river-borne frontiersmen) who had fought so brilliantly under Bradstreet, Abercromby instantly discharged 400 of them, failing to realize that they were the most effective wilderness fighters the English had. Abercromby was slow to reinforce Fort Oswego, and the strategically critical outpost fell to Montcalm on August 14, 1756. With its loss, the British yielded Lake Ontario to the French, thereby strengthening French communication with Fort Duquesne and the entire West. It was now out of the question to attack Fort Niagara, and the Iroquois, still officially neutral, inclined more sharply to the French victors. It was a blow even more severe than the defeat of Braddock had been.

In December 1756, William Pitt (the Elder) became British secretary of state for the Southern Department, which put him in charge of American colonial affairs. He took a fresh approach, ordering 2,000 additional troops to Halifax, Nova Scotia, with the intention of bringing the war into Canada, the enemy's heartland, via the Saint Lawrence Valley, and finally attacking Quebec. The first objective was the always troublesome French naval base at Louisbourg. With its defeat, New France would be largely cut off from communication with Europe. While this plan was sound, its execution suffered from massive logistical bottlenecks, which delayed its launch until August 1757, by which time the British commanders concluded that the season was too late and the enemy now too strong to attempt an assault on Louisbourg. They therefore timidly withdrew to New York.

In the meantime, on July 29, Montcalm began an advance against Fort William Henry. His objective was to gain control of the so-called Warpath of Nations, the route connecting the ocean, Hudson River, Lake George, Lake Champlain, and the Richelieu River, which leads into the Saint Lawrence. The portion of the route that lay between Lake George and Lake Champlain was a vital part of this system. In an effort to gain control of it, the French had built Forts Ticonderoga and Saint Frédéric on Lake Champlain, at the north end of Lake George, and the British had built Fort William Henry at the south end of Lake George and, south of that, Fort Edward, on the headwaters of the Hudson. For much of the war, armies fighting in the eastern theater faced one another between these sets of forts.

Fort William Henry was defended by Lieutenant Colonel George Monro with 2,372 men, of whom only 1,100 were fit for duty in August 1757, the rest being down with sickness and injury. Opposing him, Montcalm commanded 7,626 men, including 1,600 Indian allies. Despite the odds, Monro fought valiantly, holding out for a full week before capitulating on August 9, 1757. Montcalm promised the defeated com-

mandant safe conduct for his garrison, which, however, was ambushed and slaughtered by the French-allied Indians as soon as it left the fort. Some 1,500 soldiers, women, and children were massacred or taken prisoner.

The fall of Fort William Henry and the massacre that followed were the nadir of British fortunes in the French and Indian War, but as Pitt's military reform policies started to take effect, the tide began to turn. Pitt cooperated with the colonists rather than dictated to them, and he ensured that colonial assemblies had a full voice in managing funds used to prosecute the war. Perhaps most important of all, he actively recruited Indian allies, promising them that, after the war, the English would enforce a boundary line to restrict white encroachment into their lands.

Pitt personally selected Major General John Forbes, one of his best commanders, to make a new attack on Fort Duquesne. In September, Forbes led an army of 5,000 provincials, 1,400 elite Scottish Highlanders, and a handful of Indians in a march against the fort. On September 11, one of his commanders, Colonel Henry Bouquet, grew impatient with the slow pace of the advance and ordered 800 Highlanders under Major James Grant to reconnoiter in the vicinity of Fort Duquesne. The troops arrived near the fort on September 14 in the dead of night. At dawn on September 15, Major Grant ordered the drums to beat, thinking to inspire and inspirit his men. Whatever effect they had on the Highlanders, they certainly alerted the French to Grant's presence, and a sortie of French and Indians issued from the fort, overran the Highlanders, and killed a third of them, including Grant. It was a bitter blow to Forbes, yet it was also costly to the French and Indians—especially the Indians. Losses among them were so heavy that the Potawatomi, Ojibwa, and Ottawa summarily deserted the French, leaving only the Ohio tribes. What the French did not know at the time was that these Indian allies were also about to be neutralized by a treaty concluded at Easton, Pennsylvania, in October 1758. The momentous Treaty of Easton returned to the Iroquois the western lands the Six Nations had earlier ceded to Pennsylvania and further stipulated that the Iroquois would freely grant the Delaware—hitherto French allies—the right to hunt and live on these lands. The Iroquois thus became landlords to the Delaware, and insofar as most of the Iroquois were allies of the British, this relationship also meant peace between the British and the Delaware.

The Treaty of Easton was a fatal blow to the French, and while French-Indian alliances were dissolving, General Abercromby mustered 16,000 troops at Lake George for a march against Fort Ticonderoga, which the French had renamed Fort Carillon. Abercromby dispatched the highly skillful colonial commander John Bradstreet in advance, and he and his provincials readily pierced the fort's outer defenses. Hard on the heels of this success, Bradstreet asked Abercromby for permission to attack the fort itself, before Montcalm could call up reinforcements. Cautious and conventional, Abercromby ordered him to await the arrival of the main body of English troops. This timid decision gave Montcalm ample time not only to bring up reinforcements from Fort Saint Frédéric but also to construct highly effective entrenchments. Even with reinforcements, Montcalm had only 3,000 men to defend Fort Ticonderoga, but his elaborate fortification work had transformed it into a formidable position.

For their part, the British also occupied a good position, holding the high ground, called Mount Defiance, which made Fort Ticonderoga vulnerable to artillery. But, in another tactical error, Abercromby had put no artillery there, instead stationing William Johnson and 400 Mohawk atop Mount Defiance. It was a position from which they could never even be committed to battle.

Abercromby attacked on July 8 and ran into a series of French bayonet charges, in which 464 British regulars fell dead and 1,117 were wounded; provincial losses numbered 87 dead and 239 wounded. Although outnumbered more than 5 to 1, the French lost 112 officers and men, with 275 wounded. Abercromby retreated to Albany with his army thoroughly demoralized.

But Ticonderoga was to be the last major French triumph of the war. On July 26, 1758, Major General James Wolfe and Brigadier General Jeffrey Amherst made an amphibious assault on Louisbourg, Nova Scotia, capturing the great French stronghold. At the end of the next month, a provincial task force captured Fort Frontenac, near present-day Kingston, Ontario, which fell on August 27. With the loss of this fort, the French lifeline to Forts Niagara and Duquesne was severed, and France relinquished control of Lake Ontario to the British.

Fort Duquesne, which Forbes was gradually approaching, was now cut off from all sources of supplies. Commandant François-Marie Le Marchand de Lignery was also aware that he would soon be forced to release his short-term militiamen from Illinois and Louisiana, as well as his dwindling body of Indians. He therefore launched a desperate strike against Forbes's position at Loyalhanna on October 12, 1758. Quickly repulsed, Lignery withdrew into the fort. A month later, he launched another attack. This time, Forbes captured three prisoners, who revealed just how weakly Fort Duquesne was held. On November 24, as Forbes's army was preparing to move out of Loyalhanna and storm Fort Duquesne, they heard a distant explosion. Lignery had abandoned the fort and blown it up. Even reduced to ruins, Fort Duquesne was a prize: The nation that controlled the Forks of the Ohio controlled the gateway to the West. Forbes set about rebuilding the fort, renaming the rubble Fort Pitt.

If the year 1758 ended badly for the French, 1759 would prove downright disastrous. Pitt laid out a three-pronged campaign against the French, which included the capture of Fort Niagara and the reinforcement of Fort Oswego to sever the West from the Saint Lawrence River; a strike through the Lake Champlain waterway into the Saint Lawrence Valley; and an amphibious assault on Quebec itself.

Early in the year, the Fort Pitt garrison was expanded from the 200 men Forbes had left there to 350, as Brigadier General John Stanwix prepared to use it as a base for a 3,500-man strike force to operate throughout the Ohio Country. In February, William Johnson proposed an expedition against Fort Niagara via the country of the Six Nations. Indian allies could be acquired along the way. In April, the Seneca, the Iroquois tribe most inclined toward the French, at last became discouraged by the French failure to provide satisfactory trade goods and agreed to assist the British in the attack on Fort Niagara. That same month, the Oneida chief Conochquieson told William Johnson that all the Six Nations were prepared to ally themselves with the British. The balance of Indian power in the French and Indian War had finally and definitively shifted.

While Johnson recruited allies for the assault on Niagara, General Wolfe prepared to take Quebec. On May 28, 1759, Rear Admiral Philip Durrell landed a detachment on Ile-aux-Coudres in the St. Lawrence River, northeast of Quebec. His troops advanced downriver to Ile d'Orleans, nearer to Quebec, to await the main amphibious force under Wolfe and Vice Admiral Charles Saunders, which landed on June 27. By July, Wolfe's army of 9,000 men was in possession of the north shore of the Saint Lawrence above Quebec. For the next two and a half months, Wolfe probed Quebec's defenses without success. Frustrated, he turned to terrorizing the civilian population, bombarding the city day and night with his artillery, deliberately concentrating his fire on residential rather than military targets. Montcalm responded with equal ruthlessness. When, after weeks of siege and bombardment, the citizens of Quebec expressed their desire to surrender, the general threatened to turn his Indians loose upon them if they faltered.

While the siege of Quebec wore on, General Amherst decided to transfer the Niagara command to a regular British army officer, Brigadier General John Prideaux, with William Johnson relegated to a role as second in command. On July 8, Prideaux demanded the surrender of Fort Niagara. Commandant Captain Pierre Pouchot pretended not to understand English, whereupon Prideaux commenced his siege. Pouchot sent to Lignery, who was now at Fort Machault, for reinforcements, but in the meantime, as the British forces prepared to storm Niagara, an accidental shot from one of his own guns killed General Prideaux on July 19, and William Johnson again assumed command—just in time to hear of Lignery's approach with 1,000 French reinforcements. Johnson was able to surprise them, however, killing 200 and taking 100 prisoners, including the senior officers. Deprived of reinforcements, Pouchot capitulated, and Fort Niagara fell to the British on July 23.

Three days later, the French, outnumbered by Jeffrey Amherst's troops, abandoned and blew up Fort Ticonderoga. Amherst turned his attention to Fort Saint Frédéric, which fell to him on July 31. The French retreated down the Richelieu River. Only Quebec remained steadfast.

During the summer of 1759, Wolfe made several failed attempts to storm Quebec. Finally, on September 12, he took a new tack, approaching with great stealth from the Plains of Abraham, the high ground above the city. Montcalm had not anticipated an attack from this direction and accordingly fortified another position, at Beaumont. At daybreak on September 14, Montcalm, his troops, and the people of Quebec were stunned by the spectacle of a British army forming lines of battle on the Plains of Abraham. Instead of counterattacking with what he had available—while Wolfe's men were still forming up—Montcalm decided to await the arrival of his troops from Beaumont. Unaccountably, however, he did not wait for additional reinforcements from Cap Rouge. The result was military disaster, as the French commander, usually so canny, blundered by ordering a counterattack against the advancing British that was simultaneously too late and premature. Montcalm committed 4,500 troops, mostly colonials, to battle. Wolfe held his fire until the last possible moment, then delivered it into the poorly organized French ranks with horrific effect. After months of failed assaults, the climactic battle was over in a quarter of an hour, leaving 200 French troops dead and another 1,200 wounded. British losses were 60 dead and 600 wounded. Among those killed were the two commanders, Montcalm and Wolfe. Quebec formally surrendered on September 18, 1759, effectively bringing French power in North America to an end.

In military terms, the fall of the major French forts and Quebec decided the outcome of war, but the French still held Montreal and the Richelieu River as far as Isle-aux-Noix, at the bottom of Lake Champlain. The fighting therefore dragged on, the French hoping to salvage something they could bring to negotiations in order to wrest from the British the best peace terms possible. The major combat in this final phase of the war, however, was between the British and the Indians rather than between the English and the French, but Spain also entered into the picture in the final act. That kingdom had belatedly joined the Seven Years' War in Europe on the side of France, and Britain declared war on the new combatant on January 2, 1762. Britain sea power rapidly prevailed against Spain. On February 15, 1762, the French island of Martinique fell to the English, followed by Saint Lucia and Grenada. On August 12, 1762, Havana yielded to a two-month siege, and Manila fell on October 5. On November 3, France concluded the secret Treaty of San Ildefonso with Spain, in which it ceded to that country all of its territory west of the Mississippi as well as the Isle of Orleans in Louisiana. These cessions were by way of compensation for the loss of Spain's Caribbean holdings.

Both the Seven Years' War and the French and Indian War came to a formal end with with the Treaty of Paris, concluded on February 10, 1763. France ceded all of Louisiana to Spain and the rest of its North American holdings to Great Britain. Spain recovered Cuba (in compensation for the loss of territories in Florida and in the Caribbean), and France retained the Caribbean islands of Guadeloupe, Martinique, and Saint Lucia. Although the treaty decided the French-

English contest for control of North America, it did not bring an end to deep discontent among the Indians of the frontier. This meant that warfare would continue in the region for years to come.

Pontiac's Rebellion, 1763

No sooner was the Treaty of Paris concluded, formally ending the Seven Years' War and, with it, the French and Indian War, than the Ottawa tribe, led by Chief Pontiac, and other tribes— including the Delaware, some Iroquois tribes (principally the Seneca), and the Shawnee—commenced a series of raids on the western outposts the French had just surrendered to the British. This was the start of a general Indian uprising in the Ohio country, but the influence of the enormously popular, if overly romantic, 19th-century historian Francis Parkman fixed the name Pontiac's Rebellion to the entire violent episode, and so the war has been known ever since. The fact was that Pontiac, although a central figure, was but one among several Indian leaders who united, albeit temporarily, in an effort to resist English encroachment on their land.

The source of the conflict may be traced to the English capture of Detroit on November 29, 1760, during the French and Indian War, and the victorious General Jeffrey Amherst's ill-advised decision to end the custom of giving gifts to the Indians, in particular cutting off their supply of ammunition. Amherst saw this as a prudent step. Why arm a potential enemy? But the Indians had long depended on ammunition from the French for the purposes of hunting. Indeed, the French had always been generous with gifts, and the sudden loss of ammunition, arms, and other provisions was especially galling. In the months after Amherst's edict, a prophet arose among the Delaware, Neolin, who counseled the Indians to reject all the ways of the white man and return to the pure path of the ancestors. The Delaware Prophet, as he was called, insisted that his followers act in peace, but his charismatic presence alarmed traders and agents in the vicinity of Detroit and spoke of a "conspiracy" forming among the tribes.

By 1763, when France ceded virtually all of its North American territory to Britain—without, of course, consulting its Native American allies—the discontent, alarm, and desperation among the Indians in the vicinity of Detroit had mounted to what the English called "rebellion." Chief Pontiac convened a grand council on April 27, 1763, urging the Potowatomi and Huron to join his Ottawa in a joint attack on Detroit. Four days later, he visited the fort with a group of his warriors. His ostensible purpose was to entertain the garrison with a ceremonial dance, but his real object was to reconnoiter the outpost's defenses. On May 5, Pontiac outlined his plan of assault to the other chiefs. Warriors would conceal muskets, tomahawks, and knives under their blankets; enter the fort on an apparently peaceful visit; then, once inside, start the attack.

The operation was scheduled for May 7, but it was thwarted by an informant whose identity is unknown to history. Apprised of Pontiac's plan, the fort's small garrison of 120 Royal Americans and Queen's Rangers was prepared. The chief entered with 300 warriors, each with a blanket thrown over his shoulder; however, realizing that he had lost the element of surprise, Pontiac soon withdrew. This brought upon him accusations of cowardice from other leaders. On the next day, May 8, Pontiac attempted to enter the fort again, but the commandant agreed to admit only chiefs—no warriors. Frustrated, and further pressed by his followers, Pontiac led raids against the settlers in the fort's vicinity. These were followed by a combined assault by Ottawa, Wyandot, Potowatomi, and Ojibwa against the fort. After a six-hour fusillade, the attackers withdrew.

On May 11, Pontiac made a second assault on the fort, even as various Indian bands ambushed and raided settlers nearby. Pontiac appealed to the Miami and to the French living in Illinois Country for support. For their part, the French settlers in the region did not believe Pontiac would prevail. Moreover, they did not think he could control his warriors, who were beginning to raid French settlers, farmers, and trappers as well as English. Pontiac responded to their doubts with an eloquent speech made to a delegation of French settlers and succeeded in winning support from some of them.

Backed by more Indians and at least some French settlers, Pontiac and the chiefs associated with him attacked and captured Fort Michilimackinac on the southern shore of the Straits of Mackinac; in June, they struck at a number of other forts, farther east. Forts Pitt, Ligonier, and Bedford in Pennsylvania were all besieged but held out. Then, on or about June 16, 1763, a Seneca force killed the entire 15- or 16-man garrison at Fort Venango (near modern Franklin, Pennsylvania), sparing only the commandant, a Lieutenant Gordon, whom they forced to write (from dictation) a list of grievances addressed to the king of England. Once he finished this task, he was tortured to death over three days.

On June 18, the Seneca assaulted Fort LeBoeuf (at present-day Waterford, Pennsylvania), burned it, and killed six or seven of the 13 men who garrisoned it. Joined now by Ottawa, Huron, and Ojibwa, the Seneca turned against Fort Presque Isle (Erie, Pennsylvania) on June 20. The Indians fired the fort, forcing the surrender of 30 garrison soldiers, to whom they pledged safe conduct to Fort Pitt. Instead, the men were divided among the four tribes as prisoners. Most of them were subsequently killed.

When Delaware warriors demanded the surrender of Fort Pitt (at modern Pittsburgh) on June 24, Captain Simon Ecuyer, commanding, refused and, during a parley, presented the Delaware delegates with a handkerchief and two blankets from the fort's smallpox hospital. An epidemic soon swept the tribe, although whether it was the result of this early instance of biological warfare or a naturally occurring phenomenon is impossible to determine.

The Seneca hit Fort Niagara, which withstood a five-month siege from May to September at the hands of the Ottawa, Ojibwa, Potawatomi, Huron, Shawnee, Delaware, and Erie. In the meantime, Colonel Henry Bouquet led a relief column, about 460 men, to Fort Pitt. At Edge Hill, about 30 miles from the fort, on August 5, Delaware, Shawnee, Mingo, and Huron warriors ambushed the column's advance guard. Bouquet managed to force the attackers out into the open on the next day, however, and drove them off. Numerically, losses in what historians call the Battle of Bushy Run were probably equal in numbers—50 of Bouquet's men killed and 60 wounded—but the Delaware also lost two chiefs and so abandoned what might have been an important battle.

Despite the lack of any decisive battle on either side, exhaustion seems to have brought Pontiac to the peace table. The siege of Detroit was lifted in September, and on October 3, 1763, Pontiac and the other chiefs agreed to peace in return for a British pledge to halt colonial settlement at the Appalachian Mountains. King George III issued his famous Proclamation of 1763 codifying the pledge, and the limit decreed by it became known as the Proclamation Line.

Pontiac's Rebellion may be regarded as a short but intensely violent coda to the French and Indian War. Contemporary estimates calculated that some 2,000 colonists and more than 400 soldiers were killed. Indian casualties are unknown, including the numbers who succumbed to smallpox.

DOCUMENTS

THE PEQUOT WAR, 1637

Excerpts from *Narrative of the Pequot War*
John Mason
Published 1736

John Mason (ca. 1600–72) had been a professional soldier in England, holding the rank of major in the regular army by the time he immigrated to New England in 1632. He briefly lived in the Massachusetts Bay Colony but soon joined the pioneers who began to settle land along the Connecticut River. As often happened when colonists encroached on Indian country, friction developed between the settlers and the main tribe in the region, the Pequot. The Connecticut colony commissioned Mason to lead the principal expedition against the Pequot. His objective was a stronghold in what is today Mystic, Connecticut. This resulted in the so-called Mystic Massacre (May 26, 1637), in which Mason and his men killed an entire Pequot village, populated mainly by women, children, and old men.

Although Mason was largely hailed as a hero, he is at pains in his posthumously published narrative to justify the war in general and the action in Mystic in particular, especially since the attack was his idea and departed from the original mission assigned to him.

The excerpts that follow retain the original spelling.

[From the introduction by the Reverend Mr. Thomas Prince]

PSAL. XLIV. 1–3. We have heard with our Ears, O God, our Fathers have told us, what Work Thou didst in their Days, in the times of old; How Thou didst drive out the Heathen with thy Hand, and plantedst Them: how Thou did afflict the People and cast them out. For they got not the Land in Possession by their own Sword, neither did their own Arm save them: but thy right Hand, and thine Arm, and the Light of thy Countenance, because Thou hadst a Favour unto them.

PSAL. CII. 18. This shall be written for the Generation to come: and the People which shall be Created, shall praise the Lord.

. . .

The most terrible of all those [Indian] Nations [in New England] were then the Pequots; who with their depending Tribes soon entered on a Resolution to Destroy the English out of the Country. In 1634, they killed Capt. Stone and all his Company, being seven besides Himself, in and near his Bark on Connecticut River. In

This engraving depicts the Pequot encampment under attack by Captain John Mason and his men. *(New York Public Library)*

1635, they killed Capt. Oldham in his Bark at Block-Island; and at Long-Island they killed two more cast away there. In 1636, and the following Winter and March, they killed six and took seven more at Connecticut River: Those they took alive they tortured to Death in a most barbarous Manner. And on April 23, 1637, they killed nine more and carried two young Women Captive at Weathersfield.

They had earnestly solicited the Narragansetts to engage in their Confederacy: very politickly representing to them, That if they should help or suffer the English to subdue the Pequots, they would thereby make Way for their own future Ruin; and that they need not come to open Battle with the English; only Fire our Houses, kill our Cattle, lye in Ambush and shoot us as we went about our Business; so we should be quickly forced to leave this Country, and the Indians not exposed to any great Hazard. Those truly politick Arguments were upon the Point of prevailing on the Narragansetts. And had These with the Mohegans, to whom the Pequots were nearly related, joined against us; they might then, in the infant State of these Colonies, have easily accomplished their desperate Resolutions.

But the Narragansetts being more afraid of the Pequots than of the English; were willing they Should weaken each other, not in the least imagining the English could destroy them; at the same time an Agency from the Massachusetts Colony to the Narragansetts, happily Preserved their staggering Friendship. And as Uncas the Great Sachim of the Moheags [Mohegan], upon the first coming of the English, fell into an intimate Acquaintance with Capt. Mason, He from the Beginning entertained us in an amicable Manner: And though both by his Father and Mother He derived from the Royal Blood of the Pequots, and had Married the Daughter of Tatobam their then late Sachim; yet such was his Affection for us, as he faithfully adhered to us, ventured his Life in our Service, assisted at the Taking their Fort, when about Seven Hundred of them were Destroyed, and thereupon in subduing and driving out of the Country the remaining greater Part of that fierce and dangerous Nation.

. . .

[From Mason's narrative]

. . . I thought it my Duty in the Entrance to relate the first Grounds upon which the English took up Arms against the Pequots. . . . Judge of me as you please; I shall not climb after Applause, nor do I much fear a Censure; there being many Testimonies to what I shall say. . . . I desire my Name may be sparingly mentioned: My principal Aim is that God may have his due praise. . . .

To The Judicious Reader.
Gentlemen,
I NEVER had thought that this should have come to the Press, until of late: If I had, I should have endeavoured to have put a little more Varnish upon it: But being over perswaded by some Friends, I thought it not altogether amiss to present it to your courteous Disposition, hoping it might find your favourable Entertainment and Acceptance, though rude and impolished. I wish it had fallen into some better Hands that might have performed it to the life; I shall only draw the Curtain and open my little Casement, that so others of larger Hearts and Abilities may let in a

bigger Light; that so at least some small Glimmering maybe left to Posterity what Difficulties and Obstructions their Forefathers met with in their first settling these desart Parts of America; how God was pleased to prove them, and how by his wise Providence he ordered and disposed all their Occasions and Affairs for them in regard to both their Civils and Ecclesiasticals. . . .

Some Grounds of the War Against the Pequots.
ABOUT the Year 1632 one Capt. Stone arrived in the Massachusetts in a Ship from Virginia; who shortly after was bound for Virginia in a small Bark with one Capt. Norton; who sailing into Connecticut River about two Leagues from the Entrance cast Anchor; there coming to them several Indians belonging to that Place whom the Pequots Tyrannized over, being a potent and warlike People, it being their Custom so to deal with their neighbour Indians; Capt. Stone having some occasion with the Dutch who lived at a trading House near twenty Leagues up the River, procured some of those Indians to go as Pilots with two of his Men to the Dutch: But being benighted before they could come to their desired Port, put the skiff in which they went, ashoar, where the two Englishmen falling asleep, were both Murdered by their Indian Guides: There remaining with the Bark about twelve of the aforesaid Indians; who had in all probability formerly plotted their bloody Design; and waiting an opportunity when some of the English were on Shoar and Capt. Stone asleep in his Cabbin, set upon them and cruelly Murdered every one of them, plundered what they pleased and sunk the Bark.

These Indians were not native Pequots, but had frequent recourse unto them, to whom they tendered some of those Goods, which were accepted by the Chief Sachem of the Pequots: Other of the said Goods were tendered to Nynigrett Sachem of Nayanticke, who also received them.

The Council of the Massachusetts being informed of their proceedings, sent to speak with the Pequots, and had some Treaties with them: But being unsatisfied therewith, sent forth Captain John Endicot Commander in Chief, with Captain Underhill, Captain Turner, and with them one hundred and twenty Men: who were firstly designed on a Service against a People living on Block Island, who were subject to the Narragansett Sachem; they having taken a Bark of one Mr. John Oldham, Murdering him and all his Company: They were also to call the Pequots to an Account about the Murder of Capt. Stone; who arriving at Pequot had some Conference with them; but little effected; only one Indian slain and some Wigwams burnt. After which, the Pequots grew inraged against the English who inhabited Connecticut, being but a small Number, about two hundred and fifty, who were there newly arrived; as also about twenty Men at Saybrook, under the Command of Lieutenant Lyon Gardner, who was there settled by several Lords and Gentlemen in England. The Pequots falling violently upon them, slew divers Men at Saybrook; keeping almost a constant Siege upon the Place; so that the English were constrained to keep within their pallizado Fort; being so hard Beset and sometimes Assaulted, that Capt. John Mason was sent by Connecticut Colony with twenty Men out of their small Numbers to secure the Place: But after his coming, there did not one Pequot appear in view for one Month Space, which was the time he there remained.

In the Interim certain Pequots about One Hundred going to a Place called Weathersfield on Connecticut; having formerly confederated with the Indians of that Place (as it was generally thought) lay in Ambush for the English; divers of them going into a large Field adjoyning to the Town to their Labour, were there set upon by the Indians: Nine of the English were killed outright, with some Horses, and two young Women taken Captives.

At their Return from Weathersfield, they came down the River of Connecticut (Capt. Mason being then at Saybrook Fort) in three Canoes with about one hundred Men, which River of necessity they must pass: We espying them, concluded they had been acting some Mischief against us, made a Shot at them with a Piece of Ordnance, which beat off the Beak Head of one of their Canoes, wherein our two Captives were: it was at a very great distance: They then hastened, drew their Canoes over a narrow Beach with all speed and so got away.

Upon which the English were somewhat dejected: But immediately upon this, a Court was called and met in Hartford the First of May, 1637, who seriously considering their Condition, which did look very Sad, for those Pequots were a great People, being strongly fortified, cruel, warlike, munitioned, &c. and the English but an handful in comparison: But their outragious Violence against the English, having Murdered about Thirty of them, their great Pride and Insolency, constant pursuit in their malicious Courses, with their engaging other Indians in their Quarrel against the English, who had never offered them the least Wrong; who had in all likelihood Espoused all the Indians in the country in their Quarrel, had not God by more than an ordinary Providence prevented: These Things being duly considered, with the eminent Hazard and great Peril they were in; it pleased God so to stir up the Hearts of all Men in general, and the Court in special, that they concluded some Forces should forthwith be sent out against the Pequots; their Grounds being Just, and necessity enforcing them to engage in an offensive and defensive War; the Management of which War we are nextly to relate.

Captain Mason's decision to bypass the objective assigned to him, Sassacus's fort on Pequot Harbor, and to attack instead the fort on the Mystic River drew much criticism. In his narrative, Mason was at pains to explain the decision.

. . . At length we concluded, God assisting us, for Narragansett, and so to March through their Country, which Bordered upon the Enemy; where lived a great People, it being about fifteen Leagues beyond Pequot [Harbor]; The Grounds and Reasons of our so Acting you shall presently understand:

First, The Pequots our Enemies, kept a continual Guard upon the River Night and Day.

Secondly, their Numbers far exceeded ours: having sixteen Guns with Powder and Shot, as we were informed by . . . two Captives . . .

Thirdly, They were on Land, and being swift on Foot, might much impede our Landing, and possibly dishearten our Men; we being expected only by Land, there being no other Place to go on Shoar but in that River, nearer than Narragansett.

Fourthly, By Narragansett we should come upon their Backs, and possibly might surprize them unawares, at worst we should be on firm Land as well as they.

All which proved very Successful as the Sequel may evidently demonstrate. . . . What shall I say? God led his People through many Difficulties and Turnings; yet by more than an ordinary Hand of Providence he brought them to Canaan at last.

Mason then narrated the approach to and the attack on the alternate target, the Pequot fort on the Mystic River. His narrative is especially valuable for what it suggests about relations between the colonists and the "friendly" Narragansett.

On Friday Morning we set Sail for Narragansett Bay, and on Saturday towards Evening we arrived at our desired Port, there we kept the Sabbath.

On the Monday the Wind blew so hard at North-West that we could not go on Shoar; as also on the Tuesday until Sun set; at which time Capt. Mason landed and Marched up to the Place of the Chief [Narragansett] Sachem's Residence; who told the Sachem, That we had not an opportunity to acquaint him with our coming Armed in his Country sooner; yet not doubting but it would be well accepted by him, there being Love betwixt himself and us; well knowing also

that the Pequots and themselves were Enemies, and that he could not be unacquainted with those intolerable Wrongs and Injuries these Pequots had lately done unto the English; and that we were now come, God assisting, to Avenge our selves upon them; and that we did only desire free Passage through his Country.

Who returned us this Answer, That he did accept of our coming, and did also approve of our Design; only he thought our Numbers were too weak to deal with the Enemy, who were (as he said) very great Captains and Men skilful in War.

Thus he spake somewhat slighting of us.

On the Wednesday Morning, we Marched from thence to a Place called Nayanticke, it being about eighteen or twenty miles distant, where another of those Narragansett Sachems lived in a Fort; it being a Frontier to the Pequots. They carryed very proudly towards us; not permitting any of us to come into their Fort.

We beholding their Carriage and the Falsehood of Indians, and fearing least they might discover us to the Enemy, especially they having many times some of their near Relations among their greatest Foes; we therefore caused a strong Guard to be set about their Fort, giving Charge that no Indian should be suffered to pass in or out: We also informed the Indians, that none of them should stir out of the Fort upon peril of their Lives: so as they would not suffer any of us to come into their Fort, so we would not suffer any of them to go out of the Fort.

There we quartered that Night, the Indians not offering to stir out all the while.

In the Morning there came to us several of Miantomo his Men, who told us, they were come to assist us in our Expedition, which encouraged divers Indians of that Place to Engage also; who suddenly gathering into a Ring, one by one, making solemn Protestations how galliantly they would demean themselves, and how many Men they would Kill.

On the Thursday about eight of the Clock in the Morning, we Marched thence towards Pequot, with about five hundred Indians: But through the Heat of the Weather and want of Provisions some of our Men fainted: And having Marched about twelve Miles, we came to Paw-catuck River, at a Ford where our Indians told us the Pequots did usually Fish; there making an Alta, we stayed some small time: The Narragan-sett Indians manifesting great Fear, in so much that many of them returned, although they had frequently despised us, saying, That we durst not look upon a Pequot, but themselves would perform great Things; though we had often told them that we came on purpose and were resolved, God assisting, to see the Pequots, and to fight with them, before we returned, though we perished. I then enquired of Onkos [Uncas], what he thought the Indians would do? Who said, The Narragansetts would all leave us, but as for Himself He would never leave us: and so it proved: For which Expressions and some other Speeches of his, I shall never forget him. Indeed he was a great Friend, and did great Service.

And after we had refreshed our selves with our mean Commons, we Marched about three Miles, and came to a Field which had lately been planted with Indian Corn: There we made another Alt, and called our Council, supposing we drew near to the Enemy: and being informed by the Indians that the Enemy had two Forts almost impregnable; but we were not at all Dis-couraged, but rather Animated, in so much that we were resolved to Assault both their Forts at once. But understanding that one of them was so remote that we could not come up with it before Midnight, though we Marched hard; whereat we were much grieved, chiefly because the great-est and bloodiest Sachem there resided, whose name was Sassacous: We were then constrained, being exceedingly spent in our March with extream Heat and want of Necessaries, to accept of the nearest

We then Marching on in a silent Manner, the Indians that remained fell all into the Rear, who formerly kept the Van; (being possessed with great Fear) we continued our March till about one Hour in the Night: and coming to a little Swamp between two Hills, there we pitched our little Camp; much wearied with hard Travel, keeping great Silence, supposing we were very near the Fort; as our Indians informed us; which proved otherwise: The Rocks were our Pil-lows; yet Rest was pleasant: The Night proved Comfortable, being clear and Moon Light: We appointed our Guards and placed our Sentinels at some distance; who heard the Enemy Singing at the Fort, who continued that Strain until Mid-night, with great Insulting and Rejoycing, as we were afterwards informed: They seeing our Pin-naces sail by them some Days before, concluded we were afraid of them and durst not come near them, the Burthen of their Song tending to that purpose.

In the Morning, we awaking and seeing it very light, supposing it had been day, and so we might have lost our Opportunity, having purposed to make our Assault before Day; rowsed the Men with all expedition, and briefly commended our-selves and Design to God, thinking immediately to go to the Assault; the Indians shewing us a Path, told us that it led directly to the Fort. We held on our March about two Miles, wondering that we came not to the Fort, and fearing we might be deluded: But seeing Corn newly planted at the Foot of a great Hill, supposing the Fort was not far off, a Champion Country [meadow] being round about us; then making a stand, gave the Word for some of the Indians to come up: At length Onkos and one Wequash appeared; We demanded of them, Where was the Fort? They answered On the Top of that Hill: Then we demanded, Where were the Rest of the Indians? They answered, Behind, exceedingly afraid: We wished them to tell the rest of their Fellows, That they should by no means Fly, but stand at what distance they pleased, and see whether Eng-lish Men would now Fight or not. Then Capt. Underhill came up, who Marched in the Rear; and commending ourselves to God, divided our Men: There being two Entrances into the Fort, intending to enter both at once: Captain Mason leading up to that on the North East Side; who approaching within one Rod, heard a Dog bark and an Indian crying Owanux! Owanux! which is Englishmen! Englishmen! We called up our Forces with all expedition, gave Fire upon them through the Pallizado [palisade]; the Indians being in a dead indeed their last Sleep: Then we wheeling off fell upon the main Entrance, which was blocked up with Bushes about Breast high, over which the Captain passed, intending to make good the Entrance, ecouraging the rest to follow. Lieutenant Seeley endeavoured to enter; but being somewhat cumbred, stepped back and pulled out the Bushes and so entred, and with him about sixteen Men: We had formerly concluded to destroy them by the Sword and save the Plunder.

Whereupon Captain Mason seeing no Indians, entred a Wigwam; where he was beset with many Indians, waiting all opportunities to lay Hands on him, but could not prevail. At length William Heydon, espying the Breach in the Wigwam, supposing some English might be there, entred; but in his Entrance fell over a dead Indian; but speedily recovering himself, the Indians some fled, others crept under their Beds: The Captain going out of the Wigwam saw many Indians in the Lane or Street; he making towards them, they fled, were pursued to the End of the Lane, where they were met by Edward Pattison, Thomas Barber, with some others; where seven of them were Slain, as they said. The Captain facing about, Marched a slow Pace up the Lane he came down, perceiving himself very much out of Breath; and coming to the other End near the Place where he first entred, saw two Soldiers standing close to the Pallizado with their Swords pointed to the Ground: the Captain told them that We should never kill them after that manner: The Captain also said, We must Burn them; and immediately stepping into the Wigwam where he had been before, brought out a Firebrand, and putting it into the Matts with which they were covered, set the Wigwams on Fire. Lieutenant Thomas Bull and Nicholas Omsted beholding, came up; and when it was thoroughly kindled, the Indians ran as Men most dreadfully Amazed.

And indeed such a dreadful Terror did the Almighty let fall upon their Spirits, that they would fly from us and run into the very Flames, where many of them perished. And when the Fort was thoroughly Fired, Command was given, that all should fall off and surround the Fort; which was readily attended by all; only one Arthur Smith being so wounded that he could not move out of the Place, who was happily espied by Lieutenant Bull, and by him rescued.

The Fire was kindled on the North East Side to windward; which did swiftly over-run the Fort, to the extream Amazement of the Enemy, and great Rejoycing of our selves. Some of them climbing to the Top of the Pallizado; others of them running into the very Flames; many of them gathering to windward, lay pelting at us with their Arrows; and we repayed them with our small Shot: Others of the Stoutest issued forth, as we did guess, to the Number of Forty, who perished by the Sword.

What I have formerly said, is according to my own Knowledge, there being sufficient living Testimony to every Particular.

But in reference to Captain Underhill and his Parties acting in this Assault, I can only intimate as we were informed by some of themselves immediately after the Fight, Thus They Marching up to the Entrance on the South West Side, there made some Pause; a valiant, resolute Gentleman, one Mr. Hodge, stepping towards the Gate, saying; If we may not Enter, wherefore came we here; and immediately endeavoured to Enter; but was opposed by a sturdy Indian which did impede his Entrance; but the Indian being slain by himself and Sergeant Davis, Mr. Hedge Entred the Fort with some others; but the Fort being on Fire, the Smoak and Flames were so violent that they were constrained to desert the Fort.

Thus were they now at their Wits End, who not many Hours before exalted themselves in their great Pride, threatning and resolving the utter Ruin and Destruction of all the English, Exulting and Rejoycing with Songs and Dances: But God was above them, who laughed his Enemies and the Enemies of his People to Scorn, making them as a fiery Oven: Thus were the Stout Hearted spoiled, having slept their last Sleep, and none of their Men could find their Hands: Thus did the Lord judge among the Heathen, filling the Place with dead Bodies!

And here we may see the just Judgment of God, in sending even the very Night before this Assault, One hundred and fifty Men from their other Fort, to join with them of that Place, who were designed as some of themselves reported to go forth against the English, at that very Instant when this heavy Stroak came upon them where they perished with their Fellows. So that the Mischief they intended to us, came upon their own Pate: They were taken in their own snare, and we through Mercy escaped. And thus in little more than one Hour's space was their impregnable Fort with themselves utterly Destroyed, to the Number of six or seven Hundred, as some of themselves confessed. There were only seven taken captive, and about seven escaped.

Of the English, there were two Slain outright, and about twenty Wounded: Some Fainted by reason of the sharpness of the Weather, it being a cool Morning, and the want of such Comforts and Necessaries as were needful in such a Case; especially our Chyrurgeon [surgeon] was much wanting, whom we left with our Barks in Narragansett Bay, who had Order there to remain until the Night before our intended Assault.

And thereupon grew many Difficulties: Our Provision and Munition near spent; we in the enemies Country, who did far exceed us in Number, being much enraged: all our Indians, except Onkos, deserting us; our Pinnaces at a great distance from us, and when they would come we were uncertain.

But as we were consulting what Course to take, it pleased God to discover our Vessels to us before a fair Gale of Wind, sailing into Pequot Harbour, to our great Rejoycing.

We had no sooner discovered our Vessels, but immediately came up the Enemy from the other Fort; Three Hundred or more as we conceived. The Captain lead out a file or two of Men to Skirmish with them, chiefly to try what temper they were of, who put them to a stand: we being

much encouraged thereat, presently prepared to March towards our Vessels: Four or Five of our Men were so wounded that they must be carried with the Arms of twenty more. We also being faint, were constrained to put four to one Man, with the Arms of the rest that were wounded to others; so that we had not above forty Men free: at length we hired several Indians, who eased us of that Burthen, in carrying of our wounded Men. And Marching about one quarter of a Mile; the Enemy coming up to the Place where the Fort was, and beholding what was done, stamped and tore the Hair from their Heads: And after a little space, came mounting down the Hill upon us, in a full career, as if they would over run us; But when they came within Shot, the Rear faced about, giving Fire upon them: Some of them being Shot, made the rest more wary: Yet they held on running to and fro, and shooting their Arrows at Random. There was at the Foot of the Hill a small Brook, where we rested and refreshed our selves, having by that time taught them a little more Manners than to disturb us.

We then Marched on towards Pequot Harbour; and falling upon several Wigwams, burnt them: The Enemy still following us in the Rear, which was to windward, though to little purpose; yet some of them lay in Ambush behind Rocks and Trees, often shooting at us, yet through Mercy touched not one of us; And as we came to any Swamp or Thicket, we made some Shot to clear the Passage. Some of them fell with our Shot; and probably more might, but for want of Munition; But when any of them fell, our Indians would give a great Shout, and then would they take so much Courage as to fetch their Heads. And thus we continued, until we came within two Miles of Pequot Harbour; where the Enemy gathered together and left us; we Marching on to the Top of an Hill adjoining to the Harbour, with our Colours flying; having left our Drum at the Place of our Rendezvous the Night before: We seeing our Vessels there Riding at Anchor, to our great Rejoycing, and came to the Water-Side, we there sat down in Quiet.

The colonists' next—and culminating—action was against surviving Pequot, who had taken up a position in a swamp near New Haven.

About a Fortnight after our Return home, which was about one Month after the Fight at Mistick, there Arrived in Pequot River several Vessels from the Massachusetts, Captain Israel Stoughton being Commander in Chief; and with him about One hundred and twenty Men; being sent by that Colony to pursue the War against the Pequots: The Enemy being all fled before they came, except some few Straglers, who were surprised by the Moheags and others of the Indians, and by them delivered to the Massachusetts Soldiers.

Connecticut Colony being informed hereof, sent forthwith forty Men, Captain Mason being Chief Commander; with some other Gent, to meet those of the Massachusetts, to consider what was necessary to be attended respecting the future: Who meeting with them of the Massachusetts in Pequot Harbour; after some time of consultation, concluded to pursue those Pequots that were fled towards Manhatance [Manhattan], and so forthwith Marched after them, discovering several Places where they Rendezvoused and lodged not far distant from their several Removes; making but little haste, by reason of their Children, and want of Provision; being forced to dig for Clams, and to procure such other things as the Wilderness afforded: Our Vessels sailing along by the Shore. In about the space of three Days we all Arrived at New Haven Harbour, then called Quinnypiag. And seeing a great Smoak in the Woods not far distant, we supposing some of the Pequots our Enemies might be there; we hastened ashore, but quickly discovered them to be Connecticut Indians. Then we returned aboard our Vessels, where we stayed some short time, having sent a Pequot Captive upon discovery, we named him Luz; who brought us Tydings of the Enemy, which proved true: so faithful was he to us, though against his own Nation. Such was the Terror of the English upon them; that a Moheage [Mohegan] Indian

named Jack Eatow going ashore at that time, met with three Pequots, took two of them and brought them aboard.

We then hastened our march towards the Place where the Enemy was: And coming into a Corn Field, several of the English espyed some Indians, who fled from them: They pursued them; and coming to the Top of an Hill, saw several Wigwams just opposite, only a Swamp intervening, which was almost divided in two Parts. Sergeant Palmer hastening with about twelve Men who were under his Command to surround the smaller Part of the Swamp, that so He might prevent the Indians flying; Ensign Danport [Davenport], Sergeant Jeffries &c, entering the Swamp, intended to have gone to the Wigwams, were there set upon by several Indians, who in all probability were deterred by Sergeant Palmer. In this Skirmish the English slew but few; two or three of themselves were Wounded: The rest of the English coming up, the Swamp was Surrounded.

Our Council being called, and the Question propounded, How we should proceed, Captain Patrick advised that we should cut down the Swamp; there being many Indian Hatchets taken, Captain Traske concurring with him; but was opposed by others: Then we must pallizado the Swamp; which was also opposed: Then they would have a Hedge made like those of Gotham; all which was judged by some almost impossible, and to no purpose, and that for several Reasons, and therefore strongly opposed. But some others advised to force the Swamp, having time enough, it being about three of the Clock in the Afternoon: But that being opposed, it was then propounded to draw up our Men close to the Swamp, which would much have lessened the Circumference; and with all to fill up the open Passages with Bushes, that so we might secure them until the Morning, and then we might consider further about it. But neither of these would pass; so different were our Apprehensions; which was very grievous to some of us, who concluded the Indians would make an Escape in the Night, as easily they might and did: We keeping at a great distance, what better could be expected? Yet Captain Mason took Order that the Narrow in the Swamp should be cut through; which did much shorten our Leaguer. It was resolutely performed by Serjeant Davis.

We being loth to destroy Women and Children, as also the Indians belonging to that Place; whereupon Mr. Tho. Stanton a Man well acquainted with Indian Language and Manners, offered his Service to go into the Swamp and treat with them: To which we were somewhat backward, by reason of some Hazard and Danger he might be exposed unto: But his importunity prevailed: Who going to them, did in a short time return to us, with near Two Hundred old Men, Women and Children; who delivered themselves, to the Mercy of the English. And so Night drawing on, we beleaguered them as strongly as we could. About half an Hour before Day, the Indians that were in the Swamp attempted to break through Captain Patrick's Quarters; but were beaten back several times; they making a great Noise, as their Manner is at such Times, it sounded round about our Leaguer: Whereupon Captain Mason sent Sergeant Stares to inquire into the Cause, and also to assist if need required; Capt. Traske coming also in to their Assistance: But the Tumult growings to a very great Heighth, we raised our Siege; and Marching up to the Place, at a Turning of the Swamp the Indiana were forcing out upon us; but we sent them back by our small Shot.

We waiting a little for a second Attempt; the Indians in the mean time facing about, pressed violently upon Captain Patrick, breaking through his Quarters, and so escaped. They were about sixty or seventy as we were informed. We afterwards searched the Swamp, and found but few Slain. The Captives we took were about One Hundred and Eighty; whom we divided, intending to keep them as Servants, but they could not endure that Yoke; few of them continuing any considerable time with their masters.

Thus did the Lord scatter his Enemies with his strong Arm! The Pequots now became a Prey to all Indians. Happy were they that could bring in their Heads to the English: Of which there came almost daily to Winsor, or Hartford. But the Pequots growing weary hereof, sent some of the Chief that survived to mediate with the English; offering that If they might but enjoy their Lives, they would become the English Vassals, to dispose of them as they pleased. Which was granted them. Whereupon Onkos and Myantonimo were sent for; who with the Pequots met at Hartford. The Pequots being demanded, how many of them were then living? Answered, about One Hundred and Eighty, or two Hundred. There were then given to Onkos, Sachem of Monheag, Eighty; to Myantonimo, Sachem of Narragansett, Eighty; and to Nynigrett, Twenty, when he should satisfy for a Mare of Edward Pomroye's killed by his Men. The Pequots were then bound by Covenant, That none should inhabit their native Country, nor should any of them be called Pequots any more, but Moheags and Narragansetts forever.

The colonists showed no mercy to the vanquished.

[When a number of Pequot survivors] settled at Pawcatuck, a Place in Pequot Country, contrary to their late Covenant and Agreement with the English, [Connecticut authorities] sent out forty Men under the command of Captain John Mason, to supplant them, by burning their Wigwams and bringing away their Corn, except they would desert the Place: Onkos with about One Hundred of his Men in twenty Canoes, going also to assist in the Service. As we sailed into Pawcatuck-Bay We met with three of those Indians, whom we sent to inform the rest with the end of our coming, and also that we desired to speak with some of them: They promised speedily to return us an Answer, but never came to us more.

We ran our Vessel up into a small River, and by reason of Flatts were forced to land on the West Side; their Wigwams being on the East just opposite, where we could see the Indians running up and down Jeering of us. But we meeting with a narrow place in the River between two rocks, drew up our Indians Canoes, and got suddenly over sooner than we were expected or desired; Marching immediately up to their Wigwams; the Indians being all fled, except some old People that could not.

We were so suddenly upon them that they had not time to convey away their Goods: We viewed their Corn, whereof there was Plenty, it being their time of Harvest: And coming down to the Water Side to our Pinnace with half of Onkos's his Men, the rest being plundering the Wigwams; we looking towards a Hill not far remote, we espyed about sixty Indians running towards us; we supposing they were our absent Men, the Moheags that were with us not speaking one word, nor moving towards them until the other came within thirty or forty paces of them; then they ran and met them and fell on pell mell striking and cutting with Bows, Hatchets, Knives, &c. after their feeble Manner: Indeed it did hardly deserve the Name of Fighting. We then endeavoured to get between them and the Woods, that so we might prevent their flying; which they perceiving, endeavoured speedily to get off under the beach: we made no Shot at them, nor any hostile Attempt upon them. Only seven of them who were Nynigrett's Men, were taken. Some of them growing very outrageous, whom We intended to have made shorter by the Head; and being about to put it in Execution; one Otash a Sachem of Narragansett, Brother to Myantonimo stepping forth, told the Captain, They were his Brother's Men, and that he was a Friend to the English, and if he would spare their Lives we should have as many Murtherer's Heads in lieu of them which should be delivered to the English. We considering that there was no Blood shed as yet, and that it tended to Peace and Mercy, granted his Desire; and so delivered them to Onkos to secure them until his Engagement was performed, because our Prison had been very much pestered with such Creatures.

We then drew our Bark into a Creek, the better to defend her; for there were many Hundreds, within five Miles waiting upon us. There we Quartered that Night: In the Morning as soon as it was Light there appeared in Arms at least Three Hundred Indians on the other Side the Creek: Upon which we stood to our Arms; which they perceiving, some of them fled, others crept behind the Rocks and Trees, not one of them to be seen. We then called to them, saying, We desired to speak with them, and that we would down our Arms for that end: Whereupon they stood up: We then informed them, That the Pequots had violated their Promise with the English, in that they were not there to inhabit, and that we were sent to supplant them: They answered saying, The Pequots were good Men, their Friends, and they would Fight for them, and protect them: At which we were somewhat moved, and told them, It was not far to the Head of the Creek where we would meet them, and then they might try what they could do in that Respect.

They then replied, That they would not Fight with English Men, for they were Spirits, but would Fight with Onkos. We replyed, That we thought it was too early for them to Fight, but they might take their opportunity; we should be burning Wigwams, and carrying Corn aboard all that Day. And presently beating up our Drum, we Fired the Wigwams in their View: And as we Marched, there were two Indians standing upon a Hill jeering and reviling of us: Mr. Thomas Stanton our Interpreter, Marching at Liberty, desired to make a Shot at them; the Captain demanding of the Indians. What they were? Who said, They were Murtherers: Then the said Stanton having leave, let fly, Shot one of them through both his Thighs; which was to our Wonderment, it being at such a vast distance.

We then loaded our Bark with Corn; and our Indians their Canoes: And thirty more which we had taken, with Kittles, Trays, Mats, and other Indian Luggage, That Night we went all aboard, and set Sail homeward: It pleased God in a short Time to bring us all in safety to the Place of our Abode; although we strook and stuck upon a

Rock. The Way and Manner how God dealt with us in our Delivery was very Remarkable; The Story would be somewhat long to trouble you with at this time; and therefore I shall forbear.

Thus we may see, How the Face of God is set against them that do Evil, to cut off the Remembrance of them from the Earth. Our Tongue shall talk of thy Righteousness all the Day long; for they are confounded, they are brought to Shame that sought our Hurt! Blessed be the Lord God of Israel, who only doth wondrous Things; and blessed be his holy Name for ever: Let the whole Earth be filled with his Glory! Thus the Lord was pleased to smite our Enemies in the hinder Parts, and to give us their Land for an Inheritance: Who remembred us in our low Estate, and redeemed us out of our Enemies Hands: Let us therefore praise the Lord for his Goodness and his wonderful Works to the Children of Men!

Perhaps the greatest hardship of wilderness warfare in the 17th century was logistical, especially during the earliest years of the English colonies, which struggled even in the best of times to maintain a meager subsistence.

OUR Commons [rations] were very short, there being a general scarcity throughout the Colony of all sorts of Provision, it being upon our first Arrival at the Place. We had but one Pint of strong Liquors among us in our whole March, but what the Wilderness afforded; (the Bottle of Liquor being in my Hand.) and when it was empty, the very smelling to the Bottle would presently recover such as Fainted away, which happened by the extremity of the Heat: And thus we Marched on in an uncoath and unknown Path to the English, though much frequented by Indians. And was not the Finger of God in all this? By his special Providence to lead us along in the Way we should go: Nay though we knew not where their Forts were, how far it was to them, nor the Way that led to them, but by what we had from our Indian Guides; whom we could not confide in, but looked at them as uncertain:

And yet notwithstanding all our Doubts, we should be brought on the very fittest Season; nay and which is yet more, that we should be carried in our March among a treacherous and perfidious People, yea in our allodgment so near the Enemy, all Night in so populous a Country, and not the least notice of us; seemeth somewhat strange, and more than ordinary: Nay that we should come to their very Doors: What shall I say: God was pleased to hide us in the Hollow of his Hand; I still remember a Speech of Mr. Hooker at our going aboard; That they should be Bread for us. And thus when the Lord turned the Captivity of his People, and turned the Wheel upon their Enemies; we were like Men in a Dream; then was our Mouth filled with Laughter, and our Tongues with Singing; thus we may say the Lord hath done great Things for us among the Heathen, whereof we are glad. Praise ye the Lord!

A devout man, Mason was quick to see the hand of Providence in the English victory over the Pequot.

I shall mention two or three special Providences that God was pleased to vouchsafe to Particular Men; viz. two Men, being one Man's Servants, namely, John Dier and Thomas Stiles, were both of them Shot in the Knots of their Handkerchiefs, being about their Necks, and received no Hurt. Lieutenant Seeley was Shot in the Eyebrow with a flat headed Arrow, the Point turning downwards: I pulled it out myself.

Lieutenant Bull had an Arrow Shot into a hard piece of Cheese, having no other Defence: Which may verify the old Saying, A little Armour would serve if a Man knew where to place it. Many such Providences happened; some respecting my self; but since there is none that Witness to them, I shall forbear to mention them.

Source: Mason, John. *A Brief History of the Pequot War: Especially of the Memoirable Taking of Their Fort at Mistick in Connecticut in 1637.* 1736. Facsimile of the 1st ed., New York: Readex Microprint, 1966.

Excerpts from *Narrative of the Pequot War (Relation of the Pequot Warres)*

Lion Gardiner
Written 1660; published 1809, 1833

Lion Gardiner (also spelled Gardener; 1599–1663) had the distinction of founding the first English settlement in what became New York State. Born in England in 1599, he was a professional military engineer in the service of the prince of Orange in the Netherlands when the Connecticut Company hired him in 1635 to oversee construction of fortifications for its colony in New England. After completing this work, he took command of Fort Saybrook at the mouth of the Connecticut River and served in this capacity during the Pequot War. His Relation of the Pequot Warres *was written in 1660 but did not see the light of day until 1809. It was first fully published in 1833 as* Narrative of the Pequot War. *The extant edition of the* Narrative *uses the alternative spelling of Gardiner's name, Gardener. The excerpts that follow retain all original spellings.*

Gardiner objected to picking a fight with the Pequot because he believed that the Connecticut frontier outposts, including Fort Saybrook, would be imperiled.

In the year 1635, I, Lion Gardener, Engineer and Master of works of Fortification in the legers of the Prince of Orange, in the Low Countries, through the persuasion of Mr. John Davenport, Mr. Hugh Peters with some other well-affected Englishmen of Rotterdam, I made an agreement with the forenamed Mr. Peters for £100 per annum, for four years, to serve the company of patentees, namely, the Lord Say, the Lord Brooks [Brook] Sir Arthur Hazilrig, Sir Mathew Bonnington [Bonighton?], Sir Richard Saltingstone [Saltonstall], Esquire Fenwick, and the rest of their company, [I say] I was to serve them only in the drawing, ordering and making of a city, towns or forts of defence. And so I came from Holland to London, and from thence to New-England, where I was appointed to attend such orders as Mr. John Winthrop, Esquire, the present Governor of Conectecott, was to appoint, whether at Pequit [Pequot] river, or Conectecott, and that we should choose a place both for the convenience of a good harbour, and also for capableness and fitness for fortification. But I landing at Boston the latter end of November, the aforesaid Mr. Winthrop had sent before one Lieut. Gibbons, Sergeant Willard, with some carpenters, to take possession of the River's mouth, where they began to build houses against the Spring; we expecting, according to promise, that there would have come from England to us 300 able men, whereof 200 should attend fortification, 50 to till the ground, and 50 to build houses. But our great expectation at the River's mouth, came only to two men, viz. Mr. Fenwick, and his man, who came with Mr. Hugh Peters, and Mr. Oldham and Thomas Stanton, bringing with them some Otter-skin coats, and Beaver, and skeins of wampum, which the Pequits had sent for a present, because the English had required those Pequits [Pequot] that had killed a Virginean, one Capt. Stone, with his Bark's crew, in Conectecott River, for they said they would have their lives and not their presents; then I answered, Seeing you will take Mr. Winthrop to the Bay to see his wife, newly brought to bed of her first child, and though you say he shall return, yet I know if you make war with these Pequits, he will not come hither again, for I know you will keep yourselves safe, as you think, in the Bay, but myself, with these few, you will leave at the stake to be roasted, or for hunger to be starved, for Indian corn is now 12s. per bushel, and we have but three acres planted, and if they will now make war for a Virginian and expose us to the Indians, whose mercies are cruelties, they, I say, they love the Virginians better than us: for, have they stayed these four or five years, and will they begin now, we being so few in the River, and have scarce holes to put our heads in? I pray ask the Magistrates in the Bay if they have forgot what I said to them when I returned from Salem? For Mr. Winthrop, Mr. Haines, Mr. Dudley, Mr. Ludlow, Mr. Humfry, Mr. Belingam

[Bellingham], Mr. Coddington, and Mr. Nowell; these entreated me to go with Mr. Humfry and Mr. Peters to view the country, to see how fit it was for fortification. And I told them that Nature had done more than half the work already, and I thought no foreign potent enemy would do them any hurt, but one that was near. They asked me who that was, and I said it was Capt. Hunger that threatened them most, for, (said I,) War is like a three-footed Stool, want one foot and down comes all; and these three feet are men, victuals, and munition[s], therefore, seeing in peace you are like to be famished, what will or can be done if war? Therefore I think, said I, it will be best only to fight against Capt. Hunger, and let fortification alone awhile; and if need hereafter require it, I can come to do you any service: and they all liked my saying well. Entreat them to rest awhile, till we get more strength here about us, and that we hear where the seat of the war will be, may approve of it, and provide for it, for I had but twenty-four in all, men, women, and boys and girls, and not food for them for two months, unless we saved our corn-field, which could not possibly be if they came to war, for it is two miles from our home.

Mr. Winthrop, Mr. Fenwick, and Mr. Peters promised me that they would do their utmost endeavour to persuade the [Massachusetts] Bay-men to desist from war a year or two, till we could be better provided for it; and then the Pequit Sachem was sent for, and the present returned, but full sore against my will. So they three returned to Boston, and two or three days after came an Indian from Pequit, whose name was Cocommithus, who had lived at Plimoth, and could speak good English; he desired that Mr. Steven [Stephen] Winthrop would go to Pequit with an £100 worth of trucking cloth and all other trading ware, for they knew that we had a great cargo of goods of Mr. Pincheon's, and Mr. Steven Winthrop had the disposing of it. And he said that if he would come he might put off all his goods, and the Pequit Sachem would give him two horses that had been there a great while. So I sent the Shallop, with Mr.

Steven Winthrop, Sergeant Tille [Tilly], (whom we called afterward Sergeant Kettle, because he put the kettle on his head,) and Thomas Hurlbut and three men more, charging them that they should ride in the middle of the river, and not go ashore until they had done all their trade, and that Mr. Steven Winthrop should stand in the hold of the boat, having their guns by them, and swords by their sides, the other four to be, two in the fore cuddie, and two in aft, being armed in like manner, that so they out of the loop-holes might clear the boat, if they were by the Pequits assaulted; and that they should let but one canoe come aboard at once, with no more but four Indians in her, and when she had traded then another, and that they should lie no longer there than one day, and at night to go out of the river; and if they brought the two horses, to take them in at a clear piece of land at the mouth of the River, two of them go ashore to help the horses in, and the rest stand ready with their guns in their hands, if need were, to defend them from the Pequits, for I durst not trust them. So they went and found but little trade, and they having forgotten what I charged them, Thomas Hurlbut and one more went ashore to boil the kettle, and Thomas Hurlbut stepping into the Sachem's wigwam, not far from the shore, enquiring for the horses, the Indians went out of the wigwam, and Wincumbone, his mother's sister, was then the great Pequit Sachem's wife, who made signs to him that he should be gone, for they would cut off his head; which, when he perceived, he drew his sword and ran to the others, and got aboard, and immediately came abundance of Indians to the water-side and called them to come ashore, but they immediately set sail and came home, and this caused me to keep watch and ward, for I saw they plotted our destruction.

And suddenly after came Capt. Endecott, Capt. Turner, and Capt. Undrill [Underhill], with a company of soldiers, well fitted, to Seabrook and made that place their rendezvous or seat of war, and that to my great grief, for, said I, you come hither to raise these wasps about my ears, and then you will take wing and flee away; but when I had seen their commission I wondered, and made many allegations against the manner of it, but go they did to Pequit, and as they came without acquainting any of us in the River with it, so they went against our will, for I knew that I should lose our corn-field; then I entreated them to hear what I would say to them, which was this: Sirs, Seeing you will go, I pray you, if you don't load your Barks with Pequits, load them with corn, for that is now gathered with them, and dry, ready to put into their barns, and both you and we have need of it, and I will send my shallop and hire this Dutchman's boat, there present, to go with you, and if you cannot attain your end of the Pequits, yet you may load your barks with corn, which will be welcome to Boston and to me: But they said they had no bags to load them with, then said I, here is three dozen of new bags, you shall have thirty of them, and my shallop to carry them, and six of them my men shall use themselves, for I will with the Dutchmen send twelve men well provided; and I desired them to divide the men into three parts, viz. two parts to stand without the corn, and to defend the other one third part, that carried the corn to the water-side, till they have loaded what they can. And the men there in arms, when the rest are aboard, shall in order go aboard, the rest that are aboard shall with their arms clear the shore, if the Pequits do assault them in the rear, and then, when the General shall display his colours, all to set sail together.

To this motion they all agreed, and I put the three dozen of bags aboard my shallop, and away they went, and demanded the Pequit Sachem to come into parley. But it was returned for answer, that he was from home, but within three hours he would come; and so from three to six, and thence to nine, there came none. But the Indians came without arms to our men, in great numbers, and they talked with my men, whom they knew; but in the end, at a word given, they all on a sudden ran away from our men, as they stood in rank and file, and not an Indian more was to be seen: and all this while before, they carried all their stuff away, and thus was that great

parley ended. Then they displayed their colours, and beat their drums, burnt some wigwams and some heaps of corn, and my men carried as much aboard as they could, but the army went aboard, leaving my men ashore, which ought to have marched aboard first. But they all set sail, and my men were pursued by the Indians, and they hurt some of the Indians, and two of them came home wounded. The Bay-men killed not a man, save that one Kichomiquim [Cutshamequin], an Indian Sachem of the Bay, killed a Pequit; and thus began the war between the Indians and us in these parts.

So my men being come home, and having brought a pretty quantity of corn with them, they informed me (both Dutch and English) of all passages. I was glad of the corn. After this I immediately took men and went to our corn-field, to gather our corn, appointing others to come about with the shallop and fetch it, and left five lusty men in the strong-house, with long guns, which house I had built for the defence of the corn. Now these men not regarding the charge I had given them, three of them went a mile from the house a fowling; and having loaded themselves with fowl they returned. But the Pequits let them pass first, till they had loaded themselves, but at their return they arose out of their ambush, and shot them all three; one of them escaped through the corn, shot through the leg, the other two they tormented. Then the next day I sent the shallop to fetch the five men, and the rest of the corn that was broken down, and they found but three, as is above said, and when they had gotten that they left the rest; and as soon as they were gone a little way from shore, they saw the house on fire. Now so soon as the boat came home, and brought us this bad news, old Mr. Michell was very urgent with me to lend him the boat to fetch hay home from the Six-mile Island, but I told him they were too few men, for his four men could but carry the hay aboard, and one must stand in the boat to defend them, and they must have two more at the foot of the Rock with their guns, to keep the Indians from running down upon them. And in the first place, before they carry any of the cocks of hay, to scour the meadow with their three dogs, to march all abreast from the lower end up to the Rock and if they found the meadow clear, then to load their hay; but this was also neglected, for they all went ashore and fell to carrying off their hay, and the Indians presently rose out of the long grass, and killed three, and took the brother of Mr. Michell, who is the minister of Cambridge, and roasted him alive; and so they served a shallop of his, coming down the river in the Spring, having two men, one whereof they killed at Six-mile Island, the other came down drowned to us ashore at our doors, with an arrow shot into his eye through his head.

In the 22d of February, I went out with ten men, and three dogs, half a mile from the house, to burn the weeds, leaves and reeds, upon the neck of land, because we had felled twenty timber-trees, which we were to roll to the water-side to bring home, every man carrying a length of match with brimstone-matches with him to kindle the fire withal. But when we came to the small of the Neck, the weeds burning, I having before this set two sentinels on the small of the Neck, I called to the men that were burning the reeds to come away, but they would not until they had burnt up the rest of their matches. Presently there starts up four Indians out of the fiery reeds, but ran away, I calling to the rest of our men to come away out of the marsh. Then Robert Chapman and Thomas Hurlbut, being sentinels, called to me, saying there came a number of Indians out of the other side of the marsh. Then I went to stop them, that they should not get the wood-land; but Thomas Hurlbut cried out to me that some of the men did not follow me, for Thomas Rumble and Arthur Branch, threw down their two guns and ran away; then the Indians shot two of them that were in the reeds, and sought to get between us and home, but durst not come before us, but kept us in a half-moon, we retreating and exchanging many a shot, so that Thomas Hurlbut was shot almost through the thigh, John Spencer in the back, into his kidneys, myself into the thigh, two more were shot dead. But in our retreat I kept Hurlbut and Spencer still before us, we defending ourselves with our naked swords, or else they had taken us all alive, so that the two sore wounded men, by our slow retreat, got home with their guns, when our two sound men ran away and left their guns behind them. But when I saw the cowards that left us, I resolved to let them draw lots which of them should be hanged, for the articles did hang up in the hall for them to read, and they knew they had been published long before. But at the intercession of old Mr. Michell, Mr. Higgisson [Higginson], and Mr. Pell, I did forbear.

Within a few days after, when I had cured myself of my wound, I went out with eight men to get some fowl for our relief, and found the guns that were thrown away, and the body of one man shot through, the arrow going in at the right side, the head sticking fast, half through a rib on the left side, which I took out and cleansed it, and presumed to send to the Bay, because they had said that the arrows of the Indians were of no force.

Anthony Dike, master of a bark, having his bark at Rhode-Island in the winter, was sent by Mr. Vane, then Governor. Anthony came to Rhode-Island by land, and from thence he came with his bark to me with a letter, wherein was desired that I should consider and prescribe the best way I could to quell these Pequits, which I also did, and with my letter sent the man's rib as a token. A few days after, came Thomas Stanton down the River, and staying for a wind, while he was there came a troop of Indians within musket shot, laying themselves and their arms down behind a little rising hill and two great trees; which I perceiving, called the carpenter whom I had shewed how to charge and level a gun, and that he should put two cartridges of musket bullets into two sakers guns that lay about; and we levelled them against the place, and I told him that he must look towards me, and when he saw me wave my hat above my head he should give fire to both the guns; then presently came three Indians, creeping out and calling to us to speak with us: and I was glad that Thomas Stanton was there, and I sent six men down by the Garden Pales to look that none should come under the hill behind us; and having placed the rest in places convenient closely, Thomas and I with my sword, pistol and carbine, went ten or twelve pole without the gate to parley with them. And when the six men came to the Garden Pales, at the corner, they found a great number of Indians creeping behind the fort, or betwixt us and home, but they ran away.

Now I had said to Thomas Stanton, Whatsoever they say to you, tell me first, for we will not answer them directly to any thing, for I know not the mind of the rest of the English. So they came forth, calling us nearer to them, and we them nearer to us. But I would not let Thomas go any further than the great stump of a tree, and I stood by him; then they asked who we were, and he answered, Thomas and Lieutenant. But they said he lied, for I was shot with many arrows; and so I was, but my buff coat preserved me, only one hurt me. But when I spake to them they knew my voice, for one of them had dwelt three months with us, but ran away when the Bay-men came first. Then they asked us if we would fight with Niantecut Indians, or they were our friends and came to trade with us. We said we knew not the Indians one from another, and therefore would trade with none. Then they said, Have you fought enough? We said we knew not yet. Then they asked if we did use to kill women and children? We said they should see that hereafter.

So they were silent a small space, and then they said, We are Pequits, and have killed Englishmen, and can kill them as mosquetoes, and we will go to Conectecott and kill men, women, and children, and we will take away the horses, cows and hogs.

When Thomas Stanton had told me this, he prayed me to shoot that rogue, for, said he, he hath an Englishman's coat on, and saith that he hath killed three, and these other four have their cloathes on their backs. I said, No, it is not the manner of a parley, but have patience and I shall fit them ere they go. Nay, now or never, said he; so when he could get no other answer but this

last, I bid him tell them that they should not go to Conectecott, for if they did kill all the men, and take all the rest as they said, it would do them no good, but hurt, for English women are lazy, and can't do their work; horses and cows will spoil your corn-fields, and the hogs their clam-banks, and so undo them: then I pointed to our great house, and bid him tell them there lay twenty pieces of trucking cloth, of Mr. Pincheon's, with hoes, hatchets, and all manner of trade, they were better fight still with us, and so get all that, and then go up the river after they had killed all us.

Having heard this, they were mad as dogs, and ran away; then when they came to the place from whence they came, I waved my hat about my head, and the two great guns went off, so that there was a great hubbub amongst them.

Then two days after, came down Capt. Mason, and Sergeant Seely, with five men more, to see how it was with us; and whilst they were there, came down a Dutch boat, telling us the Indians had killed fourteen English, for by that boat I had sent up letters to Conectecott, what I heard, and what I thought, and how to prevent that threatened danger, and received back again rather a scoff, than any thanks, for my care and pains. But as I wrote, so it fell out to my great grief and theirs, for the next, or second day after, (as Major Mason well knows,) came down a great many canoes, going down the creek beyond the marsh, before the fort, many of them having white shirts; then I commanded the carpenter whom I had shewed to level great guns, to put in two round shot into the two sackers, and we levelled them at a certain place, and I stood to bid him give fire, when I thought the canoe would meet the bullet, and one of them took off the nose of a great canoe wherein the two maids were, that were taken by the Indians, whom I redeemed and clothed, for the Dutchmen, whom I sent to fetch them, brought them away almost naked from Pequit, they putting on their own linen jackets to cover their nakedness; and though the redemption cost me ten pounds, I am yet to have thanks for my care and charge about them: these things are known to Major Mason.

Then came from the Bay Mr. Tille, with a permit to go up to Harford [Hartford], and coming ashore he saw a paper nailed up over the gate, whereon was written, that no boat or bark should pass the fort, but that they come to an anchor first, that I might see whether they were armed and manned sufficiently, and they were not to land any where after they passed the fort till they came to Wethersfield; and this I did because Mr. Mitchel had lost a shallop before coming down from Wethersfield, with three men well armed. This Mr. Tille gave me ill language for my presumption, (as he called it), with other expressions too long here to write. When he had done, I bid him go to his warehouse, which he had built before I come, to fetch his goods from thence, for I would watch no longer over it. So he, knowing nothing, went and found his house burnt, and one of Mr. Plum's with others, and he told me to my face that I had caused it to be done; but Mr. Higgisson, Mr. Pell, Thomas Hurlbut and John Green can witness that the same day that our house was burnt at Cornfield-point I went with Mr. Higgisson, Mr. Pell, and four men more, broke open a door and took a note of all that was in the house and gave it to Mr. Higgisson to keep, and so brought all the goods to our house, and delivered it all to them again when they came for it, without any penny of charge. Now the very next day after I had taken the goods out, before the sun was quite down, and we all together in the great hall, all them houses were on fire in one instant. The Indians ran away, but I would not follow them.

Now when Mr. Tille had received all his goods I said unto him, I thought I had deserved for my honest care both for their bodies and goods of those that passed by here, at the least better language, and am resolved to order such malepert persons as you are; therefore I wish you and also charge you to observe that which you have read at the gate, 'tis my duty to God, my masters, and my love I bear to you all which is the ground of this, had you but eyes to see it; but you will not

till you feel it. So he went up the river, and when he came down again to his place, which I called Tille's folly, now called Tille's point, in our sight in despite, having a fair wind he came to an anchor, and with one man more went ashore, discharged his gun, and the Indians fell upon him, and killed the other, and carried him alive over the river in our sight, before my shallop could come to them; for immediately I sent seven men to fetch the Pink down, or else it had been taken and three men more. So they brought her down, and I sent Mr. Higgisson and Mr. Pell aboard to take an invoice of all that was in the vessel, that nothing might be lost.

Two days after came to me, as I had written to Sir Henerie Vane, then Governor of the Bay, I say came to me Capt. Undrill [Underhill], with twenty lusty men, well armed, to stay with me two months, or 'till something should be done about the Pequits. He came at the charge of my masters. Soon after came down from Harford Maj. Mason, Lieut. Seely, accompanied with Mr. Stone and eighty Englishmen, and eighty Indians, with a commission from Mr. Ludlow and Mr. Steel, and some others; these came to go fight with the Pequits. But when Capt. Undrill [Underhill] and I had seen their commission, we both said they were not fitted for such a design, and we said to Maj. Mason we wondered he would venture himself, being no better fitted; and he said the Magistrates could not or would not send better; then we said that none of our men should go with them, neither should they go unless we, that were bred soldiers from our youth, could see some likelihood to do better than the Bay-men with their strong commission last year.

Then I asked them how they durst trust the Mohegin [Mohegan] Indians, who had but that year come from the Pequits. They said they would trust them, for they could not well go without them for want of guides. Yea, said I, but I will try them before a man of ours shall go with you or them; and I called for Uncas and said unto him, You say you will help Maj. Mason, but I will first see it, therefore send you now twenty men to the Bass river, for there went yesternight six

Indians in a canoe thither; fetch them now dead or alive, and then you shall go with Maj. Mason, else not.

So he sent his men who killed four, brought one a traitor to us alive, whose name was Kiswas, and one ran away. And I gave him fifteen yards of trading cloth on my own charge, to give unto his men according to their desert. And having staid there five or six days before we could agree, at last we old soldiers agreed about the way and act, and took twenty insufficient men from the eighty that came from Harford [Hartford] and sent them up again in a shallop, and Capt. Undrill [Underhill] with twenty of the lustiest of our men went in their room, and I furnished them with such things as they wanted, and sent Mr. Pell, the sergeon, with them; and the Lord God blessed their design and way, so that they returned with victory to the glory of God, and honour of our nation, having slain three hundred, burnt their fort, and taken many prisoners.

Then came to me an Indian called Wequash, and I by Mr. Higgisson inquired of him, how many of the Pequits were yet alive that had helped to kill Englishmen; and he declared them to Mr. Higgisson, and he writ them down, as may appear by his own hand here enclosed, and I did as therein is written. Then three days after the fight came Waiandance, next brother to the old Sachem of Long Island, and having been recommended to me by Maj. Gibbons, he came to know if we were angry with all Indians. I answered No, but only with such as had killed Englishmen. He asked me whether they that lived upon Long-Island might come to trade with us. I said No, nor we with them, for if I should send my boat to trade for corn, and you have Pequits with you, and if my boat should come into some creek by reason of bad weather, they might kill my men, and I shall think that you of Long Island have done it, and so we may kill all you for the Pequits; but if you will kill all the Pequits that come to you, and send me their heads, then I will give to you as to Weakwash [Wequash], and you shall have trade with us. Then, said he, I will go to my brother, for he is the great Sachem of all

Long Island, and if we may have peace and trade with you, we will give you tribute, as we did the Pequits. Then I said, If you have any Indians that have killed English, you must bring their heads also. He answered, not any one, and said that Gibbons, my brother, would have told you if it had been so; so he went away and did as I had said, and sent me five heads, three and four heads for which I paid them that brought them as I had promised.

Then came Capt. Stoten [Stoughton] with an army of 300 men, from the Bay, to kill the Pequits; but they were fled beyond New Haven to a swamp. I sent Wequash after them, who went by night to spy them out, and the army followed him, and found them at the great swamp, who killed some and took others, and the rest fled to the Mowhakues [Mohawk], with their Sachem. Then the Mohawks cut off his head and sent it to Hartford, for then they all feared us, but now it is otherwise, for they say to our faces that our Commissioners meeting once a year, and speak a great deal, or write a letter, and there's all, for they dare not fight. But before they went to the Great Swamp they sent Thomas Stanton over to Long Island and Shelter Island to find Pequits there, but there was none, for the Sachem Waiandance, that was at Plimoth when the Commissioners were there, and set there last, I say, he had killed so many of the Pequits, and sent their heads to me, that they durst not come there; and he and his men went with the English to the Swamp, and thus the Pequits were quelled at that time. But there was like to be a great broil between Miantenomie [Miantunnomoh] and Unchus [Uncas] who should have the rest of the Pequits, but we meditated between them and pacified them; also Unchus challenged the Narraganset Sachem out to a single combat, but he would not fight without all his men; but they were pacified, though the old grudge remained still, as it doth appear.

In contrast to John Mason, Lion Gardiner took a dim view of the Pequot War, which he considered an undertaking of great folly.

Thus far I had written in a book, that all men and posterity might know how and why so many honest men had their blood shed, yea, and some flayed alive, others cut in pieces, and some roasted alive, only because Kichamokin [Cutshamequin], a Bay Indian, killed one Pequit; and thus far of the Pequit war, which was but a comedy in comparison of the tragedies which hath been here threatened since, and may yet come, if God do not open the eyes, ears, and hearts of some that I think are wilfully deaf and blind, and think because there is no change that the vision fails, and put the evil-threatened day far off, for say they, We are now twenty to one to what we were then, and none dare meddle with us. Oh! wo be to the pride and security which hath been the ruin of many nations, as woful experience has proved.

But I wonder, and so doth many more with me, that the Bay doth no better revenge the murdering of Mr. Oldham, an honest man of their own, seeing they were at such cost for a Virginian. The Narragansets that were at Block-Island killed him, and had, £50 of gold of his, for I saw it when he had five pieces of me, and put it up into a clout and tied it up all together, when he went away from me to Block Island; but the Narragansets had it and punched holes into it, and put it about their necks for jewels; and afterwards I saw the Dutch have some of it, which they had of the Narragansets at a small rate.

And now I find that to be true which our friend Waiandance told me many years ago, and that was this; that seeing all the plots of the Narragansets were always discovered, he said they would let us alone 'till they had destroyed Uncas, and him, and then they, with the Mowquakes and Mowhakues and the Indians beyond the Dutch, and all the Northern and Eastern Indians, would easily destroy us, man and mother's son. This have I informed the Governors of these parts, but all in vain, for I see they have done as those of Wethersfield, not regarding till they were impelled to it by blood; and thus we may be sure of the fattest of the flock are like to go first, if not

altogether, and then it will be too late to read Jer. XXV.—for drink we shall if the Lord be not the more merciful to us for our extreme pride and base security, which cannot but stink before the Lord; and we may expect this, that if there should be war again between England and Holland, our friends at the Dutch and our Dutch Englishmen would prove as true to us now, as they were when the fleet came out of England; but no more of that, a word to the wise is enough.

And now I am old, I would fain die a natural death, or like a soldier in the field, with honor, and not to have a sharp stake set in the ground, and thrust into my fundament, and to have my skin flayed off by piecemeal, and cut in pieces and bits, and my flesh roasted and thrust down my throat, as these people have done, and I know will be done to the chiefest in the country by hundreds, if God should deliver us into their hands, as justly he may for our sins. . . .

Source: Gardiner [Gardener], Lion. *Relation of the Pequot Warres.* 1660. Reprint, Hartford, Conn.: The Case, Lockwood & Brainard, 1901. Available online. Libraries at University of Nebraska-Lincoln, Electronic Texts in American Studies, 2007. URL: http://digitalcommons. unl.edu/cgi/viewcontent.cgi?article=context=etas. Accessed on February 8, 2010.

KIEFT'S WAR, 1643–1645

Korte Historiael Ende Journaels Aenteyckeninge (Short Historical and Journal Notes of Several Voyages)
Captain David Pietersz (or Pietersen) de Vries
Published 1655

Captain David Pietersz (or Pietersen) de Vries was born about 1593 in Hoorn, Holland, and took to the sea before becoming patroon (large landholder) of the trading company that founded the Zwaanendael Colony (in modern Lewes, Delaware) in 1631.

After establishing 33 colonists at Zwaanendael, Vries sailed back to Holland. He returned to visit the colony the following year, only to discover that most of the settlers had been massacred (as he learned) by Indians posing as friendly traders. Vries went on to establish patroonships (manors or small colonies) on Staten Island in 1639 and at Tappan in 1640. Sometime after 1643, he returned to Holland permanently, and in 1655 he published his Korte Historiael Ende Journaels Aenteyckeninge (Short Historical and Journal Notes of Several Voyages), *which was not translated into English until the 19th century. The text that follows was reprinted in* Historic Chronicles of New Amsterdam, Colonial New York and Early Long Island *(1968).*

On February 22, 1643, a large number of Wappinger Indians fled the depredations of the Mohawks (in the service of the Dutch), many of them seeking protection in Vries's house, which was near Pavonia (present-day Jersey City, New Jersey). Terrorized by no more than "eighty to ninety" Mohawks, each with a [Dutch] gun on his shoulder, . . . [t]here came flying to my house, four to five hundred Indians, desiring that I would protect them. I answered them that I could not do it, as the Indians [Mohawk] at Fort Orange were our friends, and that we could not interfere in their wars; that I now saw that they were children, that they were flying on all sides from eighty or ninety men, when they were themselves so many hundred strong; that it was displeasing to me that they should be *such* soldiers, as it was to mannetoe himself,—that is to say, the devil; but that I saw now that they were only children. As my house was full of Indians, and I had only five men with me, I made ready to go to the fort to obtain some soldiers for the purpose of having more force in my house.

Vries rowed across the Hudson to Fort Amsterdam (New Amsterdam) to request soldiers from Governor Willem Kieft, who claimed he had none to spare. The next morning, however—February 23—the Indians "came in troops on foot from my house to Pavonia, on the Oysterbank, where the great body of them encamped." In the meantime, at the governor's invitation, Vries stayed in Kieft's New Amsterdam house as his guest. Vries provides a horrific description of the unfolding of the Pavonia Massacre:

The 24th of February, sitting at table with the governor, he began to state his intentions, that he had a mind to *wipe the mouths* of the Indians; that he had been dining at the house of Jan Claesz. Damen, where Maryn Adriaensz, and Jan Claesz. Damen, together with Jacob Planck, had presented a petition to him to begin this work. I answered him that there was no sufficient reason to undertake it; that such work could not be done without the approbation of the [governing Council of] *twelve men;* that it could not take place without my assent, who was one of the twelve men; that moreover I was the first patron, and no one else hitherto had risked there so many thousands, and besides being patron, I was the first to come from Holland or Zeeland to plant a colony; and that he should consider what profit he could derive from this business, as he well knew that on account of trifling with the Indians we had lost our colony in the South river at Swanendael [Zwaanendael, at modern Lewes, Delaware], in the Hoere-kil, with thirty-two men, who were murdered in the year 1630; and that in the year 1640, the cause of my people being murdered on Staten Island was a difficulty which he had with the Raritaense [Raritan] Indians, where his soldiers had for some trifling thing killed some Indians. . . . But it appeared that my speaking was of no avail. He had, with his co-murderers, determined to commit the murder, deeming it a Roman deed, and to do it without warning the inhabitants in the open lands, that each one might take care of himself against the retaliation of the Indians, for he could not kill all the Indians. When I had expressed all these things in full, sitting at the table, and the meal was over, he told me he wished me to go to the large hall, which he had been lately adding to his

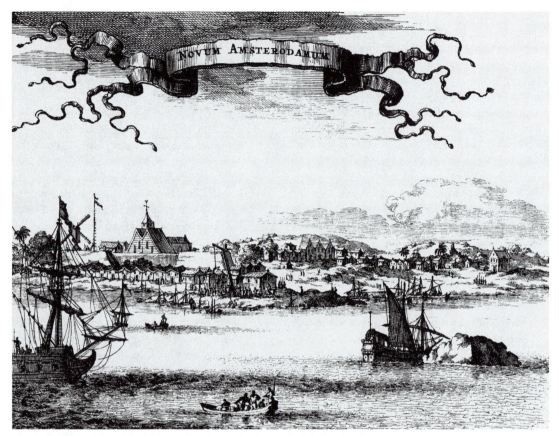

This print shows New Amsterdam's fine natural harbor, which helped make it a commercial center. *(Library of Congress)*

house. Coming to it, there stood all his soldiers ready to cross the river to Pavonia to commit the murder. Then spoke I again to Governor William [*sic*] Kieft: "Stop this work; you wish to break the mouths of the Indians, but you will also murder our own nation, for there are none of the farmers who are aware of it. My own dwelling, my people, cattle, corn, and tobacco will be lost." He answered me, assuring me that there would be no danger; that some soldiers should go to my house to protect it. But that was not done. So was this business begun between the 25th and the 26th of February in the year 1643. I remained that night at the governor's, sitting up. I went and sat in the kitchen, when, about midnight, I heard

a great shrieking, and I ran to the ramparts of the fort, and looked over to Pavonia. Saw nothing but firing, and heard the shrieks of the Indians murdered in their sleep. I returned again to the house by the fire. Having sat there awhile, there came an Indian with his squaw, whom I knew well, and who lived about an hour's walk from my house, and told me that they two had fled in a small skiff; that they had betaken themselves to Pavonia; that the Indians from Fort Orange had surprised them; and that they had come to conceal themselves in the fort [Fort Amsterdam]. I told them to go away immediately; that there was no occasion for them to come to the fort to conceal themselves; that they who had killed their people at Pavonia were not Indians, but the Swannekens, as they call the Dutch, had done it. They then asked me how they should get out of the fort. I took them to the door, and there was no sentry there, and so they betook themselves to the woods. When it was day the soldiers returned to the fort, having massacred or murdered eighty Indians, and considering that they had done a deed of Roman valour, in murdering so many in their sleep; where infants were torn from their mother s breasts, and hacked to pieces in the presence of the parents, and the pieces thrown into the fire and in the water, and other sucklings were bound to small boards, and then cut, stuck, and pierced, and miserably massacred in a manner to move a heart of stone. Some were thrown into the river, and when the fathers and mothers endeavoured to save them, the soldiers would not let them come on land, but made both parents and children drown, children from five to six years of age, and also some decrepit persons. Many fled from this scene, and concealed themselves in the neighbouring sedge, and when it was morning, came out to beg a piece of bread, and to be permitted to warm themselves; but they were murdered in cold blood and tossed into the water. Some came by our lands in the country with their hands, some with their legs cut off, and some holding their entrails in their arms, and others had such horrible cuts, and gashes, that worse than they were could never happen. And these poor simple creatures, as also many of our own people, did not know any better than that they had been attacked by a party of other Indians,—the Maquas. After this exploit, the soldiers were rewarded for their services, and Director Kieft thanked them by taking them by the hand and congratulating them. At another place, on the same night at Corler's Hook on Corler's plantation, forty Indians were in the same manner attacked in their sleep, and massacred there in the same manner as the Duke of Alva did in the Netherlands, but more cruelly. This is indeed a disgrace to our nation, who have so generous a governor in our Fatherland as the Prince of Orange, who has always endeavoured in his wars to spill as little blood as possible. As soon as the Indians understood that the Swannekens had so treated them, all the men whom they could surprise on the farm-lands, they killed; but we have never heard that they have ever permitted women or children to be killed. They burned all the houses, farms, barns, grain, haystacks, and destroyed everything they could get hold of. So there was an open destructive war begun. They also burnt my farm, cattle, corn, barn, tobacco-house, and all the tobacco. My people saved themselves in the house where I lived, which was made with embrasures, through which they defended themselves. Whilst my people were in this state of alarm, the Indian whom I had aided to escape from the fort came there, and told the other Indians that I was a good chief, that I had helped him out of the fort, and that the killing of the Indians took place contrary to my wish. Then they all cried out together to my people that they would not shoot them; that if they had not destroyed my cattle they would not do it; that they would not burn my house; that they would let my little brewery stand, though they had melted the copper-kettle, in order to make darts for their arrows; but hearing now that it (the massacre) had been done contrary to my wish, they all went away, and left my house unbesieged. When now the Indians had destroyed so many farms and men in revenge for their people, I went to Governor William Kieft, and asked him if it was not as I had said it would be, that he would only effect the spilling of Christian blood. Who would now compensate us for our losses? But he gave me no answer. He said he wondered that no Indians came to the fort. I told him that I did not wonder at it; "why should the Indians come here where you have so treated them?"

Source: Vries, David Pietersz de. "Short Historical and Journal Notes of Several Voyages . . ." In *Historic Chronicles of New Amsterdam, Colonial New York and Early Long Island,* edited by Cornell Jaray, 113–117. 2 vols. Port Washington, N.Y.: Ira J. Friedman, Inc., 1968.

KING PHILIP'S WAR, 1675–1676

The Taunton Agreement
Plymouth Colony and King Philip
April 10, 1671

In this agreement, concluded at Taunton, Massachusetts, on April 10, 1671, King Philip (Metacom) confessed to having broken his "covenant" with Plymouth Colony and pledged to renew his friendship with the colony and his submission to colonial authority. Additionally, Philip agreed to relinquish his people's arms. Far from bringing peace between the Wampanoag and the English, the humiliating terms of the Taunton Agreement proved intolerable to King Philip and certainly contributed to the outbreak of King Philip's War.

Whereas my Father, my Brother, and my self, have formally submitted ourselves and our People unto the Kings Majesty of England, and to the Colony of New Plimouth, by solemn Covenant under our Hand; but I having of late through my Indiscretion, and the Naughtiness of my Heart, violated and broken this my Covenant with my Friends, by taking up Arms, with evil intent against them, and that groundlessly; I being now deeply sensible of my Unfaithfulness and Folly, so desire at this Time solemnly to renew my Covenant with my ancient Friends, my Fathers Friends above mentioned, and do desire that this may testifie to the World against me if ever I shall again fail in my Faithfulness towards them (that I have now, and at all Times found so kind to me) or any other of the English Colonies; and as a real Pledge of my true Intentions for the Future to be Faithful and Friendly, I do freely engage to resign up unto the Government of *New Plimouth,* all my English Arms, to be kept by them for their Security, so long as they shall see Reason. For true Performance of the Premises, I have hereunto set my Hand, together with the Rest of my Council.

Source: Phillips, Charles, and Alan Axelrod. Encyclopedia of Historical Treaties and Alliances. 2nd ed. New York: Facts On File, 2006, vol. 1, p. 118.

The Wampanoag chief Metacom (King Philip)
(Library of Congress)

Excerpts from *A Brief History of the Warr with the Indians in New-England*
Increase Mather
Published 1676

Born in Dorchester, Massachusetts, Increase Mather (1639–1723) was educated at Harvard College and became a towering figure in the development of the Massachusetts Bay Colony. A conservative Puritan, he was a minister and theologian, as well as very active in governing the colony and administering his alma mater, Harvard College. An important early American historian, he wrote his account of King Philip's War, which is excerpted here, while the events were very fresh—indeed, within weeks of the killing of King Philip. In standard Puritan fashion, Mather masterfully interpreted the war in religious, symbolic, and allegorical terms.

That the Heathen People amongst whom we live, and whose Land the Lord God of our Fathers hath given to us for a rightfull Possession, have at sundry times been plotting mischievous devices against that part of the English Israel which is seated in these goings down of the Sun, no man that is an Inhabitant of any considerable standing, can be ignorant. Especially that there have been (nec injuria) jealousies concerning the Narragansets and Wompanoags, is notoriously known to all men. And whereas they have been quiet untill the last year, that must be ascribed to the wonderful Providence of God, who did (as with Jacob of old, and after that with the Children of Israel) lay the fear of the English, and the dread of them upon all the Indians. The terror of God was upon them round about. Nor indeed had they such advantages in former years as now they have, in respect of Arms and Ammunition, their bows and arrows not being comparably such weapons of death and destruction, as our guns and swords are, with which they have been unhappily furnished. Nor were our sins ripe for so dreadfull a judgment, untill the Body of the first Generation was removed, and another Generation risen up which hath not so pursued, as ought to have been, the blessed design of their Fathers, in following the Lord into this Wilderness, whilst it was a land not sown.

As for the Grounds, justness, and necessity of the present War with these barbarous Creatures which have set upon us, my design is not to *inlarge* upon that Arument, but to leav that to others whom it mostly concerns . . .

Mather provides a vivid picture of some of the Indian raids that took place early in the conflict.

June. 24 (Midsummer-day) was appointed and attended as a day of solemn Humiliation throughout that Colony, by fasting and prayer, to intreat the Lord to give success to the present

Increase Mather *(Library of Congress)*

expedition respecting the Enemy. At the conclusion of that day of Humiliation, as soon as ever the people in *Swanzy* [Swansea] were come from the place where they had been praying together, the Indians discharged a volly of shot whereby they killed one man & wounded others. Two men were sent to call a Surgeon for the relief of the wounded, but the Indians killed them by the way: and in another part of the town six men were killed, so that there were nine english men murthered this day.

Thus did the *War* begin, this being the first english blood which was spilt by the Indians in an hostile way. The Providence of God is deeply to be observed, that the sword should be first drawn upon a day of Humiliation, the Lord thereby declaring from heaven that he expects something else from his People besides fasting and prayer.

Plimouth being thus suddenly involved in trouble, send [sent] to the other united Colonyes for aid, and their desires were with all readiness complyed with.

Souldiers marched out of Boston toward *Mount-Hope, June. 26th.* and continued marching that night, when there hapned a great Eclipse of the Moon, which was totally darkned above an hour. Only it must be remembred that some dayes before any Souldiers went out of *Boston* Commissioners were sent to treat with *Philip,* that so if possible ingaging in a War might be prevented. But when the Commissioners came near to *Mount-Hope,* they found diverse english men on the ground weltring in their own blood having been newly murthered by the Indians, so that they could not proceed further. Yea the Indians killed a man of this Colony as he was travelling in the roade before such time as we took up arms: in which respect no man can doubt of the *justness* of our cause, since the enemy did shed the blood of some of ours who never did them (our enemyes themselves being judges) the least wrong before we did at all offend them, or attempt any act of hostility towards them.

June 29th. was a day of publick *Humiliation* in this Colony appointed by the Council in respect of the war which is now begun.

This morning our army would have ingaged with the enemy, The Indians shot the Pilot who was directing our Souldiers in their way to *Philips* Countrey, and wounded several of our men, and ran into Swamps, rainy weather hindred a further pursuit of the Enemy. An awfull Providence happened at this time: for a souldier (a stout man) who was sent from Watertown, seing the English *Guide* slain, and hearing many profane oathes among some of our Souldiers (namely those Privateers, who were also Volunteers) and considering the unseasonableness of the weather was such, as that nothing could be done against the Enemy; this man was possessed with a strong conceit that God was against the english, whereupon he immediately ran distracted, and so was returned home a lamentable Spectacle.

In the beginning of *July* there was another Skirmish with the Enemy, wherein several of the Indians were killed, amongst whome were *Philips* chief Captain, and one of his Counsellors.

Now it appears that *Squaw-Sachem* of *Pocasset* her men were conjoyned with the *Womponoags* (that is Philips men) in this Rebellion.

About this time they killed several English at *Taunton,* and burnt diverse houses there. Also at *Swanzy* they caused about half the Town to be consumed with merciless Flames. Likewise *Middlebury* and *Dartmouth* in *Plimouth* Colony did they burn with Fire, and barbarously murthered both men and women in those places, stripping the slain whether men or women, and leaving them in the open field as naked as in the day wherein they were born. Such also is their inhumanity as that they flay of[f] the skin from their faces and heads of those they get into their hands, and go away with the hairy Scalp of their enemyes.

July 19. Our Army pursued *Philip* who fled unto a dismal Swamp for refuge: the *English Souldiers* followed him, and killed many of his Men, also about fifteen of the *English* were then slain.The Swamp was so Boggy and thick of Bushes, as that it was judged to proceed further therein would be but to throw away Mens lives. It could not there be descerned who were *English* and who the *Indians.* Our Men when in that hideous place if they did but see a Bush stir would fire presently, whereby 'tis verily feared, that they did sometimes unhappily shoot *English men* instead of *Indians.* Wherefore a *Retreat* was Sounded, and night coming on, the Army withdrew from that place. This was because the desperate Distress which the Enemy was in was unknown to us: for the *Indians* have since said, that if the English had continued at the Swamp all night, nay, if they had but followed them but one half hour longer, Philip had come and yielded up himself. But God saw that we were not yet fit for deliverance, nor could Health be restored unto us except a great deal more Blood be first taken from us: and other places as well as *Plimouth* stood in need of such a course to be taken with them. It might rationally be conjectured that the unsuccessfulness of this

Expedition against *Philip* would embolden the *Heathen* in other parts to do as he had done, and so it came to pass. For July 14, the *Nipnep* (or *Nipmuck*) *Indians* began their mischief at a Town called *Mendam* [Mendon] (had we amended our ways as we should have done, this Misery might have been prevented) where they committed *Barbarous Murders*. This Day deserves to have a *Remark* set upon it, considering that Blood was never shed in *Massachusets Colony* in a way of Hostility before this day. Moreover the Providence of God herein is the more awful and tremendous, in that this very day the Church in *Dorchester* was before the Lord, humbling themselves by Fasting and Prayer, on account of the Day of trouble now begun amongst us.

The news of this Blood-shed came to us at *Boston* the next day in Lecture time, in the midst of the Sermon, the Scripture then improved being that, *Isai.42.24. Who gave Jacob to the spoil, and Israel to the robbers? did not the Lord, He against whom we have sinned?*

One of the war's major battles was against an Indian "fort" at Kingston, Rhode Island, on December 19, 1675. Although the colonial army killed some 600 Narragansetts (for a loss of 80 colonials, including 14 company commanders), the commander, Josiah Winslow, made the mistake of ordering that the Indians' wigwams be burned, thereby depriving his own forces of badly needed shelter from a harsh winter storm.

Decemb. 18. *Connecticut* Forces being come, a March toward the enemy was resolved upon: *Peter* Indian having informed that the *Body of Indians* (only *Ninnigret* being one of their old crafty Sachems, had with some of his men withdrawn himself from the rest, professing that he would not ingage in a *War* with the English, therefore did he goe into a place more remote) was in a Fort about eighteen miles distant from the place where our Army now was. The next day [December 19], although it were the Sabbath, yet, provisions being a[l]most spent by our Souldiers, waiting so long for Connecticut

Forces, the Councill of War resolved to give Battle to the enemy. The English Souldiers played the men wonderfully; the Indians also fought stoutly, but were at last beat out of their Fort, which was taken by the English, There were hundreds of *Wigwams* (or Indian houses) within the Fort, which our Souldiers set on fire, in the which men, women and Children (no man knoweth how many hundreds of them) were burnt to death. Night coming on, a Retreat was sounded.

Concerning the number of Indians slain in this Battle, we are uncertain: only some Indians which afterwards were taken prisoners (as also a wretched English man that apostatized to the Heathen, and fought with them against his own Country-men, but was at last taken and executed) confessed that the next day they found three hundred of their fighting men dead in their Fort, and that many men, women and children were burned in their *Wigwams*, but they neither knew, nor could conjecture how many: it is supposed that not less then a thousand Indian Souls perished at that time. *Ninnigret* whose men buried the slain, affirmeth that they found twenty & two Indian Captains among the dead bodyes. Of the English there were killed and wounded about two hundred and thirty, whereof only eighty and five persons are dead. But there was a solemn rebuke of Providence at this time, in that six of our Captains were slain, viz. Captain *Johnson* of Roxbury, Captain *Gardner* of Salem, Captain *Davenport* of Boston (son to that Captain *Davenport* who did great Service in the expedition against the Indians in the *Pequod* war, Anno 1637) Captain *Gallop* of New-London, Captain *Marshal* of Windsor, Captain *Siely* of Stratford, who dyed of his wounds some dayes after the fight was over. The three Captains first mentioned, belonged to *Mattachusets* Colony, the three last to *Connecticut*, of *Plimouth* Colony Captain *Bradford* (one of their faithfull Magistrates, and son of him that was many years Governour there) was sorely wounded, but God had mercy on him, and on his people in him, so as to spare his life, and to restore him to some measure of health, albeit the bullet shot into him is still in is body. Also Captain *Goram* of *Barnstable* in Plimouth Colony fel sick of a feaver whereof he dyed.

Thus did the Lord take away seven Captains out of that Army. Also four *Leiutenants* were wounded in that *Fort fight*, so that although the English had the better of it, yet not without solemn and humbling Rebukes of Providence. At night as the army returned to their Quarters, a great Snow fell, also part of the army missed their way, among whom was the *General* himself with his Life-guard. Had the enemy known their advantage, and pursued our Souldiers (and we have since heard that some of the Indians did earnestly move, that it might be so, but others of them through the overruling hand of Providence would not consent) when upon their retreat, they might easily have cut off the whole Army: But God would be more gracious to us. Here then was not only a *Victory*, but also a signal *Preservation*, for which let the Father of mercyes have eternal Glory.

After this God seemed to withdraw from the English, and take part with the enemy. The next day the Indians finding but few English men dead in the Fort amongst their three hundred Indians that were slain, were much troubled and amazed, supposing that no more of ours had been killed; this blow did greatly astonish them, and had the English immediately pursued the Victory begun, in all likelyhood there had been an end of our troubles: but God saw that neither yet were we fit for deliverance[.] Wherefore Connecticut Forces withdrew to Stonington, and there being so many killed and wounded amongst those that remained in the Narraganset Country, also bread for the Souldiers being wanting, by reason the extremity of the weather was such, as that the Vessels loaden with provision could not reach them, therefore the army lay still some weeks. . . .

Source: Mather, Increase. *A Brief History of the Warr with the Indians in New-England* (1676). In *So Dreadfull a Judgment: Puritan Responses to King Philip's War,* *1676–1677,* edited by Richard Slotkin and James K. Folsom, 79–206. Middletown, Conn.: Wesleyan University Press, 1978.

Excerpts from *A Narrative of the Captivity and Restoration of Mrs. Mary Rowlandson*
Mary White Rowlandson
Published 1682

By far the most famous eyewitness document to emerge from King Philip's War was The Sovereignty & Goodness of God . . . a Narrative of the Captivity and Restoration of Mrs. Mary Rowlandson. *Published in Boston in 1682, the book went through two more editions from presses in Cambridge, Massachusetts, and London, England, that same year. It continued to be very popular throughout the next century and a half, with major editions published in Boston and New London, Connecticut, in the 18th century and variously throughout the 19th century. Even today, excerpts from the* Narrative *appear in high school and college anthologies of American literature.*

Mary Rowlandson's Narrative *is a prime example of a genre of early American literature known as the captivity narrative, a first-person account of an individual's experience of being captured and held by hostile Indians. Hundreds of captivity narratives were published through at least the mid-19th century. Those written by Puritans and other devout New Englanders tended to follow a similar pattern. The captive's story almost always included suffering from hunger, pain, and even torture; typically a spouse or children are lost. In many of these narratives, an Indian seizes a baby from its mother's arms and batters it to death against a tree trunk. The captive endures everything with patient forbearance in the certain knowledge that she (or he) is in God's hands and need only await the "redemption" that comes at the end of the story. That word, redemption, has a double meaning in the captivity narratives of the Puritan era, signifying the captive's physical rescue—usually by the payment of a ran-*

som (therefore, the captive is "redeemed" from his or her captors)—as well as the captive's salvation by God's grace. As with virtually every aspect of their lives, the Puritans saw the experience of Indian captivity as both evidence of God's providence and as an allegory of that providence. The great lesson of Indian captivity, as the Puritans saw it, was that, in fact, we are all captives on earth—captives to our bodies, to our desires, to the devil, to the original sin of our first parents, Adam and Eve—and we all await the soul's redemption through the grace of God.

Mary White Rowlandson (ca. 1635–ca. 1710) was married to a minister in Lancaster, Massachusetts, and was captured in a raid during February 1676. She was carried by her captors west—that is, farther into the "wilderness," Indian territory—along with her three surviving children, after the Indians had fatally wounded one. She remained in captivity until May, when she was ransomed ("redeemed") for £20—a lordly sum. Ultimately reunited with her children, she penned the Narrative as witness to an ordeal through which God "the Redeemer" was duly glorified. For modern readers, Rowlandson's Puritan religious outlook is instructive, but what makes her narrative a truly enduring work of autobiographical literature is the vividness with which she portrays the terrifying realities of captivity. This was the nature of war on the early American frontier.

On the tenth of February 1675 [1676; at this time, the New Year was reckoned to begin on March 25; therefore, we would count the year as 1676], came the Indians with great numbers upon Lancaster: their first coming was about sun-rising; hearing the noise of some guns, we looked out; several houses were burning, and the smoke ascending to heaven. There were five persons taken in one house, the father, and the mother, and a sucking child, they knocked on the head; the other two they took and carried away alive. There were two others, who being out of their garrison upon some occasion were set upon; one was knocked on the head, the other escaped: another there was who running along was shot and wounded, and fell down; he begged of them his life, promising them money (as they told me) but they would not hearken to him but knocked him in head, and stript him naked, and split open his bowels. Another seeing many of the Indians about his barn, ventured and went out, but was quickly shot down. There were three others belonging to the same garrison who were killed; the Indians getting up upon the roof of the barn, had advantage to shoot down upon them over their fortification. Thus these murderous wretches went on, burning, and destroying before them.

At length they came and beset our own house, and quickly it was the dolefullest day that ever mine eyes saw. The house stood upon the edge of a hill; some of the Indians got behind the hill, others into the barn, and others behind any thing that could shelter them; from all which places they shot against the house, so that the bullets seemed to fly like hail; and quickly they wounded one man among us, then another, and then a third. About two hours (according to my observations, in that amazing time) they had been about the house before they prevailed to fire it (which they did with flax and hemp, which they brought out of the barn, and there being no defense about the house, only two flankers [projecting walls] at two opposite corners and one of them not finished) they fired it once and one ventured out and quenched it, but they quickly fired it again, and that took. Now is the dreadful hour come, that I have often heard of (in time of war, as it was the case of others) but now mine eyes see it. Some in our house were fighting for their lives, others wallowing in their blood, the house on fire over our heads, and the bloody heathen ready to knock us on the head, if we stirred out. Now might we hear mothers and children crying out for themselves, and one another, "Lord, what shall we do?" Then I took my children (and one of my sisters, hers) to go forth and leave the house: but as soon as we came to the door and appeared, the Indians shot so thick that the bullets rattled against the house, as if one had taken an handful of stones and threw them, so that we were fain to give back. We had six stout dogs belonging to our garrison, but none of them would stir, though another time, if any Indian had come to the door, they were ready to fly upon him and tear him down. The Lord hereby would make us the more to acknowledge His hand, and to see that our help is always in Him. But out we must go, the fire increasing, and coming along behind us roaring, and the Indians gaping before us with their guns, spears, and hatchets to devour us. No sooner were we out of the house, but my brother-in-law (being before wounded, in defending the house, in or near the throat) fell down dead, whereat the Indians scornfully shouted, and hallowed, and were presently upon him, stripping off his clothes, the bullets flying thick, one went through my side, and the same (as would seem) through the bowels and hand of my dear child in my arms. One of my elder sister's children, named William, had then his leg broken, which the Indians perceiving, they knocked him on head. Thus were we butchered by those merciless heathen, standing amazed, with the blood running down to our heels. My eldest sister being yet in the house, and seeing those woeful sights, the infidels hauling mothers one way, and children another, and some wallowing in their blood: and her elder son telling her that her son William was dead, and myself was wounded, she said, "And, Lord, let me die with them;" which was no sooner said, but she was struck with a bullet, and fell down dead over the threshold. I hope she is reaping the fruit of her good labors, being faithful to the service of God in her place. In her younger years she lay under much trouble upon spiritual accounts, till it pleased God to make that precious Scripture take hold of her heart, 2 Cor. 12. 9. "And He said unto me, my Grace is sufficient for thee." More than twenty years after I have heard her tell how sweet and comfortable that place was to her. But to return: the Indians laid hold of us, pulling me one way, and the children another, and said, "Come, go along with us;" I told them they would kill me: they answered, If I were willing to go along with them, they would not hurt me.

Oh the doleful sight that now was to behold at this house! "Come, behold the works of the Lord, what desolations He has made in the Earth." Of thirty-seven persons who were in this one house, none escaped either present death, or a bitter captivity, save only one, who might say as he, Job 1.15, "And I only am escaped alone to tell the news." There were twelve killed, some shot, some stabbed with their spears, some knocked down with their hatchets. When we are in prosperity, oh the little that we think of such dreadful sights, and to see our dear friends, and relations lie bleeding out their heart-blood upon the ground. There was one who was chopped into the head with a hatchet, and stripped naked, and yet was crawling up and down. It is a solemn sight to see so many Christians lying in their blood, some here, and some there, like a company of sheep torn by wolves, all of them stripped naked by a company of hell-hounds, roaring, singing, ranting, and insulting, as if they would have torn our very hearts out; yet the Lord by His almighty power preserved a number of us from death, for there were twenty-four of us taken alive and carried captive.

I had often before this said, that if the Indians should come, I should choose rather to be killed by them than taken alive but when it came to the trial my mind changed; their glittering weapons so daunted my spirit, that I chose rather to go along with those (as I may say) ravenous beasts, than that moment to end my days; and that I may the better declare what happened to me during that grievous captivity, I shall particularly speak of the several removes we had up and down the wilderness.

The First Remove

Now away we must go with those barbarous creatures, with our bodies wounded and bleeding, and our hearts no less than our bodies. About a mile we went that night, up upon a hill within sight of the town, where they intended to lodge. There was hard by a vacant house (deserted by the English before, for fear of the Indians). I asked them whether I might not lodge in the house that night to which they answered, "What will you love English men still?" This was the dolefullest night that ever my eyes saw. Oh, the roaring, and singing and dancing, and yelling of those black creatures in the night, which made the place a lively resemblance of hell. And as miserable was the waste, that was there made of horses, cattle, sheep, swine, calves, lambs, roasting pigs, and fowl (which they had plundered in the town) some roasting, some lying and burning, and some boiling to feed our merciless enemies; who were joyful enough though we were disconsolate. To add to the dolefulness of the former day, and the dismalness of the present night: my thoughts ran upon my losses and sad bereaved condition. All was gone, my husband gone (at least separated from me, he being in the Bay [in Boston, Massachusetts Bay Colony], and to add to my grief, the Indians told me they would kill him as he came homeward) my children gone, my relations and friends gone, our house and home and all our comforts within door, and without, all was gone (except my life) and I knew not but the next moment that might go too. There remained nothing to me but one poor wounded babe, and it seemed at present worse than death that it was in such a pitiful condition, bespeaking compassion, and I had no refreshing for it, nor suitable things to revive it. Little do many think what is the savageness and brutishness of this barbarous enemy, ay, even those that seem to profess more than others among them, when the English have fallen into their hands.

Those seven that were killed at Lancaster the summer before upon a Sabbath day, and the one that was afterward killed upon a weekday, were slain and mangled in a barbarous manner, by one-eyed John [an Indian also known as Monoco and as Apequinsah] and Marlborough's Praying Indians [supposedly Christianized Indians living in the Massachusetts town of Marlborough], which Capt. Mosely brought to Boston, as the Indians told me.

The Second Remove

But now, the next morning, I must turn my back upon the town, and travel with them into the vast and desolate wilderness, I knew not whither. It is not my tongue, or pen can express the sorrows of my heart, and bitterness of my spirit, that I had at this departure: but God was with me, in a wonderful manner, carrying me along, and bearing up my spirit, that it did not quite fail. One of the Indians carried my poor wounded babe upon a horse, it went moaning all along, "I shall die, I shall die." I went on foot after it, with sorrow that cannot be expressed. At length I took it off the horse, and carried it in my arms till my strength failed; and I fell down with it: then they set me upon a horse with my wounded child in my lap, and there being no furniture upon the horse back, as we were going down a steep hill, we both fell over the horse's head, at which they like inhumane creatures laughed, and rejoiced to see it, though I thought we should there have ended our days, as overcome with so many difficulties. But the Lord renewed my strength still, and carried me along, that I might see more of His power; yea, so much that I could never have thought of, had I not experienced it.

After this it quickly began to snow, and when night came on, they stopped: and now down I must sit in the snow, by a little fire, and a few boughs behind me, with my sick child in my lap; and calling much for water, being now (through the wound) fallen into a violent fever. My own wound also growing so stiff, that I could scarce sit down or rise up; yet so it must be, that I must sit all this cold winter night upon the cold snowy ground, with my sick child in my arms, looking that every hour would be the last of its life; and having no Christian friend near me, either to comfort or help me. Oh, I may see the wonderful power of God, that my spirit did not utterly sink under my affliction: still the Lord upheld me with His gracious and merciful spirit, and we were both alive to see the light of the next morning.

The Third Remove

The morning being come, they prepared to go on their way. One of the Indians got up upon a horse, and they set me up behind him, with my poor sick babe in my lap. A very wearisome and tedious day I had of it; what with my own wound, and my child's being so exceeding sick, and in a lamentable condition with her wound. It may be easily judged what a poor feeble condition we were in, there being not the least crumb of refreshing that came within either of our mouths, from Wednesday night to Saturday night, except only a little cold water. This day in the afternoon, about an hour by sun, we came to the place where they intended, viz. an Indian town, called Wenimesset [Menameset, Massachusetts], norward of Quabaug [Brookfield, Massachusetts]. When we were come, oh, the number of pagans (now merciless enemies) that there came about me, that I may say as David, Psal. 27. 13, "I had fainted, unless I had believed," etc. The next day was the Sabbath: I then remembered how careless I had been of God's holy time, how many Sabbaths I had lost and misspent, and how evilly I had walked in God's sight; which lay so close unto my spirit, that it was easy for me to see how righteous it was with God to cut off the thread of my life, and cast me out of His presence forever. Yet the Lord still showed mercy to me, and upheld me; and as He wounded me with one hand, so He healed me with the other. This day there came to me one Robert Pepper (a man belonging to Roxbury) who was taken in Captain Beers his fight [Beers had led militiamen in an attempt to relieve the Northfield (Massachusetts) garrison on September 4, 1675, but was killed along with most of his men] and had been now a considerable time with the Indians; and up with them almost as far as Albany, to see King Philip, as he told me, and was now very lately come into these parts. Hearing, I say, that I was in this Indian town, he obtained leave to come and see me. He told me, he himself was wounded in the leg at Captain Beers his fight; and was not able some time to go, but as they

carried him, and as he took oaken leaves and laid to his wound, and through the blessing of God he was able to travel again. Then I took oaken leaves and laid to my side, and with the blessing of God it cured me also; yet before the cure was wrought, I may say, as it is in Psal. 38. 5, 6. "My wounds stink and are corrupt, I am troubled, I am bowed down greatly, I go mourning all the day long." I sat much alone with a poor wounded child in my lap, which moaned night and day, having nothing to revive the body, or cheer the spirits of her, but instead of that, sometimes one Indian would come and tell me one hour, that your master will knock your child in the head, and then a second, and then a third, your master will quickly knock your child in the head.

This was the comfort I had from them, miserable comforters are ye all, as he said. Thus nine days I sat upon my knees, with my babe in my lap, till my flesh was raw again; my child being even ready to depart this sorrowful world, they bade me carry it out to another wigwam (I suppose because they would not be troubled with such spectacles) whither I went with a very heavy heart, and down I sat with the picture of death in my lap. About two hours in the night, my sweet babe like a lamb departed this life, on Feb. 18, 1675. It being about six years, and five months old. It was nine days from the first wounding, in this miserable condition, without any refreshing of one nature or other, except a little cold water. I cannot, but take notice, how at another time I could not bear to be in the room where any dead person was, but now the case is changed; I must and could lie down by my dead babe, side by side all the night after. I have thought since of the wonderful goodness of God to me, in preserving me in the use of my reason and senses, in that distressed time, that I did not use wicked and violent means to end my own miserable life. In the morning, when they understood that my child was dead they sent for me home to my master's wigwam: (by my master in this writing, must be understood Quanopin [Quinnapin, husband of the "squaw-sachem" Weetamoo] who was a sagamore, and married King Philip's wife's sister; not that he first took me, but I was sold to him by another Narragansett Indian, who took me when first I came out of the garrison). I went to take up my dead child in my arms to carry it with me, but they bid me let it alone: there was no resisting, but go I must and leave it. When I had been at my master's wigwam, I took the first opportunity I could get, to go look after my dead child: when I came I asked them what they had done with it? Then they told me it was upon the hill: then they went and showed me where it was, where I saw the ground was newly dug, and there they told me they had buried it: there I left that child in the wilderness, and must commit it, and myself also in this wilderness condition, to Him who is above all. God having taken away this dear child, I went to see my daughter Mary, who was at this same Indian town, at a wigwam not very far off, though we had little liberty or opportunity to see one another. She was about ten years old, and taken from the door at first by a Praying Indian and afterward sold for a gun. When I came in sight, she would fall aweeping; at which they were provoked, and would not let me come near her, but bade me be gone; which was a heart-cutting word to me. I had one child dead, another in the wilderness, I knew not where, the third they would not let me come near to: "Me" (as he said) "have ye bereaved of my children, Joseph is not, and Simeon is not, and ye will take Benjamin also, all these things are against me." I could not sit still in this condition, but kept walking from one place to another. And as I was going along, my heart was even overwhelmed with the thoughts of my condition, and that I should have children, and a nation which I knew not ruled over them. Whereupon I earnestly entreated the Lord, that He would consider my low estate, and show me a token for good, and if it were His blessed will, some sign and hope of some relief. And indeed quickly the Lord answered, in some measure, my poor prayers: for as I was going up and down mourning and lamenting my condition, my son came to me, and asked me how I did; I had not seen him before, since the destruction of the town, and I knew not where he was, till I

was informed by himself, that he was amongst a smaller parcel of Indians, whose place was about six miles off; with tears in his eyes, he asked me whether his sister Sarah was dead; and told me he had seen his sister Mary; and prayed me, that I would not be troubled in reference to himself. The occasion of his coming to see me at this time, was this: there was, as I said, about six miles from us, a small plantation of Indians, where it seems he had been during his captivity: and at this time, there were some forces of the Indians gathered out of our company, and some also from them (among whom was my son's master) to go to assault and burn Medfield: in this time of the absence of his master, his dame brought him to see me. I took this to be some gracious answer to my earnest and unfeigned desire. The next day, viz. to this, the Indians returned from Medfield, all the company, for those that belonged to the other small company, came through the town that now we were at. But before they came to us, oh! the outrageous roaring and hooping that there was: they began their din about a mile before they came to us. By their noise and hooping they signified how many they had destroyed (which was at that time twenty-three). Those that were with us at home, were gathered together as soon as they heard the hooping, and every time that the other went over their number, these at home gave a shout, that the very earth rung again: and thus they continued till those that had been upon the expedition were come up to the sagamore's wigwam; and then, oh, the hideous insulting and triumphing that there was over some Englishmen's scalps that they had taken (as their manner is) and brought with them. I cannot but take notice of the wonderful mercy of God to me in those afflictions, in sending me a Bible. One of the Indians that came from Medfield fight, had brought some plunder, came to me, and asked me, if I would have a Bible, he had got one in his basket. I was glad of it, and asked him, whether he thought the Indians would let me read? He answered yes: so I took the Bible, and in that melancholy time, it came into my mind to read first the 28. Chap. of Deut., which I did, and when I had read it, my dark heart wrought on this manner, that there was no mercy for me, that the blessings were gone, and the curses come in their room, and that I had lost my opportunity. But the Lord helped me still to go on reading till I came to Chap. 30 the seven first verses, where I found, there was mercy promised again, if we would return to Him by repentance; and though we were scattered from one end of the earth to the other, yet the Lord would gather us together, and turn all those curses upon our enemies. I do not desire to live to forget this Scripture, and what comfort it was to me.

Now the Indians began to talk of removing from this place, some one way, and some another. There were now besides myself nine English captives in this place (all of them children, except one woman). I got an opportunity to go and take my leave of them; they being to go one way, and I another, I asked them whether they were earnest with God for deliverance, they told me, they did as they were able, and it was some comfort to me, that the Lord stirred up children to look to Him. The woman viz. Goodwife Joslin told me, she should never see me again, and that she could find in her heart to run away; I wished her not to run away by any means, for we were near thirty miles from any English town, and she very big with child, and had but one week to reckon; and another child in her arms, two years old, and bad rivers there were to go over, and we were feeble, with our poor and coarse entertainment [food]. I had my Bible with me, I pulled it out, and asked her whether she would read; we opened the Bible and lighted on Psal. 27, in which Psalm we especially took notice of that, ver. ult., "Wait on the Lord, Be of good courage, and He shall strengthen thine heart, wait I say on the Lord."

The Fourth Remove

And now I must part with that little company I had. Here I parted from my daughter Mary (whom I never saw again till I saw her in Dorchester, returned from captivity) and from four little cousins and neighbors, some of which

I never saw afterward: the Lord only knows the end of them. Amongst them also was that poor woman before mentioned, who came to a sad end, as some of the company told me in my travel: she having much grief upon her spirit, about her miserable condition, being so near her time, she would be often asking the Indians to let her go home; they not being willing to that, and yet vexed with her importunity, gathered a great company together about her, and stripped her naked, and set her in the midst of them; and when they had sung and danced about her (in their hellish manner) as long as they pleased, they knocked her on head, and the child in her arms with her: when they had done that, they made a fire and put them both into it, and told the other children that were with them, that if they attempted to go home, they would serve them in like manner: the children said, she did not shed one tear, but prayed all the while. But to return to my own journey; we traveled about half a day or little more, and came to a desolate place in the wilderness, where there were no wigwams or inhabitants before; we came about the middle of the afternoon to this place, cold and wet, and snowy, and hungry, and weary, and no refreshing, for man, but the cold ground to sit on, and our poor Indian cheer.

Heartaching thoughts here I had about my poor children, who were scattered up and down among the wild beasts of the forest: my head was light and dizzy (either through hunger or hard lodging, or trouble or altogether) my knees feeble, my body raw by sitting double night and day, that I cannot express to man the affliction that lay upon my spirit, but the Lord helped me at that time to express it to Himself. I opened my Bible to read, and the Lord brought that precious Scripture to me, Jer. 31. 16. "Thus saith the Lord, refrain thy voice from weeping, and thine eyes from tears, for thy work shall be rewarded, and they shall come again from the land of the enemy." This was a sweet cordial to me, when I was ready to faint, many and many a time have I sat down, and wept sweetly over this Scripture. At this place we continued about four days.

. . .

Rowlandson's ordeal lasted nearly 12 weeks before she was ransomed. Her narrative accounts for a total of 20 wilderness "removes."

Our family being now gathered together (those of us that were living) the South Church in Boston hired an house for us: then we removed from Mr. Shepard's, those cordial friends, and went to Boston, where we continued about three quarters of a year: still the Lord went along with us, and provided graciously for us. I thought it somewhat strange to set up housekeeping with bare walls; but as Solomon says, "Money answers all things," and that we had through the benevolence of Christian friends, some in this town, and some in that, and others: and some from England, that in a little time we might look, and see the house furnished with love. The Lord hath been exceeding good to us in our low estate, in that when we had neither house nor home, nor other necessaries; the Lord so moved the hearts of these and those towards us, that we wanted neither food, nor raiment for ourselves or ours, Prov. 18. 24. "There is a friend which sticketh closer than a brother." And how many such friends have we found, and now living amongst? And truly such a friend have we found him to be unto us, in whose house we lived, viz. Mr. James Whitcomb, a friend unto us near hand, and afar off.

I can remember the time, when I used to sleep quietly without workings in my thoughts, whole nights together, but now it is other ways with me. When all are fast about me, and no eye open, but His who ever waketh, my thoughts are upon things past, upon the awful dispensation of the Lord towards us; upon His wonderful power and might, in carrying of us through so many difficulties, in returning us in safety, and suffering none to hurt us. I remember in the night season, how the other day I was in the midst of thousands of enemies, and nothing but death before me: it is then hard work to persuade myself, that ever I should be satisfied with bread again. But now we are fed with the finest of the wheat, and, as I may say, with honey out of the rock: instead of the husk, we have the fatted calf: the thoughts of these things in the particulars of them, and of the love and goodness of God towards us, make it true of me, what David said of himself, Psal. 6. 5. "I watered my couch with my tears." Oh! the wonderful power of God that mine eyes have seen, affording matter enough for my thought to run in, that when others are sleeping mine eyes are weeping.

I have seen the extreme vanity of this world: one hour I have been in health, and wealth, wanting nothing: but the next hour in sickness and wounds, and death, having nothing but sorrow and affliction.

Before I knew what affliction meant, I was ready sometimes to wish for it. When I lived in prosperity, having the comforts of the world about me, my relations by me, my heart cheerful, and taking little care for anything; and yet seeing many, whom I preferred before myself, under many trials and afflictions, in sickness, weakness, poverty, losses, crosses, and cares of the world I should be sometimes jealous lest I should have my portion in this life, and that Scripture would come to my mind, Heb. 12. 6. "For whom the Lord loveth He chasteneth, and scourgeth every son whom He receiveth." But now I see the Lord had His time to scourge and chasten me. The portion of some is to have their afflictions by drops, now one drop and then another; but the dregs of the cup, the wine of astonishment, like a sweeping rain that leaveth no food, did the Lord prepare to be my portion. Affliction I wanted, and affliction I had, full measure (I thought) pressed down and running over; yet I see, when God calls a person to anything, and through never so many difficulties, yet He is fully able to carry them through and make them see, and say they have been gainers thereby. And I hope I can say in some measure, as David did, "It is good for me that I have been afflicted." The Lord hath showed me the vanity of these outward things. That they are the vanity of vanities, and vexation of spirit; that they are but a shadow, a blast, a bubble, and things of no continuance. That we must rely on God Himself, and our whole dependence must be upon Him. If trouble from smaller matters begin to arise in me, I have something at hand to check myself with, and say, why am I troubled? It was but the other day that if I had had the world, I would have given it for my freedom, or to have been a servant to a Christian. I have learned to look beyond present and smaller troubles, and to be quieted under them, as Moses said, Exod. 14. 13. "Stand still and see the salvation of the Lord."

Source: Rowlandson, Mary White. *The Narrative of the Captivity and Restoration of Mrs. Mary Rowlandson.* 1682. Reprint, Lancaster, Mass.: Lancaster Bicentennial Commission, 1975. Available online. URL: http://www.gutenberg.org/etext/851. Accessed on February 8, 2010.

Account of the Death of King Philip
Thomas Church
Published 1716

Benjamin Church (ca. 1639–1718) was born in Plymouth Colony and lived first in Duxbury, Massachusetts, before moving to Bristol, Rhode Island. Serving as right-hand man to Governor Josiah Winslow of Plymouth Colony, he was called upon during King Philip's War to command a company in support of, but independent from, the principal army that Winslow led. From all appearances a born military leader and tactician, Church emerged as the preeminent colonial hero of the war, largely because his force was consistently the most successful, mounting highly effective counterraids against the Indians and routing them in their swamp and forest strongholds. Church was also the first colonial commander to use Indian allies effectively, and he thoroughly integrated Indian warriors into the forces he led. In contrast to the other colonial military leaders, he freely adopted and adapted Indian fighting techniques and tactics, and in American military history, he may be credited with having developed what later would be called ranger doctrine—the techniques of nonconventional warfare, including infiltration and hit-and-run guerrilla tactics. His innovative approach often put him at odds with more conventional commanders, including Governor Winslow.

Benjamin Church kept a diary of his experiences in King Philip's War, which his son, Thomas Church (1674–1746), used to compile The Entertaining History of King Philip's War, *published in 1716. The independent company Benjamin Church led ran King Philip (Metacom) to ground on August 12, 1676, effectively ending the war, except for some mop-up operations. The following excerpt from* Entertaining History *relates the end of Philip.*

Capt. *Church* being now at *Plymouth* again weary and worn, would have gone home to his Wife and Family, but the Government being Solicitous to ingage him in the Service until *Philip* was slain, and promising him satisfaction and redress for some mistreatment that he had met with: He fixes for another Expedition; he had soon Volunteers enough to make up the Company he desired and Marched thro' the Woods, until he came to *Pocasset.* And not seeing nor hearing of any of the Enemy, they went over the Ferry to *Rhode-Island* to refresh themselves. The Captain with about half a dozen in his company took Horse & rid about eight Miles down the Island, to Mr. *Sanfords* where he had left his Wife; who no sooner saw him but fainted with the surprize; and by that time she was a little revived, they spy'd two Horse men coming a great pace. Capt. *Church* told his company that those men (by their riding) came with Tydings. When they came up they prov'd to be Maj. *Sanford* and Capt. *Golding;* who immediately ask'd Capt. *Church, What he would give to hear some News of* Philip? He reply'd, *That was what he wanted.* They told him, *They had rid hard with some hopes of overtaking of him, and were now come on purpose to inform him, That there was just now Tydings from* Mount-hope; *An* Indian *came down from thence (where* Phillips Camp *now was) on to* Sand point *over against* Trips, *and hollow'd, and made signs to be fetch'd over; and being fetch'd over, he reported, That he was fled from* Philip, *who (said he) has kill'd my Brother just before I came away, for giving some advice that displeased him.* And said, *he was fled for fear of meeting with the same his Brother had met with.* Told them also, *That* Philip *was now in* Mount- hope Neck. Capt. *Church* thank'd them for their good News, and said, he hop'd by to Morrow Morning to have the Rogues head. The Horses that he and his company came on standing at the door, (for they had not been unsaddled) his Wife must content her self with a short visit, when such game was a-head; they immediately Mounted, set Spurs to their Horses, and away. The two Gentlemen that bro't him the Tydings, told him, *They would gladly wait upon him to see the event of this Expedition.* He thank'd them, and told them, he should be as fond of their company as any Mens; and (in short) they went with him. And they were soon as [at] *Trips Ferry* (with Capt. *Churches* company) where the deserter was; who was a fellow of good sense, and told his story handsomely: he offered Capt. *Church* to Pilot him to *Philip,* and to help to kill him, that he might revenge his Brothers death. Told him, That *Philip* was now upon a little spot of Upland that was in the South end of the miery Swamp just at the foot of the Mount, which was a spot of ground that Capt. *Church* was well acquainted with, By that time they were got over the Ferry, and came near the ground half the Night was spent, the Capt. commands a halt, and bringing the company together, he asked Maj *Sanford* & Capt. *Goldings* advice, what method was best to take in making the on-set, but they declining giving any advice, telling him, *That his great Experience & Success forbid their taking upon them to give advice.* Then Capt. *Church* offered Capt. *Golding,* that he should have the honour (if he would please to accept of it) to beat up *Philips* headquarters. He accepted the offer and had his alotted number drawn out to him, and the Pilot. Capt. *Churches* instructions to him were to be very careful in his approach to the Enemy, and be sure not to shew himself until by day light they might see and discern their own men from the Enemy. Told him also, That his custom in the like cases was to creep with his company on their bellies, until they came as near

as they could; and that as soon as the Enemy discovered them they would cry out; and that was the word for his Men to fire and fall on. Directed him when the Enemy should start and take into the Swamp, they should pursue with speed, every man shouting and making what noise they could; for he would give orders to his Ambuscade to fire on any that should come silently. Capt. *Church* knowing it was *Philips* custom to be foremost in the flight, went down to the Swamp and gave Capt. *Williams* of *Situate* the command of the right wing of the Ambush, and placed an *Englishman* and an *Indian* together behind such shelters of Trees, &c. that he could find, and took care to place them at such distance as none might pass undiscovered between them, charg'd 'em to be careful of themselves, and of hurting their friends: And to fire at any that should come silently thro' the Swamp: But it being some-what further thro' the Swamp than he was aware of, he wanted men to make up his Ambuscade; having placed what men he had, he took Maj. *Sanford* by the hand, said, *Sir, I have so placed them that 'tis scarce possible* Philip *should escape them.* The same moment a Shot whistled over their heads and then the noise of a Gun towards *Philips* Camp. Capt. *Church* at first tho't it might be some Gun fired by accident: but before he could speak a whole Volley followed, which was earlier than he expected. One of *Philips* gang going forth to ease himself, when he had done, look'd round him, & Capt. *Golding* thought the *Indian* looked right at him (tho' probably 'twas but his conceit) so fired at him, and upon his firing, the whole company that were with him fired upon the Enemies shelter, before the *Indians* had time to rise from their sleep, and so over-shot them. But their shelter was open on that side next the Swamp, built so on purpose for the convenience of flight on occasion. They were soon in the Swamp and *Philip* the foremost, who starting at the first Gun threw his Petunk [sling pouch] and Powder horn over his head, catch'd up his Gun and ran as fast as he could scamper, without any more clothes than his small breeches and stockings, and ran directly upon two of Capt. *Churches*

Ambush; they let him come fair within shot, and the *English mans* Gun missing fire, he bid the *Indian* fire away, and he did so to purpose, sent one Musket Bullet thro' his heart, and another not above two inches from it; he fell upon his face in the Mud & Water with his Gun under him. By this time the Enemy perceived they were way laid on the east side of the Swamp, tack'd short about. One of the Enemy who seem'd to be a great surly old fellow, hollow'd with a loud voice, & often called out, *iootash, iootash,* Capt. *Church* called to his *Indian Peter* and ask'd him, *Who that was that called so?* He answered, It was old *Annowon Philips* great Captain, calling on his Souldiers to stand to it and fight stoutly. Now the Enemy finding that place of the Swamp which was not Ambush'd, many of them made their escape in the *English* Tracks. The Man that had shot down *Philip,* ran with all speed to Capt. *Church,* and informed him of his exploit, who commanded him to be Silent about it, & let no man more know it, until they had drove the Swamp clean; but when they had drove the Swamp thro' & found the Enemy had escaped, or at least the most of them; and the Sun now up, and so the dew gone, that they could not so easily Track them, the whole Company met together at the place where the Enemies Night shelter was; and then Capt. *Church* gave them the news of *Philips* death; upon which the whole Army gave Three loud *Huzza's.* Capt. *Church* ordered his body to be pull'd out of the mire on to the Upland, so some of Capt. *Churches Indians* took hold of him by his Stockings, and some by his small Breeches, (being otherwise naked) and drew him thro' the Mud unto the Upland, and a doleful, great, naked, dirty beast, he look'd like. Capt. *Church* Then said, *That for asmuch as he had caused many an* English *mans body to lye unburied and rot above ground, that not one of his bones should be buried.* And calling his old *Indian* Executioner, bid him behead and quarter him. Accordingly, he came with his Hatchet and stood over him, but before he struck he made a small Speech directing it to *Philip;* and said, *He had been a very great Man, and had*

made many a man afraid of him, but so big as he was he would now chop his Ass for him; and so went to work, and did as he was ordered. *Philip* having one very remarkable hand being much scared, occasioned by the splitting of a Pistol in it formerly. Capt. *Church* gave the head and that hand to *Alderman,* the *Indian* who shot him, to show to such Gentlemen as would bestow gratuities upon him; and accordingly he got many a Peny by it. This being on the last day of the Week, the Captain with his Company returned to the Island, tarryed there until Tuesday; and then went off and ranged thro' all the Woods to *Plymouth,* and received their *Premium,* which was *Thirty Shillings per* head, for the Enemies which they had killed or taken, instead of all Wages; and *Philips* head went at the same price. Methinks it's scanty reward and poor incouragement; tho' it was better than what had been some time before. For this March they received *Four Shillings* and *Six Pence* a Man, which was all the Reward they had, except the honour of killing *Philip.* This was in the latter end of August, 1676.

Source: Church, Thomas. *The Entertaining History of King Philip's War.* 1716. In *So Dreadfull a Judgment: Puritan Responses to King Philip's War, 1676–1677,* edited by Richard Slotkin and James K. Folsom, 393–470. Middletown, Conn.: Wesleyan University Press, 1978.

BACON'S REBELLION, 1676

"The Declaration and Remonstrance of Sir William Berkeley His Most Sacred Majesties Governor and Captain Generall of Virginia"
Sir William Berkeley
May 19, 1676

In an effort to turn public opinion against the defiant Nathaniel Bacon, who was threatening to mount a full-scale uprising against his authority, the Virginia governor Sir William Berkeley (1605–77) published a declaration that officially "posted" Bacon as a traitor. All spellings are original.

Sheweth That about the yeare 1660 Coll. Mathews the then Governor dyed and then in consideration of the service I had don the Country, in defending them from, and destroying great numbers of the Indians, without the loss of three men, in all the time that warr lasted, and in contemplation of the equall and uncorrupt Justice I had distributed to all men, Not onely the Assembly but the unanimous votes of all the Country, concurred to make me Governor in a time, when if the Rebells in England had prevailed, I had certainly dyed for accepting itt, 'twas Gentlemen an unfortunate Love, shewed to me, for to shew myselfe gratefull for this, I was willing to accept of this Governement againe, when by my gracious Kings favour I might have had other places much more proffitable, and lesse toylesome then this hath beene. Since that time that I returned into the Country, I call the great God Judge of all things in heaven and earth to wittness, that I doe not know of any thing relateive to this Country wherein I have acted unjustly, corruptly, or negligently in distributeing equall Justice to all men, and takeing all possible care to preserve their proprietys, and defend the from their barbarous enimies.

But for all this, perhapps I have erred in things I know not of, if I have I am soe conscious of humane frailty, and my owne defects, that I will not onely acknowledge them, but repent of, and amend them, and not like the Rebell Bacon persist in an error, onely because I have comitted itt, and tells me in diverse of his Letters that itt is not for his honnor to confess a fault, but I am of opinion that itt is onely for divells to be incorrigible, and men of principles like the worst of divells, and these he hath, if truth be reported to me, of diverse of his expressions of Atheisme, tending to take away all Religion and Laws.

And now I will state the Question betwixt me as a Governor and Mr. Bacon, and say that if any enimies should invade England, any Councellor Justice of peace or other inferiour officer, might raise what forces they could to protect his Majesties subjects, But I say againe, if after the Kings knowledge of this invasion, any the greatest peere of England, should raise forces against the kings prohibition this would be now, and ever was in all ages and Nations accompted treason. Nay I will goe further, that though this peere was truly zealous for the preservation of his King, and subjects, and had better and greater abillitys then all the rest of his fellow subjects, doe his King and Country service, yett if the King (though by false information) should suspect the contrary, itt were treason in this Noble peere to proceed after the King's prohibition, and for the truth of this I appeale to all the laws of England, and the Laws and constitutions of all other Nations in the world, And yett further itt is declaried by this Parliament that the takeing up Armes for the King and Parliament is treason, for the event shewed that what ever the pretence was to seduce ignorant and well affected people, yett the end was ruinous both to King and people, as this will be if not prevented, I doe therefore againe declair that Bacon proceedeing against all Laws of all Nations modern and ancient, is Rebell to his sacred Majesty and this Country, nor will I insist upon the sweareing of men to live and dye togeather, which is treason by the very words of the Law.

Now my friends I have lived 34 yeares amongst you, as uncorrupt and dilligent as ever Governor was, Bacon is a man of two yeares amongst you, his person and qualities unknowne to most of you, and to all men else, by any vertuous action that ever I heard of, And that very action which he boasts of, was sickly and fooleishly, and as I am informed treacherously carried to the dishonnor of the English Nation, yett in itt, he lost more men then I did in three yeares Warr, and by the grace of God will putt myselfe to the same daingers and troubles againe when I have brought Bacon to acknowledge the Laws are above him, and I doubt not but by God's assistance to have better success then Bacon hath had, the reason of my hopes are, that I will take Councell of wiser men then my selfe, but Mr. Bacon hath none about him, but the lowest of the people.

Yett I must further enlarge, that I cannot without your helpe, doe any thinge in this but dye in defence of my King, his laws, and subjects, which I will cheerefully doe, though alone I doe itt, and considering my poore fortunes, I can not leave my poore Wife and friends a better legacy then by dyeing for my King and you: for his sacred Majesty will easeily distinguish betweene Mr. Bacons actions and myne, and Kinges have long Armes, either to reward or punish.

Now after all this, if Mr. Bacon can shew one precedens or example where such actings in any Nation what ever, was approved of, I will mediate with the King and you for a pardon, and excuce for him, but I can shew him an hundred examples where brave and great men have beene putt to death for gaineing Victorys against the Comand of their Superiors.

Lastly my most assured friends I would have preserved those Indians that I knew were howerly att our mercy, to have beene our spyes and intelligence, to finde out our bloody enimies, but as soone as I had the least intelligence that they alsoe were trecherous enimies, I gave out Commissions to distroy them all as the Commissions themselves will speake itt.

To conclude, I have don what was possible both to friend and enimy, have granted Mr. Bacon three pardons, which he hath scornefully rejected, suppoaseing himselfe stronger to subvert then I and you to maineteyne the Laws, by which onely and Gods assisting grace and mercy, all men must hope for peace and safety. I will add noe more though much more is still remaineing to Justifie me and condemne Mr. Bacon, but to desier that this declaration may be read in every County Court in the Country, and that a Court be presently called to doe itt, before the Assembly meet, That your approbation or dissattisfaction of this declaration may be knowne to all the Country, and the Kings Councell to whose most revered Judgments itt is submitted, Given the xxixth day of May, a happy day in the xxvith yeare of his most sacred Majesties Reigne, Charles the second, who God grant long and prosperously to Reigne, and lett all his good subjects say Amen.

Source: Berkeley, William. "The Declaration and Remonstrance of Sir William Berkeley His Most Sacred Majesties Governor and Captain Generall of Virginia." 1676. Available online. "From Revolution to Reconstruction." URL: http://www.let.rug.nl/usa/D/1651–1700/bacon_rebel/berke.htm. Accessed on February 8, 2010.

"Declaration in the Name of the People"
Nathaniel Bacon
July 30, 1676

Nathaniel Bacon (1647–76) had no scruples about declaring that he was the true representative of the people, as this declaration in their name attests— a document he signed with the title "Generall by Consent of the people." As Governor Berkeley had posted him a traitor on May 19, so now, on July 30, Bacon responded in kind, writing of how Berkeley had "traiterously . . . injured his Majesties interest here." All spellings are original.

The Declaration of the People.

1. For haveing upon specious pretences of publiqe works raised great unjust taxes upon the Comonality for the advancement of private favorites and other sinister ends, but noe visible effects in any measure adequate, For not haveing dureing this long time of his Gouvernement in any measure advanced this hopefull Colony either by fortificacons Townes or Trade.

2. For haveing abused and rendred contemptable the Magistrates of Justice, by advancing to places of Judicature, scandalous and Ignorant favorites.

3. For haveing wronged his Majesties prerogative and interest, by assumeing Monopoly of the Beaver trade, and for haveing in that unjust gaine betrayed and sold his Majesties Country and the lives of his loyall subjects, to the barbarous heathen.

4. For haveing, protected, favoured, and Imboldned the Indians against his Majesties

During Bacon's Rebellion, farmers marched to Jamestown in September 1676, took over the House of Burgesses (shown here), and passed laws for reform. *(Library of Congress)*

loyall subjects, never contriveing, requireing, or appointing any due or proper meanes of sattisfaction for theire many Invasions, robbories, and murthers comitted upon us.

5. For haveing when the Army of English, was just upon the track of those Indians, who now in all places burne, spoyle, murther and when we might with ease have distroyed them: who then were in open hostillity, for then haveing expressly countermanded, and sent back our Army, by passing his word for the peaceable demeanour of the said Indians, who imediately prosecuted theire evill intentions, comitting horred murthers and robberies in all places, being protected by the said ingagement and word past of him the said Sir William Berkeley, haveing ruined and laid desolate a greate part of his Majesties Country, and have now drawne themselves into such obscure and remote places, and are by theire success soe imboldned and confirmed, by theire confederacy soe strengthned that the cryes of blood are in all places, and the terror, and constimation of the people soe greate, are now become, not oncly a difficult, but a very formidable enimy, who might att first with ease have beene distroyed.

6. And lately when upon the loud outcryes of blood the Assembly had with all care raised and framed an Army for the preventing of further mischeife and safeguard of this his Majesties Colony.

7. For haveing with onely the privacy of some few favorites, without acquainting the people, onely by the alteracon of a figure, forged a Comission, by we know not what hand, not onely without, but even against the consent of the people, for the raiseing and effecting civill warr and distruction, which being happily and without blood shed prevented, for haveing the second time attempted the same, thereby calling downe our forces from the defence of the fronteeres and most weekely exposed places.

8. For the prevencon of civill mischeife and ruin amongst ourselves, whilst the barbarous enimy in all places did invade, murther and spoyle us, his majesties most faithfull subjects.

Of this and the aforesaid Articles we accuse Sir William Berkeley as guilty of each and every one of the same, and as one who hath traiterously attempted, violated and Injured his Majesties interest here, by a loss of a greate part of this his Colony and many of his faithfull loyall subjects, by him betrayed and in a barbarous and shamefull manner exposed to the Incursions and murther of the heathen, And we doe further declare these the ensueing persons in this list, to have beene his wicked and pernicious councellours Confederates, aiders, and assisters against the Comonality in these our Civill comotions.

Sir Henry Chichley	William Claiburne
Lieut. Coll. Christopher	Junior
Wormeley	Thomas Hawkins
Phillip Ludwell	William Sherwood
Robert Beverley	John Page Clerke
Richard Lee	John Cluffe Clerke
Thomas Ballard	John West
William Cole	Hubert Farrell
Richard Whitacre	Thomas Reade
Nicholas Spencer	Matthew Kempe
Joseph Bridger	

And we doe further demand that the said Sir William Berkeley with all the persons in this list be forthwith delivered up or surrender themselves within fower days after the notice hereof, Or otherwise we declare as followeth.

That in whatsoever place, howse, or ship, any of the said persons shall reside, be hidd, or protected, we declaire the owners, Masters or Inhabitants of the said places, to be confederates and trayters to the people and the estates of them is alsoe of all the aforesaid persons to be confiscated, and this we the Comons of Virginia doe declare, desiering a firme union amongst our selves that we may joyntly and with one accord defend our selves against the common Enimy, and lett not the faults of the guilty be the reproach of the inocent, or the faults or crimes of the oppressours devide and separate us who have suffered by theire oppressions.

These are therefore in his majesties name to command you forthwith to seize the persons above mentioned as Trayters to the King and Country and them to bring to Midle plantacon, and there to secure them untill further order, and in case of opposition, if you want any further assistance you are forthwith to demand itt in the name of the people in all the Counties of Virginia.

Nathaniel Bacon
Generall by Consent of the people.

Source: Bacon, Nathaniel. "Bacon's Declaration in the Name of the People." July 30, 1676. Available online. URL: http://www.constitution.org/bcp/baconpeo.htm. Accessed on February 8, 2010.

The Beginning, Progress, and Conclusion of Bacon's Rebellion in Virginia, in the Years 1675 and 1676
T. M.
Written 1705; published 1835

The following eyewitness account of Bacon's Rebellion was written in 1705, at the request of a British investigating commission, headed by Robert Harley, who held the title of secretary of state and was a member of the queen's Privy Council. The author,

"T. M."—Thomas Mathew—described himself as a planter who lived in Northumberland, Virginia, but was elected a member of the Virginia Assembly in 1676 for the town of Stafford. President Thomas Jefferson's minister plenipotentiary to Britain purchased the original manuscript from a London bookseller and sent it to the president, who copied it in his own hand. It was published in 1835 by the American antiquarian Peter Force. All spellings and punctuation are as in Force's text.

My dwelling was in Northumberland, the lowest county on the Potomack river, Stafford being the upmost, where, having also a plantation, servants, cattle, &c., my overseer there had agreed with one Robert Hen to come thither and be my herdsman, who then lived ten miles above it ; but on a Sabbath day morning in the summer anno 1675, people in their way to church, saw this Hen lying thwart his threshold, and an Indian without the door, both chopt on their heads, arms, and other parts, as if done with Indian hatchets, th' Indian was dead, but Hen when ask'd who did that? answered: Doegs, Doegs, and soon died, then a boy came out from under a bed, where he had hid himself, and told them, Indians had come at break of day and done those murders.

From this Englishman's bloud did (by degrees) arise Bacon's rebellion with the following mischiefs which overspread all Virginia and twice endangered Maryland, as by the ensuing account is evident. . . .

In these frightfull times the most exposed small families withdrew into our houses of better numbers, which we fortified with pallisadoes and redoubts, neighbours in bodies joined their labours from each plantation to others alternately, taking their arms into the ffields, and setting centinels; no man stirr'd out of door unarm'd, Indians were (ever and anon) espied, three 4. 5. 6 in a party lurking throughout the whole land, yet (what was remarkable) I rarely heard of any houses burnt, though abundance was forsaken, nor ever, of any corn or tobacco cut up, or other injury done, besides murders, except the killing a very few cattle and swine.

Frequent complaints of bloodshed were sent to S'r Wm. Berkeley (then Govern'r) from the heads of the rivers, which were as often answered with promises of assistance.

These at the heads of James and York rivers (having now most people destroyed by the Indians fflight thither from Potomack) grew impatient at the many slaughters of their neighbours and rose for their own defence, who chusing Mr. Bacon for their leader sent oftentimes to the Govern'r, humbly beseeching a comission to go against those Indians at their own charge which his hono'r as often promisd but did not send; the misteryes of these delays, were wondred at and which I ne're heard any coud into, other than the effects of his passion, and a new (not to be mentioned) occasion of avarice, to both which, he was (by the comon vogue) more than a little addicted: whatever were the popular surmizes and murmurings, vizt.

"that no bullets would pierce bever skins.

"rebbells forfeitures would be loyall inheritances &c."

During these protractions and people often slaine, most or all the officers, civill and military with as many dwellers next the heads of the rivers as made up 300 men taking Mr. Bacon for their coman'r, met, and concerted together, the danger of going without a comiss'n on the one part, and the continuall murders of their neighbors on th' other part (not knowing whose or how many of their own turns might be next) and came to this resolution vizt. to prepare themselves with necessaries for a march, but interim to send again for a comission, which if could or could not be obteyned by a certaine day, they woud proceed comission or no comission.

This day lapsing and no com'n come, they march'd into the wilderness in quest of these Indians after whom the Govern'r sent his proclamacon, denouncing all rebbells, who shoud not return within a limited day, whereupon those of estates obey'd; but Mr. Bacon with 57 men proceded untill their provisions were near spent, without finding enemy's when coming nigh a ffort of ffriend Indians, on the' other side a branch of

James river, they desired reliefe offering paym't. which these Indians kindly promised to help them with on the morrow, but put them off with promises untill the third day, so as having then eaten their last morsells they could not return, but must have starved in the way homeward and now 'twas suspected, these Indians had received private messages from the Govern'r. and those to be the causes of these delusive procrastinations; whereupon the English waded shoulder deep thro' that branch to the ffort pallisado's still intreating and tendering pay, for victuals ; but that evening a shot from the place they left on the other side of that branch kill'd one of Mr. Bacon's men, which made them believe, those in the ffort had sent for other Indians to come behind 'em and cut 'em off.

Hereupon they fired the palisado's, storm'd & burnt the ffort and cabins, and (with the losse of three English) slew 150 Indians.

The circumstances of this expedicn Mr. Bacon entertain'd me with, at his own chamber, at a visit I made him, the occasion whereof is hereafter menconed.

Ffom hence they return'd home where writts were come up to elect members for an assembly, when Mr. Bacon was unanimously chosen for one, who coming down the river was comanded by a ship with guns to come on board, where waited Major Hone the high sheriff of Jamestown ready to seize him, by whom he was carried down to the Govern's and by him receiv'd with a surprizing civillity in the following words "Mr. Bacon have you forgot to be a gentleman. No, may it please yo'r hon'r answer'd Mr. Bacon; then replyed the Gover'r I'll take yo'r parol, and gave him his liberty in March 1675–76 writts came up to Stafford to choose their two members for an assembly to meet in May; when Collo. Mason Capt. Brent and other gentlemen of that county, invited me to stand a candidate; a matter I little dreamt of, having never had inclinacons to tamper in the precarious intrigues of govern't. and my hands being full of my own business; they preas't severall cogent argum'ts. and I having considerable debts in that county, besides my plantation concerns, where (in one and th' other) I had much more severely suffered, than any of themselves by th' Indians disturbances in the sumer and winter foregoing. I held it not (then) discreet to disoblige the rules of it, so Coll. Mason with myself were elected without objection, he at time convenient went on horseback ; I took my sloop and the morning I arriv'd to James town after a weeks voyage, was welcom;d with the strange acclamations of All's over Bacon is taken, having not heard at home of the southern comotons, other than rumours like idle tales, of one Bacon risen up in rebellion, no body knew for what, concerning the Indians.

The next forenoon, th' assembly being met in a chamber over the generall court & our speaker chosen, the govern'r sent for us down, where his hono'r with a pathetic emphasis made a short abrupt speech wherein were these words.

"If they had killed my grandfather and grandmother, my father and mother and all my friends, yet if they come to treat of peace, they ought to have gone in peace and sat down.

The two chief comanders at the forementioned siege, who slew the ffour Indian great men, being present and part of our assembly.

The govern'r stood up againe and said "if there be joy in the presence of the angels over one sinner that repenteth, there is joy now, for we have a penitent sinner come before us, call Mr. Bacon; then did Mr. Bacon upon one knee at the bar deliver a sheet of paper confessing his crimes, and begging pardon of God the king and the govern'r. Whereto (after a short pause) he answered "God forgive you, I forgive you, thrice repeating the same words ; when Collo. Cole (one of the councill) said, "and all that were with him, Yea, said the govern'r and all that were with him, twenty or more persons being then in irons who were taking coming down in the same and other vessels with Mr. Bacon.

About a minute after this the govern'r starting up from his chair a third time said "Mr. Bacon! if you will live civilly but till next quarter court (doubling the words) but till next quarter court,

Ile promise to restore you againe to yo'r place there pointing with his hand to Mr. Bacons seat, he having been of the councill before these troubles, tho' he had been a very short time in Virginia but was deposed by the foresaid proclamacon, and in th' afternoon passing by the court door, in my way up to our chamber, I saw Mr. Bacon on this quondam seat with the govern'r and councill, which seemed a marveilous indulgence to one whom he had so lately proscribed as a rebell.

The govern'r had directed us to consider of meanes for security from th' Indian insults and to defray the charge &c. advising us to beware of two rogues amongst us, naming Laurence and Drumond both dwelling at Jamestown and who were not at the Pascataway siege . . .

Whilst some daies passed in setling the quota's of men arms and amunicon provisions &c. each county was to furnish, one morning early a bruit ran about the town Bacon is fled, Bacon is fled . . . but Bacon was escaped into the country, having intimation that the governor's generosity in pardoning him, and his followers and restoring him to his seat in council, were no other than previous weadles to amuse him and his adherents and to circumvent them by stratagem, forasmuch as the taking Mr. Bacon again into the council was first to keep him out of assembly, and in the next place the govern'r knew the country people were hastning down with dreadfull threatnings to double revenge all wrongs shoud be done to Mr. Bacon or his men, or whoever shou'd have had the least hand in 'em. . . .

In three of ffour daies after this escape, upon news that Mr. Bacon was 30 miles up the river, at the head of four hundred men, the govern'r sent to the parts adjacent, on both sides James river for the militia and all the men could be gotten to come and defend the town, espress's came almost hourly of th' army's approaches, who in less than 4 daies after the first account of 'em att 2 of the clock entered the town, without being withstood, and form'd a body upon a green, not a flight shot from the end of the state house of horse and ffoot, as well regular as veteran troops, who forthwith possess themselves of all the avenues, disarming all in town, and coming thither in boats or by land.

In half an hour after this the drum beat for the house to meet, and in less than an hour more Mr. Bacon came with a file of ffusileers on either hand near the corner of the state house where the govern'r and councill went forth to him; we saw from the window the govern'r open his breast, and Bacon strutting betwixt his two files of men with his left arm on Kenbow flinging his right arm every way both like men distracted; and if in this moment of fury, that enraged multitude had faln upon the govern'r and council we of the assembly expected the same imediate fate; I stept down and amongst the crowd of spectators found the seamen of my sloop, who pray'd me not to stir from them, when in two minutes, the govern'r walk'd towards his private apartm't. A coits cast distant at th' other end of the state house, the gentlemen of the council following him, and after them walked Mr. Bacon with outragious postures of his head arms body, and leggs, often tossing his hand from his sword to his hat and after him came a detachment of ffusileers (musketts not being there in use) who with their cocks bent presented their ffusils at a window of the assembly chamber filled with faces, repeating with menacing voices "we will have it, we will have itt, half a minute when as one of our house a person known to many of them, shook his handkercher out at the window, saying you shall have it, you shall have itt, 3 or 4 times; at these words they sate down their fusils unbent their locks and stood still untill Bacon coming back, followed him to their main body; in this hubub a servant of mine got so nigh as to hear the govern'rs words, and also followed Mr. Bacon, and heard what he said, who came and told me, that when the govern'r opened his breast he said "here! shoot me, foregod fair mark shoot, often rehearsing the same, without any other words; whereto Mr. Bacon answer'd "no may it please yo'r hono'r we will not hurt a hair of yo'r head, nor of any other mans, we are come for a comission to save our lives from th' Indians,

which you have so often promised, and now we will have it before we go.

But when Mr. Bacon followed the govern'r and councill with the forementioned impetuos (like delirious) actions whil'st that party presented their ffusils at the window full of ffaces, he said "Dam my bloud I'le kill govern'r councill assembly and all, and then I'le sheath my sword in my own heart's bloud; and afterwards 'twas said Bacon had given a signall to his men who presented their fusils at those gasing out at the window, that if he shoud draw his sword, they were on sight of it to fire, and slay us, so near was the massacre of us all that very minute, had Bacon in that paroxism of phrentick fury but drawn his sword before the pacifick handkercher was shaken out at the window.

In an hour or more after these violent concussions Mr. Bacon came up to our chamber and desired a comission from us to go against the Indians; our speaker sat silent, when one of Mr. Blayton a neighbor to Mr. Bacon and elected with him a member of assembly for the same county (who therefore durst speak to him) made answer, "'twas not in our province, or power, nor of any other, save the king's viceregent our govern'r, he press'd hard nigh half an hours harangue on the preserving our lives from the Indians, inspecting the publick revenues, th' exorbitant taxes and redressing the grievances and calamities of that deplorable country, whereto having no other answer, he went away dissatisfied. . . .

. . . I never had been conversant in military matters, and also having lived tenderly, my service cou'd be of no benefit because the hardships and fatigues of a wilderness campaigne would put a speedy period to my daies little expecting to hear of more intestine broiles, I went home to Patomack, where reports were afterwards various: we had account that Generall Bacon was march'd with a thousand men into the fforest to seek the enemy Indians, and in a few daies after our next news was, that the govern'r had sumoned together the militia of Glocester and Middlesex counties to the number of twelve hundred men, and proposed to them to follow and suppress that rebell Bacon; whereupon arose a murmuring before his face "Bacon Bacon Bacon, and all walked out of the field, muttering as they went "Bacon Bacon Bacon, leaving the governor and those that came with him to themselves, who being thus abandon'd wafted over Chesepiacke bay 30 miles to Occomack where are two countres of Virginia.

Mr. Bacon hearing of this came back part of the way, and sent out parties of horse patrolling through every county, carrying away prisoners all whom he distrusted might any more molest his Indian prosecucon yet giving liberty to such as pledg'd him their oaths to return home and live quiet; the copies or contents of which oaths I never saw, but heard were very strict, tho' little observed.

About this time was a spie detected pretending himself a deserter who had twice or thrice come and gone from party to party and was by councill of warr sentenced to death, after which Bacon declared openly to him "that if any one man in the army wou'd speak a word to save him, he shou'd not suffer, which no man appearing to do, he was execcuted, upon this manifestation of clemency Bacon was applauded for a mercifull man, not wiling to spill Christian bloud, nor indeed was it said, that he put any other man to death in cold bloud, or plunder any house; nigh the same time came Maj. Langston with his troop of horseand quarterd two nights at my house who (after high compliments from the generall) told me I was desired "to accept the lieutenancy for preserving the peace in the s. northern counties betwixt Potomack and Rappahannock rivers, I humbly thank'd his hon'r excusing myself; as I had done before on that invitation of the like nature at Jamestown, but did hear he was mightily offended at my evasions and threatened to remember me.

The govern'r made a 2d attempt coming over from Accomack with what men he could procure in sloops and boats forty miles up the river to Jamestown, which Bacon hearing of, came againe down from his fforest persuit, and finding a bank not a flight shot long, cast up thwart the neck of the peninsula there in Jamestown, he stormed it, and took the town, in which attack were 12 men slaine and wounded but the govern'r with most of his followers fled back, down the river in their vessells.

Here resting a few daies they concerted the burning of the town, wherein Mr. Lawrence and Mr. Drumond owning the two best houses save one, set fire each to his own house, which example the souldiers following laid the whole town (with church and state-house) in ashes, saying, the rogues should harbour no more there.

On these reiterated molestacons Bacon calls a convention at Midle plantation 15 miles from Jamestown in the month of August 1676, where an oath with one or more proclamations were formed, and writts by him issued for an assembly; the oaths or writs I never saw, but one proclamation comanded all men in the land on pain of death to joine him and retire into the wildernesse upon arrival of the forces expected from England, and oppose them untill they shoud propose or accept to treat of an accomodation, which we who lived comfortably could not have undergone, so as the whole land must have become an Aceldama [a dreadful place; in the New Testament, the Aceldama was a potter's field near Jerusalem that priests had purchased as a burial ground for strangers using the money Judas had received for betraying Christ] if God's exceeding mercy had not timely removed him. . . .

. . . Mr. Bacon now returns from his last expedicon sick of a fflux [presumably dysentery, a disease endemic to the frontier]; without finding any enemy Indians, having not gone far by reason of the vexations behind him, nor had he one dry day in all his marches to and fro in the fforest whilst the plantations (not 50 miles distant) had a sumer so dry as stinted the Indian corn and tobacco &c. Which the people ascribed to the pawawings i.e. the sorceries of the Indians, in a while Bacon dyes and was succeeded by his Lieuten't Genll. Ingram . . . whereupon hasten'd over the govern'r to York river, and with him they articled for themselves and whom else they could, and so all submitted and were pardoned exempting those nominated and otherwise proscribed, in a proclamation of indempnity, the principall of whom were Lawrence and Drumond. . . .

This Mr. Drumond was a sober Scotch gentleman of good repute with whome I had not a particular acquaintance, nor do I know the cause of that rancour his hono'r had against him, other than his pretensions in comon for the publick but meeting him by accident the morning I left the town, I advis'd him to be very wary, for he saw the govern'r had put a brand upon him he (gravely expressing my name) answered "I am in over shoes, I will be over boots, which I was sorry to heare and left him.

The last account of Mr. Lawrence was from an uppermost plantation, whence he and ffour others . . . with horses pistolls &c. march'd away in a snow ancle deep, who were thought to have cast themselves into a branch of some river, rather than be treated like Drumond.

Bacons body was so made away, as his bones were neverfound to be exposed on a gibbet as was purpos'd, stones being laid in his coffin, supposed to be done by Lawrence.

Near this time arrived a small ffleet with a regiment from England S'r John Berry admirall, Col. Herbert Jefferies comander of the land forces and Collo. Morrison who had one year been a former govern'r there, all three joined in comission with or to S'r William Barclay, soon after when a generall court and also an assembly were held, where some of our former assembly (with so many others) were put to death, diverse whereof were persons of honest reputations and handsome estates, as that the assembly petitioned the governour to spill no more bloud, and Mr. Presley at his coming home told me, he believed the govern'r would have hang'd half the countrey, if they had let him alone. The first was Mr. Bland whose ffriends in England had procured his pardon to be sent over with the ffleet, which he pleaded at his tryall, was in the govern'rs pocket (tho' whether 'twas so, or how it came there, I know not, yet did not hear 'twas openly contradicted,) but he was answered by Coll. Morrison that he pleaded his pardon at swords point, which was look'd upon an odd sort of reply, and he was executed; (as was talked) by private instructions from England the Duke of York having sworn "by God Bacon and Bland shoud dye.

The govern'r went in the ffleet to London (whether by comand from his majesty or spontaneous I did not hear) leaving Col. Jefferyes in his place, and by next shipping came back a person who waited on his hono'r in his voyage, and untill his death, from whom a report was whisper'd about, that the king did say "that old fool has hang'd more men in that naked country, than he had done for the murther of his ffather, whereof the governo'r hearing dyed soon after without having seen his majesty; which shuts up this tragedy.

Source: T. M. (Thomas Mathew). *The Beginning, Progress, and Conclusion of Bacon's Rebellion in Virginia, in the Years 1675 and 1676.* 1705. Reprint, Washington, D.C.: Peter Force, 1835. Available online. URL: http://memory.loc.gov/ammem/collections/jefferson_papers/tm.html. Accessed on February 28, 2010.

King William's War, 1689–1697

Account of the French Capture of Schenectady (1690)
M. de Monseignat
Written 1690

Historians have characterized King William's War as a series of murders carried out in dark corners of the American frontier. Because the war consisted for the most part of irregular or guerrilla actions—isolated raids—accounts of the action are rare. One of the most important documents, a narrative of the French capture of Schenectady in 1690, was written that same year by the comptroller-general of New France, a man named Monsieur de Monseignat, and was translated by the antiquarian E. B. O'Callahan, editor of Documents Relative to the Colonial History of the State of New-York *(Albany, 1855), in the 19th century.*

News arrived at Quebec of the success of the first party that had gone out against the English, and which had been organized at Montreal. It might have consisted of two hundred and ten men; to wit, of 80 Indians of the Fault and the Mountain sixteen Algonquins, and the remainder Frenchmen. It was commanded by Lieutenants Le Moyne de Sainte Hélène and Dailleboust de Mantet both Canadians, under whom were Sieurs Se Moyne d'Iberville and Repentigny de Montesson. The best qualified of the French were Sieurs de Bonrepos and de La Brosse, reduced lieutenants (*reformés*) Sieurs Le Moyne de Biainville, Le Bert du Chesne, and la Marque de Montigny who all served as volunteers. They took their departure from Montreal in the fore part of February. . . .

. . . they . . . experienced inconceivable difficulties . . . having been obliged to wade up to their knees in water, and to break the ice with their feet in order to find a solid footing.

They arrived within two leagues of Corlard about four o'clock in the evening, and were harangued by the Great Mohawk, the chief of the Iroquois of the Sault. He urged on all to perform their duty, and to forget their past fatigue, in the hope of taking ample revenge for the injuries they had received from the Iroquois at the solicitation of the English, and of washing them out in the blood of those traitors. This Indian was without contradiction the most considerable of his tribe, an honest man, as full of spirit, prudence and generosity as possible, and capable at the same time of the grandest undertakings. Four squaws were shortly after discovered in a wigwam who gave every information necessary for the attack on the town. The fire found in their hut served to warm those who were benumbed, and they continued their march, having previously detached Ciguières, a Canadian, with nine Indians, on the scout. They discovered no one, and returned to join the main body within one league of Corlard.

At eleven of the clock at night, they came within sight of the town, resolved to defer the assault until two o'clock of the morning. But the excessive cold admitted of no further delay.

The town of Corlard forms a sort of oblong with only two gates—one opposite where our party had halted; the other opening towards Orange, which is only six leagues distant. Messieurs de Sainte Helene and de Mantet were to enter at the first which the squaws pointed out, and which, in fact, was found wide open. Messieurs d'Iberville and de Montesson took the left with another detachment, in order to make themselves masters of that leading to Orange. But they could not discover it, and returned to join the remainder of the party. A profound silence was every where observed, until the two Commanders, who separated after having entered the town for the purpose of encircling it, met at the other extremity.

The signal of attack was given Indian fashion, and the entire force rushed on simultaneously.

M. de Mantet placed himself at the head of one detachment, and reached a small fort where the garrison was under arms. The gate was burst in after a good deal of difficulty, the whole set on fire, and all who defended the place slaughtered.

The sack of the town began a moment before the attack on the fort. Few houses made any resistance. M. de Montigny discovered several which he attempted to carry sword in hand, having tried the musket in vain. He received two thrusts of a halbert [*pertuissane*] one in the body and the other in the arm. But M. de Sainte Hélène having come to his aid, effected an entrance, and put every one who defended the place to the sword. The Massacre lasted two hours. The remainder of the night was spent in placing sentinels, and in taking some rest.

The house belonging to the Minister was ordered to be saved, so as to take him alive to obtain information from him; but as it was not known, it was not spared any more than the others. He was killed in it and his papers burnt before he could be recognized.

At day break some men were sent to the dwelling of Mr. Condre who was Major of the place, and who lived at the other side of the river. He was not willing to surrender, and put himself on the defensive with his servants and some Indians; but as it was resolved not to do him any harm, in consequence of the good treatment that the French had formerly experienced at his hands, M. d'Iberville and the Great Mohawk proceeded thither alone, promised him quarter for himself, his people and his property, whereupon he laid down his arms on their assurance entertained them in his fort, and returned with them to see the Commandants in the town.

In order to occupy the Indians, who would otherwise have taken to drink and thus rendered themselves unable for defence, the houses had already been set on fire. None were spared in the town but one belonging to Condre, and that of a widow who had six children, whither M. de Montigny had been carried when wounded. All the rest were burnt. The lives of between fifty and sixty persons, old men, women and children were spared, they having escaped the first fury of the attack; also some thirty Iroquois, in order to show them that it was the English and not they against whom the grudge was entertained. The loss on this occasion in houses, cattle and grain, amounts to more than four hundred thousand *livres.* There were upwards of eighty well built and well furnished houses in the town.

The return march commenced with thirty prisoners. The wounded, who were to be carried, and the plunder with which all the Indians and some Frenchmen were loaded, caused considerable inconvenience. Fifty good horses were brought away. Sixteen of them only reached Montreal. The remainder were killed on the road for food. . . .

Such . . . is the account of what passed at the taking of Corlard. The French lost but twenty-one men, namely four Indians and seventeen Frenchmen. Only one Indian and one Frenchman were killed at the capture of the town. The others were lost on the road.

Source: Monseignat, M. de. "The French Capture of Schenectady during King William's War." In *Documents Relative to the Colonial History of the State of New-York,* edited by E. B. O'Callahan. Available online. URL: http://www.shsu.edu/~his_ncp/Schen.html. Accessed on February 8, 2010.

QUEEN ANNE'S WAR, 1702–1713

Excerpt from *The Redeemed Captive Returning to Zion*
John Williams
Written 1706–1707

The Reverend John Williams was pastor of a congregation in the frontier village of Deerfield, Massachusetts, a settlement that, throughout the late 17th and early 18th centuries was a frequent target of Indian raids. On February 29, 1704, a mixed force of French and Indians raided Deerfield. Williams, five of his children, and most of his congregation were among the 111 captives carried off to French Canada. Like Mary Rowlandson's narrative of her captivity during King Philip's War, Williams's The Redeemed Captive Returning to Zion *is an example of the popular early American literary genre known as the captivity narrative, and, like Mrs. Rowlandson's account, it recalls the attack, the ordeal of captivity, and the snowy march to Canada as phases of a holy trial visited by God upon his faithful to test and strengthen their faith. Williams was eventually ransomed and returned to Deerfield, which he helped to rebuild. The excerpt that follows focuses on the raid and its immediate aftermath.*

On Tuesday, the 29th of February, 1703–4, not long before break of day, the enemy came in like a flood upon us; our watch being unfaithful;—an evil, the awful effects of which, in the surprisal of our fort, should bespeak all watchmen to avoid, as they would not bring the charge of blood upon themselves. They came to my house in the beginning of the onset, and by their violent endeavors to break open doors and windows, with axes and hatchets, awaked me out of sleep; on which I leaped out of bed, and, running towards the door, perceived the enemy making their entrance into the house. I called to awaken two soldiers in the chamber, and returning toward my bedside for my arms, the enemy immediately broke into the room, I judge to the number of twenty, with painted faces, and hideous acclamations. I reached up my hands to the bed-tester for my pistol, uttering a short petition to God, for everlasting mercies for me and mine, on account of the merits of our glorified Redeemer; expecting a present passage through the valley of the shadow of death; saying in myself, as Isa. xxxviii. 10, 11, "I said, in the cutting off of my days, I shall go to the gates of the grave: I am deprived of the residue of my years. I said, I shall not see the Lord, even the Lord, in the land of the living: I shall behold man no more with the inhabitants of the world." Taking down my pistol, I cocked it, and put it to the breast of the first Indian that came up; but my pistol missing fire, I was seized by three Indians, who disarmed me, and bound me naked, as I was in my shirt, and so I stood for near the space of an hour. Binding me, they told me they would carry me to Quebeck. My pistol missing fire was an occasion of my life's being preserved; since which I have also found it profitable to be crossed in my own will. The judgment of God did not long slumber against one of the three which took me, who was a captain, for by sunrising he received a mortal shot from my next neighbor's house; who opposed so great a number of French and Indians as three hundred, and yet were no more than seven men in an ungarrisoned house.

I cannot relate the distressing care I had for my dear wife, who had lain in but a few weeks before; and for my poor children, family, and Christian neighbors. The enemy fell to rifling the house, and entered in great numbers into every room. I begged of God to remember mercy in the midst of judgment; that he would so far restrain their wrath, as to prevent their murdering a us; that we might have grace to glorify his name, whether in life or death; and, as I was able, committed our state to God. The enemies who entered the house, were all of them Indians and Macquas, insulted over me awhile, holding up hatchets over my head, threatening to burn all I had; but yet God, beyond expectation, made us in a great measure to be pitied; for though some were so cruel and barbarous as to take and carry to the door two of my children and murder them, as also a negro woman; yet they gave me liberty to put on my clothes, keeping me bound with a cord on one arm, till I put on my clothes to the other; and then changing my cord, they let me dress myself, and then pinioned me again. Gave liberty to my dear wife to dress herself and our remaining children. About sun an hour high, we were all carried out of the house, for a march, and saw many of the houses of my neighbors in flames, perceiving the whole fort, one house excepted, to be taken. Who can tell what sorrows pierced our souls, when we saw ourselves carried away from God's sanctuary, to go into a strange land, exposed to so many trials; the journey being at least three hundred miles we were to travel; the snow up to the knees, and we never inured to such hardships and fatigues; the place we were to be carried to, a Popish country. Upon my parting from the town, they fired my house and barn. We were carried over the river, to the foot of the mountain, about a mile from my house, where we found a great number of our Christian neighbors, men, women, and children, to the number of an hundred, nineteen of which were afterward murdered by the way, and two starved to death, near Cowass, in a time of great scarcity, or famine, the savages underwent there. When we came to the foot of the mountain, they took away our shoes, and gave us in the room of them Indian shoes, to prepare us for our travel. Whilst we were there, the English beat out a company that remained in the town, and pursued them to the river, killing and wounding many of them; but the body of the army being alarmed, they repulsed those few English that pursued them.

I am not able to give you an account of the number of the enemy slain, but I observed after this fight no great, insulting mirth, as I expected; and saw many wounded persons, and for several days together they buried of their party, and one of chief note among the Macquas. The Governor of Canada told me, his army had that success with the loss of but eleven men; three Frenchmen, one of which was the lieutenant of the army, five Macquas, and three Indians. But after my arrival at Quebeck, I spake with an Englishman, who was taken in the last war, and of their religion; who told me, they lost above forty, and that many were wounded: I replied, "The Governor of Canada said they lost but eleven men." He answered, "It is true that there were but eleven killed outright at the taking of the fort, but many others were wounded, among whom was the ensign of the French; but," said he, "they had a fight in the meadow, and in both engagements they lost more than forty. Some of the soldiers, both French and Indians, then present, told me so," said he, adding, that the French always endeavor to conceal the number of their slain.

After this, we went up the mountain, and saw the smoke of the fires in the town, and beheld the awful desolations of Deerfield. And before we marched any farther, they killed a sucking child belonging to one of the English. There were slain by the enemy of the inhabitants of Deerfield, to the number of thirty-eight, besides nine of the neighboring towns. We travelled not far the first day; God made the heathen so to pity our children, that though they had several wounded persons of their own to carry upon their shoulders, for thirty miles, before they came to the river, yet they carried our children, incapable of travelling, in their arms, and upon their shoulders. When we came to our lodging place, the first night, they dug away the snow, and made some wigwams, cut down some small branches of the spruce-tree to lie down on, and gave the prisoners somewhat to eat; but we had but little appetite. I was pinioned and bound down that night, and so I was every night whilst I was with the army. Some of the enemy who

brought drink with them from the town fell to drinking, and in their drunken fit they killed my negro man, the only dead person I either saw at the town, or in the way.

In the night an Englishman made his escape; in the morning (March 1), I was called for, and ordered by the general to tell the English, that if any more made their escape, they would burn the rest of the prisoners. He that took me was unwilling to let me speak with any of the prisoners, as we marched; but on the morning of the second day, he being appointed to guard the rear, I was put into the hands of my other master, who permitted me to speak to my wife, when I overtook her, and to walk with her to help her in her journey. On the way, we discoursed of the happiness of those who had a right to an house not made with hands, eternal in the heavens; and God for a father and friend; as also, that it was our reasonable duty quietly to submit to the will of God, and to say, "The will of the Lord be done." My wife told me her strength of body began to fail, and that I must expect to part with her; saying, she hoped God would preserve my life, and the life of some, if not of all our children with us; and commended to me, under God, the care of them. She never spake any discontented word as to what had befallen us, but with suitable expressions justified God in what had happened. We soon made a halt, in which time my chief surviving master came up, upon which I was put upon marching with the foremost, and so made my last farewell of my dear wife, the desire of my eyes, and companion in mercies and afflictions. Upon our separation from each other, we asked for each other grace sufficient for what God should call us to. After our being parted from one another, she spent the few remaining minutes of her stay in reading the Holy Scriptures; which she was wont personally every day to delight her soul in reading, praying, meditating on, by herself, in her closet, over and above what she heard out of them in our family worship. I was made to wade over a small river, and so were all the English, the water above knee deep, the stream very swift; and after that to travel up a small mountain; my strength was almost spent, before I came to the top of it. No sooner had I overcome the difficulty of that ascent, but I was permitted to sit down, and be unburdened of my pack. I sat pitying those who were behind, and entreated my master to let me go down and help my wife; but he refused, and would not let me stir from him. I asked each of the prisoners (as they passed by me) after her, and heard that, passing through the above-said river, she fell down, and was plunged over head and ears in the water; after which she travelled not far, for at the foot of that mountain, the cruel and bloodthirsty savage who took her slew her with his hatchet at one stroke, the tidings of which were very awful. And yet such was the hard-heartedness of the adversary, that my tears were reckoned to me as a reproach. My loss and the loss of my children was great; our hearts were so filled with sorrow, that nothing but the comfortable hopes of her being taken away, in mercy to herself, from the evils we were to see, feel, and suffer under, (and joined to the assembly of the spirits of just men made perfect, to rest in peace, and joy unspeakable and full of glory, and the good pleasure of God thus to exercise us,) could have kept us from sinking under, at that time. That Scripture, Job i. 21, "Naked came I out of my mother's womb, and naked shall I return thither: the Lord gave, and the Lord hath taken away; blessed be the name of the Lord,"—was brought to my mind, and from it, that an afflicting God was to be glorified; with some other places of Scripture, to persuade to a patient bearing my afflictions.

We were again called upon to march, with a far heavier burden on my spirits than on my back. I begged of God to overrule, in his providence, that the corpse of one so dear to me, and of one whose spirit he had taken to dwell with him in glory, might meet with a Christian burial, and not be left for meat to the fowls of the air and beasts of the earth; a mercy that God graciously vouchsafed to grant. For God put it into the hearts of my neighbors, to come out as far as she lay, to take up her corpse, carry it to the town, and decently to bury it soon after. In our march they

killed a sucking infant of one of my neighbors; and before night a girl of about eleven years of age. I was made to mourn, at the consideration of my flock being, so far, a flock of slaughter, many being slain in the town, and so many murdered in so few miles from the town; and from fears what we must yet expect, from such who delightfully imbrued their hands in the blood of so many of His people. When we came to our lodging place, an Indian captain from the eastward spake to my master about killing me, and taking off my scalp. I lifted up my heart to God, to implore his grace and mercy in such a time of need; and afterwards I told my master, if he intended to kill me, I desired he would let me know of it; assuring him that my death, after a promise of quarter, would bring the guilt of blood upon him. He told me he would not kill me. We laid down and slept, for God sustained and kept us.

Source: Williams, John. *The Redeemed Captive Returning to Zion.* 1706–07. Reprint, Bedford, Mass.: Applewood Books, 1993.

THE FRENCH AND INDIAN WAR, 1754–1763

The War's First Battle: Diary Account
George Washington
May 27, 1754

Lieutenant Governor Robert Dinwiddie of Virginia sent the militia major George Washington (1732–99) with a small detachment from Williamsburg on October 31, 1753, on a mission to inform the French commandant of Fort Le Boeuf (on Lake Erie) that he and all other Frenchmen were to clear out of the Ohio territory claimed by the British. Washington delivered his message on December 12, 1753, was politely rebuffed, and returned to Williamsburg to deliver the response to Dinwiddie. The lieutenant governor reacted by ordering a fort to be built at the "forks of the Ohio," the site of modern Pittsburgh. Over the next few months, the French secretly watched construction; then they attacked, took over the stockade, and named it Fort Duquesne, after their latest governor. The date of that French victory was April 17, 1754, the very day, coincidentally, that Governor Dinwiddie sent Washington, now a year older and promoted to lieutenant colonel, with 159 militiamen to reinforce a military installation that, unknown to either man, was already lost.

On May 27, Washington's Indian scouts reported a French reconnaissance party, 33 men, camped in a secluded bower near Great Meadows (in present-day Pennsylvania). The next morning, Washington fought his maiden battle, a short, sharp exchange that touched off the French and Indian War.

Among the French dead was Joseph Coulon de Villiers, sieur de Jumonville, who (according to the prisoners Washington captured) was an ambassador of France, which made Washington not a victorious military commander but an assassin. As Washington saw it, the so-called ambassador and his "embassy" were spies. Nevertheless, the accusation of diplomatic murder somewhat curdled the savor of his victory. Moreover, Washington realized that the killing would not go unavenged.

This account was written by George Washington himself. The "Gist" referred to is Christopher Gist, a prominent British frontier trader and guide in the employ of the Ohio Company. "La Force" was the nickname universally bestowed upon Michel Pépin, the French "commissary of stores," who was responsible for distributing supplies to the French and French-allied Indians on the frontier. He was a man of great influence in the region and regarded by the British as highly treacherous. "Half-King" was Tanaghrisson, an Iroquois (Mingo) leader on whose loyalty the British counted heavily.

The 27th, Arrived Mr. *Gist*, early in the Morning, who told us, that Mr. *la Force*, with fifty Men, whose Tracks he had seen five Miles off, had been at his Plantation the Day before, towards Noon; and would have killed a Cow, and broken every Thing in the House, if two Indians, whom he had left in the House, had not persuaded

them from their Design: I immediately detached 65 Men, under the Command of Captain *Hog*, Lieut. *Mercer*, Ensign *Peronie*, three Sergeants, and three Corporals, with Instructions.

The French enquired at Mr. *Gist's*, what was become of the *Half King*? I did not fail to let the young Indians who were in our Camp know, that the French wanted to kill the *Half King;* and that had its desired Effect. They thereupon offered to accompany our People to go after the French, and if they found it true that he had been killed, or even insulted by them, one of them would presently carry the News thereof to the *Mingoes*, in order to incite their Warriors to fall upon them. One of these young Men was detached towards Mr. *Gist's*; that if he should not find the *Half King* there, he was to send a Message by a Delaware.

About eight at Night, received an Express from the *Half King*, which informed me, that, as he was coming to join us, he had seen along the Road, the Tracts of two Men, which he had followed, till he was brought thereby to a low obscure Place; that he was of Opinion the whole Party of the French was hidden there. That very Moment I sent out Forty Men, and ordered my Ammunition to be put in a Place of Safety, under a strong Guard to defend it, fearing it to be a Stratagem of the French to attack our Camp; and with the rest of my Men, set out in a heavy Rain, and in a Night as dark as Pitch, along a Path scarce broad enough for one Man; we were sometimes fifteen or twenty Minutes out of the Path, before we could come to it again, and so dark, that we would often strike one against another: All Night long we continued our Rout, and the 28th, about Sun-rise, we arrived at the Indian Camp, where, after having held a Council with the *Half King*, it was concluded we should fall on them together; so we sent out two Men to discover where they were, as also their Posture, and what Sort of Ground was thereabout; after which, we formed ourselves for an Engagement, marching one after the other, in the Indian Manner: We were advanced pretty near to them, as we thought, when they discovered us;

whereupon I ordered my Company to fire; mine was supported by that of Mr. *Wager's,* and my Company and his received the whole Fire of the French, during the greatest Part of the Action, which only lasted a Quarter of an Hour, before the Enemy was routed.

We killed Mr. *de Jumonville,* the Commander of that Party, as also nine others; we wounded one, and made Twenty-one Prisoners, among whom were M. *la Force,* M. *Drouillon,* and two Cadets. The Indians scalped the Dead, and took away the most Part of their Arms, after which we marched on with the Prisoners and the Guard, to the Indian Camp, where again I held a Council with the *Half-King;* and there informed him, that the Governor was desirous to see him, and was waiting for him at Winchester; he answered that, he could not go just then, as his People were in too eminent a Danger from the French, whom they had fallen upon; that he must send Messengers to all the allied Nations, in order to invite them to take up the Hatchet. He sent a young Delaware Indian to the Delaware Nation, and gave him also a French Scalp to carry to them. This young Man desired to have a Part of the Presents which were allotted for them, but that the remaining Part might be kept for another Opportunity: He said he would go to his own Family, and to several others, and would wait on them at Mr. *Gist's,* where he desired Men and Horses should be sent ready to bring them up to our Camp. After this I marched on with the Prisoners; They informed me that they had been sent with a Summons to order me to depart. A plausible Pretence to discover our Camp, and to obtain the Knowledge of our Forces and our Situation! It was so clear that they were come to reconnoitre what we were, that I admired at their Assurance, when they told me they were come as an Embassy; for their Instructions mentioned that they should get what Knowledge they could of the Roads, Rivers, and of all the Country as far as Potowmack: And instead of coming as an Embassador, publickly, and in an open Manner, they came secretly, and sought after the most hidden Retreats, more like Deserters than Embassadors in such Retreat they incamped, and remained hid for whole Days together, and that, no more than five Miles from us; From thence they sent Spies to reconnoitre our Camp; after this was done, they went back two Miles, from whence they sent the two Messengers spoken of in the Instruction, to acquaint M. *de Contrecour* of the Place we were at, and of our Disposition, that he might send his Detachments to inforce the Summons as soon as it should be given.

Besides, an Embassador has princely Attendants; whereas this was only a simple petty French Officer; an Embassador has no Need of Spies, his Character being always sacred: And seeing their Intention was so good, why did they tarry two Days, at five Miles distance from us, without acquainting me with the Summons, or, at least, with something that related to the Embassy? That alone would be sufficient to raise the greatest Suspicions, and we ought to do them the Justice to say, that, as they wanted to hide themselves, they could not pick out better Places than they had done.

The Summons was so insolent, and savoured the Gasconnade so much, that if it had been brought openly by two Men, it would have been an immediate Indulgence, to have suffered them to return.

It was the Opinion of the *Half-King* in this Case, that their Intentions were evil, and that it was a pure Pretence; that they never intended to come to us but as Enemies; and if we had been such Fools as to let them go, they would never help us any more to take other Frenchmen.

They say they called to us as soon as they had discovered us; which is an absolute Falshood, for I was then marching at the Head of the Company going towards them, and can positively affirm, that, when they first saw us, they ran to their Arms, without calling; as I must have heard them, had they so done.

Source: Washington, George. *George Washington's Diaries: An Abridgment,* edited by Dorothy Twohig, 41–55. Charlottesville: University Press of Virginia, 1999.

The War's First Battle:
Letter to John Augustine Washington
George Washington
May 31, 1754

Lieutenant Colonel George Washington wrote this letter to his younger brother John Augustine Washington from his camp at Great Meadows on May 31, 1754. He recounts his victory in an encounter with a small French party but also makes clear his understanding that a French reprisal will surely follow. The "Pallisado'd Fort" he describes is the tiny, makeshift fortification he named Fort Necessity, from which he would fight what is generally considered the first genuine battle of the French and Indian War.

Dr John

Since my last we have arrived at this place, where 3 days agoe we had an engagemt wth the French that is, between a party of theirs & Ours; Most of our men were out upon other detachments, so that I had scarcely 40 men under my Command, and about 10, or a doz. Indians, nevertheless we obtained a most signal Victory. The Battle lasted abt 10, or 15 minutes, sharp firing on both sides, when the French gave ground & run, but to no great purpose; there were 12 killed, among which was Monsr De Jumonville the Commandr, & taken 21 prisoners with whom are Monsieurs La Force, Druillong, together with 2 Cadets. I have sent them to his Honr the Governor at Winchester conducted by Lieut. West & a guard of 20 men. We had but one man killed, 2 or 3 wounded and a great many more within an Inch of being shott; among the wounded on our side was Lieut. Waggoner, but no danger will ensue.

We expect every Hour to be attacked by a superior Force, but shall if they stay one day longer be prepared for them; We have already got Intrenchments & are about a Pallisado'd Fort, which will I hope be finished today. The Mingo's have struck the French & I hope will give a good blow before they have done, I expect 40 odd of them here to night, wch with our Fort and some reinforcements from Colo. Fry, will enable us to exert our Noble Courage with Spirit.

I am Yr Affe Bror

Geo. Washington

I fortunately escaped without a wound, tho' the right Wing where I stood was exposed to & received all the Enemy's fire and was the part where the man was killed & the rest wounded. I can with truth assure you, I heard Bullets whistle and believe me there was something charming in the sound.

Source: Washington, George. "To John Augustine Washington, May 31, 1754." In *Writings.* New York: Library of America, 1997, p. 47.

THE BATTLE OF FORT NECESSITY, JULY 3–4, 1754

Letter to Lieutenant Governor Robert Dinwiddie
George Washington and James Mackay
July 19, 1754

After his "victory" over Jumonville's party, Washington withdrew to Great Meadows, near present-day Farmington, Pennsylvania, and there hurriedly erected a crude circular stockade just 53 feet in diameter, with projecting entrenchments. This tiny structure, which Washington christened Fort Necessity, was intended to protect some 400 men, of whom 100 were too ill even to sit up, let alone fight. Nevertheless, Washington wrote of his fort that, thanks to its protection, he would "not fear the attack of 500 men." In reality, the inexperienced Washington had poorly sited it on low, swampy ground surrounded by forest, which provided ample cover for any attacker.

On July 3, 1754, 600 French troops and 100 Indians led by Captain Louis Coulon de Villiers, the brother of the slain sieur de Jumonville, attacked Fort Necessity. Washington and his outnumbered garrison were made especially miserable by heavy rains, which flooded the low-lying fort and ruined much of their meager supply of gunpowder as well as other provisions. By the end of the day, Washington had lost 30 men killed, 70 wounded, and 19 missing. Believing that honor had been served and that further bloodshed was fruitless, Washington accepted a truce, then signed a formal capitulation the next day, July 4, 1754.

On July 19, 1754, Washington and James Mackay, captain of an "independent" company (part of the regular British army rather than the colonial militia) that fought alongside Washington's force, wrote an account of the battle and surrender for Lieutenant Governor Robert Dinwiddie.

Williamsburg 19 July 1754

The third of this Instant July, about 9 o'Clock, we received Intelligence that the French, having been reinforced with 700 Recruits, had left Monongehela, and were in full March with 900 Men to attack us. Upon this, as our Numbers were so unequal, (our whole Force not exceeding 300) we prepared for our Defence in the best Manner we could, by throwing up a small Intrenchment, which we had not Time to perfect, before our Centinel gave Notice, about Eleven o'Clock, of their Approach, by firing his Piece, which he did at the Enemy, and as we learned afterwards killed three of their Men, on which they began to fire upon us, at about 600 Yards Distance, but without any Effect: We immediately called all our Men to their Arms, and drew up in Order before our Trenches; but as we looked upon this distant Fire of the Enemy only as an Artifice to intimidate, or draw our Fire from us, we waited their nearer Approach before we returned their Salute. They then advanced in a very irregular Manner to another Point of Woods, about 60 Yards off, and from thence made a second Discharge; upon which, finding they had no Intention of attacking us in the open Field, we retired into our Trenches, and still reserved our Fire; as we expected from their great Superiority of Numbers, that they would endeavour to force our

Trenches; but finding they did not seem to intend this neither, the Colonel gave Orders to fire, which was done with great Alacrity and Undauntedness. We continued this unequal Fight, with an Enemy sheltered behind the Trees, ourselves without Shelter, in Trenches full of Water, in a settled Rain, and the Enemy galling us on all Sides incessantly from the Woods, till 8 o'Clock at Night, when the French called to Parley: From the great Improbability that such a vastly superior Force, and possessed of such an Advantage, would offer a Parley first, we suspected a Deceit, and therefore refused to consent that they should come among us; on which they desired us to send an Officer to them, and engaged their Parole for his Safety; we then sent Capt. Van Braam, and Mr. Peyronee, to receive their Proposals, which they did, and about Midnight we agreed that each Side should retire without Molestation, they back to their Fort at Monongehela, and we to Wills's Creek: That we should march away with all the Honours of War, and with all our Stores, Effects and Baggage. Accordingly the next Morning, with our Drums beating and our Colours flying, we began our March in good Order, with our Stores, &c. in Convoy; but we were interrupted by the Arrival of a Reinforcement of 100 Indians among the French, who were hardly restrained from attacking us, and did us considerable Damage by pilfering our Baggage. We then proceeded, but soon found it necessary to leave our Baggage and Stores; the great Scarcity of our Provisions obliged us to use the utmost Expedition, and having neither Waggons nor Horses to transport them. The Enemy had deprived us of all our Creatures; by killing, in the Beginning of the Engagement, our Horses, Cattle, and every living Thing they could, even to the very Dogs. The Number of the Killed on our Side was thirty, and seventy wounded; among the former was Lieutenant Mercier, of Captain Maccay's independant Company; a Gentleman of true military Worth, and whose Bravery would not permit him to retire, though dangerously wounded, till a second Shot disabled him, and a third put an End to his Life, as he was carrying to the Surgeon. Our Men behaved with singular Intrepidity, and we determined not to ask for Quarter, but with our Bayonets screw'd, to sell our Lives as dearly as possibly we could. From the Numbers of the Enemy, and our Situation, we could not hope for Victory; and from the Character of those we had to encounter, we expected no Mercy, but on Terms that we positively resolved not to submit to.

The Number killed and wounded of the Enemy is uncertain, but by the Information given by some Dutch in their Service to their Countrymen in ours, we learn that it amounted to above three hundred; and we are induced to believe it must be very considerable, by their being busy all Night in burying their Dead, and yet many remained the next Day; and their Wounded we know was considerable, by one of our Men, who had been made Prisoner by them after signing the Articles, and who, on his Return told us, that he saw great Numbers much wounded and carried off upon Litters. [Washington and Mackay's estimate of French casualties is certainly inaccurate, if not deliberately exaggerated.]

We were also told by some of their Indians after the Action, that the French had an Officer of distinguishable Rank killed. Some considerable Blow they must have received, to induce them to call first for a Parley, knowing, as they perfectly did, the Circumstances we were in.

Source: Washington, George, and James Mackay. "Letter to Lieutenant Governor Robert Dinwiddie (July 19, 1754)." In *The Papers of George Washington: Colonial Series,* edited by W. W. Abbot, 1:159–161. Charlottesville: University Press of Virginia, 1983.

Account of the Surrender of Fort Necessity
Captain Louis Coulon de Villiers
Written 1754

The French commander of the force that captured Fort Necessity recorded the details of the surrender in his journal. Coulon de Villiers was the brother of the sieur de Jumonville, whom Washington's men killed in the skirmish that had preceded the Battle of Fort Necessity. Note that Coulon de Villiers refers to

the incident as an "assassination." The appearance of this word in the Articles of Capitulation would prove a source of great embarrassment to young Washington.

They [the British] accepted the Proposal. There came a Captain to the Place where I was: I sent M. *le Mercier* to receive him, and I went to the Meadow, where I told him, that as we were not at War, we were very willing to save then from the Cruelties to which they exposed themselves, on Account of the *Indians;* but if they were stubborn, we would take away from them all Hopes of escaping; that we consented to be favourable to them at present, *as we were come only to revenge my Brother's Assassination,* and to oblige them to quit the Lands of the King our Master; and we agreed to grant them the Capitulation. . . . We considered, that nothing could be more advantageous than this Capitulation, as it was not proper to make Prisoners in a Time of Peace. We made the *English* consent to sign, that they had assassinated my Brother in his own Camp. We had Hostages for the Security of the *French* who were in their Power; we made them abandon the King's Country; we obliged them to leave us their Cannon, consisting of nine Pieces; we destroyed all their Horses and Cattle, and made them to sign, that the Favour we granted them, was only to prove, how desirous we were to use them as Friends. That very Night the Articles of Capitulation were signed, and two Hostages I had demanded, were brought to my Camp.

Source: Villiers, Captain Louis Coulon de. "Account of the Surrender of Fort Necessity." In *The Papers of George Washington: Colonial Series,* edited by W. W. Abbot, 1:163, n. 3. Charlottesville: University Press of Virginia, 1983.

Articles of Capitulation
Anonymous
July 3, 1754

The hastily drawn-up Articles of Capitulation that George Washington signed after his defeat at Fort Necessity proved highly controversial. The document was written in nearly illegible French, and the ink, exposed to rain, was runny, faded, and blurred. Captain Jacob Van Braam, a Dutch trader serving in Washington's detachment, translated. Dutch was his native language, French his second, and English a distant third; Washington spoke no French at all. In the end, Washington claimed that what he understood from Van Braam's translation was that the terms granted him and his command the "honors of war," which included safe passage out of the fort and permission to retain arms and colors. Van Braam apparently stumbled over a stipulation that the combat had not been intended to disturb the "bonne harmonie" that existed between the French and British monarchs but had served "only to avenge" what Van Braam finally decided to translate as the death or loss or killing of certain French officers (including the sieur de Jumonville). Only after Washington had signed the document, had withdrawn from the fort, and had returned to Williamsburg was it revealed that the word Van Braam had rendered in relatively innocuous English actually referred to the assassination of Jumonville and the other French officers. Thus, in the French version of these first two engagements of the French and Indian War, Lieutenant Colonel George Washington had confessed to cold-blooded political murder.

July the 3d, 1754, at 8 o'clock at Night. As our Intentions have never been to trouble the Peace and good Harmony subsisting between the two Princes in Amity, but only to revenge the Assassination ["L'assasin"] committed on one of our Officers, bearer of a Summon, as also on his Escorte, and to hinder any Establishment of the Lands of the Dominions of the King my Master: Upon these Considerations, we are willing to shew Favour to all the English who are in the said Fort, on the following Conditions, *viz.*

Article I.

We grant Leave to the English Commander, to retire with all his Garrison, and to return peaceably into his own Country; and promise to hinder his receiving any Insult from us French; and to restrain, as much as shall be in our Power, the Indians that are with us.

II.

It shall be permitted him to go out, and carry with him all that belongs to them, except the Artillery, which we reserve.

III.

That we will allow them the Honours of War; that they march out with Drums beating, and one Swivel Gun, being willing thereby to convince them, that we treat them as Friends.

IV.

That as soon as the Articles are signed by both Parties, the English Colours shall be struck.

V.

That To-morrow, at Break of Day, a Detachment of French shall go and make the Garrison file of, and take Possession of the Fort.

VI.

As the English have but few Oxen or Horses left, they are at Liberty to hide their Effects, and to come again, and search for them, when they have a Number of Horses sufficient to carry them off; and that for this End, they may have what Guards they please; on Condition, that they give their Word of Honour, to work no more upon any Buildings in this Place, or any Part on this Side the Mountains.

VII.

And as the English have in their Power, one Officer, two Cadets, and most of the Prisoners made at the Assassination of M. de Jumonville ["l'assasinat du Sr. de Jumonville"] and promise to send them back, with a safe Guard to Fort du

Quesne, situate on the Ohio. For Surety of their performing this Article as well as this Treaty, M. Jacob Vambrane and Robert Stobo, both Captains, shall be delivered to us as Hostages, till the Arrival of our French and Canadians above mentioned. We oblige ourselves on our Side, to give an Escorte to return these two Officers in Safety; and expect to have our French in two Months and a Half at farthest. A Duplicate of this being fixed upon one of the Posts of our Blockade, the Day and Year above mentioned.

Source: Anonymous. "Articles of Capitulation." In *The Papers of George Washington: Colonial Series,* edited by W. W. Abbot, 1:167. Charlottesville: University Press of Virginia, 1983.

Braddock's Defeat at Fort Duquesne, July 9, 1755

Account of Braddock's Defeat
Lieutenant Colonel William Dunbar
Written July 1755

The following is an account of Major General Edward Braddock's expedition against Fort Duquesne, culminating in his defeat on July 9, 1755. It was written by the British army lieutenant colonel William Dunbar, who assumed command after the general's death on July 13. Dunbar led the defeated column in a long retreat to Fort Cumberland, Maryland. Virginia and Pennsylvania colonial leaders beseeched Dunbar to build a defensive fort against French-backed Indian attack at Raystown (present-day Bedford, Pennsylvania), but Dunbar withdrew with his demoralized forces all the way to Philadelphia in August, leaving the frontier to suffer Indian raids.

On Wednesday the 9th Inst, We were advanced within 9 miles Fort du Quesne, & in order to reach it were to pass the Monongalhela in 2

different places. by 2 in the Morning Col: Gage with the 2 Companies of Grenadiers, to wch I belonged, with 150 Men besides was ordered with 2 six pounders, to cross the River, & cover March of the General wth the Rest of the Army. This We executed witht any disturbance from the Enemy, and when we had possession of the Bank of the sd crossing, we were remained drawn up, till the general came with the rest of the Army, & passed River in a Column. The Ground from thence to the French Fort we were told was pretty. good, & the woods open, but all upon the ascent[.] Col: Gage was then ordered with his advanced Party to march on, and was soon followed by the general. We had not marched above 800 yards from the River, when we were allarmed by the Indian Hollow [holler], & in an instant, found ourselves attacked on all sides, their methods, they immediately seise a Tree, & are certain of their Aim, so that before the Genl came to our assistance, most of our advanced Party were laid sprawling on the ground. our Men unaccustomed to that way of fighting, were quite confounded, & behaved like Poltrons, nor could the examples, nor the Intreaties of their officers prevail with them, to do any one [what was ordered]. This they denied them, when we begged of them not to throw away their fire but to follow us with fixed Bayonets to drive them from the hill & trees, they never minded us, but threw their fire away in the most confused manner, some in the air, others in the ground, & a great many destroyed their own men & officers. When the General came up to our assistance, men were seized with the same Pannic, & went into as much disorder, some Part of them being 20 deep. The officers in order to remedy this, advanced into the front, & soon became the mark of the Enemy, who scarce left one, that was not killed or wounded; when we were first attacked, It was near one o'Clock, & in this Confusion did we remain till near 5 in the Evening, our Men having then thrown away their 24 Rounds in the manner above mentioned, & scarce an officer left to head them. They then turned their backs, & left the Enemy in possession of every Thing.

The burial of Major General Edward Braddock *(Library of Congress)*

What officers were left, endeavoured to rally them at the first crossing of the River, but all to no purpose, terrified at the notion of having no Quarter & being scalped, they ran witht knowing where & most of them threw their Arms from them[.] The French & Indians not imagining our Pain & Consternation were so great, as they really were, pursued us no further than the first crossing otherwise 100 of them, might have cut the Remainder of us to Peices. We marched all night in the utmost horrour & distress, most of us wounded, without a bit of anything to eat & nothing to cover us. On Friday the 11th We arrived at Col: Dunbars Camp 56 Miles from the Place of Action. our Strength before the Engagement amounted to 1100 Men.

Killed & wounded 823.

Source: Dunbar, William. "Account of the Battle of Fort Duquesne (July 9, 1755)." Hardwicke 136, Document no. 6, Manuscripts and Archives Division, New York Public Library, Astor, Lenox and Tilden Foundations.

Letter to His Mother
George Washington
July 18, 1755

Washington's letter to his mother, Mary Ball Washington, speaks volumes of the young man's cool courage under fire. Note how he contrasts the bravery of the Virginia militiamen with the "panic," "cowardice," and "dastardly behavior" exhibited by the British "regulars." Colonial military leaders like Washington were unimpressed by the performance of British forces in the French and Indian War; doubtless, this gave them some confidence 20 years later, when they faced the British regulars in the American Revolution.

Honored Madam:

As I doubt not but you have heard of our defeat, and perhaps have it represented in a worse light (if possible) than it deserves, I've taken this earliest opportunity to give some account of the engagement as it happened, within seven miles of the French on Wednesday, the 9th inst.

We marched on to that place without any considerable loss, having only now and then a straggler picked up by the Indian scouts of the French. When we came there, we were attacked by a body of French and Indians, whose number (I am certain) did not exceed 300 men. Ours consisted of about 1,300 well-armed troops, chiefly of the English soldiers, who were struck with such a panic that they behaved with more cowardice than it is possible to conceive. The officers behaved gallantly in order to encourage their men, for which they suffered greatly, there being near 60 killed and wounded—a large proportion out of the number we had!

The Virginia troops showed a good deal of bravery, and were near all killed; for I believe out of three companies that were there, there are scarce 30 men left alive. Captain Peyrouny and all his officers, down to a corporal, were killed; Captain Polson shared near as hard a fate, for only one of his was left. In short, the dastardly behavior of those they call regulars exposed all others that were inclined to do their duty to almost certain death; and, at last, in despite of all the efforts of the officers to the contrary, they broke and ran as sheep pursued by dogs; and it was impossible to rally them.

The general was wounded; of which he died three days after. Sir Peter Halket was killed in the field, where died many other brave officers. I luckily escaped without wound, though I had four bullets through my coat, and two horses shot under me. Captains Orme and Morris, two of the general's aides de camp, were wounded early in the engagement, which rendered the duty hard upon me, as I was the only person then left to distribute the general's orders, which I was scarcely able to do as I was not half recovered from a violent illness that confined me to my bed and a wagon above ten days.

I am still in a weak and feeble condition, which induces me to halt here two or three days in hopes of recovering a little strength to enable me to proceed homeward; from whence I fear I shall not be able to stir toward September, so that I shall not have the pleasure of seeing you till then, unless it be in Fairfax. . . .

P.S. We had about 300 men killed an as many, and more, wounded.

Source: Washington, George. "George Washington to Mary Ball Washington." July 18, 1755. The George Washington Papers at the Library of Congress, 1741–1799. Available online. URL: http://memory.loc. gov/cgi-bin/query/p?mgw:3:./temp/~ammem_JzTr::. Accessed on February 8, 2010.

THE BATTLE OF LAKE GEORGE, SEPTEMBER 8, 1755

Letter to Comte d'Argenson
Jean-Armand, baron de Dieskau
September 14, 1755

The dashing French commander Jean-Armand, baron de Dieskau (1701–67) engaged the British colonial and allied Indian forces led by William Johnson in especially fierce combat. Dieskau was finally captured at the Battle of Lake George, which the French called Lake St. Sacrement. From captivity in Johnson's camp, he wrote the following account to the French politician and cofounder of the École Militaire, Marc-Pierre de Voyer de Paulmy d'Argenson, comte d'Argenson.

My Lord,

I have had the honor to report to you everything of interest to the service, up to my departure for Fort St. Frederic.

On the very vague intelligence of the designs of the English in that quartier, I proceeded thither with 3000 men, whereof 700 were Regulars, 1600 Canadians, and 700 Indians. I arrived at Fort St. Frédéric on the 16th and 17th of August; a portion of the troops had proceeded me; the remainder joined me there without delay.

Before quitting Montreal, I had already various reasons for suspecting the fidelity of the domiciliated Iroquois, both of the Sault St. Louis and that of the Lake of the Two Mountains, whose number exceeded 300, composing half of the Indians that had been given to me. I represented it repeatedly to M. de Vaudreuil, who would never admit it, but scarcely had I arrived at Fort St. Frédéric, than I had occasion to furnish him still stronger proofs thereof.

For more than 15 days that I was encamped under that fort, I encountered nothing [but] difficulties from the Indians; those who were good, were spoiled by the Iroquois. Never was I able to obtain from them a faithful scout; at one time they refused to make any; at another time, seeming to obey me, they set forth, but when a few leagues from the camp, they sent back the Frenchmen I had associated with them, and used to return within a few days without bringing me any intelligence. Such has been the conduct of the Indians, caused by the Iroquois. My letters from Fort Saint Frédéric to M. de Vaudreuil and M. Bigot, sufficiently develop the particulars of their mischievous intrigues.

At length, on the 27th of August, a Canadian named Boileau, returned from a scout and informed me that about 3000 English were encamped at Lidius' house, where they were constructing a fort [Fort Edward, New York] that was already pretty well advanced. I immediately resolved to go forward and to post myself in an advantaeous place, either to wait for the enemy, should he advance, or to anticipate him myself, by going in quest of him.

On arriving at this post, some Abenakis who had been on the scout, unknown to the Iroquois, brought me in an English prisoner, who told me that the body of the English army had moved from Lidius', and that only 500 remained there to finish the fort, but that they were expecting 2400 men, who were to march to the head of Lake St. Sacrament for the purpose of Building a fort there also.

On this intelligence I determined to leave the main body of the army where I was, and to take with me a picked force (corps d'elite) [to] march rapidly and surprise Fort Lidius, and capture the 500 men encamped without its walls. My detachement was composed of 600 Indians, 600 Canadians and 200 Regulars belonging to La Reine and Languedoc Regiments. It was four days' journey by water and across the woods to Lidius'. All exhibited an ardor which guaranteed success, but the fourth day, which ought to be favorable to the King's arms, was the commencement of our misfortune.

The Iroquois refused point blank to march to attack the fort, or rather the camp of the 500 English; but, perceiving that I was resolved to dispence with them, and that the other Indians were disposed to follow me, they sent excuses and immediately set forth to lead the van, as if to make a parade of their zeal.

Mine was a combined movement. I was to arrive at nightfall at that fort and rush to the attack; but the Iroquois, who took the lead on the march, under the pretense of zeal, caused a wrong direction to be taken; and when I was informed of the circumstance, it was no longer time to apply a remedy, so that at nightfall I was yet a league from that fort on the road leading from it to Lake St. Sacrament.

A courier that was killed, and whose despatch was brought to me, and some prisoners that were brought in, gave me the intelligence that about 3000 English were encamped near there, and that they had but a confused knowledge of the strength of my forces. I immediately gave the Indians the choice of proceeding next day to attack either the fort or this army. The vote of the Iroquois which prevailed, caused the latter course to be adopted.

On the following day, the 8th of September, I commenced my march. About 10 of the clock, after having proceeded 5 leagues, the scouts reported to me that they had seen a large body of troops on their way to the fort, which news was confirmed by a prisoner, taken at the time. They consisted of one thousand men or more, that had left the camp to reinforce the fort. I immediately made my arrangements, ordered the Indians to throw themselves into the woods, to allow the enemy to pass, so as to attack them in the rear, whilst the Canadians took them on the flank, and I should wait for them in front with the regular troops.

This was the moment of treachery. The Iroquois, who were on the left, showed themselves before the time and did not fire. The Abenakis, who occupied the right, seeing themselves discovered, alone with a few Canadians attacked the enemy in front and put them to flight. I immediately prepared to join them, in order to accompany the fugitives into their camp, though still more than a league off.

Meanwhile, the Iroquois collected on a hill, unwilling to advance. Some of them even wanted to force the Abenakis to release three Mohawks whom they had captured at the first encounter. I am ignorant of the result of that quarrel; but the Abenakis, seeing the Iroquois immovable, halted also, and the Canadians, seeing the retreat of the one and the other, were thereby intimidated.

As I was near the enemy's camp, and in front of the cannon, I marched forward with 200 Regulars to capture it, [expecting] that the Canadians would not abandon me, and that the Indians would perhaps return; but in vain. The Regulars received the whole of the enemy's fire and perished there almost to a man. I was knocked down by three shots, none of which were mortal, but I received a 4th that passed from one hip to the other, perforating the bladder.

I know not at present what will be my fate; from Monsieur Johnson, the General of the English army, I am receiving all the attention possible to be expected from a brave man, full of honor and feeling. Sieur de Bernier, my Aide de Camp, is a prisoner with me; he has been fortunate enough to receive only a slight bruise from a splinter. I know not of any other officer taken. Should the nature of my wounds destroy the hope of returning to Europe, and should Sieur Bernier go there, he will be able to give you, my Lord, the fullest details of this affair,

and of everything that my situation prevents me explaining to you.

I beg of you, my Lord, to have regard for his zeal for the service, and for his attachment to me.

I have the honor to be respectfully, My Lord,
Your most humble and
Most obedient servant,
Baron de Dieskau.

Source: Dieskau, Jean-Armand, baron de. "Letter to Count d'Argenson (September 14, 1755)." Available online. URL: http://warandgame.wordpress.com/2008/01/27/jean-armand-dieskau/. Accessed on February 8, 2010.

THE SIEGE OF QUEBEC, JUNE–SEPTEMBER 1759

A Journal of the Expedition up the River St. Lawrence
Sergeant Major of the 40th Regiment's Grenadiers
Published 1759

A Journal of the Expedition up the River St. Lawrence *was written by the sergeant major of the 40th Regiment's Grenadiers, part of the Louisbourg Grenadiers, which consisted of the grenadier companies of the 22nd, 40th, and 45th Regiments of the regular British army. On the day of the Battle of Quebec, September 13, 1759, General James Wolfe received his fatal wound while he stood next to the Louisbourg Grenadiers. When the city formally surrendered, these soldiers were the first to enter the walls of Quebec. In this account, the date of the culminating battle is incorrectly given as September 14.*

Louisbourg, June 1st, 1759
We embark'd on board the Transport Harwood, bound on the Expedition to Canada . . .

The 4th Day we set Sail for the River St. Lawerance, which we made on the 9th Day, and

Benjamin West's depiction of the death of General Wolfe *(Library of Congress)*

there we lay 'til the 16th, before we got into the River; which is very wide and Mountainous. For about forty Leagues up the River the Depth of Water is 100 Fathoms. The 16th Day we came into seventeen fathom Water; and on the 23rd we join'd Admiral Durell, who had 7 Sail of the Line, with some Frigates with him, which lay as a Guard to Protect the River, at a Place call'd the Island of Coudre. . . . This island is pleasantly situated, lies partly high, and was very well peopled before we came up: And passing this Island about a League up, we anchor'd, and two of our Boats went in Shore and was attack'd by a small Party of Canadians and Indians, and was obliged to retreat to their Ships.

The 25th we made the out End of the Island of Orleans, and on the 27th we landed on it without the loss of a Man. A small Party of Rangers were almost surrounded by a large Party of Indians; but the Rangers rush'd through them with the Loss of only one Man; what damage the Enemy sustain'd is uncertain.

On the 29th the French sent five Fire Ships down among our Fleet; but, thank God, they did no Damage. The same Day we marched about 6 miles, under the Command of Col. Carlton, and encamped that same Night in Sight of the French Army, and likewise in Sight of the Town—Gen. Monckton's Brigade and a party of Rangers landed on the South Side; we had a small Attack, by which we had 3 kill'd, 2 wounded and 4 taken Prisoners.

July 1st, the Enemy came against our Detachment on the South-side of the River with floating Batteries; but our Shipping soon drove them off;—the Damage they suffer'd is not known.

Same Day the Louisbourg Grenadiers went a Foraging; we had two kill'd and scalp'd belonging to the 22d Regiment. The same Day we marched to the West End of the Island, in order to join the Louisbourg Battalion. A Party of the Enemy fired out of the woods, and wounded two men.

July the 5th, a Barge between the Island and the main Land, to sound the Depth of Water: The French fir'd four Cannon-Shot at her, and came down on a large Bar of Sand, from whence they fir'd small arms; also five Canoes came down the River, loaded with Indians, who took the Barge, made one Man prisoner, and wounded another belonging to the 22d Regiment. On the same Day their floating Batteries attack'd our Shipping but was soon obliged to quit their Firing.—Gen. Monckton opened a small Battery upon the South Side; The first Day they canonaded and bombarded on both Sides; but lost never a Man.

The 8th, we landed on Quebeck-Shore, without any Interception, and marched up the River about two miles; when the Louisbourg Grenadiers being order'd out to get Fascines, they had scarce set down to take a small Refreshment, and detach'd a small Party of Rangers to guard the Skirts of the Wood, before a large Party of Indians surrounded them, kill'd and scalp'd 13, wounded the Captain-Lieutenant and 9 Privates; they likewise kill'd and wounded 14 of the Royal Americans, wounded 2 of the 22d and one of the 40th Regiment: we got only 3 Prisoners, and kill'd 2 of the Savages.

The third Day our Shipping was drove off by the Enemy's Shells.—We got only some few Prisoners, 'til the 12th Day, when the French built a Battery against us, but had not Time to mount any Guns on it; for we soon demolish'd it with our Field-Pieces and Hawitzers. The fourteenth Day their floating Batteries came out after our Boats, but we soon drove them back again.—The 16th, we set the Town on Fire, about 12 O'clock, which continued burning all that Day.

On the 17th we went out a Fascining, and to make Oars, with a small Party to cover us;—5 were kill'd of which 4 were scalp'd, and we was

oblig'd to quit the Wood directly; the Indians came up very close, and kill'd and scalp'd one Man close by us; the Grenadiers of the 45th Regiment fir'd upon them, and I saw one drop; but the Indians took him off in a minute. We had 5 kill'd, belonging to the 35th Regiment, and one dangerously wounded; the 15th Reg. had one wounded very bad; but our People returning upon them, made them fly so fast that they were oblig'd to leave their Blankets and Match-coats, with several other Things, behind them; but we could not get one of them Prisoners. A Deserter came to us, from whom we had an imperfect Account of their Forces; which, however, gave us some Encouragement.

July 18th, the Deserter went out with our Light-Infantry, to show them a Place where to cross the Falls; the Indians fir'd on them, but hurt none: Likewise the same Night some of our Shipping pass'd the Town, and one run ashore on the South Side of the River. The 19th Day the floating Batteries came out to attack Our Shipping round the Harbour; but our Batteries on the Land-Side drove them off, so that the Shipping receiv'd but two Shot. On the 20th an accident happen'd in the Light-Infantry's Camp; a Man sitting in his Tent, with his Firelock by him, taking hold of the Muzzle to pull it towards him, it went off and wounded him in the Thigh so that he died the same Night.

The 21st Day of July all the Grenadiers cross'd over to the Island of Orleans; the Indians attack'd us very smartly, as we was marching to the Water-Side.—Same Day the Enemy open'd two batteries on us, which raked our Camps. Our Troops, with Seamen, stormed a Battery on the S. Side, spiked the Cannon, broke the Mortars, broke into their Magazine, took all their powder, and threw all the Shot and Shells into the Water.

July 22d we set the Town on Fire, which burnt all the next Day: Some of our Shipping went to pass the Town; but they fir'd so hot, that they were oblig'd to turn back.

The 23d 300 Provincials landed on the Island of Orleans, which was some Reinforcement.

July 25th, the Louisbourg Battalion and three more Companies of Grenadiers, with 3 Companies of Light-Infantry, went round the Island of Orleans.—The 27th we arrived at our Camp; and we receiv'd News That our Forces on Montmorancy Side had been attack'd the Day before, and likewise got the Better of the Enemy; we had an Account that we kill'd 300 of them, but the Number of wounded none of us could tell: Our loss was 5 Officers and 32 Privates, 12 of whom were kill'd and the rest wounded. The same Day we went to get our Plunder, which we discovered on our march round the Island, consisting of Gowns, Shirts, Petticoats, Stockings, Coats and Waistcoats, Breeches, Shoes, and many other Articles too tedious to mention and some Cash; which, if the Things had been sold to the Value, would have fetch'd upwards of 500 £. Sterl. The same Night the French sent five Fire-Floats down, which made great Confusion among our Fleet; but the Men of War sent their Boats and tow'd them ashore, where they burnt out without further Damage.

July 29, Otway's and Hopson's Grenadiers went on board the Three-Sisters, Witmore's and Warburton's on board the Russell, the rest in flat-bottom Boats and other Vessels, with a full Intent to land on a Part of the French Shore; so as by that Means we might come at the Town:

The First Push we made was on the 31st of July: with 13 Companies of Grenadiers, supported by about 5 Thousand Battalion-men;—as soon as we landed we fixed our Bayonets and beat our Grenadier's-March, and so advanced on; during all this Time their Cannon play'd very briskly on us; but their Small-Arms, in their Trenches, lay cool 'till they were sure of their Mark; then they pour'd their Small-Shot like Showers of Hail, which caus'd our brave Grenadiers to fall very fast. Brave Gen. Wolfe saw that our attempts were in vain, so he retreated to his Boats again: The number of kill'd and wounded that Day was about 400 Men;—in our Retreat we burnt the two Ships, which we had ran ashore on that side to cover our Landing.

The 3d Day of August a Party of Capt. Danks's Rangers went from the Island of Orleans to Quebec Side, a little down the River; they were attack'd by a Party of French, and was smartly engag'd for the Space of half an Hour; but the Rangers put them to flight, kill'd several and took one Prisoner: The Rangers lost one Lieutenant, who died of his Wounds soon after, and 2 or 3 others. They got a great deal of Plunder.

Aug 4th the French made an Attempt of crossing the Falls; but our Train fir'd Hawits and Cohorns so fast, that they were oblig'd to retreat without accomplishing any Thing;—what Damage was done them I know not.

On the 6th a Victualing Ship sail'd from our Fleet, and went below the Falls, the French hove Shot and Shells in great Number at them; but did them no Harm.

The 8th of Aug. two Centinels being at the Falls, they took an Indian and bro't him Prisoner to the General, who sent him on board the Admiral. At 12 o'Clock at Night we threw a Carcass [hollow incendiary ammunition] and one Shell on the Enemy's Battery of 9 Guns, which blew up their Magazine, Platforms, and burnt with such Violence that some of the Garrison were oblig'd to get into Boats to save themselves from the Flames. The 9th Day we set the Town on Fire, being the 3d Time.

On the 10th the French floated a Thing down in the Form of a Floating-Battery; one of our Ships sent out a Boat to see what it was, and just as the Seamen were going to jump on board, it blew up and kill'd one midshipman and wounded four Sailors. The same day about 30 Sailors went a Plundering on the South-side of the River, and as they were about their Prey, they was surpriz'd by a Party of Indians and drove off; but they all got safe to their Boats, tho' not without the Loss of their Plunder.

The 11th Instant there was an Engagement between our Scouting-Parties and the Indians. Our People drove them off, we had a great Number wounded, several very badly, but the most slightly; there was but few kill'd: There was one of the 35th Reg. told me, he saw an Indian who fir'd at him, but miss'd him; that he levelled his Piece and fir'd at the Indian and miss'd him likewise; upon which the Indian immediately threw his Tommahawk at him and miss'd him; whereupon the Soldier, catching up the Tommahawk, threw it at the Indian and levell'd him, and then went to scalp him; but 2 other Indians came behind him, and one of them stuck a Tommahawk in his Back; but did not wound him so much as to prevent his Escape from them.

The 12th Day We had an Account of General Murray's going to land above the Town—He made all Attempt to land twice and was beat off; he made the third Attempt, and landed at the South-Shore with the Loss of about 100 kill'd and wounded. The same Day we had an Account from the Enemy, That Gen. Amherst's Army was taken very badly and that they were oblig'd to turn back again.

On the 13th we had an Account by one of the French Gunners, who deserted to us that Night, That the enemy had very little provisions; he likewise gave an Account what a Body of French and Indians came over the Falls, the same Side that our Army was on, and that they had four Days Provisions with them, and remain'd there still.

The 14th a Sailor belonging to the Dublin Man of War, endeavour'd to swim over to the French, over the River; but the Current ran so strong, that he was driven on Shore on the Island-Side and was taken up by one of Hopson's Grenadiers and carried to their Quarter-Guard, from whence he was carried on board his own Ship again, stark naked.

The 15th of Aug. Captain Gorham returned from an Incursion, in which Service were employ'd, under his Command, 150 Rangers, a Detachment from the different Regiments, Highlanders, Marines, &c. amounting in the whole to about 300, an arm'd Vessel, three Transports, with a Lieutenant and Seamen of the Navy to attend him, of which Expedition they gave the following Account:

"That on the 4th of August they proceeded down to St. Paul's Bay, (which is opposite to the North Side of this Island) where was a Parish containing about 200 men, who had been very active in distressing our Boats and Shipping—At 3 o 'Clock in the Morning Capt. Gorham landed and forced two of their Guards; of 20 Men each, who fired smartly for Some Time; but that in two Hours they drove them all from their Covering in the Wood, and clear'd the Village which they burnt, consisting of about 50 fine Houses and Barns; destroy'd most of their Cattle, &c. That in this one Man was kill'd and 6 wounded; but that the Enemy had two kill'd, and several wounded, who were carried off.—That from thence they proceeded to Mal Bay, 10 Leagues to the Eastward on the same Side, where they destroyed a very pretty Parish, drove off the Inhabitants and Stock without any Loss; after which, they made a Descent on the South Shore, opposite the Island of Coudre, destroyed Part of the Parish of St. Ann's and St. Roan, where were very handsome Houses with Farms, and loaded the Vessels with Cattle; after which they returned from their Expedition."

The same Day 1 of our Schooners went from the Fleet below the Fall, and the French fir'd 8 or 9 Shot at her; but miss'd her. This Day a Party of young Highlanders came to the Island of Orleans from Gen. Monckton's Encampment; on Purpose to destroy all the Canaada-Side.—The same Day our People set one of the Enemy's Floating-Batteries on Fire;—and in the Night General Monckton set the Town on Fire, (being the 4th Time) and the Flames raged so violently, that 'twas imagin'd the whole City would have been reduc'd to Ashes.

August 18th, a Sloop and Schooner went below the Falls; the French hove Shot and Shells at them, but did 'em no Damage. The same Day the Enemy hove a Bomb from the Town, which kill'd one Man and wounded 6 more,—one Man had his Arm cut off by a Piece of the same Shell.

On the 20th the Louisbourg Grenadiers began their March down the main Land of Quebeck, in order to burn and destroy all the Houses on that Side[.]—On the 24th they were attack'd by a Party of French, who had a Priest for their

Commander; but our Party kill'd and scalp'd 31 of them, and likewise the Priest, their Commander; They did our People no Damage. The three Companies of Louisbourg Grenadiers halted about 4 Miles down the River, at a Church called the Guardian-Angel, where we were order'd to fortify ourselves till further Orders; we had several small Parties in Houses, and the Remainder continued in the Church.—The 25th, began to destroy the Country, burning Houses, cutting down Corn, and the like: At Night the Indians fired several scattering Shot at the Houses, which kill'd one of the Highlanders and wounded another; but they were soon repulsed by the Heat of our Firing.—It was said that the Number of the Enemy consisted of 800 Canadians and Indians. Sept 1st we set Fire to our Houses and Fortifications, and marched to join the Grand Army at Montmorancy; the 3 Companies of Grenadiers ordered to hold themselves in Readiness to march at a Minute's Warning.

The 26th a Serjeant of the 35th Regiment deserted across the Fall, and our people fir'd several Grape-Shots after him; notwithstanding which he got clear off to the Enemy.

The 27th of August some of our Shipping went past the Town, which fir'd so hot at them with Shots and Bombs, that one would have thought Vessel to pass; but they receiv'd little or no Damage. The 29th, 5 Sail went to pass the Town, up the River; the Town fir'd very warm all the Time of their passing, and I was very well informed, That only 15 of their Shot took Place out of all their Firing; Likewise the 30th Instant four of our Ships pass'd the Town, where they kept a continual Firing; but did us very little Damage.

Sept. 1. all the Sick and Women that was on Montmorancy-Side, came over to the Island of Orleans; on the 2d Intant a large Body of Wolfe's Troops came over, with the Louisbourg Grenadiers, and encamped that Night on the same Island.

The 3d Day all the Army left Montmorancy-Side and we set all the Houses and Fortifications on Fire, and then we embark'd in flat-bottom Boats and came above the Fall; the French fir'd

very brisk all the Time of our passing, but did us no Damage, and we went over to Point Levee and encamped there.

Sept. 4th the Louisbourg Grenadiers and the Remainder of the Army, cross'd over to Point-Levee from the Island of Orleans, and encamped there.—The Same Day 4 Men came from Gen. Amherst's Army; they was 26 Days on their Journey, and inform'd us, That we had got Ticonderoga, and likewise Crown-Point.

Sept 5th about 5 or 6000 Men Marched up the River on Point-Levee Side, to go above the Town, and carried one Month's Provision up in Sloops. The same Day one of the Royal-Americans, who was taken Prisoner by the French-Indians the 31st of July last, made his Escape and came to the Porcupine Sloop of War, that lay a little below the Fall; he informs us That there is no more than about 300 Indians that carries Arms; but that there are a great number of Women and Children, that they were very scant of Provisions; likewise that he himself had been 48 Hours without any thing to eat: He further said, that the Enemy they were very numerous in their Intrenchment, consisting of at least, 14,000 Men of which 11,000 were Canadians and the rest Regulars, the latter of whom were heartily tir'd with the Siege.

Sept. 6th the Schooner Terror of France went above the Town, in the middle of the Day, as she pass'd they kept up a constant Fire at her, and she receiv'd five of their Shot; one in her Jib, two in her Mainsail and 2 in her Foresail; but lost none of her Hands, nor did she sustain any further Damage.

The whole Army being on Point-Levee Side, the main Body were order'd to get ready to march above the Town, on the South Side, and to take only one Shirt and one Pair of Stockings, besides what we had on. We marched up the River about 8 Miles, and then embark'd on board the Men of War and Transports that were up the River: the Number that embarked was 3349 Men, with a Party of the Train of Artillery.

Sept. 10. the Weather being very wet, and the Troops very much crowded on board the Men of

War and Transports, the General thought proper to land us on the South Side again; which was a great Decoy to the French: We marched to the Church of St. Nicholas, under the Command of General Monkton, where we halted. The next Day we received intelligence of a small Number of French and Indians, who were driving some Cattle; . . . we dispatched a Party of 500 Men, who took the Cattle, but the Enemy got off.

The 12th we received Orders to embarked on board our Ships again.

The 13th we had Orders to land; so we fell down the River in the Ships and Boats till we came a little above the Town, where the Enemy least suspected us (for where the Enemy thought we should have landed, they had about 600 Horse; but what Number of Foot we could not say; we could perceive that they was intrench'd and had 5 Floating-Batteries to intercept our Landing.)

On the 14th we landed, at break of Day, and immediately attacked and routed the Enemy, taking Possession of a Battery of 4 24-Pounders, and one thirteen Inch Mortar, with but an inconsiderable Loss. We then took Post on the Plains of Abraham, whither M. Montcalm (on hearing that we had landed, for he did not expect us) hasted with his whole Army (consisting of Cavalry as well as Infantry) to give us Battle; about 9 o'Clock; we observed the Enemy marching down towards us in three Columns, at 10 they formed their Line of Battle, which was at least six deep, having their Flanks covered by a thick Wood on each Side, into which they threw above 3000 Canadians and Indians, who gauled us much; the Regulars then marched briskly up to us, and gave us their first Fire, at about Fifty Yards Distance, which we did not return, as it was General Wolfe's express Orders not to fire till they came within twenty Yards of us[.]—They continued firing by Platoons, advancing in a very regular Manner till they came close up to us, and then the Action became general: In about a Quarter of an Hour the Enemy gave way on all Sides, when a terrible Slaughter ensued from the quick Fire of our Field Pieces and Musquetry with which we pursue'd them to the Walls of the Town, regardless of all excessive heavy Fire from all their Batteries. The Enemy lost in the Engagement, Lieut. Gen. Montcalm, (who was torn to Pieces by our Grape Shot) 2 Brigadier-Generals; one Colonel; 2 Lieutenant-Colonels; and at least 130 Officers and Men kill'd and 200 taken Prisoners at their very Sally-Ports, of which 58 were Officers. On our Side was killed the brave and never to be forgotten General WOLFE; with 9 Officers, 4 Serjeants and 44 Privates; wounded, Brigadier-General Monckton, Colonel Carlton, Quarter-Master-General; Major Barre, Adjutant-General; and 50 Other Officers, with 26 Serjeants and 557 privates.—This Action was the more glorious, as the Enemy were at least 12,000 strong, besides 500 Horse; whereas we, at the utmost, did not consist of above 3500, some of whom did not engage;—for at the Time of the Engagement Colonel Scott was out burning the Country with 1600 Men; Col. Burton was at Point-Levee with 2000 Men; and on the Island of Orleans there were 1500; whereas our whole Army, at our first embarking at Louisbourg, did not exceed 8240 Men.

At Ten o'Clock at Night we surpriz'd their Guard and took Possession of their Grand Hospital, wherein we found between 12 and 1500 Sick and Wounded.

We lay on our Arms all Night, and in the Morning we secured the Bridge of Boats which the Enemy had over Charles River, and possessed ourselves of all, the Posts and Avenues that was or might be of any Consequence leading to the Town, and broke Ground at 100 Yards Distance from the Walls; we likewise got up 12 heavy 24-pounders; six heavy Twelve Pounders, some large Mortars, and the 46 inch Hawitzers, to play upon the Town, and we had been employed three Days, intending to make a Breach, and storm the City Sword in hand, but we were prevented by their beating a Parley, and sending out a Flag of Truce with Articles of Capitulation, and the next Day—being the 17th of September, we took Possession of the City, where we found 250 Pieces of Cannon, a Number of mortars, from 9 to fifteen

Inches, Field-Pieces, Hawitzers, &c. with a large Quantity of Artillery-Stores.

M. Vaudreuille, the Governor-General of New-France, stole out of the City before the Capitulation; leaving only about 600 Men, under the Command of Mon. Ramsay, by whom the Capitulation was signed. The poor Remains of the French Regulars, with about 10,000 Canadians, retired to Jaques Quartiees under the Command of M. Levy; but the Canadians deserted him in great Numbers, and came in and surrendered themselves.

Sept 19th the French Garrison were embarked on board Transports: Such of the Inhabitants as would come in and take the Oaths of Allegiance, were permitted to enjoy their Estates.

Brigadier General Murray is Governor of the Town, and the whole Army left to Garrison it.

During the whole Siege from first to last, 535 Houses were burnt down, among which is the whole eastern Part of the lower Town (save 6 or 8 Houses) which make a very dismal Appearance. We also destroyed upwards of Fourteen Hundred fine Farm-Houses in the Country, &c.

FINIS

Source: Serjeant-Major of Gen. Hopson's Grenadiers. A Journal of the Expedition up the River St. Lawrence. Boston: Fowle and Draper, 1759. Available online. URL: http://openlibrary.org/b/OL7025982M/Journal_ of_the_expedition_up_the_River_St._Lawrence. Accessed on February 8, 2010.

PONTIAC'S REBELLION, 1763

Journal Entries on the Siege of Fort Pitt

William Trent
May–June 1763

Major William Trent (1715–ca. 1787) was a soldier and merchant who lived on the western Pennsylvania frontier and commanded the militia garrison at Fort Pitt during Pontiac's Rebellion. His journal records some of the particulars of the Indians' siege of the fort from June 22 to August 20, 1763, including the defenders' use of biological warfare: the presentation to the Indians of blankets from the fort's smallpox hospital.

The Indians attacked Fort Pitt on June 22, 1763, and kept it under siege throughout July and into August. On June 29, 1763, Jeffrey Amherst proposed making an attempt to disseminate smallpox among the "disaffected tribes." Colonel Henry Bouquet, preparing an expedition to relieve the siege against Fort Pitt, replied to Amherst on July 13, 1763: "I will try to inoculate the bastards with some blankets that may fall into their hands, and take care not to get the disease myself." Amherst in turn replied on July 16, 1763: "You will do well to inoculate the Indians by means of blankets, as well as every other method that can serve to extirpate this execrable race."

The fact was that officers within the fort had already done just what Amherst and Bouquet were proposing. During a truce parley at the fort on June 24, 1763, Captain Simeon Ecuyer presented representatives of the Delaware Indians a pair of blankets and a handkerchief as goodwill gifts. In reality, these were from the fort's smallpox hospital. It is known that smallpox did ravage the Delaware sometime after this, but because the disease was both endemic to and epidemic on the frontier, it is impossible to say whether the outbreak had been caused by the "gifts" or occurred naturally.

May 29

At Break of day this Morning three Men came in from Col. Claphams who was settled at the Oswegly Old Town about 25 Miles from here, on the Youghyogane River, with an account that Col. Clapham, with one of his Men, two women and a child were Merdered by Wolfe and some other Delaware Indians, about two o'Clock the day before. The 27th Wolfe with some others robed one Mr. Coleman on the Road between this and Ligonier of upwards of £50—The women that were killed at Col. Claphams, were treated in such a brutal manner that Decency forbids the Mentioning.

This Evening we had two Soldiers killed and scalped at the Sawmill.

June 1
Two Men who were sent of Express last Night to Venango returned being fired on at Shanopins Town and one of them wounded in the leg. . . .

June 5
2 o'Clock at Night one Benjamin Sutton came in who says he left Redstone two days ago and found that place evacuated and saw a number of Shoe Tracks going towards Fort Cumberland which he supposes was the Garrison: that there was with him there a White Man named Hicks and an Indian names Recois who would have burnt the Fort had he not persuaded them from it, that Hicks told him that an Indian War was broke out and that he would kill the white People wherever he found them, and went with Intention to murder Madcalfs People nine Miles from here who had removed some time before, he says they intended to have taken him Prisoner but the Wind blowing hard and it growing very dark when he came nigh the Fort made for it and called the Centinel Hicks and the Indian went by in their Bark Cannoes.

June 6
Nothing Extraordinary

June 12
An Indian was discovered from the Garden, about 11 o'Clock a Party out cutting Spelts saw two Indians and fired on them, on which a number more appeared and fired on our People, who returned it an[d] some more shot being fired from the Cannon in the Fort the Indians ran off.

June 13 and 14
Nothing worth Notice.

June 15
A Party was sent out to cut Spelts and were fired on. Serjt Miller of the Militia contrary to orders with 3 others advanced to Grants Hill and just as they had gained the Summit, Miller was shot Dead, a party advancing drove the Enemy off and prevented their scalping him.

Between 11 and 12 o'Clock at Night as an Express from Bedford was challenged by one of the Centinels from the Rampart the Enemy fired a number of Shotts at him and the Centinels in the Fort.

June 23
[A]bout 12 o'Clock at Night Two Delawares called for Mr. McKee and told him they wanted to speak to him in the Morning.

June 24
The Turtles Heart a principal Warrior of the Delawares and Mamaltee a Chief came within a small distance of the Fort Mr. McKee went out to them and they made a Speech letting us know that all our [?] as Ligonier was destroyed, that great numbers of Indians [were coming and] that out of regard to us, they had prevailed on 6 Nations [not to] attack us but give us time to go down the Country and they desired we would set of immediately. The Commanding Officer thanked them, let them know that we had everything we wanted, that we could defend it against all the Indians in the Woods, that we had three large Armys marching to Chastise those Indians that had struck us, told them to take care of their Women and Children, but not to tell any other Natives, they said they would go a speak to their Chiefs and come and tell us what they said, they returned and said they would hold fast of the Chain of friendship. Out of our regard to them we gave them two Blankets and a Handkerchief out of the Small Pox Hospital. I hope it will have the desired effect.

Source: Trent, William. "Journal Entries on the Siege of Fort Pitt, 1763." In Exploring Diversity in Pennsylvania History, published by Historical Society of Pennsylvania. Available online. URL: http://www.hsp.org/files/excerptsfromwilliamtrent.pdf. Accessed on February 8, 2010.

Proclamation of 1763
King George III
October 7, 1763

During the French and Indian War, British authorities concluded the Treaty of Easton (1758) with the Iroquois tribes and the Delaware, guaranteeing that white settlement would proceed no farther west than the Allegheny Mountains. Settlers violated this agreement almost immediately. In an effort to end Pontiac's Rebellion, King George III (1738–1820) next proclaimed a new settlement boundary, this one through the Appalachian Mountains. The so-called Proclamation Line did help to bring a brief period of peace with the Indians, but, like the earlier Easton boundary, it was soon breached by settlers, who then demanded that the royal government protect them from the resulting Indian depredations. The government often declined to protect settlers who had defied the proclamation, and the result was growing resentment toward both the eastern establishment—the colonial Tidewater—and the "mother country" itself, a situation that contributed to the spirit of rebellion that ultimately resulted in the American Revolution.

. . . And whereas it is just and reasonable, and essential to our Interest, and the Security of our Colonies, that the several Nations or Tribes of Indians with whom We are connected, and who live under our Protection, should not be molested or disturbed in the Possession of such Parts of Our Dominions and Territories as, not having been ceded to or purchased by Us, are reserved to them, or any of them, as their Hunting Grounds.—We do therefore, with the Advice of our Privy Council, declare it to be our Royal Will and Pleasure that no Governor or Commander in Chief in any of our colonies of Quebec, East Florida, or West Florida, do presume, upon any Pretence whatever, to grant Warrants of Survey, or pass any Patents for Lands beyond the Bounds of their respective Governments, as described in their Commis-

sions: as also that no Governor or Commander in Chief in any of our other Colonies or Plantations in America do presume for the present, and until our further Pleasure be known, to grant Warrants of Survey or pass Patents for any Lands beyond the Heads or Sources of any of the Rivers which fall into the Atlantic Ocean from the West and North West, or upon any Lands whatever, which, not having been ceded to or purchased by Us as aforesaid, are reserved to the said Indians, or any of them.

. . .

And We do further strictly enjoin and require all Persons whatever who have either willfully or inadvertently seated themselves upon any Lands within the Countries above described, or upon any other lands which, not having been ceded to or purchased by Us, are still reserved to the said Indians as aforesaid, forthwith to remove themselves from such Settlements.

And whereas great Frauds and Abuses have been committed in purchasing Lands of the Indians, to the great Prejudice of our Interests and to the great Dissatisfaction of the said Indians: In order, therefore, to prevent such Irregularities for the future, and to the end that the Indians may be convinced of our Justice and determined Resolution to remove all reasonable Cause of Discontent, We do, with the Advice of our Privy Council, strictly enjoin and require that no private Person do presume to make any purchase from the said Indians of any Lands reserved to the said Indians within those parts of our Colonies where We have thought proper to allow Settlement: . . .

. . .

Given at our Court at St. James's the 7th Day of October 1763. in the Third Year of our Reign.
GOD SAVE THE KING

Source: George III. "The Royal Proclamation." October 7, 1763. Available online. URL: http://www.solon.org/Constitutions/Canada/English/PreConfederation/rp_1763.html. Accessed on February 8, 2010.

The American Revolution

★

King George III (1738–1820) ascended the British throne in 1760. Encouraged by conservative ministers and the Tory faction of Parliament, he was determined to recoup from the North American colonies themselves at least some of the heavy costs of the late French and Indian War. Toward this end, he approved the enforcement of the long-dormant Navigation Acts, the earliest of which had been on the books since the mid-17th century. This legislation had developed from a policy that historians call the mercantile system, which is a form of economic nationalism that incorporated strict government regulation of trade and commerce. Under mercantilism, the chief function of colonies was the enrichment of the mother country by furnishing raw materials that the mother country used to create manufactured goods that it would sell to the colonies. Both production and consumption were monopolistic, dictated by the mother country rather than a free market. The Navigation Acts restricted much colonial export and import trade to dealing exclusively with the mother country on terms its government dictated. Until George III assumed the throne, enforcement of the existing Navigation Acts was left to local customs officials in American ports, who were readily bribed by their friends and neighbors.

For its part, the British Crown typically ignored the corruption and laxity. The pro-American British statesman Edmund Burke approvingly labeled this attitude "salutary neglect."

The first of the Navigation Acts to be revived under George III was a 1755 law authorizing royal customs officers to issue "writs of assistance" to local provincial officers, compelling them to cooperate in identifying and arresting smugglers. The writs gave officials authority to search warehouses as well as private homes without court order. Next, during the premiership of Lord Grenville (1763–65), the first of the so-called Grenville Acts imposed substantial import and export duties on various commodities. Most inflammatory of the Grenville Acts was the Sugar Act of 1764, which taxed imports of molasses from the French and Dutch West Indies. The new law authorized trial for violations by a vice admiralty court rather than by a colonial jury, thereby denying the right to trial by jury English men and women had enjoyed since the Magna Carta of 1215.

Many of the colonies banded together in 1764 to oppose the Grenville Acts through a nonimportation agreement—a boycott of British goods. At first, Parliament not only stood fast but passed the Stamp Act, which came into force on March 22, 1765. The Stamp Act taxed all manner of printed matter, from newspapers to legal documents to playing cards. Response to the act was swift. In Boston, Samuel Adams, a failed businessman but brilliant political agitator, founded one of the first of many secret societies that organized opposition to the Stamp Act. Adams's group and the others that soon followed were generically called the Sons of Liberty, and they spawned so-called committees of correspondence or committees of safety throughout the colonies, which served both to incite and coordinate protest. The organizations managed to intimidate the colonial stamp agents into resigning, with the result that the Stamp Act proved impossible to enforce.

While Sam Adams and others agitated in New England, the fiery attorney-orator Patrick Henry, a member of Virginia's House of Burgesses, introduced into that legislature the Virginia Resolves of 1765. The most important of these asserted that only the colony's legislature had the authority to tax Virginians and to legislate Virginia issues.

Almost simultaneously with passage of the Stamp Act, Parliament passed the Mutiny Act of 1765, which included provisions for quartering British troops in private houses. Parliament soon modified this with the Quartering Act, which did away with the requirement that private homeowners billet soldiers but instead required colonial authorities to furnish barracks and supplies for British troops at the colony's expense. Most colonial legislatures simply refused to allocate the required funds.

Collectively, the Stamp Act and the other legislation tended to unite the colonies—normally competitive rather than cooperative—in opposition. The union culminated in the Stamp Act Congress, which convened in New York City during October 7–25, 1765, and issued a Declaration of Rights and Grievances, which held (among other things) that Parliament had no authority to tax the colonies and that the Crown's vice-admiralty courts had no legitimate jurisdiction in the colonies. In response to eco-

nomic boycott and organized protest, Parliament repealed the Stamp Act on March 18, 1766, only to simultaneously pass the Declaratory Act, which reasserted Parliament's authority to enact laws binding on the American colonies.

In August 1766, Charles Townshend became chancellor of the exchequer and, soon after, effectively took control of the cabinet when Prime Minister William Pitt suffered a mental breakdown. Townshend ushered through Parliament the so-called Townshend Acts, which (among other things) established a new system of royal customs commissioners and suspended the New York Assembly for its rebelliousness. New duties were imposed on a variety of colonial imports, and a Revenue Act stipulated that the revenues generated would be used for military expenses in the colonies and to pay the salaries of royal colonial officials. This deprived colonial legislatures of the power of the purse, which meant that a whole host of colonial officials now answered exclusively to the Crown instead of to the people. The colonies responded with a new boycott, which was so effective that all the Townshend duties were repealed on April 12, 1770—except for the duty on tea.

In the meantime, the colonies staged their first militant protests, the best known of which resulted in the Boston Massacre of March 5, 1770. Suffering in economic hard times, a mob of Bostonians menaced a British soldier who sought part-time work at John Gray's ropewalk, a maker of ship's rope. The action grew into a riot, which provoked a detachment of soldiers to fire into the mob, killing or mortally wounding five citizens, including Crispus Attucks, a 40-year-old fugitive slave from Framingham, Massachusetts. (Many deem Attucks to be the first casualty in America's fight for independence.) Samuel Adams and others tried to fan what they called the "Boston Massacre" into the flames of full-scale revolution, but cooler heads prevailed. When a colonial court indicted the British army captain Thomas Preston and six of his men on charges of murder, two prominent colonial attorneys, Josiah Quincy and John Adams (cousin of

Samuel), volunteered to defend the accused. Although John Adams passionately believed in independence, he believed even more strongly in the rule of law. In the end, Preston and four of his men were acquitted, and two others were found guilty, not of murder but of manslaughter, and were discharged from military service with a brand on the thumb.

Repeal of the Townshend Acts shortly after the trials briefly calmed revolutionary stirrings. Indeed, by 1773, Parliament had repealed all taxes on imports, except for that on tea, a tax that made little stir among colonists, who easily evaded it by buying smuggled tea from Dutch sources. The financially ailing British East India Company was hard hit by the smuggling, and King George's latest prime minister, Lord North, was eager to aid the company, which bore all the expenses of the civil and military government of British India. North therefore engineered passage of the Tea Act of May 10, 1773, which reduced taxes levied on British East India Company tea, thereby making the East India tea cheaper even than the smuggled tea. North believed this alone would remove a principal motive for colonial protest; however, to control prices, the Tea Act also allowed the East India Company to sell directly to designated tea consignees, thereby cutting out American merchant retailers. This was sufficient to move colonial radicals to action. As they had done earlier with the stamp agents, the Sons of Liberty and others intimidated tea consignees in Philadelphia, New York, and Charleston into resigning, and American captains and harbor pilots refused to handle the East India Company cargo. Tea ships were turned back to London from Philadelphia and New York. When three tea ships dropped anchor in Boston Harbor, the Sons of Liberty prevented their being unloaded, but Massachusetts's royal governor, Thomas Hutchinson, refused to allow the ships to leave the harbor and return to London. In response, 150 colonists, their faces painted to resemble Mohawk Indians, boarded each of the ships and jettisoned 342 tea chests into Boston Harbor.

With George III's approval, Parliament responded by passing the Coercive Acts (which colonial activists dubbed the Intolerable Acts), closing the port of Boston, restricting the authority of the Massachusetts colonial government, and permanently quartering British troops in Boston. In April 1774, General Thomas Gage, a veteran of the French and Indian War, was dispatched to Boston as commander in chief of British forces in America and as royal governor of Massachusetts. The Massachusetts General Assembly, banished from Boston, defied both Parliament and Gage by convening in Salem, where they voted a proposal to convene a provincial or continental congress made up of delegates from all the colonies. Once again, the actions of king and Parliament had served to unite the colonies and push them toward rebellion.

Delegates from all of the colonies except Georgia convened in Philadelphia on September 5, 1774. The congress endorsed the Suffolk Resolves, which pronounced the Intolerable Acts unconstitutional, urged Massachusetts to form an independent government and to withhold taxes from the Crown until the acts were repealed, advised citizens to arm themselves, and recommended a general boycott of English goods.

Outbreak

On September 1, 1774, one of General Gage's Boston-based detachments seized cannon and powder from arsenals in nearby Cambridge and Charlestown. In response, what was now called the Provincial Congress, meeting in Salem, appropriated £15,627 to buy new military supplies and authorized the shipping merchant John Hancock to head a committee of safety and call out the militia, whose members were dubbed "minutemen" because these citizen-soldiers pledged themselves to be armed, assembled, and prepared for battle on a minute's notice. On December 14, 1774, the Boston silversmith Paul Revere, courier for the Boston Sons of Liberty, rode out to warn the local commander,

John Sullivan, of Gage's intention to seize munitions stored at Fort William and Mary guarding Portsmouth Harbor, New Hampshire. Sullivan led a militia force to the fort and so stunned the British guards that they surrendered without a fight, whereupon Sullivan carried off the guns and powder.

Gage now deployed and quartered his troops, but they were harassed at every turn by Patriot saboteurs. Minor acts of rebellion broke out all over New England, and the Sons of Liberty and committees of safety had established so effective a system of espionage and communication that Gage could not make a move without being observed. During this period of escalating turmoil, George III and Parliament proposed the Plan of Reconciliation, whereby Parliament would refrain from taxing the colonies if their assemblies would voluntarily contribute toward some of the costs of imperial defense. Yet, offering this concession with one hand, the Crown passed the Fishery Act with the other, restricting the trade of New England to Britain, Ireland, and the West Indies, and banning the colony from fishing in Newfoundland's rich waters. This prompted Massachusetts to transform itself into something resembling an armed camp. Gage responded on April 12, 1775, by imposing martial law, declaring all of the residents of Massachusetts to be "in treason," although he offered full pardons to one and all, save the ringleaders, John Adams and John Hancock. On April 16, Paul Revere was dispatched to ride to Lexington, Massachusetts, to warn Adams and Hancock to flee. Next, he and others set about alerting the Charlestown countryside to the movement of Gage's troops, who were headed toward Lexington, Massachusetts.

The Battles of Lexington and Concord

In the predawn hours of April 19, 1775, 600 British regulars disembarked from the whale-boats that had taken them from Boston to Lechmere Point on the north side of Boston Harbor, in Charlestown. From there, they marched northwest to the village of Lexington, which lay between Boston and Concord. At Lexington's green, they were met by some 70 minutemen. When the outnumbered minutemen defied a British demand to lay down their weapons, shots rang out, hitting one redcoat in the leg. The British opened fire, the minutemen replied, and then the redcoats charged with bayonets, scattering the Patriots. Eight minutemen, including their captain, Jonas Parker, lay dead on Lexington green; another 10 were wounded. The Battle of Lexington, which most historians consider the opening battle of the American Revolution, was over.

After the encounter at Lexington, the redcoats marched on to Concord. Here, however, militia companies from the surrounding communities had assembled, and it has been estimated that 3,763 Patriots were present, although probably no more than half this number were involved in the battle at any one time. At the moment of the redcoats' arrival, approximately 400 minutemen under Colonel James Barrett descended on the British, killing three regulars and wounding nine others, forcing the main body of troops to retreat.

In the meantime, about 1,400 British regulars, including 460 Royal Marines, drawing two six-pound cannons and led by 33-year-old Lord Hugh Percy, were beginning their march out of Boston, also bound for Concord. Along the way, the column was sniped at by militiamen crouched behind stone walls, behind trees, and even in houses. As Percy's column approached, the first wave withdrew from Concord and headed back to Lexington. Both the advancing and the retreating forces were continually harassed by snipers, and only after nearly 20 hours of a fighting retreat did the two British columns meet in Lexington. The Patriots, their numbers steadily growing, continued to harry the British retreat all the way back to Charlestown, where the redcoats found refuge within range of the big guns of their warships riding at anchor in the harbor. Seventy-three redcoats were killed, and 26 were listed as missing, presumed dead; 174 redcoats had been wounded. On the American side, 49 had died, five were reported missing, and 41 lay wounded.

Lexington and Concord: The Response

The Second Continental Congress convened in Philadelphia a month after the Battles of Lexington and Concord and moved to take control of what was now an outright revolution. Congress voted to mobilize 13,600 troops and called on local militia forces throughout New England to march to Boston in order to lay siege the British forces headquartered there.

Connecticut leaders sent Benedict Arnold, a prosperous New Haven merchant and now captain of militia, to Massachusetts. He persuaded Congress to appoint him colonel of militia and put him in charge of a mission to capture Fort Ticonderoga, strategically located at the point where Lake George drains into Lake Champlain. But the Connecticut assembly had already approved a plan to take Fort Ticonderoga, giving the assignment to Ethan Allen. Arnold agreed to a joint command with Allen, and the fort fell to a surprise assault on May 10. This gave the Patriots a gateway to Canada as well as a base from which Allen launched a successful expedition to capture the fort at Crown Point. The two victories yielded a cache of artillery and muskets—all badly needed by Patriot forces.

Back in Philadelphia, the Second Continental Congress created the Continental army under the command of George Washington, provincial hero of the French and Indian War, with Artemas Ward (already commanding the Boston militia); Israel Putnam of Connecticut; Philip Schuyler of New York; and two recently retired officers of the British army, Charles Lee and Horatio Gates, as Washington's lieutenants. By the end of 1775, Congress had 27,500 Continental soldiers on its payroll, from all the colonies.

The Battle of Bunker Hill

By the end of May 1775, approximately 1,500 colonial troops surrounded Boston and the British garrison there. On the 25th of this month, three major generals arrived from England to assist Gage in crushing the rebellion: William Howe, the senior officer; John Burgoyne; and Henry Clinton. Gage tasked Howe with making an amphibious attack to secure the high ground at Charlestown, a place called Bunker's Hill or Bunker Hill. Patriot spies quickly discovered the plan, and the local committee of safety wanted the so-called Boston army to occupy Bunker Hill before Gage could capture it. The Patriot general Israel Putnam, however, decided to concentrate his forces not on Bunker Hill but on the adjacent Breed's Hill, which was closer to Boston—although he put some men in a fortified position on Bunker Hill to hold a line of retreat. It was a fateful decision. High and steep, Bunker Hill could have been made virtually impregnable, whereas the lower Breed's Hill was more vulnerable.

Twelve hundred Patriots dug defensive positions into Breed's Hill. At dawn on June 17, the British fleet opened fire on the Patriots, and at 1:00 P.M., 2,300 redcoats disembarked from the ships at Moulton's Point, at the tip of Charlestown Peninsula, ready to assault the hill. To their shock and dismay, however, they came under heavy attack. In the meantime, the Royal Navy bombarded Charlestown itself, setting much of the town ablaze. Against this incendiary background, Howe ordered a bayonet charge into the Patriot line that fronted the Mystic River. The militia colonel William Prescott responded with one of the most memorable battle commands in American military history: "Don't fire until you see the whites of their eyes!"

This initial British charge failed, with 96 of the 350 redcoats killed. Every man in Howe's personal staff was either killed or wounded. Howe mounted a second wave, which was also cut down and repulsed. A third assault finally broke through, forcing the Patriots into a fighting retreat. Inasmuch as the Americans had been driven off both Breed's Hill and Bunker Hill, the British won the day, but they had taken much heavier losses than the Americans. Of the 2,400 men on the firing line, 1,054 had been shot, of whom 226 died.

The Invasion of Canada

After failing to persuade Canada to join in rebellion against the mother country, Congress, on June 27, 1775, ordered an invasion. The plan was for Benedict Arnold to take Quebec while General Philip Schuyler captured Montreal. After Schuyler fell ill, his second in command, Richard Montgomery, took over. He ordered Ethan Allen and another officer, John Brown, to recruit Canadians for a siege of St. Johns, a British fort and barracks. Instead, Allen and Brown launched a premature attack on Montreal, which resulted in the capture of Allen and 20 of his men. This defeat turned popular Canadian sentiment even more solidly against participation in the Revolution and also drove many Native Americans, hitherto neutral, into the camp of the British.

Montgomery eventually did take and occupy Montreal, only to find himself and his men cut off, cold, and hungry. In the meantime, Arnold experienced epic difficulties in marching his 1,100 volunteers from Cambridge, Massachusetts, to Quebec. Starvation and desertion were his greatest enemies, and by the time he reached the south bank of the St. Lawrence River on November 9, he had only 600 men left. Nevertheless, on November 14, he defeated the Canadian militia defending Quebec. Soon, however, 800 British regulars closed in against him, and he withdrew his force to Pointe aux Trembles. On December 2, Montgomery arrived, bringing the combined American invasion forces

to about 1,000. The two generals led their combined armies back to Quebec and attacked on December 31, during a blizzard. Half the remaining invasion force were killed, wounded, or captured in the unsuccessful assault. The survivors, including a badly wounded Benedict Arnold, remained outside of the city for five miserable months, from January to May 1776. Early in April 1776, reinforcements brought American strength outside of Quebec to 2,000, although sickness, desertion, and the expiration of short-term militia enlistments rapidly reduced this number to about 600 men fit for duty. With more British reinforcements en route, Congress sent more men, who, however, were intercepted and defeated before they could reach Quebec.

Having determined that the American invasion of Canada had collapsed, the British prepared a counteroffensive invasion *from* Canada. Because it was essential to gain control of the great body of water straddling Canada and the lower colonies, Lake Champlain, both the British and the remaining Americans, under Arnold, hurriedly built fleets of shallow-draft vessels. Benedict Arnold left Crown Point with 10 craft on August 24, 1776, and anchored the boats off rocky Valcour Island. By October 11, he had another five vessels ready, but when he saw the approach of no fewer than 20 British gunboats, 30 longboats, and several larger vessels, he withdrew—too late, as it turned out. Over the next three days, the two fleets battled, and by the morning of October 13, Arnold had just two large vessels left, in which he made his escape to Buttonmould Bay on the Vermont shore of Lake Champlain. He beached and burned his surviving boats there and marched his much-reduced forces overland to Crown Point. Quickly grasping the fact that he could not hold this position, he burned the fort and retreated to Fort Ticonderoga—the point from which the ill-conceived Canadian invasion had begun two years earlier. The Canadian invasion was a serious setback to the cause of the American Revolution, although Arnold's long fighting retreat did manage to sap the momentum from the British counterinvasion force and thereby averted a total catastrophe.

The Siege of Boston

By June 1775, approximately 1,500 American troops had bottled up Gage's British army of 6,500 (including Royal Navy personnel, the total came to 11,000). The American general Henry Knox supervised the transportation of British artillery captured at Fort Ticonderoga to Dorchester Heights—a distance of 300 miles—where, by January 1776, it was positioned to bombard the British garrison. Realizing that he was surrounded and outnumbered, Howe decided to abandon Boston. By secret agreement, he pledged not to burn Boston provided the Patriots did not contest his evacuation. Thus, from March 7 to March 17, 1776, the British ships were loaded. Washington assumed they would evacuate to New York; instead, Howe took his men all the way to Halifax, Nova Scotia. A Patriot army had driven the British out of Boston.

The Decision for Independence and a New British Strategy

The combat phase of the American Revolution had begun in response to Gage's attempts to seize Patriot arms, yet months after the shooting had begun, there was still no unanimity among the colonies concerning the final object of the Revolution. Long after the war was over, John Adams estimated that in 1775–76, perhaps only one-third of Americans favored independence, one-third opposed it (and many of this faction were willing to fight against the Patriots), and one-third were either undecided or indifferent. Even as the war raged, some in Congress favored reconciliation with Britain. On January

9, 1776, the publication of a 47-page pamphlet titled *Common Sense*, written by a recent British immigrant named Thomas Paine, did much to galvanize popular sentiment in favor of full independence and moved the Continental Congress on March 3 to send a representative, Silas Deane, to France to negotiate for aid and even alliance. On March 14, Congress ordered that all Tories (as colonists loyal to the Crown were called) were to be disarmed, and on April 6, Congress opened American ports to the trade of all nations save Britain. The body also created a committee to draft a declaration of independence, appointing to it John Adams, Benjamin Franklin, Robert Livingston, Roger Sherman, and Thomas Jefferson, the latter taking primary responsibility for drafting the document.

For their part, the British, having fled to Halifax, decided on a new military strategy. Instead of continuing to concentrate operations against New England, the heart of the Revolution, they decided to attack those places where the spirit of independence was weakest and where Tories outnumbered Patriots. The two most vulnerable regions were New York in the north and South Carolina in the south.

The Battles of Long Island, New York, and White Plains

Howe planned to sail from Halifax with a large army to take and occupy New York City, gateway to the Hudson River, the principal route into the American interior. From New York City, he intended to move up the Hudson to Albany, thereby cutting off New England from the rest of the colonies. Inasmuch as New England was regarded as the brains behind the Revolution, this would constitute a decapitating blow. At Albany, a British force under General Guy Carleton would join Howe, and together the two armies would defeat the rebellion in detail.

In January 1776, recognizing the strategic significance of New York, George Washington sent General Charles Lee from Boston to organize the city's defense. Lee's plan was to fortify Brooklyn Heights, which overlooked lower Manhattan. Uptown, on the island of Manhattan itself, he intended to position soldiers to defend King's Bridge, connecting Manhattan with the Bronx on the mainland. Realistically, Lee did not believe he could stop an invasion, but he thought he could effectively counterattack the British on Manhattan from the surrounding high ground.

By the end of August 1776, General William Howe had more than 30,000 troops ready to leave Halifax. They would be supported by no fewer than 30 major combat ships under the command of his brother, Admiral Richard Howe. Together, this was the largest expeditionary force England had ever assembled to that time. To oppose it, Washington had some 20,000 troops deployed on Long Island; Governor's Island in New York Harbor, off the lower tip of Manhattan; and elsewhere in and around New York City. This was almost the sum total of America's military strength. Lose this army, and the American Revolution was at an end.

Experienced in leading small units, Washington was nevertheless untrained in military theory. He made a grave error in dividing his forces between Manhattan and Long Island, with the East River and Long Island Sound separating them. The divided units were especially vulnerable to the British fleet. It is true that William Howe was no great tactician himself, but in this case, he proceeded brilliantly. Landing a large force in the Flatlands of southeast Brooklyn on the night of August 26, he marched 10,000 men to the northeast, through Bedford (today's Brooklyn neighborhood of Bedford-Stuyvesant), so that the main thrust of the attack, on the morning of August 27, came against General John Sullivan's left flank—precisely the opposite direction from which it had been expected. Then, while this main assault proceeded from the northeast, 5,000 Hessians (German mercenary troops in the British service) struck due north from the Flatlands, while another 7,000 troops—elite Highlanders—attacked from New York Bay in the west, the only direction Washington had anticipated.

Attacked by 22,000 men from three sides, the 3,100 Americans detailed to hold the ground in front of Brooklyn Heights struggled to hang on and did, indeed, exact a heavy toll on the Highlanders. Nevertheless, by noon on August 27, the American survivors of the battle had retreated into the fortifications of the Heights.

Considering his overwhelming advantages, Howe achieved remarkably little on this day. Moreover, because of adverse winds, his admiral brother, Richard Howe, could offer little support from the water. General Howe therefore dug in for an extended siege of the Brooklyn Heights fortress. At first confident that he could hold Brooklyn, Washington soon realized that it was doomed and, during the stormy night of August 29–30, carried out a remarkable evacuation of his army across the East River to Manhattan, entirely undetected by the British.

Washington had saved his army, which was now wholly deployed on Manhattan, cut off from supply, and facing the impending expiration of short-term militia enlistments. The general considered abandoning and burning the city—under the circumstances, a strategically sound idea—but Congress vetoed this. Hoping to make the best of a bad situation, on September 7 he spread his troops very thinly over 16 miles of the island, leaving the middle portion of Manhattan very weakly defended. It was yet another tactical error.

On September 15, the British fleet sailed up both the Hudson and East Rivers, flanking Manhattan and training the cannons of the men-of-war against the island along most of its length. Transport barges put in at Kip's Bay (where 34th Street today ends at FDR Drive), and redcoats landed unopposed at 11 A.M. Melting away, the Patriot militia retreated toward Harlem Heights and Fort Washington. Incredibly, however, Howe failed to pursue and attack the outnumbered and retreating Patriots but instead set up a pleasant headquarters in the Murray house (owned by a prominent Tory) in the neighborhood known today as Murray Hill. Washington thus had ample time to repair his tactical blunder by consolidating his forces at Harlem Heights. Moreover, on September 16, a small force of Connecticut Rangers engaged elements of the vaunted Black Watch Highland Regiment, forcing the Highlanders into retreat across a buckwheat field that fronted the Hudson River (on the site of today's Barnard College). It was a small American victory, but to Howe it seemed a terrible defeat, and by mid-October, he had yet to move against the Patriot forces concentrated at Fort Washington and Harlem Heights. Instead, he sent barges to probe cautiously for landing places in Westchester, north of Manhattan. Noting this, Washington concluded that Howe was slowly preparing an encirclement of his position, and on October 16, he decided to evacuate Manhattan, leaving New York City to the British in order to preserve his army. Although he was a flawed tactician, Washington was a skilled strategist. He understood that he could not defeat the army and navy of the greatest military power in the world, but he might just be able to outlast it—or, more precisely, to outlast the willingness of the British government and the British people to continue a costly war far across the Atlantic. His top priority, therefore, was the preservation of the army. As long as he could fight—even if he did not win—he brought the nation closer to independence.

Washington therefore pulled his army slowly toward White Plains, in Westchester County. There he deployed his forces on three hills—neglecting, however, to fortify the highest of them, Chatterton Hill. Sure enough, when Howe finally arrived, it was against this weak point that he focused his initial assault. Chatterton Hill fell to the British, but Howe failed to exploit his gains yet again. Instead of vigorously attacking and possibly destroying the bulk of Washington's vulnerable army, he sent the Americans into retreat farther north. Washington reached North Castle, where he had a route of communication and supply with New England. Because they now had fresh provisions and some new equipment, Washington's soldiers chose to interpret the Battle of White Plains as a victory, when the fact was that Washington had been driven from Long Island; from Manhattan; and, finally, from White Plains.

When he evacuated Manhattan, Washington left behind 2,000 men to garrison Fort Washington at the northern tip of the island. Reinforcements raised this number to nearly 3,000. Howe attacked the fort from three directions on November 16, and 2,818 American officers and men became prisoners of war. The loss of Fort Washington, the capture of so many men, and the loss of arms and ammunition were grave blows, made even worse when, four days later, Fort Lee (across the Hudson in New Jersey) also fell. In addition, all of Manhattan and a large swath along the New Jersey bank of the Hudson were now in British hands. As for the American army, what remained of it was split into three groups: Charles Lee was up in North Castle, Westchester County; General William Heath was at Peekskill, up the Hudson from Manhattan; and Washington took the main body of troops on a long retreat through New Jersey.

Retreat and Reversal

Casualties, the expiration of enlistments, desertions, and capture had reduced Washington's command to about 16,400 troops. He led his forces across New Jersey and toward the Delaware River, evading a pursuing General Charles Cornwallis. Washington reached Trenton with his main force on December 3, 1776, then evacuated across the Delaware River into Pennsylvania on December 7. With that, Cornwallis gave up the chase, settling into camp to await the arrival of spring, when he intended to finish off the American army.

As Christmas approached, Washington's army consisted of no more than 6,000 troops fit for duty. To all appearances, he had been defeated, but the American general defied appearances by launching a daring counteroffensive. On Christmas night, he loaded 2,400 veteran troops and 18 cannons into stout Durham boats and crossed the partially frozen Delaware back into New Jersey. It was three o'clock on the morning of the 26th by the time all of his men were across. He led them toward the Trenton encampment of the Hessians, mercenaries who were among the best and most feared soldiers of Europe.

Washington's forces fell upon the Hessian camp at 7:30 A.M. After a short, sharp fight, in which the Hessian commander, Colonel Johann Rall, was mortally wounded, the Hessians surrendered, giving up as well a trove of equipment and stores. Of the 1,200 Hessians engaged, 106 had been killed or wounded, and 918 became prisoners of war.

Victory at the Battle of Trenton revived the fortunes of the Continental army and reinvigorated the American Revolution. When the short-term enlistees voluntarily extended their terms of service, Washington crossed his army into New Jersey once again and achieved victory at the Battle of Princeton on January 3, 1777, but he dared not occupy the town for fear that Cornwallis would counterattack with a superior force. Nor could he afford to carry out his plan to capture New Brunswick—a major British supply depot—because his forces were just too worn out. Instead, he and his troops went west to Morristown to make winter camp. The war was essentially idled until spring.

Foreign Allies and Burgoyne's New Plan

Spring 1777 brought Washington some fresh troops and, even more gratifying, a willingness on the part of many veterans to extend their enlistments. In Paris, Benjamin Franklin and Silas Deane were making headway in securing a formal alliance between France and the United States. More immediately, however, in June, Marie-Joseph-Paul-Yves-Roch-Gilbert du Motier, marquis de Lafayette, arrived with a party of other idealistic adventurers (including the baron de Kalb), all eager to impart their European military expertise to the officers and men of the Continental army.

On the British side, General John Burgoyne proposed a new plan to wrap up the war once and for all. It would be a three-pronged attack on New York, with the main force descending from Canada, down Lake Champlain and the upper Hudson, and a smaller force operating through the New York frontier country, from Oswego through the Mohawk Valley. These two operations were to be coordinated with General Howe, who would dispatch another large force up the Hudson to meet Burgoyne's army at Albany. This meeting would constitute the culmination of a pincers movement intended to isolate New England from the rest of the colonies. It was a sound strategy, but in far-off London, Lord Germain, the minister in charge of the war's conduct, thoughtlessly approved both this plan and Howe's separate plan to capture Philadelphia. The problem? The two plans were mutually exclusive. If Howe devoted his forces to taking Philadelphia, he could not possibly rendezvous in Albany with Burgoyne.

Ticonderoga, Oriskany, and Bennington

On June 17, 1777, Burgoyne led 7,000 infantrymen from St. Johns, Newfoundland, south to Lake Champlain, where he divided his forces, sending his British regulars (plus some Loyalist militiamen) down the west side of the lake and his Brunswick mercenaries (under Baron Friedrich von Riedesel) down the east side. By the time Burgoyne reached Fort Ticonderoga, he discovered that the Americans, under General Arthur St. Clair, had abandoned it.

After taking Fort Ticonderoga, Burgoyne completed cutting a wilderness road approaching Albany, intending to meet up with General Barry St. Leger from the Mohawk Valley and Howe from the south, to deliver the contemplated crushing blow to the rebels, after which he planned to return to England in triumph. On August 3, however, he received word that Howe, engaged in taking Philadelphia, would be unable to join Burgoyne's operation.

In the meantime, Barry St. Leger, planning to attack Fort Schuyler (as the Patriots renamed Fort Stanwix after occupying it), delayed his assault after prisoners of war falsely informed him that the fort was formidably garrisoned. The delay gave the Patriot militia general Nicholas Herkimer time to intercept St. Leger at the Indian town of Oriskany, 10 miles southwest of the fort. Herkimer himself, however, was ambushed at Oriskany on August 6 before he could begin his attack. In what was undoubtedly the fiercest backwoods battle of the war, Herkimer was mortally wounded but nevertheless continued to direct the fight. Combat ended when a sudden thunderstorm made further fighting impossible for either side. The result was a very bloody draw in which all combatants—American militia, British regulars, Loyalist militia, and British-allied Indians—suffered heavy casualties. St. Leger nevertheless demanded the surrender of Fort Schuyler/Stanwix. The commandant, Colonel Marinus Willet, refused to yield and held out until a Massachusetts brigade and the First New York Regiment (under General Benedict Arnold) arrived to lift the siege on August 22. St. Leger's withdrawal persuaded most of his Indian allies to desert him, and thus the British forces along the Hudson were put at a great disadvantage.

Worse was to come for the British. Burgoyne detailed Hessian troops under Lieutenant Colonel Friedrich Baum to capture Bennington, Vermont. Opposing Baum were 800 Vermont militiamen, who, on August 16, made a preemptive attack from the front, rear, and flanks. After Baum fell, mortally wounded, his dispirited men surrendered, even as more Hessians arrived. Met at the outskirts of Bennington by elements of the Patriot militia, they were quickly defeated, along with some British regulars. In the end, of the combined British and German forces, 207 lay dead and another 700 had been taken prisoner. Thirty Americans had fallen in battle, and perhaps 40 more were wounded. The Battle of Bennington ended any possibility Burgoyne had of cutting off New England from the rest of the colonies.

The Battle of Brandywine, the Fall of Philadelphia, and the Battle of Germantown

William Howe chose not to join forces with Burgoyne in upstate New York so that he could devote his forces to taking Philadelphia, seat of the Continental Congress. At best, he hoped the capture of the city would deal a decapitating blow to the Revolution, but at the least he believed it would lure Washington into the trap of exposing his forces in defense of the city.

Howe's army numbered about 15,000 troops to the 11,000 Washington was able to muster. On September 11, 1777, Washington sent his principal forces to intercept British troops sighted near Kennett Square, Pennsylvania. Too late, he realized that they were merely a diversionary force, and he had been tricked into leaving the upstream fords across Brandywine Creek undefended. It was here that Howe's main force attacked the Americans from the right rear. All along the Brandywine, the thin American line crumbled, and by nightfall, Washington withdrew to Chester, Pennsylvania, to regroup and take up a new position to block Howe's route into Philadelphia. Of the 11,000 American troops engaged at Brandywine, as many as 1,300 had been killed, wounded, or captured.

After resting the night at Chester, Washington took a defensive position even closer to Philadelphia. Nevertheless, on September 18, the Continental Congress fled, first to Lancaster, Pennsylvania, and then to York. In the meantime, Washington dispatched General Anthony Wayne with 1,500 men and four cannons to Warren's Tavern, near the town of Paoli, Pennsylvania, to harass the British rear guard; however, during the night of September 20–21, the redcoats made a surprise bayonet raid on Wayne's camp so fierce that locals dubbed it the "Paoli massacre." Despite losing some 150 casualties, Wayne saved most of his men—and his precious artillery.

Shaken by the Paoli massacre, Washington moved his troops to Pott's Grove (present-day Pottstown), Pennsylvania—a tactical error that allowed Howe's subordinate Charles Cornwallis to march across the Schuylkill River and into Philadelphia, unopposed, on September 23. He bedded down his four British and two Hessian units in Germantown, just north of the city.

Instead of accepting ignominious defeat, Washington audaciously mounted a counterattack precisely where Cornwallis had concentrated his troops—at Germantown—at dawn on October 4. He threw 8,000 Continentals and 3,000 militiamen against 9,000 British and Hessians, but the British 40th Regiment, taking cover in the great stone house of Benjamin Chew, poured fire on the attackers, creating sufficient confusion to blunt the entire operation, which was also hampered by dense fog. Regarded from a strictly tactical point of view, Germantown was yet another of Washington's fiascoes: 150 Americans died, 521 were wounded, and 400 were captured. Yet, from a strategic point of view, Germantown was a triumph. French observers of the battle were so impressed by Washington's aggressive audacity in responding to defeat with an attack that they advised their government to make a full alliance with the Patriots. As for the "defeated" American army, its officers and men regarded the battle not as a failure but as a narrowly missed victory, and they took heart from it.

The Saratoga Campaign

Howe's capture of Philadelphia did not bring the Revolution closer to an end, and without Howe's aid, Burgoyne reeled from one blow after another even as he continued his advance toward Albany, the original objective of his grand plan. Local Patriots harassed his columns along the way. On September 16, 1777, Burgoyne attempted to draw the main body of American forces into open combat at a place called Freeman's Farm, outside of Saratoga, New York. So anxious was the British commander for a single decisive battle that he made the elementary tactical blunder of dividing his forces in the face of the enemy, sending three separate columns toward Freeman's Farm. The American commander, Horatio Gates, ordered riflemen under the skilled frontiersman Daniel Morgan and light infantry under Henry Dearborn to make contact. Acting from ambush, Morgan's riflemen killed every British officer in the advance line, then charged into the line, causing it to stampede in panic. When Morgan's men collided with the main body of the British center column, his soldiers retreated in disarray. Morgan efficiently reformed them, however, sending the British back in panic. They likewise reformed, along the northern edge of Freeman's Farm, whereupon Morgan and Dearborn, along with seven more American regiments sent down from Bemis Heights, just south of the farm, battled for four hours. The British suffered heavy losses but retained discipline and returned effective fire. When Burgoyne's Hessians arrived, the Americans fell back, albeit in good order, as darkness fell. In this first battle of the Saratoga campaign, Burgoyne had lost some 600 men, whereas American losses totaled 319, including 65 killed, 208 wounded, and 36 missing.

The Saratoga campaign next moved from Freeman's Farm to Bemis Heights after a lull of several days during which Gates received reinforcements, so that he now outnumbered Burgoyne, 11,000 to 5,000. Burgoyne also awaited reinforcements, but when they had not arrived by October 7, fearing that he was about to be attacked, he sent a reconnaissance force of 1,650 men to ascertain just what he was facing. Morgan and another Patriot general, Enoch Poor, advanced to intercept it. Benedict Arnold, whose impetuosity had prompted the cautious and conventional Gates to expel him from camp, acted without orders from Gates and led a detachment to attack the breastworks behind which some of Burgoyne's men had taken shelter. After this, he assaulted "Breymann's redoubt," a strong position held by the Hessians. Arnold was badly wounded in the leg in these actions, and without his leadership, the Patriot charge dissolved—but not before Burgoyne's army had been badly battered. Six hundred of Burgoyne's men (including Hessians) had been killed or wounded, for American casualties of fewer than 150. Burgoyne retreated, but on October 12, Gates maneuvered around him, cutting off his access to the Hudson. Trapped, Burgoyne surrendered his army on October 13. Combined with Washington's audacious demonstration at Germantown, the American victory at Saratoga prompted the government of France at last to proclaim a full and open alliance with a nation that now called itself the United States.

Valley Forge

The Franco-American alliance was officially established on December 17, 1777, and proved critically vital to the Patriot cause. Yet Washington had to fend off a movement among a handful of his officers to unseat him as commander in chief, and he was faced with the increasingly daunting task of holding his threadbare Continental army together in their encampment at Valley Forge, Pennsylvania, during the winter of 1777–78. The Continental Congress provided little to feed, clothe, and shelter the army, and starvation was a real possibility. Some 2,500 men died during the six months in camp, mainly from exposure and privation. Yet those who survived benefited from a winter of rigorous training to

European military standards by Baron Friedrich Wilhelm von Steuben (a Prussian general in volunteer service to the Patriot cause), Lafayette, and other foreign officers.

Spring not only brought relief from the cold and misery, it also brought the first substantial fruits of the new Franco-American alliance. The British high command ordered the transfer of many troops to the French West Indies, a move that took much pressure off Patriot forces. Even more dramatic was the transfer of the British garrison holding Philadelphia, which left for New York City in March 1778. The capital was relinquished to the rebels.

The Battle of Monmouth Courthouse

In June 1778, Washington's spies reported unusual movements that suggested to the American commander that the British were preparing for some major operation in New Jersey. He ordered General Charles Lee to intercept certain British regiments, but Lee bungled the assignment, Washington relieved him and then took over personally. On June 28, he positioned his forces near Monmouth Courthouse and fought a fierce battle in which the biggest enemy for both sides was the intense summer heat. Both sides, exhausted, ultimately withdrew without a decision; 356 Americans were killed, wounded, or missing, and 358 British killed or wounded (some historians believe that British losses were much higher). The Americans held the field, but the British kept their army intact and completed the evacuation from Philadelphia.

The Frontier War

Although the American Revolution spanned nearly eight years, battles between formally constituted, regular army units were relatively few. Much of the fighting took place on the frontier between the Euro-Americans and the Native Americans. In the course of the war, most Indian tribes remained neutral, but among those who chose sides, the majority sided with the British. The major British-allied tribes included the Mohawk, Seneca, Cayuga, and Onondaga, most of the so-called Iroquois Confederacy. Of the Iroquois tribes, only the Oneida and the Tuscarora allied themselves with the Americans. Also fighting on the side of Americans were the Mahican (also called the Stockbridge Indians).

Major engagements involving Indians were fought in Cherry Valley, some 40 miles west of Schenectady, New York, during 1778 and later, and in the Wyoming Valley of Pennsylvania at about the same time. Patriot settlements in the New York and Pennsylvania frontier were so hard hit that in June 1779 George Washington authorized an ambitious campaign of retaliation against the Iroquois confederation, committing forces in a three-pronged punitive expedition. General John Sullivan was assigned to lead 2,500 men from Easton, Pennsylvania, through the Susquehanna and up to the southern border of New York, while General James Clinton (no relation to the British general Henry Clinton), with 1,500 troops, swept through the Mohawk Valley to Lake Otsego and then headed down the Susquehanna. Simultaneously, Colonel Daniel Brodhead led 600 men from Fort Pitt up the Allegheny. At Tioga, Pennsylvania, Sullivan and Clinton were to join forces, move north to Niagara, and meet Brodhead at Genesee, New York. Throughout their long marches, all commanders were to sweep away whatever Indian presence they encountered.

While Sullivan and the others attacked British-allied warriors in the Northeast, George Rogers Clark was given the task of dealing with widespread Indian raids in the "Old Northwest" (the frontier region north of the Ohio River and east of the Mississippi) and Kentucky. In July 1776, a council of Shawnee, Iroquois, Delaware, Ottawa, Cherokee, Wyandot, and Mingo warriors united under Chief Cornstalk to ally themselves with the British. By the end of Janu-

ary 1777, they had driven most settlers out of Kentucky when George Rogers Clark persuaded Virginia authorities to make Kentucky a county of that state and commission him to command a Kentucky militia. Clark planned to attack the British western forts in what is today Illinois and Indiana, then to march to Detroit and capture that important stronghold. In the meantime, Shawnee, Wyandot, Mingo, and Cherokee raided the area of Wheeling (in present-day West Virginia) during midsummer 1777. The Continental Congress responded by sending General Edward Hand to attack a key British-run Indian supply depot on the Cuyahoga River, near present-day Cleveland, Ohio.

On February 8, 1778, the Shawnee chief Blue Jacket captured the already legendary frontiersman Daniel Boone at Blue Licks, Kentucky. Boone pretended to turn traitor, accepted adoption into the Shawnee tribe, and offered to cooperate with Henry Hamilton, Britain's chief liaison with the Indians. By feigning cooperation, Boone managed to delay an attack on Fort Pitt and to gather information on an attack planned against Boonesboro, Kentucky. He escaped just in time to mount a successful resistance at the settlement named for him, and his brilliant undercover work helped save the frontier during the American Revolution.

By the end of May 1778, Clark had begun his conquest of the British western forts, but their fall only seemed to make the Indians more desperate, and raiding throughout the Old Northwest became so severe in 1780 that Clark had to abandon his objective of taking Detroit in order to suppress the raiders directly.

While Clark fought in the West, General Sullivan ravaged Indian settlements throughout upstate New York. Yet, as with Clark's triumphs, this action served only to exacerbate Indian hostility by 1780. In May of that year, the Loyalist leader Sir John Johnson organized a massive assault on the Patriot forts of the Mohawk Valley while the British-allied Indian leader Joseph Brant raided the settlements of Caughnawaga and Canajoharie, then started down the Ohio, destroying a force of Pennsylvania militia. After this, Brant and his men turned back to New York, where they rejoined Johnson's Tories and a Seneca chief named Cornplanter. With a combined force of 1,800, they descended upon New York's Scoharie Valley on October 15, then progressed up the Mohawk River, burning everything they encountered. In the space of five days, Johnson and Brant destroyed as much as General Sullivan had in a monthlong campaign.

With Patriot fortunes now in deep crisis, Colonel Marinus Willett was assigned command of the upstate New York region and, skillfully wielding just 130 Continental troops and a handful of militiamen, he put an end to raiding by the summer of 1781. When attacks resumed in October, Willett squared off against Tories and Indians led by the charismatic Loyalist Walter Butler, who was fatally wounded in the engagement. With his death, the raiders dispersed.

British Progress in the South

After the British were driven out of Boston at the beginning of the war, they focused much of their effort on two regions where Patriot strength was perceived as weak and Loyalist sentiment ran high: New York (especially in and around New York City) and the South. On June 4, 1776, 10 British warships and 30 troop transports dropped anchor off Charleston Bar preparatory to an invasion of Charleston. To the stunned chagrin of the British commander, Henry Clinton, Patriot resistance was so effective that the invasion had to be quickly canceled, and the British largely turned away from the South for the next two years until the creation of a Franco-American alliance in 1778 prompted British strategy to change once again. From the end of 1778 to the end of the war, the South became a principal focus of the British war effort.

On November 27, 1778, British troops sailed from Sandy Hook, New Jersey, en route to Savannah, Georgia. On December 23, the invasion force of 3,500 anchored off Tybee Island at the mouth of the Savannah River, and six days later they brushed aside some 1,000 defenders and marched into Savannah. In September–October 1779, a fleet under the French admiral Jean-Baptiste-Charles-Henri-Hector, comte d'Estaing, acting in concert with American units, bungled an attempt to recapture the city, which remained in British hands until July 1782.

As of 1779, Charleston was still in Patriot hands, but in December of that year, Henry Clinton dispatched a force of more than 11,000 from New York to take the city. Bad weather delayed the arrival of the invaders until February 11, 1780, and the British set up a siege. The city managed to hold out until May 12, 1780, when not only did this key American port fall, but 5,000 Continental soldiers became prisoners of war, and 400 precious artillery pieces were lost to the enemy. It was the costliest Patriot defeat of the Revolution.

The Revolution at Sea

By the period of the American Revolution, the Royal Navy had suffered a decline from its glory days earlier in the 18th century, but it was still the most powerful navy in the world, with (in 1783) a total fleet of 468 major warships. At the start of the Revolution, the United States had no navy at all. Merchant vessels were pressed into service, and the Continental Congress authorized construction of 13 frigates. By 1783, the end of the war, the U.S. Navy had 53 ships, a fleet variously augmented by state navies and by privateers (armed commercial vessels authorized to prey on enemy shipping).

During March 3–4, 1776, "Commodore" Esek Hopkins led a Continental navy squadron in a surprise assault on Nassau (then called Providence or New Providence), Bahamas, and captured Fort Montagu as well as the governor of the island, Monfort Browne. On April 6, 1776, just a little over a month after his triumph at

Nassau, Hopkins led five Continental navy ships back from the West Indies and was intercepted by the 20-gun British frigate *Glasgow,* which inflicted 24 casualties among the American sailors and disabled one of the fleet's ships. Worse, the encounter disheartened the infant American navy, which simply fell apart. Hopkins was censured by Congress and then relieved of command, as was the captain of the USS *Providence,* who was promptly replaced by one of Hopkins's junior officers, a young Scots immigrant named John Paul Jones.

Jones quickly proved himself one of history's great naval heroes. Commanding the *Providence* and a small flotilla, he quickly captured or sank 21 British warships, transports, and commercial vessels, as well as one Tory privateer by the end of 1776. On April 10, 1778, commanding the sloop *Ranger,* Jones left the French port of Brest and, during April 27–28, raided Whitehaven on the coast of northwest England, spiking the guns of two forts and burning three British ships. After unsuccessfully attempting to abduct the earl of Selkirk at Kirkcudbright Bay, Scotland, Jones crossed the Irish Sea to Carrickfergus, where he captured the British sloop *Drake.* By the time he returned to Brest, on May 8, he had seven prizes and a good many prisoners.

In summer 1779, Jones assumed command of a refitted French merchant ship, the *Duras,* and renamed it *Bonhomme Richard* (in homage to Benjamin Franklin's Poor Richard of his popular *Poor Richard's Almanac*). He used it as his flagship in a patrol around the British Isles, during which he captured 17 British ships. On September 23, 1779, off Flamborough Head, along the York coast, in the North Sea, Jones sighted two warships convoying 40 British merchant vessels. The warships were the 44-gun *Serapis* and the 20-gun *Countess of Scarborough.* Jones pursued *Serapis* while his three other vessels—*Vengeance, Pallas,* and *Alliance*—chased the *Countess.* In the opening moments of this moonlit battle, two of Jones's largest cannons exploded; he was therefore critically outgunned, but he nevertheless outmaneuvered *Serapis* and

then rammed her stern. When the captain of *Serapis* demanded Jones's surrender, the American captain replied with perhaps the single most famous utterance in U.S. military history: "I have not yet begun to fight." After two more hours of mutual pounding, the *Serapis* surrendered, and Jones took it as a prize.

The Tide Turns in the South

After the British capture of Charleston, Lieutenant Colonel Banastre Tarleton was put in charge of mixed British regular, Tory, and Indian forces and was assigned to mop up Patriot resistance in the Carolina backcountry. Throughout the spring and summer of 1780, he did this with singular ruthlessness. Against George Washington's recommendation, the Continental Congress sent the excessively cautious and resolutely conventional General Horatio Gates to take command of Patriot forces in the beleaguered South. He marched first against Camden, South Carolina, held by 2,200 troops under Cornwallis. Along the way, Gates acquired militia reinforcements to augment his Continentals, amassing a force of more than 4,000, but by the time he was ready to attack, an epidemic of dysentery had greatly reduced the number of troops fit for combat. The Battle of Camden, fought on August 16, 1780, dissolved into a rout in which as many as 1,900 Americans died, and nearly 1,000 were taken prisoner. British losses were 68 killed and 350 wounded. Gates himself fled the field.

On September 8, 1780, the victorious Cornwallis moved from Camden on to North Carolina, dividing his advance into three columns. While he personally led the main force, Tarleton headed up the British Legion (a Tory unit) and the regular light infantry, and Major Patrick Ferguson led the another Tory unit. Charlotte fell to the British on September 26, 1780, but Cornwallis, having taken substantial casualties, found it difficult to maintain communication with his base in Camden. The result was that the war in the Carolinas dissolved into scattered guerrilla clashes. Cornwallis tasked Ferguson with consolidating local Tory efforts by leading a force of Tories along the Carolina foothills. Patriot militia attacked Ferguson's column, forcing him to a stand on October 7, 1780, at King's Mountain, on the border between North and South Carolina. Surrounded, Ferguson was killed in battle, and his force surrendered. Four hundred Tories were killed or wounded, and 700 became prisoners.

After so many southern defeats, King's Mountain was a welcome triumph for the Continental army. Not only was Cornwallis stopped dead in his tracks, he was forced to retreat back into South Carolina. Even more important, the battle put an end to Tory influence in North Carolina. Before and after King's Mountain, South Carolina partisans continually harried the British forces. When the Continental general Nathanael Greene replaced Gates in the South, he commenced a productive working relationship with the American guerrillas, and he assigned their most effective leader, Daniel Morgan, to harass British positions in the western wilderness of South Carolina while he supported the operation of partisans in the north-central portion of the state. Cornwallis responded by sending Tarleton to deal with Morgan while he personally led an attack on Greene.

On January 16, 1781, Morgan, commanding 1,000 men, learned that Tarleton was nearby with 1,100 Tories and regulars. He decided to make a stand at the Cowpens, little more than a backwoods South Carolina cattle pasturage. Purposely positioning his men so that the Broad River cut off any avenue of retreat, Morgan set up a kill-or-be-killed proposition for his militia. He also violated accepted military practice by putting his least experienced militiamen in the front line, backing them up with the Continentals and seasoned men from Virginia. Farthest to the rear, he held his cavalry in reserve, the very troops that are conventionally employed in the front line.

Tarleton commenced the Battle of Cowpens with a fierce bayonet charge, to which Morgan's front line responded with surprisingly effective musket fire. After shooting, they sheared off to the left and around to the rear, putting the best troops in position to fire on Tarleton's overconfident men. As Tarleton's troops continued their charge, Morgan sent his green troops, who had returned to the American rear, to a position behind Tarleton's left and set his cavalry into motion around the rear of Tarleton's right. This double envelopment cost Tarleton and Cornwallis 100 killed, 229 wounded (and captured), and 600 captured (unwounded). Of 66 British officers engaged in the battle, 39 were killed. American losses were 12 killed and 60 wounded. The American victory at Cowpens turned the tide of the war in the South.

After Cowpens, Cornwallis stripped his remaining troops of all the baggage that had for so long encumbered British armies in the American wilderness. He then led his streamlined force in hot pursuit of Greene's army, pushing north, all the way to the Dan River, near the Virginia border. Greene crossed the Dan, taking all available boats with him, leaving Cornwallis on the opposite bank, so desperately low on supplies (his baggage having been shed) that he had to withdraw to Hillsboro for resupply. Now Greene seized the initiative, crossing back into North Carolina to attack Cornwallis's lines of communication. In the meantime, guerrilla operations against local Tories deprived Cornwallis of the last vestiges of Loyalist support in the region.

On March 15, 1781, Greene forced Cornwallis to a stand at Guilford Courthouse, North Carolina. He hoped to replicate Morgan's victory at Cowpens by setting up a double envelopment, but his men proved unable to execute the complex movements required, and the Battle of Guilford Courthouse ended in a draw. Cornwallis held the field but lost a quarter of his army. He evacuated the interior of North Carolina, withdrawing to Wilmington, on the Carolina coast, and thence into Virginia.

Now the focus of the southern theater shifted north to Virginia. Benedict Arnold—who, dissatisfied with lack of recognition and promotion in the Continental army, had turned traitor in May 1779—led a costly Tory raid into Virginia beginning in December 1780. General Friedrich Wilhelm von Steuben, who now commanded Patriot forces in Virginia, attempted to ambush Arnold but was counterattacked and routed. A French fleet was supposed to carry three light infantry regiments to join the campaign against Arnold in Virginia, but a British blockade of Newport, Rhode Island, delayed the departure of the French fleet and forced it into battle with the British fleet in Chesapeake Bay on March 16, 1781. The result was a very narrow French victory, which nevertheless prompted the French admiral Charles-René-Dominique Destouches to abandon the plan of joining the Virginia expedition. In the meantime, the British commander in chief Henry Clinton sent 2,000 reinforcements to Arnold. This, combined with the abortive failure of the Franco-American mission to Virginia, put the Patriot cause in peril. Steuben had nothing more than a handful of Continentals and militia to defend all of Virginia against 3,000 British regulars and Tory auxiliaries. The marquis de Lafayette and his three light infantry regiments were still on the Chesapeake, 150 miles from Richmond, Virginia. As for Washington, he faced the prospect of watching his principal army disband for want of food and supplies.

On April 30, 1781, General William Phillips and Benedict Arnold reached the James River and were poised to capture Richmond. All that stood in their way was the freshly arrived Lafayette with a total of 3,000 troops. Determined to destroy Lafayette and his small army, Cornwallis consolidated a force of 7,200 men, including that commanded by Phillips and Arnold. When Phillips suddenly succumbed to typhoid fever, Cornwallis assumed direct command of all British and Tory forces in Virginia and, turning away from Richmond, began to chase Lafayette northward. Incredibly, the Frenchman managed to elude his pursuers. Cornwallis then broke

off the pursuit and turned the Tories of John G. Simcoe and Banastre Tarleton loose on the Virginia countryside.

As the Virginia frontier reeled under Tory raids, Lafayette used his reprieve to accept reinforcements—three Pennsylvania regiments under no less a commander than Anthony Wayne—so that he now controlled 4,500 men. With these, he counterattacked Cornwallis's army. The Battle of Jamestown Ford (July 6, 1781) resulted in a narrow British victory, but Cornwallis decided not to pursue Lafayette and Wayne and instead proceeded to Portsmouth, Virginia, apparently in obedience to an order from Henry Clinton to send reinforcements to New York. No sooner did Cornwallis break off his engagement of Lafayette and Wayne, however, than Clinton issued new orders, directing Cornwallis to continue to hold a position in Virginia. Toward this end, Cornwallis decided to occupy Yorktown, a sleepy tobacco port on the Yorktown peninsula, which, he believed, would allow him access to support from the Royal Navy. It was, however, a grave strategic blunder: Cornwallis had put his army in a cul de sac.

The Yorktown Campaign

Combining his Continental forces with a large French army under General Jean-Baptiste Rochambeau, George Washington decided to reinforce Lafayette and Wayne against Cornwallis while the French admiral Francois-Joseph-Paul, comte de Grasse attacked the British fleet to prevent its making contact with Cornwallis at the Yorktown peninsula. On August 21, 1781, the Franco-American army began its march to Virginia. In the meantime, on September 5, 1781, in Chesapeake Bay, at the Battle of the Capes, Grasse defeated the British fleet, which withdrew from the Chesapeake and returned to New York, leaving Cornwallis stranded at Yorktown. By September 9, another French fleet joined Grasse in Chesapeake Bay, allowing him to land additional troops at Williamsburg,

Virginia, bringing the Franco-American army to 16,000 men, which now marched against Cornwallis's 6,000 men bottled up within the fortifications of Yorktown.

On September 17, Washington and Rochambeau met aboard the *Ville de Paris* to plan the siege of Yorktown. While Grasse maintained control of the sea, the two generals would encircle and bombard Yorktown, and engineers would dig siege trenches to attack and breach the English fortifications. The American batteries opened fire, beginning on October 1, 1781. On October 6, Washington personally broke ground for the first approach trench. On October 14, Alexander Hamilton and a French officer led a gallant nighttime bayonet attack against defenders of two redoubts near the York River. With these objectives secured, the approach trenches were extended to the river, completely cutting Cornwallis off. In desperation, on October 16, Cornwallis sent out a sortie of 350 men against a line of allied trenches, but the sortie was repulsed. Cornwallis then attempted a nighttime breakout across the York River, to Gloucester Point, which was followed by a forced march northward, all the way to New York. A sudden storm foiled the attempt, and Cornwallis agreed to unconditional surrender on October 17, 1781. The formal surrender took place two days later.

Victory and Independence

The defeat of Cornwallis hardly wiped out the British in the United States, but it effectively ended the British will to continue resisting the Patriots. On December 20, 1781, Parliament concluded that it was no longer feasible to continue to fight to hold America. Although combat continued sporadically in the South, peace negotiations commenced in Paris on April 12, and on November 30, 1782, a provisional treaty was drawn up. On September 3, 1783, the Treaty of Paris was signed, and the American Revolution ended with the independence of the United States.

DOCUMENTS

THE BOSTON TEA PARTY, DECEMBER 16, 1773

Letter to William Barrell
John Andrews
December 18, 1773

In 1859, Captain George Gibson, Jr., U.S. Army, was posted at the U.S. Arsenal on the banks of Schuylkill River in Philadelphia. In a "garret room" of the arsenal, he discovered a bundle of letters written by a prominent Boston merchant named John Andrews to William Barrell, a Philadelphia merchant. The Bostonian described the arrival of the redcoats into Boston and their occupation of the city, the chronic fighting between Bostonians and soldiers, and—in the letter that follows—the Boston Tea Party. Andrews's account is dated just two days after the event, which took place on December 16, 1873.

Boston, December 18, 1773

However precarious our situation may be, yet such is the present calm composure of the people that a stranger would hardly think that ten thousand pounds sterling of the East India Company's tea was destroyed the night, or rather the evening before last, yet it's a serious truth; and if yours, together with the other Southern provinces, should rest satisfied with their quota being stored, poor Boston will feel the whole weight of ministerial vengeance. However, it's the opinion of most people that we stand an equal chance now whether troops are sent in consequence of it or not; whereas, had it been stored, we should inevitably have had them to enforce the sale of it.

The affair was transacted with greatest regularity and despatch. Mr. Rotch [captain of the tea ship *Dartmouth*] finding he exposed himself not only to the loss of his ship but for the value of the tea, in case he sent her back with it

This early 19th-century painting depicts the Boston Tea Party of December 16, 1773. *(Library of Congress)*

without a clearance from the custom house, as the Admiral kept a ship in readiness to make a seizure of it whenever it should sail under those circumstances, therefore declined complying with his former promises [to return to England without unloading his cargo of tea] and absolutely declared his vessel should not carry it without a proper clearance could be procured or he to be indemnified for the value of her: when a general muster was assembled, from this and all the neighboring towns, to the number of five or six thousand, at 10 o'clock Thursday morning in the Old South Meeting House, where they passed a unanimous vote that the tea should go out of the harbour that afternoon, and sent a committee with Mr. Rotch to the Custom house to demand a clearance, which the collector told them was not in his power to give, without the duties being first paid. They then sent Mr. Rotch to Milton to ask a pass from the Governor, who sent for answer that "consistent with the rules of government and his duty to the King he could not grant one without they produced a previous clearance from the office."

By the time he returned with this message the candles were light in the house, and upon reading it, such prodigious shouts were made

that induced me, while drinking tea at home, to go out and know the cause of it. The house was so crowded I could get no farther than the porch, when I found the moderator was just declaring the meeting to be dissolved, which caused another general shout, out doors and in, and three cheers. What with that, and the consequent noise of breaking up the meeting, you'd thought that the inhabitants of the infernal regions had broke loose. For my part, I went contentedly home and finished my tea, but was soon informed what was going forward: but still not crediting it without ocular demonstration, I went and was satisfied.

They mustered, I'm told, upon Fort Hill, to the number of about two hundred, and proceeded, two by two, to Griffin's wharf, where Hall, Bruce and Coffin lay, each with 114 chests of the ill-fated article on board; the two former with only that article, but the latter, arrived at the wharf only the day before, was freighted with a large quantity of other goods, which they took the greatest care not to injure in the least, and before nine o'clock in the evening, every chest from on board the three vessels was knocked to pieces and flung over the sides. They say the actors were Indians from Narragansett. Whether they were or not, to a transient observer they appeared as such, being cloathed in blankets with the heads muffled, and copper-colored countenances, being each armed with a hatchet or axe, and pair pistols, nor was their dialect different from what I conceive these geniusses to speak, as their jargon was unintelligible to all but themselves. . . .

Should not have troubled you with this, by this post, hadn't I thought you would be glad of a more particular account of so important a transaction than you could have obtained by common report; and if it affords my brother but a temporary amusement, I shall be more than repaid for the trouble of writing it. . . .

Source: Andrews, John. *Letters of John Andrews, Esq., of Boston, 1772–1776.* Edited by Winthrop Sargent. Cambridge, Mass.: J. Wilson and Sons, 1866.

Account of the Boston Tea Party
George Robert Twelve Hewes
Published 1834

George Robert Twelve Hewes (1742–1840) was a Boston shoemaker who took part in many of the events leading up to the outbreak of rebellion in Boston. More than half a century after the Boston Tea Party, Hewes recalled for a writer named James Hawkes how he had led one of the groups of Bostonians who disguised themselves as Mohawk Indians, boarded the ships in Boston Harbor on December 16, 1773, and dumped a large and valuable cargo of tea overboard. Hawkes published the account in an 1834 book titled A Retrospect of the Boston Tea-Party.

The tea destroyed was contained in three ships, lying near each other at what was called at that time Griffin's wharf, and were surrounded by armed ships of war, the commanders of which had publicly declared that if the rebels, as they were pleased to style the Bostonians, should not withdraw their opposition to the landing of the tea before a certain day, the 17th day of December, 1773, they should on that day force it on shore, under the cover of their cannon's mouth. On the day preceding the seventeenth, there was a meeting of the citizens of the county of Suffolk, convened at one of the churches in Boston, for the purpose of consulting on what measures might be considered expedient to prevent the landing of the tea, or secure the people from the collection of the duty. At that meeting a committee was appointed to wait on Governor Hutchinson, and request him to inform them whether he would take any measures to satisfy the people on the object of the meeting. To the first application of this committee, the Governor told them he would give them a definite answer by five o'clock in the afternoon. At the hour appointed, the committee again repaired to the Governor's house, and on inquiry found he had gone to his country seat at Milton, a distance of about six miles. When the committee returned and informed the meeting of the absence of the Governor, there was a confused murmur among the members, and the meeting was immediately dissolved, many of them crying out, "Let every man do his duty, and be true to his country"; and there was a general huzza for Griffin's wharf.

It was now evening, and I immediately dressed myself in the costume of an Indian, equipped with a small hatchet, which I and my associates denominated the tomahawk, with which, and a club, after having painted my face and hands with coal dust in the shop of a blacksmith, I repaired to Griffin's wharf, where the ships lay that contained the tea. When I first appeared in the street after being thus disguised, I fell in with many who were dressed, equipped and painted as I was, and who fell in with me and marched in order to the place of our destination.

When we arrived at the wharf, there were three of our number who assumed an authority to direct our operations, to which we readily submitted. They divided us into three parties, for the purpose of boarding the three ships which contained the tea at the same time. The name of him who commanded the division to which I was assigned was Leonard Pitt. The names of the other commanders I never knew. We were immediately ordered by the respective commanders to board all the ships at the same time, which we promptly obeyed. The commander of the division to which I belonged, as soon as we were on board the ship, appointed me boatswain, and ordered me to go to the captain and demand of him the keys to the hatches and a dozen candles. I made the demand accordingly, and the captain promptly replied, and delivered the articles; but requested me at the same time to do no damage to the ship or rigging. We then were ordered by our commander to open the hatches and take out all the chests of tea and throw them overboard, and we immediately proceeded to execute his orders, first cutting and splitting the chests with our tomahawks, so as thoroughly to expose them to the effects of the water.

In about three hours from the time we went on board, we had thus broken and thrown overboard every tea chest to be found in the ship, while those in the other ships were disposing of the tea in the same way, at the same time. We were surrounded by British armed ships, but no attempt was made to resist us.

We then quietly retired to our several places of residence, without having any conversation with each other, or taking any measures to discover who were our associates; nor do I recollect of our having had the knowledge of the name of a single individual concerned in that affair, except that of Leonard Pitt, the commander of my division, whom I have mentioned. There appeared to be an understanding that each individual should volunteer his services, keep his own secret, and risk the consequence for himself. No disorder took place during that transaction, and it was observed at that time that the stillest night ensued that Boston had enjoyed for many months.

During the time we were throwing the tea overboard, there were several attempts made by some of the citizens of Boston and its vicinity to carry off small quantities of it for their family use. To effect that object, they would watch their opportunity to snatch up a handful from the deck, where it became plentifully scattered, and put it into their pockets. One Captain O'Connor, whom I well knew, came on board for that purpose, and when he supposed he was not noticed, filled his pockets, and also the lining of his coat. But I had detected him and gave information to the captain of what he was doing. We were ordered to take him into custody, and just as he was stepping from the vessel, I seized him by the skirt of his coat, and in attempting to pull him back, I tore it off; but, springing forward, by a rapid effort he made his escape. He had, however, to run a gauntlet through the crowd upon the wharf, each one, as he passed, giving him a kick or a stroke.

Another attempt was made to save a little tea from the ruins of the cargo by a tall, aged man who wore a large cocked hat and white wig, which was fashionable at that time. He had sleightly slipped a little into his pocket, but being detected, they seized him and, taking his hat and wig from his head, threw them, together with the tea, of which they had emptied his pockets, into the water. In consideration of his advanced age, he was permitted to escape, with now and then a slight kick.

The next morning, after we had cleared the ships of the tea, it was discovered that very considerable quantities of it were floating upon the surface of the water; and to prevent the possibility of any of its being saved for use, a number of small boats were manned by sailors and citizens, who rowed them into those parts of the harbor wherever the tea was visible, and by beating it with oars and paddles so thoroughly drenched it as to render its entire destruction inevitable.

Source: Hawkes, James. *A Retrospect of the Boston Tea-Party, with a Memoir of George R. T. Hewes, a Survivor of the Little Band of Patriots Who Drowned the Tea in Boston Harbor in 1773.* New York: S. S. Bliss, 1834.

KING AND PARLIAMENT PUNISH BOSTON, 1774–1775

Letters to William Barrell
John Andrews
May 1774–January 1775

The Boston merchant John Andrews wrote a series of letters to his friend William Barrell, a merchant living in Philadelphia, narrating the particulars of life in his city after Parliament passed the Port Bill, closing the port of Boston in an effort to strangle the rebellion in its infancy.

May 18th, 1774
Imagine to yourself the horror painted in the faces of a string of slaves condemned by the Inquisition to perpetual drudgery at the oar!

Such is the dejection imprinted on every countenance we meet in this once happy, but now totally ruined town.

Yes, Bill, nothing will save us but an entire stoppage of trade, both to England and the West Indies, throughout the continent: and that must be determined as speedily as absolutely. The least hesitancy on your part *to the southerd,* and the matter is over; we must acknowledge and ask forgiveness for all past offences, whether we have been guilty of any or no; give up the point so long contested, and acknowledge the right of Parliament to d—n us whenever they please; and to add to all this, we must pay for an article unjustly forced upon us with a sole view to pick our pockets (not that I would by any means justify the destruction of that article). When that is done, where are we? Why, in much the same situation as before, without one flattering hope of relief: entirely dependant on the will of an arbitrary Minister, who'd sacrifice the Kingdom to gratify a cursed revenge. A more convincing proof we can't have than in the present Act for blocking up our Port, which could not have been more severely and strongly expressed if all the Devils in the infernal regions had had a hand in the draughting it.

Shall endeavor to content myself to stay here till I see what turn affairs will take. If to my liking, well; if not, shall look out for some other place of residence, as I sincerely believe they intend to put their threats in execution; which is, to make the town a desolate wilderness, and the grass to grow in our streets.

Our Militia was yesterday mustered for the reception of General Gage, who was proclaimed Governor amid the acclamations of the people. He expressed himself as sensible of the unwelcome errand he came upon, but as a servant of the Crown he was obliged to see the Act put in execution; but would do all in his power to serve us. Whether they were only words of course or not, can't say; am a little doubtful. There was an elegant entertainment provided for him at Faneuil Hall, and after a number of toasts gave by him, in which the prosperity of the town

of Boston was included, he gave "Governor Hutchinson," which was received by a general hiss. Such is the detestation in which that tool of tyrants is held among us. . . . The damned arch traitor, as he is called, is very much chagrined at being superseded, as it's only last Thursday when he gave orders for repairs to his houses in town and country, and upon the workman's suggestions that he would be succeeded soon, he said it was like many other reports that prevailed, for that he had all the satisfaction he could wish for or expect from home, and every part of his conduct was entirely approved of, and left to his option whether to enjoy the Government or go to England. But now a guilty conscience has induced him to take refuge at the Castle.

It's reported here that your Government, as well as New York, is to be changed and removed, the one to Burlington and the other to Amboy, with requisitions made upon both, and more particularly upon Rhode Island.

June 12th, 1774

If my last was in a desponding stile, I'm sure I have much more reason to be so now; as ought else than poverty and distress stare us in the face. . . . Animosities run higher than ever, each party charging the other as bringing ruin upon their country; that unless some expediency is adopted to get the Port open by paying for the tea (which seems to be the only one) am afraid we shall experience the worst of evils, a civil war, which God avert!

The trading part promised themselves a general compliance with the tenor of the Act . . . but . . . those who have governed the town for years past and were in a great measure the authors of all our evils by their injudicious conduct are grown more obstinate than ever, and seem determined to bring total destruction upon us: which may be sufficiently evinced by all their conduct. They not only intend to deprive us of trade in future, but render us utterly incapable of contributing that assistance which will be absolutely necessary for the support of the indigent the approaching fall and winter, by their cruel endeavors to stop the little inland trade we expected.

Our wharfs are intirely deserted; not a topsail vessel to be seen either there or in the harbour, save the ships of war and transport, the latter of which land their passengers in this town tomorrow. Four regiments are already arrived, and four more are expected. How they are to be disposed of, can't say. It's gave out that if the General Court don't provide barracks for them, they are to be quartered on the inhabitants in the fall: if so, am determined not to stay in it. The executors of the Act seem to strain points beyond what was ever intended, for they make all the vessels, both with grain and wood, entirely unload at Marblehead before they'll permit them to come in here, which conduct, in regard to the article of wood, has already greatly enhanced the price, and the masters say they won't come at all, if they are to be always put to such trouble, as they are obliged to hire another vessel to unload into, and then to return it back again, as they have no wharves to admit of their landing it on. Nor will they suffer any article of merchandize to be brought or carried over Charles River ferry, [so] that we are obliged to pay for 28 miles land carriage to get our goods from Marblehead or Salem.

Could fill up a number of sheets to enumerate all our difficulties.

September 2nd, 1774
The country people, being vastly more vigilant and spirited than the town, did not fail to visit Brattle and Sewall's house last evening, but not finding either of 'em at home, they quietly went off. But a report having prevailed through the country (by reason of the seizure of the powder yesterday) that the same game had been played here, and the inhabitants disarmed, has raised such a spirit as will require the utmost prudence to allay; for they are in arms at all quarters, being determined to see us redressed.

At eight o'clock this morning there were about three thousand under their regular leaders at Cambridge common, and continually increas-

ing; had left their arms at a little distance, when Judge Lee and Danforth waited upon 'em, and gave them the fullest assurances that they had resigned their seats at the board and would not act in any capacity whatever that was disagreeable to the people.

Lieutenant Governor Oliver is come to town and Brattle is gone to the Castle, which, I believe, is the only place of safety for him in the province.

Four or five expresses have come down to Charlestown and here, to acquaint us that between Sudbury and this, above ten thousand men are in arms, and are continually coming down from the country back: that their determination is to collect about forty or fifty thousand by night (which they are sure of accomplishing) when they intend to fling in about fifteen thousand by the way of the Neck, and as many more over the ferry: when once got possession, to come in like locusts and rid the town of every soldier. But such a scheme is so big with mischief and calamity that the committee of correspondence, selectmen and every prudent man in the town of Charlestown set off to appease 'em early in the morning; and the committee of correspondence from this town also went at the same time. Since which, accounts have been so alarming that between ten and eleven o'clock the selectmen set out from here, to try what they could do to satisfy and disperse 'em.

Ruthy set out this morning for Hingham, in company with my mother, Mr. Breck and Ben. Am rejoiced that she is out of the way, just at this time.

A guard of soldiers is set upon the powder house at the back of the Common, so that people are debarred from selling their own property; and the guard upon the Neck is doubled, as well as that the whole battalions have had new flints, etc., delivered out to them.

September 25th, 1774
. . . The example of our worthy brethren of New York in not letting their vessels for Government service, as well as that their carpenters would

not engage in any work for 'em, has induced the country people to think seriously whether they were right in supplying with timber, joice and straw for the barracks here. They accordingly met and determined in the negative; sent committees to the several contractors to let them know if they supplied any further they would incur the resentment of the whole country; and at the same time signified to our committee of correspondence that they did not think it eligible for the workmen here to go on with building barracks or preparing houses for the reception of the troops, as we might possibly, by persisting, not only incur blame from our sister colonies, but essentially affect the union now subsisting between town and country; which circumstance caused the committee to get together Saturday P.M., when they passed a vote that it was not prudent for the workmen to go on with the frames, etc., nor in any shape to contribute towards the accomodation of the soldiery, as they might themselves give offence to their country brethren.

The purport of which coming to the Governor, he sent his compliments to the selectmen, and begged their attendance at six o'clock this evening, when he requested of them that they would not take any measures to prevent the workmen from going on with the barracks.

They replied it was not in their power to influence the country, and it lay principally with them whether the workmen should proceed or not: that they themselves were disposed to have the barracks go on, as they conceived it much more for the benefit of the town (if the soldiery must be here) to have them kept together, rather than to be scattered over the town, as in that case it would be a very difficult matter to keep them in order.

The Governor seemed a great deal worried about the affair, and am told that in the course of the conversation he expressed himself thus—"Good G—d! for G—d's sake, Gentlemen! they have got two months work to do, and the soldiers ought to be in barracks in one. Do consider, Gentlemen!"

Thus the tables are in some measure turned. Formerly they solicited the Governor, but now it seems he solicits them. A pretty good mess for Sunday, Bill, don't you think it is?

October 1, 1774

It's common for the soldiers to fire at a target fixed in the stream at the bottom of the common. A countryman stood by a few days ago, and laughed very heartily at a whole regiment's firing, and not one being able to hit it. The officer observed him, and asked why he laughed.

"Perhaps you'll be affronted if I tell you," replied the countryman. No, he would not, he said.

"*Why then*," says he, "I laugh to see how awkward they fire. Why, I'll be bount I hit it ten times running."

"Ah! will you?" replied the officer. "Come try. Soldiers, go and bring five of the best guns, and load 'em for this honest man."

"Why, you need not bring so many: let me have any one that comes to hand," replied the other, "but I chuse to load *myself*." He accordingly loaded, and asked the officer where he should fire. He replied, "To the right,"—when he pulled tricker, and drove the ball as near the right as possible. The officer was amazed—and said he could not do it again, as that was only by chance.

He loaded again. "Where shall I fire?"

"*To the left*,"—when he performed as well as before.

"Come! Once more," says the officer.

He prepared the third time. "Where shall I fire *naow*?"

"*In the center.*"

He took aim, and the ball went as exact in the middle as possible. The officers as well as soldiers stared, and thought the Devil was in the man. "Why," says the countryman, "I'll tell you *naow*. I have got a boy at home that will toss up an apple and shoot out all the seeds as it's coming down."

The country towns, in general, have chose their own officers and muster for exercise once a week at least—when the parson as well as the squire stands in the ranks with a firelock. In particular at Marblehead, they turn out three or four times a week, when Col. Lee as well as the clergymen there are not ashamed to appear in the ranks, to be taught the manual exercise in particular.

One more anecdote, and I'll close this barren day. When the 59th Regiment came from Salem and were drawn up on each side the Neck, a remarkable tall countryman, near eight feet high, struted between 'em at the head of his waggon, looking very sly and contemptuously on one side and t'other, which attracted the notice of the whole regiment.

"Ay, ay," says he, "you don't know what boys we have got in the country. I am near nine feet high, and one of the smallest among 'em"— which caused much merriment to the spectators, as well as surprise to the soldiers.

Indeed, Bill! were I to tell you of all the jokes and wittisisms of the country people, I would have little else to do.

January 21st, 1775

Last evening a number of drunken officers attacked the town house watch between eleven and 12 o'clock, when the assistance of the New Boston watch was called, and a general battle ensued; some wounded on both sides. A party from the main guard was brought up with their captain together with another party from the Governor's. Had it not been for the prudence of two officers that were sober, the captain of the main guard would have acted a second tragedy to the 5th March, as he was much disguised with liquor and would have ordered the guard to fire on the watch had he not been restrained. His name is Gore, being a captain in the 5th or Earl Peircy's [Percy's] Regiment. He was degraded not long since for some misdemeanour.

This afternoon there was a general squabble between the butchers in the market and a number of soldiers. It first began by a soldier's tripping up the heals of a fisherman who was walking through the market with a piece of beef in his hands. A guard from the 47th barracks appered and carried off the soldiers, together with one butcher who was most active, the officer taking him by the collar. He was able to have crushed

the officer, but was advised to be quiet. Young Ned Gray insisted on it that he should not be carried into the guard house, upon which many hard words passed between him and the captain of the guard. However, Gray prevailed, and they carried the man into Miss Foster's store close by the barracks, from whence the officer dismissed him after finding upon deliberation that his conduct was not justifiable—and seemed to be much afraid lest the butcher should take advantage of him by law or complaint.

Source: Andrews, John. *Letters of John Andrews, Esq., of Boston, 1772–1776.* Edited by Winthrop Sargent. Cambridge, Mass.: J. Wilson and Sons, 1866.

Paul Revere's "Midnight Ride," April 18–19, 1775

Letter to Dr. Jeremy Belknap
Paul Revere
Written 1798

The story of the "Midnight Ride of Paul Revere" was most famously related in Henry Wadsworth Longfellow's poem of that title, written in 1860 and published the following year. Revere himself recalled the particulars—less romantically—in a letter to the clergyman and historian Dr. Jeremy Belknap in 1798.

In the fall of 1774 and winter of 1775, I was one of upwards of thirty, chiefly mechanics [artisans and tradespeople], who formed ourselves into a committee for the purpose of watching the movements of the British soldiers, and gaining every intelligence of the movements of the Tories. We held our meetings at the Green Dragon tavern. We were so careful that our meetings should be kept secret that every time we met, every person swore upon the Bible that they would not discover any of our transactions but to Messrs. Hancock, Adams, Doctors Warren, Church and one or two more.

. . . In the winter, towards the spring, we frequently took turns, two and two, to watch the soldiers by patrolling the streets all night. The Saturday night preceding the 19th of April, about 12 o'clock at night, the boats belonging to the transports were all launched and carried under the sterns of the men-of-war. (They had been previously hauled up and repaired.) We likewise found that the grenadiers and light infantry were all taken off duty.

From these movements we expected something serious was to be transacted. On Tuesday evening, the 18th, it was observed that a number of soldiers were marching towards the bottom of the Common. About 10 o'clock, Dr. Warren sent in great haste for me and begged that I would immediately set off for Lexington, where Messrs. Hancock and Adams were, and acquaint them of the movement, and that it was thought they were the objects.

When I got to Dr. Warren's house, I found he had sent an express by land to Lexington—a Mr. William Daws [Dawes]. The Sunday before, by desire of Dr. Warren, I had been to Lexington, to Messrs. Hancock and Adams, who were at the Rev. Mr. Clark's. I returned at night through Charlestown; there I agreed with a Colonel Conant and some other gentlemen that if the British went out by water, we would show two lanthorns in the North Church steeple; and if by land, one, as a signal; for we were apprehensive it would be difficult to cross the Charles River or get over Boston Neck. I left Dr. Warren, called upon a friend and desired him to make the signals.

I then went home, took my boots and surtout, went to the north part of the town, where I had kept a boat; two friends rowed me across Charles River, a little to the eastward where the *Somerset* man-of-war lay. It was then young flood, the ship was winding, and the moon was rising. They landed me on the Charlestown side. When I got into town, I met Colonel Conant and several others; they said they had seen our signals. I told them

The midnight ride of Paul Revere, April 18, 1775 *(Library of Congress)*

what was acting, and went to get me a horse; I got a horse of Deacon Larkin. While the horse was preparing, Richard Devens, Esq., who was one of the Committee of Safety, came to me and told me that he came down the road from Lexington after sundown that evening; that he met ten British officers, all well mounted, and armed, going up the road.

I set off upon a very good horse; it was then about eleven o'clock and very pleasant. After I had passed Charlestown Neck . . . I saw two men on horseback under a tree. When I got near them, I discovered they were British officers. One tried to get ahead of me, and the other to take me. I turned my horse very quick and galloped towards Charlestown Neck, and then pushed for the Medford Road. The one who chased me, endeavoring to cut me off, got into a clay pond near where Mr. Russell's Tavern is now built. I got clear of him, and went through Medford, over the bridge and up to Menotomy. In Medford, I awaked the captain of the minute men; and after that, I alarmed almost every house, till I got to Lexington. I found Messrs. Hancock and Adams at the Rev. Mr. Clark's; I told them my errand and enquired for Mr. Daws; they said he had not been there; I related the story of the two officers, and supposed that he must have been stopped, as he ought to have been there before me.

After I had been there about half an hour, Mr. Daws came; we refreshed ourselves, and set off for Concord. We were overtaken by a young Dr. Prescott, whom we found to be a high Son of Liberty. I told them of the ten officers that Mr. Devens met, and that it was probable we might be stopped before we got to Concord; for I supposed that after night they divided themselves, and that two of them had fixed themselves in such passages as were most likely to stop any intelligence going to Concord. I likewise mentioned that we had better alarm all the inhabitants till we got to Concord. The young doctor much approved of it and said he would stop with either of us, for the people between that and Concord knew him and would give the more credit to what we said.

We had got nearly half way. Mr. Daws and the doctor stopped to alarm the people of a house. I was about one hundred rods ahead when I saw two men in nearly the same situation as those officers were near Charlestown. I called for the doctor and Mr. Daws to come up. In an instant I was surrounded by four. They had placed themselves in a straight road that inclined each way; they had taken down a pair of bars on the north side of the road, and two of them were under a tree in the pasture. The doctor being foremost, he came up and we tried to get past them; but they being armed with pistols and swords, they forced us into the pasture. The doctor jumped his horse over a low stone wall and got to Concord.

I observed a wood at a small distance and made for that. When I got there, out started six officers on horseback and ordered me to dis-

mount. One of them, who appeared to have the command, examined me, where I came from and what my name was. I told him. He asked me if I was an express. I answered in the affirmative. He demanded what time I left Boston. I told him, and added that their troops had catched aground in passing the river, and that there would be five hundred Americans there in a short time, for I had alarmed the country all the way up. He immediately rode towards those who stopped us, when all five of them came down upon a full gallop. One of them, whom I afterwards found to be a Major Mitchel, of the 5th Regiment, clapped his pistol to my head, called me by name and told me he was going to ask me some questions, and if I did not give him true answers, he would blow my brains out. He then asked me similar questions to those above. He then ordered me to mount my horse, after searching me for arms. He then ordered them to advance and to lead me in front. When we got to the road, they turned down towards Lexington. When we had got about one mile, the major rode up to the officer that was leading me, and told him to give me to the sergeant. As soon as he took me, the major ordered him, if I attempted to run, or anybody insulted them, to blow my brains out.

We rode till we got near Lexington meeting-house, when the militia fired a volley of guns, which appeared to alarm them very much. The major inquired of me how far it was to Cambridge, and if there were any other road. After some consultation, the major rode up to the sergeant and asked if his horse was tired. He answered him he was—he was a sergeant of grenadiers and had a small horse. "Then," said he, "take that man's horse." I dismounted, and the sergeant mounted my horse, when they all rode towards Lexington meeting-house.

I went across the burying ground and some pastures and came to the Rev. Mr. Clark's house, where I found Messrs. Hancock and Adams. I told them of my treatment, and they concluded to go from that house towards Woburn. I went with them and a Mr. Lowell, who was a clerk to Mr. Hancock.

When we got to the house where they intended to stop, Mr. Lowell and myself returned to Mr. Clark's, to find what was going on. When we got there, an elderly man came in; he said he had just come from the tavern, that a man had come from Boston who said there were no British troops coming. Mr. Lowell and myself went towards the tavern, when we met a man on a full gallop, who told us the troops were coming up the rocks. We afterwards met another, who said they were close by. Mr. Lowell asked me to go to the tavern with him, to get a trunk of papers belonging to Mr. Hancock. We went up chamber, and while we were getting the trunk, we saw the British very near, upon a full march. We hurried towards Mr. Clark's house. In our way we passed through the militia. There were about fifty. When we had got about one hundred yards from the meeting-house, the British troops appeared on both sides of the meeting-house. In their front was an officer on horseback. They made a short halt; *when I saw, and heard, a gun fired,* which appeared to be a pistol. Then I could distinguish two guns, and then a continual roar of musketry; when we made off with the trunk.

Source: Revere, Paul. "Letter of Paul Revere to Dr. Belknap." Edited by Charles Deane. *Proceedings of the Massachusetts Historical Society* 16 (1879): 370–376.

THE BATTLE OF LEXINGTON, APRIL 19, 1775

Letter to William Barrell
John Adams
April 19, 1775

John Adams (1735–1826), one of the leading architects of the American Revolution, was a prolific letter writer and a keen observer of his times, especially the unfolding of the rebellion. He sent the following account of the first battle of the revolution to the prominent Philadelphia merchant William Barrell, who had many business contacts and personal friends in Boston.

April 19 [1775]

Yesterday produced a scene the most shocking New England ever beheld. Last Saturday P.M. orders were sent to the several regiments quartered here not to let their Grenadiers or Light Infantry do any duty till further orders, upon which the inhabitants conjectured that some secret expedition was on foot, and being on the look out, they observed those bodies upon the move between ten and eleven o'clock the evening before last, observing a perfect silence in their march towards a point opposite Phip's farm, where [boats?] were in waiting that conveyed 'em over.

The men appointed to alarm the country upon such occasions got over by stealth as early as they [could] and took their different routs. The first advice we had was about eight o'clock in the morning, when it was reported that the troops had fired upon and killed five men in Lexington—previous to which an officer came express to his Excellency Governor Gage, when between eight and nine o'clock a brigade marched out under the command of Earl Piercy, consisting of the Marines, the Welch Fusileers, the 4th Regiment, the 47th, and two field pieces.

About twelve o'clock it was gave out by the general's aide camps that no person was killed, and that a single gun had not been fired, which report was variously believed—but between one and two, certain accounts came that eight were killed outright and fourteen wounded of the inhabitants of Lexington—who had about forty men drawn out early in the morning near the meeting house to exercise. The party of the Light Infantry and Grenadiers, to the number of about eight hundred, came up to them and ordered them to disperse. The commander of 'em replied that they were only innocently amusing themselves with exercise, that they had not any ammunition with 'em, and therefore should not molest or disturb them. Which answer not satisfying, the troops fired upon and killed three or four, the others took to their heels and the troops continued to fire. A few took refuge in the meeting, when the soldiers shoved up the windows and pointed their guns in and killed three there. Thus much is best account I can learn of the beginning of this fatal day.

You must naturally suppose that such a piece would rouse the country (allowed the report to be true). The troops continued their march to Concord, entered the town, and refreshed themselves in the meeting and town house. In the latter place they found some ammunition and stores belonging to the country, which they found they could not bring away by reason that the country people had occupied all the posts around 'em. They therefore set fire to the house, which the people extinguished. They set fire a second time, which brought on a general engagement at about eleven o'clock. The troops took two pieces [of] cannon from the peasants, but their numbers increasing they soon regained 'em, and the troops were obliged to retreat towards town.

About noon they were joined by the other brigade under Earl Piercy [Percy], when another very warm engagement came on at Lexington, which the troops could not stand; therefore were obliged to continue their retreat, which they did with the bravery becoming British soldiers—but the country were in a manner desperate, not regarding their cannon (any more) in the least, and followed 'em till seven in the evening, by which time they got into Charlestown, when they left off the pursuit, least they might injure the inhabitants.

I stood upon the hills in town and saw the engagement very plain. It was very bloody for seven hours. It's conjectured that one half the soldiers at least were killed. The last brigade was sent over the ferry in the evening to secure their retreat—where they are this morning entrenching themselves upon Bunker's Hill [to] get a safe retreat to this town. It's impossible to learn any particulars, as the communication between town and country is at present broken off. They were till ten o'clock last night bringing over their wounded, several of which are since [dead], two officers in particular.

When I reflect and consider that the fight was between those whose parents but a few generations ago were brothers, I shudder at the thought, and there's no knowing where our calamities will end.

Source: "'A Scene the Most Shocking New England Ever Beheld': John Adams." In *The Spirit of Seventy Six: The Story of the American Revolution as Told by Participants,* edited by Henry Steele Commager and Richard B. Morris, 75–76. New York: Da Capo Press, 1995.

Sermon
Reverend Jonas Clarke [also spelled Clark]
April 19, 1776

The Reverend Jonas Clarke (1730–1805), pastor of the Congregationalist church at Lexington, delivered this account as part of his sermon of April 19, 1776, the first anniversary of the Battle of Lexington. Clarke had firsthand reports of the battle. At the time, he was harboring both John Hancock and Samuel Adams at his Lexington parsonage, and he compiled his sermon from them as well as from his neighbors' accounts of what they experienced.

Between the hours of twelve and one, on the morning of the nineteenth of April, we received intelligence, by express, from the Honorable Joseph Warren, Esq., at Boston, "that a large body of the king's troops (supposed to be a brigade of about 12 or 1500) were embarked in boats from Boston, and gone over to land on Lechmere's Point (so called) in Cambridge; and that it was shrewdly suspected that they were ordered to seize and destroy the stores belonging to the colony, then deposited at Concord." , , ,

Upon this intelligence, as also upon information of the conduct of the officers as above-mentioned, the militia of this town were alarmed and ordered to meet on the usual place of parade; not with any design of commencing hostilities upon the king's troops, but to consult what might be done for our own and the people's safety; and also to be ready for whatever service providence might call us out to, upon this alarming occasion, in case overt acts of violence or open hostilities should be committed by this mercenary band of armed and blood-thirsty oppressors. . . .

The militia met according to order and waited the return of the messengers, that they might order their measures as occasion should require. Between 3 and 4 o'clock, one of the expresses returned, informing that there was no appearance of the troops on the roads either from Cambridge or Charlestown; and that it was supposed that the movements in the army the evening before were only a feint to alarm the people. Upon this, therefore, the militia company were dismissed for the present, but with orders to be within call of the drum—waiting the return of the other messenger, who was expected in about an hour, or sooner, if any discovery should be made of the motions of the troops. But he was prevented by their silent and sudden arrival at the place where he was waiting for intelligence. So that, after all this precaution, we had no notice of their approach till the brigade was actually in the town and upon a quick march within about a mile and a quarter of the meeting house and place of parade.

However, the commanding officer thought best to call the company together, not with any design of opposing so superior a force, much less of commencing hostilities, but only with a view to determine what to do, when and where to meet, and to dismiss and disperse.

Accordingly, about half an hour after four o'clock, alarm guns were fired, and the drums beat to arms, and the militia were collecting together. Some, to the number of about 50 or 60, or possibly more, were on the parade, others were coming towards it. In the mean time, the troops having thus stolen a march upon us and, to prevent any intelligence of their approach, having seized and held prisoners several persons whom they met unarmed upon the road, seemed to come determined for murder and bloodshed—and that whether provoked to it or not! When within about half a quarter of a mile

of the meeting-house, they halted, and the command was given to prime and load; which being done, they marched on till they came up to the east end of said meeting-house, in sight of our militia (collecting as aforesaid) who were about 12 or 13 rods distant.

Immediately upon their appearing so suddenly and so nigh, Capt. Parker, who commanded the militia company, ordered the men to disperse and take care of themselves, and not to fire. Upon this, our men dispersed—but many of them not so speedily as they might have done, not having the most distant idea of such brutal barbarity and more than savage cruelty from the troops of a British king, as they immediately experienced! For, no sooner did they come in sight of our company, but one of them, supposed to be an officer of rank, was heard to say to the troops, "Damn them! We will have them!" Upon which the troops shouted aloud, huzza'd, and rushed furiously towards our men.

About the same time, three officers (supposed to be Col. Smith, Major Pitcairn and another officer) advanced on horse back to the front of the body, and coming within 5 or 6 rods of the militia, one of them cried out, "Ye villains, ye Rebels, disperse! Damn you, disperse!"—or words to this effect. One of them (whether the same or not is not easily determined) said, "Lay down your arms! Damn you, why don't you lay down your arms?" The second of these officers, about this time, fired a pistol towards the militia as they were dispersing. The foremost, who was within a few yards of our men, brandishing his sword and then pointing towards them, with a loud voice said to the troops, "Fire! By God, fire!"—which was instantly followed by a discharge of arms from the said troops, succeeded by a very heavy and close fire upon our party, dispersing, so long as any of them were within reach. Eight were left dead upon the ground! Ten were wounded. The rest of the company, through divine goodness, were (to a miracle) preserved unhurt in this murderous action! . . .

One circumstance more before the brigade quitted Lexington, I beg leave to mention, as what may give a further specimen of the spirit and character of the officers and men of this body of troops. After the militia company were dispersed and the firing ceased, the troops drew up and formed in a body on the common, fired a volley and gave three huzzas, by way of triumph and as expressive of the joy of victory and glory of conquest! Of this transaction, I was a witness, having, at that time, a fair view of their motions and being at the distance of not more than 70 or 80 rods from them.

Source: Clark, Jonas. The Battle of Lexington: A Sermon and Eyewitness Narrative. 1776. Reprint, Ventura, Calif.: Nordskog, 2007.

Account of the Battle
Sylvanus Wood
June 17, 1826

Sylvanus Wood (1748–1840) was a member of the Lexington militia, a minuteman who answered the summons to arms on the morning of April 29, 1775. He was 23 at the time. Years later, on June 17, 1826, he recounted his experience of the battle to a local justice of the peace. The account remained in manuscript until it was published in 1858.

I, Sylvanus Wood, of Woburn, in the county of Middlesex, and commonwealth of Massachusetts, aged seventy-four years, do testify and say that on the morning of the 29th of April, 1775, I was an inhabitant of Woburn, living with Deacon Obadiah Kendall; that about an hour before the break of day on said morning, I heard the Lexington bell ring, and fearing there was difficulty there, I immediately arose, took my gun and, with Robert Douglass, went in haste to Lexington, which was about three miles distant. When I arrived there, I inquired of Captain Parker, the commander of the Lexington company, what was the news. Parker told me he did not know what to believe, for a man had come up about half an hour before and informed him that the British troops were not on the road. But while we were talking, a messenger came up and told the captain that the British troops were within half a mile. Parker immediately turned to his drummer, William Diman, and ordered him to beat to arms, which was done. Captain Parker then asked me if I would parade with his company. I told him I would. Parker then asked me if the young man with me would parade. I spoke to Douglass, and he said he would follow the captain and me.

By this time many of the company had gathered around the captain at the hearing of the drum, where we stood, which was about half way between the meeting-house and Buckman's tavern. Parker says to his men, "Every man of you, who is equipped, follow me; and those of you who are not equipped, go into the meeting-house and furnish yourselves from the magazine, and immediately join the company." Parker led those of us who were equipped to the north end of Lexington Common, near the Bedford Road, and formed us in single file. I was stationed about in the centre of the company. While we were standing, I left my place and went from one end of the company to the other and counted every man who was paraded, and the whole number was thirty-eight, and no more.

Just as I had finished and got back to my place, I perceived the British troops had arrived on the spot between the meeting-house and Buckman's, near where Captain Parker stood when he first led off his men. The British troops immediately wheeled so as to cut off those who had gone into the meeting-house. The British troops approached us rapidly in platoons, with a general officer on horseback at their head. The officer came up to within about two rods of the centre of the company, where I stood, the first platoon being about three rods distant. They there halted. The officer then swung his sword, and said, "Lay down your arms, you damned rebels, or you are all dead men. Fire!" Some guns were fired by the British at us from the first platoon, but no person was killed or hurt, being probably charged only with powder.

Just at this time, Captain Parker ordered every man to take care of himself. The company immediately dispersed; and while the

A fanciful early 20th-century book illustration of the Battle of Lexington—the first battle of the American Revolution *(National Archives)*

company was dispersing and leaping over the wall, the second platoon of the British fired and killed some of our men. There was not a gun fired by any of Captain Parker's company, within my knowledge. I was so situated that I must have known it, had any thing of the kind taken place before a total dispersion of our company. I have been intimately acquainted with the inhabitants of Lexington, and particularly with those of Captain Parker's company, and, with one exception, I have never heard any of them say or pretend that there was any firing at the British from Parker's company, or any individual in it, until within a year or two. One member of the company told me, many years since, that, after Parker's company had dispersed, and he was at some distance, he gave them "the guts of his gun." . . .

Source: Wood, Sylvanus. "Eyewitness Accounts: Sylvanus Wood. June 17, 1826, Testimony." *Revolutionary Viewpoints.* Available online. URL: http://www.cyber-bee.com/viewpoints/wood.html. Accessed on February 8, 2010.

THE BATTLE OF CONCORD, APRIL 19, 1775

Diary Entry
Reverend William Emerson of Concord
April 19, 1775

The Reverend William Emerson (1769–1811) of Concord—grandfather of Ralph Waldo Emerson, the 19th-century American essayist, philosopher, and poet—left this account of the Battle of Concord in his diary on the day of the battle.

This morning, between 1 and 2 o'clock, we were alarmed by the ringing of the bell, and upon examination found that the troops, to the number of 800, had stole their march from Boston, in boats and barges, from the bottom of the Common over to a point in Cambridge, near to Inman's farm, and were at Lexington Meeting-house, half an hour before sunrise, where they had fired upon a body of our men, and (as we afterward heard) had killed several.

This intelligence was brought us at first by Dr. Samuel Prescott, who narrowly escaped the guard that were sent before on horses, purposely to prevent all posts and messengers from giving us timely information. He, by the help of a very fleet horse, crossing several walls and fences, arrived at Concord at the time above mentioned; when several posts were immediately despatched, that returning confirmed the account of the [British] regulars' arrival at Lexington, and that they were on their way to Concord.

Upon this, a number of our minute men belonging to this town, and Acton and Lyncoln, with several others that were in readiness, marched out to meet them, while the alarm company were preparing to receive them in the town. Capt. Minot, who commanded them, thought it proper to take possession of the hill above the meeting-house, as the most advantageous situation. No sooner had our men gained it than we were met by the companies that were sent out to meet the troops, who informed us that they were just upon us, and that we must retreat, as their number was more than treble ours.

We then retreated from the hill near the Liberty Pole and took a new post back of the town upon an eminence, where we formed into two battalions and waited the arrival of the enemy. Scarcely had we formed before we saw the British troops at the distance of a quarter of a mile, glittering in arms, advancing towards us with the greatest celerity. Some were for making a stand, notwithstanding the superiority of their number; but others more prudent thought best to retreat till our strength should be equal to the enemy's by recruits from neighboring towns that were continually coming to our assistance.

Accordingly we retreated over the bridge, when the troops came into the town, set fire to several carriages for the artillery, destroyed 60 barrels flour, rifled several houses, took possession of the town-house, destroyed 500 lb. of balls, set a guard of 100 men at the North Bridge, and sent up a party to the house of Col. Barrett, where they were in expectation of finding a quantity of warlike stores. But these were happily secured just before their arrival, by transportation into the woods and other by-places.

In the meantime, the guard set by the enemy to secure the pass at the North Bridge were alarmed by the approach of our people, who had retreated, as mentioned before, and were now advancing with special orders not to fire upon the troops unless fired upon. These orders were so punctually observed that we received the fire of the enemy in three several and separate discharges of their pieces before it was returned by our commanding officer; the firing then soon became general for several minutes, in which skirmish two were killed on each side, and several of the enemy wounded.

It may here be observed, by the way, that we were the more cautious to prevent beginning a rupture with the King's troops, as we were then uncertain what had happened at Lexington, and knew [not] that they had begun the quarrel there by first firing upon our people and killing eight men upon the spot.

The three companies of troops soon quitted their post at the bridge and retreated in the greatest disorder and confusion to the main body, who were soon upon the march to meet them. For half an hour, the enemy, by their marches and countermarches, discovered great fickleness and inconstancy of mind, sometimes advancing, sometimes returning to their former posts; till at length they quitted the town and retreated by the way they came. In the meantime, a party of our men (150) took the back way through the Great Fields into the east quarter and had placed themselves to advantage, lying in ambush behind walls, fences and buildings, ready to fire upon the enemy on their retreat.

Source: Emerson, William. "Diary." In *Miscellanies,* by Ralph Waldo Emerson. Boston: Houghton Mifflin, 1888, pp. 91–93.

Diary Entry
Lieutenant Frederick Mackenzie
April 19, 1775

Frederick Mackenzie, the son of a Dublin merchant and his Huguenot wife, was commissioned in the 23rd Regiment, the Royal Welsh Fusiliers, in 1743. He was promoted to captain shortly after the Battles of Lexington and Concord and went on to become a major in 1780 and, in 1787, lieutenant colonel of his new regiment, the 37th Foot. Mackenzie began keeping a diary in 1748 and maintained it through 1791. Eight volumes survive, and they include accounts of some major battles of the American Revolution, which provide a rare British perspective on the events. The diary entry that follows is dated the day of the battles that began the Revolutionary War.

19 April. At 7 o'clock this morning a brigade order was received by our regiment, dated at 6 o'clock, for the 1st Brigade to assemble at 1/2 past 7 on the grand parade. We accordingly assembled the regiment with the utmost expedition, and with the 4th and 47th were on the parade at the hour appointed, with one days provisions. By some mistake the Marines did not receive the order until the other regiments of the brigade were assembled, by which means it was half past 8 o'clock before the brigade was ready to march. Here we understood that we were to march out of town to support the troops that went out last night.

A quarter before 9, we marched in the following order: advanced guard of a captain and 50 men; 2 six-pounders, 4th Regiment, 47th Regi-

ment, 1st Battalion of Marines, 23rd Regiment or Royal Welch Fusiliers; rear guard of a captain and 50 men; the whole under the command of Brigadier General Earl Percy. We went out of Boston by the Neck and marched thro' Roxbury, Cambridge and Menotomy, towards Lexington. In all the places we marched through, and in the houses on the road, few or no people were to be seen; and the houses were in general shut up.

When we arrived near Lexington, some persons who came from Concord informed that the Grenadiers and Light Infantry were at that place, and that some persons had been killed and wounded by them early in the morning at Lexington. As we pursued our march, about 2 o'clock we heard some straggling shots fired about a mile in our front. As we advanced we heard the firing plainer and more frequent, and at half after 2, being near the church at Lexington, and the fire encreasing, we were ordered to form the line, which was immediately done by extending on each side of the road, but by reason of the stone walls and other obstructions it was not formed in so regular a manner as it should have been. The Grenadiers and Light Infantry were at this time retiring towards Lexington, fired upon by the Rebels, who took every advantage the face of the country afforded them. As soon as the Grenadiers and Light Infantry perceived the 1st Brigade drawn up for their support, they shouted repeatedly, and the firing ceased for a short time.

The ground we first formed upon was something elevated and commanded a view of that before us for about a mile, where it was terminated by some pretty high grounds covered with wood. The village of Lexington lay between both parties. We could observe a considerable number of the Rebels, but they were much scattered, and not above 50 of them to be seen in a body in any place. Many lay concealed behind the stone walls and fences. They appeared most numerous in the road near the church, and in a wood in the front, and on the left flank of the line where our regiment was posted. A few cannon shot were fired at those on and near the road, which dispersed them.

The flank companies now retired and formed behind the brigade, which was soon fired upon by the Rebels most advanced. A brisk fire was returned, but without much effect. As there was a piece of open morassy ground in front of the left of our regiment, it would have been difficult to have passed it under the fire of the Rebels from behind the trees and walls on the other side. Indeed no part of the brigade was ordered to advance; we therefore drew up near the morass, in expectation of orders how to act, sending an officer for one of the 6-pounders. During this time the Rebels endeavored to gain our flanks, and crept into the covered ground on either side and as close as they could in front, firing now and then in perfect security. We also advanced a few of our best marksmen who fired at those who shewed themselves.

About 1/4 past 3, Earl Percy having come to a resolution of returning to Boston, and having made his disposition for that purpose, our regiment received orders to form the rear guard. We immediately lined the walls and other cover in our front with some marksmen, and retired from the right of companies by files to the high ground a small distance in our rear, where we again formed in line, and remained in that position for near half an hour, during which time the flank companies and the other regiments of the brigade began their march in one column on the road towards Cambridge.

As the country for many miles round Boston and in the neighbourhood of Lexington and Concord had by this time had notice of what was doing, as well by the firing as from expresses which had been [sent] from Boston and the adjacent places in all directions, numbers of armed men on foot and on horseback were continually coming from all parts guided by the fire, and before the column had advanced a mile on the road, we were fired at from all quarters, but particularly from the houses on the roadside, and the adjacent stone walls. Several of the troops were killed and wounded in this way, and the soldiers were so enraged at suffering from an unseen enemy that they forced open many of the houses from which the fire proceeded, and put to death all those found in them. Those houses would certainly have been burnt had any fire been found in them, or had there been time to kindle any; but only three or four near where we first formed suffered in this way.

As the troops drew nearer to Cambridge the number and fire of the Rebels increased, and altho they did not shew themselves openly in a body in any part, except on the road in our rear, our men threw away their fire very inconsiderately and without being certain of its effect; this emboldened them and induced them to draw nearer, but whenever a cannon shot was fired at any considerable number, they instantly dispersed. Our regiment, having formed the rear guard for near 7 miles and expended a great part of its ammunition, was then relieved by the Marines which was the next battalion in the column. . . .

During the whole of the march from Lexington the Rebels kept an incessant irregular fire from all points at the column, which was the more galling as our flanking parties, which at first were placed at sufficient distances to cover the march of it, were at last, from the different obstructions they occasionally met with, obliged to keep almost close to it. Our men had very few opportunities of getting good shots at the Rebels, as they hardly ever fired but under cover of a stone wall, from behind a tree, or out of a house; and the moment they had fired they lay down out of sight until they had loaded again or the column had passed. In the road indeed in our rear, they were most numerous and came on pretty close, frequently calling out, "King Hancock forever!"

Many of them were killed in the houses on the road side from whence they fired; in some of them 7 or 8 men were destroyed. Some houses were forced open in which no person could be discovered, but when the column had passed, numbers sallied out from some place in which they had lain concealed, fired at the rear guard, and augmented the number which followed us. If we had had time to set fire to those houses many Rebels must have perished in them, but as night drew on Lord Percy thought it best to continue the march. Many houses were plundered by the soldiers, notwithstanding the efforts of the officers to prevent it. I have no doubt this inflamed the Rebels, and made many of them follow us farther than they would otherwise have done. By all accounts some soldiers who staid too long in the houses were killed in the very act of plundering by those who lay concealed in them. We brought in about ten prisoners, some of whom were taken in arms. One or two more were killed on the march, while prisoners, by the fire of their own people.

Few or no women or children were to be seen throughout the day. As the country had undoubted intelligence that some troops were to march out, and the Rebels were probably determined to attack them, it is generally supposed they had previously removed their families from the neighbourhood. . . .

Source: Mackenzie, Frederick. *Diary of Frederick Mackenzie, Giving a Daily Narrative of His Military Service as an Officer of the Regiment of Royal Welsh Fusiliers during the Years 1775–1781.* Cambridge, Mass.: Harvard University Press, 1930.

Letter to General Gage
General Lord Percy
April 20, 1775

Hugh Percy, later second duke of Northumberland (1742–1817), commanded the British 5th Regiment of Foot in Boston as its brigadier general. In the letter that follows, he wrote to his commanding officer, General Thomas Gage, about his leadership of the relief column in the Battles of Lexington and Concord and the grueling withdrawal from Concord. Percy was a skilled commander who kept the demoralized redcoats together and probably saved them from incurring even heavier casualties than they did.

20 April, 1775
Sir—In obedience to your Excellency's orders I marched yesterday morning at 9 o'clock, with the

First Brigade and 2 field-pieces, in order to cover the retreat of the Grenadiers and Light Infantry, on their return from the expedition to Concord.

As all the houses were shut up and there was not the appearance of a single inhabitant, I could get no intelligence concerning them till I had passed Menotomy, when I was informed that the Rebels had attacked His Majesty's troops, who were retiring, overpowered by numbers, greatly exhausted and fatigued, and having expended almost all their ammunition. And about 2 o'clock I met them retiring through the town of Lexington.

I immediately ordered the 2 fieldpieces to fire at the Rebels, and drew up the brigade on a height. The shot from the cannon had the desired effect and stopped the Rebels for a little time, who immediately dispersed and endeavoured to surround us, being very numerous. As it began now to grow pretty late, and we had 15 miles

Engraving of Thomas Gage, commander in chief of British forces in America and military governor of Massachusetts at the outbreak of the Revolution *(National Archives)*

to retire, and only our 36 rounds, I ordered the Grenadiers and Light Infantry to move off first, and covered them with my brigade, sending out very strong flanking parties, which were absolutely necessary, as there was not a stone-wall or house, though before in appearance evacuated, from whence the Rebels did not fire upon us.

As soon as they saw us begin to retire, they pressed very much upon our rear-guard, which for that reason I relieved every now and then. In this manner we retired for 15 miles under an incessant fire all round us, till we arrived at Charlestown between 7 and 8 in the even, very much fatigued with a march of above 30 miles, and having expended almost all our ammunition.

We had the misfortune of losing a good many men in the retreat, tho' nothing like the number which, from many circumstances, I have reason to believe were killed of the Rebels.

His Majesty's troops during the whole of the affair behaved with their usual intrepidity and spirit. Nor were they a little exasperated at the cruelty and barbarity of the Rebels who scalped and cut off the ears of some of the wounded men who fell into their hands.

Source: Percy, Hugh. "To Governor Gage, April 20, 1775." In *Letters of Hugh Earl Percy, from Boston and New York, 1774–1776,* edited by Charles Knowles Bolton, 1902. Reprint, Boston: Gregg Press, 1972, pp. 49–51.

THE CAPTURE OF FORT TICONDEROGA, MAY 10, 1775

Account of the Fort's Capture
Ethan Allen
Published 1779

The popular Vermont guerrilla leader Ethan Allen (1738–89) was tapped by Connecticut militia leaders to assist in the capture of Fort Ticonderoga, New York, which was lightly held by a British garrison. On May 2, 1775, 60 militiamen from Massachusetts and Connecticut rendezvoused with Allen in Bennington, and on May 7, this contingent linked up with 130 of Allen's famed Green Mountain Boys, intending to raid the fort on May 10. On the 9th, however, Benedict Arnold arrived, bearing a commission from the Massachusetts Committee of Safety and disputing Allen's command of the raiding force. When Allen's men refused to fight under Arnold, however, the two divided the command.

The attack on the fort was made in the early dawn of May 10. After surprising the single sentry guarding the place, Allen approached the commandant's quarters, where he was met by Lieutenant Jocelyn Feltham, aide to Captain William Delaplace. To the lieutenant's imperious demand to know by what authority he had entered the fort, Allen declared that he had come "In the name of the great Jehovah and the Continental Congress!" (Allen falsely claimed that he spoke these words directly to Captain Delaplace.) The fort surrendered without resistance. The following excerpt is from Allen's A Narrative of Colonel Ethan Allen's Captivity, *first published in 1779.*

Ever since I arrived to a state of manhood and acquainted myself with the general history of mankind, I have felt a sincere passion for liberty. The history of nations doomed to perpetual slavery, in consequence of yielding up to tyrants their natural born liberties, I read with a sort of philosophical horror; so that the first systematical and bloody attempt at Lexington to enslave America thoroughly electrified my mind and fully determined me to take part with my country.

And while I was wishing for an opportunity to signalize myself in its behalf, directions were privately sent to me from the then colony (now state) of Connecticut to raise the Green Mountain Boys, and (if possible) with them to surprise and take the fortress Ticonderoga. This enterprise I cheerfully undertook; and, after first guarding all the several passes that led thither, to cut off all intelligence between the garrison and the country, made a forced march from

Bennington and arrived at the lake opposite to Ticonderoga on the evening of the ninth day of May, 1775, with two hundred and thirty valiant Green Mountain Boys; and it was with the utmost difficulty that I procured boats to cross the lake. However, I landed eighty-three men near the garrison, and sent the boats back for the rear guard commanded by Col. Seth Warner. But the day began to dawn, and I found myself under a necessity to attack the fort before the rear could cross the lake; and, as it was viewed hazardous, I harangued the officers and soldiers in the manner following:

"Friends and fellow soldiers, you have, for a number of years past, been scourge and terror to arbitrary power. Your valour has been famed abroad and acknowledged, as appears by the advice and orders to me (from the general assembly of Connecticut) to surprise and take the garrison now before us. I now propose to advance before you and in person conduct you through the wicket-gate; for we must this morning either quit our pretensions to valour, or possess ourselves of this fortress in a few minutes; and, in as much as it is a desperate attempt (which none but the bravest of men dare undertake), I do not urge it on any contrary to his will. You that will undertake voluntarily, poise your firelocks!"

The men being (at this time) drawn up in three ranks, each poised his firelock. I ordered them to face to the right, and, at the head of the centre-file, marched them immediately to the wicket gate aforesaid, where I found a centry

Ethan Allen captures Fort Ticonderoga, May 10, 1775. Copy of engraving after Alonzo Cappel *(National Archives)*

posted, who instantly snapped his fusees at me. I ran immediately toward him, and he retreated through the covered way into the parade within the garrison, gave a halloo and ran under a bomb-proof. My party who followed me into the fort, I formed on the parade in such a manner as to face the two barracks which faced each other. The garrison being asleep (except the centries), we gave three huzzas which greatly surprised them. One of the centries made a pass at one of my officers with a charged bayonet and slightly wounded him. My first thought was to kill him with my sword; but, in an instant, altered the design and fury of the blow to a slight cut on the side of the head; upon which he dropped his gun and asked quarter, which I readily granted him, and demanded of him the place where the commanding officer kept. He shewed me a pair of stairs in the front of a barrack, on the west part of the garrison, which led up to a second story in said barrack, to which I immediately repaired, and ordered the commander (Capt. Delaplace) to come forth instantly, or I would sacrifice the whole garrison; at which the captain came immediately to the door with his breeches in his hand, when I ordered him to deliver to me the fort instantly, who asked me by what authority I demanded it; I answered, "In the name of the great Jehovah and the Continental Congress."

The authority of the Congress being very little known at that time, he began to speak again; but I interrupted him and, with my drawn sword over his head, again demanded an immediate surrender of the garrison; to which he then complied, and ordered his men to be forthwith paraded without arms, as he had given up the garrison. In the mean time some of my officers had given orders, and in consequence thereof, sundry of the barrack doors were beat down, and about one third of the garrison imprisoned, which consisted of the said-commander, a Lieut. Feltham, a conductor of artillery, a gunner, two serjeants and forty-four rank and file; about one hundred pieces of cannon, one 13-inch mortar and a number of swivels.

This surprise was carried into execution in the gray of the morning of the 10th day of May, 1775. The sun seemed to rise that morning with a superior lustre; and Ticonderoga and its dependencies smiled on its conquerors, who tossed about the flowing bowl and wished success to Congress and the liberty and freedom of America. . . . Col. Warner with the rear guard crossed the lake and joined me early in the morning, whom I sent off without loss of time, with about one hundred men, to take possession of Crown Point, which was garrisoned with a serjeant and twelve men; which he took possession of the same day, as also upwards of one hundred pieces of cannon.

But one thing now remained to be done to make ourselves complete masters of Lake Champlain: This was to possess ourselves of a sloop of war, which was then laying at St. John's; to effect which, it was agreed in a council of war to arm and man out a certain schooner, which lay at South Bay, and that Capt. (now General) Arnold should command her, and that I should command the batteaux. The necessary preparations being made, we set sail from Ticonderoga in quest of the sloop, which was much larger and carried more guns and heavier metal than the schooner.

General Arnold, with the schooner sailing faster than the batteaux, arrived at St. John's and by surprise possessed himself of the sloop before I could arrive with the batteaux. He also made prisoners of a serjeant and twelve men, who were garrisoned at that place. It is worthy [of] remark that as soon as General Arnold had secured the prisoners on board and had made preparation for sailing, the wind which but a few hours before was fresh in the south and well served to carry us to St. John's, now shifted and came fresh from the north; and in about one hour's time General Arnold sailed with the prize and schooner for Ticonderoga. When I met him with my party, within a few miles of St. John's, he saluted me with a discharge of cannon, which I returned with a volley of small arms. This being repeated three times, I went on board the sloop with my party, where several loyal Congress healths were drank.

We were now masters of Lake Champlain and the garrisons depending thereon.

Source: Allen, Ethan. *A Narrative of Colonel Ethan Allen's Captivity, Written by Himself.* 3d ed. Burlington, Vt.: H. Johnson & Co., 1838.

THE SIEGE OF BOSTON, APRIL 19, 1775– MARCH 17, 1776

Letter to His Brother
Peter Oliver
June 1, 1775

Peter Oliver was the son of the chief justice of Massachusetts, a Crown official much despised by the Patriots. On June 1, 1775, Oliver, who was naturally a Loyalist, wrote to his brother (in Bath, England) to describe the "rebel" siege of Boston, which had begun on April 19, 1775, and would endure until long after Oliver's letter, ending on March 17, 1776, with the withdrawal of the British troops from the city.

Boston, June 1st, 1775
Dear Brother,
We learn by the *Cerberus* man-of-war, which arrived last Thursday the 25th of May, that you have done with the thoughts of coming to Boston at present, which rejoices your friends.

I received yours dated at Bath, and am much obliged to you.

Our situation here, without any exaggeration, is beyond description almost; it is such as eye has not seen nor ear heard, nor hath it ever entered into the heart of man to conceive Boston ever to arrive at.

We are besieged this moment with 10 or 15000 men, from Roxbury to Cambridge; their rebell sentrys within call of the troops' sentrys on the Neck. We are every hour expecting an attack by land or water. All marketing from the country stopt ever since the battle. Fire and slaughter hourly threatened, and not out of danger from some of the inhabitants within, of setting the town of [on] fire. All the interest the Judge and I ound [owned] in Middleborough exposed to the ravage of a set of robbers, Mr. Conant at the head of them. Poor Jenny and Phoebe, and children, we can't hear of, or get any word to; whether they are all living or not, or whether the works and buildings are left standing is rather a doubt with me, for we have heard since the battle that a number set out to destroy and burn our interest, but that the selectmen interposed and saved them.

You seem in England to be entirely ignorant of the temper of our people. They are as much determined from Florida to Hallifax to oppose you at home, do what you will, as I hear the Ministry are determined to pursue their plan. I am in no doubt but you will be able to conquer America at last, but a horrid bloody scene will be opened here as never was in New England before. What comfort or satisfaction do you think we take now, or can take, when the dreadful scene opens?

Your wife is in Plymouth, yet we can't get any intelligence of her, good or bad. It is said by the rebels at Roxbury that Col. Watson has given his quota to support the people.

Good God! Do thou avert the impending calamity that threatens this former happy land, and turn the hearts of those deluded wretches from the power of sin and Satan to thy unerring precepts, and then, and then only, shall we be once more a happy people favoured of Heaven. . . .

O tempora! O mores! Yrs as usual,
PETER OLIVER, JUNR.

Source: Oliver, Peter. "Peter Oliver to His Brother." Available online. URL: http://www.historycarper.com/resources/articles/poliver.htm. Accessed on February 8, 2010.

THE BATTLE OF BUNKER [BREED'S] HILL, JUNE 17, 1775

Diary Entries
Corporal Amos Farnsworth
June 16–17, 1775

Amos Farnsworth, the eldest son of Amos Farnsworth and Lydia (Longley) Farnsworth, was born in Groton, Connecticut, on April 28, 1754. After the Battles of Lexington and Concord (April 19, 1775), he joined a company of minutemen led by Captain Henry Farnwell and marched to Cambridge. As a corporal, he fought at the Battle of Bunker Hill in Charlestown. He recorded the account that follows in diary entries dated June 16 and June 17.

Friday June 16. Nothing done in the forenoon; in the afternoon we had orders to be redy to march. At six agreable to orders our regiment preadid [paraded] and about sun-set we was drawn up and herd prayers; and about dusk marched for Bunkers Hill under command of our own Col Prescott. Just before we turned out of the rode to go up Bunkers-Hill, Charlestown, we was halted; and about sixty men was taken out of our batallion to go into Charlestown, I being one of them. Capt Nutten heded us down to the town house; we sot our centres by the waterside; the most of us got in the town house but had orders not to shut our eyes. Our men marched to Bunker-Hill and begun thair intrenchment and careed it on with the utmost viger all night. Early in the morning I joined them.

Saturday June 17. The enemy appeared to be much alarmed on Saturday morning when

This contemporary engraving depicts the Battle of Bunker Hill and the bombardment of Charlestown by the British fleet. *(National Archives)*

thay discovered our operations and immediately began a heavy cannonading from a batery on Corps-Hill, Boston, and from the ships in the harbour. We with little loss continued to carry on our works till 1 o'clock when we discovered a large body of the enemy crossing Charles-River from Boston. Thay landed on a point of land about a mile eastward of our intrench-ment and immediately disposed thair army for an attack, previous to which thay set fire to the town of Charlestown. It is supposed that the enemy intended to attack us under the cover of the smoke from the burning houses, the wind favouring them in such a design; while on the other side their army was extending northward towards Mistick-River with an apparant design of surrounding our men in the works, and of cutting of[f] any assistance intended for our relief. Thay ware however in some measure counteracted in this design, and drew their army into closer order.

As the enemy approached, our men was not only exposed to the attack of a very numerous musketry, but to the heavy fire of the battery on Corps-Hill, 4 or 5 men of war, several armed boats or floating batteries in Mistick River, and a number of field pieces. Notwithstanding we within the intrenchment, and at a breast work without, sustained the enemy's attacks with great bravery and resolution, killed and wounded great numbers, and repulsed them several times; and after bearing, for about 2 hours, as sever and heavy a fire as perhaps ever was known, and many having fired away all their ammunition, and having no reinforcement, althoe thare was a great boddy of men nie by, we ware over-powered by numbers and obliged to leave the intrenchment, retreating about sunset to a small distance over Charlestown Neck.

N.B. I did not leave the intrenchment until the enemy got in. I then retreated ten or fifteen rods; then I receved a wound in my rite arm, the bawl gowing through a little below my elbow breaking the little shel bone. Another bawl struk my back, taking a piece of skin about as big as a penny. But I got to Cambridge that night. The

town of Charlestown supposed to contain about 300 dwelling-houses, a great number of which ware large and elegant, besides 150 or 200 other buildings, are almost all laid in ashes by the bar-barity and wanton cruelty of that infernal villain Thomas Gage.

Oh, the goodness of God in preserving my life althoe thay fell on my right hand and on my left! O, may this act of deliverance of thine, Oh God, lead me never to distrust the[e]; but may I ever trust in the[e] and put confodence in no arm of flesh! I was in great pane the first night with my wound.

Source: Farnsworth, Amos. "Diary." Edited by Dr. Samuel A. Greene. *Massachusetts Historical Society Proceedings* 2nd ser., 12 (1899): 74–107.

Letter to His Mother
Private Peter Brown
June 25, 1775

Massachusetts militia private Peter Brown, from Westford, Massachusetts, served at Bunker Hill under Colonel William Prescott. He wrote a letter to his mother, Sarah Brown, in Newport, Rhode Island, that provides a uniquely personal perspective on the battle, replete with detail and emotion.

. . . Friday the 16th of June we were orderd to parade at six o'Clock with one days provisions and Blankets ready for a March somewhere but we knew not where but we readily and cheer-fully obey'd the whole that were call'd for, were these three Collo Prescotts, Frys, and Nicksons Regiments—after tarrying on parade till Nine at Night, we march'd down, on to Charlston Hill against Copts [Copp's] hill in Boston, where we entrench'd & made a Fort, ten rod long, and eight wide, with a Breastwork of about eight more, we work'd there undiscovered till about five in the Morning, when we saw our danger, being against Ships of the Line, and all Boston fortified against us. The danger we where in made us think there was treachery and that we were brought there to be all slain, and I must and will say that there was treachery oversight or presumption in the Conduct of our Officers, for about 5 in the morning, we not having more than half of our fort done, they began to fire (I suppose as soon as they had orders) pretty briskly for a few minutes then ceas'd but soon begun again, and fird to the number of twenty minutes (they killed but one of our men) then ceas'd to fire till about eleven o'clock when they began to fire as brisk as ever, which caus'd many of our young Country people to desert, apprehending the danger in a clearer manner than others who were more diligent in digging & fortifying ourselves against them. We began to be almost beat out, being fatigued by our Labour, having no sleep the night before, very little to eat, no drink but rum, but what we hazzarded our lives to get, we grew faint, Thirsty, hungry and weary.—The enemy fir'd very warm from Boston, and from on board their Ships till about 2 o'clock when they begain to fire from Ships that lay in Ferry way and from a Ship that lay in the river against us, to stop our reinforcement, which they did in some Measure one cannon cut three men in two on the neck, Our officers sent time after time for Cannon from Cambridge in the Morning & could get but four, the Captn of which fir'd a few times then swung his hat three times round to the enemy and ceas'd to fire, then about three o'clock there was a cessation of the Cannons roaring, soon after we espied as many as 40, boats or barges coming over, full of troops it is supposed there were 3000 of them, and about 700 of us left, not deserted, besides 500 reinforcement that could not get nigh enough to us to do us any good till they saw that we must all be cut off of some of them then they ventur'd to advance.—When our Officers porceivd that the enemy intended to Land, they ordered the Artillery to go out of the fort & prevent, it if possible from whence the Artillery Captn took his pieces and return'd home to Cambridge with much haste, for which he is now confined and it is expected must suffer death.—The enemy landed, fronted before us,

and form'd themselves in an oblong square, in order to surround, which they did in part. After they were well form'd they advanced towards us, in order to swallow us up, but they found a Choaky mouthful of us, 'tho we could do nothing with our small arms as yet for distance, and had but two cannon, and no gunner, and they from Boston, and from the shipping firing and throwing Bombs, keeping us down, till they almost surrounded us.—But God in Mercy to us fought our battle, and tho' we were but few in number, and suffer'd to be defeated by our enemy, yet we were preserv[ed] in a most wonderful manner, far beyond our expectation and to our admiration for out of our Regiment there were but 37 kill'd 4 or 5 taken captive, about forty seven Wounded & Oh may I never forget Gods distinquishing Mercy to me, in sparing my Life, when they fell on my right hand, and on my left, and close by me, they were to the eye of reason no more expos'd than myself.—When the Arrows of death flew thick around me, I was preserv'd while others were suffer'd to fall a prey to our cruel enemies O may that God whose Mercy was so far extended in my preservation, grant me his grace to devote my future Life to his devine service.—Nor do I conclude that the danger is yet over, unless God in his Mercy either remove our enemy, or heal the breach—but if we should be call'd again to action I hope to have courage and strength to act my part valiently in defence of our Liberties & Country trusting in him who hath hitherto kept me, and hath cover'd my head in the day of battle, and altho' we have lost four out of our Company & several taken captive by the enemy of America, I was not suffer'd to be touched I was in the fort when the enemy came in, Jump'd over the wall and ran half a Mile, where balls flew like hail stones and Cannon roared like thunder, but tho I escap'd then it may be my turn next after asking your Prayers must conclude wishing you the best of Blessings, still remain your Dutiful Son Peter Brown . .

Source: Westford Colonial Minutemen. "A Letter from Peter Brown of Westford to His Mother, Sarah Brown of Rhode Island, Following the Battle of Bunker Hill." Available online. URL: http://lacroixfam.home.comcast.net/~lacroixfam/wmm/Peter_Brown.html. Accessed on February 8, 2010.

Account of the Battle
Reverend Peter Thacher
Late June 1775

About two weeks after the Battle of Bunker Hill, the Massachusetts Committee of Safety appointed the Reverend Peter Thacher (and others) to write an official eyewitness account of the Battle of Bunker Hill. Thacher had watched the action from the vantage point of the Mystic River.

In consequence of undoubted information received from Boston by the commanders of the Continental Army at Cambridge that Genl Gage with a part of his troops purposed the next day to take possession of Bunker's Hill, a promontory just at the entrance of the peninsula of Charlestown, they determined with the advice of the Committee of Safety of the Massachusetts Province to send a party who might erect some fortifications upon the hill and prevent this design.

Accordingly on the 16th of June, orders were issued that a party of about one thousand men should that evening march to Charlestown and entrench upon the hill. About 9 o'clock in the evening the detachment marched upon the design to Breed's hill situated on the further part of the peninsula next to Boston, for by a mistake of orders this hill was marked out for the entrenchment instead of the other. As there were many things necessary to be done preparatory to the entrenchments being thrown up which could not be done before lest the enemy should observe them, it was nearly twelve o'clock before the work was entered upon, for the clocks in Boston were heard to strike about 10 minutes after the men first took their tools into their hands. The work was carried on in every animation and success so that by the dawn of the day they had

nearly completed a small redoubt about eight rods square.

At this time an heavy fire began from 3 men of war, a number of floating batteries and from a fortification of the enemys on Cops hill in Boston directly opposite to our little redoubt. These kept up an incessant shower of shot and bombs, by which one man pretty soon fell. Not discouraged by the melancholly fate of their companion, the soldiers laboured indefatigably till they had thrown up a small breastwork extending from the north side of the redoubt . . . to the bottom of the hill but were prevented by the intolerable fire of the enemy from completing them whol[ly] in such a manner as to make them defensible.

Having laboured thus between 12 and 1 o'clock a number of boats and barges filled with soldiers were observed approaching towards Charlestown. These landed their troops at a place called Moretons Point, situated a little to the eastward of our works. The brigade formed upon their landing tho they were something galled by the fire of two small field pieces which we had placed at the end of the intrenchments. They stood thus formed till a second brigade arrived from Boston to join them.

Having sent out large flank guards in order to surround them they began a very slow march towards our lines. At this instant flames and smoke were seen to arise in large clouds from the town of Charlestown [which] had been set on fire from some of the enemys batterys with a design to favour their attack upon our lines by the smoke which they imagined would have been blown directly that way and thence covered them in their attack, but the wind changing at this instant it was carried another way.

The provincials in the redoubt and the lines reserved their fire till the enemy had come within about 10 or 12 yards and then discharged at once upon them. The fire threw their body into very great confusion, and all of them after having kept a fire for some time retreated in very great disorder down to the point where they landed, and there some of them even into their boats.

At this time their officers were observed by spectators on the opposite shore to come there and then use the most passionate gestures and even to push forward the men with their swords. At length by their exertions the troops were again rallied and marched up to the entrenchments. The Americans reserved their fire and a second time put the regulars to flight who once more retreated in precipitation to their boats.

The same or greater exertions were now again observed to be made by their officers, and having formed once more they brought some cannon to bear in such a manner as to rake the inside of the breastwork, and having drove the provincials thence into the redoubt they determined now, it appeared, to make a decisive effort. The fire from the ships and batteries as well as from the cannon in front of their army was redoubled. Innumerable bombs were sent into the fort. The officers behind the army of the regulars were observed to goad forward their men with renewed exertion. The breastwork on the side of the entrenchment without the redoubt was abandoned, the ammunition of the provincials was expended, the enemy advanced on three sides of the fort at once and scaled the walls.

Can it be wondered at then that the word was given to retreat? But even this was not done till the redoubt was half filled with regulars, and the provincials had for some time kept up an engagement with the but ends of their muskets which unfortunately were not fixed with bayonets. . . .

With very great signs of exultation the British troops again took possession of the hill whither they had fled after their retreat from Concord, and it was expected that they would have prosecuted the advantage which they had gained by marching immediately to Cambridge which was then indeed in an almost defenceless state; they did not however do this, but kept firing with their cannon from the hill and from their ships and batteries across the Neck. The wonder which was excited and the conduct of them soon ceased when a certain account arrived from Boston that of 3 thousand who marched out on the expedition, no less than 1500, among which were 92 commission officers, were killed and wounded, a more severe blow than the British troops had ever before met with in proportion to the number who were engaged, and the time the engagement lasted from the first fire of the musketry to the last was exactly an hour and an half.

Source: Thacher, Peter. "Eyewitness Narrative Prepared about Two Weeks after the Battle of Bunker Hill." Available online. URL: http://www.historycentral.com/documents/BunkerHill.html. Accessed on February 8, 2010.

Letter to an Unidentified Correspondent
General Sir William Howe
June 22 and 24, 1775

General Sir William Howe (1729–1814), who commanded the British assault on Bunker Hill, wrote of the battle to an unidentified correspondent on June 22 and June 24. Not only does the letter reflect Howe's shock and dismay at the ferocity of the resistance at Bunker Hill, it also reveals his pessimistic understanding of the "rebel" strategy— "to fortify every post in our way; wait to be attacked at every one, having their rear secure, destroying as many of us as they can before they set out to their next strong situation."

. . . The troops were no sooner ashore than it was instantly perceived the enemy were very strongly posted, the redoubt upon their right being large and full of men with cannon. To the right of the redoubt they had troops in the houses of Charles Town, about 200 yards distant from the redoubt, the intermediate space not occupied, being exposed to the cannon of the Boston side battery.

From the left of the redoubt, they had a line cannon-proof, about 80 yards in length; and from thence to their left, close upon the Mystic River, they had a breast work made with strong railing taken from the fences and stuffed with hay, which effectually secured those behind it from musquettry. This breast work about 300 yards in extent—they had made the whole in the night of the 16th.

As a specimen of our knowledge of service, the centrys on the Boston side had heard the Rebels at work all night without making any other report of it, except mentioning it in conversation in the morning. The first knowledge the General had of it was by hearing one of the ships firing at the workmen, and going to see what occasioned the firing. Their works when we landed were crowded with men, about 500 yards from us.

From the appearance of their situation and numbers, and seeing that they were pouring in all the strength they could collect, I sent to General Gage to desire a reinforcement, which he immediately complied with, the remaining Light Companies and Grenadiers, with the 47th Battalion and 1st of the Marines landing soon after. Our strength being then about 2200 rank and file, with six field pieces, two light 12-pounders and two howitzers, we begun the attack (the troops in two lines, with Pigott upon the left) by a sharp cannonade, the line moving slowly and frequently halting to give time for the artillery to fire.

The Light Companies upon the right were ordered to keep along the beach to attack the left point of the enemy's breast work, which being carried, they were to attack them in flank. The Grenadiers being directed to attack the enemy's left in front, supported by the 5th and 52d, their orders were executed by the Grenadiers and 2 battalions with a laudable perseverance, but not with the greatest share of discipline, for as soon as the order with which they set forward to the attack with bayonets was checked by a difficulty they met with in getting over some very high fences of strong railing, under a heavy fire, well kept up by the Rebels, they begun firing, and by crowding fell into disorder, and in this state the 2d line mixt with them. The Light Infantry at the same time being repulsed, there was a moment that I never felt before, but by the gallantry of the officers it was all recovered and the attack carried.

Upon the left, Pigott met with the same obstruction from the fences, and also had the troops in the houses to combat with, before he could proceed to assail the redoubt, or to turn it to his left, but the town being set on fire by order at this critical time by a carcass from the battery on the Boston side, Pigott was relieved from his enemies in that quarter, and at the 2d onset he carried the redoubt in the handsomest manner, tho' it was most obstinately defended to the last. Thirty of the Rebels not having time to get away were killed with bayonets in it. The little man is worthy of Our Master's favour.

But I now come to the fatal consequences of this action—92 officers killed and wounded—a most dreadful account. I have lost my aid de camp Sherwin, who was shot thro' the body and died the next day. Our friend Abercrombie is also gone—he had only a flesh wound, but is said to have been in a very bad habit of body. The General's returns will give you the particulars of what I call this unhappy day. I freely confess to you, when I look to the consequences of it, in the loss of so many brave officers, I do it with horror. The success is too dearly bought. Our killed, serjeants and rank and file, about 160; 300 wounded and in hospital, with as many more incapable of present duty. The Rebels left near 100 killed and 30 wounded, but I have this morning learnt from a deserter from them that they had 300 killed and a great number wounded.

We took five pieces of cannon, and their numbers are said to have been near 6000, but I do not suppose they had more than between 4 and 5000 engaged.

The corps remained upon their arms the night of the action, where we are now encamped in a strong situation, with redoubts commanding the isthmus in our front, the enemy being in two corps about one mile and a half distant from us and both well entrenched; the principal body being upon a height called Summer Hill commanding the way from thence to Cambridge; the other called Winter Hill upon the road to Midford (or Mystich) on the side of Roxbury—they are also entrenched and have artillery at all their posts.

Entre nous, I have heard a bird sing that we can do no more this campaign than endeavour to preserve the town of Boston, which it is supposed the Rebels mean to destroy by fire or sword or both—and it is my opinion, with the strength we shall have collected here upon the arrival of the 4 battalions last from Ireland (one of which, with Bailey of the 23d, came in the day before yesterday), that we must not risk the endangering the loss of Boston tho' should anything offer in our favour, I should hope we may not let pass the opportunity.

The intentions of these wretches are to fortify every post in our way; wait to be attacked at every one, having their rear secure, destroying as many of us as they can before they set out to their next strong situation, and, in this defensive mode (the whole country coming into them upon every action), they must in the end get the better of our small numbers. We can not (as the General tells us) muster more now than 3400 rank and file for duty, including the Marines and the three last regiments from Ireland.

Source: "General Sir William Howe Concludes That 'Success Was Too Dearly Bright.'" In *The Spirit of Seventy Six: The Story of the American Revolution as Told by Participants,* edited by Henry Steele Commager and Richard B. Norris, 131–133. New York: Da Capo Press, 1995.

Letter to Lord Barrington
General Thomas Gage
June 26, 1775

Following his bitter Pyrrhic victory at Bunker Hill, General Gage wrote to Lord Barrington, Britain's secretary of state for war, in an effort to make the desperate nature of the situation clear. Like other highly placed British officials, Gage was stunned by the ferocity of the Patriots' resistance. He recommended two courses of action, which the British high command did eventually follow. The first was to recruit "foreign" troops—that is, the mercenary forces knowns as the Hessians. The second was a strategy of withdrawing from Patriot strongholds such as New England and concentrating instead on regions where the British were more likely to find support from "friends"—that is, Loyalists, or so-called Tories.

My Lord: You will receive an account of some success against the Rebels, but attended with a long list of killed and wounded on our side; so many of the latter that the hospital has hardly hands sufficient to take care of them. These people shew a spirit and conduct against us they never shewed against the French, and every body has judged of them from their formed appearance and behaviour when joyned with the Kings forces in the last war; which has led many into great mistakes.

They are now spirited up by a rage and enthousiasm as great as ever people were possessed of, and you must proceed in earnest or give the business up. A small body acting in one spot will not avail. You must have large armys, making divertions on different sides, to divide their force.

The loss we have sustained is greater than we can bear. Small armys cant afford such losses, especially when the advantage gained tends to little more than the gaining of a post—a material one indeed, as our own security depended on it. The troops are sent out too late, the Rebels were at least two months before-hand with us, and your Lordship would be astonished to see the tract of country they have entrenched and fortifyed; their number is great, so many hands have been employed.

We are here, to use a common expression, taking the bull by the horns, attacking the enemy in their strong parts. I wish this cursed place was burned. The only use is its harbour, which may be said to be material; but in all other respects it is the worst place either to act offensively from, or defencively. I have before wrote your Lordship my opinion that a large army must at length be employed to reduce these people, and mentioned the hiring of foreign troops. I fear it must come to that, or else to avoid a land war and make use only of your fleet. I dont find one province in appearance better disposed than another, tho' I think if this army was in New York, that we should find many friends, and be able to raise forces in that province on the side of Government. . . .

Source: "General Thomas Gage: 'The Loss Is Greater Than We Can Bear.'" In *The Spirit of Seventy Six: The Story of the American Revolution as Told by Participants,* edited by Henry Steele Commager and Richard B. Morris, 134–135. New York: Da Capo Press, 1995.

BENEDICT ARNOLD'S MARCH TO QUEBEC, 1775

Diary Entries
Private Abner Stocking
September–October 1775

Of all aspects of the ill-fated, ill-advised American attempt to invade Canada, none was more miserable or more heroic than the epic march Benedict Arnold led from Cambridge, Massachusetts, to Quebec. Abner Stocking (1726–1816), a private in Arnold's army, kept a journal of the march; it was first published in 1810.

Sept. 13. 1775. All things being in readiness for our departure, we set out from Cambridge, near Boston, on the 13th Sept. at sunset, and encamped at Mistick at eight o'clock at night. We were all in high spirits, intending to endure with fortitude all the fatigues and hardships that we might meet with in our march to Quebec.

September 14th. This morning we began our march at 5 o'clock and at sunset encamped at Danvers, a place twenty miles distant from Mistick.

The weather through the day was very sultry and hot for the season of the year. The country through which we passed appeared barren and but thinly inhabited.

September 15th. This morning we marched very early, and encamped at night within five miles of Newbury Port. The inhabitants who visited us in our encampment expressed many good wishes for our success in our intended enterprise.

September 16th. Zealous in the cause, and not knowing the hardships and distresses we were to encounter, we as usual began our march very early. At eight o'clock we arrived at Newbury Port where we were to tarry several days and make preparations for our voyage. We were here to go on board vessels which we found lying ready to receive us and carry us to the mouth of the Kennebeck. The mouth of the Kennebeck River is about thirty leagues to the eastward of Newbury Port.

September 17th. We are still in Newbury Port and are ordered to appear at a general review.

We passed the review with much honor to ourselves. We manifested great zeal and animation in the cause of liberty and went through the manual exercise with much alacrity.

The spectators, who were very numerous, appeared much affected. They probably thought we had many hardships to encounter and many of us should never return to our parents and families.

September 18th. We this day embarked at six o'clock in the afternoon. Our fleet consisted of eleven sail, sloops and schooners. Our whole number of troops was 1100—11 companies of musketmen and three companies of riflemen. We hauled off into the road and got ready to weigh anchor in the morning if the wind should be favorable.

September 19th. This morning we got under way with a pleasant breeze, our drums beating, fifes playing and colours flying.

Many pretty girls stood upon the shore, I suppose weeping for the departure of their sweethearts.

At eleven o'clock this day we left the entrance of the harbor and bore away for Kennebeck River. In the latter part of the night, there came on a thick fog and our fleet was separated. At break of day we found ourselves in a most dangerous situation, very near a reef of rocks. The rocks indeed appeared on all sides of us, so that we feared we should have been dashed to pieces on some of them. We were brought into this deplorable situation by means of liquor being dealt out too freely to our pilots. Their intemperance much endangered their own lives and the lives of all the officers and soldiers on board; but through the blessing of God we all arrived safe in Kennebeck River.

September 20. This day was very pleasant, and with a gentle breeze we sailed and rowed 30 miles up the Kennebeck River. By the evening tide we floated within six miles of Fort Western, where we were obliged to leave our sloops and take to our bateaus.

September 21. This day we arrived at Fort Western, where we tarried until the 25th in order to make farther preparation for our voyage up the river, and our march through the wilderness. . . .

September 25th. Early this morning, we embarked on board our batteaus and proceeded on our way. We labored hard through the day and found ourselves at night but about 7 miles from the place of our departure. The current began to be swift. We encamped at night by the edge of a cornfield and fared very sumptuously.

September 26th. This day we started very early and made our encampment at evening 4 miles below Fort Halifax. We began to experience great difficulty from the increasing rapidity of the current, and the water becoming shoal.

September 27th. This day we carried our batteaus and baggage round Ticonnick Falls. The land carriage was only about 40 rods. After launching in again and getting our provisions and baggage on board, we pushed against the stream on our way about three miles.

September 28th. This day we proceeded 8 miles but with great difficulty. The stream was in some places very rapid and shoal, and in others so deep that those who dragged the boats were obliged to nearly swim. We encountered these hardships and fatigues with great courage and perseverance from the zeal we felt in the cause. When night came on, wet and fatigued as we were, we had to encamp on the cold ground. It was at this time that we inclined to think of the comfortable accommodations we had left at home.

September 29th. This day we arrived to the second carrying place, called Skowhegan Falls. Though this was only 60 rods over, it occasioned much delay and great fatigue. We had to ascend a ragged rock, near on 100 feet in height and almost perpendicular. Though it seemed as though we could hardly ascend it without any burden, we succeeded in dragging our batteaus and baggage up it.

September 30th. After getting over the carrying place, we found the water more still. We proceeded 5 miles and at sundown encamped in a most delightful wood, where I thought I could have spent some time agreeably in solitude, in contemplating the works of nature. The forest was stripped of its verdure, but still appeared to me beautiful. I thought that though we were in a thick wilderness, uninhabited by human beings, yet we were as much in the immediate presence of our divine protector as when in the crowded city.

October 1st. This day we proceeded with unusual perseverance, but as the water was exceedingly rapid, we could advance but slowly. It was but a small part of the way that any thing could be done by rowing or setting.

While one took the batteau by the bow, another kept hold of the stern to keep her from upsetting or filling with water. Thus our fatigues seemed daily to encrease. But what we most dreaded was the frost and cold from which we began to suffer considerably.

October 2d. This day we carried over Norridge-wock Falls, one mile and a quarter. At night we encamped at a place formerly inhabited by the natives and afterwards by the French and Indians; the former had erected a mass house for their devotions, but had deserted it at the time the New England forces made great slaughter among them in the French [and Indian] war. A few inhabitants were now living here, who rendered us some assistance. The temple of worship contained some curiosities, such as crosses, etc. We took up our lodgings here for the night and were much pleased with our accommodations. The place had the appearance of once having been the residence of a considerable number of inhabitants.

October 3d. Having had some better refreshment than usual, we pushed on our way with increased resolution. We had now taken leave of the last inhabitants. The remainder of our route was to be through a trackless wilderness. We now entered a doleful barren woods; the timber mostly pine and hemlock—some thick patches of spruce and fir, and some groves of sugar-maple.

Source: Stocking, Abner. *An Interesting Journal of Abner Stocking of Chatham, Connecticut, Detailing the Distressing Events of the Expedition against Quebec.* 1810. Reprint, Tarrytown, N.Y.: W. Abbatt, 1921.

Diary Entries
Dr. Isaac Senter
October–November 1775

Dr. Isaac Senter (1753–99) was born in Londonderry, New Hampshire, and moved to Rhode Island when he was still a youth. There he studied medicine under Dr. Thomas Moffat and began practicing in Cranston. After the Battle of Lexington, he joined Rhode Island militia forces marching to Boston. Appointed surgeon for Colonel Benedict Arnold's covert 1775 expedition to Quebec, Senter found himself in the midst of a disaster. All the troops of his regiment were killed or captured. He was charged with caring for the sick and wounded in captivity. Released after several months, Senter returned to Cranston and served as surgeon general of Rhode Island in 1776 and from 1778 to 1780, though he resigned from the Continental army in 1779. His journal reflects the misery of the ill-fated expedition to Canada.

Tuesday, October 24th. Approaching necessity now obliged us to double our diligence. Three miles only had we proceeded ere we came to a troublesome water-fall in the river, distant half a mile. Not more than the last mentioned distance before we were brought up by another, distance the same. As the number of falls increased, the water became consequently more rapid. The heights of land upon each side of the river, which had hitherto been inconsiderable, now became prodigiously mountainous, closing as it were up the river with an aspect of an immense height. The river was now become very narrow, and such a horrid current as rendered it impossible to proceed in any other method than by hauling the batteaux up by the bushes, painters, etc.

Here we met several boats returning loaded with invalids, and lamentable stories of the inaccessibleness of the river, and the impracticability of any further progress into the country; among which was Mr. Jackson . . . , complaining of the gout most severely, joined to all the terrors of approaching famine. I was now exhorted in the most pathetic terms to return, on pain of famishing upon contrary conduct, and the army were all returning except a few who were many miles forward with Col. Arnold. However his elocution did not prevail; I therefore bid him adieu and proceeded.

Not far had I proceeded before I discovered several wrecks of batteaux belonging to the front division of riflemen, etc., with an increased velocity of the water. A direful howling wilderness, not describable. With much labour and difficulty I arrived with the principal part of my baggage (leaving the batteaux made fast) to the encampment. Two miles from thence I met the informants last mentioned, where were Col. Greene's division, etc., waiting for the remainder of the army to come up, that they might get some provisions, ere they advanced any further. Upon enquiry I found them almost destitute of any eatable whatever, except a few candles, which were used for supper, and breakfast the next morning, by boiling them in water gruel, etc.

Wednesday, 25. Every prospect of distress now came thundering on with a twofold rapidity. A storm of snow had covered the ground of nigh six inches deep, attended with very severe weather. We now waited in anxious expectation for Col. Enos' division to come up, in order that we might have a recruit of provisions ere we could start off the ground. An express was ordered both up and down the river, the one up the river in quest of Col. Arnold, that he might be informed of the state of the army, many of whom were now entirely destitute of any sustenance. The colonel had left previous orders for the two divisions, viz.: Greene's and Enos', to come to an adjustment of the provisions, send back any who were indisposed, either in body or mind, and pursue him with the others immediately. The other express went down the river to desire Col. Enos and officers to attend in consultation. They accordingly came up before noon, when a council of war was ordered. Here sat a number of grimacers—melancholy aspects who had been preaching to their men the doctrine of impenetrability and non-perseverance. Col. Enos in the chair. The matter was debated upon the expediency of proceeding on for Quebec. The party against going urging the impossibility, averring the whole provisions, when averaged, would not support the army five days.

The arrangements of men and provisions being made at Fort Western, in such a manner as to proceed with the greater expedition. For this end it was thought necessary that Capt. Morgan's company with a few pioneers should advance in the first division, Col. Greene's in the second, and Enos, with Capt. Colbourn's company of artificers, to bring up the rear. The advantage of the arrangement was very conspicuous, as the rear division would not only have the roads cut, rivers cleared passible for boats, etc., but stages of encampments formed and the bough huts remaining for the rear. The men being thus arranged, the provisions were distributed according to the supposed difficulty or facility attending the different dispositions. Many of the first companies took only two or three barrels of flour with several of bread, most in a small proportion, while the companies in the last division had not less than fourteen of flour and ten of bread. The bread, as mentioned before, was condemned in consequence of the leaky casks, therefore the proportion of bread being much greater in the first division, their loss was consequently the greater.

These hints being premised, I now proceed to the determination of the council of war. After debating upon the state of the army with respect to provisions, there was found very little in the division then encamped at the falls (which I shall name *Hydrophobus*). The other companies not being come up, either through fear that they should be obliged to come to a divider, or to shew their disapprobation of proceeding any further. The question being put whether all to return, or only part, the majority were for part only returning. . . .

According to Col. Arnold's recommendation the invalids were allowed to return, as also the timorous. One batteau only for each company to proceed, in order to carry the military stores, medicines, etc, . . . The officers who were for going forward requested the division of the provisions, and that it was necessary they should have the far greater quantity in proportion to the number of men, as the supposed distance that they had to go ere they arrived into the inhabitants was greater than what they had come, after leaving the Cenebec inhabitants. To this the returning party (being predetermined) would not consent. . . . To compel them to a just division we were not in a situation, as being the weakest party. Expostulations and entreaties had hitherto been fruitless. Col. Enos, who more immediately commanded the division of returners, was called upon to give positive orders for a small quantity, if no more. He replied that his men were out of his power, and that they had determined to keep their possessed quantity whether they went back or forward. They finally concluded to spare 2 1/2 barrels of flour, if determined to pursue our destination. . . .

Thus circumstanced, we were left the alternative of accepting their small pittance, and proceed or return. The former was adopted, with a determined resolution to go through or die. Received it, put it on board of our boats, quit the few tents we were in possession of, with all other camp equipage, took each man to his duds on his back, bid them adieu, and away—passed the river, passed over falls and encamped.

Thursday, 26th. We were now within 154 computed miles of the Canadian inhabitants; every man made the best of his way to the Chaudière pond, the place of rendezvous for all the forward party except Col. Arnold. Passed three carrying places on the river. Passed over several rocky mountains and monstrous precipices, to appearance inaccessible; fired with more than Hannibalian enthusiasm, American Alps nor Pyrenees were obstacles. Passed a pond which the river ran through, lodged on a promontory of another. Only Jack Wright was in company. Came to us in the night Maj. Ogden, volunteer, who being lost spied our fire, and came on shore in his boat in which were military stores, etc.

Friday, 27th. Our bill of fare for last night and this morning consisted of the jawbone of a swine destitute of any covering. This we boiled in a quantity of water, that with a little thickening constituted our sumptuous eating. For covering, the atmosphere only, except a blanket. . . .

Saturday, 28th. A letter per express from General Arnold, at 4 o'clock, P.M., requesting as speedy a procedure as possible. That one of his expresses (Jackquith) had returned from the Canadian inhabitants, informing of their amicable disposition towards us, that he had received their pledge of friendship in a loaf of bread, etc. By this time our men were all arrived, embodied, and the glad tidings promulgated among them, to the unspeakable joy of the whole camp. In consequence of this news we were ordered to be in motion immediately. The provisions were ordered into one fund, in order that every man might be acquainted with what he had to depend upon to carry him into the inhabitants, computed at about a hundred miles. Upon a division of the provisions there [were] five pints per man. Pork, though the only meat, was not properly divisible, as the whole amount would not have been an ounce per man. The officers in general were generous enough to dispense with [it] for the better satisfaction and encouragement of the soldiers. Decamped this evening and marched a mile and a half.

Sunday, 29th. Not less than 14 days had our detachment been upon half allowance ere yesterday's division took place. That several of the men devoured the whole of their flour the last evening, determined (as they expressed it) to have a full meal, letting the morrow look out for itself. The ground being overflowed with water before the little stream emptied into the Chaudière, it was thought best by the majority to go to the southeast of the stream upon the higher land and so pass round the lake; however, there were three or four companies proceeded down the stream as far as they could, then leaving it to the southward, and taking the north-westerly shore round the lake. While Col. Greene and most of his officers including myself took our course N. E. and by E. for the Chaudière. Deluded by a pretended pilot, we found our error ere night closed upon us.

From the first appearance of daylight this morn we picked up our small affairs and beat a march. Not long had we marched this course before we came into a spruce and cedar swamp and arrived at a small pond at 11 o'clock, through the most execrable bogmire, impenetrable Pluxus of shrubs, imaginable. This pond we pursued till coming to an outlet rivulet, [which] we followed to a lake much larger than the first, and notwithstanding the most confident assertions of our pilot, we pursued this pond the most of the day, but no Chaudière. . . . This day's march was computed at eighteen miles. Capt. Morgan's company, with seven batteaux, followed the 7 mile stream, with a purpose of passing the south lake, which they effected. These old woodsmen had resolutely persevered in carrying that number of boats over the mountains, with an intent to still preserve a certain quantity of the military stores, which by no other means could be conveyed any further than the Chaudière.

Monday, 30th. . . . This was the third day we had been in search of the Chaudière, who were only seven computed miles distant the 28th inst. Nor were we possessed of any certainty that our course would bring us either to the lake or river, not knowing the point it lay from where we started. However we came to a resolution to continue it. In this state of uncertainty we wandered through hideous swamps and mountainous precipices, with the conjoint addition of cold, wet and hunger, not to mention our fatigue—with the terrible apprehension of famishing in this desert. The pretended pilot was not less frightened than many of the rest; added to that the severe execrations he received, from the front of the army to the rear, made his office not a little disagreeable.

Several of the men towards evening were ready to give up any thoughts of ever arriving at the desired haven. Hunger and fatigue had so much the ascendancy over many of the poor fellows, added to their despair of arrival, that some of them were left in the river, nor were heard of afterwards. In turn with Col. Greene, I carried the compass the greater part of this day. In this condition we proceeded with as little knowledge of where we were or where we should get to, as if we had been in the unknown interior of Africa, or the deserts of Arabia.

Just as the sun was departing, we brought a pond or lake, which finally proved to be Chaudière, and soon the small footpath made by the other division of the army, whose choice turned to their account. Our arrival here was succeeded with three huzzas, and then came to our encampment.

Tuesday, 31. The appearance of daylight roused us as usual, and we had advanced with all possible speed till about 11 o'clock, ere we saw the Chaudière River, which we last night imagined within a mile. Animated afresh with the sight of a stream, which we very well knew would conduct us into the inhabitants if our strength continued, we proceeded with renewed vigour. The emptying of the Chaudière is beautiful, and formed a very agreeable ascent, though the stream is somewhat rapid. The land was now much descending, yet very difficult travelling. The spruce, cedar and hemlock were the chief growth of the earth, and these were in tolerable plenty, almost impenetrably so in many places.

We now began to discover the wrecked batteaux of those who conducted the ammunition, etc. These were seven in number, who followed the seven mile stream into the Chaudière lake, river, etc., and soon came to an encampment, where I found Capt. Morgan and most of the boatmen who were wrecked upon a fall in the river, losing every thing except their lives, which they all saved by swimming, except one of Morgan's riflemen. This was the first man drowned in all the dangers we were exposed to, and the third [lost] by casualties, except some lost in the wilderness, the number unknown. At this encampment was Lieut. McCleland, of Morgan's company, almost expiring with a violent peripneumonia. Necessaries were distributed as much as possible, with two lads of the company in charge of him. Nor was this poor fellow the only one left sick upon this river. Life depending upon a vigorous push for the inhabitants, and that did not admit of any stay for any person; nor could the two lads have been prevailed upon had not provisions been dealt out sufficient to conduct them to the inhabitants, with the promising to send them relief as soon as possible from the settlements.

In this general wreck my medicine box suffered the fate of the rest, with a set of capital instruments, etc. Though little was to be feared from either my chirurgical [surgical] apparatus or physical portions, I had, however, a few necessaries in that way in my knapsack, etc., with a lancet in my pocket, which enabled me at least to comply with the Sangradoine method.

Continued our march about five miles further.

Wednesday, Nov. 1st. Our greatest luxuries now consisted in a little water, stiffened with flour, in imitation of shoemakers' paste, which was christened with the name of Lillipu. Instead of the diarrhea, which tried our men most shockingly in the former part of our march, the reverse was now the complaint, which continued for many days. We had now arrived, as we thought, to almost the zenith of distress. Several had been entirely destitute of either meat or bread for many days. These chiefly consisted of those who devoured their provision immediately, and a number who were in the boats. The voracious disposition many of us had now arrived at rendered almost any thing admissible. Clean and unclean were forms now little in use. In company was a poor dog [who had] hitherto lived through all the tribulations, became a prey for the sustenance of the assassinators. This poor animal was instantly devoured, without leaving any vestige of the sacrifice. Nor did the shaving soap, pomatum, and even the lip salve, leather of their shoes, cartridge boxes, etc., share any better fate. Passed several poor fellows, truly commiserating [them].

Thursday, 2d. Long ere this necessity had obliged us to dismiss all our encamping equipage, excepting a small light tin kettle among a number; but nothing to cut our wood, etc. According to our strength and spirits, we were scattered up and down the river at the distance of perhaps twenty miles. Not more than eight

miles had we marched when a vision of horned cattle, four-footed beasts, etc., rode and drove by animals resembling Plato's two footed featherless ones. Upon a nigher approach our vision proved real! Exclamations of joy, echoes of gladness resounded from front to rear with a [*Te Deum*]. Three horned cattle, two horses, eighteen Canadians and one American. A heifer was chosen as victim to our wants, slain and divided accordingly. Each man was restricted to one pound of beef. Soon arrived two more Canadians in b[irch] canoes, ladened with a coarse kind of meal, mutton, tobacco, etc. Each man drew likewise a pint of this provender. The mutton was destined for the sick. They proceeded up the river in order to the rear's partaking of the same benediction. We sat down, eat our rations, blessed our stars, and thought it luxury. Upon a general computation we marched from 20 to 30 miles per day. Twenty miles only from this to the settlements. Lodged at the great falls this night.

Source: Senter, Isaac. "The Journal of Isaac Senter, M.D., on a Secret Expedition against Quebec, 1775." Philadelphia: Historical Society of Pennsylvania, 1846. Reprint, Tarrytown, N.Y.: William Abbatt, 1915.

THE REPULSE OF THE BRITISH AT CHARLESTON, SOUTH CAROLINA, JUNE 27–29, 1776

Letter to an Unidentified Correspondent
Royal Navy Surgeon
July 9, 1776

The Royal Navy anticipated little difficulty in capturing Charleston, South Carolina, but as this letter from an unidentified Royal Navy surgeon to an also unidentified correspondent attests, the treacherous harbor was skillfully defended by well-placed batteries. The Patriot defenders also benefited from the careless seamanship of the British commanders, who managed to run three ships aground on the shoals of James and Sullivan's Islands. The letter is dated July 9, 1776.

We left Cape-Fear on the 27th of May, and anchored the same evening off the bar. The camp was struck at the same time, and the troops embarked the same evening on board the several transports. All our motions were so languid and so innervate that it was the 9th of June before the *Bristol* and *Pigot* passed the bar of Charlestown; the *Bristol* in passing struck, which alarmed us all exceedingly; but, as it wanted two hours of high water, she soon floated again. The *Prince of Piedmont,* a victualling ship, was totally lost on the north breakers of the bar. General Clinton and Lord Cornwallis were both on board when she struck; but as the weather was very fine, they were not in the least danger.

By our delays we gave the people every opportunity they could have asked for to extend their lines, etc.: they were not idle—every hour gave us astonishing proofs of their industry. As we anchored at one league distance from Sullivan's Island, we could see all that was going on with the help of our glasses. The fort of this island is exceedingly strong (or rather the battery); it is built of palm trees and earth, and on it are mounted eighteen of the lower deck guns of the *Foudroyant:* I never could distinguish more than seventeen; others imagined they could see nineteen—however, that is immaterial.

The signal for attacking was made by Sir Peter Parker on the 27th of June; but the wind coming suddenly to the northward, the ships were obliged again to anchor. The troops have been encamped on Long-Island since the 15th, and it was intended that General Clinton should pass the neck that divides Long-Island from Sullivan's Island, and attack by land while Sir Peter attacked by sea. General Lee had made such a disposition of masked batteries, troops, etc., that it is the opinion of all the officers of the Army

The British withdrew from Charleston on June 28, 1776, after 10 hours of battle. *(U.S. Army Center of Military History)*

whom I have heard mention this circumstance, that if our troops had attacked, they must have been cut off; but this assertion does not satisfy the Navy, for they certainly expected great assistance from the Army. Excuse this necessary digression.

On the morning of the 28th, the wind proved favourable; it was a clear fine day, but very sultry. The *Thunder,* bomb, began the attack at half past eleven by throwing shells while the ships were advancing. The ships that advanced to attack the battery were the *Bristol* and *Experiment,* two fifty-gun ships; the *Solebay, Active, Acteon* and *Syren,* of twenty-eight guns; the *Sphinx,* of twenty, and the *Friendship,* an armed ship of twenty-eight guns. With this force what might not have been expected?

Unfortunately the bomb was placed at such a distance that she was not of the least service. This

Colonel James, the principal engineer, immediately perceived; to remedy which inconvenience, an additional quantity of powder was added to each mortar: the consequences were the breaking down the beds and totally disabling her for the rest of the day.

The *Bristol* and *Experiment* have suffered most incredibly: the former very early had the spring of her cable shot away—of course she lay end on to the battery and was raked fore and aft; she lost upwards of one hundred men killed and wounded. Captain Morris, who commanded her, lost his arm; the worthy man, however, died a week after on board the *Pigot*. Perhaps an instance of such slaughter cannot be produced; twice the quarter-deck was cleared of every person except Sir Peter, and he was slightly wounded. She had nine thirty-two-pound shot in her mainmast, which is so much damaged as to be obliged to be shortened; the mizzen had seven thirty-two-pound shot and was obliged, being much shattered, to be entirely cut away.

It is impossible to pretend to describe what our shipping have suffered. Captain Scott, of the *Experiment*, lost his right arm, and the ship suffered exceedingly; she had much the same number killed and wounded as the *Bristol*. Our situation was rendered very disagreeable by the *Acteon*, *Syren* and *Sphinx* running foul of each other, and getting on shore on the middle ground. The *Sphinx* disengaged herself by cutting way her bowsprit; and, as it was not yet flood-tide, the *Sphinx* and *Syren* fortunately warped off. The *Acteon* was burnt next morning by Captain Atkins, to prevent her falling into the hands of the Provincials, as fine a new frigate as I ever saw.

Our ships, after laying nine hours before the battery, were obliged to retire with great loss. The Provincials reserved their fire until the shipping were advanced within point-blank shot; their artillery was surprisingly well served, it is said, under the command of a Mr. Masson and DeBrahm; it was slow, but decisive indeed; they were very cool, and took great care not to fire except their guns were exceedingly well directed.

But there was a time when the battery appeared to be silenced for more than an hour; the Navy say, had the troops been ready to land at this time, they could have taken possession. How that is I will not pretend to say. I will rather suppose it; but the fire became exceedingly severe when it was renewed again, and did amazing execution after the battery had been supposed to have beeen silenced.

This will not be believed when it is first reported in England. I can scarcely believe what I myself saw on that day—a day to me one of the most distressing of my life. The Navy, on this occasion, have behaved with the usual coolness and intrepidity; one would have imagined that no battery could have resisted their incessant fire.

Source: "The Batteries of Charlestown Repel the British Navy: A British Surgeon." In *The Spirit of Seventy Six: The Story of the American Revolution as Told by Participants,* edited by Henry Steele Commager and Richard B. Morris, 1,065–1,067. New York: Da Capo Press, 1995.

THE BATTLE OF LONG ISLAND, AUGUST 27–30, 1776

Diary Entry
Reverend Ewald G. Shewkirk
July 12, 1776

In his diary on July 12, 1776, the Reverend Mr. Ewald G. Shewkirk, pastor of the Moravian Church of New York, recorded the arrival of the first of the British fleet in preparation for the attack on New York City. The fleet, under Admiral Richard Howe, was so large that many who witnessed its approach spoke of a "forest" of masts appearing over the horizon. Had Admiral Howe and his brother, General William Howe, moved more quickly and vigorously, they might well have brought the American Revolution to an abrupt end. As it was, they drove

The Battle of Brooklyn, August 27, 1776, was a major tactical victory for the British. *(U.S. Army Center of Military History)*

George Washington out of Long Island as well as Manhattan.

A few more ships came in through the Narrows, and it was reported that the great fleet from England began to arrive. In the afternoon about 3 o'clock there was unexpectedly a smart firing. Two men of war, with some tenders, came up. They fired all the batteries, but did little execution. The wind and tide being their favor, the ships sailed fast of the North River [that is, the lower Hudson River, between New York and New Jersey], and soon were out of sight. When they came this side of Trinity Church [at Broadway and Wall Streets in lower Manhattan], they began to fire smartly. The balls and bullets went through several houses between here and Green-

wich [Street]. Six men were killed, either some or all by ill-managing the [city's defensive] cannons, though it is said that a couple were killed by the ship's firing; one man's leg was broke, etc. The six were put this evening into one grave on the Bowling Green. The smoke of the firing drew over our street like a cloud, and the air was filled with the smell of powder.

This affair caused a great fright in the city. Women and children and some with their bundles came form the lower parts, and walked to the Bowery, which was lined with people. Mother Bosler had been brought down into their cellar. Phil. Sypher's, with their child, which was sick, came again to our house. Not long after this affair was over, the fleet below fired a salute, Admiral Howe coming in from England.

Source: "Diary of Rev. Mr. Shewkirk, Pastor of the Moravian Church, New York." In *The Campaign of 1776 around New York and Brooklyn*, by Henry P. Johnston, 110–111. Brooklyn: Long Island Historical Society, 1878.

Diary Entry
Chaplain Philip Vickers Fithian
August 22, 1776

Philip Vickers Fithian (1747–76), was born and raised in New Jersey and educated at the College of New Jersey (modern Princeton University). He postponed his ordination as a Presbyterian minister to tutor the family of Robert Carter III in Virginia's Northern Neck and here began his extensive diary. Toward the end of 1775, he was appointed chaplain to the New Jersey militia and was stationed in Brooklyn with his regiment when the British began to land in overwhelming numbers on the morning of August 22, 1776, after a stormy night. The chaplain recorded the event in his diary on the day of the landing.

Fithian retreated with Washington from Brooklyn to Manhattan, contracted a sickness in camp at Harlem Heights, and died on October 8, 1776, near Fort Washington.

We had last night a most terrible storm of wind, thunder and lightening! So violent as I have not seen since about this time in August 1773. We expect it must have damaged the shipping. It has done a little injury in the harbour tho not so much as from a most furious sudden wind, lasting an hour and a half, might be expected! These two days past many of the ships have gone out. And this morning, before seven, thirteen weighed and went out. It is said by express those which went yesterday were fitted with troups.

Several hundred men are making a breastwork still along the river only as a defence from musquetry. It runs close by our lodging so that we shall have only to step into the trench, load, fire, etc!

Crack! Crack! An alarm from Red-Hook. Crack! Crack! Crack! The alarm repeated from Cobble-Hill. Orders are given for the drums to beat to arms. The enemy have been landing for some time down at the Narrows, and, it is said, have now ashore several thousand. The battalions of riffle-men stationed there, on the enemy's landing, left their camp and came up the island, setting on fire, all the way, the stacks of grain; this is the first degree of ravage occasioned by this unworthy and unchristian assault of our enemies that I have been witness to.

Every battalion, for the present, was ordered to repair to its proper alarm-post. Ours, however, soon had orders to enter Fort-Box. I equipt myself for an action with my gun, canteen, knapsack, blanket, and with the regiment entered the fort and waited for further orders.

Three battalions were ordered off immediately to intercept them and annoy their march.

The alarm guns were fired a little before twelve o'clock.

Before four two brigades were over from New-York, the greater number of which marched on to meet the enemy. Generals Sullivan and Green rode on to gain some intelligence of their place and numbers. Word soon came back that they are within a few miles.

Our battalion all turned out and made a formidable piquet round our little fortification, in order to retard the approach of the enemy and hinder their surrounding us, especially their horse. The men work with vigor; a sense of necessity and the security of life are strong springs to industry.

About eight in the evening the generals returned into camp, and inform that the enemy have made a halt at Flat-Bush, about four miles distance—that the several battalions advanced are in ambush and otherways arranged to annoy them—and that our battalions, after the guards are taken out, may repair to quarters til two in the morning, when all without fail are to be at their post. No officer or soldier is to take off his clothes, and all are to lye on their arms.

Source: "Storm and Alarm as the British Land: Philip Vickers Fithian." In *The Spirit of Seventy Six: The Story of the American Revolution as Told by Participants,* edited by Henry Steele Commager and Richard B. Morris, 428–430. New York: Da Capo Press, 1995.

Letter to a Friend
British Officer
September 3, 1776

In a letter to a friend, written on September 3, 1776, an unidentified British officer gave his impressions of the victory at Long Island. Howe enjoyed tremendous superiority of numbers over Washington, and the writer may be forgiven for believing that the victory had dealt the "Rebels a d——d crush." In fact, Washington managed a nearly miraculous withdrawal across the East River to Manhattan, thereby keeping his battered army intact and viable as a force.

Rejoice, my friend, that we have given the Rebels a d——d crush. We landed on Long-Island the 22d ult., without opposition. On the 27th we had a very warm action, in which the Scots regiments behaved with the greatest bravery and carried the day after an obstinate resistance on the Rebel side. But we flanked and overpowered them with numbers. The Hessians and our brave Highlanders gave no quarters; and it was a fine sight to see with what alacrity they despatched the Rebels with their bayonets after we had surrounded them so that they could not resist. Multitudes were drowned and suffocated in morasses—a proper punishment for all Rebels. Our battalion out-marched all the rest, and was always first up with the Rebel fugitives. A fellow they call Lord Stirling [Major General William Alexander, popularly known as Lord Stirling], one of their generals, with two others, is prisoner, and a great many of their officers, men, artillery, and stores. It was a glorious achievement, my friend, and will immortalize us and crush Rebel colonies. Our loss was nothing. We took care to tell the Hessians that the Rebels had resolved to give no quarters to them in particular, which made them

fight desperately and put all to death that fell into their hands. You know all stratagems are lawful in war, especially against such vile enemies to their King and country. The island is all ours, and we shall soon take New-York, for the Rebels dare not look us in the face. I expect the affair will be over this campaign, and we shall all return covered with American laurels and have the cream of American lands allotted us for our services.

Source: British Officer. Letter, September 3, 1776. In *American Archives: Fifth Series,* edited by Peter Force, 1:1,259–1,260. Washington, D.C.: St. Clair and Force, 1848.

Account of the Battle
Colonel Benjamin Tallmadge
Published 1858

Benjamin Tallmadge (1754–1835) was probably born on Long Island, New York. He attended Yale College (graduating in 1773), where he was a classmate of Nathan Hale, and lived his adult life in Connecticut. From 1773 to 1776, Tallmadge served as superintendent of Wethersfield High School, leaving in June 1776 to accept a commission as a major in the 2nd Regiment Light Dragoons, Continental army. He was promoted to colonel within a short time and served as George Washington's principal intelligence officer and spymaster. He was with Washington throughout the harrowing evacuation of the Continental army from Long Island to Manhattan on the stormy night of August 29, 1776, an event he recalled in his Memoir of Col. Benj. Tallmadge, Prepared by Himself, at the Request of His Children *(1858), which is excerpted here.*

This was the first time in my life that I had witnessed the awful scene of a battle, when man was engaged to destroy his fellow-man. I well remember my sensations on the occasion, for they were solemn beyond description, and very hardly could I bring my mind to be willing to attempt the life of a fellow-creature. Our army having retired behind their intrenchment, which extended from Vanbrunt's Mills on the west to the East River, flanked occasionally by redoubts, the British army took their position, in full array, directly in front of our position. Our intrenchment was so weak that it is most wonderful the British general did not attempt to storm it soon after the battle in which his troops had been victorious.

Gen. Washington was so fully aware of the perilous situation of this division of his army that he immediately convened a council of war, at which the propriety of retiring to New York was decided on. After sustaining incessant fatigue and constant watchfulness for two days and nights, attended by heavy rain, exposed every moment to an attack from a vastly superior force in front, and to be cut off from the possibility of a retreat to New York by the fleet which might enter the East River, on the night of the 29th of August Gen. Washington commenced recrossing his troops from Brooklyn to New York.

To move so large a body of troops, with all their necessary appendages, across a river a full mile wide, with a rapid current, in the face of a victorious, well disciplined army nearly three times as numerous as his own, and a fleet capable of stopping the navigation so that not one boat could have passed over, seemed to present most formidable obstacles. But in face of these difficulties, the Commander-in-Chief so arranged his business that on the evening of the 29th, by 10 o'clock, the troops began to retire from the lines in such a manner that no chasm was made in the lines, but as one regiment left their station on guard, the remaining troops moved to the right and left and filled up the vacancies, while Gen. Washington took his station at the ferry and superintended the embarkation of the troops.

It was one of the most anxious, busy nights that I ever recollect, and being the third in which hardly any of us had closed our eyes in sleep, we were all greatly fatigued. As the dawn of the next day approached, those of us who remained in the trenches became very anxious for our own safety, and when the dawn appeared there were several regiments still on duty. At this time a very dense fog began to rise, and it seemed to settle in a peculiar manner over both encampments. I recollect this peculiar providential occurrence perfectly well; and so very dense was the atmosphere that I could scarcely discern a man at six yards' distance.

When the sun rose we had just received orders to leave the lines, but before we reached the ferry, the Commander-in-Chief sent one of his aids to order the regiment to repair again to their former station on the lines. Col. Chester immediately faced to the right about and returned, where we tarried until the sun had risen, but the fog remained as dense as ever. Finally, the second order arrived for the regiment to retire, and we very joyfully bid those trenches a long adieu. When we reached Brooklyn ferry, the boats had not returned from their last trip, but they very soon appeared and took the whole regiment over to New York; and I think I saw Gen. Washington on the ferry stairs when I stepped into one of the last boats that received the troops. I left my horse tied to a post at the ferry.

The troops having now all safely reached New York, and the fog continuing as thick as ever, I began to think of my favorite horse and requested leave of volunteers to go with me, and guiding the boat myself, I obtained my horse and got off some distance into the river before the enemy appeared in Brooklyn.

As soon as they reached the ferry we were saluted merrily from their musketry, and finally by their field pieces; but we returned in safety. In the history of warfare I do not recollect a more fortunate retreat. After all, the providential appearance of the fog saved a part of our army from being captured, and certainly myself, among others who formed the rear guard. Gen. Washington has never received the credit which was due to him for this wise and most fortunate measure.

Source: Tallmadge, Benjamin. *Memoir of Col. Benj. Tallmadge, Prepared by Himself, at the Request of His Children.* New York: Privately printed, 1858.

Letter to John Page
Brigadier General George Weedon
September 20, 1776

Brigadier General George Weedon (1734–93) wrote to John Page, president of the Virginia Council, on September 20, 1776, to complain of the poor performance of American troops at Kip's Bay, Manhattan, in the face of the British landings on September 15.

Since my last we have evacuated New York, a step that was found absolutely necessary for the preservation of the army, as we held it on very precarious terms, and might have been attended with the worst of consequences at this time, the General not haveing an army that he could depend upon, and so circumstanced from the situation of the place that a safe retreat could not be made had the enemy have landed above us, which was easy to effect.

We should have got of[f] all the stores and troops on Sunday night, but believe the enemy suspected a thing of the sort, and early on Sunday morning sent several frigates up the East and North Rivers, and landed two considerable armies near the same time on the shores of each. General Putnam commanded in York, and had time to bring the troops out whilst our batteries amused the shipping. Two brigades of northern troops were to oppose their landing, and engage them. They run of[f] without fireing a gun, tho' General Washington was himself present, and all he, his aide de camps and other general officers could do, they were not to be rallied till they had got some miles.

The General was so exasperated that he struck several officers in their flight, three times dashed his hat on the ground, and at last exclaimed, "Good God, have I got such troops as those!" It was with difficulty his friends could get him to quit the field, so great was his emotions. He however got of[f] safe, and all the troops as you may think. Nothing was left in York but about 700 barrels of flower and some old come of little consequence. . . .

Two days after the Patriot rout at Kip's Bay, it was the turn of the British to receive a stunning repulse from Washington's troops, who had withdrawn to fortifications in Harlem Heights. Weedon reported this in his letter to John Page.

The enemy, elated at this piece of success [the virtually unopposed landing at Kip's Bay], formed next morning and advanced in three columns. A disposition was made at this place to check them, in which your 3d Virginia Regiment made part. I was ordered to defend a pass at a val[l]ey that divides those flights from New York and the country below. The brave Major Leitch was detached with 3 rifle companies commanded by Captains Thornton, West and Ashby to flank the enemy that were then makeing for it. I soon got engaged, as did the major and his party. How we behaved it does not become me to say. Let it suffice to tell you that we had the Generals thanks in publick orders for our conduct. We were reinforced by some Maryland troops and others who behaved well. The poor major received three balls through his body before he quitted the field, and so lucky are their direction that I am in hopes he will do well. At present he is in a fair way.

I lost with his party and my own three killed and 12 wounded. The other cores that joined us lost in proportion. The enemies loss was at first supposed to be 97, but a deserter that came in today makes them to have lost between 2 and 3 hundred. This is partly confirmed by an old countryman to whose barn they carried their wounded. He declares they had at one time 97 wounded that was brought in, and that night sent it to their main army in waggons, several of which the deserter says is since dead. Upon the whole they got cursedly thrashed and have since declared they did not think the Virginians had got up.

We are now very near neighbours, and view each other every hour in the day. The two armies lay within two miles of each other and a general action is every hour expected. I am more easy in my mind since we have got elbow room, and had the army first thrown up lines here it would have saved vast labour and expence. Indeed, I could wish we were three miles further back yet, as it's not our business to run any risque of being surrounded, an advantage that this country affords the enemy by the number of navigable rivers and creeks that make into it, and in many places do not leave the land more than a mile or two [wide]. . . .

Source: "'Upon the Whole They Got Cursedly Thrashed': George Weedon." In *The Spirit of Seventy Six: The Story of the American Revolution as Told by Participants,* edited by Henry Steele Commager and Richard B. Morris, 470. New York: Da Capo Press, 1995.

THE EXECUTION OF NATHAN HALE, SEPTEMBER 22, 1776

Diary Entry
Captain Frederick Mackenzie
September 22, 1776

After the Battle of Harlem Heights, a Connecticut officer, a former schoolmaster named Nathan Hale, volunteered to conduct espionage behind the British lines to secure intelligence concerning troop movements. He was captured on Long Island, identified as a spy (some sources say that he was fingered by his own cousin, Samuel Hale—but it is also true that he carried incriminating documents on his person), and summarily hanged on September 22, 1776. There is considerable difference of opinion as to the site of his execution, which may have been at the present intersection of 66th Street and Third Avenue in Manhattan; at City Hall Park in Lower Manhattan, or at the present location of the Yale Club at 44th Street and Vanderbilt Avenue, across from Grand Central Terminal. Frederick Mackenzie, a British captain, recorded the execution in his diary on the day of the event.

Sept. 22. A person named Nathaniel Hales [*sic*], a lieutenant in the Rebel army and a native of Connecticut, was apprehended as a spy last night upon Long Island; and having this day made a full and free confession to the Commander in Chief of his being employed by Mr Washington in that capacity, he was hanged at 11 o'clock in front of the park of artillery. He was about 24 years of age, and had been educated at the College of Newhaven [Yale College] in Connecticut. He behaved with great composure and resolution, saying he thought it the duty of every good officer to obey any orders given him by his Commander in Chief; and desired the spectators to be at all times prepared to meet death in whatever shape it might appear.

Source: Mackenzie, Frederick. *Diary of Frederick Mackenzie, Giving a Daily Narrative of His Military Service as an Officer of the Regiment of Royal Welsh Fusiliers during the Years 1775–1781.* Cambridge, Mass.: Harvard University Press, 1930.

Account of the Execution of Nathan Hale
Captain William Hull
Published 1848

William Hull (1753–1825) became infamous during the War of 1812 as the American general who surrendered Fort Detroit to the British without firing a shot. During the American Revolution, he was a Connecticut militia officer (eventually achieving the rank of lieutenant colonel) who fought in the battles of White Plains, Trenton, Princeton, Stillwater, Saratoga, Fort Stanwix, Monmouth, and Stony Point. A friend to fellow Connecticut man Nathan Hale, he tried unsuccessfully to talk him out of undertaking espionage. Hull heard the story of Hale's execution and his speech from John Montresor (1736–99), a British officer who witnessed the hanging. Hull's narrative is excerpted from an unpublished memoir quoted in a biography by Maria Hull Campbell.

In a few days an officer came to our camp, under a flag of truce, and informed [Alexander] Hamilton, then a captain of artillery, but afterwards the aid[e] of General Washington, that Captain Hale had been arrested within the British lines, condemned as a spy, and executed that morning.

I learned the melancholy particulars from this officer, who was present at his execution and seemed touched by the circumstances attending it.

He said that Captain Hale had passed through their army, both of Long Island and [New] York Island. That he had procured sketches of the fortifications, and made memoranda of their number and different positions. When apprehended, he was taken before Sir William Howe, and these papers, found concealed about his person, betrayed his intentions. He at once declared his name, his rank in the American army, and his object in coming within the British lines.

Sir William Howe, without the form of a trial, gave orders for his execution the following morning. He was placed in the custody of the Provost Marshal, who was a refugee and hardened to human suffering and every softening sentiment of the heart. Captain Hale, alone, without sympathy or support, save that from above, on the near approach of death asked for a clergyman to attend him. It was refused. He then requested a Bible; that too was refused by his inhuman jailer.

"On the morning of his execution," continued the officer, "my station was near the fatal spot, and I requested the Provost Marshal to permit the prisoner to sit in my marquee, while he was making the necessary preparations. Captain Hale entered: he was calm, and bore himself with gentle dignity, in the consciousness of rectitude and high intentions. He asked for writing materials, which I furnished him: he wrote two letters, one to his mother and one to a brother officer." He was shortly after summoned to the gallows. But a few persons were around him, yet his characteristic dying words were remembered. He said, "I only regret that I have but one life to lose for my country."

Source: Hull, William. Account of the Execution of Nathan Hale. In *Revolutionary Services and Civil Life of General William Hull,* by Maria Hull Campbell, 37–38. New York: D. Appleton, 1848.

THE BATTLE OF WHITE PLAINS, OCTOBER 28, 1776

Letter to Caesar Rodney
Colonel John Haslet
November 12, 1776

John Haslet (ca. 1727–77), colonel of the 1st Delaware Regiment of the Continental army, described the fight for Chatterton's Hill, key high ground in the Battle of White Plains, New York. He wrote to Caesar Rodney, president of Delaware, on November 12, 1776.

I received his Excellency's [George Washington's] orders to take possession of the hill [Chatterton's Hill] beyond our lines, and the command of the Militia regiments there posted; which was done. We had not been many minutes on the ground when the cannonade began, and the second shot wounded a militia-man in the thigh, upon which the whole regiment broke and fled immediately, and were not rallied without much difficulty. Soon after, General McDougall's brigade took post behind us. Some of our officers expressed much apprehension from the fire of our friends so posted. On my application to the general, he ordered us to the right, formed his own brigade on the left, and ordered Brooks's Massachusetts Militia still farther to the right, behind a stone fence.

The troops being thus disposed, I went up to the top of the hill, in front of our troops, accompanied by Major McDonough, to reconnoitre the enemy, I plainly perceived them marching to the White-Plain, in eight columns, and stop in the wheat-fields a considerable time. I saw their General Officers on horse back assemble in council, and soon their whole body face about and in one continued column march to the hill opposite to our right. I then applied to General McDougall again to vary his disposition, and advised him to order my regiment farther onward, and replace it with Colonel Smallwood's, or order the colonel forward, for there was no dependence to be placed on the Militia. The latter measure was adopted.

On my seeing the enemy's march to the creek begin in a column of their main body, and urging the necessity of bringing our field-pieces immediately forward to bear upon them, the general ordered one, and that so poorly appointed, that myself was forced to assist in dragging it along the rear of the regiment. While so employed, a cannon-ball struck the carriage, and scattered the shot about, a wad of tow blazing in the middle. The artillerymen fled. One alone was prevailed upon to tread out the blaze and collect the shot. The few that returned made not more than two discharges, when they retreated with the field-piece.

At this time the Maryland battalion was warmly engaged, and the enemy ascending the hill. The cannonade from twelve or fifteen pieces, well served, kept up a continual peal of reiterated thunder. The Militia regiment behind the fence fled in confusion, without more than a random, scattering fire. Colonel Smallwood in a quarter of an hour afterwards gave way also. The rest of General McDougall's brigade never came up to the scene of action. Part of the first three Delaware companies also retreated in disorder, but not till after several were wounded and killed. The left of the regiment took post behind a fence on the top of the hill with most of the officers, and twice repulsed the Light Troops and Horse of the enemy; but seeing ourselves deserted on all hands, and the continued column of the enemy advancing, we also retired. Covering the retreat of our party, and forming at the foot of the hill, we marched into camp in the rear of the body sent to reinforce us.

Source: Haslet, John. Letter to Caesar Rodney (November 12, 1776). In *Letters to and from Caesar A. Rodney,* edited by George H. Ryden, 142–143. Philadelphia: University of Pennsylvania Press, 1933.

THE CAPTURE OF FORT WASHINGTON, NOVEMBER 16, 1776

Memoirs of His Own Time, with Reminiscences of the Men and Events of the Revolution
Captain Alexander Graydon
Published 1811

Captain Alexander Graydon (1752–1818), captured with his regiment in the fall of Fort Washington, wrote this account of the catastrophe in his Memoirs of His Own Time, with Reminiscences of the Men and Events of the Revolution, *first published in 1811 and later republished in 1822, 1828, and 1846.*

At ten o'clock in the morning, a large body of the enemy appeared on Haerlem plains, preceded by their field pieces, and advanced with their whole body towards a rocky point of the height, which skirted the plains in a southern direction from the first line, and at a considerable distance from it—and, commencing a brisk fire on the small work constructed there, drove out the party which held it, consisting of twenty men, and took possession of it, the men retiring with the picket guard to the first line. The enemy, having gained the heights, advanced in column on open ground towards the first line; whilst a party of their troops pushed forward and took possession of a small unoccupied work in front of the first line; from whence they opened their fire with some field pieces and a howitzer, upon the line, but without effect. When the column came within proper distance, a fire from the six-pounder was directed against it; on which, the whole column inclined to their left and took post behind a piece of woods, where they remained. As it was suspected that they would make an attempt on the right of the line, under cover of the wood, that part was strengthened.

Things remained in this position for about an hour and a half, during which interval General Washington, with Generals Putnam, Greene, Mercer and other principal officers, came over the North [Hudson] River from Fort Lee and crossed the island to Morris's house; whence they viewed the position of our troops and the operations of the enemy in that quarter. Having remained there a sufficient time to observe the arrangement that had been made for the defence of that part of the island, they retired by the way they came, and returned to Fort Lee, without making any change in the disposition of the troops or communicating any new orders. It is a fact not generally known that the British troops took possession of the very spot on which the Commander-in-chief, and the general officers with him, had stood, in fifteen minutes after they left it.

Colonel Rawlings was some time late in the morning attacked by the Hessians, whom he fought with great gallantry and effect, as they were climbing the heights, until the arms of the riflemen became useless from the foulness they contracted from the frequent repetition of their fire. From this incident, and the great superiority of the enemy, Colonel Rawlings was obliged to retire into the fort. The enemy, having gained the heights, immediately pushed forward towards the fort and took post behind a large store-house within a small distance of it.

But to return to what passed at the first line towards New York. Intelligence having been received by Colonel Cadwalader that the enemy were coming down Haerlem River in boats to land in his rear, he detached Captain Lenox with fifty men to oppose them, and, on farther information, a hundred more, with Captains Edwards and Tudor. This force, with the addition of about the same number from Fort Washington, arrived on the heights near Morris's house, early enough to fire on the enemy in their boats, which was done with such effect that about ninety were killed and wounded. The great superiority, how-

ever, of the enemy (their numbers amounting to about eight hundred men) prevailed over the bravery and good conduct of our troops, who, with some loss, retired to Fort Washington.

This body of the enemy immediately advanced and took possession of the grounds in advance of and a little below Morris's house, where some soldiers' huts had been left standing, not far from the second line. This position of the enemy being observed, it was expected they would march down and take possession of the second line (which, from the want of men, was entirely without defence) and thereby place the troops in the first line between two fires. This important movement did not, however, take place, owing, as was afterwards learned, to the apprehension they entertained that the enclosed bastions concealed therein a number of men whose fire would greatly annoy them. They hesitated; and this being perceived from the delay that took place, Colonel Cadwalader, to avoid the fatal consequences that must have resulted from the expected movement, immediately resolved to retire to the fort with the troops under his command; and as the measure required promptness and activity, he sent orders to the right and left of the line to move off towards Fort Washington, on the signal being given; which, after a proper interval of time, being made, the whole was put in motion (those on the left retiring obliquely towards the centre of the second line) past the second line, and when they came opposite to the body of the enemy posted at the huts, received their fire, which was returned in an irregular manner; and, pursuing the road which led to the fort, under the heights by the North River, arrived there with little or no loss.

The militia under Colonel Baxter, posted on Haerlem River, were attacked by the British guards and light infantry, who landed on the island of New York, protected by the fire from the work on the heights on the opposite side of the river. A short contest ensued; but our troops, overpowered by numbers, and leaving behind them Colonel Baxter who was killed by a British officer as he was bravely encouraging his men, retired to the fort. The guards and light infantry then crossed the island to the heights on the North River, a little below the fort, under which Colonel Cadwalader with his party, but a few minutes before, had passed in his way to the fort.

Source: Graydon, Alexander. *Memoirs of His Own Time, with Reminiscences of the Men and Events of the Revolution,* edited by John Stockton Littell, 191–202. 1811. Reprint, Philadelphia: Lindsay & Blakiston, 1846.

Diary Entry
John Reuber
November 17, 1776

John Reuber, a soldier in Colonel Johann Rall's "Hessian" army regiment, which participated in the British attack on Fort Washington, wrote an account of the battle in his diary.

17 November, in the morning before day-break, all the regiments and corps were assembled, the Hessians on the right wing at the north haven; the English troops upon the left wing at the south haven. When it was now day and the Americans perceived us, but nothing more very plainly, at once these two ships of war, on both sides, made their master-strokes upon the fort, and we began at the same time on the land with cannon, and all the regiments marched forward up the hill and were obliged to creep along up the rocks, one falling down alive, another being shot dead. We were obliged to drag ourselves by the beech-tree bushes up the height where we could not really stand.

At last, however, we got about on the top of the hill where there were trees and great stones. We had a hard time of it there together. Because they now had no idea of yielding, Col. Rall gave the word of command, thus: "All that are my grenadiers, march forwards!" All the drummers struck up the march, the hautboy-players blew. At once all that were yet alive shouted, "Hurrah!" Immediately all were mingled together, Americans and Hessians. There was no more firing, but all ran forward pell-mell upon the fortress. Before we came up, the Americans had a trench about the fortress, as soon as we were within

which, the order came to halt. Then the Americans had a mind to run out through us, but then came the command: "Hold! you are all prisoners of war." The fort was at once demanded by Gen. V. Kniphausen. The Rebels were allowed two hours for capitulating; when they were expired, the fort was surrendered to General V. Kniphausen with all the munitions of war and provisions belonging thereto within and without the fort; all guns and arms were to be laid down, and when all this was done, Rall's regiment and the old Lossberg [Regiment], being made to form into two lines facing each other, they were required to march out between the two regiments and deposit their guns and other weapons.

Then came the English and took them to New York into custody, and when the first transport was off, the second marched out of the citadel and was as strong as the first, and they also were conducted to New York into confinement. And when all this was got through with, it was night. Thus the Hessians took possession of the fort, and the rest marched again round to Kingsbridge into our old camp we had before stopped so long. Then came the order that the fort should be called Fort Kniphausen.

Source: "Thus the Hessians Took Possession of the Fort: John Reuber." In *The Spirit of Seventy-Six: The Story of the American Revolution as Told by Participants,* edited by Henry Steele Commager and Richard Morris, 494. New York: Da Capo Press, 1995.

THE CAPTURE OF FORT LEE, NOVEMBER 19, 1776

Letter to Robert Auchmuty
Francis Rawdon-Hastings
November 25, 1776

Francis Rawdon-Hastings, Lord Rawdon (1754–1826), served in the British army at the capture of Fort Washington and Fort Lee (among other engagements). Then a lieutenant, he wrote the following account in a letter of November 25, 1776, to Robert Auchmuty, the prominent Boston Loyalist who had aided John Adams and Josiah Quincy in defending the soldiers accused in the Boston Massacre of 1770. Lord Rawdon would later become governor-general of British India and first marquess of Hastings.

. . . This grand point [Fort Washington] being gained, by which [New] York Island and a great part of the province was cleared from the rebels, General Howe, I think on the morning of the 20th instant, landed 5,000 men under the command of Lord Cornwallis up the North [Hudson] River on the Jersey shore, a few miles above the other famous fortification, called Fort Constitution or Fort Lee. His Lordship immediately marched to attack this place, and got to it by 1 o'clock the same day, but found it had been evacuated by the rebels so precipitately that the pots were left absolutely boiling on the fire, and the tables spread for dinner of some of their officers. In the fort they found but twelve men, who were all dead drunk. There were forty or fifty pieces of cannon found loaded, with two large iron sea mortars and one brass one, with a vast quantity of ammunition, provision and stores, with all their tents standing.

His Lordship, finding this, pressed forward as quick as he could toward Hackinsack new bridge. But the people belonging to the fort had the heels of him. However, on the road he met with 3 or 4,000 fresh hands coming from Newark to assist in garrisoning the forts. To these gentry the troops distributed a couple of rounds, and set them a scampering, leaving behind them several brass field pieces and their baggage; and as they marched along, found the roads thick strewed with muskets, knapsacks, etc. But the number of cattle taken in the Hackinsack meadows, which had been driven from Pensylvania and some parts of the Jerseys for the use of the grand rebel army, is truly astonishing, and amount to many thousands.

His Lordship's face seems to be set towards Philadelphia, where he will meet with no kind of opposition. I hope he will be at Amboy or Brunswick to-morrow or next day, if it will leave off raining. You see, my dear sir, that I have not been mistaken in my judgement of this people. The southern people will no more fight than the Yankees. The fact is that their army is broken all to pieces, and the spirits of their leaders and their abettors is also broken. However, I think one may venture to pronounce that it is well nigh over with them.

Source: "The Fall of Fort Lee: 'Their Army Is Broken to Pieces': Lord Francis Rawdon." In *The Spirit of Seventy Six: The Story of the American Revolution as Told by Participants,* edited by Henry Steele Commager and Richard B. Morris, 496. New York: Da Capo Press, 1995.

THE BATTLE OF TRENTON, DECEMBER 26, 1776

Account of the Delaware River Crossing
Sergeant Elisha Bostwick
Undated

Elisha Bostwick (1749–1834) was a native of New Milford, Connecticut, who enlisted in the 7th Connecticut Regiment, Continental army, in 1775. A sergeant and clerk of the regiment, he wrote a memoir covering the early years of the war, including the famous Christmas crossing of the Delaware in 1776 and the subsequent Battle of Trenton. It was first published in 1949 in William S. Powell, "A Connecticut Soldier under Washington: Elisha Bostwick's Memoirs of the First Years of the Revolution" (William and Mary Quarterly, Third Series, Vol. 6, No. 1 [Jan. 1949], pp. 94–107).

. . . [O]ur army passed through Bethleham and Moravian town and so on to the Delaware which we crossed 9 miles north of Trenton and encamped on the Pennsylvania side and there remaind to the

24th December. [O]ur whole army was then set on motion and toward evening began to recross the Delaware but by obstructions of ice in the river did not all get across till quite late in the evening, and all the time a constant fall of snow with some rain, and finally our march began with the torches of our field pieces stuck in the exhalters. [They] sparkled and blazed in the storm all night and about day light a halt was made, at which time his Excellency and aids came near to front on the side of the path where the soldiers stood.

I heard his Excellency as he was comeing on speaking to and encourageing the soldiers. The words he spoke as he passed by where I stood and in my hearing were these:

"Soldiers, keep by your officers. For God's sake, keep by your officers!" Spoke in a deep and solemn voice.

While passing a slanting, slippery bank his Excellencys horse's hind feet both slipped from under him, and he siezed his horse's mane and the horse recovered. Our horses were then unharnessed and the artillery men prepared. We marched on and it was not long before we heard the out centries of the enemy both on the road we were in and the eastern road, and their out gards retreated fireing, and our army, then with a quick step pushing on upon both roads, at the same time entered the town. Their artilery taken, they resigned with little opposition, about nine hundred all Hessians, with 4 brass field pieces; the remainder crossing the bridge at the lower end of the town escaped. . . .

Marched the next day with our prisoners back to an encampment. I will here make a few remarks as to the personal appearance of the Hessians. They are of a moderate stature, rather broad shoulders, their limbs not of equal proportion, light complexion with a blueish tinge, hair cued as tight to the head as possible, sticking straight back like the handle of an iron skillet. Their uniform blue with black facings, brass drums which made a tinkling sound, their flag or standard of the richest black silk and the devices upon it and the lettering in gold leaf. . . .

When crossing the Delaware with the prisoners in flat bottom boats the ice continually stuck to the boats, driving them down stream; the boatmen endevering to clear off the ice pounded the boat, and stamping with their feet, bec[k]oned to the prisoners to do the same, and they all set to jumping at once with their cues flying up and down, soon shook off the ice from the boats, and the next day recrossed the Delaware again and returned back to Trenton, and there on the first of January 1777 our yeers service expired, and then by the pressing solicitation of his Excellency a part of those whose time was out consented on a ten dollar bounty to stay six weeks longer, and altho desirous as others to return home, I engaged to stay that time and made every exertion in my power to make as many of the soldiers stay with me as I could, and quite a number did engage with me who otherwise would have went home. . . .

Source: "'For God's Sake, Keep by Your Officers!': Elisha Bostwick." In The Spirit of Seventy Six: The Story of the American Revolution as Told by Participants, *edited by Henry Steele Commager and Richard B. Morris, 511. New York: Da Capo Press, 1995.*

Emanuel Leutze's *Washington Crossing the Delaware* is one of the most widely reproduced of American 19th-century paintings. It depicts the perilous crossing from Pennsylvania to New Jersey, where Washington made a daring, desperate, and triumphant counterattack on the Hessian camp at Trenton. *(National Archives)*

Letter to His Wife
General Henry Knox
December 28, 1776

Before the American Revolution, Henry Knox (1750–1806) was a prosperous bookseller in his native Boston. Largely self-educated, he was especially interested in military history and joined the colonial militia when he was only 18. Two years after witnessing the Boston Massacre (March 5, 1770), he joined the Boston Grenadier Corps. In 1775, he fought at the Battle of Bunker Hill. When George Washington assumed command of the Boston army, absorbing it into the Continental army, he gave Knox command of the Regiment of Artillery.

Knox and Washington greatly admired one another, and in 1785, President Washington appointed Knox as his secretary of war. The following text is an excerpt from Knox's letter to his wife of December 28, 1776, describing the Battle of Trenton.

. . . Trenton is an open town, situated nearly on the banks of the Delaware, accessible on all sides. Our army was scattered along the river for nearly twenty-five miles. Our intelligence agreed that the force of the enemy in Trenton was from two to three thousand, with about six field cannon, and that they were pretty secure in their situation, and that they were Hessians—no British troops. A hardy design was formed of attacking the town by storm. Accordingly a part of the army, consisting of about 2,500 or 3,000, passed the river on Christmas night, with almost infinite difficulty, with eighteen field-pieces. The floating ice in the river made the labor almost incredible. However, perseverance accomplished what at first seemed impossible. About two o'clock the troops were all on the Jersey side, we then were about nine miles from the object. The night was cold and stormy; it hailed with great violence; the troops marched with the most profound silence and good order.

They arrived by two routes at the same time, about half an hour after daylight, within one mile of the town. The storm continued with great violence, but was in our backs, and consequently in the faces of our enemy. About half a mile from the town was an advanced guard on each road, consisting of a captain's guard. These we forced, and entered the town with them pell-mell; and here succeeded a scene of war of which I had often conceived, but never saw before.

The hurry, fright and confusion of the enemy was [not] unlike that which will be when the last trump shall sound. They endeavored to form in streets, the heads of which we had previously the possession of with cannon and howitzers; these, in the twinkling of an eye, cleared the streets. The backs of the houses were resorted to for shelter. These proved ineffectual: the musketry soon dislodged them. Finally they were driven through the town into an open plain beyond. Here they formed in an instant.

During the contest in the streets measures were taken for putting an entire stop to their retreat by posting troops and cannon in such passes and roads as it was possible for them to get away by. The poor fellows after they were formed on the plain saw themselves completely surrounded; the only resource left was to force their way through numbers unknown to them. The Hessians lost part of their cannon in the town: they did not relish the project of forcing, and were obliged to surrender upon the spot, with all their artillery, six brass pieces, army colors, etc. A Colonel Rawle [Rall] commanded, who was [mortally] wounded. The number of prisoners was above 1,200, including officers—all Hessians. There were few killed or wounded on either side. After having marched off the prisoners and secured the cannon, stores, etc., we returned to the place, nine miles distant, where we had embarked.

Providence seemed to have smiled upon every part of this enterprise. Great advantages may be gained from it if we take the proper steps. At another post we have pushed over the river 2,000 men, to-day another body, and to-morrow the whole army will follow. It must give a sensible pleasure to every friend of the rights of man to think with how much intrepidity our people pushed the enemy and prevented their forming in the town.

Source: Drake, Francis Samuel. *Life and Correspondence of Henry Knox, Major-General in the American Revolutionary Army.* Boston: S. G. Drake, 1873, pp. 36–37.

Letter to Caesar Rodney
Thomas Rodney
December 30, 1776

Thomas Rodney (1744–1811) was active in Delaware politics before the American Revolution and, in 1774, served as a delegate to the state convention that elected his older brother, Caesar (1728–84), as Delaware's delegate to the Continental Congress. Thomas Rodney had been colonel of a local militia before the war and was an officer in the 1st Delaware Regiment of the Continental army during it. He wrote to Caesar Rodney, at that time president of Delaware, on December 30, 1776, with the following concise account of the Delaware River crossing and the Battle of Trenton.

. . . On the 25th inst. in the evening, we received orders to be at Shamony ferry as soon as possible. We were there according to orders in two hours, and met the rifle-men, who were the first from Bristol; we were ordered from thence to Dunk's Ferry, on the Delaware, and the whole army of about 2000 men followed as soon as the artillery got up. The three companies of Philadelphia infantry and mine were formed into a body, under the command of Captain Henry (myself second in command), which were embarked immediately to cover the landing of the other troops.

We landed with great difficulty through the ice, and formed on the ferry shore, about 200 yards from the river. It was as severe a night as ever I saw, and after two battalions were landed, the storm increased so much, and the river was so full of ice, that it was impossible to get the artillery over; for we had to walk 100 yards on the ice to get on shore. Gen. Cadwallader therefore ordered the whole to retreat again, and we had to stand at least six hours under arms—first to cover the landing and till all the rest had retreated again—and, by this time, the storm of wind, hail, rain and snow, with the ice, was so bad that some of the infantry could not get back till next day. This design was to have surprised the enemy at Black Horse and Mount Holley, at the same time that Washington surprised them at Trenton; and had we succeeded in getting over, we should have finished all our troubles. Washington took 910 prisoners, with 6 pieces of fine artillery, and all their baggage in Trenton.

The next night I received orders to be in Bristol before day; we were there accordingly, and about 9 o'clock began to embark one mile above Bristol, and about 3 o'clock in the afternoon got all our troops and artillery over, consisting of about 3000 men and began our march to Burlington—the infantry, flanked by the rifle-men, making the advanced guard. We got there about 9 o'clock and took possession of the town, but found the enemy had made precipitate retreat the day before, bad as the weather was, in a great panic. The whole infantry and rifle-men were then ordered to set out that night and make a forced march to Bordentown (which was about 11 miles), which they did, and took possession of the town about 9 o'clock, with a large quantity of the enemy's stores, which they had not time to carry off. We stayed there till the army came up; and the general, finding the enemy were but a few miles ahead, ordered the infantry to proceed to a town called Croswick's, four miles from Bordentown, and they were followed by one of the Philadelphia and one of the New England battalions. We got there about 8 o'clock, and at about 10 (after we were all in quarters) were informed that the enemy's baggage was about 16 miles from us, under a guard of 300 men.

Some of the militia colonels applied to the infantry to make a forced march that night and overhaul them. We had then been on duty four

General Washington receives the surrender of the Hessians following the Battle of Trenton. *(National Archives)*

nights and days, making forced marches, without six hours sleep in the whole time; whereupon the infantry officers of all the companies unanimously declared it was madness to attempt, for that it would knock up all our brave men, not one of whom had yet gave out, but every one will suppose were much fatigued. . . .

The enemy have fled before us in the greatest panic that ever was known; we heard this moment that they have fled from Princeton, and that they were hard pressed by Washington. Never were men in higher spirits than our whole army is; none are sick, and all are determined to extirpate them from the Jersey, but I believe the enemy's fears will do it before we get up with them. The Hessians, from the general to the common soldier, curse and imprecate the war, and swear they were sent here to be slaughtered; that they never will leave New-York again till they sail for Europe. Jersey will be the most whiggish colony on the continent: the very Quakers declare for taking up arms. You cannot imagine the distress of this country. They have stripped every body almost without distinction—even of all their cloths, and have beat and abused men, women and children in the most cruel manner ever heard of.

We have taken a number of prisoners in our route, Hessians and British, to the amount of about twenty. It seems likely through the blessing of Providence that we shall retake Jersey again without the loss of a man, except one Gen. Washington lost at Trenton. The enemy seem to be bending their way to Amboy with all speed, but I hope we shall come up with the Princeton baggage yet, and also get a share of their large stores at Brunswick. I hope, if I live, to see the conquest of Jersey, and set off home again in two weeks. Some of my men have complained a little, but not to say sick; they are all now well here.

Source: Rodney, Thomas. Letter to Caesar Rodney (December 30, 1776). In *Letters to and from Caesar A. Rodney,* edited by George H. Ryden, 248–249. Philadelphia: University of Pennsylvania Press, 1933.

THE BATTLE OF PRINCETON, JANUARY 3, 1777

Letter to an Unidentified Correspondent
"Sergeant R——"
March 24, 1832

In a letter dated March 24, 1832, a revolutionary veteran known to history only as "Sergeant R——" left this account of the Battle of Princeton, which followed Washington's victory at Trenton.

Three or four days after the victory at Trenton, the American army recrossed the Delaware into New Jersey. At this time our troops were in a destitute and deplorable condition. The horses attached to our cannon were without shoes, and when passing over the ice they would slide in every direction and could advance only by the assistance of the soldiers. Our men, too, were without shoes or other comfortable clothing; and as traces of our march towards Princeton, the ground was literally marked with the blood of the soldiers' feet. Though my own feet did not bleed, they were so sore that their condition was little better. While we were at Trenton, on the last of December, 1776, the time for which I and most of my regiment had enlisted expired. At this trying time General Washington, having now but a little handful of men and many of them new recruits in which he could place but little confidence, ordered our regiment to be paraded, and personally addressed us, urging that we should stay a month longer. He alluded to our recent victory at Trenton; told us that our services were greatly needed, and that we could

now do more for our country than we ever could at any future period; and in the most affectionate manner entreated us to stay. The drums beat for volunteers, but not a man turned out. The soldiers, worn down with fatigue and privations, had their hearts fixed on home and the comforts of the domestic circle, and it was hard to forego the anticipated pleasures of the society of our dearest friends.

The General wheeled his horse about, rode in front of the regiment and addressing us again said, "My brave fellows, you have done all I asked you to do, and more than could be reasonably expected; but your country is at stake, your wives, your houses and all that you hold dear. You have worn yourselves out with fatigues and hardships, but we know not how to spare you. If you will consent to stay only one month longer, you will render that service to the cause of liberty and to your country which you probably never can do under any other circumstances."

A few stepped forth, and their example was immediately followed by nearly all who were fit for duty in the regiment, amounting to about two hundred volunteers. (About half of these volunteers were killed in the battle of Princeton or died of the small pox soon after.) An officer enquired of the General if these men should be enrolled. He replied: "No! men who will volunteer in such a case as this need no enrolment to keep them to their duty."

Leaving our fires kindled to deceive the enemy, we decamped that night and by a circuitous route took up our line of march for Princeton. General Mercer commanded the front guard of which the two hundred volunteers composed a part. About sunrise of the 3rd January, 1777, reaching the summit of a hill near Princeton, we observed a light-horseman looking towards us, as we view an object when the sun shines directly in our faces. Gen. Mercer, observing him, gave orders to the riflemen who were posted on the right to pick him off. Several made ready, but at that instant he wheeled about and was out of their reach. Soon after this as we were descending a hill through an orchard, a party of the enemy who were entrenched behind a bank and fence rose and fired upon us. Their first shot passed over our heads, cutting the limbs of the trees under which we were marching. . . . Our fire was most destructive; their ranks grew thin and the victory seemed nearly complete when the British were reinforced. Many of our brave men had fallen, and we were unable to withstand such superior numbers of fresh troops.

I soon heard Gen. Mercer command in a tone of distress, "Retreat!" He was mortally wounded and died shortly after. I looked about for the main body of the army which I could not discover, discharged my musket at part of the enemy, and ran for a piece of wood at a little distance where I thought I might shelter. At this moment Washington appeared in front of the American army, riding towards those of us who were retreating, and exclaimed, "Parade with us, my brave fellows! There is but a handful of the enemy, and we will have them directly." I immediately joined the main body, and marched over the ground again.

. . . The British were unable to resist this attack, and retreated into the College, where they thought themselves safe. Our army was there in an instant, and cannon were planted before the door, and after two or three discharges a white flag appeared at the window, and the British surrendered. They were a haughty, crabbed set of men, as they fully exhibited while prisoners on their march to the country. In this battle my pack, which was made fast by leather strings, was shot from my back, and with it went what little clothing I had. It was, however, soon replaced by one which had belonged to a British officer and was well furnished. It was not mine long, for it was stolen shortly afterwards. . . .

Source: "'The Ground Was Marked with the Blood of Soldiers' Feet': Sergeant R——." In *The Spirit of Seventy Six: The Story of the American Revolution as Told by Participants,* edited by Henry Steele Commager and Richard B. Morris, 519–520. New York: Da Capo Press, 1995.

THE AMERICANS ABANDON FORT TICONDEROGA, JULY 5, 1777

Diary Entries
Lieutenant William Digby
July 1777

Beyond the fact that he was a lieutenant in the British army's Shropshire Regiment and kept a remarkable diary of his service in General Burgoyne's army, nothing is known of William Digby. His regiment was one of the relatively few that were not newly arrived in America. Its service on the continent began during the French and Indian War. In the excerpts that follow, Digby describes how the Americans abandoned Fort Ticonderoga, New York.

[*July*] *4th.* Before day light, we shifted our camp farther back a small way from the range of their shot, until our 12-pounders could come up to play on them in return; by their not throwing shells, we supposed they had none, which from our camp being on a rocky eminence would have raked us much; as to their balls we did not much mind them being at too great a distance to suffer from any point blank shot from their cannon.

About noon we took possession of Sugar Loaf Hill [Fort Defiance] on which a battery was immediately ordered to be raised. It was a post of great consequence, as it commanded a great part of the works of Ticonderoga, all their vessels, and likewise afforded us the means of cutting off their communication with Fort Independent, a place also of great strength and the works very extensive. But here the commanding officer was reckoned guilty of a great oversight in lighting fires on that post, tho I am informed it was done by the Indians, the smoak of which was soon perceived by the enemy in the fort; as he should have remained undiscovered till night, when he was to have got two 12-pounders up, tho their getting there was almost a perpendicular ascent, and drawn up by most of the cattle belonging to the Army.

They no sooner perceived us in possession of a post which they thought quite impossible to bring cannon up to, than all their pretended boastings of holding out to the last, and choosing rather to die in their works than give them up, failed them, and on the night of the 5th they set fire to several parts of the garrison, kept a constant fire of great guns the whole night, and under the protection of that fire and clouds of smoke they evacuated the garrison, leaving all their cannon, amunition and a great quantity of stores. They embarked what baggage they could during the night in their battows, and sent them up to Skeensborough under the protection of five schooners, which Captain Carter of the Artillery with our gun boats followed and destroyed with all their baggage and provisions.

As I happened to be one of the lieutenants of the Grenadiers piquet that night, when we perceived the great fires in the fort, the general was immediately made acquainted with it and our suspicion of their abandoning the place, who with many other good officers imagined it was all a feint in them to induce us to make an attack, and seemingly with a great reason of probability, tho to me, who could be but a very poor judge, it seemed quite the contrary, as I never before saw such great fires.

About 12 o'clock we were very near committing a most dreadful mistake. At that hour of the night, as I was going my rounds to observe if all the sentrys were alert on their different posts, one sentry challenged a party of men passing under his post, which was situated on the summit of a ravine or gully, and also heard carriages dragging in the same place, who answered friends, but on his demanding the countersign, they did not give it, and by their hesitating appeared at a loss; when the fellow would have instantly fired upon them according to his orders, had not I come up at the time, on which I caused him to challenge them again; they not answering, I called to the piquet to turn out and stand to their arms, still lothe to fire. Just at the time, Captain

Walker came up in great haste and told me it was a party of his Artillery with two 12-pounders going to take post on Sugar Loaf Hill, and his orders to them was to cause it to be kept as secret as possible, which by their too strictly attending to in not answering our challenge, which could never be the intention of their orders, was near involving us all in a scene of the greatest confusion, which must have arose from our piquet firing on them. I own I was somewhat alarmed, still thinking the great fires in their lines a feint and their coming to attack us with more security, imagine- ing we gave in to that feint.

[July] 6th. At the first dawn of light, 3 deserters came in and informed that the enemy were retreating the other side of Mount Independent. The general was, without loss of time, made acquainted with it, and the picquets of the army were ordered to march and take possession of the garrison and hoist the King's colors, which was immediately done, and the Grenadiers and Light Infantry were moved under the command [of] Brigadier General Frazier, if possible to come up with them with the greatest expedition. From the fort we were obliged to cross over a boom of boats between that place and Mount Independent, which they, in their hurry, attempted to burn without effect, as the water quenched it, though in some places we could go but one abreast, and had they placed one gun so as the grape shot [could] take the range of the bridge—and which surprised us they did not, as two men could have fired it, and then made off—they would, in all probability, have destroyed all or most of us on the boom. We continued the pursuit the whole day without any sort of provisions, and, indeed, I may say, we had very little or none, excepting one cow we happened to kill in the woods, which, without bread, was next to nothing among so many for two days after; a few hours rest at night in the woods was absolutely necessary.

Source: Digby, William. The British Invasion from the North, edited by James Phinney Baxter, 204–209. Albany: Joel Munsell's Sons, 1887.

THE BATTLE OF ORISKANY, AUGUST 6, 1777

Letter to General John Burgoyne
Colonel Barry St. Leger
August 27, 1777

On August 27, the British lieutenant colonel Barry St. Leger (1733–89) reported to General John Burgoyne on the Battle of Oriskany. St. Leger portrayed it as a British victory. In reality, it was a costly draw that sent many of Burgoyne's Indian allies running.

On the 5th [of August], in the evening, intelligence arrived by my discovering parties on the Mohawk River, that a reinforcement of eight hundred militia, conducted by General Herkimer, were on their march to relieve the garrison [of Fort Schuyler], and were actually at that instant at Oriska[ny], an Indian settlement twelve miles from the fort. The garrison being apprised of their march by four men, who were seen to enter the fort in the morning through what was thought an impenetrable swamp, I did not think it prudent to wait for them and thereby subject myself to be attacked by a sally from the garrison in the rear, while the reinforcement employed me in front. I therefore determined to attack them on the march, either openly or covertly, as circumstances should offer. At this time I had not two hundred and fifty of the King's troops in camp, the various and extensive operations I was under an absolute necessity of entering into having employed the rest; and therefore could not send above eighty white men, rangers and troops included, with the whole corps of Indians.

Sir John Johnson put himself at the head of this party, and began his march that evening at five o'clock, and met the rebel corps at the same hour next morning. The impetuosity of the Indians is not to be described; on the sight of the enemy (forgetting the judicious disposition formed by Sir John, and agreed to by themselves, which was to suffer the attack to begin with the troops in front, while they should be on both flanks and rear), they rushed in, hatchet in hand, and thereby gave the enemy's rear an opportunity to escape.

In relation to the victory, it was equally complete as if the whole had fallen; nay, more so, as the two hundred who escaped only served to spread the panic wider; but it was not so with the Indians; their loss was great (I must be understood Indian computation, being only about thirty killed, and the like number wounded, and in that number some of their favorite chiefs and confidential warriors were slain). On the enemy's side, almost all their principal leaders were slain. General Herkimer has since died of his wounds.

It is proper to mention that the four men detached with intelligence of the march of the reinforcement set out the evening before the action, and consequently the enemy could have no account of the defeat, and were in possession only of the time appointed for their arrival; at which, as I suspected, they made a sally with two hundred and fifty men towards Lieutenant Bird's post, to facilitate the entrance of the relieving corps, or bring on a general engagement, with every advantage they could wish.

Captain Hoyes was immediately detached to cut in upon their rear, while they engaged the lieutenant. Immediately upon the departure of Captain Hoyes, having learned that Lieutenant Bird, misled by the information of a cowardly Indian that Sir John was pressed, had quitted his post to march to his assistance, I marched the detachment of the King's Regiment in support of Captain Hoyes by a road in sight of the garrison, which, with executive fire from his party, immediately drove the enemy into the fort, without any farther advantage than frightening some squaws and pilfering the packs of the warriors which they left behind them.

After this affair was over, orders were immediately given to compleat a two-gun battery and mortar beds, with three strong redoubts in their rear, to enable me, in case of another attempt to relieve the garrison by their regimented troops, to march out a larger body of the King's troops.

Source: "Herkimer's Relief Force Is Routed at Oriskany." In *The Spirit of Seventy Six: The Story of the American Revolution as Told by Participants,* edited by Henry Steele Commager and Richard B. Morris, 564–565. New York: Da Capo Press, 1995.

THE BATTLE OF BENNINGTON, AUGUST 16, 1777

Letter to General Horatio Gates
General John Stark
August 22, 1777

General John Stark (1728–1822), the principal commander at the Battle of Bennington, Vermont, wrote to his commanding officer, General Horatio Gates, on August 22, 1777, to describe the circumstances of his victory over the Hessians.

I shall now give Your Honour a short and brief account of the action on the 13th inst. I was informed that there was a party of Indians in Cambridge on their march to this place. I sent Lieut. Colonel Greg of my brigade to stop them with 200 men. In the night I was informed by express that there was a large body of the enemy on their march in the rear of the Indians. I rallied all my brigade and what Militia was at this place in order to stop their proceedings. Likewise sent to Manchester to Colonel Warner's regiment that was stationed there; also sent expresses for the Militia to come in with all speed to our assistance, which was punctually obeyed. I then marched in company with Colonels Warner, Williams, Herrick and Brush, with all the men that were present. About 5 miles from this place I met Colonel Greg on his retreat and the enemy in close pursuit after him.

I drew up my little army in order of battle, but when the enemy hove in sight, they halted on a very advantageous hill or piece of ground. I sent out small parties in their front to skirmish with them, which scheme had a good effect. They killed and wounded thirty of the enemy without any loss on our side, but the ground that I was upon did [not] suit for a general action. I marched back about one mile and incamped. Called a counsel, and it was agreed that we should send two detachments in their rear, while the others attacked them in front. But the 15th it rained all day; therefore, had to lay by, could do nothing but skirmish with them.

On the 16th in the morning was joined by Colonel Simons with some Militia from Berkshire County. I pursued my plan, detached Colonel Nichols with 200 men to attack them in the rear. I also sent Colonel Herrick with 300 men in the rear of their right, both to join, and when joined to attack their rear. I likewise sent the Colonels Hubbard and Whitney with 200 men on their right, and sent 100 men in their front, to draw away their attention that way, and about 3 o'clock we got all ready for the attack. Colonel Nichols began the same, which was followed by all the rest. The remainder of my little army I pushed up in the front, and in a few minutes the action began. In general it lasted 2 hours, the hotest I ever saw in my life. It represented one continued clap of thunder. However the enemy was obliged to give way, and leave their field pieces and all their baggage behind them. They were all invironed within two breastworks, with their artillery. But our martial courage proved too hard for them.

I then gave orders to rally again, in order to secure the victory, but in a few minutes was informed that there was a large reinforcement on their march within two miles of us. Lucky for us, that moment Colonel Warner's regiment came up fresh, who marched on and began the attack afresh. I pushed forward as many of the men as I could to their assistance. The battle continued obstinate on both sides till sunset. The enemy was obliged to retreat. We pursued them till dark. But had daylight lasted one hour longer,

General John Stark strategically surrounds an unsuspecting Hessian force and leads another Patriot victory at the Battle of Bennington, August 16, 1777. *(National Guard Bureau)*

we should have taken the whole body of them. We recovered 4 pieces of brass cannon, some hundred stands of arms, 8 brass barrells, drums, several Hessian swords, about seven hundred prisoners. 207 dead on the spot. The number of wounded is as yet unknown. That part of the enemy that made their escape marched all night, and we returned to our camp.

Too much honor cannot be given to the brave officers and soldiers for gallant behaviour. They fought through the midst of fire and smoke, mounted two breastworks that was well fortified and supported with cannon. I can't particularize any officer as they all behaved with the greatest spirit and bravery.

Colonel Warner's superior skill in the action was of extraordinary service to me. I would be glad he and his men could be recommended by Congress.

As I promised in my orders that the soldiers should have all the plunder taken in the enemy's camp, would be glad your Honour would send me word what the value of the cannon and the other artillery stores above described may be. Our loss was inconsiderable, about 40 wounded and thirty killed. I lost my horse, bridle and saddle in the action.

Source: "'How a "Little Army" of Farmers Beat Professional Troops': John Stark." In *The Spirit of Seventy Six: The Story of the American Revolution as Told by Participants,* edited by Henry Steele Commager and Richard B. Morris, 572–573. New York: Da Capo Press, 1995.

Account of the Battle
"Glich"
August 16, 1777

Eyewitness accounts by Hessian troops are extremely rare. In this excerpt, a Hessian officer known to history only as "Glich" recorded his version of the Battle of Bennington in a narrative dated on the day of the battle, August 16, 1777. Friedrich Adolf Riedesel, Freiherr zu Eisenbach (1738–1800) was the commanding officer of one of the so-called Hessian—his men were actually from Braunschweig—regiments deployed in the British service during the Revolution.

The dispersal of the troops after what was for them a disastrous battle undermines the legendary image of the Hessians as the best-disciplined of European soldiery. It is believed that about one-third of the Hessians who fought in the American Revolution chose not to return to Europe but stayed in America and were integrated into the communities where they had formerly fought.

The morning of the sixteenth rose beautifully serene; and it is not to the operation of the elements alone that my expression applies. All was perfectly quiet at the outposts, not an enemy having been seen nor an alarming sound heard for several hours previous to sunrise. So peaceable, indeed, was the aspect which matters bore that our leaders felt warmly disposed to resume the offensive without waiting the arrival of the additional corps for which they had applied; and orders were already issued for the men to eat their breakfasts, preparatory to more active operations. But the arms were scarcely piled and the haversacks unslung when symptoms of a state of affairs different from that which had been anticipated began to show themselves, and our people were recalled to their ranks in all haste, almost as soon as they had quitted them. From more than one quarter scouts came in to report that columns of armed men were approaching—though whether with friendly or hostile intention, neither their appearance nor actions enabled our informants to ascertain.

It has been stated that during the last day's march our little corps was joined by many of the country people, most of whom demanded and obtained arms, as persons friendly to the royal cause. How Colonel Baume became so completely duped as to place reliance on these men, I know not; but having listened with complacency to their previous assurances that in Bennington a large majority of the populace were our friends, he was somehow or other persuaded to believe that the armed bands, of whose approach he was warned, were loyalists on their way to make tender of their services to the leader of the king's troops. Filled with this idea, he dispatched positive orders to the outposts that no molestations should be offered to the advancing columns, but that the pickets retiring before them should join the main body, where every disposition was made to receive either friend or foe. Unfortunately for us, these orders were but too faithfully obeyed. About half past nine o'clock, I, who was not in the secret, beheld, to my utter amazement, our advanced parties withdraw without firing a shot from thickets which might have been maintained for hours against any superiority of numbers; and the same thickets occupied by men whose whole demeanor, as well as their dress and style of equipment, plainly and incontestably pointed them out as Americans.

I cannot pretend to describe the state of excitation and alarm into which our little band was now thrown. With the solitary exception of our leader, there was not a man among us who appeared otherwise than satisfied that those to whom he had listened were traitors, and that unless some prompt and vigorous measures were adopted, their treachery would be crowned with its full reward. . . .

We might have stood about half an hour under arms, watching the proceedings of a column of four or five hundred men, who, after dislodging the pickets, had halted just at the edge of the open country, when a sudden trampling of feet in the forest on our right, followed by the report of several muskets, attracted our attention. A patrol was instantly sent in the direction of the sound, but before the party composing it had proceeded many yards from the lines, a loud shout, followed by a rapid though straggling fire of musketry, warned us to prepare for a meeting the reverse of friendly. Instantly the Indians came pouring in, carrying dismay and confusion in their countenances and gestures. We were surrounded on all sides; columns were advancing everywhere against us, and those whom we had hitherto trusted as friends had only waited till the arrival of their support might justify them in advancing.

There was no falsehood in these reports, though made by men who spoke rather from their fears than their knowledge. The column in our front no sooner heard the shout than they replied cordially and loudly to it; then, firing a volley with deliberate and murderous aim, rushed furiously towards us. Now then, at length, our leader's dreams of security were dispelled. He found himself attacked in front and flanked by thrice his number, who pressed forward with the confidence which our late proceedings were calculated to produce, whilst the very persons in whom he had trusted, and to whom he had given arms, lost no time in turning them against him. These followers no sooner heard their comrades' cry than they deliberately discharged their muskets among Reidesel's dragoons and, dispersing before any steps could be taken to seize them, escaped, excepting one or two, to their friends.

If Col. Baume had permitted himself to be duped into a great error, it is no more than justice to confess that he exerted himself manfully to remedy the evil and avert its consequences. Our little band, which had hitherto remained in column, was instantly ordered to extend, and the troops lining the breastworks replied to the fire of the Americans with extreme celerity and considerable effect. So close and destructive, indeed, was our first volley that the assailants recoiled before it, and would have retreated, in all probability, within the woods; but ere we could take advantage of the confusion produced, fresh attacks developed themselves, and we were warmly engaged on every side and from all quarters. It became evident that each of our detached posts were about

to be assailed at the same instant. No one of our dispositions had been concealed from the enemy, who, on the contrary, seemed to be aware of the exact number of men stationed at each point, and they were one and all threatened with a force perfectly adequate to bear down opposition, and yet by no means disproportionately large or such as to render the main body inefficient. All, moreover, was done with the sagacity and coolness of veterans, who perfectly understood the nature of the resistance to be expected and the difficulties to be overcome, and who, having well considered and matured their plans, were resolved to carry them into execution at all hazards and at every expense of life.

It was at this moment, when the heads of columns began to show themselves in rear of our right and left, that the Indians, who had hitherto acted with spirit and something like order, lost all confidence and fled. Alarmed at the prospect of having their retreat cut off, they stole away, after their own fashion, in single files, in spite of the strenuous remonstrances of Baume and of their own officers, leaving us more than ever exposed by the abandonment of that angle of the intrenchments which they had been appointed to maintain. But even this spectacle, distressing as it doubtless was, failed in affecting our people with a feeling at all akin to despair.

The vacancy which the retreat of the savages occasioned was promptly filled up by one of our two field pieces, whilst the other poured destruction among the enemy in front, as often as they showed themselves in the open country or threatened to advance. In this state of things we continued upwards of three quarters of an hour. Tho' repeatedly assailed in front, flank and rear, we maintained ourselves with so much obstinacy as to inspire a hope that the enemy might even yet be kept at bay till the arrival of Breyman's corps, now momentarily expected; when an accident occurred, which at once put an end to this expectation and exposed us, almost defenceless, to our fate.

The solitary tumbril which contained the whole of our spare ammunition became ignited and blew up with a violence which shook the very ground under our feet and caused a momentary cessation in firing, both on our side and that of the enemy. But the cessation was only for a moment. The American officers, guessing the extent of our calamity, cheered their men to fresh exertions. They rushed up the ascent with redoubled ardor, in spite of the heavy volley which we poured in to check them, and, finding our guns silent, they sprang over the parapet and dashed within our works.

For a few seconds the scene which ensued defies all power of language to describe. The bayonet, the butt of the rifle, the sabre, the pike, were in full play, and men fell, as they rarely fall in modern war, under the direct blows of their enemies. But such a struggle could not, in the nature of things, be of long continuance. Out-numbered, broken and somewhat disheartened by late events, our people wavered and fell back, or fought singly and unconnectedly, till they were either cut down at their posts, obstinately defending themselves, or compelled to surren-der. Of Reidesel's dismounted dragoons, few survived to tell how nobly they had behaved; Col. Baume, shot through the body by a rifle ball, fell mortally wounded; and all order and discipline being lost, flight or submission was alone thought of.

For my own part, whether the feeling arose from desperation or accident I cannot tell, but I resolved not to be taken. As yet I had escaped almost unhurt, a slight flesh wound in the left arm having alone fallen to my share; and gathering around me about thirty of my comrades, we made a rush where the enemy's ranks appeared weakest, and burst through. This done, each man made haste to shift for himself without pausing to consider the fate of his neighbor; and losing one third of our number from the enemy's fire, the remainder took refuge, in groups of two or three, within the forest.

Source: "Glich." "Account of the Battle of Benning-ton." *Vermont Historical Society Collections* 1 (1870): 211–213.

THE BATTLE OF BRANDYWINE, SEPTEMBER 11, 1777

Diary Entry
Private Joseph Clark
September 11, 1777

George Washington's army suffered a harsh defeat at Brandywine, as General Howe drove through to capture the Revolutionaries' capital, Philadelphia. Joseph Clark, a young Continental soldier from Princeton, New Jersey, kept a diary account.

Sept. 11. The cannonading began in the morning. At the upper ford the enemy sent a great part of their force about noon. Three divisions of our army were sent immediately to oppose them, viz: Sterling's, Sullivan's and Stephens'; but as there were no heights at this ford, on our side, to prevent their landing by cannon from batteries, we were obliged to oppose them after they had crossed; but as their number was larger than was expected, they stretched their line beyond ours and flanked our right wing shortly after the action began.

This occasioned the line to break, to prevent being surrounded, though the firing, while the action lasted, was the warmest, I believe, that has been in America since the war began; and, as our men on the left of the line were pretty well stationed, they swept off great numbers of the enemy before they retreated, and from the best accounts I could collect from the officers in the action, the enemy must have suffered very much from our people before they broke, though, indeed, our people suffered much in this action, and would have suffered more if Gen'l Green had not been detached to their assistance, by whose timely aid they made a safe retreat of the men, though we lost some pieces of artillery; he, however, got up too late to form in a proper line and give our party that was broken time to recover. Notwithstanding this repulse, which was the most severe upon the 3d Virginia Regiment, who, through mistake, was fired upon by our own men, our whole body got off with but an inconsiderable loss in men, though something considerable in artillery.

When the action began at the upper ford, the batteries at the middle ford opened upon each other with such fury as if the elements had been in convulsions; the valley was filled with smoke, and now I grew seriously anxious for the event. For an hour and a half this horrid sport continued, and about sunset I saw a column of the enemy advance to one of our batteries and take it. Under cover of their cannon they had crossed at the ford, and were advancing in a large body. What we lost at our batteries I have not yet heard. As all our militia were at the lower ford, where was no action, and Gen'l Green sent to reinforce at the upper ford, we had not a very large party to oppose the enemy at the middle ford. The body stationed across the valley drew off to the right, and formed farther back on an eminence, when an engagement began with musketry, and the enemy gave way; but, as night was spreading its dusky shade through the gloomy valley, and our army was something broke, it was necessary to leave the field of action and take care of the troops.

Accordingly, after sunset, the party at the middle ford drew off and marched down to Chester, where the whole army, by appointment, met. The sun was set when I left the hill from whence I saw the fate of the day. His Excellency [George Washington] I saw within 200 yards of the enemy, with but a small party about him, and they drawing off from their station, our army broke at the right, and night coming on, adding a gloom to our misfortunes, amidst the noise of cannon, the hurry of people, and wagons driving in confusion from the field, I came off with a heart full of distress. In painful anxiety I took with hasty step the gloomy path from the field, and travelled 15 miles to Chester, where I slept two hours upon a couple of chairs. . . .

Source: Clark, Joseph. "Diary." *New Jersey Historical Society Proceedings* 7 (1855): 95–110.

THE SARATOGA CAMPAIGN, SEPTEMBER 19– OCTOBER 7, 1777

Diary Entry
Lieutenant William Digby
September 19, 1777

William Digby was a British officer of the Shropshire Regiment (see "The Americans Abandon Fort Ticonderoga, July 5, 1777"). He described the Battle of Freeman's Farm in his journal, written on the day of the battle.

[*September*] 19th. At day break intelligence was received that Colonel Morgan, with the advance party of the enemy consisting of a corps of rifle men, were strong about 3 miles from us; their main body amounting to great numbers encamped on a very strong post about half a mile in their rear; and about 9 o'clock we began our march, every man prepared with 60 rounds of cartridge and ready for instant action. We moved in 3 columns, ours to the right on the heights and farthest from the river in thick woods. A little after 12 our advanced picquets came up with Colonel Morgan and engaged, but from the great superiority of fire received from him—his numbers being much greater—they were obliged to fall back, every officer being either killed or wounded except one, when the line came up to their support and obliged Morgan in his turn to retreat with loss.

About half past one, the fire seemed to slacken a little; but it was only to come on with double force, as between 2 and 3 the action became general on their side. From the situation of the ground, and their being perfectly acquainted with it, the whole of our troops could not be brought to engage together, which was a very material disadvantage, though everything possible was tried to remedy that inconvenience, but to no effect. Such an explosion of fire I never

The fighting at Saratoga between the Americans and the British went on for weeks. A turning point came with the death of Britain's General Fraser, causing General Burgoyne to withdraw and the Americans to proclaim victory on October 17, 1777. *(U.S. Army Center of Military History)*

had any idea of before, and the heavy artillery joining in concert like great peals of thunder, assisted by the echoes of the woods, almost deafened us with the noise. To an unconcerned spectator, it must have had the most awful and glorious appearance, the different battalions moving to relieve each other, some being pressed and almost broke by their superior numbers. The crash of cannon and musketry never ceased till darkness parted us, when they retired to their camp, leaving us masters of the field; but it was a dear-bought victory if I can give it that name, as we lost many brave men. The 62nd had scarce 10 men a company left, and other regiments suffered much, and no very great advantage, honor excepted, was gained by the day.

On its turning dusk we were near firing on a body of our Germans, mistaking their dark clothing for that of the enemy. General Burgoyne was every where and did every thing [that] could be expected from a brave officer, and Brig. Gen. Frazier gained great honour by exposing himself to every danger. During the night we remained in our ranks, and tho we heard the groans of our wounded and dying at a small distance, yet could not assist them till morning, not knowing the position of the enemy, and expecting the action would be renewed at day break. Sleep was a stranger to us, but we were all in good spirits and ready to obey with cheerfulness any orders the general might issue before morning dawned.

Source: Digby, William. *The British Invasion from the North,* edited by James Phinney Baxter, 243–245. Albany: Joel Munsell's Sons, 1887.

Account of the Battle of Freeman's Farm, September 19, 1777
Captain E. Wakefield
Published 1885

Horatio Gates (ca. 1727–1806) possessed something few officers in the Continental army had: experience as a professional soldier. Born in Essex, England, he served in the British army in Nova Scotia during 1749–50 and then in the French and Indian War, in which he was badly wounded during the attack on Fort Duquesne in 1755. A conservative commander, he seemed often to verge on outright defeatism. Thanks largely to the aggressive efforts of Benedict Arnold and Daniel Morgan, Gates prevailed in the Saratoga Campaign—then attempted to seize all credit for a victory his overly cautious and conventional approach would probably have failed to win. In the brief excerpt that follows, a Continental army captain known to history only as E. Wakefield records his impressions of Arnold and Morgan at Freeman's Farm in order to counter the "persistent effort" to "rob Arnold of the glory" he deserved.

A persistent effort has been made from the day of the battle to rob Arnold of the glory. Being attached to Dearborn's Light Infantry, which had a conspicuous part in the battles of the 19th of September and the 7th of October, I had the opportunity of witnessing the principal movements of both, and therefore speak from personal knowledge.

I shall never forget the opening scene of the first day's conflict. The riflemen and light infantry were ordered to clear the woods of the Indians. Arnold rode up, and with his sword pointing to the enemy emerging from the woods into an opening partially cleared, covered with stumps and fallen timber, addressing Morgan, he said,

"Colonel Morgan, you and I have seen too many redskins to be deceived by that garb of paint and feathers; they are asses in lions' skins, Canadians and Tories; let your riflemen cure them of their borrowed plumes."

And so they did; for in less than fifteen minutes the "Wagon Boy," with his Virginia riflemen, sent the painted devils with a howl back to the British lines. Morgan was in his glory, catching the inspiration of Arnold, as he thrilled his men; when he hurled them against the enemy, he astonished the English and Germans with the deadly fire of his rifles.

Nothing could exceed the bravery of Arnold on this day; he seemed the very genius of war. Infuriated by the conflict and maddened by Gates' refusal to send reinforcements, which he repeatedly called for, and knowing he was meeting the brunt of the battle, he seemed inspired with the fury of a demon.

Source: Wakefield, E. Undated Account of the Battle of Freeman's Farm. In *Chaplain Smith and the Baptists; or, Life, Journals, Letters, and Addresses of the Rev. Hezekiah Smith,* by Reuben Aldridge Guild, 213. Philadelphia: American Baptist Publication Society, 1885.

Letter to General Philip Schuyler
Ebenezer Mattoon
October 7, 1777

The Saratoga Campaign culminated in the Battle of Bemis Heights on October 7, 1777. That same day, Ebenezer Mattoon, an officer in the Continental army, reported to General Philip Schuyler on Benedict Arnold's assault against Breymann's Redoubt—which was carried out against the orders of his commanding officer, Horatio Gates.

About one o'clock of this day, two signal guns were fired on the left of the British army which indicated a movement. Our troops were immediately put under arms, and the lines manned. At this juncture Gens. Lincoln and Arnold rode with great speed towards the enemy's lines. While they were absent, the picket guards on both sides were engaged near the river. In about half an hour, Generals Lincoln and Arnold returned to headquarters, where many of the officers collected to hear the report, General Gates standing at the door.

Gen. Lincoln says, "Gen. Gates, the firing at the river is merely a feint; their object is your left. A strong force of 1500 men are marching circuitously, to plant themselves on yonder height. That point must be defended, or your camp is in danger."

Gates replied, "I will send Morgan with his riflemen, and Dearborn's infantry."

Arnold says, "That is nothing; you must send a strong force."

Gates replied, "Gen. Arnold, I have nothing for you to do; you have no business here."

Arnold's reply was reproachful and severe.

Gen. Lincoln says, "You must send a strong force to support Morgan and Dearborn, at least three regiments."

Two regiments from Gen. Larned's brigade, and one from Gen. Nixon's, were then ordered to that station and to defend it at all hazards. Generals Lincoln and Arnold immediately left the encampment and proceeded to the enemy's lines.

In a few minutes, Capt. Furnival's company of artillery, in which I was lieutenant, was ordered to march towards the fire, which had now opened upon our picket in front, the picket consisting of about 300 men. While we were marching, the whole line, up to our picket or front, was engaged. We advanced to a height of ground which brought the enemy in view, and opened our fire. But the enemy's guns, eight in number, and much heavier than ours, rendered our position untenable.

We then advanced into the line of infantry. Here Lieutenant M'Lane joined me. In our front there was a field of corn, in which the Hessians were secreted. On our advancing towards the corn field, a number of men rose and fired upon us. M'Lane was severely wounded. While I was removing him from the field, the firing still continued without abatement.

During this time, a tremendous firing was heard on our left. We poured in upon them our canister shot as fast as possible, and the whole line, from left to right, became engaged. The smoke was very dense, and no movements could be seen; but as it soon arose, our infantry appeared to be slowly retreating, and the Hessians slowly advancing, their officers urging them on with their hangers. . . .

The troops continuing warmly engaged, Col. Johnson's regiment, coming up, threw in a heavy fire and compelled the Hessians to retreat. Upon this we advanced with a shout of victory. At the same time Auckland's corps gave way. We proceeded but a short distance before we came upon four pieces of brass cannon, closely surrounded with the dead and dying; at a few yards further we came upon two more. Advancing a little further, we were met by a fire from the British infantry, which proved very fatal to one of Col. Johnson's companies, in which were killed one sergeant, one corporal, fourteen privates—and about twenty were wounded.

They advanced with a quick step, firing as they came on. We returned them a brisk fire of canister shot, not allowing ourselves time even to sponge our pieces. In a short time they ceased firing and advanced upon us with trailed arms. At this juncture Arnold came up with a part of Brooks's regiment, and gave them a most deadly fire, which soon caused them to face about and retreat with a quicker step than they advanced.

The firing had now principally ceased on our left, but was brisk in front and on the right. At this moment Arnold says to Col. Brooks (late governor of Massachusetts), "Let us attack Balcarras's works."

Brooks replied, "No. Lord Auckland's detachment has retired there, we can't carry them."

"Well, then, let us attack the Hessian lines."

Brooks replies, "With all my heart."

We all wheeled to the right and advanced. No fire was received, except from the cannon, until we got within about eight rods, when we received a tremendous fire from the whole line. But a few of our men, however, fell. Still advancing, we received a second fire, in which a few men fell, and Gen. Arnold's horse fell under him, and he himself was wounded. He cried out, "Rush on, my brave boys!" After receiving the third fire, Brooks mounted their works, swung his sword, and the men rushed into their works. When we entered the works, we found Col. Bremen dead, surrounded with a number of his companions, dead or wounded. We still pursued slowly, the fire, in the mean time, decreasing. Nightfall now put an end to this day's bloody contest. During the day we had taken eight cannon and broken the centre of the enemy's lines.

We were ordered to rest until relieved from the camps. The gloom of the night, the groans and shrieks of the wounded and dying, and the horrors of the whole scene baffle all description.

Source: Mattoon, Ebenezer. Letter to General Philip Schuyler (October 7, 1777). Quoted in *Campaign of Lieut. Gen. John Burgoyne, and the Expedition of Lieut. Col. Barry St. Leger,* by William L. Stone, 371–375. Albany: Joel Munsell, 1877.

Diary Entry
Captain Georg Pausch
October 7, 1777

The Hessian captain Georg Pausch, in command of the Hanau Artillery unit, recorded the defeat of his unit in his journal on October 7, 1777. The account is especially interesting for two things. Pausch praises an English officer who served under him, which reveals that Hessian "mercenary" units and British regulars were not always as rigorously separated as many historians have assumed. Additionally, Pausch delivers one of the most concise evocations of the American style of fighting, which was much better suited to the frontier than European methods designed for open battlefields. He writes of "the bushes . . . full of" the enemy, who "were hidden behind the trees; and bullets in plenty received us."

At this junction, our left wing retreated in the greatest possible disorder, thereby causing a simi-

lar rout among our German command, which was stationed behind the fence in line of battle. They retreated—or to speak more plainly—they left their position without informing me, although I was but fifty paces in advance of them. Each man for himself, they made for the bushes. Without knowing it, I kept back the enemy for a while with my unprotected cannon loaded with shells. How long before this the infantry had left its position, I cannot tell, but I saw a great number advance towards our now open left wing within a distance of about 300 paces. I looked back towards the position still held, as I supposed, by our German infantry, under whose protection I, too, intended to retreat—but not a man was to be seen. They had all run across the road into the field and thence into the bushes, and had taken refuge behind the trees. Their right wing was thus in front of the house I have so often mentioned, but all was in disorder, though they still fought the enemy which continued to advance.

In the mean time, on our right wing, there was stubborn fighting on both sides, our rear, meanwhile, being covered by a dense forest, which, just before, had protected our right flank. The road by which we were to retreat lay through the woods and was already in the hands of the enemy, who accordingly intercepted us. Finding myself, therefore, finally in my first mentioned position—alone, isolated, and almost surrounded by the enemy, and with no way open but the one leading to the house where the two 12-pound cannon stood, dismounted and deserted—I had no alternative but to make my way along it with great difficulty if I did not wish to be stuck in a *damned* crooked road.

After safely reaching the house under the protection of a musketry fire—which, however, owing to the bushes, was fully as dangerous to me as if the firing came from the enemy—I presently came across a little earth-work, 18 feet long by 5 feet high. This I at once made use of by posting my two cannon, one on the right, and the other on the left, and began a fire alternately with balls and with shells, without, however, being able to discriminate in favor of our men who were in the bushes; for the enemy, without troubling them, charged savagely upon my cannon, hoping to dismount and silence them. . . .

A brave English Lieutenant of Artillery, by the name of Schmidt, and a sergeant were the only two who were willing to serve the cannon longer. He came to me and asked me to let him have ten artillery-men and one subaltern from my detachment to serve these cannon. But it was impossible for me to grant his request, no matter how well disposed I might have been towards it. Two of my men had been shot dead; three or four were wounded; a number had straggled off, and all of the infantry detailed for that purpose either gone to the devil or run away. Moreover, all I had left, for the serving of each cannon, were four or five men and one subaltern. A six-pound cannon, also, on account of its rapidity in firing, was more effectual than a twelve-pounder, with which only one-third the number of shots could be fired; and furthermore, I had no desire to silence my own cannon, which were still in my possession, and thereby contribute to raise the honors of another corps. Three wagons of ammunition were fired away by my cannon, which became so heated that it was impossible for any man to lay his hands on them. In front, and also to the right and left of my guns, I had conquered, for myself and for those who were in the same terrain, a pretty comfortable fort. But this state of things lasted only a short time, the fire behind us coming nearer. Finally, our right wing was repulsed in our rear; its infantry, ever, fortunately retreating in better order than our left wing had done.

I still could see, as far as the plain and clearing reached, the road, on which had marched to this second position, open, and a chance, therefore, to retreat. Accordingly, myself, the artillery-man Hausemann and two other artillery-men, hoping to save one of the cannon, dragged it towards this road. The piece of wood on the cannon made the work for us four men very difficult and, in fact, next to impossible. Finally, a subaltern followed with the other cannon and placed it on the carriage. We now brought up the other carriage, on which I quickly placed the remaining gun, and

marched briskly along the road, hoping to meet a body of our Infantry and with them make a stand. But this hope proved delusive and was totally dispelled; for some ran in one, and others in another direction; and by the time that I came within gunshot of the woods, I found the road occupied by the enemy. They came towards us on it; the bushes were full of them; they were hidden behind the trees; and bullets in plenty received us.

Seeing that all was irretrievably lost, and that it was impossible to save anything, I called to the few remaining men to save themselves. I myself took refuge through a fence, in a piece of dense underbrush on the right of the road, with the last ammunition wagon, which, with the help of a gunner, I saved with the horses. Here I met all the different nationalities of our division running pell-mell—among them Capt. Schoel, with whom there was not a single man left of the Hanau Regiment. In this confused retreat all made for our camp and our lines. The entrenchment of Breymann was furiously assailed; the camp in it set on fire and burned, and all the baggage-horses and baggage captured by the enemy. The three 6-pound cannon of my brigade of artillery were also taken, the artillery-men, Wachler and Fintzell, killed, and artillery-man Wall (under whose command were the cannon) severely, and others slightly, wounded. The enemy occupied this entrenchment and remained in it during the night. The approaching darkness put an end to further operations on the part of the Americans.

Source: Pausch, Captain. *Journal of Captain Pausch, Chief of the Hanau Artillery during the Burgoyne Campaign.* Translated by William L. Stone. Albany, N.Y.: Joel Munsell's Sons, 1886.

Diary Entry
Lieutenant William Digby
October 7, 1777

In his diary entry for October 7, the Shropshire Regiment's Lieutenant William Digby (see "The

Americans Abandon Fort Ticonderoga, July 5, 1777") set down the particulars of the British catastrophe at Saratoga. The ferocity of the American attack is vividly present in this account, as is General Burgoyne's failure of leadership, a failure that seems surprising in a distinguished veteran of the Seven Years' War until one considers that the American frontier presented very different conditions from the battlefields of Europe. Some commanders had evident difficulty in adapting.

Brigadier General Frazier was mortally wounded, which helped to turn the fate of the day. When General Burgoyne saw him fall, he seemed then to feel in the highest degree our disagreeable situation. He was the only person we could carry off with us. Our cannon were surrounded and taken—the men and horses being all killed—which gave them additional spirits, and they rushed on with loud shouts, when we drove them back a little way with so great loss to ourselves that it evidently appeared a retreat was the only thing left for us.

They still advanced upon our works under a severe fire of grape shot, which in some measure stopped them by the great execution we saw made among their columns; during which another body of the enemy stormed the German lines after meeting with a most shameful resistance, and took possession of all their camp and equipage, baggage, etc., etc., Colo. Bremen fell nobly at the head of the foreigners, and by his death blotted out part of the stain his countrymen so justly merited from that day's behaviour.

On our retreating, which was pretty regular, considering how hard we were pressed by the enemy, General Burgoyne appeared greatly agitated as the danger to which the lines were exposed was of the most serious nature at that particular period. . . . He said but little, well knowing we could defend the lines or fall in the attempt. Darkness interposed (I believe fortunately for us), which put an end to the action.

General Frazier was yet living, but not the least hopes of him. He that night asked if Genl. Burgoyne's army were not all cut to pieces, and being informed to the contrary, appeared for a moment pleased, but spoke no more. Captn. Wight (53rd Grenadiers), my captain, was shot in the bowels early in the action. In him I lost a sincere friend. He lay in that situation between the two fires, and I have been since informed lived till the next day and was brought into their camp. Major Ackland was wounded and taken prisoner with our Quartermaster General and Major Williams of the Artillery. Sir Francis Clerk fell, Aid de camp to the general, with other principal officers.

Our grenadier company, out of 20 men going out, left their captain and 16 men on the field.

Some here did not scruple to say General Burgoyne's manner of acting verified the rash stroke hinted at by General Gates in his orders of the 26th; but that was a harsh and severe insinuation, as I have since heard his intended design was to take post on a rising ground, on the left of their camp—the 7th—with the detachment, thinking they would not have acted on the offensive, but stood to their works, and on that night our main body was to move, so as to be prepared to storm their lines by day break of the 8th; and it appears by accounts since that Gen Gates would have acted on the defensive, only for the advice of Brigadier General Arnold, who assured him from his knowledge of the troops a vigorous sally would inspire them with more courage than waiting behind their works for our attack, and also their knowledge of the woods would contribute to ensure the plan he proposed.

During the night we were employed in moving our cannon, baggage, etc., nearer to the river. It was done with silence, and fires were kept lighted to cause them not to suspect we had retired from our works where it was impossible for us to remain, as the German lines commanded them, and were then in possession of the enemy, who were bringing up cannon to bear on ours at day break. It may easily be supposed we had no thought for sleep, and some time before day we retreated nearer to the river. Our design of retreating to Ticonderoga then became public.

Source: Digby, William. In *The British Invasion from the North,* edited by James Phinney Baxter, 317–323. Albany: Joel Munsell's Sons, 1887.

THE PAOLI MASSACRE, SEPTEMBER 20–21, 1777

Diary Entry
Major John André
September 20, 1777

Major John André (1750–80), the British officer who would enter history on October 2, 1780, when he was executed after having been captured carrying the plans of the American fort at West Point given him by the turncoat Benedict Arnold, recorded details of the Paoli massacre in his journal.

Intelligence having been received of the situation of General Wayne and his design of attacking our rear, a plan was concerted for surprising him, and the execution entrusted to Major General Grey. The troops for this service were the 40th and 55th Regiments, under Colonel Musgrave, and the 2d Battalion Light Infantry, the 42d and 44th Regiments under General Grey. General Grey's detachment marched at 10 o'clock at night, that under Colonel Musgrave at 11.

No soldier of either was suffered to load; those who could not draw their pieces took out the flints. We knew nearly the spot where the Rebel corps lay, but nothing of the disposition of their camp. It was represented to the men that firing discovered us to the enemy, hid them from us, killed our friends and produced a confusion favorable to the escape of the Rebels and perhaps productive of disgrace to ourselves. On the other hand, by not firing we knew the foe to be wherever fire appeared and a charge ensured his destruction; that amongst the enemy those in the rear would direct their fire against whoever fired in front, and they would destroy each other.

General Grey's detachment marched by the road leading to White Horse, and took every inhabitant with them as they passed along. About three miles from camp they turned to the left and proceeded to the Admiral Warren [Tavern], where, having forced intelligence from a blacksmith, they came in upon the out sentries, piquet and camp of the Rebels. The sentries fired and ran off to the number of four at different intervals. The piquet was surprised and most of them killed in endeavoring to retreat. On approaching the right of the camp we perceived the line of fires, and the Light Infantry being ordered to form to the front, rushed along the line putting to the bayonet all they came up with, and overtaking the main herd of the fugitives, stabbed great numbers and pressed on their rear till it was thought prudent to order them to desist.

Near 200 must have been killed, and a great number wounded. Seventy-one prisoners were brought off; forty of them badly wounded were left at different houses on the road. A major, a captain and two lieutenants were amongst the prisoners. We lost Captain Wolfe killed and one or two private men; four or five were wounded, one an officer, Lieut. Hunter of the 52d Light Company.

It was about 1 o'clock in the morning when the attack was made, and the Rebels were then assembling to move towards us, with the design of attacking our baggage.

Source: André, John. *Major André's Journal.* Tarrytown, N.Y.: W. Abbatt, 1930, pp. 45–47.

Letter to Colonel William Irvine
Major Samuel Hay
September 29, 1777

Samuel Hay, a major in the 7th Pennsylvania Regiment of the Continental army, survived the Paoli massacre to write about it to Colonel (later Brigadier General) William Irvine on September 29, 1777. The Irish-born Irvine (1741–1804) had personal experience with military massacres, having survived

Braddock's defeat at the Battle of the Wilderness (July 9, 1755) in the French and Indian War.

Since I had the pleasure of seeing you, the division under the command of General Wayne has been surprised by the enemy, with considerable loss. We were ordered by his Excellency [George Washington] to march from the Yellow Springs down to where the enemy lay, near the Admiral Warren [Tavern], there to annoy their rear. We marched early on the 17th instant, and got below the Paoli that night. On the next day fixed on a place for our camp.

We lay the 18th and 19th undisturbed, but, on the 20th, at 12 o'clock at night, the enemy marched out, and so unguarded was our camp that they were amongst us before we either formed in any manner for our safety, or attempted to retreat, notwithstanding the General had full intelligence of their designs two hours before they came out.

I will inform you in a few words of what happened. The annals of the age cannot produce such a scene of butchery. All was confusion. The enemy amongst us, and your regiment the most exposed, as the enemy came on the right wing. The 1st Regiment (which always takes the right) was taken off and posted in a strip of woods, stood only one fire and retreated. Then we were next the enemy, and, as we were amongst our fires, they had great advantage of us. I need not go on to give the particulars, but the enemy rushed on with fixed bayonets and made the use of them they intended. So you may figure to yourself what followed.

The party lost 300 privates in killed, wounded and missing, besides commissioned and non-commissioned officers. Our loss is Col. Grier, Captain Wilson and Lieutenant Irvine wounded (but none of them dangerously) and 61 non commissioned and privates killed and wounded, which was just half men we had on the ground fit for duty.

The 22d, I went to the ground to see the wounded. The scene was shocking—the poor men groaning under their wounds, which were all by stabs of bayonets and cuts of Light-Horsemen's swords. Col. Grier is wounded in the side

by a bayonet, superficially slanting to the breast bone. Captain Wilson's stabbed in the side, but not dangerous, and it did not take the guts or belly. He got also a bad stroke on the head with the cock nail of the locks of musket. Andrew Irvine was ran through the fleshy part of the thigh with the bayonet. They are all lying near David Jones' tavern. I left Captain McDowell with them to dress and take care of them, and they all are in a fair way of recovery. Major La Mar, of the 4th Regiment, was killed, and some other inferior officers. The enemy lost Captain Wolf, killed, and four or five Light-Horsemen, and about 20 privates, besides a number wounded.

Source: Hay, Samuel. "Letter." *Pennsylvania Archives* 2nd ser., 1 (1879): 598–599.

THE CAPTURE OF PHILADELPHIA, SEPTEMBER 26, 1777

Diary Entries
Elizabeth Sandwith Drinker
September–October 1777

Elizabeth Sandwith Drinker (1735–1807), a prominent Philadelphian, was eyewitness to the British capture and occupation of the Revolutionary capital. Modern accounts of the fall of Philadelphia emphasize the absence of Patriot opposition. Drinker's account from her diary shows that there was violence, gunfire, and the arrest and intimidation of certain citizens.

September 25, 1777.—This has been a day of great confusion in the city. Enoch Story was the first to inform us that the English were within 4 or 5 miles of us. We have since heard they were by John Dickinson's place and are expected tonight. Most of our warm people have gone off. G. Napper brings word that he spoke with Galloway, who told him that the inhabitants must take care of the city tonight, and they would be in in the morning. As it rained, they fixed their camp within 2 miles of the city. Numbers met at the State House since 8 o'clock to form themselves into different companies to watch the city.

Sept. 26.—Well! here are the English in earnest! About 2 or 300 came in through Second Street without opposition. Cornwallis came with the troops. Gen. Howe has not arrived.

Sept. 27.—About 9 o'clock this morning the *Province* and *Delaware* frigates, with several gondollas, came up the river with a design to fire on the city, but they were attacked by a battery which the English had erected at the lower end of the city. The engagement lasted about half an hour. Many shots were exchanged; one house struck, but not much damaged, and no body that I have heard, hurt on shore. The cook on the *Delaware*, 'tis said, had his head shot off, and a man wounded. She ran aground, and by some means took fire, which occasioned her to strike her colors. The English boarded her and the others drew off. Admiral Alexander and his men were taken prisoners. Part of this scene we witnessed from the little window in our loft.

Sept. 29.—Some officers are going about this day numbering the houses with chalk on the doors. A number of the citizens taken up and imprisoned, among them are John Hall, Jacob Bright, Tom Leech, Jacob Douche and William Moulder.

Oct. 1.—Several fire-rafts which were sent down the river in order to annoy the fleet, ran ashore and were burnt.

Oct. 4.—Before I arose this morning I heard cannon firing; understood from inquiry that a part of Washington's army had attacked the English picket guards near Chestnut Hill. This has been a sorrowful day in Philadelphia, and much more so at Germantown and thereabouts. It was reported in the forenoon that 1000 of the English were slain, but Chalkley James told us that he had been as far as B. Chew's place and could not learn of more than 30 of the Eng-

lish being killed, though a great number were wounded and brought to the city. He counted 18 of the Americans lying dead in the lane from the road to Chew's house, and the house is very much damaged as a few of the English troops had taken shelter there and were fired upon from the road. The last accounts towards evening was that the English were pursuing Washington's troops, who were numerous, and that they were flying before them. The Americans are divided into three divisions, one over Schuy[l]kill, another near Germantown, and the third I know not where, so that the army with us are chiefly called off, and a double guard this night is thought necessary. Washington is said to be wounded in the thigh. [This proved to be a false rumor.]

Oct. 6.—The heaviest firing I think I ever heard was this evening for upwards of two hours; supposed to be the English troops engaged with Mud Island battery. An officer called this afternoon to ask if we could take in a sick or wounded captain, but I put him off by saying that as my husband was from me, I should be pleased if he could obtain some other place. Two of the Presbyterian meeting-houses are made hospitals for the wounded soldiers, of which there are great numbers.

Source: Drinker, Mrs. Henry. "Extracts from the Journal of Mrs. Henry Drinker." *Pennsylvania Magazine of History and Biography* 13 (1889): 298–308.

THE BATTLE OF GERMANTOWN, OCTOBER 4, 1777

Account of the Battle
Lieutenant Sir Martin Hunter
Published 1894

General Washington's response to defeat at the Battle of the Brandywine and to the loss of Philadelphia was to counterattack the British encampment at Germantown (now part of Philadelphia). Lieutenant Sir Martin Hunter (1757–1846) recorded with shame how the British light infantry retreated from the Americans' initial onslaught.

General [Anthony] Wayne commanded the advance, and fully expected to be revenged for the surprise we had given him [at Paoli]. When the first shots were fired at our pickets, so much had we all Wayne's affair [the Paoli massacre] in remembrance that the battalion was out and under arms in a minute. At this time the day had just broke; but it was a very foggy morning and so dark we could not see a hundred yards before us. Just as the battalion had formed, the pickets came in and said the enemy were advancing in force.

They had hardly joined the battalion, when we heard a loud cry of "Have at the bloodhounds! Revenge Wayne's affair!" and they immediately fired a volley. We gave them one in return, cheered, and charged. As it was near the end of the campaign, it was very weak; it did not consist of more than three hundred men, and we had no support nearer than Germantown, a mile in our rear. On our charging, they gave way on all sides, but again and again renewed the attack with fresh troops and greater force. We charged them twice, till the battalion was so reduced by killed and wounded that the bugle was sounded to retreat; indeed had we not retreated at the very time we did, we should all have been taken or killed, as two columns of the enemy had nearly got round our flank. But this was the first time we had retreated from the Americans, and it was with great difficulty we could get our men to obey our orders.

The enemy were kept so long in check that the two brigades had advanced to the entrance of Biggenstown when they met our battalion retreating. By this time General Howe had come up, and seeing the battalion retreating, all broken, he got into a passion and exclaimed: "For shame, Light Infantry! I never saw you retreat before. Form! form! It's only a scouting party."

However, he was soon convinced it was more than a scouting party, as the heads of the enemy's columns soon appeared. One coming through Biggenstown, with three pieces of cannon in their front, immediately fired with grape at the crowd that was standing with General Howe under a large chestnut-tree. I think I never saw people enjoy a discharge of grape before; but we really all felt pleased to see the enemy make such an appearance, and to hear the grape rattle about the commander-in-chief's ears, after he had accused the battalion of having run away from a scouting party. He rode off immediately, full speed, and we joined the two brigades that were now formed a little way in our rear; but it was not possible for them to make any stand against Washington's whole army, and they all retreated to Germantown, except Colonel Musgrave, who, with the 40th Regiment, nobly defended Howe's house till we were reinforced from Philadelphia.

Source: Hunter, Sir Martin. The Journal of Gen. Sir M. Hunter . . . and Some Letters of His Wife, Lady Hunter, edited by Miss A. Hunter and Miss Bell, 346–347. Edinburgh: Edinburgh Press, 1894.

Letter to Lieutenant Colonel John Lamb
T. Will Heth
October 12, 1777

Continental army officer T. Will Heth wrote to Lieutenant Colonel John Lamb on October 12, 1777, to lament what he regarded as a victory at Germantown that "we gave away." Little is known about Heth, but Lamb, the son of an Englishman "transported" to America following a burglary conviction, was a prominent Continental army officer who would go on to command the major portion of the American artillery at the Battle of Yorktown in 1781. Heth's letter captures the ambivalence with which Patriots viewed their defeat at Germantown. It was a loss, yet one that exposed the British forces as highly vulnerable.

Before this reaches you, the news of our late action at German Town, no doubt will have come to hand. It was a grand enterprize, an inimitable plan, which nothing but its God-like author could equal. Had the execution of it been equal to its formation, it must have been attended with the most happy success. The following are the outlines of the orders, and the assault, which had nearly completed the total ruin of the British army. In fact, we had gained a victory, had we known it.

On Friday evening the 3d inst. the whole army marched from their encampment (about 11 miles from the enemys), disposed of in such a manner as to march by several ranks, so as to arrive at the enemys picquets by 2 o'c[lock]— there wait till the hour of 3, and then to advance with charged bayonets upon their front, flank and rear, but from short marches and frequent halts it was near 6 before the first volley of small arms were heard, when Genls. Green and Stephen's divisions, who were to oppose the enemys right, were then, from some mismanagement, only forming at more than a mile's distance. However our troops who made the attack were successful. They drove the enemy from field to field, and through part of German Town.

In the mean time [ou]r wing, by another piece of bad conduct, attempted to march in line of battle, till that order was found impracticable, which from the great number of post and rail fences, thickets and in short [ev]ery thing that could obstruct our march, threw us frequently into the greatest disorder, and as the heavy fire before us urged us on to a dog trot, we were nearly exhausted before we came to the first field of action, when unfortunately a strong stone house, in which the enemy had taken post, drew the attention of ten times the number that would have been sufficient to have kept them snug, and from which we received considerable damage. And after we had brought some artillery to play upon opposite parts of the house, each party took [the] other for the enemy. About this time an opinion prevailed among some general officers that the house was occupied by our own men, when part of our troops were accordingly ordered

off. The heavy smoke, added to a thick fog, was of vast injury to us. It undoubtedly increased the fear of some to fancy themselves flanked and surrounded, wh[ich] like an electrical shock seized some thousands, who fled in confusion, without the appearance of an enemy.

What makes this inglorious retreat more grating is that we now know the enemy had orders to retreat and rendevouz at Chester, and that upwards of 2000 Hessians had actually crossed the Schuylkill for that purpose; that the Torys were in the utmost distress and moveing out of the city; that our friends confined in the New-Gaol made it ring with shouts of joy; that we passed, in pursuing them, upwards of twenty pieces of cannon, their tents standing filled with that choicest baggage. In fine, everything was as we could wish, when the above flight took place.

Tho we gave away a complete victory, we have learned this valuable truth: [that we are able] to beat them by vigorous exertion, and that we are far superior [in] point of swiftness. We are in high spirits. Every action [gives] our troops fresh vigor and a greater opinion of their own strength. Another bout or two must make their [the British] situation very disagreeable.

Source: "'We Had Gained a Victory Had We Known It': T. Will Heth." In *The Spirit of Seventy Six: The Story of the American Revolution as Told by Participants,* edited by Henry Steele Commager and Richard B. Morris, 629. New York: Da Capo Press, 1995.

VALLEY FORGE, WINTER 1777–1778

Diary Entries
Dr. Albigence Waldo
December 1777

Dr. Albigence Waldo (1750–94), surgeon of the Continental army's Connecticut Line and personal physician to General George Washington, was expected to treat men who were forced to endure the harsh conditions of winter encampment at Valley Forge, Pennsylvania. Food and clothing were in short supply, and the unheated, uninsulated 16 feet × 14 feet log huts the men shared, sleeping on dirt floors, offered scant protection from the cold.

December 11.—At four o'clock the whole army were ordered to march to Swedes Ford on the River Schuylkill, about 9 miles N. W. of Chestnut Hill, and 6 from White Marsh, our present encampment. At sun an hour high the whole were moved from the lines and on their march with baggage. This night encamped in a semi circle nigh the ford. The enemy had marched up the west side of Schuylkill—Potter's brigade of Pennsylvania Militia were already there and had several skirmishes with them with some loss on his side and considerable on the enemies. . . .

I am prodigious sick and cannot get any thing comfortable. What in the name of Providence am I to do with a fit of sickness in this place where nothing appears pleasing to the sickened eye and nausiating stomach? But I doubt not Providence will find out a way for my relief. But I cannot eat beef if I starve, for my stomach positively refuses to entertain such company, and how can I help that?

December 12.—A bridge of waggons made across the Schuylkill last night consisting of 36 waggons, with a bridge of rails between each. Some skirmishing over the river. Militia and dragoons brought into camp several prisoners. Sun set— We were ordered to march over the river—It snows—I'm sick—eat nothing—no whiskey—no forage—Lord—Lord—Lord. The army were till sun rise crossing the river—some at the waggon bridge and some at the raft bridge below. Cold and uncomfortable.

December 13.—The army marched three miles from the west side [of] the river and encamped near a place called the Gulph and not an improper name neither, for this Gulph seems well adapted by its situation to keep us from the pleasures and enjoyments of this world, or being conversant with any body in it. It is an excellent place to raise the ideas of a philosopher beyond the glutted thoughts and reflexions of an Epicurian. His reflexions will be as different from the common reflexions of mankind as if he were unconnected with the world and only conversant with immaterial beings. It cannot be that our superiors are about to hold consultations with spirits infinitely beneath their order, by bringing us into these utmost regions of the terraqueous sphere.

No, it is, upon consideration, for many good purposes since we are to winter here: 1st, there is plenty of wood and water. 2ndly, there are but few families for the soldiery to steal from—tho' far be it from a soldier to steal. 41y, there are warm sides of hills to erect huts on. 5ly, they will be heavenly minded like Jonah when in the belly of a great fish. 61y, they will not become home sick as is sometimes the case when men live in the open world—since the reflections which will naturally arise from their present habitation will lead them to the more noble thoughts of employing their leisure hours in filling their knapsacks with such materials as may be necessary on the Journey to another Home.

December 14.—Prisoners and deserters are continually coming in. The army, which has been surprisingly healthy hitherto, now begins to grow sickly from the continued fatigues they have suffered this campaign. Yet they still show a spirit of alacrity and contentment not to be expected from so young troops. I am sick—discontented—and out of humour. Poor food—hard lodging—cold weather—fatigue—nasty cloathes—nasty cookery—vomit half my time—smoked out of my senses—the Devil's in't—I can't endure it—Why are we sent here to starve and freeze?—What sweet felicities have I left at home: A charming wife—pretty children—good beds—good food— good cookery—all agreeable—all harmonious! Here all confusion—smoke and cold—hunger and filthyness—a pox on my bad luck! There comes a bowl of beef soup, full of burnt leaves and dirt, sickish enough to make a Hector spue—

away with it, boys!—I'll live like the chameleon upon air.

Poh! Poh! crys Patience within me, you talk like a fool. Your being sick covers your mind with a melancholic gloom, which makes everything about you appear gloomy. See the poor soldier when in health—with what cheerfulness he meets his foes and encounters every hardship. If barefoot, he labours thro' the mud and cold with a song in his mouth extolling War and Washington. If his food be bad, he eats it notwithstanding with seeming content—blesses God for a good stomach and whistles it into digestion.

But harkee, Patience, a moment. There comes a soldier; his bare feet are seen thro' his worn out shoes, his legs nearly naked from the tattered remains of an only pair of stockings, his breeches not sufficient to cover his nakedness, his shirt hanging in strings, his hair dishevelled, his face meagre; his whole appearance pictures a person forsaken and discouraged. He comes, and crys with an air of wretchedness and despair, I am sick, my feet lame, my legs are sore, my body covered with this tormenting itch. My cloaths are worn out, my constitution is broken, my former activity is exhausted by fitigue, hunger and cold. I fail fast, I shall soon be no more! and all the rewtard I shall get will be: "Poor Will is dead."

People who live at home in luxury and ease, quietly possessing their habitations, enjoying their wives and families in peace, have but a very faint idea of the unpleasing sensations and continual anxiety the man endures who is in a camp, and is the husband and parent of an agreeable family. These same people are willing we should suffer every thing for their benefit and advantage, and yet are the first to condemn us for not doing more!!

December 5.—Quiet. Eat pessimmens, found myself better for their lenient opperation. Went to a house, poor and small, but good food within—eat too much from being so long abstemious, thro' want of palatables. Mankind are never truly thankfull for the benefits of life until they have experienced the want of them. The man who has seen misery knows best how to enjoy good. He who is always at ease and has enough of the blessings of common life is an impotent judge of the feelings of the unfortunate. . . .

December 16.—Cold rainy day. Baggage ordered over the Gulph of our division, which were to march at ten, but the baggage was ordered back and for the first time since we have been here the tents were pitched, to keep the men more comfortable.

"Good morning, Brother Soldier," says one to another, "how are you?" "All wet I thank'e, hope you are so," says the other.

The enemy have been at Chestnut Hill opposite to us near our last encampment the other side Schuylkill, made some ravages, killed two of our horsemen, taken some prisoners. We have done the like by them. . . .

December 21.—Preparations made for huts [soldiers' shelters]. Provisions scarce. Mr. Ellis went homeward—sent a letter to my wife. Heartily wish myself at home. My skin and eyes are almost spoiled with continual smoke. A general cry thro' the camp this evening among the soldiers, "No meat! No meat!" The distant vales echoed back the melancholly sound—"No meat! No meat!" Immitating the noise of crows and owls, also, made a part of the confused musick.

What have you for your dinners, boys? "Nothing but fire cake and water, Sir." At night: "Gentlemen, the supper is ready." What is your supper, lads? "Fire cake and water, Sir."

Very poor beef has been drawn in our camp the greater part of this season. A butcher bringing a quarter of this kind of beef into camp one day who had white buttons on the knees of his breeches, a soldier cries out: "There, there, Tom, is some more of your fat beef. By my soul I can see the butcher's breeches buttons through it."

December 22.—Lay excessive cold and uncomfortable last night. My eyes are started out from their orbits like a rabbit's eyes, occasioned by a great cold and smoke.

What have you got for breakfast, lads? "Fire cake and water, Sir." The Lord send that our Commissary of Purchases may live [on] fire cake and water till their glutted gutts are turned to pasteboard.

Our division are under marching orders this morning. I am ashamed to say it, but I am tempted to steal fowls if I could find them, or even a whole hog, for I feel as if I could eat one. But the impoverished country about us affords but little matter to employ a thief, or keep a clever fellow in good humour. But why do I talk of hunger and hard usage, when so many in the world have not even fire cake and water to eat?

Source: Waldo, Albigence. "Valley Forge, 1777–1778. Diary of Surgeon Albigence Waldo, of the Connecticut Line." *Pennsylvania Magazine of History and Biography* 21 (1897): 299–323.

THE BATTLE OF MONMOUTH COURTHOUSE, JUNE 28, 1778

Testimony in the Court-Martial of General Charles Lee
Lieutenant Colonel Richard Harrison
July 15, 1778

Washington hoped to achieve a major victory over the British regulars at Monmouth Courthouse, but the battle ended as a tactical draw, although the Americans retained the field. Washington had ordered General Charles Lee to attack the retreating British. Instead, Lee retreated—colliding with Washington and his advancing troops. Washington ordered Lee's arrest and court-martial for insubordination. Found guilty, the general was relieved of command for one year. Continental army lieutenant colonel Richard Harrison delivered this testimony at Lee's court-martial.

On the 28th of June, as one of His Excellency's [Washington's] suite, I marched with him till we passed the Meetinghouse near Monmouth. . . . When we came to where the roads forked, His Excellency made a halt for a few minutes, in order to direct a disposition of the army. The wing under General Greene was the ordered to go to the right to prevent the enemy's turning our right flank.

After order was given in this matter, and His Excellency was proceeding down the road, we met a fifer, who appeared to be a good deal frighted. The General asked him whether he was a soldier belonging to the army, and the cause of his returning that way; he answered that he was a soldier, and that the Continental troops that had been advanced were retreating. On this answer the General seemed to be exceedingly surprized, and rather more exasperated, appearing to discredit the account, and threatened the man, if he mentioned a thing of the sort, he would have him whipped.

We then moved on a few paces forward (perhaps about fifty yards) where we met two or three persons more on that road; one was, I think, in the habit of a soldier. The General asked them from whence they came, and whether they belonged to the army; one of them replied that he did, and that all the troops that had been advanced, the whole of them, were retreating. His Excellency still appeared to discredit the account, having not heard any firing except a few cannon a considerable time before. However, the General, or some gentleman in company, observed that, as the report came by different persons, it might be well not wholly to disregard it.

Upon this I offered my services to the General to go forward and to bring him a true account of the situation of matters, and requested that Colonel Fitzgerald might go with me. After riding a very short distance, at the bridge in front of the line that was afterwards formed on the heights, I met part of Colonel Grayson's regiment, as I took it, from some of the officers that I knew. As I was in pursuit of information, I addressed myself to Captain Jones of that regiment and asked him

The Battle of Monmouth Courthouse, June 28, 1778. Mass confusion on the part of the American soldiers led to the court-martial and dismissal of General Charles Lee. *(U.S. Army Center of Military History)*

the cause of the retreat, whether it was general, or whether it was only a particular part of the troops that were coming off. I do not precisely recollect the answer that he gave me; but I think, to the best of my knowledge, he said, "Yonder are a great many more troops in the same situation."

I proceeded and fell in with Lieutenant-Colonel Parke. These troops were rather disordered. The next officer that I was acquainted with was Lieutenant-Colonel William Smith. I addressed myself to Colonel Smith and asked him what was the cause of the troops retreating, as I had come to gain information? who replied that he could not tell, that they had lost but one man. I then proceeded down the line, determined to go to the rear of the retreating troops, and met with Colonel Ogden. I asked him the same question, whether he could assign the cause or give me any information why the troops retreated. He appeared to be exceedingly exasperated and said, "By God! they are flying from a shadow."

I fell in immediately after with Captain Mercer, who is aid-de-camp to Major-General Lee, and, expecting to derive some information from him, I put the same question to him. Captain Mercer seemed, by the manner of his answer (as I addressed myself to him, saying, "For God's sake, what is the cause of this retreat?"), to be displeased; his answer was, "If you will proceed, you will see the cause; you will see several columns of foot and horse." I replied to Captain Mercer that I presumed that the enemy was not in greater force than when they left Philadelphia, and we came to that field to meet columns of foot and horse.

The next field-officer I met was Lieutenant-Colonel Rhea, of New Jersey, who appeared to be conducting a regiment. I asked him uniformly the same question for information, and he appeared to be very much agitated, expressed his disapprobation of the retreat, and seemed to be equally concerned (or perhaps more) that he had no place assigned to go where the troops were to halt.

About this time I met with General Maxwell; and, agreeable to the General's direction to get intelligence, I asked him the cause. He appeared to be as much at a loss as Lieutenant-Colonel Rhea or any other officer I had met with; and intimated that he had received no orders upon the occasion and was totally in the dark what line of conduct to pursue.

I think nearly opposite to the point of wood where the first stand was made, I saw General Lee. I do not recollect that anything passed between us, but General Lee's asking me where General Washington was, and my telling him that he was in the rear advancing.

I then went to the extreme of the retreating troops, which were formed of Colonel Stewart's regiment, and found them in the field where the enemy retreated to, just beyond the defile. I addressed myself to General Wayne, General Scott and, I believe, to Colonel Stewart, and to several other officers who were there; and asked General Wayne the cause of the retreat, who seemed no otherwise concerned than at the retreat itself, told me he believed it was impossible to tell the cause; and while we were standing together, which I supposed might be three or four minutes, the enemy's light infantry and grenadiers came issuing out of the wood, pressing very hard upon us at about two or three or four hundred yards distance. The troops that had been halted were put in motion.

I had some conversation with General Wayne relative to a disposition of the troops, if nothing could be done to check the advance of the enemy, who seemed to consider the matter exceedingly practicable, provided any effort or exertion was made for the purpose, alledging that a very select body of men had been that day drawn off from a body far inferior in number. General Wayne then told me that as General Washington might not be perfectly well acquainted with the country, it might be well to advise him of a road, if I met him, that led by Taylor's Tavern, on which it would be necessary to throw a body of troops, in

case the enemy should attempt to turn our right flank.

I, upon this, left General Wayne and galloped down the line to meet General Washington, to report to him the state of our troops and the progress of the enemy. I met General Washington at the point of wood, or near it, where the first stand was made, and reported to him what I had seen, adding that the enemy was pressing hard and would be upon him in a march of fifteen minutes; which (I have since understood) was the first information he received of the enemy being so close upon our retreating troops. We remained there a few minutes until the extreme rear of our retreating troops got up.

Source: Harrison, Richard. "Testimony of Lieutenant Colonel Richard Harrison." *New York Historical Society Collections* 6 (1783): 71–75.

Account of Molly Pitcher
Sergeant Joseph P. Martin
Published 1830

The Battle of Monmouth Courthouse produced the celebrated legend of "Molly Pitcher," the sobriquet bestowed on a woman who may have fought in the battle, or who may be a composite of more than one woman. It is also possible that she is entirely fictional.

The nickname "Molly Pitcher" may have been applied to any number of women who volunteered to carry water to men on the battlefield—not for the purpose of drinking, but to swab out cannon barrels between shots so as to prevent glowing embers from prematurely igniting the powder as the cannon was being loaded. If the Molly Pitcher associated with the Battle of Monmouth Courthouse was a real figure, she was probably Mary Ludwig Hays McCauley, wife of the artilleryman William Hays. When Hays was wounded or felled by sunstroke at Monmouth, Mary Hays reportedly took his place at his cannon. Legend has it that, after the battle, Washington personally issued the warrant of a noncommissioned officer in her name.

Whatever this woman's role in the war, in 1822 the state of Pennsylvania awarded her an annual pension of $40 in recognition of her service. She died in 1832, at age 78.

Sergeant Joseph P. Martin, who fought at Monmouth, left the following sketch of "Molly Pitcher."

One little incident happened during the heat of the cannonade, which I was eye-witness to, and which I think would be unpardonable not to mention. A woman whose husband belonged to the Artillery, and who was then attached to a piece in the engagement, attended with her husband at the piece the whole time. While in the act of reaching a cartridge and having one of her feet as far before the other as she could step, a cannon shot from the enemy passed directly between her legs without doing any other damage than carrying away all the lower part of her petticoat. Looking at it with apparent unconcern, she observed that it was lucky it did not pass a little higher, for in case it might have carried away something else, and continued her occupation.

Source: Martin, Joseph Plumb. *A Narrative of Some of the Adventures, Dangers and Sufferings of a Revolutionary Soldier*. Hallowell, Me.: Privately printed, 1830, pp. 96–97.

THE CAPTURE OF KASKASKIA, JULY 4, 1778

Letter to George Mason
George Rogers Clark
November 19, 1779

While General John Sullivan and others fought the Indians on the northeastern frontier, the Virginia militia leader George Rogers Clark (1752–1818) attacked them throughout the Old Northwest—the Ohio Country. One of his key triumphs was the capture of the British frontier stronghold at Kas-

kaskia in what is now Illinois. Clark reported the circumstances of the event in a letter of November 19, 1779, to George Mason of Virginia.

I set out from Red Stone the 12th of May, 1778, leaving the country in great confusion, much distressed by the Indians. General Hand, pleased with my intentions, furnished me with every necessary I wanted, and the —— of May I arrived at the Canoweay (Kanawha) to the joy of the garrison, as they were very weak and had the day before been attacted by a large body of Indians. Being joined by Capt. Oharrads company on his way to the Osark, after spending a day or two we set out and had a very pleasant voyage to the Falls of Ohio, having sent expresses to the stations on Kentucky from the mouth of the river for Capt. Smith to join me immediately, as I made no doubt but that he was wateing for me. But you may easily guess at my mortification on being informed that he had not arrived; that all his men had been stopt by the incessant labours of the populace, except part of a company that had arrived under the command of one Capt. Delland, some on their march being threatened to be put in prison if they did not return. This information made me as desperate as I was before determined. . . .

I knew that my case was desperate, but the more I reflected on my weakness the more I was pleased with the enterprise. Joined by a few of the Kentuckians, under Col. Montgomery, to stop the desertion I knew would ensue on troops knowing their destination, I had encamped on a small island in the middle of the Falls, kept strict guard on the boats, but Lieutenant Hutchings of Dillards Company contrived to make his escape with his party after being refused leave to return. Luckily a few of his men was taken the next day by a party sent after them. On this island I first began to discipline my little army, knowing that to be the most essential point towards success. Most of them determined to follow me. The rest seeing no probability of making their escape, I soon got that subbordination as I could wish for. About twenty families that had followed me much against my inclination I found now to be of service to me in guarding a block house that I had erected on the island to secure my provisions.

I got every thing in readiness on the 26th of June, set off from the Falls, double manned our oars and proceeded day and night until we run into the mouth of the Tenesse River. The fourth day landed on an island to prepare ourselves for a march by land. A few hours after we took a boat of hunters but eight days from Kaskaskias; before I would suffer them to answer any person a question after their taking the oath of allegiance, I examined them particularly. They were Englishmen, and appeared to be in our interest; their intiligence was not favourable; they asked leave to go on the expedition granted it, . . .

In the evening of the same day I run my boats into a small creek about one mile above the old Fort Missack, reposed ourselves for the night, and in the morning took a rout to the northwest and had a very fatigueing journey for about fifty miles, until we came into those level plains that is frequent throughout this extensive country. As I knew my success depended on secrecy, I was much afraid of being discovered in these meadows, as we might be seen in many places for several miles. Nothing extraordinary happened dureing our route excepting my guide loosing himself and not being able, as we judged by his confusion, of giving a just account of himself; it put the whole troops in the greatest confusion.

I never in my life felt such a flow of rage—to be wandering in a country where every nation of Indians could raise three or four times our number, and a certain loss of our enterprise by the enemie's getting timely notice. I could not bear the thoughts of returning; in short every idea of the sort served to put me in that passion that I did not master for some time; but in a short time after our circumstance had a better appearance, for I was in a moment determined to put the

guide to death if he did not find his way that evening. He begged that I would not be hard with him, that he could find the path that evening; he accordingly took his course and in two hours got within his knowledge.

On the evening of the 4th of July we got within three miles of the town Kaskaskias, having a river of the same name to cross to the town. After making ourselves ready for anything that might happen, we marched after night to a farm that was on the same side of the river about a mile above the town, took the family prisoners, and found plenty of boats to cross in; and in two hours transported ourselves to the other shore with the greatest silence.

I learned that they had some suspician of being attacted and had made some preparations, keeping out spies, but they, making no discoveries, had got off their guard. I immediately divided my little army into two divisions, ordered one to surround the town, with the other I broke into the fort, secured the Governour Mr. Rochblave, in 15 minutes had every street secured, sent runners through the town ordering the people on the pane of death to keep close to their houses, which they observed and before daylight had the whole disarmed; nothing could excell the confusion these people seemed to be in, being taught to expect nothing but savage treatment from the Americans. Giving all for lost, their lives were all they could dare beg for, which they did with the greatest fervancy; they were willing to be slaves to save their families. I told them it did not suit me to give an answer at that time. They repared to their houses, trembling as if they were led to execution; my principal would not suffer me to distress such a number of people, except through policy it was necessary. A little reflection convinced me that it was my interest to attach them to me, according to my first plan; for the town of Cohos [Cahokia] and St. Vincents [Vincennes] and the numerous tribes of Indians attached to the French was yet to influence, for I was too weak to treat them any other way. . . .

As soon as they were a little moderated they told me that they had always been kept in the dark as to the dispute between America and Britain; that they had never heard any thing before but what was prejuditial and tended to insence them against the Americans, that they were now convinced that it was a cause they ought to espouse; that they should be happy of an opportunity to convince me of their zeal, and think themselves the happyest people in the world if they were united with the Americans. . . .

The priest that had lately come from Canada had made himself a little acquainted with our dispute; contrary to the principal of his brother in Canada was rather prejudiced in favour of us. He asked if I would give him liberty to perform his duty in his church. I told him that I had nothing to do with churches more than to defend them from insult; that by the laws of the state his religion had as great previledges as any other. This seemed to compleat their happiness. They returned to their families, and in a few minutes the scean [scene] of mourning and destress was turned to an excess of joy, nothing else seen nor heard—addorning the streets with flowers and pavilians of different colours, compleating their happiness by singing, etc.

In meantime I prepared a detachment on horseback, under Capt. Bowman, to make a descent on Cohos, about sixty miles up the country. The inhabitants told me that one of their townsmen was enough to put me in possession of that place by carrying the good news that the people would rejoice. However, I did not altogether chuse to trust them, dispatched the captain, attended by a considerable number of the inhabitants, who got into the middle of the town before they were discovered; the French gentlemen calling aloud to the people to submit to their happier fate, which they did with very little hesitation. . . .

Source: Clark, George Rogers. Letter to George Mason, November 19, 1779. George Rogers Clark Papers, 1771–1781. Collections of the Illinois State Historical Library 8 (1912).

SULLIVAN'S PUNITIVE CAMPAIGN ON THE INDIAN FRONTIER, SUMMER 1779

Diary Entries
Lieutenant William Barton
June–August 1779

Raids by mixed forces of Tories and British-allied Indians in Pennsylvania's Wyoming Valley and New York's Cherry Valley prompted George Washington to send General John Sullivan on punitive expedition in the region. Sullivan's assignment was to kill as many hostile Indians as he encountered and to destroy their villages, livestock, and stocks of food. One of his officers, Lieutenant William Barton (1754–1829), kept a journal of the expedition.

Tuesday, June 8th, 1779.—Took leave of my friends and set out to join the regiment at Wyoming: arrived at Easton the same evening where I found the second and third Jersey regiments and one company of our regiment which was left behind to take care of the baggage belonging to it, and was the next day to proceed with it on horses to Wyoming. . . .

[July] 31st.—The army marched at 12 o'clock, after signals being given by a discharge of cannon from the fort, which were immediately answered from the boats, which carried all the artillery and stores, excepting some kegs of flour, which were carried on horses—Gen. Hand, having previously advanced about one mile, being appointed to the light corps on this expedition. The whole proceeded, only our regiment, which composed the rear guard, having in charge stragglers, cattle, etc., which occasioned us to march very slow. After a tedious march, came to some cleared fields one mile distant from Lackawannah, then 11 P.M. . . .

[*August*] *26th.*—At half past 12 P.M. began our march with several pieces of cannon, which caused us to move very slowly, as we had formed a hollow square, in which the pack horses and cattle were all driven together with the cannon. This day received information that Col. Broadhead, with six hundred troops, was within forty miles of the Senakee [Seneca] castle, and had destroyed almost one whole tribe of Indians by strategem; he painted his men like Indians, with cutting their hair, etc. We this day likewise received intelligence of Count De Estaing's victory over the British fleet, and having taken the island of St. Vincents. This day marched about four miles and encamped at 5 P.M. near a large flat, on the north-east side of Cahuga Creek. This day's march through a level land, but very poor, excepting the flats, which are good, grown up with grass of great height.

Sunday, 29th.—Proceeded very slowly two miles, occasioned by the roughness of the way, which we had to clear for the artillery, baggage, etc., to pass. Here we halted for one hour and a half, until the artillery, etc., should raise a difficult height, at which time an advanced party of our riflemen discovered the enemy throwing up some works on the other side of a morass, and a difficult place through which we had to pass. It appears this was intended for an ambuscade, it being on a small height, where some logs, etc., were laid up, covered with green bushes; which extended half a mile. On the right was a small town which they had destroyed themselves, making use of the timber, etc., in the above works. After the ground was well reconnoitered, the artillery was advanced on their left. At the same time Gen'l Poor with his brigade was endeavoring to gain their rear around their left; Gen'l Hand's brigade was following in rear of Poor. Our brigade was kept us a reserve, as also Gen'l Clinton's, until their rear should be gained; but they having a party posted on a very considerable height, over which our right flank had to pass, we were discovered by them.

Previous to this, some shells and round shot were thrown among them in their works, which caused them to give several yells, and doubtless intimidated them much. But at this discovery they gave a most hideous yell and quit their works, endeavoring to prevent Gen'l Poor's ascending the height by a loose scattering fire; but our troops, pressing forward with much vigor, made them give way, leaving their dead behind (amounting to eleven or twelve), which were scalped immediately. We likewise took one white man, who appeared to be dead, and was stripped, when an officer came up and examined him, said he was not wounded, gave him a stroke and bade him get up; he immediately rose up and implored mercy, and was kept a prisoner some time. In the evening a Negro was taken. Their number wounded not known. Two or three of ours killed, and thirty-four or five wounded. Among the latter Major Titcomb, Capt. Cloise, and Lt. Allis.

At half after three the firing ceased, and the army proceeded one mile and a half to a considerable town consisting of about twenty huts. The number of the enemy uncertain, but from the best intelligence from the prisoners, the whites were about two hundred, the Indians five. They were commanded by Butler and Brant, who had been waiting some days for our approach. It appears their expectations were great, from their numbers, situation, etc. The prisoners likewise inform us they had been kept on an allowance of seven ears of corn per day each although there is a very great abundance of corn, beans, potatoes, squashes, etc., for several miles on the creek, upon which our whole army has subsisted for days. We had nevertheless to destroy some hundred bushels. Here was found a deal of plunder of theirs, such as blankets, brass kettles, etc.

Monday [*September*] *13th.*—At half past four, morning, proceeded one mile and a half; came to a considerable town, Canesaah, consisting of from sixteen to twenty huts, and halted for the troops to get some refreshment and to build a bridge across a creek; meantime a party of twenty-six men, commanded by Lt. Boyd, was sent out to a town about six miles for discovery, at which place he arrived without molestation.

Here an Indian was killed and scalped by his party. He then dispatched two men to inform us what had happened; after they had gone two miles they saw five Indians. They immediately ran back and told the lieutenant what they had seen, who marched on to the place with all speed, when he discovered some few of them who retreated; he pursued and killed one of them. The men then went to scalp him, which caused some dispute who should have it; at the same instant the enemy rose up from their ambuscade, when the action commenced, but they being much superior in numbers, caused him and one or two others to surrender, though not until the rest were all killed and got off.

About the same time, Capt. Lodge, surveyor of the road, with a small party, was discovered about one mile beyond, where the party was building a bridge. They were fired on by the Indians and one of his men wounded. The rest ran off and were pursued so closely that one of them drew out his tomahawk and was close on the heels of one of our men, when a sentinel from the party at the bridge fired at the Indian, which caused them all to run off. Major Poor immediately pushed on, hearing the firing, and found the knapsacks, etc., of the Indians, who had all run off on his approach.

At two o'clock the bridge being completed, we marched on to a town, Casawavalatetah, where we arrived about dark, in expectation of an attack, and encamped. Land continuing very fertile; at both of these places was a large quantity of corn; at the former we did not destroy all.

Tuesday, 14th.—Early in the morning was ordered to destroy the corn, which we did by throwing the ears into the creek, which runs close to the town and is a branch of the Canisee [Genesee] River, which empties into the Lake Ontario about fourteen miles hence. At 2 P.M. marched and crossed the creek, and forded the main branch of Canisee, and proceeded four miles down to the Chenisee castle, where we arrived about four P.M. At this place was Lieut. Boyd and one soldier found, with their heads

cut off; the Lieutenants head lay near his body; his body appeared to have been whipped and pierced in many different places. The others head was not found. A great part of his body was skinned, leaving the ribs bare.

Wednesday, 15th.—The whole army employed until 3 o'clock in gathering the corn, and burning it in their huts, which were in number about eighty or a hundred, and much the largest quantity of corn I have yet seen in any one place since I have been out. Here came in a white woman with a young child, who was almost starved, having made her escape two or three nights before from the enemy. She informs us they were in great confusion, the Indians some times agreeing to treat with us, but it was made void by Butler and Johnson, who promised to supply them with provisions. One of the Indians at this cocked his gun and was about to shoot Johnson, but was prevented. This woman was taken from Wyoming in '77, where her husband was killed. At half past two P.M. we began our march for returning, and proceeded as far as the fording place of the creek, crossed onto, encamping near the town Casawavalatetah. This place very rich and good. Distance from here to Niagaree said to be about eighty miles, whither the Indians carry all their furs, etc., for sale. They go and return in canoes in five or six days.

Thursday, 23rd.—Proceeded to Catharine town, at which place we arrived at twelve o'clock, finding the old squaw here which was left as we went up, with a paper that had many lines of Indian wrote underneath, a protection that was given her by the general, the contents of which I did not hear. We likewise found the corpse of a squaw who appeared to have been shot three or four days, which lay in a mud hole, supposed to have came there since our departure to take care of the old brute. Who killed her I cannot ascertain, but it is generally believed to be three men of ours who were sent up from Tioga express a few days before. At our departure from here the General ordered there should be left a keg of pork and some biscuit, etc., for the old creature to subsist on, although it was so scare an article that no officer under the rank of a field officer had tasted any since leaving Tioga, and a very scant allowance of half a pound of poor beef and a like quantity of flour.

Proceeded at two o'clock about three miles through a swamp of exceeding bad road for the pioneers to repair them and halted for the army's arrival, which was at five o'clock P.M., on a small flat of cleared ground, and encamped. Distance of day's march from 16 to 18 miles. This evening we, the advance guard, had orders to march at reveille for the purpose of having the roads repaired through a most notorious swamp of five miles, and appearance of rain, which would render the swamp almost impassable.

Sunday, 26th.—Still remained at Fort Reed. In the morning there was a detachment of three hundred men ordered to be sent up the river Kihuga [Cayuga] for the purpose of destroying a town or two, but was defered by reason of rain coming. At one in the afternoon the detachment under Col. Durbin, that came down the south of the Kihuga lake, arrived with two squaws, and inform us they burnt three or four towns. They likewise say they found one Indian and one other squaw, the latter so old as not to be able to be brought off; the Indian man young but decrepid to such a degree that he could not walk. I have since heard it said, the Colonel left one house standing for them to stay in, and would not suffer them to be hurt, but some of the soldiers taking an opportunity when not observed set the house on fire, after securing and making the door fast. The troops having got in motion and marched some distance, the house was consumed together with the savages, in spite of all exertions.

Monday, 27th.—The morning clear. The detachment yesterday detained by rain has gone out with an addition of two hundred men more, and divided into two parties, one under the command of Col. Courtland, and the other under Col. D'Hart; one going up the north side, and the other the south of the Kihuga Creek. In the

evening the detachments came in, after destroying a considerable quantity of corn, etc.

Tuesday, 28th.—The same detachment again sent out an account of a small party being sent farther up, who say there is a large quantity of corn yet standing on the creek. About ten o'clock A.M. the detachment under Col. Butler came in from the north of Kihuga Lake, who say they have destroyed vast quantities of corn and several very considerable of their towns. . . .

Source: New York (State) Secretary of State. *Journals of the Military Expedition of Major General John Sullivan against the Six Nations of Indians in 1779 with Records of the Centennial Celebrations,* edited by Frederick Cook, 3–13. Augburn, N.Y.: Knapp, Peck & Thomson, 1887.

Diary Entry
Major Jeremiah Fogg
September 30, 1779

Jeremiah Fogg was born in 1749, the son of Reverend Jeremiah Fogg of Kensington, New Hampshire. He graduated from Harvard College in 1768, taught school, and then studied law before joining the staff of Colonel Enoch Poor at the outbreak of the Revolutionary War in 1775. His journal, kept during his service with the Sullivan expedition, was published privately in Exeter, New Hampshire, in 1879 in an edition of 150 copies. Fogg makes it clear that Sullivan's army visited great destruction on the Indians yet had achieved nothing strategically definitive.

[*September*] *30th, 1779.* Arrived at Tioga about 3 o'clock, where we were saluted by thirteen cannon from the fort. From hence we have water carriage to Wyoming, a most fortunate affair as our horses are worn down and our men are naked.

Although we are, now, one hundred and twenty miles from peaceful inhabitants, yet we consider ourselves at home, and the expedition ended; having fulfilled the expectations of our country by beating the enemies and penetrating and destroying their whole country. The undertaking was great and the task arduous. The multiplicity of disappointments, occasioning a long delay at the beginning, foreboded a partial, if not a total frustration of our design; but the unbounded ambition and perseverance of our commander and army led him to the full execution contrary to our most sanguine expectations.

The army marched from Tioga, with twenty pounds of beef and twenty seven pounds of flour per man, with which they marched twenty days out through an enemy's country yet unexplored with five pieces of artillery; having a road to clear, through swamps and over mountains a hundred and fifty miles; after having marched three hundred [miles] from their winter quarters; a cruel, subtle and desultory foe to contend with; void of hospital stores and conveniences for the sick and wounded; scarcely able to move for want of means of transportation. One battle, at the extent of our route, must have been attended with consequences such as nothing but the event itself could ascertain; yet a march of three hundred miles was performed, a battle was fought and a whole country desolated in thirty days.

But let us not arrogate too much, for "The battle is not to the strong" is a proverb fully verified in this expedition; the special hand and smiles of Providence being so apparently manifested that he who views the scene with indifference is worse than an infidel. The dimest eye must observe through the whole a succession of most unfortunate events. The very evils that at first predicted a defeat were a chain of causes in our favor. (I mean our delay.) Had we marched when we wished we could not have had a general engagement; for a great scarcity amounting almost to a famine the preceding year had prevented their embodying until the growth of the present crop, and we must therefore have been harassed daily by small parties much to our disadvantage. The artillery, which at first seemed a clog and totally useless, served a noble purpose. The action being general, their total rout together with the thunder of our artillery impressed them with such a terrific idea of our importance that a universal panic struck both the sachem and the warrior, each finding full employment in removing his little ones from threatening danger.

The place of action was likewise remarkable, having water carriage for our wounded. Not a single gun was fired for eighty miles on our march out, or an Indian seen on our return. Then we expected the greatest harassment—a hundred might have saved half their country by retarding us until our provisions were spent; and a like number hanging on our rear in the return would have occasioned the loss of much baggage and taught us an Indian dance. Their corn and vegetables were half our support, which we should have been deprived of had our march been earlier. And to say no more, the extraordinary continuance of fair weather has infinitely facilitated our expectations, having never been detained a single day, nor has there been an hour's rain since the thirtieth day of August.

The question will naturally arise, What have you to show for your exploits? Where are your prisoners? To which I reply that the rags and emaciated bodies of our soldiers must speak for our fatigue, and when the querist will point out a mode to tame a partridge, or the expediency of hunting wild turkeys with light horse, I will show them our prisoners. The nests are destroyed, but the birds are still on the wing.

Source: New York (State) Secretary of State. *Journals of the Military Expedition of Major General John Sullivan against the Six Nations of Indians in 1779 with Records of the Centennial Celebrations,* edited by Frederick Cook, 101. Augburn, N.Y.: Knapp, Peck & Thomson, 1887.

BONHOMME RICHARD V. HMS *SERAPIS,* SEPTEMBER 23, 1779

Account of the Battle
Lieutenant Richard Dale
Published 1825

Richard Dale (1756–1826) was born near Norfolk, Virginia; went to sea when he was 12, became a lieutenant in the Virginia state navy in 1776; and, captured by the British, briefly joined the Royal Navy. Wounded, he convalesced ashore in America and resolved "never again to put himself in the way of the bullets of his own countrymen," according to the author John Henry Sherburne. He enlisted as a midshipman on the American brig Lexington; was captured; escaped; was recaptured; escaped again; and, disguised as a British naval officer, reached France, where he joined John Paul Jones's squadron as master's mate. Quickly promoted to first lieutenant of the Bonhomme Richard, he fought alongside Jones in the battle with the Serapis on September 23, 1779.

On the 23d of September, 1779, being below, was roused by an unusual noise upon deck. This induced me to go upon deck when I found the men were swaying up the royal yards, preparatory to making sail for a large fleet under our lee. I asked the coasting pilot what fleet it was?

He answered, "The Baltic fleet under convoy of the Serapis of 44 guns and the Countess of Scarborough of 20 guns."

A general chase then commenced of the Bon Homme Richard, the Vengeance, the Pallas and the Alliance, the latter ship being then in sight after a separation from the squadron of nearly three weeks, but which ship, as usual, regarded the private signals of the Commodore. At this time our fleet headed to the northward with a light breeze, Flamborough Head being about o leagues distant. At 7 P.M. it was evident the Baltic fleet perceived we were in chace from the signal of the Serapis to the merchantmen to stand in shore. At the same time the Serapis and Countess of Scarborough tacked ship and stood off shore, with the intention of drawing off our attention from the convoy. When these ships had separated from the convoy about two miles, they again tacked and stood in shore after the merchantmen.

Engagement between the Bonhomme Richard and the Serapis, September 23, 1779 (Naval Historical Foundation)

At about eight, being within hail, the *Serapis* demanded, "What ship is that?"

He was answered, "I can't hear what you say."

Immediately after, the *Serapis* hailed again, "What ship is that? Answer immediately, or I shall be under the necessity of firing into you."

At this moment I received orders from Commodore Jones to commence the action with a broadside, which indeed appeared to be simultaneous on board both ships. Our position being to windward of the *Serapis* we passed ahead of her, and the *Serapis* coming up on our larboard quarter, the action commenced abreast of each other. The *Serapis* soon passed ahead of the *Bon Homme Richard*, and when he thought he had gained a distance sufficient to go down athwart the fore foot to rake us, found he had not enough distance, and that the *Bon Homme Richard* would be aboard him, put his helm a-lee, which brought the two ships on a line, and the *Bon Homme Richard*, having head way, ran her bows into the stern of the *Serapis*.

We had remained in this situation but a few minutes when we were again hailed by the *Serapis*, "Has your ship struck?" [that is, struck colors—surrendered]

To which Captain Jones answered, "I have not yet begun to fight!"

As we were unable to bring a single gun to bear upon the *Serapis* our topsails were backed, while those of the *Serapis* being filled, the ships separated. The *Serapis* bore short round upon her heel, and her jibboom ran into the mizen rigging of the *Bon Homme Richard*. In this situation the ships were made fast together with a hawser, the bowsprit of the *Serapis* to the mizenmast of the *Bon Homme Richard*, and the action recommenced from the starboard sides of the two ships. With a view of separating the ships, the *Serapis* let go her anchor, which manoeuver brought her head and the stern of the *Bon Homme Richard* to the wind, while the ships lay closely pressed against each other.

A novelty in naval combats was now presented to many witnesses, but to few admirers. The rammers were run into the respective ships to enable the men to load after the lower ports of the *Serapis* had been blown away, to make room for running out their guns, and in this situation the ships remained until between 10 and 11 o'clock P.M., when the engagement terminated by the surrender of the *Serapis*.

From the commencement to the termination of the action there was not a man on board the *Bon Homme Richard* ignorant of the superiority of the *Serapis*, both in weight of metal and in the qualities of the crews. The crew of that ship was picked seamen, and the ship itself had been only a few months off the stocks, whereas the crew of the *Bon Homme Richard* consisted of part Americans, English and French, and a part of Maltese, Portuguese and Malays, these latter contributing by their want of naval skill and knowledge of the English language to depress rather than to elevate a just hope of success in a combat under such circumstances. Neither the consideration of the relative force of the ships, the fact of the blowing up of the gundeck above them by the bursting of two of the 18-pounders, nor the alarm that the ship was sinking, could depress the ardor or change the determination of the brave Captain Jones, his officers and men. Neither the repeated broadsides of the *Alliance*, given with the view of sinking or disabling the *Bon Homme Richard*, the frequent necessity of suspending the combat to extinguish the flames, which several times were within a few inches of the magazine, nor the liberation by the master-at-arms of nearly 500 prisoners, could charge or weaken the purpose of the American commander. At the moment of the liberation of the prisoners, one of them, a commander of a 20-gun ship taken a few days before, passed through the ports on board the *Serapis* and informed Captain Pearson that if he would hold out only a little while longer, the ship alongside would either strike or sink, and that all the prisoners had been released to save their lives. The combat was accordingly continued with renewed ardor by the *Serapis*.

The fire from the tops of the *Bon Homme Richard* was conducted with so much skill and effect as to destroy ultimately every man who appeared upon the quarter deck of the *Serapis*, and induced her commander to order the survivors to go below. Nor even under the shelter of the decks were they more secure. The powder-monkies of the *Serapis*, finding no officer to receive the 18-pound cartridges brought from the magazines, threw them on the main deck and went for more. These cartridges being scattered along the deck and numbers of them broken, it so happened that some of the hand-grenades thrown from the main-yard of the *Bon Homme Richard*, which was directly over the main-hatch of the *Serapis*, fell upon this powder and produced a most awful explosion. The effect was tremendous; more than twenty of the enemy were blown to pieces, and many stood with only the collars of their shirts upon their bodies. In less than an hour afterward, the flag of England, which had been nailed to the mast of the *Serapis*, was struck by Captain Pearson's *own hand*,° as none of his people would venture aloft on this duty; and this too when more than 1500 persons were witnessing the conflict, and the humiliating termination of it, from Scarborough and Flamborough Head.

Upon finding that the flag of the *Serapis* had been struck, I went to Captain Jones and asked whether I might board the *Serapis*, to which he consented, and jumping upon the gun-wale, seized the main-brace pennant and swung myself upon her quarter-deck. Midshipman Mayrant followed with a party of men and was immediately run through the thigh with a boarding pike by some of the enemy stationed in the waist, who were not informed of the surrender of their ship.

I found Captain Pearson standing on the leeward side of the quarter-deck and, addressing myself to him, said, "Sir, I have orders to send you on board the ship alongside." The first lieutenant of the *Serapis* coming up at this moment inquired of Captain Pearson whether the ship alongside had struck to him. To which I replied, "No, Sir, the contrary: he has struck to us."

The lieutenant renewed his inquiry, "Have you struck, Sir?"

"Yes, I have."

The lieutenant replied, "I have nothing more to say," and was about to return below when I informed him he must accompany Captain Pearson on board the ship alongside. He said, "If you will permit me to go below, I will silence the firing of the lower-deck guns."

This request was refused, and with Captain Pearson, he was passed over to the deck of the *Bon Honnne Richard*. Orders being sent below to cease firing, the engagement terminated, after a most obstinate contest of three hours and a half.

Upon receiving Captain Pearson on board the *Bon Homme Richard*, Captain Jones gave orders to cut loose the lashings, and directed me to follow him with the *Serapis*. Perceiving the *Bon Homme Richard* leaving the *Serapis*, I sent one of the quartermasters to ascertain whether the wheel-ropes were cut away, supposing something extraordinary must be the matter, as the ship would not pay off, although the head sails were aback, and no after sail; the quartermaster, returning, reported that the wheel-ropes were all well, and the helm hard a-port. Excited by this extraordinary circumstance, I jumped off the binnacle, where I had been sitting, and falling upon the deck, found to my astonishment I had the use of only one of my legs. A splinter of one of the guns had struck and badly wounded my leg without my perceiving the injury until this moment. I was replaced upon the binnacle, when the sailing-master of the *Serapis* coming up to me observed that from my orders he judged I must be ignorant of the ship being at anchor. Noticing the second lieutenant of the *Bon Homme Richard*, I directed him to go below and cut away the cable, and follow the *Bon Homme Richard* with the *Serapis*. I was then carried on board the *Bon Homme Richard* to have my wound dressed.

°Captain Pearson subsequently stated: "I found it in vain, and indeed impracticable from the situation we were in, to stand out any longer with the least prospect to success. I therefore struck." [original footnote]

Source: Sherburne, John Henry. *Life and Character of the Chevalier John Paul Jones, a Captain in the Navy of the United States, during Their Revolutionary War.* Washington, D.C.: Wilder and Campbell, 1825, pp. 126–129.

Memoirs
Nathaniel Fanning
Published 1806 and 1808

Nathaniel Fanning (1755–1805), an officer in the Continental navy and later a lieutenant the U.S. Navy, served as a midshipman on the Bonhomme Richard *during its 1779 battle with HMS* Serapis. *Born in Stonington, Connecticut, Fanning was the son of a merchant sea captain who was a key provisioner of the Continental army during the American Revolution. He was captured in 1778 by the British and exchanged the following year. He ended up in France, where he met John Paul Jones and agreed to serve as a midshipman as well as Jones's private secretary. The narrative that follows is excerpted from Fanning's memoirs, which were published posthumously in 1806 and again in 1808. This passage was printed in* The Spirit of Seventy-Six, *edited by Henry Steele Commager and Richard B. Morris.*

The battle had now continued about three hours, and as we, in fact, had possession of the *Serapis's* top, which commanded her quarter-deck, upper gun-deck and forecastle, we were well assured that the enemy could not hold out much longer, and were momently expecting that they would strike [surrender] to us, when the following farcical piece was acted on board our ship.

It seems that a report was at this time circulated among our crew between deck, and was credited among them, that Captain Jones and all his principal officers were slain, the gunners were now the commanders of our ship, that the ship had four or five feet of water in her hold, and that she was then sinking. They therefore advised the gunner to go up on deck, together with the carpenter and master at arms, and beg of the enemy quarters, in order, as they said, to save their lives.

These three men, being thus delegated, mounted the quarter-deck, and bawled out as loud as they could, "Quarters, quarters, for God's sake, quarters! Our ship is sinking!" and immediately got upon the ship's poop with a view of hauling down our colours.

Hearing this in the top, I told my men that the enemy had struck and was crying out for quarters, for I actually thought that the voices of these men sounded as if on board of the enemy; but in this I was soon undeceived. The three poltroons, finding the ensign and ensign-staff gone, they proceeded upon the quarter-deck, and were in the act of hauling down our pennant, still bawling for "quarters!" when I heard our commodore say in a loud voice, "What d——d rascals are them?—Shoot them!—Kill them!" He was upon the forecastle when these fellows first made their appearance upon the quarter-deck where he had just discharged his pistols at some of the enemy. The carpenter and the master-at-arms, hearing Jones's voice, sculked below, and the gunner was attempting to do the same when Jones threw both of his pistols at his head, one of which struck him in the head, fractured his skull and knocked him down at the foot of the gang-way ladder, where he lay till the battle was over.

Both ships now took fire again; and on board of our ship it communicated to and set our main top on fire, which threw us into the greatest consternation imaginable for some time, and it was not without some exertions and difficulty that it was overcome. The water which we had in a tub, in the fore part of the top, was expended without extinguishing the fire. We next had recourse to our clothes, by pulling off our coats and jackets, and then throwing them upon the fire and stamping upon them, which in a short time smothered it. Both crews were also now, as before, busily employed in stopping the progress of the flames, and the firing on both sides ceased.

The enemy now demanded of us if we had struck, as they had heard the three poltroons halloo for quarters. "If you have," said they, "why don't you haul down your pendant?" as they saw our ensign was gone.

"Ay, ay," said Jones, "we'll do that when we can fight no longer, but we shall see yours come down the first; for you must know that Yankees do not haul down their colours till they are fairly beaten."

The combat now recommenced again with more fury if possible than before, on the part of both, and continued for a few minutes, when the cry of fire was again heard on board of both ships. The firing ceased, and both crews were once more employed in extinguishing it, which was soon effected, when the battle was renewed with redoubled vigour, with what cannon we could manage, hand grenadoes, stink pots, etc., but principally, towards the closing scene, with lances and boarding pikes. With these the combatants killed each other through the ship's port holes, which were pretty large; and the guns that had been run out at them becoming useless, as before observed, had been removed out of the way.

At three quarters past 11 P.M. the *Alliance* frigate hove in sight, approached within pistol shot of our stern and began a heavy and well-directed fire into us as well as the enemy, which made some of our officers as well as men believe that she was an English man of war. (The moon at this time, as though ashamed to behold this bloody scene any longer, retired behind a dark cloud.) It was in vain that some of our officers hailed her and desired them not to fire any more; it was in vain they were told they had slain a number of our men; it was in vain also that they were told that the enemy was fairly beaten, and that she must strike her colours within a few minutes. The *Alliance,* I say, notwithstanding all this, kept a position either ahead of us or under our stern, and made a great deal of havock and confusion on board of our ship; and she did not cease firing entirely till the signal of recognisance was displayed in full view on board of our ship; which was three lighted lanthorns ranged in a horizontal line about fifteen feet high, upon the fore, main and

mizzen shrouds, upon the larboard side. This was done in order to undeceive the *Alliance,* and which had the desired effect, and the firing from her ceased.

And at thirty-five minutes past 12 at night, a single hand grenado having been thrown by one of our men out of the main top of the enemy, designing it to go among the enemy who were huddled together between her gun decks, it on its way struck on one side of the combings of her upper hatchway,° and rebounding from that, it took a direction and fell between their decks, where it communicated to a quantity of loose powder scattered about the enemy's cannon; and the hand grenado bursting at the same time made a dreadful explosion and blew up about twenty of the enemy.

This closed the scene, and the enemy now in their turn (notwithstanding the gasconading of Capt. Parsons [*sic*]) bawled out "Quarters, quarters, quarters, for God's sake!"

It was, however, some time before the enemy's colours were struck. The captain of the *Serapis* gave repeated orders for one of his crew to ascend the quarter-deck and haul down the English flag, but no one would stir to do it. They told the captain they were afraid of our rifle-men, believing that all our men who were seen with muskets were of that description. The captain of the *Serapis* therefore ascended the quarter-deck, and hauled down the very flag which he had nailed to the flag-staff a little before the commencement of the battle, and which flag he had at that time, in the presence of his principal officers, swore he never would strike to that infamous pirate J. P. Jones.

The enemy's flag being struck, Captain Jones ordered Richard Dale, his first lieutenant, to select out of our crew a number of men and take

---

°The hatchways are generally taken off during an action; for this reason, that if anything thrown on board, such as a hand grenado and the like, happens to fall in through the hatchway, it descends down upon the haul-up-deck, where if it bursts it will injure nobody. [original footnote]

possession of the prize, which was immediately put in execution. Several of our men (I believe three) were killed by the English on board of the *Serapis* after she had struck to us, for which they afterwards apologized by saying that the men who were guilty of this breach of honour did not know at the time that their own ship had struck her colours.

Thus ended this ever memorable battle, after a continuance of a few minutes more than four hours. The officers, headed by the captain of the *Serapis* now came on board of our ship; the latter (Captain Parsons) enquired for Captain Jones, to whom he was introduced by Mr. Mase, our purser. They met, and the former accosted the latter, in presenting his sword, in this manner: "It is with the greatest reluctance that I am now obliged to resign you this, for it is painful to me, more partciularly at this time, when compelled to deliver up my sword to a man who may be said to fight with a halter around his neck!"

Jones, after receiving his sword, made this reply: "Sir, you have fought like a hero, and I make no doubt but your sovereign will reward you in a most ample manner for it."

Captain Parsons then asked Jones what countrymen his crew principally consisted of.

The latter said, "Americans."

"Very well," said the former, "it has been diamond cut diamond with us."

Captain Parsons's officers had, previous to coming on board of our ship, delivered their side arms to Lieutenant Dale. Captain Parsons in his conversation with Captain Jones owned that the Americans were equally as brave as the English. The two captains now withdrew into the cabin and there drank a glass or two of wine together. . . .

Source: "'Jones Wins His Greatest Victory Over Again in Lavish Style': Nathaniel Fanning." In *The Spirit of Seventy Six: The Story of the American Revolution as Told by Participants,* edited by Henry Steele Commager and Richard B. Morris, 954–956. New York: Da Capo Press, 1995.

The Siege of Charleston, April 11–May 12, 1780

Diary Entry
Captain Johann Hinrichs
April 24, 1780

Johann Hinrichs was a captain on the staff of a regiment of jägers, *elite Hessian light cavalry troops who collaborated closely with the 42nd Regiment of Foot in the second British campaign to capture Charleston. This diary entry is a rare close-up account of an 18th-century assault operation.*

I was ordered by Major General Leslie at three o'clock this morning to take thirty men and occupy the left of the advanced work, while Lieutenant von Winzingeroda with thirty jägers was to proceed to the right. When I arrived at the part thrown up last night, I had my jägers halt, while I myself and two men inspected the work, for I was aware of our light way of building and knew that we were right under the enemy's outer works. There was not a single traverse in a trench four hundred paces long. I went as far as the enemy's gatework. But as day was breaking, the enemy sent two enfilading shots from their left front redoubt into our trench, one of them enfilading *en flanc* down the entire trench as far as the sap, while the other, *en revers,* struck the back of the parapet a hundred paces this side of the gatework.

I had my two jägers halt at the end of the trench to watch the gatework while I ran back to the British grenadiers in the second parallel. I brought one noncommissioned officer and twelve men (of the grenadier company of the 42nd Regiment) and had a traverse made approximately in the center of the trench. General Leslie came and was surprised that no infantry was here yet. He thanked me for my labors. In the meantime I had my jägers fetch sandbags and lay them on the parapet. While in the trench, which was barely six feet deep where

I stood, I heard a loud yelling in the center, i.e. in the space that was still between the right and the left section of the third parallel. At the same moment the double post I had left standing above fired, and the workmen on the other side of the traverse came running over crying, "D——me, the rebels are there!"

I jumped on the parapet and when I saw the enemy, who were already pressing upon our right wing from a barrier situated at their left-wing front redoubt and were also rushing out of the gatework, I had my workmen seize their muskets, withdrew the two jägers this side of the traverse, and opened a continuous fire along the unoccupied part of the parallel as far as the gatework. The enemy, having penetrated our right wing, were already more than fifty paces behind us, partly between the third and second parallels. I ordered some jägers and Corporal Rübenkönig behind the traverse and had them fire behind the trench across the plain. Now our second parallel began to fire. This made many bullets fall in our rear. But when the second parallel pressed forward on our right wing, the enemy withdrew, leaving twenty muskets behind. But they covered their retreat with so excessive a shower of canisters which were loaded with old burst shells, broken shovels, pickaxes, hatchets, flat-irons, pistol barrels, broken locks, etc., etc. (these pieces we found in our trench), and so enfiladed us at the same time from the front redoubt of their left wing (fifteen balls were embedded in the traverse I had thrown up) that one could hardly hear another close beside him.

It was still dark, and the smoke of the powder was so thick that one could not tell friend from enemy. Since I could not know that the enemy had with drawn, I jumped on the parapet and had my jägers and grenadiers keep up such a hot fire along the trench and upon their embrasures that after half an hour's cannonade the enemy's batteries were silent. A deserter told us in the evening that Colonel Parker and several artillerymen were killed in an embrasure. I suffered no loss except one Englishman slightly wounded with a bayonet. The entire parapet where I stood with my men was razed more than one foot by the enemy's battery. What luck!

Our right wing, where Lieutenant von Winzingeroda was stationed with thirty jägers and twenty-five light infantry, did not get off so well. One light-infantryman was killed, five wounded; two jägers had bayonet wounds and three, one of whom had a bullet wound in the abdomen, were taken prisoners. They were compelled to repair to the second parallel because through the negligence of the English the enemy was upon them too quickly, and without support they could not make a stand with discharged rifles against bayonets.

From Captain Lawson of the artillery I had borrowed two pieces resembling cohort's, taken on the Delaware frigate, which he had changed into swivels. They were made of brass and had a chamber. They served me splendidly today, for my jägers had no more cartridges. (At ten o'clock fifteen fresh men and two companies of light infantry came to support me.) These Lawsons, as I shall call them, threw a hand grenade 1,800 feet. I also fired 100-bullet canisters, 3-pound case shot, and one-half-pound bogy shot, firing in the course of the day 130 shots. The enemy tried to silence me with cannon, a sign that our fire was effective. However, I moved from one place to another with my pieces and sometimes fired three to four 100-bullet canisters into the enemy's embrasures. During the night this part of the parallel, which was pretty well shot to pieces, was repaired again and provided with several traverses. Likewise, a new sap was begun on the left wing of the left section of the third parallel.

The signal that the enemy was making a sortie along the whole line was a threefold "Hurray!" on our side—a fatal signal, indeed! About twenty to thirty of the enemy were seen at the gatework. Our nearest infantry post on guard gave the signal and fired. Everyone repeated the signal; the workmen ran back; the second parallel saw them coming, heard the "Hurray!" believed they were enemies, and fired. Within a short time there was a tremendous fire of musketry, cannon and shell on both sides. It was two o'clock in the morning before everyone realized that it was a mistake. We had an officer killed (71st) and more than fifty [enlisted men] killed and wounded. Besides, our working parties could accomplish little or nothing during the night.

Source: Hinrichs, Johann. Journal. Quoted in *The Siege of Charleston,* edited and translated by Bernard A. Uhlendorf, 117–125. Ann Arbor: University of Michigan Press, 1938.

THE BATTLE OF CAMDEN, AUGUST 16, 1780

Account of the Battle
Deputy Adjutant General Otho Williams
Published 1822

The defeat at Camden, South Carolina, was one of the Patriot humiliations of the war. Colonel Otho Williams (1749–94), deputy adjutant general of the southern army under General Horatio Gates, wrote of the desertion of the militia in his account of the Battle of Camden. It is not known when Williams wrote the narrative, which was first published 28 years after his death.

It has been observed that the direct march of the American army towards Camden and the prospect of considerable re-enforcements of militia had induced the commanding officer, Lord Rawdon, to collect there all the forces under his direction. And it is certain that the seeming confidence of the American general had inspired him with apprehensions for his principal post. Lord Cornwallis, at Charlestown, was constantly advised of the posture of affairs in the interior of the country; and, confident that Lord Rawdon could not long resist the forces that might, and probably would, be opposed to him, in a very short time resolved to march himself, with a considerable re-enforcement, to Camden. He

arrived on [August] 14th and had the discernment at once to perceive that delay would render that situation dangerous, even to his whole force; the disaffection from his late assumed, arbitrary and vindictive power having become general through all the country above General Gates' line of march, as well as to the eastward of Santee and to the westward of Wateree Rivers. He, therefore, took the resolution of attacking the new constituted American army in their open irregular encampment at Clermont. Both armies, ignorant of each other's intentions, moved about the same hour of the same night and, approaching each other, met about half way between their respective encampments at midnight.

The first revelation of this new and unexpected scene was occasioned by a smart, mutual salutation of small arms between the advanced guards. Some of the cavalry of Armand's legion were wounded, retreated and threw the whole corps into disorder; which, recoiling suddenly on the front of the column of infantry, disordered the First Maryland Brigade and occasioned a general consternation through the whole line of the army. The light infantry under Porterfield, however, executed their orders gallantly; and the enemy, no less astonished than ourselves, seemed to acquiesce in a sudden suspension of hostilities.

Some prisoners were taken on both sides. From one of these, the deputy adjutant general of the American army extorted information respecting the situation and numbers of the enemy. He informed that Lord Cornwallis commanded in person about three thousand regular British troops, which were in line of march, about five or six hundred yards in front. Order was soon restored in the corps of infantry in the American army, and the officers were employed in forming a front line of battle when the deputy adjutant general communicated to General Gates the information which he had from the prisoner. The general's astonishment could not be concealed. He ordered the deputy adjutant general to call another council of war. All the general officers immediately assembled in the rear of the line. The unwelcome news was communicated to them.

General Gates said, "Gentlemen, what is best to be done?"

All were mute for a few moments, when the gallant Stevens exclaimed, "Gentlemen, is it not too late now to do any thing but fight?"

No other advice was offered, and the general desired the gentlemen would repair to their respective commands.

The Baron de Kalb's opinion may be inferred from the following fact: When the deputy adjutant general went to call him to council, he first told him what had been discovered. "Well," said the baron, "and has the general given you orders to retreat the army?" The baron, however, did not oppose the suggestion of General Stevens, and every measure that ensued was preparatory for action.

Lieutenant Colonel Porterfield, in whose bravery and judicious conduct great dependence was placed, received in the first rencontre a mortal wound (as it long afterwards proved) and was obliged to retire. His infantry bravely kept the ground in front; and the American army were formed in the following order: The Maryland division, including the Delawares, on the right—the North Carolina militia in the center—and the Virginia militia on the left. It happened that each flank was covered by a marsh, so near as to admit the removing of the First Maryland Brigade to form a second line, about two hundred yards in the rear of the first. The artillery was removed from the center of the brigades and placed in the center of the front line; and the North Carolina militia (light infantry) under Major Armstrong, which had retreated at the first rencontre, was ordered to cover a small interval between the left wing and the swampy grounds on that quarter.

Frequent skirmishes happened during the night between the advanced parties—which served to discover the relative situations of the two armies—and as a prelude to what was to take place in the morning.

At dawn of day (on the morning of the 16th of August) the enemy appeared in front, advancing in column. Captain Singleton, who commanded some pieces of artillery, observed to Colonel Williams that he plainly perceived the ground of the British uniform at about two hundred yards in front. The deputy adjutant general immediately ordered Captain Singleton to open his battery, and then rode to the general, who was in the rear of the second line, and informed him of the cause of the firing which he heard. He also observed to the general that the enemy seemed to be displaying their column by the right; the nature of the ground favored this conjecture, for yet nothing was clear.

The general seemed disposed to wait events— he gave no orders. The deputy adjutant general observed that if the enemy, in the act of displaying, were briskly attacked by General Stevens' brigade, which was already in line of battle, the effect might be fortunate, and first impressions were important.

"Sir," said the general, "that's right—let it be done."

This was the last order that the deputy adjutant general received. He hastened to General Stevens, who instantly advanced with his brigade, apparently in fine spirits. The right wing of the enemy was soon discovered *in line*—it was too late to attack them displaying. Nevertheless, the business of the day could no longer be deferred. The deputy adjutant general requested General Stevens to let him have forty or fifty privates, volunteers, who would run forward of the brigade and commence the attack. They were led forward within forty or fifty yards of the enemy, and ordered to take trees and keep up as brisk a fire as possible. The desired effect of this expedient, to extort the enemy's fire at some distance in order to the rendering it less terrible to the militia, was not gained.

General Stevens, observing the enemy to rush on, put his men in mind of their bayonets; but the impetuosity with which they advanced, firing and huzzaing, threw the whole body of the militia into such a panic that they generally threw down their loaded arms and fled in the utmost consternation. The unworthy example of the Virginians was almost instantly followed by the North Carolinians; only a small part of the brigade commanded by Brigadier General Gregory made a short pause. A part of Dixon's regiment of that brigade, next in the line to the Second Maryland Brigade, fired two or three rounds of cartridge. But a great majority of the militia (at least two-thirds of the army) fled without firing a shot. The writer avers it of his own knowledge, having seen and observed every part of the army, from left to right, during the action.

He who has never seen the effect of a panic upon a multitude can have but an imperfect idea of such a thing. The best disciplined troops have been enervated and made cowards by it. Armies have been routed by it, even where no enemy appeared to furnish an excuse. Like electricity, it operates instantaneously—like sympathy, it is irresistible where it touches. But, in the present instance, its action was not universal. The regular troops, who had the keen edge of sensibility rubbed off by strict discipline and hard service, saw the confusion with but little emotion. They engaged seriously in the affair; and, notwithstanding some irregularity, which was created by the militia breaking pell mell through the second line, order was restored there—time enough to give the enemy a severe check, which abated the fury of their assault and obliged them to assume a more deliberate manner of acting. The Second Maryland Brigade, including the battalion of Delawares, on the right, were engaged with the enemy's left, which they opposed with very great firmness. They even advanced upon them and had taken a number of prisoners when their companions of the First Brigade (which formed the second line), being greatly outflanked and charged by superior numbers, were obliged to give ground.

At this critical moment the regimental officers of the latter brigade, reluctant to leave the field without orders, inquired for their commanding officer (Brigadier General Smallwood) who, however, was not to be found. Notwithstanding, Colonel Gunby, Major Anderson and a number of other brave officers, assisted by the deputy adjutant general and Major Jones, one of Smallwood's aids, rallied the brigade and renewed the contest. Again they were obliged to give way, and were again rallied. The Second Brigade were still warmly engaged. The distance between the two brigades did not exceed two hundred yards, their opposite flanks being nearly upon a line perpendicular to their front.

At this eventful juncture, the deputy adjutant general, anxious that the communication between them should be preserved, and wishing that, in the almost certain event of a retreat, some order might be sustained by them, hastened from the First to the Second Brigade, which he found precisely in the same circumstances. He called upon his own regiment (the 6th Maryland) not to fly, and was answered by the Lieutenant Colonel, Ford, who said, "They have done all that can be expected of them. We are outnumbered and outflanked. See the enemy charge with bayonets!"

The enemy having collected their corps and directing their whole force against these two devoted brigades, a tremendous fire of musketry was for some time kept up on both sides with equal perseverance and obstinacy, until Lord Cornwallis, perceiving there was no cavalry opposed to him, pushed forward his dragoons, and his infantry charging at the same moment with fixed bayonets put an end to the contest.

His victory was complete. All the artillery and a very great number of prisoners fell into his hands. Many fine fellows lay on the field, and the rout of the remainder was entire. Not even a company retired in any order. Every one escaped as he could. If in this affair the militia fled too soon, the regulars may be thought almost as blamable for remaining too long on the field, especially after all hope of victory must have been despaired of. Let the commandants of the brigades answer for themselves. Allow the same privilege to the officers of the corps comprising those brigades, and they will say that they never received orders to retreat, nor any order from any general officer, from the commencement of the action until it became desperate. The brave Major General, the Baron de Kalb, fought on foot with the Second Brigade and fell, mortally wounded, into the hands of the enemy, who stripped him even of his shirt: a fate which probably was avoided by other generals only by an opportune retreat.

The torrent of unarmed militia bore away with it Generals Gates, Caswell and a number of others, who soon saw that all was lost. General Gates at first conceived a hope that he might rally, at Clermont, a sufficient number to cover the retreat of the regulars; but the farther they fled the more they were dispersed, and the generals soon found themselves abandoned by all but their aids. Lieutenant Colonel Senf, who had been on the expedition with Colonel Sumpter, returned and, overtaking General Gates, informed him of their complete success—that the enemy's redoubt on Wateree, opposite to Camden, was first reduced, and the convoy of stores, etc., from Charleston was decoyed and became prize to the American party almost without resistance. That upwards of one hundred prisoners and forty loaded waggons were in the hands of the party, who had sustained very little loss; but the general could avail himself nothing of this trifling advantage. The detachment under Sumpter was on the opposite side of the Wateree, marching off as speedily as might be to secure their booty—for the course of the firing in the morning indicated unfavorable news from the army.

The militia, the general saw, were in air, and the regulars, he feared, were no more. The dreadful thunder of artillery and musketry had ceased, and none of his friends appeared. There was no existing corps with which the victorious detachment might unite, and the Americans had no post in the rear. He, therefore, sent orders to Sumpter to retire in the best manner he could; and proceeded himself with General Caswell towards Charlotte, an open village on a plain,

about sixty miles from the fatal scene of action. The Virginians, who knew nothing of the country they were in, involuntarily reversed the route they came, and fled, most of them, to Hillsborough. General Stevens pursued them, and halted there as many as were not sufficiently refreshed before his arrival to pursue their way home. Their terms of service, however, being very short, and no prospect presenting itself to afford another proof of their courage, General Stevens soon afterwards discharged them.

The North Carolina militia fled different ways, as their hopes led or their fears drove them. Most of them, preferring the shortest way home, scattered through the wilderness which lies between Wateree and Pee Dee rivers, and thence towards Roanoke. Whatever these might have suffered from the disaffected, they probably were not worse off than those who retired the way they came; wherein they met many of their insidious friends, armed and advancing to join the American army; but, learning its fate from the refugees, they acted decidedly in concert with the victors, and, captivating some, plundering others and maltreating all the fugitives they met, returned, exultingly, home. They even added taunts to their perfidy. One of a party who robbed Brigadier General Butler of his sword consoled him by saying, "You'll have no further use of it."

The regular troops, it has been observed, were the last to quit the field. Every corps was broken and dispersed; even the boggs and brush, which in some measure served to screen them from their furious pursuers, separated them from one another. Major Anderson was the only officer who fortunately rallied, as he retreated, a few men of different companies, and whose prudence and firmness afforded protection to those who joined his party on the rout. . . .

The general order for moving off the heavy baggage, etc., to Waxaws was not put in execution, as directed to be done on the preceding evening. The whole of it, consequently, fell into the hands of the enemy, as well as all that which followed the army except the waggons of the Generals Gates and De Kalb; which, being furnished with the stoutest horses, fortunately escaped under the protection of a small quarter guard. Other waggons also had got out of danger from the enemy; but the cries of the women and the wounded in the rear and the consternation of the flying troops so alarmed some of the wag-goners that they cut out their teams and, taking each a horse, left the rest for the next that should come. Others were obliged to give up their horses to assist in carrying off the wounded, and the whole road, for many miles, was strewed with signals of distress, confusion and dismay.

What added not a little to this calamitous scene was the conduct of Armand's Legion. They were principally foreigners, and some of them, probably, not unaccustomed to such scenes. Whether it was owing to the disgust of the colonel at general orders, or the cowardice of his men, is not with the writer to determine; but certain it is, the Legion did not take any part in the action of the 16th. They retired early and in disorder, and were seen plundering the bag-gage of the army on their retreat. One of them cut Captain Lemar, of the Maryland infantry, over the hand for attempting to reclaim his own portmanteau, which the fellow was taking out of the waggon. Captain Lemar was unarmed, hav-ing broke his sword in action, and was obliged to submit both to the loss and to the insult. The tent covers were thrown off the waggons, generally, and the baggage exposed, so that one might take what suited him to carry off. General Caswell's mess waggon afforded the best refreshment; very unexpectedly to the writer, he there found a pipe of good Madeira, broached, and surrounded by a number of soldiers, whose appearance led him to inquire what engaged their attention. He acknowledges that in this instance he shared in the booty and took a draught of wine, which was the only refreshment he had received that day.

Source: Williams, Otho. Account of the Battle of Camden. Quoted in *Sketches of the Life and Correspondence of Nathanael Greene, Major General of the Armies of the United States,* by William Johnson, 1:494–498. Charleston, S.C.: A. E. Miller, 1822.

THE BATTLE OF KING'S MOUNTAIN, OCTOBER 7, 1780

Account of the Battle
Ensign Robert Campbell
October or November 1780

After the catastrophe of Camden, the resounding Patriot victory at King's Mountain, on the border of North and South Carolina, was especially sweet—and it served to turn the tide in the South. North Carolina ensign Robert Campbell recalled the battle in a document preserved in The State Records of North Carolina. *It is one of several firsthand reports written by North Carolina officers shortly after the battle.*

[British major Patrick] Ferguson, [commanding one section of General Cornwallis's army,] find-ing that he must inevitably be overtaken, chose his ground and waited for the attack on King's Mountain. On the 7th of October, in the after-noon, after a forced march of forty-five miles on that day and the night before, the volunteers came up with him. The forenoon of the day was wet, but they were fortunate enough to come on him undiscovered and took his pickets, they not having it in their power to give an alarm. They were soon formed in such order as to attack the enemy on all sides. The Washington and Sul-livan regiments were formed in the front and on the right flank; the North and South Carolina troops, under Cols. Williams, Sevier, Cleveland, Lacey and Brandon, on the left. The two armies being in full view, the centre of the one nearly opposite the centre of the other, the British main guard posted nearly half-way down the moun-tain, the commanding officer gave the word of command to raise the Indian war-whoop and charge. In a moment King's Mountain resounded with their shouts, and on the first fire the guard retreated, leaving some of their men to crimson the earth. The British beat to arms and immediately formed on top of the mountain behind a chain of rocks that appeared impregnable, and had their wagons drawn up on their flank across the end of the mountain, by which they made a strong breast work.

Thus concealed, the American army advanced to the charge. In ten or fifteen minutes the wings came round, and the action became general.

The enemy annoyed our troops very much from their advantageous position. Col. Shelby, being previously ordered to reconnoitre their position, observing their situation and what a destructive fire was kept up from behind those rocks, ordered Robert Campbell['s men] to advance and post themselves opposite to the rocks and near to the enemy, and then return to assist in bringing up the men in order, who had been charged with the bayonet. These orders were punctually obeyed, and they kept up such a galling fire as to compel Ferguson to order a company of regulars to face them, with a view to cover his men that were posted behind the rocks.

At this time a considerable fire was drawn to this side of the mountain by the repulse of those on the other, and the Loyalists not being permitted to leave their post. This scene was not of long duration, for it was the brave Virginia volunteers and those under Col. Shelby, on their attempting rapidly to ascend the mountain, that were charged with the bayonet. They obstinately stood until some of them were thrust through the body, and having nothing but their rifles by which to defend themselves, they were forced to retreat. They were soon rallied by their gallant commanders, Campbell, Shelby and other brave officers, and by a constant and well-directed fire of their rifles drove them back in their turn, strewing the face of the mountain with their assailants, and kept advancing until they drove them from some of their posts.

Ferguson, being heavily pressed on all sides, ordered Capt. DePeyster to reinforce some of the extreme post with a full company of British regulars. He marched, but to his astonishment, when he arrived at the place of destination, he had almost no men, being exposed in that short distance to the constant fire of their rifles. He then ordered his cavalry to mount, but to no purpose. As quick as they were mounted they were taken down by some bold marks-man. Being driven to desperation by such a scene of misfortune, Col. Ferguson endeavored to make his escape, and, with two colonels of the Loyalists, mounted his horse and charged on that part of the line which was defended by the party who had been ordered round the mountain by Col. Shelby where it appeared too weak to resist them. But as soon as he got to the line he fell, and the other two officers, attempting to retreat, soon shared the same fate.

It was about this time that Col. Campbell advanced in front of his men and climbed over a steep rock close by the enemy's lines to get a view of their situation, and saw that they were retreating from behind the rocks that were near to him.

As soon as Capt. DePeyster observed that Col. Ferguson was killed, he raised a flag and called for quarters. It was soon taken out of his hand by one of the officers on horse back and raised so high that it could be seen by our line, and the firing immediately ceased. The Loyalists, at the time of their surrender, were driven into a crowd, and being closely surrounded, they could not have made any further resistance.

In this sharp action, one hundred and fifty of Col. Ferguson's party were killed, and something over that number were wounded. Eight hundred and ten, of whom one hundred were British regulars, surrendered themselves prisoners, and one thousand five hundred stand of arms were taken. The loss of the American army on this occasion amounted to thirty killed and something over fifty wounded, among whom were a number of brave officers. Col. Williams, who has been so much lamented, was shot through the body, near the close of the action, in making an attempt to charge upon Ferguson. He lived long enough to hear of the surrender of the British army. He then said, "I die contented, since we have gained the victory," and expired.

Source: North Carolina, State of. *The State Records of North Carolina,* edited by Walter Clark, 15:101–103. Winston: M. I. and J. C. Stewart, 1895.

Account of the Battle
James P. Collins
Published 1859

James Potter Collins (1763–1844) was a 17-year-old South Carolinian who fought with General Thomas Sumter and other militia leaders after Charleston fell to the British. He kept a journal—published as his autobiography in 1859—in which he wrote of the British and Loyalist depredations and their comeuppance at the Battle of King's Mountain and the Battle of Cowpens.

The enemy was posted on a high, steep and rugged ridge—very difficult of access. . . . The plan was to surround the mountain and attack them on all sides, if possible. In order to do this, the left had to march under the fire of the enemy to gain the position assigned to them on the stream on the right of the enemy, while the right was to take possession of the other stream. In doing this they were not exposed, the cliff being so steep as to cover them completely.

Each leader made a short speech in his own way to his men, desiring every coward to be off immediately. Here I confess I would willingly have been excused, for my feelings were not the most pleasant. This may be attributed to my youth, not being quite seventeen years of age—but I could not well swallow the appellation of coward. I looked around. Every man's countenance seemed to change. Well, thought I, fate is fate; every man's fate is before him and he has to run it out. . . .

We were soon in motion, every man throwing four or five balls in his mouth to prevent thirst, also to be in readiness to reload quick. The shot of the enemy soon began to pass over us like hail. The first shock was quickly over, and for my own part, I was soon in profuse sweat. My lot happened to be in the center, where the severest part of the battle was fought. We soon attempted to climb the hill, but were fiercely charged upon and forced to fall back to our first position. We tried a second time, but met the same fate; the fight then seemed to become more furious. Their leader, Ferguson, came in full view, within rifle shot as if to encourage his men, who by this time were falling very fast. He soon disappeared. We took to the hill a third time; the enemy gave way.

When we had gotten near the top, some of our leaders roared out, "Hurrah, my brave fellows! Advance! They are crying for quarter."

By this time, the right and left had gained the top of the cliff; the enemy was completely hemmed in on all sides, and no chance of escaping—besides, their leader had fallen. They soon threw down their arms and surrendered. After the fight was over, the situation of the poor Tories appeared to be really pitiable; the dead lay in heaps on all sides, while the groans of the wounded were heard in every direction. I could not help turning away from the scene before me with horror and, though exulting in victory, could not refrain from shedding tears. . . .

On examining the dead body of their great chief, it appeared that almost fifty rifles must have been leveled at him at the same time; seven rifle balls had passed through his body, both of his arms were broken, and his hat and clothing were literally shot to pieces. Their great elevation above us had proved their ruin. They overshot us altogether, scarce touching a man, except those on horseback, while every rifle from below seemed to have the desired effect. . . .

Next morning, which was Sunday, the scene became really distressing; the wives and children of the poor Tories came in, in great numbers. Their husbands, fathers and brothers lay dead in heaps, while others lay wounded or dying—a melancholy sight indeed! while numbers of the survivors were doomed to abide the sentence of a court martial, and several were actually hanged. . . .

We proceeded to bury the dead, but it was badly done. They were thrown into convenient piles and covered with old logs, the bark of old trees, and rocks; yet not so as to secure them from becoming a prey to the beasts of the forest or the vultures of the air; and the wolves became so plenty that it was dangerous for any one to be out at night, for several miles around; also, the hogs in the neighborhood gathered in to the place to devour the flesh of men, inasmuch as numbers chose to live on little meat rather than eat their hogs, though they were fat. Half of the dogs in the country were said to be mad and were put to death. I saw, myself, in passing the place a few weeks after, all parts of the human frame lying scattered in every direction. . . .

Source: Collins, James Potter. *Autobiography of a Revolutionary Soldier.* Clinton, La.: Feliciana *Democrat,* 1859, 259–261.

THE MUTINY OF THE PENNSYLVANIA LINE, JANUARY 1, 1781

Letter to an Unidentified Correspondent
Lieutenant Enos Reeves
January 2, 1781

George Washington never believed he could definitively defeat Great Britain, the greatest military power in the world, but he held fast to the hope that he could outlast the British will to continue the fight—provided that he could keep his army together and in the field. The great problem was that the soldiers of the Continental army were ill-clothed and nearly starved. In May 1780, two Connecticut regiments mutinied in a demand for their long overdue pay. In January, the Pennsylvania Line followed suit. They had not been paid for months, their clothes were falling off their backs in rags, and they subsisted on a ration of bread and water. The mutinous Pennsylvanians sent a spokesman to

Congress, which agreed to most of their demands; however, three New Jersey regiments mutinied a few weeks later—and, this time, Washington responded by force of arms and the execution of the chief mutineers.

Lieutenant Enos Reeves, an officer in the Pennsylvania Line, told the story of the mutiny in a letter of January 2, 1781.

Mount Kemble, N. J., January 2, 1781
Yesterday being the last time we (the officers of the regiment) expected to be together, as the arrangement was to take place this day, we had an elegant regimental dinner and entertainment, at which all the field and other officers were present, with a few from the German regiment, who had arrived with the men of their regiment that belong to the Penna. Line. We spent the day very pleasantly and the evening till about ten o'clock as cheerfully as we could wish, when we were disturbed by the huzzas of the soldiers upon the Right Division, answered by those on the Left.

I went on the Parade and found numbers in small groups whispering and busily running up and down the line. In a short time a gun was fired upon the right and answered by one on the right of the Second Brigade, and a skyrocket thrown from the center of the first, which was accompanied by a general huzza throughout the line, and the soldiers running out with their arms, accoutrements and knapsacks.

I immediately found it was a mutiny, and that the guns and skyrocket were the signals. The officers in general exerted themselves to keep the men quiet, and keep them from turning out. We each applied himself to his own company, endeavored to keep them in their huts and lay by their arms, which they would do while we were present, but the moment we left one but to go to another, they would be out again. Their excuse was they thought it was an alarm and the enemy coming on.

Next they began to move in crowds to the Parade, going up to the right, which was the place appointed for their rendezvous. Lieut.

White of our regiment, in endeavoring to stop one of those crowds, was shot through the thigh, and Capt. Samuel Tolbert in opposing another party was shot through the body, of which he is very ill. They continued huzzaing and fireing in a riotous manner, so that it soon became dangerous for an officer to oppose them by force. We then left them to go their own way.

Hearing a confused noise to the right, between the line of huts and Mrs. Wicks, curiosity led me that way, and it being dark in the orchard I mixed among the crowd and found they had broken open the magazine and were preparing to take off the cannon. In taking possession of the cannon they forced the sentinel from his post and placed one of their own men. One of the mutineers coming officiously up to force him away (thinking him to be one of our sentinels) received a ball through the head and died instantly.

A dispute arose among the mutineers about firing the alarms with the cannon, and continued for a considerable time—one party aledging that it would arouse the timid soldiery, the other objected because it would alarm the in habitants. For a while I expected the dispute would be decided by the bayonet, but the gunner in the meantime slipped up to the piece and put a match to it, which ended the affair. Every discharge of the cannon was accompanied by a confused huzza and a general discharge of musketry.

About this time Gen. Wayne and several field officers (mounted) arrived. Gen. Wayne and Col. Richard Butler spoke to them for a considerable time, but it had no effect. Their answer was, they had been wronged and were determined to see themselves righted. He replied that he would right them as far as in his power. They rejoined, it was out of his power; their business was not with the officers, but with Congress and the Governor and Council of the State; 'twas they had wronged and they must right. With that, several platoons fired over the General's head. The General called out, "If you mean to kill me, shoot me at once—here's my breast!" opening his coat. They replied that it was not their intention to hurt or disturb an officer of the Line (two or three individuals excepted); that they had nothing against their officers, and they would oppose any person that would attempt anything of the kind.

A part of the Fourth Regiment was paraded and led on by Capt. Campbell, to recapture the cannon; they were ordered to charge and rush on. They charged but would not advance, then dispersed and left the officer alone. Soon after a soldier from the mob made a charge upon Lieut. Col. William Butler, who was obliged to retreat between the huts to save his life. He went around one hut and the soldier around another to head him, met Capt. Bettin who was coming down the alley, who seeing a man coming towards him on a charge, charged his espontoon to oppose him, when the fellow fired his piece and shot the captain through the body and he died two hours later.

About twelve o'clock they sent parties to relieve or seize the old camp guard, and posted sentinels all round the camp. At one o'clock they moved off towards the left of the line with the cannon and when they reached the centre they fired a shot. As they came down the line, they turned the soldiers out of every hut, and those who would not go with them were obliged to hide till they were gone. They continued huzzaing and a disorderly firing till they went off, about two o'clock, with drums and fifes playing, under command of the sergeants, in regular platoons, with a front and rear guard.

Gen. Wayne met them as they were marching off and endeavored to persuade them back, but to no purpose; he then inquired which way they were going, and they replied either to Trenton or Philadelphia. He begged them not to attempt to go to the enemy. They declared it was not their intention, and that they would hang any man who would attempt it, and for that, if the enemy should come out in consequence of this revolt, they would turn back and fight them. "If that is your sentiments," said the General, "I'll not leave you, and if you wont allow me to march in your front, I'll follow in your rear."

This day Col. Stewart and Richard Butler joined Gen. Wayne in hopes they could turn them when they grew cooler, being much agitated with liquor when they went off; it being New Years Day, they had drawn half a pint per man. The men have continued going off in small parties all day. About one o'clock one hundred head of cattle came in from the eastward, which they drove off to their main body, which lay in a wood near Vealtown, leaving a behind for the use of the officers.

When we came to draw provisions and State stores this day, we found that half of the men of our regiment had remained.

The men went off very civily last night to what might have been expected from such a mob. They did not attempt to plunder our officers' huts or insult them in the least, except those who were obstinate in opposing them. They'd not attempt to take with them any part of the State stores, which appears to me a little extraordinary, for men when they get but little want more.

The militia are called out—they are to assemble at Chatham—in order to oppose the enemy if they come out, or the mutineers if they attempt going them.

Source: Reeves, Enos. "Extracts from the Letter-Books of Lieutenant Enos Reeves, of the Pennsylvania Line." *Pennsylvania Magazine of History and Biography* 21 (1897): 72–75.

THE BATTLE OF COWPENS, JANUARY 17, 1781

Letter to General Nathanael Greene
Colonel Daniel Morgan
January 19, 1781

Daniel Morgan (1736–1802) was a teamster during the French and Indian War, and after running afoul of General John Burgoyne in the advance against Fort Duquesne, he was sentenced to 499 lashes.

No one was expected to survive such punishment, but Morgan did, and the experience left him with a bitter hatred for the British and the British army. At the Cowpens, therefore, he was determined to destroy the forces arrayed against him. He was able to entrap the British in a double envelopment, which resulted in the total defeat of the 1,076 men under Lieutenant Colonel Banastre Tarleton. Of the British and Loyalist troops, 110 were killed and 830 captured (of whom about 200 were also wounded). On January 19, 1781, Morgan wrote to his commanding officer, General Nathanael Greene, to report the particulars of what many military historians consider the most brilliant battle of the American Revolution.

The troops I have the honor to command have been so fortunate as to obtain a complete victory over a detachment from the British army, commanded by Lieut. Col. Tarleton. The action happened on the 17th inst., about sunrise, at the Cowpens. It, perhaps, would be well to remark, for the honor of the American arms, that although the progress of this corps was marked with burning and devastation, and although they waged the most cruel warfare, not a man was killed, wounded or even insulted after he surrendered. Had not Britons during this contest received so many lessons of humanity, I should flatter myself that this might teach them a little. But I fear they are incorrigible.

To give you a just idea of our operations, it will be necessary to inform you that on the 14th inst., having received certain intelligence that Lord Cornwallis and Lieut. Col. Tarleton were both in motion, and that their movements clearly indicated their intentions of dislodging me, I abandoned my encampment on Grindall's Ford on the Pacolet, and on the 16th, in the evening, took possession of a post about seven miles from the Cherokee Ford on Broad River. My former position subjected me at once to the operations of Cornwallis and Tarleton, and in case of a defeat, my retreat might easily have been cut off. My situation at the Cowpens enabled me to improve any advantages I might gain, and to provide better for my own security should I be unfortunate. These reasons induced me to take this post, at the risk of its wearing the face of a retreat.

I received regular intelligence of the enemy's movements from the time they were first in motion. On the evening of the 16th inst., they took possession of the ground I had removed from in the morning, distant from the scene of action about twelve miles. An hour before daylight one of my scouts returned and informed me that Lieut. Col. Tarleton had advanced within five miles of our camp. On this information, I hastened to form as good a disposition as circumstances would admit, and from the alacrity of the troops we were soon prepared to receive him.

The light infantry, commanded by Lieut. Col. Howard, and the Virginia militia, under the command of Maj. Triplett, were formed on a rising ground and extended a line in front. The third regiment of dragoons, under Lieut. Col. Washington, were posted at such a distance in their rear as not to be subjected to the line of fire directed at them, and to be so near as to be able to charge the enemy should they be broken. The volunteers of North Carolina, South Carolina and Georgia, under the command of the brave and valuable Col. Pickens, were situated to guard the flanks. Maj. McDowell, of the North Carolina volunteers, was posted on the right flank in front of the line, one hundred and fifty yards; and Maj. Cunningham, of the Georgia volunteers, on the left, at the same distance in front. Cols. Brannon and Thomas, of the South Carolinians, were posted in the right of Maj. McDowell, and Cols. Hays and McCall, of the same corps, on the left of Maj. Cunningham. Capts. Tate and Buchanan, with the Augusta riflemen, to support the right of the line.

The enemy drew up in single line of battle, four hundred yards in front of our advanced corps. The first battalion of the 71st Regiment was opposed to our right, the 7th Regiment to our left, the infantry of the [Tory] Legion to our centre, the light companies on their flanks. In front moved two pieces of artillery. Lieut. Col.

A portrait, engraved from a painting by Alonzo Chappel, of the militia commander Daniel Morgan (*National Archives*)

Tarleton, with his cavalry, was posted in the rear of his line.

The disposition of battle being thus formed, small parties of riflemen were detached to skirmish with the enemy, upon which their whole line moved on with the greatest impetuosity, shouting as they advanced. McDowell and Cunningham gave them a heavy and galling fire and retreated to the regiments intended for their support. The whole of Col. Pickens's command then kept up a fire by regiments, retreating agreeably to their orders. When the enemy advanced to our line, they received a well-directed and incessant fire. But their numbers being superior to ours, they gained our flanks, which obliged us to change our position. We retired in good order about fifty paces, formed, advanced on the enemy and gave them a fortunate volley, which threw them into disorder. Lieut. Col. Howard, observing this, gave orders for the line to charge bayonets, which was done with such address that they fled with the utmost precipitation, leaving their fieldpieces in our possession. We pushed our advantage so effectually that they never had an opportunity of rallying, had their intentions been ever so good.

Lieut. Col. Washington, having been informed that Tarleton was cutting down our riflemen on the left, pushed forward and charged them with such firmness that instead of attempting to recover the fate of the day, which one would have expected from an officer of his splendid character, [they] broke and fled.

The enemy's whole force were now bent solely in providing for their safety in flight—the list of their killed, wounded and prisoners will inform you with what effect. Tarleton, with the small remains of his cavalry and a few scattering infantry he had mounted on his wagon-horses, made their escape. He was pursued twenty-four miles, but, owing to our having taken a wrong trail at first, we never could overtake him.

As I was obliged to move off of the field of action in the morning to secure the prisoners, I cannot be so accurate as to the killed and wounded of the enemy as I could wish. From the reports of an officer whom I sent to view the ground, there were one hundred non-commissioned officers and privates and ten commissioned officers killed and two hundred rank and file wounded. We have now in our possession five hundred and two non-commissioned officers and privates prisoners, independent of the wounded, and the militia are taking up stragglers continually. Twenty-nine commissioned officers have fell into our hands. Their rank, etc., you will see by an enclosed list. The officers I have paroled; the privates I am conveying by the safest route to Salisbury.

Two standards, two fieldpieces, thirty-five wagons, a travelling forge and all their music are ours. Their baggage, which was immense, they have in a great measure destroyed.

Our loss is inconsiderable, which the enclosed return will evince. I have not been able to ascer-

tain Col. Pickens' loss, but know it to be very small.

From our force being composed of such a variety of corps, a wrong judgment may be formed of our numbers. We fought [deployed] only eight hundred men, two-thirds of which were militia. The British, with their baggage-guard, were not less than one thousand one hundred and fifty, and these veteran troops. Their own officers confess that they fought [deployed] one thousand and thirty-seven.

Such was the inferiority of our numbers that our success must be attributed to the justice of our cause and the bravery of our troops. My wishes would induce me to mention the name of every sentinel in the corps I have the honor to command. In justice to the bravery and good conduct of the officers, I have taken the liberty to enclose you a list of their names, from a conviction that you will be pleased to introduce such characters to the world. . . .

Source: Graham, James. *Life of General Daniel Morgan.* New York: Denby and Jackson, 1859, pp. 467–470.

THE BATTLE OF GUILFORD COURTHOUSE, MARCH 15, 1781

Letter to Joseph Reed
General Nathanael Greene
March 18, 1781

The Continental general Nathanael Greene (1742–86) hoped to score an absolute victory against General Cornwallis at Guilford Courthouse in North Carolina. In the end, however, it was Greene who was forced from the field, although Cornwallis lost nearly a quarter of his men. Technically, the battle was yet another bloody draw, yet in the larger strategic picture, it resulted in Cornwallis's fateful deci-

sion to abandon the Carolinas for Virginia, setting up the circumstances in which Washington and Rochambeau cornered Cornwallis at Yorktown, the culminating battle of the American Revolution. On March 18, 1781, Greene wrote about Guilford Courthouse in a dispatch to Joseph Reed, president of Pennsylvania.

Our force was so small and Lord Cornwallis's movements were so rapid that we got no reinforcements of militia, and therefore were obliged to retire out of the State, upon which the spirits of the people sunk, and almost all classes of the inhabitants gave themselves up for lost. They would not believe themselves in danger until they found ruin at their doors. The foolish prejudice of the formidableness of the militia being a sufficient barrier against any attempts of the enemy prevented the Legislature from making any exertions equal to their critical and dangerous situation. Experience has convinced them of their false security.

It is astonishing to me how these people could place such a confidence in a militia scattered over the face of the whole earth, and generally destitute of everything necessary to their own defence. The militia in the back country are formidable, the others are not, and all are very ungovernable and difficult to keep together. As they have generally come out, twenty thousand might be in motion, and not five hundred in the field.

After crossing the Dan and collecting a few Virginia militia, finding the enemy had erected their standard at Hillsborough and the people began to flock to it from all quarters, either for protection or to engage in their service, I determined to recross at all hazards, and it was very fortunate that I did, otherwise Lord Cornwallis would have got several thousand recruits. Seven companies were enlisted in one day. Our situation was desperate at the time we recrossed the Dan; our numbers were much inferior to the enemy, and we were without ammunition,

The Battle of Guilford Courthouse, March 15, 1781 *(U.S. Army Center of Military History)*

provisions or stores of any kind, the whole having retired over the Stanton River. However, I thought it was best to put on a good face and make the most of appearances. Lieutenant Colonel Lee's falling in with the Tories upon the Haw almost put a total stop to their recruiting service.

Our numbers were, doubtless, greatly magnified, and pushing on boldly towards Hillsborough led Lord Cornwallis into a belief that I meant to attack him wherever I could find him. The case was widely different. It was certain I could not fight him in a general action without almost certain ruin. To skirmish with him was my only chance. Those happened daily, and the enemy suffered considerably; but our militia coming out principally upon the footing of volunteers, they fell off daily after every skirmish and went home to tell the news. In this situation, with an inferior force, I kept constantly in the neighbourhood of Lord Cornwallis until the 6th, when he made a rapid push at our Light Infantry, commanded by Colonel Williams, who very judiciously avoided the blow. This manoeuvre of the enemy obliged me to change my position. Indeed, I rarely ever lay more than two days in a place. The country, being much of a wilderness, obliged the enemy to guard carefully against a surprise and rendered it difficult to surprise us. We had few wagons with us—no baggage, and only tents enough to secure our arms in case of a wasting rain.

Here has been the field for the exercise of genius and an opportunity to practise all the great and little arts of war. Fortunately, we have blundered through without meeting with any capital misfortune. On the 11th of this month I formed a junction, at the High Rock Ford, with a considerable body of Virginia and North Carolina militia, and with a Virginia regiment of eighteen months' men. Our force being now much more considerable than it had been and upon a more permanent footing, I took the determination of giving the enemy battle without loss of time and made the necessary dispositions accordingly.

The battle was fought at or near Guilford Court-House, the very place from whence we began our retreat after the Light Infantry joined the army from the Pedee. The battle was long, obstinate and bloody. We were obliged to give up the ground and lost our artillery, but the enemy have been so soundly beaten that they dare not move towards us since the action, notwithstanding we lay within ten miles of him for two days. Except the ground and the artillery, they have gained no advantage. On the contrary, they are little short of being ruined. The enemy's loss in killed and wounded cannot be less than between six and seven hundred, perhaps more.

Victory was long doubtful, and had the North Carolina militia done their duty, it was certain. They had the most advantageous position I ever saw, and left it without making scarcely the shadow of opposition. Their general and field officers exerted themselves, but the men would not stand. Many threw away their arms and fled with the utmost precipitation, even before a gun was fired at them. The Virginia militia behaved nobly and annoyed the enemy greatly. The horse, at different times in the course of the day, performed wonders. Indeed, the horse is our great safeguard, and without them the militia could not keep the field in this country. . . . Never did an army labour under so many disadvantages as this; but the fortitude and patience of the officers and soldiery rise superior to all difficulties. We have little to eat, less to drink, and lodge in the woods in the midst of smoke. Indeed, our fatigue is excessive. I was so much overcome night before last that I fainted.

Our army is in good spirits, but the militia are leaving us in great numbers to return home to kiss their wives and sweethearts.

I have never felt an easy moment since the enemy crossed the Catawba until since the defeat of the 15th, but now I am perfectly easy, being persuaded it is out of the enemy's power to do us any great injury. Indeed, I think they will retire as soon as they can get off their wounded. My love to your family and all friends.

Source: Reed, William B. *Life and Correspondence of Joseph Reed, Military Secretary of Washington.* Philadelphia: Lindsay and Blakiston, 1847, 2:348–351.

ANDREW JACKSON AS A YOUNG SOLDIER, 1781

Account of His War Experience
Andrew Jackson
Published 1904

The future president Andrew Jackson was 13 years old when he was unofficially enlisted in a local Carolina regiment as a courier. He and his brother Robert were captured and held as prisoners of war under brutal conditions of semistarvation. When Andrew Jackson refused to clean the boots of a British officer, he received a blow of the man's sword, which left him with deep scars on his left hand and head. In captivity, both Jackson brothers contracted smallpox, from which Robert died. Jackson's mother died shortly afterward, leaving Andrew an orphan at 14. Jackson related his war experience to Francis P. Blair, an influential journalist who served on Jackson's celebrated "Kitchen Cabinet" of unofficial advisers, sometime between 1831 and 1837.

I witnessed two battles, Hanging Rock and Hobkirk's Hill, but did not participate in either. I was in one skirmish—that of Sands House—and there they caught me, along with my brother Robert and my cousin, Tom Crawford. A lieutenant of Tarleton's Light Dragoons tried to make me clean his boots and cut my arm with his sabre when I refused. After that they kept me in jail at Camden about two months, starved me nearly to death and gave me the small-pox. Finally my mother succeeded in persuading them to release Robert and me on account of our extreme youth and illness. Then Robert died of the small-pox and I barely escaped death. When it left me I was a skeleton—not quite six feet long and a little over six inches thick! It took me all the rest of that year [1781] to recover my strength and get flesh enough to hide my bones. By that time Cornwallis had surrendered and the war was practically over in our part of the country.

I was never regularly enlisted, being only fourteen when the war practically ended. Whenever I took the field it was with Colonel Davie, who never put me in the ranks, but used me as a mounted orderly or messenger, for which I was well fitted, being a good rider and knowing all the roads in that region. The only weapons I had were a pistol that Colonel Davie gave me and a small fowling-piece that my Uncle Crawford lent to me. This was a light gun and would kick like sixty when loaded with a three-quarter-ounce ball or with nine buckshot. But it was a smart little gun and would carry the ball almost as true as a rifle fifteen or twenty rods, and threw the buckshot spitefully at close quarters—which was the way I used it in the defence of Captain Sands's house, where I was captured.

I was as sorry about losing the gun there as about the loss of my own liberty, because Uncle Crawford set great store by the gun, which he had brought with him from the old country; and, besides, it was the finest in that whole region. Not long afterward—while I was still in the Camden jail or stockade—some of Colonel Davie's men under Lieutenant Curriton captured a squad of Tories, one of whom had that gun in his possession, together with my pistol that Colonel Davie had given to me. This Tory's name was Mulford. The gun and pistol cost him his life. Davie's men regarded his possession of them as prima facie evidence that he had been a member of the party that captured Captain Sands's house, sacked and burned it and insulted the womenfolks of his family. He pleaded that he was not there; that he had bought the gun and pistol from another Tory. Davie's men told him it would do him no good to add lying to his other crimes, hanged him forthwith and afterward restored the gun and pistol to their proper owners.

The Tories also got the horse I had when captured. He was a three-year-old colt—fine fellow—belonging to Captain Sands himself. He was hid in the woods when they attacked the house, but they [the Tories] found him the next morning. This colt was also retaken about six weeks afterward. The Tory who had him was not hanged, because he had been shot through the stomach before he surrendered and was already dying.

Take it altogether, I saw and heard a good deal of war in those days, but did nothing toward it myself worth mention.

Source: Buell, Augustus C. *History of Andrew Jackson, Pioneer, Patriot, Soldier, Politician, President*. 2 vols. New York: Scribner's, 1904, 1:51–53.

THE SIEGE OF YORKTOWN, SEPTEMBER 28– OCTOBER 19, 1781

Account of the Siege
Sergeant Joseph Plumb Martin
Published 1830

Although the American Revolution would not officially end until the Treaty of Paris was signed on September 3, 1783, the Franco-American victory against Cornwallis at Yorktown, Virginia, brought an end to the main phase of the fighting and ensured that the British would look for an end to the war. Sergeant Joseph Plumb Martin (1760–1850) of Connecticut was impressed by Washington's presence in the front lines of the Yorktown siege, as he recorded in a book published in 1830.

We now began to make preparations for laying close siege to the enemy. We had holed him and nothing remained but to dig him out. Accordingly, after taking every precaution to prevent his escape, settled our guards, provided fascines and gabions, made platforms for the batteries, to be laid down when needed, brought on our battering pieces, ammunition, etc., on the fifth of October we began to put our plans into execution.

One third part of all the troops were put in requisition to be employed in opening the trenches. A third part of our sappers and miners were ordered out this night to assist the engineers in laying out the works. It was a very dark and rainy night. However, we repaired to the place and began by following the engineers and laying laths of pine wood end to end upon the line marked out by the officers for the trenches. We had not proceeded far in the business before the engineers ordered us to desist and remain where we were, and be sure not to straggle a foot from the spot while they were absent from us.

In a few minutes after their departure, there came a man alone to us, having on a surtout, as we conjectured (it being exceeding dark), and inquired for the engineers. We now began to be a little jealous for our safety, being alone and without arms, and within forty rods of the British trenches. The stranger inquired what troops we were; talked familiarly with us a few minutes, when, being informed which way the officers had gone, he went off in the same direction, after strictly charging us, in case we should be taken prisoners, not to discover to the enemy what troops we were. We were obliged to him for his kind advice, but we considered ourselves as standing in no great need of it; for we knew as well as he did that sappers and miners were allowed no quarters, at least are entitled to none by the laws of warfare, and of course should take care, if taken and the enemy did not find us out, not to betray our own secret.

In a short time the engineers returned and the aforementioned stranger with them; they discoursed together sometime, when, by the officers often calling him "Your Excellency," we discovered that it was Gen. Washington. Had we dared, we might have cautioned him for exposing himself so carelessly to danger at such a time, and doubtless he would have taken it in good part if we had. But nothing ill happened to either him or ourselves.

It coming on to rain hard, we were ordered back to our tents, and nothing more was done that night. The next night, which was the sixth of October, the same men were ordered to the lines that had been there the night before. We this night completed laying out the works.

General Washington and the comte de Grasse surrounded British forces under General Cornwallis at Yorktown, leading to the eventual surrender of Cornwallis and a decisive victory for the Americans in their Revolution. *(U.S. Army Center of Military History)*

The troops of the line were there ready with entrenching tools and began to entrench, after General Washington had struck a few blows with a pickaxe, a mere ceremony, that it might be said, "Gen. Washington with his own hands first broke ground at the siege of Yorktown." The ground was sandy and soft, and the men employed that night eat no "idle bread" (and I question if they eat any other), so that by daylight they had covered themselves from danger from the enemy's shot, who, it appeared, never mistrusted that we were so near them the whole night, their attention being directed to another quarter. There was upon the right of their works a marsh; our people had sent to the western side of this marsh a detachment to make a number of fires, by which, and our men often passing before the fires, the British were led to imagine that we were about some secret mischief there, and consequently directed their whole fire to that quarter, while we were entrenching literally under their noses.

As soon as it was day they perceived their mistake and began to fire where they ought to have done sooner. They brought out a fieldpiece or two without their trenches and discharged several shots at the men who were at work erecting a bomb-battery; but their shot had no effect and they soon gave it over. They had a large bull-dog, and every time they fired he would follow their shots across our trenches. Our officers wished to catch him and oblige him to carry a message from them into the town to his masters, but he looked too formidable for any of us to encounter.

I do not remember, exactly, the number of days we were employed before we got our batteries in readiness to open upon the enemy, but think it was not more than two or three. The French, who were upon our left, had completed their batteries a few hours before us, but were not allowed to discharge their pieces till the American batteries were ready. Our commanding battery was on the near bank of the river and contained ten heavy guns; the next was a bomb-battery of three large mortars; and so on through the whole line; the whole number, American and French, was ninety-two cannon, mortars and howitzers. Our flagstaff was in the ten-gun battery, upon the right of the whole.

I was in the trenches the day that the batteries were to be opened; all were upon the tiptoe of expectation and impatience to see the signal given to open the whole line of batteries, which was to be the hoisting of the American flag in the ten-gun battery. About noon the much-wished-for signal went up. I confess I felt a secret pride swell my heart when I saw the "star-spangled banner" waving majestically in the very faces of our implacable adversaries; it appeared like an omen of success to our enterprize, and so it proved in reality. A simultaneous discharge of all the guns in the line followed, the French troops accompanying it with "Huzza for the Americans!"

It was said that the first shell sent from our batteries entered an elegant house, formerly owned or occupied by the Secretary of State under the British government, and burnt directly over a table surrounded by a large party of British officers at dinner, killing and wounding a number of them,—this was a warm day to the British.

Source: Martin, Joseph Plumb. *A Narrative of Some of the Adventures, Dangers and Sufferings of a Revolutionary Soldier.* Hallowell, Me.: Privately printed, 1830, pp. 166–169.

Account of the Siege and Surrender
Dr. James Thacher
Published 1823

Dr. James Thacher (1754–1844) was born and raised in Barnstable, Massachusetts, and served from 1775 to 1783 as surgeon to the Massachusetts 16th Regiment of the Continental army. After the war, he spent the rest of his long life in private practice, but he found time to write A Military Journal during the American Revolutionary War *(1823; 2nd edition, 1827) as well as an 1834 account of the execution of Major John André, the ill-fated courier to whom turncoat Benedict Arnold gave the plans of West Point. Thacher also wrote an important book for medical practitioners,* American New Dispensatory *(1810). In the following excerpt from his* Military Journal, *he recorded the ferocity of the Franco-American artillery bombardment against General Cornwallis's defensive position at Yorktown.*

From the 10th to the 15th, a tremendous and incessant firing from the American and French batteries is kept up, and the enemy return the fire, but with little effect. A red-hot shell from the French battery set fire to the *Charon*, a British 44-gun ship, and two or three smaller vessels at anchor in the river, which were consumed in the night. From the bank of the river I had a fine view of this splendid conflagration. The ships were enwrapped in a torrent of fire, which, spreading with vivid brightness among the combustible rigging, and running with amazing rapidity to the tops of the several masts, while all around was thunder and lightning from our numerous cannon and mortars, and in the darkness of night, presented one of the most sublime and magnificent spectacles which can be imagined. Some of our shells, overreaching the town, are seen to fall into the river and, bursting, throw up columns of water like the spouting of the monsters of the deep.

We have now made further approaches to the town by throwing up a second parallel line and batteries within about three hundred yards; this was effected in the night, and at day-light the enemy were roused to the greatest exertions; the engines of war have raged with redoubled fury and destruction on both sides, no cessation day or night. The French had two officers wounded and fifteen men killed and wounded, and among the Americans, two or three were wounded. I assisted in amputating a man's thigh.

The siege is daily becoming more and more formidable and alarming, and his lordship must view his situation as extremely critical, if not desperate. Being in the trenches every other night and day, I have a fine opportunity of witnessing the sublime and stupendous scene which is continually exhibiting. The bombshells from the besiegers and the besieged are incessantly crossing each others' path in the air. They are clearly visible in the form of a black ball in the day, but in the night they appear like a fiery meteor with a blazing tail, most beautifully brilliant, ascending majestically from the mortar to a certain altitude and gradually descending to the spot where they are destined to execute their work of destruction.

It is astonishing with what accuracy an experienced gunner will make his calculations, that a shell shall fall within a few feet of a given point, and burst at the precise time, though at a great distance. When a shell falls, it whirls round, burrows, and excavates the earth to a considerable extent and, bursting, makes dreadful havoc around. I have more than once witnessed fragments of the mangled bodies and limbs of the British soldiers thrown into the air by the bursting of our shells; and by one from the enemy, Captain White, of the Seventh Massachusetts Regiment, and one soldier were killed and another wounded near where I was standing. About twelve or fourteen men have been killed or wounded within twenty-four hours. I attended at the hospital, amputated a man's arm and assisted in dressing a number of wounds.

The enemy having two redoubts, about three hundred yards in front of their principal works, which enfiladed our intrenchment and impeded our approaches, it was resolved to take possession of them both by assault. The one on the left of the British garrison, bordering on the banks of the river, was assigned to our brigade of light-infantry, under the command of the Marquis de la Fayette. The advanced corps was led on by the intrepid Colonel Hamilton, who had commanded a regiment of light-infantry during the campaign, and assisted by Colonel Gimat.

The assault commenced at eight o'clock in the evening, and the assailants bravely entered the fort with the point of the bayonet without firing a single gun. We suffered the loss of eight men killed and about thirty wounded, among whom Colonel Gimat received a slight wound in his foot, and Major Gibbs, of his excellency's guard, and two other officers were slightly wounded. Major Campbell, who commanded in the fort, was wounded and taken prisoner, with about thirty soldiers; the remainder made their escape. I was desired to visit the wounded in the fort even before the balls had ceased whistling about my ears, and saw a sergeant and eight men dead in the ditch. A captain of our infantry, belonging to New Hampshire, threatened to take the life of Major Campbell to avenge the death of his favorite, Colonel Shammel; but Colonel Hamilton interposed, and not a man was killed after he ceased to resist.

During the assault, the British kept up an incessant firing of cannon and musketry from their whole line. His Excellency General Washington, Generals Lincoln and Knox, with their aids, having dismounted, were standing in an exposed situation waiting the result.

Colonel Cobb, one of General Washington's aids, solicitous for his safety, said to His Excellency, "Sir, you are too much exposed here. Had you not better step a little back?"

"Colonel Cobb," replied His Excellency, "if you are afraid, you have liberty to step back."

The other redoubt on the right of the British lines was assaulted at the same time by a detachment of the French, commanded by the gallant Baron de Viomenil. Such was the ardor displayed by the assailants that all resistance was soon overcome, though at the expense of nearly one hundred men killed and wounded. Of the defenders of the redoubt, eighteen were killed, and one captain and two subaltern officers and forty-two rank and file captured.

Our second parallel line was immediately connected with the two redoubts now taken from the enemy, and some new batteries were thrown up in front of our second parallel line, with a covert way and angling work approaching to less than three hundred yards of their principal forts. These will soon be mantled with cannon and mortars, and when their horrid thundering commences, it must convince his lordship that his post is not invincible, and that submission must soon be his only alternative. Our artillery-men, by the exactness of their aim, make every discharge take effect, so that many of the enemy's guns are entirely silenced, and their works are almost in ruins.

Dr. Thacher described the surrender of the British on October 19, 1781.

This is to us a most glorious day, but to the English, one of bitter chagrin and disappoint-ment. Preparations are now making to receive as captives that vindictive, haughty commander and that victorious army, who, by their robber-ies and murders, have so long been a scourge to our brethren of the Southern states. Being on horseback, I anticipate a full share of satisfaction in viewing the various movements in the interest-ing scene.

The stipulated terms of capitulation are simi-lar to those granted to General Lincoln at Charleston the last year. The captive troops are to march out with shouldered arms, colors cased and drums beating a British or German march, and to ground their arms at a place assigned for the purpose. The officers are allowed their side-arms and private property, and the generals and such officers as desire it are to go on parole to England or New York. The marines and sea-men of the king's ships are prisoners of war to the navy of France; and the land forces to the United States. All military and artillery stores to be delivered up unimpaired. The royal prisoners

to be sent into the interior of Virginia, Maryland and Pennsylvania in regiments, to have rations allowed them equal to the American soldiers, and to have their officers near them. Lord Corn-wallis to man and despatch the *Bonetta* sloop-of-war with despatches to Sir Henry Clinton at New York without being searched, the vessel to be returned and the hands accounted for.

At about twelve o'clock, the combined army was arranged and drawn up in two lines extend-ing more than a mile in length. The Americans were drawn up in a line on the right side of the road, and the French occupied the left. At the head of the former, the great American com-mander, mounted on his noble courser, took his station, attended by his aids. At the head of the latter was posted the excellent Count Rochambeau and his suite. The French troops, in complete uniform, displayed a martial and noble appearance; their bands of music, of which the timbrel formed a part, is a delightful novelty and produced while marching to the ground a most enchanting effect. The Americans, though not all in uniform, nor their dress so neat, yet exhibited an erect, soldierly air, and every countenance beamed with satisfaction and joy. The concourse of spectators from the country was prodigious, in point of numbers was probably equal to the mili-tary, but universal silence and order prevailed.

It was about two o'clock when the captive army advanced through the line formed for their reception. Every eye was prepared to gaze on Lord Cornwallis, the object of peculiar interest and solicitude; but he disappointed our anxious expectations; pretending indisposition, he made General O'Hara his substitute as the leader of his army. This officer was followed by the con-quered troops in a slow and solemn step, with shouldered arms, colors cased and drums beat-ing a British march. Having arrived at the head of the line, General O'Hara, elegantly mounted, advanced to his excellency the commander-in-chief, taking off his hat, and apologized for the non-appearance of Earl Cornwallis. With his usual dignity and politeness, his excellency pointed to Major-General Lincoln for directions, by whom the British army was conducted into a spacious field, where it was intended they should ground their arms.

The royal troops, while marching through the line formed by the allied army, exhibited a decent and neat appearance, as respects arms and clothing, for their commander opened his store and directed every soldier to be furnished with a new suit complete, prior to the capitulation. But in their line of march we remarked a disorderly and unsoldierly conduct, their step was irregular, and their ranks frequently broken.

But it was in the field, when they came to the last act of the drama, that the spirit and pride of the British soldier was put to the severest test: here their mortification could not be concealed. Some of the platoon officers appeared to be exceedingly chagrined when giving the word "ground arms," and I am a witness that they performed this duty in a very unofficer-like manner; and that many of the soldiers manifested a sullen temper, throwing their arms on the pile with violence, as if determined to render them useless. This irregularity, however, was checked by the authority of General Lincoln. After having grounded their arms and divested themselves of their accoutrements, the captive troops were conducted back to Yorktown and guarded by our troops till they could be removed to the place of their destination.

The British troops that were stationed at Gloucester surrendered at the same time and in the same manner to the command of the Duke de Luzerne [Lauzun].

This must be a very interesting and gratifying transaction to General Lincoln, who, having himself been obliged to surrender an army to a haughty foe the last year, has now assigned him the pleasing duty of giving laws to a conquered army in return, and of reflecting that the terms which were imposed on him are adopted as a basis of the surrender in the present instance. It is a very gratifying circumstance that every degree of harmony, confidence and friendly intercourse subsisted between the American and French troops during the campaign—no contest,

except an emulous spirit to excel in exploits and enterprise against the common enemy, and a desire to be celebrated in the annals of history for an ardent love of great and heroic actions.

We are not to be surprised that the pride of the British officers is humbled on this occasion, as they have always entertained an exalted opinion of their own military prowess and affected to view the Americans as a contemptible, undisciplined rabble. But there is no display of magnanimity when a great commander shrinks from the inevitable misfortunes of war; and when it is considered that Lord Cornwallis has frequently appeared in splendid triumph at the head of his army, by which he is almost adored, we conceive it incumbent on him cheerfully to participate in their misfortunes and degradations, however humiliating; but it is said he gives himself up entirely to vexation and despair.

Source: Thacher, Dr. James. *A Military Journal during the American Revolutionary War.* Boston: Cotton & Bernards, 1827, pp. 288–290.

FRONTIER WARFARE: THE DEATH OF A TORY TERRORIST, OCTOBER 29, 1781

Letter to Governor George Clinton
Colonel Marinus Willett
November 2, 1781

The war on the frontier consisted not so much of battles as stealthy murders and massacres. Both sides used Indians as agents of terror. One of the most effective leaders of Indian warriors on the New York frontier was the "Tory ranger" Walter Butler. His death put an end to the mixed Tory-Indian campaign of terror in the northern frontier, as Marinus Willett reported in a letter to New York's governor George Clinton.

Fort Rensselaer, 2nd November, 1781

Dear Sir, I am just returned from a most fatiguing pursuit of the enemy, and tho it has not been in my power to take or kill the whole of the detachment that lately made their appearance in this quarter, yet I flatter myself they are little better off, as those that are not among the killed and taken are in a famis[h]ing situation, scattered throughout the wilderness on the rout to Buck Island, where any of them that may arrive will have tales of horror only to relate.

After the affair at Johnstown, which happened on the 25th ultimo, and which would at once have proved fatal to them had the right wing of the small number of troops I had engaged behaved half as well as the left, the enemy took to the wilderness and, finding it out of their power to pass us so as to get to the Oneida Creek where they had left their boats, they directed their rout towards Buck Island, keeping far back in the wilderness. This determined me to cut across from the German Flatts in order to intercept them on that rout. Accordingly, on the evening of the 28th, having furnished near 400 men and sixty Indians, who had just joined me, with four days and a half provisions, which was all I could procure, I crossed the Mohawk from Fort Herkimer and incamped in the woods.

The 29th we marched north upwards of twenty miles in a snow storm, and at eight oclock A.M. of the 30th we fell in with the enemy, who, without making any resistance worth mentioning, fled from that time until night. We pursued them closely and warmly as possible. Nor did they ever attempt to check us in our advance except at one difficult ford in Canada Creek, where they lost several of their men. Amongst those killed at that place was Walter Butler, the person who commanded the massacre at Cherry Valley in November 1778. He was called Major, but by the commission found in his pocket appears to be no more than a captain.

A number of prisoners have been taken and many were killed in our intercourse with those gentry.

To pursue them any farther was thought improper; many of the troops as well as the Indians had laid aside their blankets and provisions

in order to pursue with greater ease. And in the evening we find ourselves at least twenty miles from those packs. The woods was strewed with the packs of the enemy; provision they had none. The few horses they had amongst them when we first fell in with them, they were obliged to leave; except five, which were sent a considerable way in front, with some of their wounded and a few prisoners. Their flight was performed in an Indian file upon a constant trott, and one man's being knocked in the head or falling off into the woods never stoped the progress of his neighbour. Not even the fall of their favorite Butler could attract their attention so much as to induce them to take even the money or anything else out of his pocket, altho he was not dead when found by one of our Indians, who finished his business for him and got a considerable booty.

Strange as it may appear, yet it is true, that notwithstanding the enemy had been four days with only half a pound of horseflesh for each man per day, yet they did not halt from the time we began to pursue them untill they had proceeded more than thirty miles (and they continued their rout a considerable part of the night). In this situation to the compassion of a starving wilderness, we left them in a fair way of receiving a punishment better suited to their merit than a musquet ball, a tomahawk or captivity. . . .

Source: Willett, Marinus. *A Narrative of the Military Actions of Colonel Marinus Willett, Taken Chiefly from His Manuscript.* New York: Carvill, 1831, pp. 431–433.

THE GNADENHÜTTEN MASSACRE, MARCH 8, 1782

Diary Entry
David Zeisberger
March 7, 1782

The Tory-allied Mohawk war leader Joseph Brant tried to recruit the so-called Moravian Indians— Delaware who had been christianized by Moravian missionaries—to join him in his fight against the Patriots. Try as he might, however, he was unable to persuade them, which prompted British authorities to order their removal from Pennsylvania westward to the Ohio country. Accordingly, they set out for the banks of the Sandusky River, but their trek was interrupted early in 1782 by a terrible winter famine. They secured permission to move back temporarily to their western Pennsylvania mission towns on the Tuscarawas River.

They returned at precisely the wrong time. Mohawk and Delaware had just finished an especially horrific series of raids, and Colonel Daniel Brodhead, who now commanded the Continental army in the area, sent Colonel David Williamson with a contingent of men to conduct reprisals. Williamson encountered the Moravian Indians at the mission town of Gnadenhütten (in present-day Ohio). He told their leader, known as Abraham, and the 48 men, women, and boys who were with him that they were to follow him to Fort Pitt, where they would find shelter and protection from all harm. Williamson asked Abraham to send runners to Salem, a nearby missionary-Indian town, and bring the Indians from there to Gnadenhütten. All, he said, would be taken to the safety of Fort Pitt.

No sooner did the Salem Indians arrive, however, than Williamson sent his troops to bind the wrists of every Indian—now about 90 in all. The next morning, Williamson announced that, as reprisal for the Delaware raids, they would all be put to death, and at the end of the day, each was struck with a single mallet blow to the back of the head. Somehow, two boys evaded death and lived to tell the tale. The Moravian missionary David Zeisberger (1721–1808) recorded details of the atrocity in his journal.

The militia, some 200 in number, as we hear, came first to Gnadenhütten. A mile from town they met young Schebosh in the bush, whom they at once killed and scalped, and, near the houses, two friendly Indians, not belonging to us, but who had gone there with our people from Sandusky, among whom were several other friends who perished likewise. Our Indians were mostly on the plantations and saw the militia

come, but no one thought of fleeing, for they suspected no ill. The militia came to them and bade them come into town, telling them no harm should befall them. They trusted and went, but were all bound, the men being put into one house, the women into another.

The Mohican, Abraham, who for some time had been bad in heart, when he saw that his end was near, made an open confession before his brethren, and said: "Dear brethren, according to appearances we shall all very soon come to the Saviour, for as it seems they have so resolved about us. You know I am a bad man, that I have much troubled the Saviour and the brethren, and have not behaved as becomes a believer, yet to him I belong, bad as I am; he will forgive us all and not reject me; to the end I shall hold fast to him and not leave him."

Then they began to sing hymns and spoke words of encouragement and consolation one to another until they were all slain, and the above mentioned Abraham was the first to be led out, but the others were killed in the house. The sisters also afterwards met the same fate, who also sang hymns together. Christina, the Mohican, who well understood German and English, fell upon her knees before the captain, begging for life, but got for answer that he could not help her. Two well-grown boys, who saw the whole thing and escaped, gave this information. One of these lay under the heaps of slain and was scalped, but finally came to himself and found opportunity to escape. The same did Jacob, Rachel's son, who was wonderfully rescued. For they came close upon him suddenly outside the town, so that he thought they must have seen him, but he crept into a thicket and escaped their hands. . . . He went a long way about and observed what went on.

John Martin went at once to Salem when the militia came, and thus knew nothing about how the brethren in Gnadenhütten fared. He told them there the militia were in Gnadenhütten, whereupon they all resolved not to flee, but John Martin took with himself two brethren and turned back to Gnadenhütten, and told them there were still more Indians in Salem, but he did not know [how] it had gone with them in Gnadenhütten. A part of the militia went there on the 8th with a couple of Indians, who had come to Salem and brought the brethren away, after they had first taken away their arms, and when they came to Gnadenhütten, before they led them over the stream, they bound them, took even their knives from them. The brethren and the sisters alike 10 were bound, led into town, and slain. They made our Indians bring all their hidden goods out of the bush, and then took them away; they had to tell them where in the bush the bees were, help get the honey out; other things also they had to do for them before they were killed. Prisoners said that the militia themselves acknowledged and confessed they had been good Indians. They prayed and sang until the tomahawks struck into their heads. The boy who was scalped and got away said the blood flowed in streams in the house. They burned the dead bodies, together with the houses, which they set on fire.

Source: Zeisberger, David. *Diary of David Zeisberger, a Moravian Missionary among the Indians of Ohio.* Cincinnati: Clarke, 1885, pp. 79–81.

The War of 1812

For many students of American history, the War of 1812 is a subject of great controversy. Some have deemed it the nation's "second war of independence," defining it as a struggle to assert, protect, and enforce the sovereignty of the still-young United States, whereas others have condemned it as a war of choice rather than necessity and, at that, a war of poor choice and high cost.

Those who justify the war as an assertion and defense of sovereignty point out that Great Britain repeatedly attacked U.S. sovereignty in three ways. First, the British violated both the Treaty of Paris, which ended the American Revolution, and Jay's Treaty, which resolved (however imperfectly) certain territorial disputes. In violation of these treaties, British commercial interests, mostly fur trappers and traders, repeatedly "invaded" U.S. territory on the western frontier. Second, British traders and other commercial interests incited Indian tribes of the Ohio country and Old Northwest (much of the upper Midwest between the Appalachian Mountains and the Mississippi River) to acts of hostility against American traders and other commercial interests in an effort to evict them and thereby perpetuate British mercantile dominance on the frontier. Third, the British Royal Navy made it a practice to impress—that is, to abduct for Royal Navy

service—American merchant sailors. On the high seas, British warships would routinely intercept U.S. vessels and board them, the boarding parties seizing any sailor the commander of the party unilaterally deemed a deserter from the Royal Navy or a British subject liable for service.

Traditionally, this third issue, impressment, has been cited as the principal cause of the War of 1812. There is some basis for this. Great Britain was at war with Napoleonic France during this period, and the Royal Navy was certainly in urgent need of sailors to man its warships. It is also true that British navy vessels frequently intercepted and boarded the ships of neutrals, including merchant vessels of the United States, for the purpose of impressing men deemed (often arbitrarily) to be British subjects. However, it is also the case that the United States declared war on Great Britain on June 18, 1812, even though two days earlier, on June 16, Great Britain had agreed to end impressment on the high seas, effective June 23. In beating the drum for war, the "war hawk" faction of the U.S. Congress continued to speak of impressments, yet it is a measure of the degree to which impressment had become a nonissue that the Treaty of Ghent (which ended the War of 1812 on December 24, 1814) is silent on the subject.

In truth, the more pressing causes of the War of 1812 were, from the U.S. point of view, issues relating to the sovereignty and peace of the western frontier territories and, perhaps most compelling of all, an urge to satisfy the young republic's ravenous appetite for new territory. By the time of the war, so-called Spanish Florida (which extended as far west as the Mississippi River) loomed for residents of the South as well as the West as an especially attractive parcel. Because Spain was allied with Great Britain against Napoléon, the congressional war hawks—legislators who favored war—believed that to defeat Great Britain would entail the acquisition of its ally's territory; Spanish Florida would be wedded to the vast western territories acquired by the Louisiana Purchase of 1803.

Much of the fighting in the War of 1812 took place along the U.S.-Canadian frontier between Detroit and Lake Champlain. Although the United States claimed to be defending its sovereignty, the initial American strategy was aggressively offensive. As in the American Revolution, an invasion of Canada was mounted with the twin objectives of confining the war to British Canadian territory and acquiring new, economically productive territory for the United States. The invasion, however, proved abortive, and the war was fought mainly in the United States. Forces transported from England rapidly expanded the theater of operations to encompass the mid-Atlantic coast as well as U.S. territories along much of the Gulf of Mexico. The theater of war thus included territory from Canada and the Canadian borderlands south to New Orleans.

As they had in the American Revolution, the British made extensive use of Indian allies and auxiliaries, especially in the Old Northwest (the territory corresponding to the upper Midwest between the Appalachians and the Mississippi River). In the South, especially in territory adjacent to the Gulf Coast, warfare between U.S. forces and Native Americans evolved into a separate conflict fought, for the most part, simultaneously with the War of 1812. This was the Creek War.

Unpreparedness

The United States embarked on the War of 1812 with grandiose and unrealistic assumptions. A major issue of the American Revolution had been revulsion at the notion of maintaining and quartering a large standing army. In consequence, the United States had a federal force of only 12,000 regulars with which to prosecute a war against a great European power that, moreover, was fully mobilized because of the ongoing Napoleonic Wars. To make matters worse, the U.S. Army was very thinly distributed over a vast territory, its mission less that of a conventional army than as a kind of rural constabulary, struggling to control hostile Indian tribes. Nor was this an elite force led by professional military officers. For the most part, American generals had attained their rank through political connections rather than military training or aptitude. Conditions were better in the U.S. Navy, many of whose officers were of a significantly higher caliber than those of the army. Yet, like the U.S. Army, the U.S. Navy was a puny force, especially compared to the Royal Navy, the biggest in the world and a force that had been significantly expanded over the period of the British struggle against Napoléon.

American military planners relied heavily on short-term militia units to build up a force for the invasion of Canada. As if oblivious to the realities of manpower and logistics, however, the U.S. high command laid out a three-pronged invasion plan, to include a penetration from Lake Champlain to Montreal; another across the Niagara frontier; and a third into Upper Canada from Detroit. All three were destined to fail and to fail at great cost.

American Defeats

To serve as commander of the "Army of the Northwest"—all American forces north of the Ohio River, 300 regulars and 1,200 militiamen from Kentucky and Ohio (most of whom deserted almost immediately and had to be replaced at the last minute by Michigan volunteers)—Secretary of War William Eustis tapped the governor of Michigan Territory, William Hull. He had as impressive a military background as any U.S. officer in 1812, having fought in the American Revolution at the battles of White Plains, Trenton, Princeton, Stillwater, Saratoga, Fort Stanwix, Monmouth, and Stony Point, but he was nearly 60 years old when he led the Army of the Northwest across the Detroit River into Canada on July 12, 1812.

Hull's assigned objective was to capture Fort Malden, guarding the entrance to Lake Erie. The closer he approached the fort, however, the more convinced he became that he was badly outnumbered. In fact, he was not, but his doubts caused him to delay his advance repeatedly, giving the highly capable British commander, Major General Isaac Brock, more than enough time to bring up his regulars, all of whom were seasoned veterans of the wars against Napoléon. While Brock mustered his forces, a mixed force of Canadians and Indians overran the American garrison occupying Fort Michilimackinac, which controlled the Mackinac Straits connecting Lake Huron and Lake Michigan. The garrison surrendered without a fight on July 17, 1812.

On August 2, the Shawnee political and war leader Tecumseh began a series of harassing attacks on the Army of the Northwest. Believing these attacks involved far more than the 700 warriors Tecumseh actually led, Hull retreated from Canada and fell back on Fort Detroit. Seeing his opportunity, Brock united his 600 regulars with Tecumseh's warriors and pursued the retreating Americans to the fort. There, Brock simply intimidated Hull into capitulating. As the Fort Michilimackinac garrison had done, Hull surrendered without firing a shot—giving up both the fort and the entire Army of the Northwest on August 16. (Hull would subsequently be convicted by court-martial of cowardice; sentenced to death by firing squad, he was pardoned by President James Madison.)

There was yet more disaster. On August 15, the day before the fall of Detroit, Fort Dearborn (at the site of present-day Chicago) surrendered to a mixed force of British and Potawatomi Indians. Although promised safe conduct out of the fort, troops as well as settlers were set upon by Indian warriors about a mile and a half south of the fort. Some 50 men, women, and children were killed, most of them by torture. Most of the rest were captured, then sold to the British as slaves. British authorities immediately released them.

In the Northeast, Stephen Van Rensselaer, a general of militia, led 2,270 New York militiamen and 900 U.S. Army regulars against Queenston Heights, Canada, on the Canadian bank of the Niagara River. Most of the regulars had crossed the river before British general Brock, having rushed to Queenston from Detroit, counterattacked on October 13, 1812. Brock's men held the regulars at bay. Had the militia effected a Niagara River crossing at this time, it is likely that Brock would have been forced to retire; however, the bulk of the militia simply refused to cross the international boundary, arguing that the terms of their militia service were strictly domestic. They stood by as 600 British regulars and 400 Canadian militiamen overran the U.S. regulars. It was another costly and humiliating American defeat, in which 250 regulars died and 700 became prisoners of war; British losses were 14 killed and 96 wounded. Among those 14, however, was Isaac Brock, the most thoroughly capable and aggressive British commander in North America at the time. This single loss was a heavy blow for the British.

With two major American forces defeated, Major General Henry Dearborn set out with his 5,000 men, chiefly militia, in a march down Lake Champlain. By November 19, 1812, he was poised to cross into Canada when, suddenly, the militiamen asserted what they declared as their "constitutional rights," refusing to cross the border for a fight in a foreign country. Dearborn had no choice but to withdraw without having engaged the enemy. Thus was the third of the three prongs of the Canadian offensive defeated—before it had really begun.

The loss of Forts Detroit and Dearborn, along with the ignominious collapse of the Canadian campaign, exposed the entire upper Midwest (the Old Northwest) to raids by British-allied Indians and a general invasion of British regulars. Guerrilla warfare, mostly conducted by Shawnee warriors, was intense along the frontier, yet neither the Indians nor regular British forces decisively exploited the many gains they made.

The Victories of Taylor, Harrison, and Perry

On September 5, 1812, U.S. commander Zachary Taylor beat off a Potawatomi attack on Fort Wayne, Indiana Territory—a rare major American victory, which did not, however, prevent most of the Old Northwest from falling under the hatchet. Still, the fully coordinated British-Indian campaign through the region, which surely would have brought the War of 1812 to a quick and (for the Americans) devastating end, failed to materialize. The problem was with the regulars and their new commander, Colonel Henry Procter, who replaced the slain Isaac Brock. Whereas Brock had been both brilliant and aggressive, Procter was the typical British officer of the period: dull and overly cautious—far more concerned with avoiding loss than gaining victory. He repeatedly refused to support Tecumseh, who was always eager to advance the fight.

Procter's hesitation and his failure to coordinate with Tecumseh gave U.S. general William Henry Harrison sufficient time to mount a series of effective counterattacks. In the waning days of 1812, Harrison razed the Miami villages near Fort Wayne (never mind that the Miami had proclaimed themselves neutral) and raided what amounted to Indian refugee camps near

present-day Peru, Indiana. In January 1813, he moved against British-held Fort Malden, boldly advancing across a frozen Lake Erie, but when one of his subordinate officers made a premature attack at the River Raisin on January 21, Harrison suffered a disastrous defeat. Of 960 Americans engaged in the attack, Procter's regulars and a unit of Red Stick Creek under Little Warrior killed 400 and captured virtually all of the survivors. A mere 33 men evaded death or capture.

Remarkably, Procter again declined to exploit his victory. In July 1813, he passed up an opportunity to capture Fort Stephenson, a key American supply depot on the Sandusky River. Procter commanded some 3,000 troops (mixed British and Indian forces), whereas the fort was defended by no more than 150 men under Major George Croghan. This notable absence of aggression prompted many of Procter's Indian allies to desert him. Although this gave the Americans a reprieve on the frontier, it remained a gloomy fact that, by late 1813, 4,000 American soldiers had been killed or captured, whereas combined British and Indian losses amounted to 500 or less.

Through all of 1812 and much of 1813, U.S. land forces fared miserably, whereas the miniscule U.S. Navy managed to achieve some remarkable results against the vastly superior Royal Navy. The British brought to bear a total of 1,048 Royal Navy craft to blockade American shipping. To oppose this vast armada, the U.S. Navy had but 14 seaworthy warships in addition to a variable number of privateers (civilian vessels commissioned to raid enemy shipping). Despite the staggering odds, U.S. Navy frigates (all superbly built and ably commanded) were victorious in a series of single-ship engagements, the most famous of which were the battles between the USS *Constitution* (the fabled "Old Ironsides") and HMS *Guerriere,* off the coast of Massachusetts on August 19, 1812; and between the *Constitution* and HMS *Java,* off the Brazilian coast on December 29–30, 1812. These victories did much to boost American morale, but they accomplished nothing to relieve the stranglehold of a blockade that had effectively destroyed American trade, bringing the U.S. economy to the brink of collapse.

As noted, in 1813, new American attempts to invade Canada ended in failure, but in the West, the American outlook brightened somewhat. After the January defeat of his Fort Malden campaign on the River Raisin, William Henry Harrison rebuilt and expanded his army into a force of 8,000, which was prepared for combat by the late summer of 1813. Simultaneously, the U.S. Navy's Oliver Hazard Perry rushed to cobble together an inland navy at Presque Isle (present-day Erie), Pennsylvania. By August, Perry was ready to sail onto Lake Erie, and on September 10, he engaged the British Lake Erie squadron in a battle so brutally punishing that he was forced to transfer his flag from the severely damaged brig *Lawrence* to the *Niagara*. It was from this new flagship that he directed the destruction of the entire British squadron, after which he sent to General Harrison the celebrated message: "We have met the enemy and they are ours."

Perry's triumph severed British lines of supply and communication, forcing not only the abandonment of Fort Malden but a general British evacuation of the Detroit region and a general retreat eastward. Harrison was quick to exploit the opportunity Perry had provided. Pursuing the retreating British, he overtook them and their Indian allies on October 5, 1813, forcing them to a stand at the Battle of the Thames. Tecumseh himself fell in this battle, leaving the Native Americans without an effective political and military leader. Although American forces achieved no other major victories during 1813, the Battle of Lake Erie and the Battle of the Thames pushed the British toward negotiating an end to the war; however, in Europe, the fall of Paris on March 30, 1814, followed by the mutiny of Napoléon's marshals on April 1, the emperor's abdication on April 4, and his exile to Elba, seemed to spell the end of the Napoleonic Wars. This freed up the British to release more men for service in North America.

A Renewed British Offensive

Feeling they had gained a fresh purchase on the struggle, British high command drew up plans to attack in three principal areas: in New York, along Lake Champlain and the Hudson River, which would sever New England from the rest of the union; at New Orleans, which would block the vital Mississippi artery; and in Chesapeake Bay, to threaten Washington, D.C., and to create a diversion that would draw off and pin down U.S. manpower. The objective of this grand campaign was to pummel the already battered and economically ailing United States into making vast territorial concessions in return for peace. Despite the victories of 1813, the American situation looked bleak indeed by late summer 1814. In New England, opponents of the war even began talking of secession from the Union.

On August 24, 1814, a large British column under Major General Robert Ross swept aside inept resistance in Maryland at the Battle of Bladensburg, then marched into Washington, putting to the torch most of the public buildings, including the Capitol and the White House, as President James Madison and much of the rest of the government fled into the countryside. After sacking the nation's capital, Ross advanced north, setting his sights on the conquest of Baltimore. His amphibious forces bombarded Fort McHenry, in Baltimore Harbor, during the night of September 13–14, 1814—an event witnessed by a young Washington lawyer, Francis Scott Key, who was being detained on a British warship. Key composed verses to commemorate his anxious nightlong vigil, which ended when, by "dawn's early light," he saw that the

"Star-Spangled Banner" still waved over the fort. Indeed, meeting much stiffer resistance here than they had in Maryland and Washington, Ross was forced to break off the attack.

To be sure, the salvation of Baltimore was a hopeful sign, but, at this very time, some 10,000 British regulars—all veterans of the Napoleonic Wars—marched into the United States from Montreal. Although the American land forces opposing this advance were outnumbered, on September 11, 1814, U.S. Navy captain Thomas MacDonough intercepted and engaged the British squadron on Lake Champlain, defeating it decisively. Yet again, the British army had lost its line of communication and supply and was forced to withdraw.

"Status Quo Antebellum"

Costly to both sides, the fighting continued in the War of 1812 even though, as early as March 1813, President Madison had accepted a Russian offer to mediate an armistice. The British rejected the mediation in July 1813 but then made separate peace overtures, which Madison welcomed in January 1814. Talks did not actually commence until July of that year, in Ghent, Belgium. Initially, the British demanded the establishment of an Indian buffer state in the U.S. Northwest as well as extensive territorial cessions along the Canadian border. Emboldened by victory at the Battle of Lake Champlain, U.S. negotiators flatly rejected these demands. Weary of an epoch of war in North America as well as Europe and elsewhere, the British government at length resolved to forgo its demands for the buffer state and territorial cessions, which prompted the United States to withdraw its demand that Britain recognize American neutral rights—thereby renouncing the chief stated reason for having gone to war in the first place. These concessions enabled the conclusion of the Treaty of Ghent on December 24, 1814, which restored the status quo antebellum (prewar conditions).

Other than ending the war, little was resolved by the Treaty of Ghent, although it did call for a joint U.S.-British commission to set a definitive boundary between the United States and Canada. Nevertheless, the United States did not emerge from the War of 1812 the same nation that it had been when it entered the war. Economic depression was severe, yet the withdrawal of British support for the frontier Native Americans offered much opportunity for western expansion.

It is important to note that the treaty did not bring an immediate end to the war. Word of the transaction at Ghent did not reach the American general Andrew Jackson or the British general Edward Pakenham before the two engaged in the Battle of New Orleans. Pakenham advanced on the city with 5,300 British regulars and was supported by Royal Navy forces under Vice Admiral Sir Alexander Cochrane. Jackson commanded 3,100 Tennessee and Kentucky volunteers, in addition to New Orleans militiamen and a collection of locals (including "free colored" volunteers), which brought his total strength to about 4,700 men.

On December 23, 1814, Jackson first engaged the British forces but failed to drive them off. On December 28 and, again, on January 1, 1815, Pakenham jabbed at Jackson's defenses. At last, on January 8, the British commander launched his principal attack against Jackson's line on the east bank of the Mississippi, while making a smaller attack against positions on the west bank of the river. Although his secondary attack succeeded, his main assault failed, the British ranks melting under Jackson's well-coordinated artillery fire. Pakenham lost 2,400 killed and wounded—and then was himself killed, along with his two senior subordinates. Jackson's losses amounted to no more than 70 men. The badly mauled British withdrew.

To the majority of Americans, it mattered little that the Battle of New Orleans had been fought after the war had officially ended. This triumph made the whole mostly disastrous conflict *feel* like a great victory, raising the level of American national sentiment.

DOCUMENTS

THE FORT DEARBORN MASSACRE, AUGUST 15, 1812

Account of the Massacre
Linai T. Helm
Written 1814; published 1912

Defeated at Fort Detroit, General William Hull also ordered the evacuation of Fort Dearborn, on the site of modern Chicago. The fort's commander, Captain Nathan Heald, negotiated its surrender to the British-allied Indians, and although he had agreed to leave behind all of the fort's ample stores of whiskey and gunpowder, he ordered these destroyed just before evacuating on August 15, 1812. This may have provoked the ambush that followed.

Heald led a column of 148 soldiers, women, and children out of the fort, but they were ambushed by Potawatomi warriors after marching about a mile and a half south. Some 50 were killed in the ambush, and survivors were taken as prisoners to be sold to the British as slaves. British authorities did purchase the prisoners but released them immediately. As for Fort Dearborn, it was burned. One of the survivors of the Fort Dearborn Massacre, a militia lieutenant named Linai T. Helm, wrote the following narrative.

Some time in April, about the 7th–10, a party of Winnebagoes came to Chicago and murdered 2 men. This gave sufficient ground to suppose the Indians hostile, as they have left every sign by scalping them and leaving a weapon, say a war mallet, as a token of their returning in June. Mr. Kinzie sent a letter from the Interior of the Indian Country to inform Capt. Heald that the Indians were hostile inclined and only waiting the Declaration of War to commence open hostilities. This they told Kinzie in confidence on the loth of July. Capt. Heald got the information of War being declared, and on the 8th of August got Gen. Hull's order to evacuate the Post of Fort Dearborn by the route of Detroit, or Fort Wayne, if practicable. This letter was brought by a Potowautemie [Potowatomi] Chief Winnemeg, and he informed Capt. Heald, through Kenzie, to evacuate immediately the next day, if possible, as the Indians were hostile and that the troops should change the usual routes to go to Fort Wayne. On the 12th August, Capt. William Wells arrived from Fort Wayne with 27 Miamis, and after a council being held by him with the tribes there assembled to amount of 500 warriors 179 women and children. He after council declared them hostile and that his opinion was that they would interrupt us on our route. Capt. Wells enquired into the State of the arms, ammunition and provisions. We had 200 stand of arms, four pieces of artillery, 6,000 lbs. of powder and a sufficient quantity of shot lead, etc. 3 months provisions taken in Indian corn and all this on the 12th of August, having prior to this expended 3 months provisions at least in the interval between the 7th and 12th of August, exclusive of this we had at our command 200 head of horned cattle and 27 barrels of salt. After this survey, Wells demanded of Capt. Heald if he intended to evacuate. His answer was he would. Kenzie then, with Lt. Helm, called on Wells and requested him to call on Capt. Heald and cause the ammunition and arms to be destroyed, but Capt. Wells insisted on Kenzie and Helm to join with him. This being done, Capt. Heald hesitated and observed that it was not sound policy to tell a lie to an Indian; that he had received a positive order from Gen. Hull to deliver up to those Indians all the public property of whatsoever nature particularly to those Indians that would take in the Troops and that he could not alter it, and that it might irritate the Indians and be the means of the destruction of his men. Kenzie volunteered

Many warriors of the so-called Iroquois Confederation (also known as the Six Nations) fought on the British side during the War of 1812. This studio portrait of surviving Six Nations warriors was made in July 1882, many years after the conflict. Pictured right to left are Sakawaraton, a.k.a. John Smoke Johnson (born ca. 1792); John Tutela (born ca. 1797); and Young Warner (born ca. 1794). *(Library and Archives Canada)*

to take the responsibility on himself, provided Capt. Heald would consider the method he would point out a safe one, he agreed. Kenzie wrote an order as if from Genl. Hull, and gave it into Capt. Heald. It was supposed to answer and accordingly was carried into effect. The ammunition and muskets were all destroyed the night of the 13th. The 15th, we evacuated the Garrison, and about one and half mile from the Garrison we were informed by Capt. Wells that we were surrounded and the attack by the Indians began about 10 of the clock morning. The men in a few minutes were, with the exception of 10, all killed and wounded. The Ensign and Surgeons Mate

were both killed. The Capt. and myself both badly wounded during the battle. I fired my piece at an Indian and felt confident I killed him or wounded him badly. I immediately called to the men to follow me in the pirara [pirogue, a lake boat], or we would be shot down before we could load our guns. We had proceeded under a heavy fire about an hundred and five paces when I made a wheel to the left to observe the motion of the Indians and avoid being shot in the back, which I had so far miraculously escaped. Just as I wheeled I received a ball through my coat pocket, which struck the barrel of my gun and fell in the lining of my coat. In a few seconds, I received a ball in my right foot, which lamed me considerably. The Indians happened immediately to stop firing and never more renewed it. I immediately ordered the men that were able to load their guns and commenced loading for them that were not able. I now discovered Capt. Heald for the first time to my knowledge during the battle. He was coming towards the Indians and to my great surprise they never offered to fire on him. He came up and ordered the men to form; that his intentions were to charge the body of Indians that were on the bank of the Lake where we had just retreated from. They appeared to be about 300 strong. We were 27, including all the wounded. He advanced about 5 steps and not at all to my surprise was the first that halted. Some of the men fell back instead of advancing. We then gained the only high piece of ground that was near. We now had a little time to reflect and saw death in every direction. At this time an interpreter from the Indians advanced towards us and called for the Captain, who immediately went to meet him (the interpreter was a half Indian and had lived a long time within a few yards of the fort and bound to Mr. Kinzie; he was always very friendly with us all). A chief by the name of Blackbird advanced to the interpreter and met the Captain, who after a few words of conversation delivered him his sword, and in a few minutes returned to us and informed me he had offered 100 dollars for every man that was then living. He said they were then deciding on what to do. They, however, in a few minutes, called him again and talked with him some time, when he returned and informed me they had agreed if I and the men would surrender by laying down our arms they would lay down theirs, meet us half way, shake us by the hand as friends and take us back to the fort. I asked him if he knew what they intended doing with us then. He said they did not inform him. He asked me if I would surrender. The men were at this time crowding to my back and began to beg me not to surrender. I told them not to be uneasy for I had already done my best for them and was determined not to surrender unless I saw better prospects of us all being saved and then not without they were willing. The Captain asked me the second time what I would do, without an answer. I discovered the interpreter at this time running from the Indians towards us, and when he came in about 20 steps the Captain put the question the third time. The Interpreter called out, "Lieut, don't surrender for if you do they will kill you all, for there has been no general council held with them yet. You must wait, and I will go back and hold a general council with them and return and let you know what they will do." I told him to go, for I had no idea of surrender. He went and collected all the Indians and talked for some time, when he returned and told me the Indians said if I would surrender as before described they would not kill any, and said it was his opinion they would do as they said, for they had already saved Mr. Kinzie and some of the women and children. This enlivened me and the men, for we well knew Mr. Kinzie stood higher than any man in that country among the Indians, and he might be the means of saving us from utter destruction, which afterwards proved to be the case. We then surrendered, and after the Indians had fired off our guns they put the Captain and myself and some of the wounded men on horses and marched us to the bank of the lake, where the battle first commenced. When we arrived at the bank and looked down on the sand beach I was struck with horror at the sight of men, women and children lying naked with principally all their heads off, and in passing over the bodies I was confident I saw my wife with her head off about two feet from her shoulders. Tears for the first time rushed in my eyes, but I consoled myself with a firm belief that I should soon follow her. I now began to repent that I had ever surrendered, but it was too late to recall, and we had only to look up to Him who had first caused our existence. When we had arrived in half a mile of the Fort they halted us, made the men sit down, form a ring around them, began to take off their hats and strip the Captain. They attempted to strip me, but were prevented by a Chief who stuck close to me. I made signs to him that I wanted to drink, for the weather was very warm. He led me off towards the Fort and, to my great astonishment, saw my wife sitting among some squaws crying. Our feelings can be better judged than expressed. They brought some water and directed her to wash and dress my wound, which she did, and bound it up with her pocket handkerchief. They then brought up some of the men and tommyhawked one of them before us. They now took Mrs. Helm across the river (for we were nearly on its banks) to Mr. Kinzie's. We met again at my fathers in the State of New York, she having arrived seven days before me after being separated seven months and one week. She was taken in the direction of Detroit and I was taken down to Illinois River and was sold to Mr. Thomas Forsyth, half brother of Mr. Kinzie's, who, a short time after, effected my escape. This gentleman was the means of saving many lives on the warring frontier. I was taken on the 15th of August and arrived safe among the Americans at St. Louis on the 14th of October.

Capt. Heald, through Kenzie, sending his two negroes, got put on board an Indian boat going to St. Joseph, and from that place got to Makenac by Lake Michigan in a birch canoe.

The night of the 14th, the Interpreter and a Chief (Black Partridge) waited on Capt. Heald. The Indian gave up his medal and told Heald to beware of the next day, that the Indians would destroy him and his men. This Heald never communicated to one of his officers. There was but Capt. Wells that was acquainted with it. You will observe, sir, that I did, with Kenzie, protest against destroying the arms, ammunition and provisions until that Heald told me positively that he would evacuate at all hazards.

15th of August, we evacuated the Fort. The number of soldiers was 52 privates and musicians (2), 4 officers and physicians, 14 citizens, 18 children and 9 women, the baggage being in front with the citizens, women and children and on the margin of the lake, we having advanced to gain the Prairie. I could not see the massacre, but Kinzie, with Doctor Van Vorees, being ordered by Capt. Heald to take charge of the women and

children, remained on the beach, and Kinzie since told me he was an eye witness to the horrid scene. The Indians came down on the baggage wagons for plunder. They butchered every male citizen but Kinzie, two women and 12 children in the most inhuman manner possible, opened them, cutting off their heads and taken out their hearts; several of the women were wounded but not dangerously.

Source: Helm, Linai Taliaferro. The Fort Dearborn Massacre. Written in 1814 by Lieutenant Linai T. Helm. . . . Edited by Nelly Kinzie Gordon, 15–26. Chicago and New York: Rand McNally, 1912.

Account of the Massacre
Nellie Kinzie Gordon
Published 1912

John Kinzie, generally regarded as the first permanent white settler in what is now Chicago, married his second wife, Eleanor Lytle McKillip, in 1800 and settled in Chicago in 1804. The Kinzies survived the Fort Dearborn Massacre. Nellie Kinzie Gordon, an early 20th-century descendant of the Kinzies, drew on the eyewitness narratives of Mrs. Linai Helm and Mrs. John Kinzie to create the following account.

Captain Heald was struck with the inadvisability of furnishing the enemy (for such they must now consider their old neighbors) with arms against himself, and determined to destroy all the ammunition except what should be necessary for the use of his own troops.

On August 13 the goods, consisting of blankets, broadcloths, calicoes, paints, and miscellaneous supplies were distributed, as stipulated. The same evening part of the ammunition and liquor was carried into the sally port, and there thrown into a well which had been dug to supply the garrison with water in case of emergency. The remainder was transported, as secretly as possible, through the northern gate; the heads of the barrels were knocked in, and the contents poured into the river. The same fate was shared by a large quantity of alcohol belonging to Mr. Kinzie, which had been deposited in a warehouse near his residence opposite the fort.

The Indians suspected what was going on, and crept, serpent-like, as near the scene of action as possible; but a vigilant watch was kept up, and no one was suffered to approach but those engaged in the affair. All the muskets not necessary for the command on the march were broken up and thrown into the well, together with bags of shot, flints, gunscrews; in short, everything relating to weapons of defense.

Some relief to the general feeling of despondency was afforded by the arrival, on August 14, of Captain Wells with fifteen friendly Miami. Of this brave man, who forms so conspicuous a figure in our frontier annals, it is unnecessary here to say more than that he had resided from boyhood among the Indians, and hence possessed a perfect knowledge of their character and habits.

At Fort Wayne [in present-day Indiana] he had heard of the order to evacuate the fort at Chicago, and, knowing the hostile determination of the Potowatomi, had made a rapid march across the country to prevent the exposure of his relative, Captain Heald, and his troops to certain destruction. But he came "all too late." When he reached the post he found that the ammunition had been destroyed, and the provisions given to the Indians. There was, therefore, no alternative, and every preparation was made for the march of the troops on the following morning.

On the afternoon of the same day a second council was held with the Indians. They expressed great indignation at the destruction of the ammunition and liquor. Notwithstanding the precautions that had been taken to preserve secrecy, the noise of knocking in the heads of the barrels had betrayed the operations of the preceding night; indeed, so great was the quantity of liquor thrown into the river that next morning the water was, as one expressed it, "strong grog."

Murmurs and threats were everywhere heard among the savages. It was evident that the first moment of exposure would subject the troops to some manifestation of their disappointment and resentment.

Among the chiefs were several who, although they shared the general hostile feeling of their tribe towards the Americans, yet retained a personal regard for the troops at this post and for the few white citizens of the place. These chiefs exerted their utmost influence to allay the revengeful feelings of the young men, and to avert their sanguinary designs, but without effect.

On the evening succeeding the council Black Partridge, a conspicuous chief, entered the quarters of the commanding officer.

"Father," said he, "I come to deliver up to you the medal I wear. It was given me by the Americans, and I have long worn it in token of our mutual friendship. But our young men are resolved to imbrue their hands in the blood of the whites. I cannot restrain them, and I will not wear a token of peace while I am compelled to act as an enemy."

Had further evidence been wanting, this circumstance would have sufficiently justified the devoted band in their melancholy anticipations. Nevertheless, they went steadily on with the necessary preparations; and, amid the horrors of the situation there were not wanting gallant hearts who strove to encourage in their desponding companions the hopes of escape they themselves were far from indulging.

Of the ammunition there had been reserved but twenty-five rounds, besides one box of cartridges, contained in the baggage wagons. This must, under any circumstances of danger, have proved an inadequate supply; but the prospect of a fatiguing march, in their present ineffective state, forbade the troops embarrassing themselves with a larger quantity.

The morning of August 15 arrived. Nine o'clock was the hour named for starting and all things were in readiness.

Mr. Kinzie, having volunteered to accompany the troops in their march, had intrusted his family to the care of some friendly Indians, who promised to convey them in a boat around the head of Lake Michigan to a point on the St. Joseph River, there to be joined by the troops, should their march be permitted.

Early in the morning Mr. Kinzie received a message from To-pee-nee-bee, a chief of the St. Joseph band, informing him that mischief was intended by the Potowatomi who had engaged to escort the detachment, and urging him to relinquish his plan of accompanying the troops by land, promising him that the boat containing his family should be permitted to pass in safety to St. Joseph.

Mr. Kinzie declined this proposal, as he believed his presence might restrain the fury of the savages, so warmly were the greater number of them attached to him and his family.

Seldom does one find a man who, like John Kinzie, refuses safety for himself in order to stand or fall with his countrymen, and who, as stern as any Spartan, bids farewell to his dear ones to go forward to almost certain destruction.

The party in the boat consisted of Mrs. Kinzie and her four younger children, their nurse Josette, a clerk of Mr. Kinzie's, two servants, and the boatmen, besides the two Indians who were to act as their protectors. The boat started, but had scarcely reached the mouth of the river, which, it will be recalled, was here half a mile below the fort, when another messenger from To-pee-nee-bee arrived to detain it. There was no mistaking the meaning of this detention.

In breathless anxiety sat the wife and mother. She was a woman of unusual energy and strength of character, yet her heart died within her as she folded her arms about her helpless infants and gazed upon the march of her husband and eldest child to what seemed certain death.

As the troops left the fort, the band struck up the Dead March. On they came, in military array, but with solemn mien, Captain Wells in the lead at the head of his little band of Miami. He had blackened his face before leaving the garrison, in token of his impending fate. The troops took their route along the lake shore; but when they reached the point where the range of sand hills intervening between the prairie and the beach commenced, the escort of Potowatomi, in number about five hundred, took the level of the prairie, instead of continuing along the shore with the Americans and Miami.

They had marched perhaps a mile and a half when Captain Wells, who had kept somewhat in advance with his Miami, came riding furiously back.

"They are about to attack us," shouted he; "form instantly, and charge upon them."

Scarcely were the words uttered, when a volley was showered from among the sand hills. The troops, brought hastily into line, charged up the bank. One man, a veteran of seventy winters, fell as they ascended. The remainder of the scene is best described in the words of an eyewitness and participator in the tragedy, Mrs. Helm, the wife of Captain (then Lieutenant) Helm, and stepdaughter of Mr. Kinzie.

"After we had left the bank the firing became general. The Miami fled at the outset. Their chief rode up to the Potowatomi, and said: 'You have deceived us and the Americans. You have done a bad action, and (brandishing his tomahawk) I will be the first to head a party of Americans to return and punish your treachery.' So saying, he galloped after his companions, who were now scurrying across the prairies.

"The troops behaved most gallantly. They were but a handful, but they seemed resolved to sell their lives as dearly as possible. Our horses pranced and bounded, and could hardly be restrained as the balls whistled among them. I drew off a little, and gazed upon my husband and father, who were yet unharmed. I felt that my hour was come, and endeavored to forget those I loved, and prepare myself for my approaching fate.

"While I was thus engaged, the surgeon, Dr. Van Voorhees, came up. He was badly wounded. His horse had been shot under him, and he had received a ball in his leg. Every muscle of his face was quivering with the agony of terror. He said to me, 'Do you think they will take our lives? I am badly wounded, but I think not mortally. Perhaps we might purchase our lives by promising them a large reward. Do you think there is any chance?'

"'Dr. Van Voorhees,' said I, 'do not let us waste the moments that yet remain to us in such vain hopes. Our fate is inevitable. In a few moments we must appear before the bar of God. Let us make what preparation is yet in our power.'

"'Oh, I cannot die!' exclaimed he, 'I am not fit to die—if I had but a short time to prepare—death is awful!'

"I pointed to Ensign Ronan, who, though mortally wounded and nearly down, was still fighting with desperation on one knee.

"'Look at that man!' said I. 'At least he dies like soldier.'

"'Yes,' replied the unfortunate surgeon, with a convulsive gasp, 'but he has no terrors of the future—he is an atheist.'

"At this moment a young Indian raised his tomahawk over me. Springing aside, I partially avoided the blow, which, intended for my skull, fell on my shoulder. I seized the Indian around the neck, and while exerting my utmost strength to get possession of his scalping-knife, hanging in a scabbard over his breast, I was dragged from his grasp by another and older Indian.

"The latter bore me struggling and resisting towards the lake. Despite the rapidity with which I was hurried along, I recognized, as I passed, the lifeless remains of the unfortunate surgeon. Some murderous tomahawk had stretched him upon the very spot where I had last seen him.

"I was immediately plunged into the water and held there with a forcible hand, notwithstanding my resistance. I soon perceived, however, that the object of my captor was not to drown me, for he held me firmly in such a position as to keep my head above water. This reassured me, and, regarding him attentively, I soon recognized, in spite of the paint with which he was disguised, the Black Partridge.

"When the firing had nearly subsided, my preserver bore me from the water and conducted me up the sand banks. It was a burning August morning, and walking through the sand in my drenched condition was inexpressibly painful and fatiguing. I stooped and took off my shoes to free them from the sand with which they were nearly filled, when a squaw seized and carried them off, and I was obliged to proceed without them.

"When we had gained the prairie, I was met by my father, who told me that my husband was safe and but slightly wounded. I was led gently back towards the Chicago River, along the southern bank of which was the Potowatomi encampment. Once I was placed upon a horse without a saddle, but, finding the motion insupportable, I sprang off. Assisted partly by my kind conductor, Black Partridge, and partly by another Indian, Pee-so-tum, who held dangling in his hand a scalp which by the black ribbon around the queue I recognized as that of Captain Wells, I dragged my fainting steps to one of the wigwams.

"The wife of Wau-bee-nee-mah, a chief from the Illinois River, was standing near. Seeing my exhausted condition, she seized a kettle, dipped up some water from a stream that flowed near, threw into it some maple sugar, and, stirring it with her hand, gave it to me to drink. This act of kindness, in the midst of so many horrors, touched me deeply. But my attention was soon diverted to other things.

"The fort, since the troops marched out, had become a scene of plunder. The cattle had been shot as they ran at large, and lay about, dead or dying. This work of butchery had commenced just as we were leaving the fort. I vividly recalled a remark of Ensign Ronan, as the firing went on. 'Such,' turning to me, 'is to be our fate—to be shot down like brutes!'

"'Well, sir,' said the commanding officer, who overheard him, 'are you afraid?'

"'No,' replied the high-spirited young man, 'I can march up to the enemy where you dare not show your face.' And his subsequent gallant behavior showed this was no idle boast.

"As the noise of the firing grew gradually fainter and the stragglers from the victorious party came dropping in, I received confirmation of what my father had hurriedly communicated in our meeting on the lake shore: the whites had surrendered, after the loss of about two thirds of their number. They had stipulated, through the interpreter, Peresh Leclerc, that their lives and those of the remaining women and children be spared, and that they be delivered in safety at certain of the British posts, unless ransomed by traders in the Indian country. It appears that the wounded prisoners were not considered as included in the stipulation, and upon their being brought into camp an awful scene ensued.

"An old squaw, infuriated by the loss of friends, or perhaps excited by the sanguinary scenes around her, seemed possessed by a demoniac ferocity. Seizing a stable fork she assaulted one miserable victim, already groaning and writhing in the agony of wounds aggravated by the scorching beams of the sun. With a delicacy of feeling scarcely to have been expected under such circumstances, Wau-bee-nee-mah stretched a mat across two poles, between me and this dreadful scene. I was thus in some degree shielded from its horrors, though I could not close my ears to the cries of the sufferer. The following night five more of the wounded prisoners were tomahawked."

After the first attack, it appears the Americans charged upon a band of Indians concealed in a sort of ravine between the sand banks and the prairie. The Indians gathered together, and after hard fighting, in which the number of whites was reduced to twenty-eight, their band succeeded in breaking through the enemy and gaining a rise of ground not far from Oak Woods. Further contest now seeming hopeless, Lieutenant Helm sent Peresh Leclerc, the half-breed boy in the service of Mr. Kinzie, who had accompanied the troops and fought manfully on their side, to propose terms of capitulation. It was stipulated, as told in Mrs. Helm's narrative, that the lives of all the survivors should be spared, and a ransom permitted as soon as practicable.

But in the meantime horrible scenes had indeed been enacted. During the engagement near the sand hills one young savage climbed into the baggage wagon which sheltered the twelve children of the white families, and tomahawked

the entire group. Captain Wells, who was fighting near, beheld the deed, and exclaimed:

"Is that their game, butchering the women and children? Then I will kill, too!"

So saying, he turned his horse's head and started for the Indian camp, near the fort, where the braves had left their squaws and children.

Several Indians followed him as he galloped along. Lying flat on the neck of his horse, and loading and firing in that position, he turned occasionally on his pursuers. But at length their balls took effect, killing his horse, and severely wounding the Captain. At this moment he was met by Winnemeg and Wau-ban-see, who endeavored to save him from the savages who had now overtaken him. As they helped him along, after having disengaged him from his horse, he received his deathblow from Pee-sotum, who stabbed him in the back.

The heroic resolution shown during the fight by the wife of one of the soldiers, a Mrs. Corbin, deserves to be recorded. She had from the first expressed the determination never to fall into the hands of the savages, believing that their prisoners were invariably subjected to tortures worse than death.

When, therefore, a party came upon her to make her prisoner, she fought with desperation, refusing to surrender, although assured, by signs, of safety and kind treatment. Literally, she suffered herself to be cut to pieces, rather than become their captive.

There was a Sergeant Holt, who early in the engagement received a ball in the neck. Finding himself badly wounded, he gave his sword to his wife, who was on horseback near him, telling her to defend herself. He then made for the lake, to keep out of the way of the balls.

Mrs. Holt rode a very fine horse, which the Indians were desirous of possessing, and they therefore attacked her in the hope of dismounting her. They fought only with the butt ends of their guns, for their object was not to kill her. She hacked and hewed at their pieces as they were thrust against her, now on this side, now that. Finally, she broke loose and dashed out into the prairie, where the Indians pursued her, shouting and laughing, and now and then calling out, "The brave woman! do not hurt her!"

At length they overtook her, and while she was engaged with two or three in front, one succeeded in seizing her by the neck from behind, and in dragging her from her horse, large and powerful woman though she was. Notwithstanding their guns had been so hacked and injured, and they themselves severely cut, her captors seemed to regard her only with admiration. They took her to a trader on the Illinois River, who showed her every kindness during her captivity, and later restored her to her friends.

Meanwhile those of Mr. Kinzie's family who had remained in the boat, near the mouth of the river, were carefully guarded by Kee-po-tah and another Indian. They had seen the smoke, then the blaze, and immediately after, the report of the first tremendous discharge had sounded in their ears. Then all was confusion. They knew nothing of the events of the battle until they saw an Indian coming towards them from the battle ground, leading a horse on which sat a lady, apparently wounded.

"That is Mrs. Heald," cried Mrs. Kinzie. "That Indian will kill her. Run, Chandonnai," to one of Mr. Kinzie's clerks, "take the mule that is tied there, and offer it to him to release her."

Mrs. Heald's captor, by this time, was in the act of disengaging her bonnet from her head, in order to scalp her. Chandonnai ran up and offered the mule as a ransom, with the promise of ten bottles of whisky as soon as they should reach his village. The whisky was a strong temptation.

"But," said the Indian, "she is badly wounded—she will die. Will you give me the whisky at all events?"

Chandonnai promised that he would, and the bargain was concluded. The savage placed the lady's bonnet on his own head, and, after an ineffectual effort on the part of some squaws to rob her of her shoes and stockings, she was brought on board the boat, where she lay moaning with pain from the many bullet wounds in her arms.

Having wished to possess themselves of her horse uninjured, the Indians had aimed their shots so as to disable the rider, without in any way harming her steed.

Mrs. Heald had not lain long in the boat when a young Indian of savage aspect was seen approaching. A buffalo robe was hastily drawn over her, and she was admonished to suppress all sound of complaint, as she valued her life.

The heroic woman remained perfectly silent while the savage drew near. He had a pistol in his hand, which he rested on the side of the boat, while, with a fearful scowl, he looked pryingly around. Black Jim, one of the servants, who stood in the bow of the boat, seized an ax that lay near and signed to him that if he shot he would cleave his skull, telling him that the boat contained only the family of Shaw-nee-aw-kee. Upon this, the Indian retired. It afterwards appeared that the object of his search was Mr. Burnett, a trader from St. Joseph with whom he had some account to settle.

When the boat was at length permitted to return to the house of Mr. Kinzie, and Mrs. Heald was removed there, it became necessary to dress her wounds.

Mr. Kinzie applied to an old chief who stood by, and who, like most of his tribe, possessed some skill in surgery, to extract a ball from the arm of the sufferer.

"No, father," replied the Indian. "I cannot do it—it makes me sick here," placing his hand on his heart.

Mr. Kinzie himself then performed the operation with his penknife.

At their own house, the family of Mr. Kinzie were closely guarded by their Indian friends, whose intention it was to carry them to Detroit for security. The rest of the prisoners remained at the wigwams of their captors.

On the following morning, the work of plunder being completed, the Indians set fire to the fort. A very equitable distribution of the finery appeared to have been made, and shawls, ribbons, and feathers fluttered about in all directions. The ludicrous appearance of one young fellow arrayed in a muslin gown and a lady's bonnet would, under other circumstances, have been a matter of great amusement.

Black Partridge, Wau-ban-see, and Kee-po-tah, with two other Indians, established themselves in the porch of the Kinzie house as sentinels, to protect the family from any evil that the young men might be incited to commit, and all remained tranquil for a short space after the conflagration.

Very soon, however, a party of Indians from the Wabash made their appearance. These were, decidedly, the most hostile and implacable of all the tribes of the Potowatomi.

Being more remote, they had shared less than some of their brethren in the kindness of Mr. Kinzie and his family, and consequently their friendly regard was not so strong.

Runners had been sent to the villages to apprise these Indians of the intended evacuation of the post, as well as of the plan to attack the troops.

Thirsting to participate in such an event, they had hurried to the scene, and great was their mortification, on arriving at the river Aux Plaines, to meet a party of their friends with their chief, Nee-scot-nee-meg, badly wounded, and learn that the battle was over, the spoils divided, and the scalps all taken. Arriving at Chicago they blackened their faces, and proceeded toward the dwelling of Mr. Kinzie.

From his station on the piazza Black Partridge had watched their approach, and his fears were particularly awakened for the safety of Mrs. Helm, Mr. Kinzie's stepdaughter, who had recently come to the post, and was personally unknown to the more remote Indians. By his advice she was made to assume the ordinary dress of a Frenchwoman of the country—a short gown and petticoat with a blue cotton handkerchief wrapped around her head. In this disguise she was conducted by Black Partridge himself to the house of Ouilmette, a Frenchman with a half-breed wife, who formed a part of the establishment of Mr. Kinzie and whose dwelling was close at hand.

It so happened that the Indians came first to this house in their search for prisoners. As they approached, the inmates, fearful that the fair complexion and general appearance of Mrs. Helm might betray her as an American, raised a large feather bed and placed her under the edge of it upon the bedstead, with her face to the wall. Mrs. Bisson, a half-breed sister of Ouilmette's wife, then seated herself with her sewing upon the front of the bed.

It was a hot day in August, and the feverish excitement of fear and agitation, together with her position, which was nearly suffocating, became so intolerable that Mrs. Helm at length entreated to be released and given up to the Indians.

"I can but die," said she; "let them put an end to my misery at once."

Mrs. Bisson replied, "Your death would be the destruction of us all, for Black Partridge has resolved that if one drop of the blood of your family is spilled, he will take the lives of all concerned in it, even his nearest friends; and if once the work of murder commences, there will be no end of it, so long as there remains one white person or half-breed in the country."

This expostulation nerved Mrs. Helm with fresh courage.

The Indians entered, and from her hiding place she could occasionally see them gliding about and stealthily inspecting every part of the room, though without making any ostensible search, until, apparently satisfied that there was no one concealed, they left the house.

All this time Mrs. Bisson had kept her seat upon the side of the bed, calmly sorting and arranging the patchwork of the quilt on which she was engaged, and preserving an appearance of the utmost tranquillity, although she knew not but that the next moment she might receive a tomahawk in her brain. Her self-command unquestionably saved the lives of all who were present.

From Ouilmette's house the party of Indians proceeded to the dwelling of Mr. Kinzie. They entered the parlor in which the family were assembled with their faithful protectors, and seated themselves upon the floor, in silence.

Black Partridge perceived from their moody and revengeful looks what was passing in their minds, but he dared not remonstrate with them. He only observed in a low tone to Wau-ban-see, "We have endeavored to save our friends, but it is in vain—nothing will save them now."

At this moment a friendly whoop was heard from a party of newcomers on the opposite bank of the river. As the canoes in which they had hastily embarked touched the bank near the house, Black Partridge sprang to meet their leader.

"Who are you?" demanded he.

"A man. Who are you?"

"A man like yourself. But tell me who you are,"—meaning, Tell me your disposition, and which side you are for.

"I am a Sau-ga-nash!"

"Then make all speed to the house—your friend is in danger, and you alone can save him."

Billy Caldwell, for it was he, entered the parlor with a calm step, and without a trace of agitation in his manner. He deliberately took off his accouterments and placed them with his rifle behind the door, then saluted the hostile savages.

"How now, my friends! A good day to you. I was told there were enemies here, but I am glad to find only friends. Why have you blackened your faces? Is it that you are mourning for the friends you have lost in battle?" purposely misunderstanding this token of evil designs. "Or is it that you are fasting? If so, ask our friend, here, and he will give you to eat. He is the Indian's friend, and never yet refused them what they had need of."

Thus taken by surprise, the savages were ashamed to acknowledge their bloody purpose. They, therefore, said modestly that they had come to beg of their friends some white cotton in which to wrap their dead before interring them. This was given to them, with some other presents, and they peaceably took their departure from the premises.

With Mr. Kinzie's party was a noncommissioned officer who had made his escape in a singular manner. As the troops had been about to leave the fort, it was found that the baggage horses of the surgeon had strayed off. The quartermaster sergeant, Griffith, was sent to find and bring them on, it being absolutely necessary to recover them, since their packs contained part of the surgeon's apparatus and the medicines for the march.

For a long time Griffith had been on the sick report and for this reason was given charge of the baggage, instead of being placed with the troops. His efforts to recover the horses proved unsuccessful, and, alarmed at certain appearances of disorder and hostile intention among the Indians, he was hastening to rejoin his party when he was met and made prisoner by To-pee-nee-bee.

Having taken his arms and accouterments from him, the chief put him into a canoe and paddled him across the river, bidding him make for the woods and secrete himself. This Griffith did; and in the afternoon of the following day, seeing from his lurking place that all appeared quiet, he ventured to steal cautiously into Ouilmette's garden, where he concealed himself for a time behind some currant bushes.

At length he determined to enter the house, and accordingly climbed up through a small back window into the room where the family were, entering just as the Wabash Indians had left the house of Ouilmette for that of Mr. Kinzie. The danger of the sergeant was now imminent. The family stripped him of his uniform and arrayed him in a suit of deerskin, with belt, moccasins, and pipe, like a French engagé. His dark complexion and heavy black whiskers favored the disguise. The family were all ordered to address him in French, and, although utterly ignorant of this language, he continued to pass for a Weemtee-gosh, and as such remained with Mr. Kinzie and his family, undetected by his enemies, until they reached a place of safety.

On the third day after the battle, Mr. Kinzie and his family, with the clerks of the establishment, were put into a boat, under the care of Francois, a half-breed interpreter, and conveyed to St. Joseph, where they remained until the following November, under the protection of To-pee-nee-bee's band. With the exception of Mr. Kinzie they were then conducted to Detroit, under the escort of Chandonnai and their trusty Indian friend, Kee-po-tah, and delivered as prisoners of war to Colonel McKee, the British Indian Agent.

Mr. Kinzie himself was held at St. Joseph and did not succeed in rejoining his family until some months later. On his arrival at Detroit he was paroled by General Proctor.

Lieutenant Helm, who was likewise wounded, was carried by some friendly Indians to their village on the Au Sable and thence to Peoria, where he was liberated through the intervention of Mr. Thomas Forsyth, the half brother of Mr. Kinzie. Mrs. Helm accompanied her parents to St. Joseph, where they resided for several months in the family of Alexander Robinson, receiving from them all possible kindness and hospitality.

Source: Helm, Linai Taliaferro. *The Fort Dearborn Massacre. Written in 1814 by Lieutenant Linai T. Helm. . . .* Edited by Nellie Kinzie Gordon, 47–77. Chicago and New York: Rand McNally, 1912.

THE FALL OF DETROIT, AUGUST 16, 1812

Account of an Incident following the Fall of Detroit
Peter Buell Porter
Late September 1812

The surrender of Fort Detroit by General William Hull on August 16, 1812, was deeply demoralizing to Americans, especially the war hawks in Congress. One of these, who also served as New York's quartermaster general (the manager of supply for New York militia units), was Peter Buell Porter (1773–1844), who was present at the American

camp near Lewiston, New York, and watched Hull's defeated troops march north along the Canadian shore of the Niagara River.

Three days ago we witnessed a sight which made my heart sick within me, and the emotions it excited throughout the whole of our troops along the line . . . are not to be described. The heroes of Tippecanoe, with the garrisons of Detroit and Michilimackinac . . . were marched like cattle from Fort Erie to Fort George, guarded by General Brock's regular troops with all the parade and pomp of British insolence, and we were incapacitated by the armistice and our own weakness from giving them the relief which they seemed anxiously to expect, and could only look on and sicken at the sight . . .

Source: War of 1812, Events & Locations. "Eyewitness Accounts of Hull's Defeated Army." Available online. URL: http://www.galafilm.com/1812/e/events/detroit_eyewit.html. Accessed on February 5, 2010.

Account of the Aftermath of the Fall of Detroit
Anonymous
1812

An anonymous Briton visited Montreal when he was 11 years old and years later recalled the sight of General Hull's captured troops paraded ignominiously through the streets of the city. Hull and his troops were soon paroled (released), and Hull faced court-martial.

In a few days, General Hull's army, which had been captured by General Brock at Detroit, arrived as prisoners of war at Lachine, a village nine miles above Montreal; and as I felt a strong desire to see them, I set out, with my brother and a gentleman of the 49th regiment, to meet them. On our way we met a calash [a barouche carriage], in which we had the unexpected satisfaction to recognize my father and the Colonel of his regiment, who had come down from Kingston, attached to the escort of the prisoners, the latter having the command.

We returned to town with them, and about nine o'clock in the evening we had the pleasure of witnessing the arrival of the first fruits of this useless and too disastrous war. I was a very young boy at the time; and, having been born and brought up in the army, it is natural to suppose that my ideas ran early upon military exploits. Scenes of war, conquered enemies, etc. had long been familiar to me in idea, but in reality had always been remote from me; and I had been in the habit, when thinking of a foreign enemy, to picture to my mind something very unlike what I had daily before my eyes.

Upon this occasion, however, I witnessed the reality; and my youthful heart, big with warlike achievements, and too inconsiderate to sympathize in misfortunes of this description, triumphantly exalted in the sight of a fallen enemy. . . . Though after a long journey, as prisoners, it is natural to suppose that their appearance was not very brilliant; yet it is evident, from its shabbiness, that their appointments had not been, at any time, of the most splendid description.

The band of the 8th regiment marched at the head of them, playing the well known air, "Yankee Doodle." General Hull, a venerable looking old gentleman, and his son with the other officers, in calashes, followed the band; and were succeeded by the soldiers, guarded on either side by a rank of our own troops. As it was dark when they reached the town, the streets they passed through were quite illuminated by numbers of candles, held out from the windows of all the houses which were crowded with people assembled to witness the scene.

Source: War of 1812, Events & Locations. "Eyewitness Accounts of Hull's Defeated Army." Available online. URL: http://www.galafilm.com/1812/e/events/detroit_ eyewit2.html. Accessed on February 5, 2010.

USS *CONSTITUTION* V. HMS *JAVA*, OFF THE BRAZILIAN COAST, DECEMBER 29–30, 1812

Diary Entries
Commodore William Bainbridge
December 29–30, 1812

One of the most illustrious victories of the USS Constitution *came on December 29, 1812, against the HMS* Java. *The following document presents the battle from the American point of view. This is an excerpt from the journal of Commodore William Bainbridge, captain of the* Constitution. *The original spellings have been retained in this document.*

Tuesday 29th December 1812

At 9 AM, discovered two Strange Sails on the weather bow, at 10. AM. discovered the strange sails to be Ships, one of them stood in for the land, and the other steered off shore in a direction towards us. At 10.45. we tacked ship to the Nd & Wd and stood for the sail standing towards us,—At 11 tacked to the Sd & Ed hauld up the mainsail and took in the Royals. At 11.30 AM made the private signal for the day, which was not answered, & then set the mainsail and royals to draw the strange sail off from the neutral Coast.

Wednesday 30th December 1812, (Nautical Time) Commences with Clear weather and moderate breezes from E.N.E. Hoisted our Ensign and Pendant. At 15 minutes past meridian, The ship hoisted her colours, an English Ensign,— having a signal flying at her Main Red Yellow-Red At 1.26 being sufficiently from the land, and finding the ship to be an English Frigate, took in the Main Sail and Royals, tacked Ship and stood for the enemy

At 1.50. P.M, The Enemy bore down with an intention of rakeing us, which we avoided by wearing. At 2, P.M, the enemy being within half a mile, of us, and to wind ward, & having hawled down his colours to dip his Gafft, and not hoisting them again except an Union Jack at the Mizen Mast head, (we having hoisted on board the *Constitution* an American Jack forward Broad Pendant at Main, American Ensign at Mizen Top Gallant Mast head and at the end of The Gafft) induced me to give orders to the officer of the 3rd Division to fire one Gun ahead of the enemy to make him show his Colours, which being done brought on a fire from us of the whole broadside, on which he hoisted an English Ensign at the Peak, and another in his weather Main Rigging, besides his Pendant and then immediately returned our fire, which brought on a general action with round and grape.

The enemy Kept at a much greater distance than I wished, but Could not bring him to closer action without exposing ourselves to several rakes.—Considerable Manoeuvers were made by both Vessels to rake and avoid being raked.

The following Minutes Were Taken during the Action

At 2.10. P.M, Commenced The Action within good grape and Canister distance. The enemy to windward (but much farther than I wished).

At 2.30. P.M, our wheel was shot entirely away

At 2.40. determined to close with the Enemy, notwithstanding her rakeing, set the Fore sail & Luff'd up close to him.

At 2.50, The Enemies Jib boom got foul of our Mizen Rigging

At 3 The Head of the enemies Bowsprit & Jib boom shot away by us

At 3.5 Shot away the enemies foremast by the board

At 3.15 Shot away The enemies Main Top mast just above the Cap

At 3.40 Shot away Gafft and Spunker boom

At 3.55 Shot his mizen mast nearly by the board

At 4.5 Having silenced the fire of the enemy completely and his colours in main Rigging being [down] Supposed he had Struck, Then hawl'd about the Courses to shoot ahead to repair our rigging, which was extremely cut, leaving the enemy a complete wreck, soon after discovered that The enemies flag was still flying hove too to repair Some of our damages.

At 4.20. The Enemies Main Mast went by the board.

At 4.50 [Wore] ship and stood for the Enemy

At 5.25 Got very close to the enemy in a very [effective] rakeing position, athwart his bows & was at the very instance of rakeing him, when he most prudently Struck his Flag.

Had The Enemy Suffered the broadside to have raked him previously to strikeing, his additional loss must have been extremely great laying like a log upon the water, perfectly unmanageable, I could have continued rakeing him without being exposed to more than two of his Guns, (if even Them)

After The Enemy had struck, wore Ship and reefed the Top Sails, hoisted out one of the only two remaining boats we had left out of 8 & sent Lieut [George] Parker 1st of the Constitution on board to take possession of her, which was done about 6. P.M, The Action continued from the commencement to the end of the Fire, 1 H 55 m our sails and Rigging were shot very much, and some of our spars injured-had 9 men Killed and 26 wounded. At 7 PM. the boat returned from the Prize with Lieut. [Henry D.] Chads the 1st of the enemies Frigate (which

I then learnt was the *Java* rated 38—had 49 Guns mounted—)—and Lieut Genl [Thomas] Hislop—appointed to Command in the East Indies,—Major Walker and Capt Wood, belonging to his Staff.—Capt [Henry] Lambert of the *Java* was too dangerously wounded to be removed immediately.

The Cutter returned on board the Prize for Prisoners, and brought Capt [John] Marshall, Master & Commander of The British Navy, who was passenger on board, as also Several other Naval officers destined for ships in the East Indies. The *Java* had her whole number complete and nearly an hundred supernumeraries. The number she had on board at the commencement of the Action, The officers have not candour to say; from the different papers we collected, such as a muster book, Watch List and quarter Bills, she must have had upwards of 400 souls, she had one more man stationed at each of her Guns on both Decks than what we had The Enemy had 83 wounded & 57 Kill'd.

The *Java* was an important ship fitted out in the compleatest manner to [carry out] the Lieut. Genl & dispatches. She had Copper &c. on board for a 74 building at Bombay, and, I suspect a great many other valuables, but every thing was blown up, except the officers baggage when we set her on fire on the 1st of January 1813 at 3 P.M. Nautical Time.

Source: Naval Historical Center, Selected Naval Documents. "Defeat of HMS *Java*." Available online. URL: http://www.history.navy.mil/docs/war1812/const6htm. Accessed on February 6, 2010.

Letter to Secretary of the Admiralty John W. Croker

Lieutenant Henry D. Chads
December 31, 1812

A report from Lieutenant Henry D. Chads, Royal Navy first officer of the defeated HMS Java, *written to Secretary of the Admiralty John W. Croker, giving the British viewpoint of the battle.*

Triplicate
United States Frigate *Constitution*
off St Salvador Decr 31st 1812

Sir

It is with deep regret that I write you for the information of the Lords Commissioners of the Admiralty that His Majesty's Ship *Java* is no more, after sustaining an action on the 29th Inst for several hours with the American Frigate *Constitution* which resulted in the Capture and ultimate destruction of His Majestys Ship. Captain Lambert being dangerously wounded in the height of the Action, the melancholy task of writing the detail devolves on me.

On the morning of the 29th inst at 8 AM off St Salvador (Coast of Brazil) the wind at NE. we perceived a strange sail, made all sail in chace and soon made her out to be a large Frigate; at noon prepared for action the chace not answering our private Signals and backing towards us under easy sail; when about four miles distant she made a signal and immediately tacked and made all sail away upon the wind, we soon found we had the advantage of her in sailing and came up with her fast when she hoisted American Colours. she then bore about three Points on our lee bow at 1:50 PM the Enemy shortened Sail upon which we bore down upon her, at 2:10 when about half a mile distant she opened her fire giving us her larboard broad-side which was not returned till we we were close on her weather bow; both Ships now manoeuvered to obtain advantageous positions; our opponent evidently avoiding close action and firing high to disable our masts in which he succeeded too well having shot away the head of our bowsprit with the Jib boom and our running rigging so much cut as to prevent our preserving the weather gage At 3:5 finding the Enemys raking fire extreemly heavy Captain Lambert ordered the Ship to be laid on board, in which we should have succeeded had not our foremast been shot away at this moment, the remains of our bowsprit passing over his taffrail, shortly after this the main topmast went leaving the Ship totally unmanageable with most of our Starboard Guns rendered useless from the wreck laying over them At 3:30 our Gallant Captain received a dangerous wound in the breast and was carried below, from this time we could not fire more than two or three guns until 4:15 when our Mizen mast was shot away the Ship then fell off a little and brought many of our Starboard Guns to bear, the Enemy's rigging was so much cut that he could not now avoid shooting ahead which brought us fairly Broadside and Broadside. Our Main yard now went in the slings both ships continued engaged in this manner till 4:35 we frequently on fire in consequence of the wreck laying on the side engaged. Our opponent now made sail ahead out of Gun shot where he remained an hour repairing his damages leaving us an unmanageable wreck with only the mainmast left, and that toterring; Every exertion was made by us during his interval to place this Ship in a state to renew the action. We succeeded in clearing the wreck of our Masts from our Guns. a Sail was set on the stumps of the Foremast & Bowsprit the weather half of the Main Yard remaining aloft, the main tack was got forward in the hope of getting the Ship before the Wind, our helm being still perfect. the effort unfortunately proved ineffectual from the Main mast falling over the side from the heavy rolling of the Ship, which nearly covered the whole of our Starboard Guns. We still waited the attack of the Enemy, he now standing toward us for that purpose. on his coming nearly within hail of us & from his manouvre perceiving he intended a position a head where he could rake us without a possibility of our returning a shot. I then consulted the Officers who agreed with myself that on having a great part of our Crew killed & wounded our Bowsprit and three masts gone, several guns useless, we should not be justified in waisting the lives of more of those remaining whom I hope their Lordships & Country will think have bravely defended His Majestys Ship. Under these circumstances, however reluctantly at

5:50 our Colours were lowered from the Stump of the Mizen Mast and we were taken possession a little after 6. by the American Frigate *Constitution* commanded by Commodore Bainbridge who immediately after ascertaining the state of the Ship resolved on burning her which we had the satisfaction of seeing done as soon as the Wounded were removed. Annexed I send you a return of all killed and wounded and it is with pain I perceive it so numerous also a statement of the comparative force of the two Ships when I hope their Lordships will not think the British Flag tarnished although success has not attended us. It would be presumptive in me to speak of Captain Lamberts merit, who, though still in danger from his wound we still entertain the greatest hopes of his being restored to the service & his Country. It is most gratifying to my feelings to notice the general gallantry of every Officer, Seaman & Marine on board. In justice to the Officers I beg leave to mention them individually. I can never speak too highly of the able exertions of Lieuts. [William A.] Herringham & Buchanan and also Mr. [Batty] Robinson Master who was severely wounded and Lieuts Mercer and Davis [David Davies] of the Royal Marines the latter of whom was also severly wounded. To Capt Jno Marshall RN who was a passenger I am particular]y obliged to for his exertions and advice throughout the action. To Lieutt Aplin who was on the Main Deck and Lieutt Sanders who commanded on the Forecastle, I also return my thanks. I cannot but notice the good conduct of the Mates, & Midshipmen. many of whom are killed & the greater part wounded. To Mr T. C. [Thomas Cooke] Jones Surgeon and his Assistants every praise is due for their unwearied assiduity in the care of the wounded. Lieutt General [Thomas] Hislop, Major Walker and Captain [J. T.] Wood of his Staff the latter of whom was severly wounded were solicitous to assist & remain on the quarter Deck I cannot conclude this letter without expressing my grateful acknowledgement thus publicly for the generous treatment Captain Lambert and his

Officers have experienced from our Gallant Enemy Commodore Bainbridge and his Officers. I have the honor to be [&c.]

W [H] D Chads, 1st Lieut
of His Majestys late Ship *Java*

To John Wilson Croker Esquire
Secretary
Admiralty.

PS. The *Constitution* has also suffered severly, both in her rigging and men having her Fore and Mizen masts, main topmast, both main topsailyards, Spanker boom, Gaff & trysail mast badly shot, and the greatest part of the standing rigging very much damaged with ten men killed. The Commodore, 5 Lieuts and 46 men wounded four of whom are since dead.

Source: Naval Historical Center, Selected Naval Documents. "Defeat of HMS *Java*." Available online. URL: http://www.history.navy.mil/docs/war1812/const6.htm. Accessed on February 5, 2010.

THE RIVER RAISIN MASSACRE, JANUARY 23, 1812

Accounts of the Raisin River Massacre
Anonymous
Published 1813; republished 1871

After General William Hull surrendered Fort Detroit, General William Henry Harrison led the Army of the Northwest in what he hoped would be a successful effort to retake the fort. Harrison divided his forces into two columns, personally leading one and placing the other under General James Winchester. Harrison ordered Winchester to remain within supporting distance of his own column. Instead of following this order, however, Winchester advanced to Frenchtown, along the River Raisin. He routed a much smaller Canadian and Indian force on January 18 and occupied Frenchtown, but four days later, the main British and Indian force attacked, pushing Winchester's column into a disastrous rout. Fearing retaliation from Harrison's column, the British withdrew, leaving their American prisoners to the mercy of the Indians, who killed 68 wounded prisoners and ransomed the few who had not been injured. These men, including militia officer George Madison, soon to become Kentucky's sixth governor, returned to tell the tale of the "River Raisin Massacre." Their story was related to the editor of the Frankfort (Kentucky) Mercury *in 1813 and was reprinted on March 23, 1871, in the* Monroe (Michigan) *commercial.*

Since the publication of the last *Mercury*, a number of the brave fellows who were made prisoners at the battle of Frenchtown on the 22nd of January, under Gen. Winchester, have passed through this place on their way to Kentucky. They were paroled at Fort George, not to serve during the war against his Britannic majesty, or his allies, unless regularly exchanged. They came down the Canadian side from Malden to Fort George, crossed over the Niagara, and proceeded direct to Pittsburgh. They have since gone on by water for Kentucky. The best wishes of their country go with them.

These men are generally of the first respectability and intelligence, the flower of Kentucky, and they reflect the highest honor on the State from which they came and on their country. The easy gracefulness of manner, the manly independence of sentiment, and the ardent love of country which they have displayed, under all the reverses of fortune, entitle them to the first place in the hearts of their countrymen.

Notwithstanding the unparalleled fatigues they have undergone, in a dreary wilderness, the dangers to which they have been exposed, and the numerous privations they have suffered, still are their noble spirits unbroken—not a murmur has escaped their lips—no imbecile apprehensions are entertained by them for the safety of their brethren in arms—but their honest hearts spring forward with elastic hope that their wrongs will be avenged, and the day of retribution is at hand.

The Editor has the pleasure of conversing with a number of these gentlemen. He therefore offers this honest tribute to their merit. From this source he lays the following facts before his readers:

"The advance of General Winchester to the River Raisin, or rather Frenchtown, arose from the ardent solicitation of the inhabitants of the place, and was undertaken with the approbation and at the desire of the whole army. The inhabitants of the town, being citizens of the United States solicited the protection of Gen. Winchester from the violence and outrages of the hordes of savages with which they were surrounded, and to whose brutalities they were daily exposed. The Wednesday succeeding the march of Gen. Winchester for Frenchtown, had been fixed on by these merciless allies of Britain for the burning of the town and the butchery of its inhabitants. Gen. Winchester, yielding to the calls of humanity, and desirous of protecting American citizens from savage violence, advanced to their relief. The expedition under Colonel Lewis was, as is known, completely successful, and put our troops in possession of the town. On the 20th Gen. Winchester concentrated his troops, amounting to 750 men, at Frenchtown, 600 of which were posted in pickets. The picket was formed in a half circle.

"The attack commenced on the right wing, on the morning of the 22nd, at the beating of the reveille. Our troops were immediately ready for the reception of the enemy. Scarcely a minute had elapsed from the firing of the alarm till the first discharge. The right wing sustained the shock for about 20 minutes, when, overpowered by numbers, they retreated across the river, and fell in with a large body of Indians stationed at the rear, and were cut off or taken prisoners. Two companies of 50 men each, from the pickets, sallied out and unfortunately joined the retreating party. The fate of the whole is uncertain but our principal loss was in this quarter.

"The left wing, with Spartan valor, maintained their ground within the pickets. The enemy's regulars made three different charges upon them. The shocks were received with distinguished coolness and intrepidity, and the enemy was always repulsed. Out of 400 regulars of the enemy 150 were slain. We have had 5 killed within the pickets and about 40 wounded. Gen. Winchester and Col. Lewis had been taken prisoners early in the action, in attempting to rally the retreating party. About 11 o'clock Gen. Winchester sent in a flag informing that he had capitulated for the troops. The firing had in a great measure ceased at this time; and when the flag came in, so confidant were the men of their success, that they merely expected it as a proffer for a cessation of arms. Thus this brave little band maintained this tremendous action, which lasted from daybreak till 11 o'clock, with their honor untarnished. It ought not, however, to be understood as attaching any blame to Gen. Winchester for entering into the capitulation. Opposed by the overwhelming force of the enemy, these brave fellows must otherwise have fallen a sacrifice.

"The British force consisted of about 2,000, including Indians. In the rear were stationed a large body of Indians with a design to cut off a retreat, should it be attempted, but the left wing bravely kept their ground, and thus obtained that security which their valor deserved.

"We come now to relate the tragic part of the story, at which every honorable and feeling heart must recoil, and which demands the prompt attention of government. After the capitulation, the American commanding officer remonstrated with the British officer on the necessity of protecting the wounded prisoners from the fury of the savages. The officer pledged himself to attend to it, and thus they should be removed out the following day. But they were left without the promised protection, and on the morning of the 23rd, the savage allies of a Christian King stripped and murdered all of them who were unable to march. If the vengeance of our country can sleep after such an act as this, then indeed may we weep over the ruins of the republic.

"The fate of Capt. Hart, one of the wounded, is peculiarly distressing. This gentleman had greatly signalized himself by his undaunted bravery. After the capitulation, a British officer, a Captain Elliot, who had been a classmate with him at Princeton College, waited on Captain Hart and unsolicited promised him his protection, declaring that the next morning he would have him taken to Malden, where he should remain until his recovery. But Elliot broke his promise and left him to his fate. On the next day a band of savages came into the house where he lay, and ruthlessly tore him from his bed. A brother officer caught him in his arms and carried him to another apartment. Here he was again assailed by the monsters. At length he bargained with one of them and gave him a considerable sum of money to have himself taken to Malden. They set off, and after traveling about four or five miles, were met by a fresh band of the hell hounds, who shot the Captain on his horse, and tomahawked and scalped him! Such are the allies of his Britannic majesty; and such the righteousness of his cause.

"The prisoners were generally stripped of their clothing, rifled of their cash, and the swords of the officers given to the savages, notwithstanding a promise that the swords should be returned to them again at Malden; and, as if all honorable warfare must cease, men whose education, talents, and general respectability ought to have entitled them to respect, were treated by the enemy with all the haughty superciliousness which characterizes ignoble minds.

"Gen. Winchester and the field officers are, it is supposed, ordered on to Quebec.

"Several interesting incidents serving to display the bravery and good conduct of the troops deserve to be noticed. On their march from Fort Defiance to the Rapids, the horses were worn out and nearly famished for the want of forage. The men themselves were destitute of many articles of the first necessity. Yet these circumstances did not in the least dampen the ardor and the spirits of the troops. When the horses were not longer able to draw, these gallant fellows hitched themselves to the sleds, and, in this manner, with the greatest cheerfulness and alacrity, coveyed their baggage a distance of more than sixty miles, through frost and snow-thus manifesting an intrepidity of character which rivals of Greece or Rome.

"In the battle of the 18th, on the first onset the savages raised their accustomed and horrid yell. But the noise was drowned in the returning shouts of the brave assailants. They advanced boldly to the charge, and drove the enemy in all directions. On the first fire, sixteen of the savages were distinctly seen to fall.

"In the battle of the 22nd, the British advanced in platoons to charge the pickets, keeping up a street fire. The men within the pickets, with the most determined bravery and presence of minds, reserved their fire until the enemy advanced with point-blank shot. They then opened a cross fire upon the enemy—their pieces well leveled—and they thus mowed down the ranks in such a manner as rendered all his efforts in vain, and compelled him to retire. Well may the enemy acknowledge that he had a dear-bought victory.

"We have said that the British officers treated their prisoners with haughty superciliousness. We might have gone further, perhaps, and said with provoking insolence. When an American office urged the necessity of having the wounded put under the care of suitable surgeons, he was tauntingly answered, 'The Indians are excellent doctors!' 'Yes,' replied the American with spirit, you have proven it on the morning of the 23rd, alluding to the massacre of the wounded.

"Although our brave men were made captives and disarmed, their spirits were unbroken. When offered the parole for their signatures, they demanded to know who 'were his Majesty's allies.' Even British effrontery was staggered at the pertinency of the inquiry. The 'compunctious' visiting of nature, deferred them from acknowledging the savage, and they alluded a direct reply by answering 'his Majesty's allies are known!' Yes, truly are they known. They are recorded in letters of blood!

"Why are the disclosures made? To show the people of the United States the merciless enemy they have had to contend with. To awaken the dormant spirit of the nation. To steel their hearts and nerve their arms, for an awful display of that retribution which the cruelties of our unrelenting enemy justly entitles him to."

We close this article with the following statement furnished us by a gentleman in the staff department; who was an eye-witness to the massacre of the wounded:

"On the morning of the 22nd of January at reveille beating, the detachment under Gen. Winchester at the River Raisin, were attacked by a party of British and Indians. The officers and men were ready at their posts to receive them, insomuch as they were informed the preceding evening an attack would be made. The detachment consisted of about 750 men, of whom 500 were protected by a temporary breastwork, composed of rails and garden paling. The remainder who had joined us the day preceding the action were encamped on the right, somewhat detached, and unprotected by any kind of shelter. The attack was made with great violence on the troops without the shelter, who maintained their ground about fifteen minutes, when an order was given to retreat with the picketing. In the confusion that order was mistaken for a general retreat. On their retreat they were attacked by a large body of Indians who had been stationed on our rear and in adjacent wood previous to the attack. The retreating party were thrown into considerable confusion. Gen. Winchester, Cols. Lewis and Allen, pursued and endeavored to rally them, which proved ineffectual. The party finding a retreat was in vain, resolved to sell their lives at the dearest rate, and fired until the last. Few of them arrived safe at camp. Gen. Winchester and aide and his son, and Col. Lewis were taken prisoners. The party who remained in the breastwork kept up a constant and warm fire until eleven o'clock, when a flag was brought in by General Winchester's aide, informing us he had surrendered us prisoners of war, and requested our compliance. A surrender took place and the men immediately marched off. About 456 capitulated. The wounded, amounting to 65 were left on the ground, under the care of Drs. Todd and Bowers, the two surviving surgeons, with a promise of protection from the commanding officer, Colonel Proctor, and that the wounded should be carried on the next morning to Malden. On the morning of the 23rd, about sunrise a large body of Indians came, plundered the wounded of their clothing, and everything of value, and tomahawked and scalped all that were unable to march; among them were some valuable officers, particularly Captain Hickman. The remainder were taken prisoners, as they termed it, and many are either killed or are still in their possession. Our loss is estimated at about 200 killed. Kentucky has lost some her choicest sons, particularly Col. Allen. Among the officers killed, we recollect Capt. Simpson, (a member of Congress) Captain Mead, Edwards, Price, and McCracken, and many very valuable subalterns. The loss of officers was considerable. The loss of the enemy could not be ascertained. They acknowledged the victory a dear one. Their loss of regulars of the 41st regiment was estimated at 150, in making three unsuccessful charges. The force of the enemy was estimated by many of the British officers at 2,000, and several assured me their loss exceeded ours. During the whole of the action, a heavy cannonade was kept up by six pieces of artillery.

"After Madison's command had marched out of the pickets to pile their arms, the Indians rushed around them and commenced plundering and menacing the men. Major Madison, addressing Gen. Proctor said to him: 'Is this the way, sir, you observe the terms on which we surrendered?' Proctor replied that they were Indians and he couldn't help it. 'Then, sir,' said Madison, 'I can. Boys, stand to your guns.' And his men would have died with them in their hands, but Proctor spoke to the Indians, and they desisted. One, a little more daring than the rest, seized Major Madison's saddle, but the Major gave him a whack with his sword that made him scamper quickly." . . .

Source: Monroe County [Michigan] Library System. "Bygones of Monroe." Available online. URL: http://monroe.lib.mi.us/eresearch/recommended_sites/history/bygones_monroe/war_1812.htm. Accessed on February 5, 2010.

THE BATTLE OF LAKE ERIE, SEPTEMBER 10, 1813

Eyewitness Account of the Battle
Anonymous
Published 1834

After the defeat of his campaign on the River Raisin in January, General William Henry Harrison rebuilt and expanded his army into a force of 8,000, which was prepared for combat by late summer 1813. Simultaneously, the U.S. Navy's Oliver Hazard Perry hurriedly built an inland navy at Presque Isle (present-day Erie), Pennsylvania. By August, Perry was ready to sail onto Lake Erie, and on September 10, he engaged the British Lake Erie squadron. The two fleets pounded one another until Perry's flagship, the USS Lawrence, *was a virtual wreck, four-fifths of her crew killed or wounded. Perry remained on board until the last gun on the* Lawrence *could no longer be fired. He then transferred his flag to the USS* Niagara. *By this time, the British flotilla had been decimated, and Perry led the remaining ships of his flotilla against the few British vessels still able to fight. By late in the afternoon, they surrendered. The cost to the Royal Navy was 41 killed and 94 wounded out of 451 engaged. Perry lost 27 killed and 96 wounded, of whom two subsequently died.*

The battle won, Perry wrote to Harrison the words that entered American history: "We have met the enemy and they are ours. Two ships, two brigs, one schooner and one sloop." Bereft of support from the water, the British land forces withdrew.

In 1834, Archibald Duncan, a collector of maritime history, included what he identified only as a "minute and interesting account of the naval conflict on Lake Erie . . . by an eye witness" in his The Mariner's Chronicle.

Commodore Perry arrived at Erie in June, with five small vessels from Black Rock. The [HMS] *Queen Charlotte* and [HMS] *Lady Prevost* were cruising off Long Point to intercept him—he passed them in the night unperceived. The [USS] *Lawrence* and [USS] *Niagara* were then on the stocks—every exertion was made to expedite their building and equipment, and early in August they were ready to sail. But it was necessary to pass the bar at the entrance of the harbor, over which there was but six feet of water, and the brigs drew nine. The British fleet appeared off the harbor, for the purpose of preventing ours from going to lake!—The means employed by our officers to take the brigs over the bar, were ingenious and deserve mention. Two large scows, fifty feet long, ten feet wide, and eight feet deep, were prepared—they were first filled with water and then floated along side one of the vessels in a parallel direction; they were then secured by means of large pieces of hewn timber placed athwart ship, with both ends projecting from the port holes across the scows; the space between the timbers and the boat, being secured by other pieces properly arranged; the water was then bailed from the scows, thereby giving them an astonishing lifting power. It was thus that the bar was passed before the enemy had taken any steps to oppose it. One obstacle was surmounted, but the fleet was not in a condition to seek the enemy at Malden. There was not at this time more than half sailors enough to man the fleet. However, a number of Pennsylvania militia having volunteered their services, the Commodore made a short cruize off Long Point, more perhaps for the purpose of exercising his men than seeking an enemy.

About the last of August, Commodore Perry left Erie, to co-operate with General Harrison in the reduction of Malden. He anchored off the

In this painting, Oliver Hazard Perry stands in a small boat after being forced to abandon his flagship, the *Lawrence,* in the Battle of Lake Erie. *(Library of Congress)*

mouth of Sandusky river, and had an interview with General Harrison, who furnished him with about seventy volunteers, principally Kentuckians, to serve as marines on board the fleet. Captain Dobbin, in the [USS] *Ohio,* was ordered to return to Erie for provisions. The [USS] *Amelia* had been left there for want of men to man her. Exclusive of these he had nine sail, mounting in all fifty-four guns. The British fleet at Malden, consisted of six sail, and mounted sixty six guns.

Commodore Perry appeared before Malden, offered battle, reconnoitered the enemy and retired to Put-in-Bay, thirty-five miles distant from his antagonist. Both parties remained a few days inactive; but their repose was that of the lion.

On the morning of the 10th of September, at sunrise, the enemy were discovered bearing down from Malden for the evident purpose of attacking our squadron, then at anchor at Put-in-Bay. Not a moment was to be lost. Perry's squadron immediately got under way, and stood out to meet the British fleet, which at this time had the weather gage. At 10 a.m. the wind shifted from S.W. to S.E. which brought our squadron to windward. The wind was light, the day beautiful—not a cloud obscured the horizon. The line was formed at 11, and Commodore Perry caused an elegant flag, which he had privately prepared, to be hoisted at the masthead of the *Lawrence;* on this flag was painted, in characters legible to the whole fleet, the dying words of the immortal

LAWRENCE:—"DON'T GIVE UP THE SHIP." Its effect is not to be described—every heart was electrified. The crews cheered—the exilerating can was passed. Both fleets appeared eager for the conflict, on the result of which so much depended. At 15 minutes before twelve, the [HMS] *Detroit,* the head-most ship of the enemy, opened upon the *Lawrence,* which for ten minutes, was obliged to sustain a well directed and heavy fire from the enemy's two large ships. without being able to return it with carronades; at five minutes before twelve the *Lawrence* opened upon the enemy—the other vessels were ordered to support her, but the wind was at this time too high to enable them to come up. Every brace and bowline of the *Lawrence* being soon shot away, she became unmanageable, and in this situation sustained the action upwards of two hours, within canister distance, until every gun was rendered useless, and but a small part of her crew left unhurt upon deck.

At half past two the wind increased and enabled the [USS] *Niagara* to come into close action—the gun-boats took a nearer position. Commodore Perry left his ship in charge of Lt. Yarnel, and went on board the *Niagara.* Just as he reached that vessel, the flag of the *Lawrence* came down; the crisis had arrived. Captain Elliot at this moment anticipated the wishes of the commodore, by volunteering his services to bring the schooners into close action.

At forty-five minutes past two the signal was made for close action. The *Niagara* being very little injured, and her crew fresh, the commodore determined to pass through the enemy's line; he accordingly bore up and passed ahead of the *Detroit, Queen Charlotte* and *Lady Prevost,* pouring a terrible raking fire into them from the starboard guns, and on the [HMS] *Chippeway* and [HMS] *Little Belt,* from the larboard side at half pistol shot distance. The small vessels at this time having got within grape and canister distance, kept up a well directed and destructive fire. The action now raged with the greatest fury—the *Queen Charlotte,* having lost her commander and several of her principal officers, in a

moment of confusion got foul of the *Detroit*—in this situation the enemy in their turn had to sustain a tremendous fire without the power of returning it with much effect; the carnage was horrible—the flags of the *Detroit, Queen Charlotte* and *Lady Prevost,* were struck in rapid succession. The brig [HMS] *Hunter,* and schooner *Chippeway,* were soon compelled to follow their example. The *Little Belt* attempted to escape to Malden, but she was pursued by two of the gunboats and surrendered about three miles distant from the scene of action.

The writer of this account, in company with five others, arrived at the head of Put-in-Bay island, on the evening of the 9th, and had a view of the action, at the distance of only ten miles. The spectacle was truly grand and awful. The firing was incessant for the space of three hours, and continued at short intervals forty-five minutes longer. In less than one hour after the battle began, most of the vessels of both fleets were enveloped in a cloud of smoke, which rendered the issue of the action uncertain, till the next morning, when we visited the fleet in the harbor on the opposite side of the island. The reader will easily judge of our solicitude to learn the result. There is no sentiment more painful than suspense, when it is excited by the uncertain issue of an event like this.

If the wind had continued at S. W. it was the intention of Admiral Barclay to have boarded our squadron; for this purpose he had taken on board of his fleet about 200 of the famous 41st regiment; they acted as marines and fought bravely, but nearly two thirds of them were either killed or wounded.

The carnage on board the prizes was prodigious—they must have lost 200 in killed besides wounded. The sides of the *Detroit* and *Queen Charlotte* were shattered from bow to stem; there was scarcely room to place one's hand on their larboard sides without touching the impression of a shot—a great many balls, canister and grape, were found lodged in their bulwarks, which were too thick to be penetrated by our carronades, unless within pistol shot distance. Their masts were so much shattered, that they fell overboard soon after they got into the bay.

The loss of the Americans was severe, particularly on board the *Lawrence*. When her flag was struck she had but nine men fit for duty remaining on deck. Her sides were completely riddled by the shot from the long guns of the British ships. Her deck, the morning after the conflict, when I first went on board, exhibited a scene that defies description—for it was literally covered with blood, which still adhered to the plank in clots—brains, hair and fragments of bones were still sticking to the rigging and sides. The surgeons were still busy with the wounded—enough! horror appalled my senses.

Among the wounded were several brave fellows, each of whom had lost a leg or an arm—they appeared cheerful and expressed a hope that they had done their duty. Rome and Sparta would have been proud of these heroes.

It would be invidious to particularize instances of individual merit, where every one so nobly performed his part. Of the nine seamen remaining unhurt at the time the *Lawrence* struck her flag, five were immediately promoted for their unshaken firmness in such a trying situation. The most of these had been in the actions with the *Guerriere* and *Java*.

Every officer of the *Lawrence*, except the commodore and his little brother, a promising youth, 13 years old, were either killed or wounded.

The efficacy of the gun-boats was fully proved in this action, and the sterns of all the prizes bear ample testimony of the fact. They took raking positions and galled the enemy severely. The *Lady Prevost* lost twelve men before either of the brigs fired on her. Their fire was quick and precise. Let us hear the enemy. The general order of Adjutant General Baynes, contains the following words: 'His [Perry's] numerous gun boats [four], which had proved the greatest annoyance during the action, were all uninjured.'

The undaunted bravery of Admiral Barclay entitled him to a better fate; to the loss of the day was superadded grievous and dangerous wounds: he had before lost an arm; it was now his hard fortune to lose the use of the other, by a shot which carried away the blade of the right shoulder; a canister shot made a violent contusion in his hip: his wounds were for some days considered mortal. Every possible attention was paid to his situation. When Commodore Perry sailed for Buffalo, he was so far recovered that he took passage on board our fleet. The fleet touched at Erie. The citizens saw the affecting spectacle of Harrison and Perry leading the wounded British hero, still unable to walk without help, from the beach to their lodgings.

The British officers had domesticated a bear at Malden. Bruin accompanied his comrades to battle—was on the deck of the *Detroit* during the engagement, and escaped unhurt.

On board the *Detroit,* twenty-four hours after her surrender, were found snugly stowed away in the hold, two Indian Chiefs, who had the courage to go on board at Malden, for the purpose of acting as sharp shooters to kill our officers. One had the courage to ascend into the round top and discharged his piece, but the whizzing of shot, splinters, and bits of rigging, soon made the place too warm for him—he descended faster than he went up; at the moment he reached the deck, the fragments of a seamen's head struck his comrade's face and covered it with blood and brains. He vociferated the savage interjection "*qvoh!*" and both sought safety below.

Commodore Perry treated the prisoners with humanity and indulgence; several Canadians, having wives at Malden were permitted to visit their families on parole.

The killed of both fleets were thrown overboard as fast as they fell. Several were washed ashore upon the island and the main during the gales that succeeded the action.

The British were superior in the length and number of their guns, as well as in the number of men. The American fleet was manned with a motley set of beings, Europeans, Africans, Americans from every part of the United States. Full one fourth were blacks. I saw one Russian, who could not speak a word of English. They were brave—and who could be otherwise under the command of Perry?

The day after the battle, the funeral obsequies of the American and British officers, who had fallen in the action, were performed, in an appropriate and affecting manner. An opening on the margin of the bay was selected for the interment of the bodies. The crews of both fleets attended. The weather was fine—the elements seemed to participate in the solemnities of the day, for every breeze was hushed, and not a wave ruffled the surface of the water. The procession of boats—the neat appearance of the officers and men—the music—the slow and regular motion of the oars, striking in exact time with the notes of the solemn dirge—the mournful waving of the flags—the sound of the minute guns from the different ships in the harbor—the wild and solitary aspect of the place, the stillness of nature, gave to the scene an air of melancholy grandeur, better felt than described—all acknowledged its influence—all were sensibly affected. What a contrast did it exhibit to the terrible conflict of the preceding day. Then the people of the two squadrons were engaged la the deadly strife of arms. Now they associated like brothers, to pay the last sad tribute of respect to the dead of both nations.

Five officers were interred, two American and three British. Lt. Brooks and Midshipman Laub of the *Lawrence;* Captain Finnis and Lt. Slokoe of the *Queen Charlotte,* and Lt. Garland of the *Detroit.* The graves are but a few paces from the beach, and the future traveler of either nation, will find no memento whereby he may distinguish the American from the British hero.

The marines of our fleet were highly complimented by the commodore, for their good conduct; although it was the first time that most of them had seen a square rigged vessel, being fresh from Harrison's army. The Kentuckians proved, on this occasion, as has the commodore since, that they can fight on both elements.

Source: Duncan, Archibald. "Battle of Lake Erie." In *The Mariner's Chronicle: Containing Narratives of the* *Most Remarkable Disasters at Sea.* New Haven, Conn.: E. M. Treadway, 1834, pp. 485–490.

THE BATTLE OF THE THAMES, OCTOBER 5, 1813

Account of the Battle
William Greathouse
Published 1927

On October 5, 1813, William Henry Harrison led some 3,500 infantry and cavalry against 800 soldiers under the British general Henry Procter. An additional force of 500 British-allied Native Americans was under the command of the Shawnee chief Tecumseh. Procter's plan was to ambush and trap Harrison on the banks of the Thames, but Harrison preempted this with a bold frontal attack, which sent the British fleeing from the field. Tecumseh and his warriors kept fighting, but their resolve quickly dissolved after the great Indian leader was killed. In conjunction with Oliver H. Perry's naval victory on Lake Erie, Harrison's triumph on the banks of the Thames opened the way to the reestablishment of American control over the Old Northwest.

All that is known of William Greathouse is that he enlisted in a rifle company of the 5th Kentucky Regiment (Martin H. Wickliffe, captain) and fought in all phases of the campaign that culminated in the Battle of the Thames.

I entered the service as a volunteer, the 24th of August in Bardstown, Nelson county, Kentucky, for the purpose of exterminating the savage foe and the British armies that were committing woeful depredations on the frontiers of Ohio and Michigan in the northwest, and to reinforce General Harrison. We rendezvoused at Newport opposite Cincinnati, crossed the Ohio river, then marched north until we struck the Miami river; kept up that stream to the mouth of the Mad river to a small town called Dayton, then through a densely heavy timbered country to a little town called Urbana, then northeast to the Sandusky river to the bay that empties into Lake Erie. On the west of the bay one mile and a half empties a river by the name of Carion river into the lake. There we built a fence out of poles from river to river, fencing and enclosing about ten thousand acres, and made use of that as pasture for our horses.

After we left upper Sandusky fort about ten miles, we passed through General Crawford's battle ground where General Crawford perhaps fought the severest and most blood contest with the Indians that was ever fought in the United States. General Crawford had four hundred mounted volunteers, the Indians had fourteen hundred. They fought for days and nights, hand to hand. The Americans were completely defeated. On the fourth night Crawford gave orders for every man for himself. My father was in that desperate battle. He and about sixty men reached home, traveling seven days without food. My Grandfather Greathouse was a prisoner at that time seven years with the Indians.

At that time, General Crawford was taken prisoner and burned at the stake. Dr. Night, whom I was well acquainted with, informed me some years later that he was in that most bloody contest with General Crawford and was taken prisoner with him, and was to have been burned the same day at a little Indian village with a guard of two very large Indians. The mosquitoes were very bad and they built a good fire. The Dr. was a very small man, and as the mosquitoes were so very bad the Dr. prevailed on the Indians to untie him so he could knock the mosquitoes off, So when the fire burned down, the Dr. seized hold of the fire end of a stick that had been burned in two and knocked one of the Indians in the head. The other Indian ran off and left the Doctor to himself. He traveled for sixteen days without food except two little birds he took out of the nest of their mother and she complained most desperately so that he gave her back one and ate the other raw. He reached within four miles of home and could go no further—perfectly given out. Four hunters came across him. He could

not walk and they tied a blanket to a pole and put him in it and carried him home. He lived in Shelby county, Kentucky, raised a respected family of sons and daughters.

When I reached home, I was telling my father that I passed through General Crawford's battleground that he had with the Indians. He told me all the particulars in relation to the battle. I digressed a little in relating Crawford's defeat with the Indians. I do think it should never he lost from the American people. When we left Sandusky bay we embarked in small bateau boats that would hold about seventy five men. What the boats could not take, Commodore Perry's fleet took the balance. There were about eleven thousand: Our first landing was on Put-in-Bay Island about twenty five miles from our horse pasture. We left about five hundred men to [take] care of our horses, We staid two or three days on the Island, then our next move was at the Three Sisters Island. Stayed there two days. From this Island we could see [Fort] Moulden [Malden]. The British burned the fort and all their military stores that they could not take. Our next move was to Fort Moulden. We found it vacant and stayed there one night and pursued the enemy with a forced march. There were about seventy five or perhaps a hundred of those bateau boats to take the sick and the baggage up the Detroit river to Detroit where Hull surrendered to the British. I was very sick at Fort Moulden. I was unable to march in the morning. By twelve o'clock I felt very much better and felt very willing to stay there in the midst of the enemies of my country. I walked down to the bay at the mouth of the Detroit river to see if all the small boats were gone. To my joy, I found two just ready to push off. I asked the privilege of going on one of the boats, the first refused me. Then I called on the second and last one. They also refused me. I then remonstrated with them, telling them that I was very sick and thought they were very unkind and ungrateful to a brother soldier who was not able to help himself. By this time they were a good rod from shore. He said to me if I would wade in, I might go. A man stood in the bow, cursed the fellow and told him to push the boat to shore and I got in and laid down as the sight of the water made me deathly sick. I moaned terribly and the man who stood at the bow of the boat said to them, that man, poor fellow, was very sick. I lay there till in the evening. I suppose we had gone some fifteen or twenty miles and there we had a little scrimmage with the rear guard of the British army.

The boats all landed on a sand beach. I had an occasion to crawl out on the beach and lay down with my head on my knapsack. We lay there perhaps some two hours and when the men were returning to their boats, an old friend of my Father's and also my friend saw me lying on the beach. He came to me and asked me what was the matter. I told him. He picked me up in his arms and took me to his boat and took the best care of me he possibly could.

That night we landed in shallow water so that our boat could not get near the shore. My friend took me up on his back, knapsack, gun and all of his own luggage and packed me to the shore and made me as comfortable as he could. That night there was an alarm gun fired so that all the camp was called to arms and I was left solitary and alone. Some time in the night an old cow hauled my knapsack out from under my head, waked me and I thought I was gone, that I would be scalped in a little time. But I thank my God that it was nothing but an old cow, perhaps wanted a little salt instead of my scalp. So the next morning I was carried by my friend to the boat and the next night we landed at a little Canadian town called Sandwich opposite Detroit. By this time I had recovered from my sickness and felt able to perform my duty as a soldier. Here the officers held a council of war and were determined to pursue the enemy. Here my friends tried to prevail on me to stay at Fort Detroit. We left something like 1,000 men here that professed to be sick. But I told them I was determined to go so long as I could lift one leg past the other. So, the next morning we took a forced march after the enemy upon the Canadian side of the Detroit river to the head and struck Lake Sinclair, around

it until we came to the river Thames which is very deep and quite crooked. The British ran up several small ships loaded with military goods, seeing the ships sailing in full sail, looking across a farm you would think the ships were moving on dry land, for you would not see or know that there was any river there until you came upon it. We had several skrimmages while going up the Thames. Whenever we would get too close to the ships they would set fire to them, leaving bombs on board so that we never dared attempt to go on board. We marched a forced march all the time in a good dog trot. Sometimes we would be a mile or two in the rear, and we would hear the bombs booming at considerable rate. I often thought that when we could come up that we would have some tall fighting, but when we came up we found to our satisfaction that there was no fighting. The British one day in a forced march, came on a barge, [and] landed on the opposite of the river. The soldiers were unloading. Our adjutant was present with us. He ordered us to take a deliberate aim and try to kill several of them. I took a good rest and had one fair fire at a red coat, but my ball fell some distance between me and the object I shot at. I shot up the river and saw the ball strike the water, so they were taken prisoner without killing any. On the second day we crossed the river Thames at a large flour mill and went up on the west side of the river Thames. That day about three or four o'clock we brought the enemy to a halt. We came up to an old field which seemed to have been cleared a long time and well set in blue grass. At the upper edge of this field we came to a large bottom, very heavily timbered, but very little undergrowth in this timber, the British and Indians were formed for battle. There was a range of mountains about half a mile from the river. Under this mountain was a swamp, The Indians were formed running from the river to the mountains. Our men were formed in three divisions running from the river towards the mountain. [Johnson's Regiment] was commanded to charge on the British lines and form in their rear, but their horses revolted and none but Colonel Johnson and two or three were able to make their horses stand the fire of the enemy, and in their retreat back Johnson received five wounds. I passed over his feet or legs. He seemed to be in great pain and calling for water. I saw close by some men running with a hat full of water for him. His gray mare was close by badly wounded and was very bloody and died that night.

The British made but one fire and surrendered. They marched their prisoners down by divisions. An officer called on my Captain for a file of men to take charge of the prisoners. The Captain ordered me to take a file of men and take charge of the prisoners. I begged to be excused as the Indians were firing very sharply and I wanted to have a hand in it. My Captain ordered me to obey. I took the file of men and went about fifty yards and I handed the prisoners over to one of my men and told him to take good care of them and I returned to my Captain and by that time the Indians had outflanked my company and we wheeled to the left and passed the Indians. By that time their Chief fell and they gave the loudest yells I ever heard from human beings and that ended the fight. The first division fought the British; the second division fought the Indians; the third had no hand in the fight. Tecumseh fell by some man, but it was not known by whom. It was thought he fell by the hand of an old man. We called him Colonel Weekley. They lay close together. Weekley that day shot an Indian on the other side of the river Thames, swam over and scalped him and swam back. He was one of the advance guards. He was a brave old man. After the battle I went to see who and how many were killed. I think the British killed none and wounded seven. I found General Harrison in person ordering and providing for the poor fellows that were wounded. I intended visiting Tecumseh but learned that the boys had taken several razor strops from his person, so I did not go where he lay.

That night the drum and fife were beating around for volunteers to go up the river about two miles to a Moravian town. It was said or thought the Indians and what British were left would be in that little town. Our company had about one hundred and fifty men. I was the only man that turned out and I was chosen for the advance guard. About dark we marched. We went but a little ways before I tumbled over a dead Indian. I passed on and in about half a mile I stumbled over, I thought, a second, but it happened to be a large leather valise well packed with clothing which turned out to my interest very much as I had my clothing stolen from me. There was everything that a man wanted, but money there was none.

We marched up to the town and found several hundred Indian women and children—the soldier's wives. In the morning I and one of our soldiers took a little ramble to see what we could spy out. I found a silver coin that an Indian had worn in his nose. It had a small hole in it and there was a large leather string about three foot in it. It had caught in a brush and torn out. It had the lion and unicorn on one side and the King and Queen on the other side. In the morning we marched the women and children down to the camp. The advance with several men pursued Proctor, the British general, and made him leave his carriage and take the brush. They brought the carriage into camp. We then made a move for our homes. Just before the main army made a move, myself, lieutenant and three other men jumped into a canoe and started down the little Thames to the mouth, then in the Lake Sinclair. We made tolerable progress. About dark a considerable gale of wind arose so high that we had to abandon our canoe and take it afoot. I took the lead. It rained intolerable. The sand was very soft, so much so, that we sunk shoe mouth deep every step we made, not knowing what minute we might receive a tomahawk from an Indian. The country was full of them. We traveled with undeviating zeal. In the course of an hour's hard marching, one of my men passed me, and after some time the second passed me. At this time the Lieutenant was behind me. I thought my time was close at hand for I felt like I would certainly give out and if the lieutenant should pass me, I should slip out in the brush and camp for the night. When the lieutenant came up to my side I said to him, "Don't leave me, I am giving out." He responded, "I am giving out and felt like I could not go much further." So we slacked our gait and took our time to get into the settlement. We found our companions waiting our arrival. We spent a comfortable night. In the morning my companions took it afoot to Detroit and I mingled my fate with six men, all strangers, but brother soldiers. We jumped into an elm bark canoe and put out for Detroit which was not more than six or eight miles. We had not progressed a great ways before a gale of wind sprung up and threw us on an island right at the head of Detroit river. There we lay two days and one night and the wind blew very strong and quite cold. The second clay a Frenchman came across us. He was hunting ducks and took us over the little neck of the Detroit river for $1.50 each, which took him about an hour to make two trips. I thought in crossing we should all be cast in the deep, but the Frenchman called out never fear, we would reach the shore safely. By dark we had all landed safely with our conductor at his home, tarried with him all night. In the morning we marched down to Detroit. We found the army all in motion. Picking the sick from the able-bodied men who were able to wade creeks, lakes and rivers to their chins, many times, the sick were piled into vessels thick as three in a bed, suffering much with cold, landed where our horses were late in the evening the second day and found our horses doing very well. We lay there two or three days and marched home. We marched in good order until we reached Maysville, Kentucky, on the Ohio river. There we were turned loose to go home the best way we could, without money or provisions. Our uniforms were blue trimmed with red. Our arms, American rifles, caliber from 16 to 25 to the pound, belt with tomahawk and butcher knife buckled around us.

Source: "The Battle of the Thames." In *Stories of 1812: Prize Winning Reminiscences,* edited by Margaret Shotwell. Omaha, Nebr.: Privately printed, 1927, pp. 11–17.

THE BATTLE OF LUNDY'S LANE, JULY 25, 1814

Account of the Battle with Eyewitness Reports
Edgerton Ryerson
Published 1880

American troops under the command of Major General Jacob Brown advanced on the Portage Road toward Queenston, Ontario, to make a preemptive strike against British forces believed to be preparing on the U.S. side of the Niagara River. At Lundy's Lane (today a street in Niagara Falls, Ontario), the American and British forces met. Although Brown determined that the British force was larger than his, he decided to attack, sending 1,500 men against 1,700 British troops at six o'clock on the evening of July 25, 1814. The opening American attack was repulsed by cannon fire, but a stealthy U.S. counterattack overran the British gunners and captured their cannons.

The fighting continued well after dark, until about 11:00, at which point Brown began an orderly withdrawal to Fort Erie. Although the Americans were driven from the field, the losses to both sides were so great that the battle cannot be declared an outright British victory. British and Canadian losses were 878 killed and wounded; the Americans suffered 860 killed and wounded. Seven out of 10 of the U.S. regimental commanders engaged were either killed or wounded. It was the bloodiest single battle of the War of 1812 and, like the war itself, proved indecisive.

Edgerton Ryerson (1803–82), who served as the chief superintendent of education for Upper Canada from 1844 to 1876, drew on eyewitness accounts to present the Canadian Loyalist side of the bloody Battle of Lundy's Lane, in a book that was published in 1880.

Of all the battles fought during the war, the most sanguinary and obstinate was that of Lundy's Lane . . . the battle fought the last few months of the war, the 25th of July, 1814. It was the most formidable and final effort of the American General Brown to get permanent footing in Canada. The smallest number of American soldiers engaged in the battle, according to General Brown's report, was upwards of 5,000; and the largest number of British soldiers and Canadian militia engaged, according to the British General Drummond's report, was 2,800, although the greater part of the battle was fought with a force not exceeding 1,600. I shall not attempt to describe the order, or narrate the incidents of the battle; I will only say, that the high ground, near the east end of Lundy's Lane, was the centre of interest, and the position contended for by both parties in deadly strife for several hours. In no battle during the war did the Americans fight with such heroism and obstinacy; and in no battle was the courage, steadiness and perseverance of the British soldiers and Canadian volunteers put to so severe a test. The enemy was drawn up in order of battle within 600 yards of the coveted eminence, when General Drummond arrived on the ground, and he had barely time to plant his artillery on the brow of the hill, when the enemy concentrated all his power and efforts to obtain the key of the battle-field. An eyewitness says: "Columns of the enemy, not unlike the surge of the adjacent cataract, rushed to the charge in close and impetuous succession." The curtain of night soon enveloped the scene, now drenched with blood; but the darkness seemed to intensify the fury of the combatants, and the rage of the battle increased as the night advanced. An eye-witness truly observes, that "nothing could have been more awful than this midnight contest. The desperate charges of the enemy were succeeded by a dead silence, interrupted only by the groans of the dying, and the dull sounds of the stupendous Falls of Niagara, while the adverse lines were now and then dimly discerned through the moonlight, by the dismal gleam of their arms. Those anxious pauses were succeeded by a blaze of musketry along the lines, and by a repetition of the most desperate charges from the enemy, which the British received with the most unshaken firmness." General Drummond, in his official report of the battle, says:—"In so determined a manner were these attacks directed against our guns, that our artillerymen were bayoneted by the enemy in the act of loading, and the muzzles of the enemy's guns were advanced within a few yards of ours. The darkness of the night, during this extraordinary conflict, occasioned several uncommon incidents; our troops having, for a moment, been pushed back, some of our guns remained for a few minutes in the enemy's hands; they were, however, not only quickly recovered, but the two pieces, a six-pounder and a five-and-a-half-inch howitzer, which the enemy had brought up, were captured by us, together with several tumbrils. About nine o'clock (the action having commenced at six) there was a short intermission of firing, during which it appears the enemy was employed in bringing up the whole of his remaining force; and he shortly afterwards renewed the attack with fresh troops, but was everywhere repelled with equal gallantry and success. The enemy's efforts to carry the hill were continued until about midnight, when he had suffered so severely from the superior steadiness and discipline of his Majesty's troops, that he gave up the contest, and retreated with great precipitation to his camp beyond the Chippewa. On the following day he abandoned his camp, threw the greatest part of his baggage, camp equipage and provisions into the Rapids; and having set fire to Street's Mills, and destroyed the bridge at Chippewa, he continued his retreat in great disorder towards Fort Erie."

In this bloody battle, the Canadian militia fought side by side with the regular soldiers; and General Drummond said, "the bravery of the militia on this occasion could not have been excelled by the most resolute veterans."

Such was the loyalty of our grandfathers and fathers, and such their self-devotion and courage in the darkest hour of our country's dangers and sufferings, and though few in number in comparison of their invaders, they had

Hearts resolved and hands prepared
The blessings they enjoyed to guard.

There was doubtless as much true courage among the descendants of Great Britain and Ireland in the United States as in Canada; but the former fought for the oppressor of Europe, the latter fought for the freedom of Europe; the former fought to prostrate Great Britain in her death struggle for the liberties of mankind, and to build up the United States upon her ruin, the latter fought in the glorious cause of the mother country, and to maintain our own unity with her; the former fought for the conquest of Canada, the latter fought in her defence; the fire that kindled the military ardour of the former was the blown-up embers of old enmities against Great Britain, the gross misrepresentations of President Madison, the ambition of adventure, and the lust of booty—the fire that burned in the hearts of the latter, and animated them to deeds of death or freedom, was the sacred love of hearth and home, the patriotic love of liberty, and that hallowed principle of loyalty to truth, and law, and liberty combined, which have constituted the life, and development, and traditions, and strength, and unity, and glory of British institutions, and of the British nation, from the resurrection morn of the Protestant Reformation to the present day. . . .

Source: Ryerson, Edgerton. *The Loyalists of America and Their Times: From 1620 to 1816.* Toronto: William Briggs, 1880, pp. 455–458.

THE BURNING OF WASHINGTON, D.C., AUGUST 24, 1814

Account of the Burning of Washington, D.C.
Reverend George Robert Gleig
Published 1821

Some 4,250 British troops under the command of Major General Robert Ross, having defeated weak American forces at Bladensburg, Maryland, occupied Washington, D.C., and set fire to many of the capital's public buildings, including the White House and the original Capitol. It is believed that the raid was in revenge for the American sack of York (modern Toronto) in 1813, in which the Parliament Buildings of Upper Canada were razed. Ross ordered his troops to confine their arson to public buildings only. No private houses were burned. After the raid, the British withdrew. No one on either side was killed or wounded.

The Reverend George Robert Gleig (1796–1888) served in the British army during the War of 1812 and witnessed the capture, sack, and burning of Washington, D.C. He published the following account in 1821.

Towards morning, a violent storm of rain, accompanied with thunder and lightning, came on, which disturbed the rest of all those who were exposed to it. Yet, in spite of the disagreeableness of getting wet, I cannot say that I felt disposed to grumble at the interruption, for it appeared that what I had before considered as superlatively sublime, still wanted this to render it complete. The flashes of lightning seemed to vie in brilliancy, with the flames which burst from the roofs of burning houses, while the thunder drowned the noise of crumbling walls, and was only interrupted by the occasional roar of cannon, and of large depots of gunpowder, as they one by one exploded.

. . . [T]he consternation of the inhabitants was complete, and . . . to them this was a night of terror. So confident had they been of the success of their troops, that few of them had dreamt of quitting their houses, or abandoning the city; nor was it till the fugitives from the battle began to rush in, filling every place as they came with dismay, that the President himself thought of providing for his safety. That gentleman, as I was credibly informed, had gone forth in the morning with the army, and had continued among his troops till the British forces began to make their appearance. Whether the sight of his enemies cooled his courage or not, I cannot say, but, according

BRITISH BURN THE CAPITOL · 1814

British Burn the Capitol, 1814, by Allyn Cox, an oil-on-canvas painting applied to the ceiling of the Hall of Capitols, a corridor in the House side of the United States Capitol, depicts the burning of the original Capitol by British troops on August 24, 1814. *(Courtesy of the Architect of the Capitol)*

to my informer, no sooner was the glittering of our arms discernible, than he began to discover that his presence was more wanted in the senate than with the army; and having ridden through the ranks, and exhorted every man to do his duty, he hurried back to his own house, that he might prepare a feast for the entertainment of his officers, when they should return victorious. For the truth of these details, I will not be answerable; but this much I know, that the feast was actually

prepared, though, instead of being devoured by American officers, it went to satisfy the less delicate appetites of a party of English soldiers. When the detachment, sent out to destroy Mr. Maddison's house, entered his dining parlour, they found a dinner-table spread, and covers laid for forty guests. . . .

They sat down to it, therefore, not indeed in the most orderly manner, but with countenances which would not have disgraced a party of aldermen at a civic feast; and having satisfied their appetites with fewer complaints than would have probably escaped their rival gourmands, and partaken pretty freely of the wines, they finished by setting fire to the house which had so liberally entertained them.

But, as I have just observed, this was a night of dismay to the inhabitants of Washington. They were taken completely by surprise; nor could the arrival of the flood be more unexpected to the natives of the antediluvian world, than the arrival of the British army to them. The first impulse of course tempted them to fly, and the streets were in consequence crowded with soldiers and senators, men, women and children, horses, carriages, and carts loaded with household furniture, all hastening towards a wooden bridge which crosses the Potomac. The confusion thus occasioned was terrible, and the crowd upon the bridge was such as to endanger its giving away. But Mr. Maddison, having escaped among the first, was no sooner safe on the opposite bank of the river, than he gave orders that the bridge should be broken down; which being obeyed, the rest were obliged to return, and to trust to the clemency of the victors. In this manner was the night passed by both parties; and at day-break next morning, the light brigade moved into the city, while the reserve fell back to a height, about half a mile in the rear. Little, however, now remained to be done, because every thing marked out for destruction, was already consumed. Of the senate-house, the President's palace, the barracks, the dock-yard, &c. nothing could be seen, except heaps of smoking ruins; and even the bridge, a noble structure upwards of a mile in length, was almost wholly demolished. There was, therefore, no farther occasion to scatter the troops, and they were accordingly kept together as much as possible on the Capitol hill.

Sources: Gleig, George Robert. *A Narrative of the Campaigns of the British Army at Washington and New Orleans.* London: J. Murray, 1821; Hart, Albert Bushnell. *Source-Book of American History.* New York: Macmillan, 1899, pp. 218–220.

THE BATTLE OF BALTIMORE, SEPTEMBER 12–15, 1814

"The Star-Spangled Banner"
Francis Scott Key
Published September 17, 1814

"The Star-Spangled Banner" is certainly the most famous and enduring eyewitness "account" of battle ever to emerge from an American war. The verses were written by a young Washington attorney, Francis Scott Key (1779–1843), who was detained on a British warship in Baltimore Harbor during the night of September 13–14, 1814, as the British fleet bombarded Fort McHenry, which defended the city of Baltimore. Key anxiously watched the night-long assault, both fearing and expecting to find, "at dawn's early light," the fort reduced and Baltimore in the hands of the British. Instead, sunrise brought a glimpse of the tattered Stars and Stripes still flying over the fort. At the sight of this, Key penned his account of the battle, which was published on September 17 under the title "Defence of Fort McHenry." His verses were not intended to be set to music. However, the simple meter readily lent itself to an existing popular tune attributed to John Stafford Smith, "To Anacreon in Heaven," originally composed for the members of a London drinking club, the Anacreontic Society, but so popular in the United States that, by 1820, some 84 different poems were sung to it.

"The Star-Spangled Banner," as it eventually became known, was long popular as a patriotic air and was even adopted informally as the anthem of the Union army during the Civil War. When it shipped out to France in April 1917, during World War I, the U.S. Army officially claimed it as a marching song, but it did not become the U.S. national anthem legally until March 3, 1931, when President Herbert Hoover signed its status into law.

O say, can you see, by the dawn's early light,
What so proudly we hailed at the twilight's
last gleaming?

Whose broad stripes and bright stars,
    through the perilous fight,
O'er the ramparts we watched, were so gal-
    lantly streaming?
And the rocket's red glare, the bombs burst-
    ing in air,
Gave proof through the night that our flag
    was still there.
O say does that star spangled banner yet
    wave
O'er the land of the free, and the home of
    the brave?

On the shore dimly seen through the mists
    of the deep.
Where the foe's haughty host in dread
    silence reposes,
What is that which the breeze, o'er the tow-
    ering steep,

As it fitfully blows, half conceals, half
    discloses?
Now it catches the gleam of the morning's
    first beam,
In full glory reflected now shines in the
    stream:
'Tis the Star-Spangled Banner! O long may
    it wave
O'er the land of the free and the home of
    the brave.

And where is that band who so vauntingly
    swore
That the havoc of war and the battle's
    confusion
A home and a country should leave us no
    more?
Their blood has washed out their foul foot-
    steps' pollution.
No refuge could save the hireling and slave
From the terror of flight, or the gloom of the
    grave:
And the Star-Spangled Banner, in triumph
    doth wave
O'er the land of the free and the home of
    the brave.

O thus be it ever when freemen shall stand
Between their loved homes and the war's
    desolation!
Blest with vict'ry and peace, may the
    Heaven-rescued land
Praise the Power that hath made and pre-
    served us a nation.
Then conquer we must when our cause it is
    just
And this be our motto: "In God is our
    Trust."
And the Star-Spangled Banner in triumph
    shall wave
O'er the land of the free and the home of
    the brave

Francis Scott Key, who observed the British attack on Fort McHenry in Baltimore Harbor, was inspired by the sight of the American flag that remained flying to write "The Star-Spangled Banner." *(Library of Congress)*

The source melody, "To Anacreon in Heaven," was first published in London about 1780. The original lyrics, by Anacreontic Club member Ralph Tomlinson, were remote from Key's anxious patriotism:

To Anacreon in heaven where he sat in full
    glee,
A few sons of harmony sent a petition,
That he their inspirer and patron would be,
When this answer arrived from the jolly old
    Grecian:
Voice, fiddle and flute, no longer be mute,
I'll lend you my name and inspire you to
    boot!
And besides I'll instruct you like me to
    entwine
The myrtle of Venus and Bacchus's vine.

The news through Olympus immediately flew,
When old Thunder pretended to give himself airs,
If these mortals are suffered their scheme to
    pursue,
The devil a goddess will stay above stairs,
Hark! already they cry, in transports of joy,
A fig for Parnassus, to Rowley's we'll fly,
And there my good fellows, we'll learn to
    entwine
The myrtle of Venus and Bacchus's vine.

The yellow-haired god, and his nine fusty
    maids,
To the hill of old Lud will incontinent flee,
Idalia will boast but of tenantless shades,
And the biforked hill a mere desert will be,
My thunder, no fear on't, will soon do its
    errand,
And, damn me I'll swinge the ringleaders, I
    warrant
I'll trim the young dogs, for thus daring to
    twine
The myrtle of Venus with Bacchus's vine.

Apollo rose up and said, "Prythee ne'er
    quarrel,
Good king of the gods, with my votaries
    below

Your thunder is useless—then showing his
    laurel,
Cried, *Sic evitabile fulmen,* you know!
Then over each head my laurels I'll spread,
So my sons from your crackers no mischief
    shall dread
Whilst snug in their club-room, they jovially
    twine
The myrtle of Venus and Bacchus's vine.

Sources: Wikipedia. "The Star-Spangled Banner." Available online. URL: http://en.wikipedia.org/wiki/The_Star-Spangled_Banner. Accessed on February 5, 2010; PotW.org. "The Anacreontic Song as Sung at the Crown and Anchor Tavern in the Strand." Available online. URL: http://www.potw.org/archive/potw234.html. Accessed on February 5, 2010.

THE BATTLE OF NEW ORLEANS, JANUARY 8, 1815

Eyewitness Account of the Battle
Anonymous
Published 1926

At dawn on January 8, 1815, a motley American army of 4,000 men under Andrew Jackson confronted a British force, commanded by Sir Edward Pakenham, of eight or nine thousand veterans of the Napoleonic Wars. This was to be the culminating exchange in a battle that had begun on December 23, 1814, when Jackson made a preemptive attack against a British force that had landed eight miles south of the city. Jackson was forced into retreat, but he dug in just three miles closer to New Orleans. It was here that he and his men took their stand on January 8.

The British forces performed poorly and could not operate effectively in the swampy terrain Jackson had chosen to defend. Incredibly, after less than

General Andrew Jackson, on horseback, commanding the American troops in their victory over the British forces at the Battle of New Orleans. *(Library of Congress)*

an hour, the British surrendered, having lost some 300 killed and 1,200 wounded. Jackson's losses were light: 13 killed and 52 wounded or missing.

For good reason, the Battle of New Orleans was embraced as a great American victory, even though the January exchange was fought two weeks after the signing of the Treaty of Ghent, which ended the war, news of the treaty having failed to reach either the British commanders or Jackson. General Pakenham was among those killed in the battle.

The eyewitness account of the Battle of New Orleans that follows was written by an unknown American soldier fighting from the top of the breastworks (spelled "brestwork" in this document) defending the city.

Col. Smiley, from Bardstown, was the first one who gave us orders to fire from our part of the line; and then, I reckon, there was a pretty considerable noise. There were also brass pieces on our right, the noisiest kind of varmints, that began blaring away as hard as they could, while the heavy iron cannon, toward the river, and some thousands of small arms, joined in the chorus and made the ground shake under our feet. Directly after the firing began, Capt. Patterson, I think he was from Knox County, Kentucky, but an Irishman born, came running along. He jumped upon the brestwork and stooping a moment to look through the darkness as well as he could, he shouted with a broad North of Ireland brogue, "shoot low, boys! shoot low! rake them—rake them! They're comin' on their all fours!"

The official report said the action lasted two hours and five minutes, but it did not seem half that length of time to me. It was so dark that little could be seen, until just about the time the battle ceased. The morning had dawned to be sure, but the smoke was so thick that every thing seemed to be covered up in it. Our men did not seem to apprehend any danger, but would load and fire as fast as they could, talking, swearing, and joking all the time. All ranks and sections were soon broken up. After the first shot, everyone loaded and banged away on his own hook.

Henry Spillman did not load and fire quite so often as some of the rest, but every time he did fire he would go up to the brestwork, look over until he could see something to shoot at, and then take deliberate aim and crack away. Lieut. Ashby was as busy as a nailor and it was evident that, the River Raisin [Massacre of January 22–23, 1813, near Frenchtown, Michigan] was uppermost in his mind all the time. He kept dashing about and every now and then he would call out, with an oath, "We'll pay you now for the River Raisin! We'll give you something to remember the River Raisin!" When the British came up to the opposite side of the brestwork, having no gun, he picked up an empty barrel and flung it at them. Then finding an iron bar, he jumped up on the works and hove that at them.

At one time I noticed, a little on our right, a curious kind of a chap named Ambrose Odd, one of Captain Higdon's company, and known among the men by the nickname of "Sukey," standing coolly on the top of the brestworks and peering into the darkness for something to shoot at. The balls were whistling around him and over our heads, as thick as hail, and Col. Slaughter coming along, ordered him to come down.

The Colonel told him there was policy in war, and that he was exposing himself too much. Sukey turned around, holding up the flap of his old broad brimmed hat with one hand, to see who was speaking to him, and replied: "Oh! never mind Colonel—here's Sukey—I don't want to waste my powder, and I'd like to know how I can shoot until I see something?" Pretty soon after, Sukey got his eye on a red coat, and, no doubt, made a hole through it, for he took delib-

erate aim, fired and then coolly came down to load again.

During the action, a number of the Tennessee men got mixed up with ours. One of them was killed about five or six yards from where I stood. I did not know his name. A ball passed through his head and he fell against Ensign Weller. I always thought, as did many others who were standing near, that he must have been accidently shot by some of our own men. From the range of the British balls, they could hardly have passed over the breastwork without passing over our heads, unless we were standing very close to the works, which were a little over brest high, and five or six feet wide on the top.

This man was standing a little back and rather behind Weller. After the battle, I could not see that any of the balls had struck the oak tree lower than ten or twelve feet from the ground. Above that height it was thickly peppered. This was the only man killed near where I was stationed. It was near the close of the firing. About the time that I observed three or four men carrying his body away or directly after, there was a white flag raised on the opposite side of the brestwork and the firing ceased.

The white flag, before mentioned, was raised about ten or twelve feet from where I stood, close to the brestwork and a little to the right. It was a white handkerchief, or something of the kind, on a sword or stick. It was waved several times, and as soon as it was perceived, we ceased firing. Just then the wind got up a little and blew the smoke off, so that we could see the field. It then appeared that the flag had been raised by a British Officer wearing epaulets. It was told he was a Major. He stepped over the brestwork and came into our lines. Among the Tennesseans who had got mixed with us during the fight, there was a little fellow whose name I do not know; but he was a cadaverous looking chap and went by that of Paleface. As the British Officer came in, Paleface demanded his sword. He hesitated about giving it to him, probably thinking it was derogatory to his dignity, to surrender to a private all over begrimed with dust and powder and that some Officer should show him the courtesy to receive it. Just at that moment, Col. Smiley came up and cried, with a harsh oath, "Give it up—give it up to him in a minute!" The British Officer quickly handed his weapon to Paleface, holding it in both hands and making a very polite bow.

A good many others came in just about the same time. Among them I noticed a very neatly dressed young man, standing on the edge of the breastwork, and offering his hand, as if for some one to assist him. He appeared to be about nineteen or twenty years old, and, as I should judge from his appearance, was an Irishman. He held his musket in one hand, while he was offering the other. I took hold of his musket and set it down, and then giving him my hand, he jumped down quite lightly. As soon as he got down, he began trying to take off his cartouch[e] box, and then I noticed a red spot of blood on his clean white under jacket. I asked him if he was wounded, he said that he was and he feared pretty badly. While he was trying to disengage his accounterments, Capt. Farmer came up, and said to him, "Let me help you my man!" The Captain and myself then assisted him to take them off. He begged us not to take his canteen, which contained his water. We told him we did not wish to take anything but what was in his way and cumbersome to him. Just then one of the Tennesseans, who had run down to the river, as soon as the firing ceased, for water, came along with some in a tin coffeepot. The wounded man observed him, asked if he would please give him a drop. "O! Yes," said the Tenneessean, "I will treat you to anything I've got." The young man took the coffeepot and swallowed two or three mouthfuls out of the spout. He then handed back the pot, and in an instant we observed him sinking backwards. We eased him down against the side of a tent, when he gave two or three gasps and was dead. He had been shot through the breast.

On the opposite side of the brestwork there was a ditch about ten feet wide, made by the excavation of the earth, of which the work was formed. In it, was about a foot or eighteen inches of water, and to make it the more difficult of passage, a quantity of thornbush had been cut and thrown into it. In this ditch a number of British soldiers were found at the close under the brestwork, as a shelter from our fire. These, of course, came in and surrendered.

When the smoke had cleared away and we could obtain a fair view of the field, it looked, at the first glance, like a sea of blood. It was not blood itself which gave it this appearance but the red coats in which the British soldiers were dressed. Straight out before our position, for about the width of space which we supposed had been occupied by the British column, the field was entirely covered with prostrate bodies. In some places they were laying in piles of several, one on the top of the other. On either side, there was an interval more thinly sprinkled with the slain; and then two other dense rows, one near the levee and the other towards the swamp. About two hundred yards off, directly in front of our position, lay a large dapple gray horse, which we understood to have been [Major General Sir Edward] Pakenham's [commander of British forces at the Battle of New Orleans].

Something about half way between the body of the horse and our breastwork there was a very large pile of dead, and at this spot, as I was afterward told, Pakenham had been killed; his horse having staggered off to a considerable distance before he fell. I have no doubt that I could not have walked on the bodies from the edge of the ditch to where the horse was laying, without touching the ground. I did not notice any other horse on the field.

When we first got a fair view of the field in our front, individuals could be seen in every possible attitude. Some laying quite dead, others mortally wounded, pitching and tumbling about in the agonies of death. Some had their heads shot off, some their legs, some their arms. Some were laughing, some crying, some groaning, and some screaming. There was every variety of sight and sound. Among those that were on the ground, however, there were some that were neither dead nor wounded. A great many had thrown themselves down behind piles of slain, for protection. As the firing ceased, these men were every now and then jumping up and either running off or coming in and giving themselves up.

Among those that were running off, we observed one stout looking fellow, in a red coat, who would every now and then stop and display some gestures toward us, that were rather the opposite of complimentary. Perhaps fifty guns were fired at him, but he was a good way off, without effect. "Hurra, Paleface! load quick and give him a shot. The infernal rascal is patting his butt at us!" Sure enough, Paleface rammed home his bullet, and taking a long sight, he let drive. The fellow, by this time, was from two to three hundred yards off, and somewhat to the left of Pakenham's horse. Paleface said as he drew sight on him and then run it along up his back until the sight was lost over his head, to allow for the sinking of the ball in so great a distance, and then let go. As soon as the gun cracked, the fellow was seen to stagger. He ran forward a few steps, and then pitched down on his head, and moved no more. As soon as he fell, George Huffman, a big stout Dutchman, belonging to our Company, asked the Captain if he might go and see where Paleface hit him. The Captain said he didn't care and George jumping from the breastwork over the ditch, ran over the dead and wounded until he came to the place where the fellow was lying. George rolled over the body until he could see the face and then, turning round to us, shouted at the top of his voice, "Mine Gott! he is a nagar!" He was a mulatto and he was quite dead. Paleface's ball had entered between the shoulders, and passed out through his breast.

George, as he came back, brought three or four muskets which he had picked up. By this time, our men were running out in all directions, picking up muskets and sometimes watches and other plunder. One man who had got a little too far out on the field was fired at from the British brestwork and wounded in the arm. He came running back a good deal faster than he had gone out. He was not much hurt but pretty well scared.

Source: "They're Comin' on Their All Fours." *Louisiana Historical Quarterly* 9, no. 1 (January 1926): 1–5.

The Creek War

By the early 19th century, throughout Georgia, Tennessee, and the Mississippi Territory, the so-called Creek confederacy, a loose amalgam of tribes, was torn by conflict between those who advocated cooperation with non-Indians and those determined to expel white settlers from Creek lands. During the War of 1812, this rupture resulted in the formation of Creek factions who decided to ally with the Americans and others who sided with the British. The former were the Lower Creek, also called the White Sticks, who lived mainly in Georgia; the latter were the Upper Creek, or Red Sticks, who lived west of the White Sticks, at a farther remove from the white frontier. The Red Sticks reasoned that allying themselves with the British would drive the Americans farther east, away from their frontier, and since the British did not intend to occupy the land from which the Americans were driven, there was little risk of replacing one set of white settlers with another. The White Sticks, in contrast, enjoyed close and profitable trade and cultural relations with white settlers and wanted to perpetuate this state of affairs.

The Red Stick chief Little Warrior participated directly in the War of 1812, taking part in the River Raisin Massacre (near present-day Monroe, Michigan) on January 21, 1813, and raiding settlers along the Ohio as he and his warriors made their way home from the River Raisin engagement. While Little Warrior was en route, the White Stick chief, Big Warrior, captured and executed him. This escalated the conflict between the White and Red Sticks.

The Battle of Burnt Corn

In Pensacola, Florida, a Red Stick warrior leader known as Peter McQueen received weapons and other equipment from the Spanish. Learning of this, the commander of the U.S. Army garrison at Fort Mims, Alabama, sent a poorly organized force to intercept McQueen and his warriors. The result was the Battle of Burnt Corn, about 80 miles north of Pensacola, near modern Monroeville, Alabama, on July 27, 1813. Initially, the Americans prevailed, forcing the Red Sticks to run for the nearby swamps. However, the undisciplined troops fell to looting the pack horses the Red Sticks had left behind. This allowed McQueen to counterattack later in the day, catching the Americans off guard and forcing them to scatter.

The Fort Mims Massacre and Jackson's Campaign

On August 30, 1813, McQueen and another Red Stick war chief, William "Red Eagle" Weatherford, led a major attack on Fort Mims itself, killing most of the whites as well as mixed-blood Creek who had taken refuge there. Some 500 persons, militiamen and civilians, were killed—although the Red Sticks deliberately spared most of the African-American slaves, who subsequently became the Red Sticks' slaves.

The Fort Mims Massacre moved the Tennessee legislature to authorize $300,000 to outfit a large army under Major General Andrew Jackson. Quickly mustering his forces, Jackson marched deep into Red Stick country with 5,000 Tennessee militiamen, 19 Cherokee warrior companies, and 200 White Sticks. Early in November 1813, a detachment from Jackson's force under Colonel John Coffee (which included in its number the already legendary Davy Crockett) fell upon a large contingent of Red Sticks at Tallushatchee, Calhoun County, Alabama. Red Stick losses were 186 killed, whereas Coffee lost five killed and 41 wounded. Later in the month, Jackson himself marched to the relief of Talladega (a few miles south of Tallusahatchee), where a White Stick fort had been held under Red Stick siege. Reportedly, 290 Red Sticks fell in this engagement, while Jackson incurred losses of 15 killed and 85 wounded.

After the Talladega battle, Jackson and General William Claiborne coordinated what proved to be a fruitless two-month pursuit of McQueen, Red Eagle, and their men. During this period, Jackson's forces dwindled as a result of desertions and the expiration of short-term militia enlistments. Fortunately, in January 1814, he received 800 fresh troops, which he used to resume the offensive, engaging Red Sticks at Emuckfaw and at Enotachopco Creek, both in Alabama. In a campaign that spanned October 7, 1813 to March 27, 1814, Jackson's tactics were those of total warfare, namely the ruthless destruction of Red Stick towns and food stores.

The Battle of Horseshoe Bend

In March 1814, the U.S. Army sent 600 regulars from the 39th Infantry to augment Jackson's militia forces. Now with some 1,400 men, Jackson struck against Horseshoe Bend, a peninsula on the Tallapoosa River, fighting a daylong battle on March 27, 1814. Jackson laid siege against the Red Sticks' position on the peninsula, which was accompanied by a merciless artillery bombardment. By the time the Red Sticks surrendered, some 750 of their 900 warriors engaged lay dead. Jackson's losses were 32 killed and 99 wounded; his Cherokee allies lost 18 killed and 36 wounded, and his White Stick allies five dead and 11 wounded. As a result of the battle, William "Red Eagle" Weatherford walked into Jackson's camp a few days after the defeat and gave himself up. Apparently respecting his fighting prowess and wary of giving the Red Sticks a martyr, Jackson accepted his surrender and allowed him to leave in return for his word to lay down arms permanently.

Andrew Jackson was not as generous to any of the other Native Americans involved in the Creek War, whether enemy or ally. The Treaty of Horseshoe Bend, which followed the battle and formally ended the war, extorted 23 million acres from Red Sticks and White Sticks alike. Two-thirds of all Creek tribal lands changed hands, and white American settlement was instantly extended from the Tennessee River to the Gulf of Mexico. As for the faithful Cherokee allies, Tennessee militiamen turned against them, stealing their ponies and their food and then, with gratuitous malevolence, vandalized their property and generally abused Cherokee women, children, and old men.

DOCUMENTS

THE BATTLE OF BURNT CORN, JULY 27, 1813

Account of the Battle
Published 1895

The Battle of Burnt Corn took place on July 27, 1813, in what is today southern Alabama, near Monroeville. Earlier in the month, Peter McQueen had led a large party of Red Stick warriors to Pensacola, Florida, where he presented the Spanish governor with $400 and a letter from the British commandant of Fort Malden (Amherstburg, Ontario), asking him to furnish the Indians with munitions. The governor complied. In the meantime, the American commandant of Fort Mims, Alabama, hearing of McQueen's mission, sent a force to intercept McQueen's party, which they did at Burnt Corn. Initially, the Red Sticks retreated into the swamps, whereupon the undisciplined force from Fort Mims set about looting the pack horses the Red Sticks had abandoned. This prompted the Creek to regroup and attack the Americans. From the point of view of the Red Sticks, the Battle of Burnt Corn constituted a declaration of war against them and prompted the massacre at Fort Mims that followed.

The following account was published in 1895 in The Creek War of 1813 and 1814, *by Henry S. Halbert and T. H. Ball. The authors quote from Generals Wilkinson and Woodward, as well as from* History of Alabama *(1851), by Albert James Pickett.*

From [a] letter of General James Wilkinson, we learn that more than three hundred hostile Creeks, under the Prophet Francis, were camped, on the 25th of June, at the Holy Ground. General Wilkinson writes: "The last information received of their doings was on Wednesday [the 23d of June], by Ward's wife, who has been forced from him with her children. She reported that the party, thus encamped, were about to move down the river to break up the half-breed settlements, and those of the citizens in the fork of the rivers." While this was, no doubt, the real and ultimate design of the hostile Creeks, it was first necessary to put themselves on a thorough war footing by procuring supplies of arms and ammunition from Pensacola.

With this object in view, at some period in the early part of July, a party of Creeks, comprising a portion, if not all, of the hostile camp at the Holy Ground, with many pack-horses, took up the line of march for Pensacola. This party was under the command of Peter McQueen, at the head of the Tallassee warriors, with Jim Boy, as principal war chief, commanding the Atossees, and Josiah Francis, commanding the Alibamos. [The Alabama historian Albert James] Pickett gives the entire force as amounting to three hundred and fifty warriors; Colonel Carson, in a letter to General Claiborne, estimates them at three hundred; but General Woodward, in his *Reminiscences*, simply states that their numbers have been greatly overrated. "On their way," writes Pickett, "they beat and drove off every Indian that would not take the war-talk." On their arrival at Burnt Corn Spring, situated at the crossing of the Federal and the Pensacola roads, they burned the house and corn crib of James Cornells, seized his wife and carried her with them to Pensacola, where she was sold to Madame Baronne, a French lady, for a blanket. A man, named Marlowe, living with Cornells, was also carried prisoner to Pensacola. Cornells, it seems, was absent from home, at the time of this outrage. We hear of him, soon afterwards, at Jackson, on the Tombigbee, "mounted on a fast-flying grey horse," bringing to the settlers the tidings of Creek hostilities.

The perilous condition of the southern frontier at this period, the early part of July, is well portrayed in the following passages from Pickett: "The inhabitants of the Tombigbee and the Tensaw had constantly petitioned the Governor for an army to repel the Creeks, whose attacks they hourly expected. But General Flournoy, who had succeeded Wilkinson in command, refused to send away of the regular or volunteer troops. The British fleet was seen off the coast, from which supplies, arms, ammunition, and Indian emissaries, were sent to Pensacola and other Spanish ports in Florida. Everything foreboded the extermination of the Americans in Alabama, who were the most isolated and defenceless people imaginable." When Colonel Joseph Carson, commanding at Fort Stoddart, was informed that the above mentioned force of Creek warriors had gone to Pensacola, he despatched David Tate and William Pierce to the town to ascertain the intentions of the Creeks and whether [the Spanish] Governor Manique would grant them a supply of ammunition. The information gained by these spies and reported on their respective returns, all summed up, was that the Creeks, on their arrival in Pensacola, had called upon the Governor and presented him a letter from a British general in Canada. This letter had been given to Little Warrior when he was in Canada and at his death was saved by his nephew and afterwards given to Josiah Francis, The Creeks, whether right or wrong, supposed that this letter requested or authorized the Governor to supply them with ammunition. The Governor, in reply, assured them that it was merely a letter of recommendation, and at first refused to comply with their demands. He, however, appointed another meeting for them, and the Creeks, in the meanwhile, made every exertion to procure powder and lead by private purchase. According to Tate's information, which he received from some of the prisoners whom the Creeks had brought down with them, their language breathed out vengeance against the white people and they dropped some hints of attacking the Tensaw settlers on their return. The Creeks finally succeeded in their negotiation with the Governor, who issued an order supplying them with three hundred pounds of powder and a proportionate quantity of lead. To obtain this large supply, McQueen handed the Governor a list of the towns ready to take up arms, making four

thousand eight hundred warriors. Even this large amount of ammunition was not satisfactory to the Creeks; they demanded more, but it seems that Manique yielded no further to their demands. The Creeks now openly declared that they were going to war against the Americans; that on their return to the nation they would be joined by seven hundred warriors at the Whet Stone Hill, where they would distribute their ammunition and then return against the Tombigbee settlers. They now held their war-dance, an action equivalent to a formal declaration of war.

As the descriptions of the Burnt Corn battle ground given by Meek and Pickett are somewhat vague and inaccurate, a more correct account of the topography, gained from personal observation, is here given to the reader. Burnt Corn Creek, near which the battle was fought, runs southward for several hundred yards, then making an abrupt bend, runs southeastward for half a mile or more. Right at the elbow of the bend is the crossing of the old Pensacola road. The low pine barren enclosed in this bend—not a peninsula as called by Pickett—is enveloped by a semicircular range of hills, which extends from the creek bank on the south some half a mile below the crossing, and terminates on the west at the bank, some three hundred yards above the crossing. This western terminus is now locally known as the Bluff Landing. The Pensacola road from the crossing runs northward some two hundred yards, then turning runs eastward half a mile, making a continuous and gradual ascent up the slope of the hills, and then again turns northward. The spring, now known as Cooper's Spring, is situated about half a mile nearly east of the crossing, and about one hundred and fifty yards south of the road. It gushes forth at the base of a steep hill and is the fountain head of a small reed-brake branch, which empties into the creek about two hundred yards below the crossing. The hill, at the base of which the spring is situated, is about the centre of the semicircular range of hills which envelops the pine barren.

About sixty yards northwest of the spring, between the spring and the road, is a comparatively level spot of land, about an acre in extent. This spot, we conjecture, was the Creek camp, or at least where the main body was encamped, as it is the only place immediately near the spring suitable for a camp. The hill here rises steep and abruptly to the northeast, and a hostile force could well approach and charge down this hill within close gunshot of the camp before being seen. This locality famed as the battle ground of Burnt Corn is in Escambia County, one-half a mile from the line of Conecuh County, on the north. As reported by the scouts, the Creek camp was near the spring, and their pack-horses were grazing around them. No rumor of the foe's advance had reached their ears; all were careless, off their guard and enjoying themselves, for good cheer was in the Muscogee camp. Their martial spirits, as we may well imagine, were not now stirred by thoughts of war and bloodshed, but were concentrated on the more peaceful delights of cooking and feasting, the pleasures of the pot, the kettle, and the bowl. . . .

Colonel Callers troops, as we may conjecture, must have turned to the left, off the road, perhaps near the Red Hollow, about a mile distant from the spring, and thence approached the Creek camp from the northeast and east, as from the nature of the country this was the only route they could have taken so as to surprise the Red Stick camp. The troops moved cautiously and silently onward until they reached the rear of the hill that overlooked the Creek camp. Here, Pickett says, they dismounted; but Meek says the main body dismounted; yet neither Pickett nor Meek makes any statement as to the disposition of their horses—whether they were tied or were consigned to the care of a guard, or whether each trooper, as he dismounted, left his horse to shift for himself. From the fact that many of the horses fell into the hands of the enemy, one is led to the conjecture that no regular system was employed, but that every man did that which was right in his own eyes. After dismounting, the troops moved silently to the crest of the hill, whence they made a rapid charge down its slope and opened fire upon the Creek camp, as the red warriors stood, sat, or reclined in scattered groups over the ground. The Creeks, though startled by this sudden and unexpected onset, quickly sprang to arms, returned the fire, and for several minutes bravely withstood the charge of the whites, then gave way and retreated in wild confusion to the creek. Early in the fight a Creek woman and a negro man were slain. It is stated that the latter, who was busily engaged in cooking, had ample time to make his escape, but being a slave and non-combatant he doubtless apprehended no danger from the whites. A portion of the troops pursued the Indians to the creek—Meek says they even drove them across the creek into a reed-brake beyond—but we think this latter statement exceedingly doubtful.

While these were performing this soldierly duty, the more numerous party devoted their energies to capturing and leading off the pack-horses. This led to a disastrous reverse. The Creeks in the cane and reed-brakes soon saw the demoralization of the greater part of the whites and the fewness of the assailants confronting them. They rallied, and, with guns, tomahawks and war clubs, rushed forth from the swamp, and with the fiercest cries of vengeance charged upon their foes and drove them headlong before them. Colonel Caller acted bravely, but unable to restore order, he commanded the troops to fall back to the hill so as to secure a stronger position and there to renew the battle. The plundering party, misconstruing this order, and seeing the fighting portion of the troops falling back before the enemy, were now seized with a panic, and fled in wild confusion, still, however, notwithstanding their terror, driving their horses before them, some even mounting their prizes so as to more quickly escape from the fatal field. In vain did Colonel Caller, Captain Bailey and other officers endeavor to rally them and persuade them to make a stand against the foe. Terror and avarice proved more potent than pride and patriotism, and the panic-stricken throng surged to the rear. Only about eighty fighting men now remained, and these had taken a stand in the open woods at the foot of the hill. Commanded by Captains

Dale, Bailey, and Smoot, they fought with laudable courage for an hour or more under the fire poured upon them by McQueen's warriors from the cover of the thick and sheltering reeds. The battle may now be briefly described as "a series of charges and retreats, irregular skirmishes and frequent close and violent encounters of individuals and scattered squads." It was noticed that the Creek marksmanship was inferior to that of the Americans. It was in the fight at the foot of the hill that Captain Dale was wounded by a rifle ball, which struck him in the left side, glanced around and lodged near the back bone. The captain continued to fight as long as his strength permitted, and then threw aside his double barrel into the top of a fallen tree. This gun, we may here state, Dale recovered after the war from an Indian, at Fort Barancas. About the same time that Dale was wounded, Elijah Glass, a twin brother of David Glass, was slain. He was standing behind another soldier, who was in a stooping position, when a rifle ball struck him fatally in the upper part of the breast.

The battle now at last began to bear hard upon the Americans. Two-thirds of the command were in full retreat, and no alternative lay before the fighting portion but to abandon the field, which they did in the greatest disorder. Many of them had lost their horses, some of which had been appropriated by the fugitives, and others, in some manner, had fallen into the hands of the enemy, among these, the horses belonging to Colonel Caller and Major Wood. The troops now fled in all directions. Some succeeded in reaching and mounting their own horses; others mounted the first horses they came to; in some cases, in their eagerness to escape, two mounting the same horse; while others actually ran off afoot. It was a disgraceful rout. "After all these had left the field," writes Pickett, "three young men were found, still fighting by themselves on one side of the peninsula, [bend,] and keeping at bay some savages who were concealed in the cane. They were Lieutenant Patrick May, a private named Ambrose Miles, and Lieutenant Girard W. Creagh. A warrior presented his tall

form. May and the savage discharged their guns at each other. The Indian fell dead in the cane; his fire, however, had shattered the Lieutenant's piece near the lock. Resolving, also to retreat, these intrepid men made a rapid rush for their horses, when Creagh, brought to the ground by the effects of a wound which he received in the hip, cried out 'Save me, Lieutenant, or I am gone.' May instantly raised him up, bore him off on his back, and placed him in the saddle, while Miles held the bridle reins. A rapid retreat saved their lives. Reaching the top of the hill, they saw Lieutenant Bradberry, bleeding with his wounds, and endeavoring to rally some of his men." This was the last effort made to stem the tide of disaster.

Two young men were slain in the battle, —— Ballard and Elijah Glass, both it is believed, being members of Dale's company. Ballard had fought with great bravery. Just before the final retreat, he was wounded in the hip. He was able to walk, but not fast enough to reach his horse, which in the meantime, had been appropriated by one of the fugitives. A few of the soldiers returned and successively made efforts to mount Ballard behind them on their horses, but the Indians pressed them so closely that this could not be done. Ballard told them to leave him to his fate and not to risk their own lives in attempting to save him. At last the Indians reached him, and for some moments, he held them at bay, fighting desperately with the butt of his musket, but he was soon overpowered and slain. Several Indians now sprang forward, scalped him and began to beat him with their war clubs. Two of the retreating soldiers, David Glass and Lenoir, saw this. Glass was afoot, Lenoir mounted. "Is your gun loaded," asked Glass of Lenoir. "Yes," was the reply. "Then shoot those Indians that are beating that man yonder." Lenoir hesitating, Glass quickly spoke, "Then lend me your gun." Exchanging guns, Glass then advanced a few paces and fired at two or three of the Indians whose heads happened to be in a line, and at the discharge one of them fell, as Glass supposed, slain or wounded. This was the last shot fired in the battle of Burnt Corn, which had lasted from about midday until about three o'clock in the afternoon. The Creeks pursued the whites nearly a mile in the open woods and nothing but their inability to overtake them saved the fugitives from a general slaughter. Pickett writes: "The retreat continued all night in the most irregular manner, and the trail was lined from one end to the other with small squads, and sometimes one man by himself. The wounded travelled slowly, and often stopped to rest."

Such was the result of the battle of Burnt Corn, the first engagement in the long and bloody Creek War. Most of the Creek pack-horses, about two hundred pounds of powder and some lead was all the success the Americans could claim from this engagement. Their loss was two men killed, Ballard and Glass. Fifteen were wounded, Captain Sam. Dale, Lieutenant G. W. Creagh, Lieutenant William Bradberry, shot in the calf of the leg; Armstrong, wounded in the thigh; Jack Henry, wounded in the knee; Robert Lewis, Alexander Hollinger, William Baldwin, and seven others whose names have not been preserved.

The Creek loss is not positively known. Colonel Carson, in a letter to General Claiborne, written a few days after the battle, states that from the best information it was ten or twelve killed and eight or nine wounded. As to the numbers engaged at Burnt Corn, we know that the American force numbered one hundred and eighty. General Woodward, in his Reminiscences, states, on the authority of Jim Boy, that the Creek force was two-thirds less. He writes. "Jim Boy [a Red Stick warrior] said that the war had not fairly broke out, and that they never thought of being attacked; that he did not start [from Pensacola] with a hundred men, and all of those he did start with were not in the fight. I have heard Jim tell it often that if the whites had not stopped to gather up the pack horses, and had pursued the Indians a little further, they, the Indians, would have quit and gone off. But the Indians discovered the very great confusion the whites were in searching for plunder, and they fired a few guns from the creek

swamp, and a general stampede was the result. McGirth always corroborated Jim Boy's statement as to the number of Indians in the Burnt Corn battle."

The above, perhaps, may be regarded, in some measure, as the Creek version of Burnt Corn. If possession of the battlefield may be considered a claim to victory, then Burnt Corn may well be regarded a Creek victory. After the battle, a part of the Red Sticks retraced their steps to Pensacola for more military supplies, and a part returned to the nation. Their antagonists, Colonel Caller's troopers, were never reorganized after the battle. They returned home, in scattered bands, by various routes, and each man mustered himself out of service. About seventy of them on the retreat collected together at Sizemore's Ferry, where, for a while, they had much difficulty in making their horses swim the river. David Glass finally plunged into the stream and managed to turn the horses' heads towards the other shore. After the horses had all landed on the further bank, the men crossed over in canoes.

Colonel Caller and Major Wood, as we have related, both lost their horses at Burnt Corn. As the fugitives shifted, every man for himself, these two officers were left in the rear. They soon became bewildered and lost their way in the forest, and as they did not return with the other soldiers, their friends became very apprehensive as to their safety. "When General Claiborne arrived in the country, he wrote to Bailey, Tate, and Moniac, urging them to hunt for these unfortunate men. They were afterwards found, starved almost to death, and bereft of their senses." When found, Colonel Caller had on nothing but his shirt and drawers. After the war, the Colonel, with some difficulty, recovered his fine horse from the Creeks. But Major Wood was not so fortunate.

Colonel J. F. H. Claiborne, in his "Life of Sam Dale," writes: "Colonel Caller was long a conspicuous man in the politics of Mississippi Territory, often representing Washington County in the legislature. No one who knew Caller and

Wood intimately doubted their courage; but the disaster of Burnt Corn brought down on them much scurrility. Major Wood, who was as sensitive as brave, bad not the fortitude to despise the scorn of the world, and sought forgetfulness, as too many men often do, in habitual intemperance."

Source: Halbert, Henry S., and T. H. Ball. *The Creek War of 1813 and 1814.* Chicago: Donohue & Henneberry; and Montgomery, Ala.: White, Woodruff & Fowler, 1895, pp. 125–141.

THE PUNITIVE EXPEDITION FOLLOWING THE FORT MIMS MASSACRE, NOVEMBER 1813– JANUARY 1814

Account of the Punitive Expedition following the Fort Mims Massacre
David "Davy" Crockett
Published 1834

The Tennessee backwoodsman, hunter, Indian fighter, congressman, and Alamo martyr David "Davy" Crockett (1786–1836) had his baptism of fire during the Creek War phase of the War of 1812 when he joined Andrew Jackson's punitive expedition in retaliation for the Creek massacre of the garrison at Fort Mims, Alabama, on August 30, 1813. Crockett provides a vivid eyewitness account of part of the expedition.

When we marched from Fort Montgomery, we went some distance back towards Pensacola, then we turned to the left, and passed through a poor piny country, till we reached the Scamby river, near which we encamped. We had about one thousand men, and as a part of that number, one hundred and eighty-six Chickasaw and Choctaw Indians with us. That evening a boat landed from Pensacola, bringing many articles that were both good and necessary; such as sugar and coffee, and liquors of all kinds. The same evening, the Indians we had along proposed to cross the river, and the officers thinking it might be well for them to do so, consented; and Major Russell went with them, taking sixteen white men, of which number I was one. We camped on the opposite bank that night, and early in the morning we set out. We had not gone far before we came to a place where the whole country was covered with water, and looked like a sea. We didn't stop for this, tho', but just put in like so many spaniels, and waded on, sometimes up to our armpits, until we reached the pine hills, which made our distance through the water about a mile and a half. Here we struck up a fire to warm ourselves, for it was cold, and we were chilled through by being so long in the water. We again moved on, keeping our spies out; two to our left near the bank of the river, two straight before us, and two others on our right. We had gone in this way about six miles up the river, when our spies on the left came to us leaping the brush like so many old bucks, and informed us that they had discovered a camp of Creek Indians, and that we must kill them. Here we paused for a few minutes, and the prophets pow-wowed over their men awhile, and then got out their paint, and painted them, all according to their custom when going into battle. They then brought their paint to old Major Russell, and said to him, that as he was an officer, he must be painted too. He agreed, and they painted him just as they had done themselves. We let the Indians understand that we white men would first fire on the camp, and then fall back, so as to give the Indians a chance to rush in and scalp them. The Chickasaws marched on our left hand, and the Choctaws on our right, and we moved on till we got in hearing of the camp, where the Indians were employed in beating up what they called chainy briar root. On this they mostly subsisted. On a nearer approach we found they were on an island, and that we could not get to

After the massacre of settlers at Fort Mims (pictured here), Davy Crockett was among the Tennessee frontiersmen who joined General Andrew Jackson in the Creek War. *(Library of Congress)*

them. While we were chatting about this matter, we heard some guns fired, and in a very short time after a keen whoop, which satisfied us, that where ever it was, there was war on a small scale. With that we all broke, like quarter horses, for the firing; and when we got there we found it was our two front spies, who related to us the following story: As they were moving on, they had met with two Creeks who were out hunting their horses; as they approached each other, there was a large cluster of green bay bushes exactly between them, so that they were within a few feet of meeting before either was discovered. Our spies walked up to them, and speaking in the Shawnee tongue, informed them that General Jackson was at Pensacola, and they were making their escape, and wanted to know where

they could get something to eat. The Creeks told them that nine miles up the Conaker, the river they were then on, there was a large camp of Creeks, and they had cattle and plenty to eat; and further that their own camp was on an island about a mile off, and just below the mouth of the Conaker. They held their conversation and struck up a fire, and smoked together, and shook hands, and parted. One of the Creeks had a gun, the other had none, and as soon as they had parted, our Choctaws turned round and shot down the one that had the gun, and the other attempted to run off. They snapped several times at him, but the gun still missing fire, they took after him, and overtaking him, one of them struck him over the head with his gun, and followed up his blows till he killed him.

The gun was broken in the combat, and they then fired off the gun of the Creek they had killed, and raised the war-whoop. When we reached them, they had cut off the heads of both the Indians; and each of those Indians with us would walk up to one of the heads, and taking his war club would strike on it. This was done by every one of them; and when they had got done, I took one of their clubs, and walked up as they had done, and struck it on the head also. At this they all gathered round me, and patting me on the shoulder, would call me "Warrior—warrior."

They scalped the heads, and then we moved on a short distance to where we found a trace leading in towards the river. We took this trace and pursued it, till we came to where a Spaniard had been killed and scalped, together with a woman, who we supposed to be his wife, and also four children. I began to feel mighty ticklish along about this time, for I knowed if there was no danger then, there had been; and I felt exactly like there still was. We, however, went on till we struck the river, and then continued down it till we came opposite to the Indian camp, where we found they were still beating their roots.

It was now late in the evening, and they were in a thick cane brake. We had some few friendly Creeks with us, who said they could decoy them. So we all hid behind trees and logs, while the attempt was made. The Indians would not agree that we should fire, but pick'd out some of their best gunners, and placed them near the river.

Our Creeks went down to the river's side, and hailed the camp in the Creek language. We heard an answer, and an Indian man started down towards the river, but didn't come in sight. He went back and again commenced beating his roots, and sent a squaw. She came down, and talked with our Creeks until dark came on. They told her they wanted her to bring them a canoe. To which she replied, that their canoe was on our side; that two of their men had gone out to hunt their horses and hadn't yet returned. They

were the same two we had killed. The canoe was found, and forty of our picked Indian warriors were crossed over to take the camp. There was at last only one man in it, and he escaped; and they took two squaws, and ten children, but killed none of them, of course.

We had run nearly out of provisions, and Major Russell had determined to go up the Conaker to the camp we had heard of from the Indians we had killed. I was one that he selected to go down the river that night for provisions, with the canoe, to where we had left our regiment. I took with me a man by the name of John Guess, and one of the friendly Creeks, and cut out. It was very dark, and the river was so full that it overflowed the banks and the adjacent low bottoms. This rendered it very difficult to keep the channel, and particularly as the river was very crooked. At about ten o'clock at night we reached the camp, and were to return by morning to Major Russell, with provisions for his trip up the river; but on informing Colonel Blue of this arrangement, he vetoed it . . . and said, if Major Russell didn't come back the next day, it would be bad times for him. I found we were not to go up the Conaker to the Indian camp, and a man of my company offered to go up in my place to inform Major Russell. I let him go; and they reached the major, as I was told about sunrise in the morning, who immediately returned with those who were with him to the regiment, and joined us where we crossed the river, as hereafter stated.

The next morning we all fixed up, and marched down the Scamby to a place called Miller's Landing, where we swam our horses across, and sent on two companies down on the side of the bay opposite to Pensacola, where the Indians had fled when the main army first marched to that place. One was the company of Captain William Russell, a son of the old major, and the other was commanded by a Captain Trimble. They went on, and had a little skirmish with the Indians. They killed some, and took all the balance prisoners, though I don't remember the numbers. We again met those companies in a day or two, and sent the prisoners they had taken on to Fort Montgomery, in charge of some of our Indians.

I did hear that after they left us, the Indians killed and scalped all the prisoners and I never heard the report contradicted. I cannot positively say it was true but I think it entirely probable for it is very much like the Indian character.

Source: Crockett, David "Davy." *A Narrative of the Life of David Crockett.* Philadelphia: Carey, Hart & Co., 1834, pp. 106–113.

The U.S.-Mexican War

★

Following a brief war in 1835–36, Texas—since the early 1820s a province of Mexico colonized chiefly by Americans—won its independence and, failing to obtain immediate annexation to the United States, proclaimed itself a republic. Nearly a decade later, on March 1, 1845, the U.S. Congress finally voted to admit Texas into the Union. Predictably, this prompted the Mexican government, which had repudiated the 1836 Treaty of Velasco (by which Mexico's dictator Antonio López de Santa Anna had recognized Texas's independence), to sever diplomatic relations with the United States. The U.S. president, James Polk, sought to avert war with Mexico by negotiating U.S. claims to Texas as well as to Alta (Upper) California, whose American residents had (in the so-called Bear Flag Rebellion) recently initiated a militant movement to win independence from Mexico. Nevertheless, Polk anticipated the war would break out, and on July 4, 1845, after the government of the Texas republic formally accepted U.S. annexation, he ordered Brigadier General Zachary Taylor to deploy on or near the Rio Grande in order to repel any attempted invasion of Texas by Mexican forces.

Throughout the summer and fall of 1845, some 4,000 Americans assembled on the plain at the mouth of the Nueces River near Corpus Christi. When negotiations between the U.S. and Mexican governments broke down in February 1846, Polk ordered Taylor to advance 100 miles down the coast to the Rio Grande. Accordingly, he established a supply camp on the coast at Point Isabel and deployed most of his men along the Rio Grande, 18 miles to the southwest. Just opposite the Mexican border town of Matamoros, he established Fort Texas.

The Battle of Palo Alto

On April 25, 1846, the Mexican general Mariano Arista invaded Texas with a substantial force, crossing the Rio Grande and attacking an advance detachment of 60 U.S. dragoons under Captain Seth B. Thornton. Eleven Americans were killed, and the others were captured. Reporting to President Polk that hostilities had commenced, Taylor appealed to Texas and Louisiana for 5,000 militia volunteers, then fell back with his main force to Point Isabel in order to guard his supplies. On May 7, after strengthening his fortifications there and resupplying his army, he set out with 2,300 troops to reoccupy Fort Texas.

On May 8, 1846, at Palo Alto, Texas, U.S. and Mexican forces fought the first major battle of the war. *(Library of Congress)*

On May 8, while en route to the fort, Taylor encountered 4,000 troops of Arista's advancing Mexican army at Palo Alto. Outnumbered 2 to 1, Taylor nevertheless possessed superior artillery and excellent young officers, including a pair of new lieutenants, Ulysses S. Grant and George G. Meade. The general skillfully deployed his artillery to fire a deadly combination of antipersonnel canister shot and solid shells. Despite his superior numbers, Arista had only obsolete Napoleonic-era artillery, which lacked sufficient range to do much damage. The Mexicans were thus thoroughly outgunned, and the American barrage was so intense that the dry grass of Palo Alto burst into flames, forcing a pause in the battle. By the time action resumed, the Mexicans were in full retreat, having lost 320 killed and 380 wounded. Taylor's losses were nine killed and 47 wounded. A cautious commander,

Taylor did not immediately pursue the retreating Mexican forces but first strengthened defenses around his supply train and only then set off after Arista's army.

The Battle of Resaca de la Palma

On May 9, Taylor reached a dry riverbed called Resaca de la Palma, five miles' distant from Palo Alto. When scouts reported the Mexican forces entrenched in a nearby ravine called Resaca de la Guerra, Taylor deployed a highly mobile "flying artillery" detachment to dislodge them. The Battle of Resaca de la Palma seesawed for a time, the rugged terrain rendering Taylor's artillery less effective than it had been on the open plain at Palo Alto. Soon, combat turned fiercely hand-to-hand. Demoralized by their defeat at Palo Alto, Arista's troops showed little stomach for close fighting and fell back on Matamoros after 547 Mexicans had been killed or wounded at a cost to Taylor of 33 killed and 89 wounded.

Yet even as the battle ended, Mexican soldiers continued to fall, either drowned in the Rio Grande or victims of guns fired from nearby Fort Texas. That installation had been held under siege for two days during the Palo Alto and Resaca de la Palma fights, but it had held out, suffering the loss of two men, including Major Jacob Brown, the commanding officer. The fort was renamed for him accordingly.

The Battle of Resaca de la Palma and its aftermath constituted a major victory for Taylor; however, yet again he chose not to press his advantage. Instead of pursuing the defeated Arista across the Rio Grande—where he almost certainly would have bagged the entire Mexican army—he paused until May 18, a delay that allowed the enemy to withdraw far into Mexican territory.

American Strategy

On May 12, 1846, with a shooting war now well under way, President Polk signed the formal declaration of war Congress had voted following a bitter debate. The strength of the regular army was increased from about 8,500 men to 15,540, and a call-up of 50,000 one-year volunteers was also authorized. Polk's war aim was to take all Mexican territory north of the Rio Grande and Gila River, all the way west to the Pacific Ocean. He turned to the U.S. Army's most senior commander, Major General Winfield Scott, to create a strategy. Scott's plan was for General Taylor to advance west from Matamoros to Monterrey, Mexico; once Monterrey was taken, all of northern Mexico would be exposed and vulnerable. Simultaneously, Brigadier General John E. Wool (1784–1869) was to march from San Antonio to Chihuahua, Mexico, and then advance farther south, to Saltillo, to a position near Taylor's force at Monterrey. Finally, Colonel Stephen Watts Kearny would be ordered to commence a long march out of Fort Leavenworth, Kansas, to capture Santa Fe, New Mexico, and then press on, all the way to San Diego, California. This phase of the plan would later be modified when part of Kearny's force, under Colonel Alexander W. Doniphan, was detached to make a remarkable advance deep into Mexico, via Chihuahua to Parras.

As Polk and Scott initially conceived the strategy, there was no intention to make a deeper invasion for the purpose of taking the Mexican capital, Mexico City. It was hoped that the shallow advance would quickly prompt Mexico to surrender, yielding the territory the United States coveted. By July 1846, however, Polk became increasingly ambitious in his strategic view and, with Secretary of War William L. Marcy, laid out a plan to penetrate far into Mexico, capturing the capital, Mexico City, by means of a bold amphibious landing at Veracruz. This plan was held in abeyance, however, pending progress of the initial strategy.

The Battle of Monterrey

Carrying out the three-pronged strategy was no easy task. Taylor's problems had less to do with the enemy than with logistics and transportation. He needed to move 6,000 men to Monterrey via Camargo, a town on the San Juan River, where he would set up a base of supply. A road connected Camargo to Monterrey, 125 miles away. While he assembled the means of transportation, Taylor was joined by short-term militiamen, who brought his strength at Camargo to 15,000 by August 1846. Heat and illness there reduced his army to just 3,080 regulars and 3,150 militiamen fit for duty by the time they were ready to begin their advance to Monterrey, which they reached on September 19. The city was defended by 7,000 Mexican troops who occupied strong positions and (in contrast to

Arista's forces) possessed modern British-made artillery. Sending his engineers ahead to survey the Mexican fortifications, Taylor carefully formulated a plan of attack and, on September 20, sent a division of regulars, accompanied by 400 Texas Rangers, to cut off the road to Saltillo. This was achieved by the next day, September 21, whereupon Taylor commenced a full-scale artillery bombardment, then moved in with his main forces from the east. By September 22, Taylor's men had breached Monterrey's defenses and were fighting in the city's streets. Within 24 hours, the defenders had been pushed into the town's central plaza. Taylor fired upon them with his heaviest siege gun, a 10-inch mortar, which soon brought a plea for terms. The defeated Mexican commander asked for an eight-week armistice. Taylor was clearly in a position to dictate unconditional surrender, but instead he agreed to the terms requested on the grounds that he, too, had taken heavy casualties, especially with so many soldiers sick. He also hoped that his generosity would encourage the Mexican government to negotiate peace.

There was reason to believe that it would. President Polk had recently agreed to a peace-making proposal from none other than Antonio López de Santa Anna, the very general who had led the massacre against the Alamo during the Texas War for Independence and who was now living in Cuba as an exile after a rebellion had toppled his dictatorship in Mexico. Santa Anna promised to aid the United States to negotiate a favorable peace, including a Rio Grande boundary for Texas and the possession of California, in return for $30,000,000 and safe conduct from Cuba to Mexico. Polk withheld the money, but he did permit Santa Anna to return via the United States to Mexico. Unknown to the president, no sooner was Santa Anna restored to his

The last day of the siege of Monterrey, September 24, 1846 *(National Archives)*

homeland than he began raising an army to lead personally against Zachary Taylor.

In the meantime, Polk was not pleased by the terms Taylor had granted his enemy. On October 11, the president ordered an immediate end to the armistice, and accordingly, on November 13, Taylor sent a thousand of his men to Saltillo to seize control of the only road to Mexico City from the north as well as the road to Chihuahua. Two days after this, U.S. Navy forces captured the town of Tampico, and, the following month, Brigadier General John E. Wool arrived from San Antonio with 2,500 men. He started off for Chihuahua, but learning that the town had been abandoned, he joined his forces to those of Taylor at Monterrey.

The Battle of Buena Vista

In accordance with the original invasion plan, Taylor proposed setting up a defensive line connecting Parras, Saltillo, Monterrey, and Victoria. At this point, however, he received word that President Polk had authorized Winfield Scott to make an amphibious assault on Veracruz—in preparation for the invasion and capture of Mexico City—and 8,000 of Taylor's troops were summarily ordered to join Scott's force. Left with just 7,000 men, mostly volunteers, Taylor was now ordered to evacuate Saltillo and assume a defensive posture in Monterrey. He chose to interpret this order as nothing more than "advice," so that he could act more aggressively. Leaving small garrisons at Monterrey as well as Saltillo, he sent 4,650 men 18 miles south of Saltillo to Agua Nueva.

On February 21, 1847, scouts attached to the forces approaching Agua Nueva observed the approach of Santa Anna's entire army, which outnumbered the American force three to one. Taylor responded with a strategic withdrawal to Buena Vista, just south of Saltillo, a position from which he knew that he could make a strong defensive stand. Nevertheless, on February 22, Santa Anna demanded Taylor's surrender. When

General John E. Wool (1784–1869), in addition to General Zachary Taylor, commanded the U.S. forces in their successful two-day battle at Buena Vista, February 22–23, 1847. *(Library of Congress)*

he refused, the Mexican commander lobbed a few artillery shells at him, and the two armies jockeyed for position. The Battle of Buena Vista did not begin in earnest until February 23. At first, it went badly for the Americans, but a rally led by the future Confederate president Jefferson Davis forced Santa Anna to fall back. The Mexican commander brought up his reserves and counterattacked vigorously, but Taylor's forces made a surprise counterattack of their own, forcing Santa Anna, who had lost perhaps as many as 2,000 men killed or wounded, to fall back on San Luis Potosí. American casualties were 264 men killed and 450 wounded. Defeated at Buena Vista, the Mexican army was no longer a threat to the lower Rio Grande.

The Campaigns of Kearny and Doniphan

While Taylor was moving from victory to victory in Mexico, Colonel Stephen Watts Kearny was leading the long march from Fort Leavenworth, Kansas, to Santa Fe, New Mexico. At Santa Fe, the provincial governor, Manuel Armijo, had set up an ambush in steep-walled Apache Canyon, only to see his poorly disciplined troops scatter in panic as Kearny's column approached. The result was that Santa Fe fell without a shot having to be fired. From the New Mexico capital, Kearny advanced into California, but by the time he reached San Diego in December 1846, he discovered that a U.S. Navy squadron had already secured this key California port.

In the meantime, in November 1846, Colonel Alexander Doniphan was assigned to lead a detachment of 856 Missouri Indians from Kearny's main force and to march with them from Santa Fe south on a mission to "pacify" the upper Rio Grande region. Crossing the river at El Paso, he quickly engaged and defeated a force of 1,200 Mexicans, but as his 800-plus Missourians approached Chihuahua on February 27, 1847, they encountered 2,700 Mexican regulars augmented by perhaps a thousand civilian volunteers. Instead of withdrawing, Doniphan deployed his outnumbered forces with utmost tactical skill, handily outflanking the defenders. The resulting two-hour Battle of Sacramento resulted in the defeat of nearly 4,000 Mexicans. At least 300 of the enemy were killed for a loss to the Doniphan's detachment of one dead and five wounded.

The Veracruz Campaign

By March 2, 1847, when Scott began operations leading to the Veracruz landing, Taylor and Doniphan had achieved control of all northern Mexico. On March 9, Scott landed 10,000 men at Veracruz, and on March 22 he commenced bombardment of the city. His mortars failing to induce surrender, Scott called in a more intensive naval bombardment from the fleet of Commodore Matthew C. Perry. This brought Veracruz to its knees by March 27.

The Battle of Cerro Gordo

From Veracruz, Scott marched to Xalapa, 74 miles inland along the National Highway leading to Mexico City. Major General David E. Twiggs was in the lead with 2,600 men and artillery. On April 11, his scouts reported that Mexican artillery covered the pass near the village of Cerro Gordo. In fact, Santa Anna had deployed not only artillery but some 12,000 infantrymen there and intended to make a devastating ambush. Premature firing tipped his hand, however, prompting Twiggs to make a strategic withdrawal. After being reinforced to a strength of 8,500 by the arrival of Scott on April 14, Scott sent Captain Robert E. Lee to survey the passes. Lee discovered that the main Mexican artillery emplacement was on a high hill called El Telegrafo, and he also found a rugged, entirely undefended pass by which Scott could bring up his own artillery to fire on the Mexican rear, without having to traverse the National Highway, which was thoroughly covered by the Mexican artillery. Accordingly, the Americans cut their way through thick forest and brush, hoisting heavy siege artillery into position. On April 17, Scott installed a rocket battery on a hill to the right of El Telegrafo, and the next morning he commenced his attack. More than 1,000 Mexicans were killed or wounded in the Battle of Cerro Gordo, whereas Scott incurred 417 casualties, including 64 killed. Santa Anna had no choice but to fall back toward Mexico City.

The Battle of Contreras

Scott now moved from Cerro Gordo to Xalapa and then to Puebla, the second largest city in

Mexico, which surrendered to him without resistance on May 15, 1847. While the general now prepared to march out of Puebla and on to Mexico City, a State Department official, Nicholas P. Trist, opened treaty negotiations with Santa Anna. President Polk ordered Scott to advance to the capital as quickly as possible in order to pressure the Mexicans to make a prompt and favorable peace. Accordingly, Scott boldly decided to commit almost all of his troops to the advance, save for an occupation force in Puebla, even though this meant leaving his line of communication, from Veracruz to Puebla, undefended. He began his advance on August 7. Reaching Ayolta on August 10, 14 miles from Mexico City, Scott discovered that the direct road was heavily defended. He therefore shifted to the south so that he could approach from the west, by way of a 15-mile-wide lava bed called Pedregal. The Mexicans having judged this to be impassable, they had left it undefended. Captain Lee, however, discovered a mule path across it to the village of Contreras, from which the invasion could be mounted. An initial assault on Contreras, under Brevet Major General Gideon J. Pillow, was defeated on August 19, but the arrival of reinforcements enabled a new attack at dawn on August 20. Seven hundred Mexicans fell in the Battle of Contreras, and 800 were captured, among them four generals. American casualties were 60 killed or wounded.

The Battle of Churubusco

In contrast to Taylor, Scott was an uncompromisingly bold and energetic commander. He pressed his pursuit of the retreating Mexicans, but Santa Anna managed to keep his army intact and took a defensive position at Churubusco, effectively transforming a stone-walled church and convent into twin fortresses. Santa Anna now conducted a very vigorous defense, which slowed Scott substantially, but by late afternoon, with Santa Anna's ammunition running low, Scott made a final push. In the end, the Battle of Churubusco

cost nearly 4,000 Mexican casualties, killed or wounded; Scott suffered losses of 155 killed and 876 wounded.

The Battle of Chapultepec and the Capture of Mexico City

The lopsided American victory at Churubusco brought a renewed request from Santa Anna to reopen peace negotiations. When this latest round of negotiations stalled, Scott recommenced his advance to Mexico City on September 6. He now commanded about 8,000 men against Santa Anna's 15,000. Although outnumbered, he proceeded methodically yet always boldly. On September 8, he stormed and seized El Molino del Rey, a cannon foundry just west of Chapultepec Castle, the old fortress defending the capital. On September 13, he attacked Chapultepec, overrunning it by 9:30 that the morning. It is estimated that 1,800 Mexicans were killed or wounded in the Battle of Chapultepec, whereas U.S. casualties were 130 killed and 703 wounded. Falling back on the capital itself, the Mexicans defended it in bitter house-to-house combat, finally surrendering on September 14, 1847.

The Siege of Puebla and Peace

Even with Mexico City occupied by the Americans, U.S.-held Puebla was besieged by Mexican forces from September 14 to October 12, 1847, but by that time, peace negotiations were already under way. Polk urged Scott to continue fighting all-out, so as to force the most extreme terms upon the Mexicans, but both the general and the negotiator Trist were convinced that the Mexican government was in a most precarious condition. If negotiations were protracted, it was likely that there would be nothing left of a government with which to negotiate. Turning a deaf ear to Polk, Trist and Scott continued to negotiate, producing the Treaty of Guadalupe Hidalgo, which was signed on February 2, 1848, and ratified by the U.S. Senate on March 10. The two nations exchanged final ratifications on May 30.

In return for the cession to the United States of "New Mexico"—the present state of New Mexico and portions of the present states of Utah, Nevada, Arizona, and Colorado—and California, as well as Mexican renunciation of claims to Texas above the Rio Grande, Mexico was to be paid $15 million. In addition, the United States would assume all claims of U.S. citizens against Mexico, which (as later determined) amounted to an additional $3.25 million. The treaty further established a boundary line separating Mexico and the United States, and both sides pledged eternal "peace and friendship." In 1853, the Treaty of Guadalupe Hidalgo was modified by the Gadsden Treaty, which formalized the U.S. acquisition through the purchase of additional territory from Mexico.

DOCUMENTS

THE BATTLE OF PALO ALTO, MAY 8, 1846

"Taylor's official report of the Battle of Palo Alto"
Major General Zachary Taylor
May 16, 1846

On May 8, 1846, the vanguard of Major General Zachary Taylor's 2,300-man force sighted General Mariano Arista's advancing Mexican army at Palo Alto, Texas. With about 4,000 troops, Arista out-numbered Taylor nearly two to one. He took up a blocking position on the road to Fort Texas (present-day Brownsville) along a broad front.

In addition to being outnumbered, Taylor was marching on terrain favorable to cavalry, which Arista possessed in abundance. Taylor, however, had superior artillery and superb subordinate commanders, including Lieutenants Ulysses S. Grant and George G. Meade, fresh out of West Point. Taylor and his officers expertly positioned two 18-pounder siege guns in the American line, then deployed the lighter field pieces everywhere they could be brought to bear rapidly. He loaded his siege guns not with heavy solid shot but with canister, antipersonnel ammunition; his lighter guns fired solid shells nonstop. The effect of the artillery was overwhelming. The Mexicans returned fire with their obsolescent bronze four- and eight-pounders, which lacked sufficient range to do significant damage. In contrast, the American barrage was so fierce that the dry grass of Palo Alto burst into flames, forcing a halt to the battle. When the fires died out, the battle resumed, and Arista was soon driven into retreat.

Taylor sent this report of the battle to Roger Jones, adjutant general of the U.S. Army, more than a week after the event.

Headquarters Army of Occupation
Camp near Matamoras, May 16, 1846.

Sir:—I have now the honor to submit a more detailed report of the action of the 8th instant.

The main body of the army of occupation marched under my immediate orders from Point Isabel, on the evening of the 7th May, and bivouacked 7 miles from that place.

Our march was resumed the following morning. About noon, when our advance of cavalry had reached the water-hole of "Palo Alto," the Mexican troops were reported in our front, and were soon discovered occupying the road in force. I ordered a halt upon reaching the water, with a view to rest and refresh the men, and form deliberately our line of battle. The Mexican line was now plainly visible across the prairie, and about three-quarters of a mile distant. Their left, which was composed of a heavy force of cavalry, occupied the road resting upon a thicket of chapparal, while masses of infantry were discovered in succession on the right, greatly outnumbering our own force.

Our line of battle was now formed in the following order, commencing on the extreme right: 5th infantry, commanded by Lieutenant Colonel McIntosh; Major Ringgold's artillery; 3d infantry, commanded by Captain L. M. Morris; two 18-pounders, commanded by Lieutenant Colonel Garland; and all the above corps, together with two squadrons of dragoons under captains Ker and May, composed the right wing, under the orders of Colonel Twiggs. The left was formed by the battalion of artillery, commanded by Lieutenant Colonel Childs, Captain Duncan's light artillery, and the 8th infantry, under Captain Montgomery—all forming the 1st brigade, under command of Lieutenant Colonel Belknap. The train was parked near the water, under direction of Captains Crosman and Myers, and protected by Captain Ker's squadron.

About 2 o'clock we took up the march by heads of columns, in the direction of the enemy, the 18-pounder battery following the road. While the columns were advancing, Lieutenant Blake, topographical engineers, volunteered a reconnoisance of the enemy's line, which was handsomely performed, and resulted in the discovery of at least two batteries of artillery in the intervals of their cavalry and infantry. These batteries were soon opened upon us, when I ordered the columns halted and deployed into line, and the fire to be returned by all our artillery. The 8th infantry, on our extreme left, was thrown back to secure that flank. The first fires of the enemy did little execution, while our 18-pounders and Major Ringgold's artillery soon dispersed the cavalry which formed his left. Captain Duncan's battery, thrown forward in advance of the line, was doing good execution at this time. Captain May's squadron was now detached to support that battery and the left of our position. The Mexican cavalry, with two pieces of artillery, were

now reported to be moving through the chapparal to our right, to threaten that flank or make a demonstration against the train. The 5th infantry was immediately detached to check this movement, and supported by Lieutenant Ridgely, with a section of Major Ringgold's battery and Captain Walker's company of volunteers, effectually repulsed the enemy—the 5th infantry repelling a charge of lancers, and the artillery doing great execution in their flanks. The 3d infantry was now detached to the right as a still further security to that flank yet threatened by the enemy. Major Ringgold, with the remaining section, kept up his fire from an advanced position, and was supported by the 4th infantry.

The grass of the prairie had been accidentally fired by our artillery, and the volumes of smoke now partially concealed the armies from each other. As the enemy's left had evidently been driven back and left the road free, and as the cannonade has been suspended, I ordered forward the 18-pounders on the road nearly to the position first occupied by the Mexican cavalry, and caused the 1st brigade to take up a new position still on the left of the 18-pounder battery. The 5th was advanced from its former position, and occupied a point on the extreme right of the new line. The enemy made a change of position corresponding to our own, and, after a suspension of nearly an hour, the action was resumed.

The fire of artillery was now most destructive; openings were constantly made through the enemy's ranks by our fire, and the constancy with which the Mexican infantry sustained this severe cannonade was a theme of universal remark and admiration. Capt. May's squadron was detached to make a demonstration on the left of the enemy's position, and suffered severely from the fire of artillery to which it was for some time exposed.

The 4th infantry, which had been ordered to support the 18-pounder battery, was exposed to a most galling fire of artillery, by which several men were killed, and Capt. Page dangerously wounded. The enemy's fire was directed against our 18-pounder battery, and the guns under Major Ringgold in its vicinity. The Major himself, while cooly directing the fire of his pieces, was struck by a cannon ball and mortally wounded.

In the mean time the battalion of artillery under Lieut. Col. Childs had been brought up to support the artillery on our right. A strong demonstration of cavalry was now made by the enemy against this part of our line, and the column continued to advance under a severe fire from the 18-pounders. The battalion was instantly formed in square, and held ready to receive the charge of cavalry; but when the advancing squadrons were within close range, a deadly fire of cannister from the 18-pounders dispersed them. A brisk fire of small arms was now opened upon the square, by which one officer, Lieut. Luther, 2d artillery, was slightly wounded; but a well-directed volley from the front of the square silenced all further firing from the enemy in this quarter. It was now nearly dark, and the action was closed on the right of our line—the enemy having been completely driven back from his position, and foiled in every attempt against our line.

While the above was going forward on our right, and under my own eye, the enemy had made a serious attempt against the left of our line. Captain Duncan instantly perceived the movement, and, by the bold and brilliant maneuvering of his battery, completely repulsed several successive efforts of the enemy to advance in force upon our left flank. Supported in succession by the 8th infantry and by Capt. Ker's squadron of dragoons, he gallantly held the enemy at bay, and finally drove him with immense loss from the field. The action here, and along the whole line, continued until dark, when the enemy retired into the chapparal in rear of his position. Our army bivouacked on the ground it occupied. During the afternoon the train had been moved forward about half a mile and was parked in rear of the new position.

Our loss this day was nine killed, forty-four wounded, and two missing. Among the wounded were Major Ringgold, who has since died, and Captain Page, dangerously wounded; Lieut.

Luther slightly so. I annex a tabular statement of the casualties of the day.

Our own force engaged is shown by the field report (herewith) to have been 177 officers and 2,111 men; aggregate 2,288. The Mexican force, according to the statements of their own officers taken prisoner in the affair of the 9th, was not less than 6,000 regular troops, with 10 pieces of artillery, and probably exceeded that number; the irregular force not known. Their loss was not less than 200 killed and 400 wounded—probably greater. This estimate is very moderate, and formed upon the number actually counted upon the field, and upon the reports of their own officers.

As already reported in my first brief despatch, the conduct of our officers and men was everything that could be desired. Exposed for hours to the severest trial, a cannonade of artillery, our troops displayed a coolness and constancy which gave me, throughout, the assurance of victory.

I purposely defer the mention of individuals until my report of the action of the 9th, when I will endeavor to do justice to the many instances of distinguished conduct on both days. In the mean time I refer, for more minute details, to the reports of individual commanders.

I am, sir, very respectfully, your obedient servant, Z. TAYLOR,

Brevet Brig. Gen. U.S.A., commanding.

Source: Documents of the U.S.-Mexican War. "Brigadier-General Zachary Taylor, at camp near Matamoras, to Roger Jones, Adjutant-General of the Army at Washington, D.C. Taylor's official report of the Battle of Palo Alto." Available online. URL: http://www.dmwv.org/mexwar/documents/paloalto.htm. Accessed on February 5, 2010.

Account of the Battle
Ulysses S. Grant
Published 1885

The future commander of the Union armies in the Civil War was a freshly minted West Point second lieutenant during the U.S.-Mexican War, attached

to the 4th Infantry. In this extract from his memoirs, Grant is careful to point out the outmoded weapons of the Mexican cavalry, and he devotes close attention to the American artillery, which he contrasts with that of the Mexicans. Not only were the Mexican guns lacking in range, but their powder was defective—a problem that dogged the Mexican army throughout the war. Like several others who wrote of their combat experience in the U.S.-Mexican War, Grant notes the way in which Mexican cannonballs fell short and then rolled harmlessly through the U.S. ranks.

Early in the forenoon of the 8th of May as Palo Alto was approached, an army, certainly outnumbering our little force, was seen, drawn up in line of battle just in front of the timber. Their bayonets and spearheads glistened in the sunlight formidably. The force was composed largely of cavalry armed with lances. Where we were the grass was tall, reaching nearly to the shoulders of the men, very stiff, and each stock was pointed at the top, and hard and almost as sharp as a darning-needle. General Taylor halted his army before the head of column came in range of the artillery of the Mexicans. He then formed a line of battle, facing the enemy. His artillery, two batteries and two eighteen-pounder iron guns, drawn by oxen, were placed in position at intervals along the line. A battalion was thrown to the rear, commanded by Lieutenant-Colonel Childs, of the artillery, as reserves. These preparations completed, orders were given for a platoon of each company to stack arms and go to a stream off to the right of the command, to fill their canteens and also those of the rest of their respective companies. When the men were all back in their places in line, the command to advance was given. As I looked down that long line of about three thousand armed men, advancing towards a larger force also armed, I thought what a fearful responsibility General Taylor must feel, commanding such a host and so far away from friends. The Mexicans immediately opened fire upon us, first with artillery and then with infantry. At first their shots did not reach us, and the advance was continued. As we got nearer, the cannon balls commenced going through the ranks. They hurt no one, however, during this advance, because they would strike the ground long before they reached our line, and ricochetted through the tall grass so slowly that the men would see them and open ranks and let them pass. When we got to a point where the artillery could be used with effect, a halt was called, and the battle opened on both sides.

The infantry under General Taylor was armed with flint-lock muskets, and paper cartridges charged with powder, buck-shot and ball. At the distance of a few hundred yards a man might fire at you all day without your finding it out. The artillery was generally six-pounder brass guns throwing only solid shot; but General Taylor had with him three or four twelve-pounder howitzers throwing shell, besides his eighteen-pounders before spoken of, that had a long range. This made a powerful armament. The Mexicans were armed about as we were so far as their infantry was concerned, but their artillery only fired solid shot. We had greatly the advantage in this arm.

The artillery was advanced a rod or two in front of the line, and opened fire. The infantry stood at order arms as spectators, watching the effect of our shots upon the enemy, and watching his shots so as to step out of their way. It could be seen that the eighteen-pounders and the howitzers did a great deal of execution. On our side there was little or no loss while we occupied this position. During the battle Major Ringgold, an accomplished and brave artillery officer, was mortally wounded, and Lieutenant Luther, also of the artillery, was struck. During the day several advances were made, and just at dusk it became evident that the Mexicans were falling back. We again advanced, and occupied at the close of the battle substantially the ground held by the enemy at the beginning. In this last move there was a brisk fire upon our troops, and some execution was done. One cannon-ball passed through our ranks, not far from me. It took off the head of an enlisted man, and the under jaw of Captain Page of my regiment, while the splinters from the musket of the killed soldier, and his brains and bones, knocked down two or three others, including one officer, Lieutenant Wallen,—hurting them more or less. Our casualties for the day were nine killed and forty-seven wounded.

Source: Grant, Ulysses S. *Personal Memoirs of U.S. Grant.* 1885. Reprint, New York: Da Capo Press, 1982, pp. 43–45.

THE BATTLE OF RESACA DE LA PALMA, MAY 9, 1846

Description of the Battle's Action
Sergeant Milton
Published 1847

At 2:00 in the afternoon of May 9, 1846, Zachary Taylor halted his march at a dry riverbed called Resaca de la Palma, five miles from the scene of the previous day's battle at Palo Alto. When his scouts reported the Mexicans entrenched in Resaca de la Guerra, a nearby ravine, and pointed out that the terrain—ponds and chaparral—effectively protected the enemy's flanks, Taylor called up his "flying artillery" (a mobile light artillery detachment) to dislodge the Mexicans. A Mexican battery returned fire but was soon overrun by a contingent of U.S. dragoons in the action that one dragoon, a Sergeant Milton, describes in the following extract from a biography of Taylor. The dragoons, in turn, were swept by infantry crossfire as they returned to the American lines. The Mexicans quickly retook their artillery position, which would be recaptured late in the battle.

Unlike the flat terrain at Palo Alto, Resaca de la Palma presented a rugged landscape, which reduced the effectiveness of the American artillery. Taylor therefore relied more heavily on his infantry, and the battle was soon fought hand to hand. Demoralized from their drubbing at Palo Alto, the Mexicans, who still outnumbered the Americans, withdrew to Matamoros—but not before 547 had *been killed or wounded. (Many historians believe the casualty count was even higher.) Taylor lost 33 killed and 89 wounded.*

There is no incident connected with this brilliant action that has created so much admiration throughout the country, and which, in reality, displayed such daring courage, as the charge of Captain May upon the Mexican batteries. Though this bold and hazardous achievement has already been incidentally referred to, it is believed the following more detailed account, by an eyewitness and actor in the charge, will possess interest. It is by Sergeant Milton, an officer of May's dragoons:

"At Palo Alto," says he, "I took my rank in the troop as second sergeant, and while upon the field my horse was wounded in the jaw by a grape-shot, which disabled him for service. While he was plunging in agony I dismounted, and the quick eye of Captain May observed me as I alighted from my horse. He inquired if I was hurt. I answered no—that my horse was the sufferer. 'I am glad it is not yourself,' replied he; 'there is another,' (pointing at the same time to a steed without a rider, which was standing with dilated eye, gazing at the strife,) 'mount him.' I approached the horse, and he stood still until I put my hand upon the rein and patted his neck, when he rubbed his head alongside of me, as if pleased that some human being was about to become his companion in the affray. He was a noble bay, which had, with a number of others, been purchased for the troop in St. Louis. I bestrode him, and we passed through the first day unharmed.

"On the second day, at Resaca de la Palma, our troop stood anxiously waiting for the signal to be given, and never had I looked upon men on whose countenances were more clearly expressed a fixed determination to win. The lips of some were pale with excitement, and their eyes wore that fixed expression which betokens mischief; others, with shut teeth, would quietly laugh, and catch a tighter grip of the rein, or seat themselves with care and firmness in the saddle, while quiet words of confidence and encouragement were passed from each to his neighbor. All at once Captain May rode to the front of his troop—every rein and sabre was tightly grasped. Raising himself and pointing at the battery, he shouted, 'Men, follow!' There was now a clattering of hoofs and a rattling of sabre sheaths—the fire of the enemy's guns was partly drawn by Lieutenant Ridgeley, and the next moment we were sweeping like the wind up the ravine. I was in a squad of about nine men, who were separated by a shower of grape from the battery, and we were in advance, May leading. He turned his horse opposite the breastwork, in front of the guns, and with another shout 'to follow,' leaped over them. Several of the horses did follow, but mine, being new and not well trained, refused; two others balked, and their riders started down the ravine to turn the breastwork where the rest of the troop had entered. I made another attempt to clear the guns with my horse, turning him around—feeling all the time secure at thinking the guns discharged—I put his head towards them and gave him spur, but he again balked; so turning his head down the ravine, I too started to ride round the breastwork.

"As I came down a lancer dashed at me with lance in rest. With my sabre I parried his thrust, only receiving a slight flesh-wound from its point in the arm, which felt at the time like the prick of a pin. The lancer turned and fled; at that moment a ball passed through my horse on the left side and shattered my right side. The shot killed the horse instantly, and he fell upon my left leg, fastening me by his weight to the earth. There I lay, right in the midst of the action, where carnage was riding riot, and every moment the shot, from our own and the Mexican guns, tearing up the earth around me. I tried to raise my horse so as to extricate my leg, but I had already grown so weak with my wound that I was unable, and from the mere attempt, I fell back exhausted. To add to my horror, a horse, who was careering about, riderless, within a few yards of me, received a wound, and he commenced struggling and rearing with pain. Two

or three times, he came near falling on me, but at length, with a scream of agony and a bound, he fell dead—his body touching my own fallen steed. What I had been in momentary dread of now occurred—my wounded limb, which was lying across the horse, received another ball in the ankle.

"I now felt disposed to give up; and, exhausted through pain and excitement, a film gathered over my eyes, which I thought was the precursor of dissolution. From this hopeless state I was aroused by a wounded Mexican, calling out to me, 'Bueno Americano,' and turning my eyes towards the spot, I saw that he was holding a certificate and calling to me. The tide of action now rolled away from me, and hope again sprung up. The Mexican uniforms began to disappear from the chapparal, and squadrons of our troops passed in sight, apparently in pursuit. While I was thus nursing the prospect of escape, I beheld, not far from me, a villainous-looking ranchero, armed with an American sergeant's short sword, dispatching a wounded American soldier, whose body he robbed—the next he came to was a Mexican, whom he served the same way, and thus I looked on while he murderously slew four. I drew an undischarged pistol from my holsters, and, laying myself along my horse's neck, watched him, expecting to be the next victim; but something frightened him from his vulture-like business, and he fled in another direction. I need not say that had he visited me I should have taken one more shot at the enemy, and would have died content, had I succeeded in making such an assassin bite the dust. Two hours after, I had the pleasure of shaking some of my comrades by the hand, who were picking up the wounded. They lifted my Mexican friend, too, and I am pleased to say he, as well as myself, live to fight over again the sanguine fray of Resaca de la Palma.

Source: Montgomery, H. *The Life of Major General Zachary Taylor.* 1847. Reprint, Auburn, N.Y.: Derby, Miller & Company, 1850, pp. 160–163.

THE BATTLE OF MONTERREY, SEPTEMBER 21–23, 1846

Account of the Battle

Brevet Major William Seaton Henry
Published 1847

On September 19, 1846, Zachary Taylor marched to the outskirts of Monterrey, Mexico. It presented a formidable objective, defended by 7,000 troops who were equipped with heavier, modern British-made artillery instead of the inferior pieces they had had at Palo Alto. Taylor sent out his engineers to survey Monterrey's fortifications. On September 20, he sent a division of U.S. Army regulars augmented by 400 Texas Rangers to seize the road to Saltillo. While this preparatory phase was nearing an end on September 21, Taylor opened an artillery bombardment against the fortifications. This was followed by an attack with his principal forces from the east.

By September 22, U.S. Army soldiers were fighting in the streets of Monterrey. They pushed the defenders into the town's central plaza on September 23, whereupon Taylor used his 10-inch mortar to shell the concentration of Mexican troops. This brought surrender.

William Seaton Henry (1816–51) graduated from West Point in 1835 and entered the U.S.-Mexican War as a captain but was breveted to major for his gallantry at Monterrey. His Campaign Sketches of the War with Mexico *(1847) was his only book.*

September 21st. During the night an express was received from General Worth, stating he had arrived in position, and would storm two heights to the southwest of the castle before storming the height directly west of it. About 7 A.M. the 1st and Volunteer Divisions were ordered under arms, and advanced toward the city. The mortar and howitzer batteries opened, but with little or no effect. General Taylor directed the 1st Division to be moved toward the east of the city to support Major Mansfield in a close reconnaissance of the enemy's works. The division (owing

to the indisposition of General Twiggs, who had no idea the action was to be brought on, and was at first in camp, but immediately repaired to the field) was under the command of Colonel Garland, 4th Infantry. The 4th Infantry, under Major Allen, being at the mortar battery, the division went into action with the 3d Infantry, commanded by Major Lear, the 4th Brigade, commanded by Colonel Wilson, consisting of the 1st Infantry, commanded by Major Abercrombie, and the Baltimore Battalion under Colonel Watson, and Bragg's and Ridgely's batteries. Major Mansfield was directed by General Taylor to bring on the action, if he thought the works could be carried. The reconnoitering party was first supported by Company C., 3d Infantry, under the command of Lieutenant Hazlitt, and re-enforced, upon application, by Company H., 3d Infantry, under the command of Captain Field.

The division was formed in line of battle out of reach of the guns of the enemy, when orders were brought for us to advance (by Lieutenant Pope, topographical engineer, and Colonel Kinney, who was acting as volunteer aid-de-camp), make our way into the city, and storm battery No. 1, at the extreme eastern end. As we advanced, battery No. 1 opened upon us. The first shot fired struck immediately in front of our line and ricoched over it. An enfilading fire was opened upon us from the citadel. The line steadily but rapidly advanced, regardless of all fire; important work was to be performed, and we had made up our minds to carry all before us at the point of the bayonet.

For five hundred yards we advanced across a plain under fire of the two batteries. We rushed into the streets. Unfortunately, we did not turn soon enough to the left, and had advanced but a short distance when we came suddenly upon an unknown battery, which opened its deadly fire upon us. From all its embrasures, from every house, from every yard, showers of balls were hurled upon us. Being in utter ignorance of our locality, we had to stand and take it; our men, covering themselves as well as they could, dealt death and destruction on every side; there was no resisting the deadly, concealed fire, which appeared to come from every direction. On every side we were cut down. Major Barbour was the first officer who was shot down; he fell, cheering his men. He was killed by an escopet ball passing through his heart. He never spoke; his most intimate friend, standing by his side, never received one kind look—one "God bless you!" but his spirit, in the twinkling of lightning, winged its way to his Maker.

We retired into the next street, under cover of some walls and houses. Into this street the body of Major Barbour was carried. Here were lying the dead, wounded, and dying. Captain Williams, of the topographical corps, lay on one side of the street, wounded; the gallant Major Mansfield, wounded in the leg, still pressed on with unabated ardor, cheering the men, and pointing out places of attack. It was in this street I saw the gallant Colonel Watson, followed by a few of his men (some of them were persuading him to retire). Never shall I forget the animated expression of his countenance when, in taking a drink from the canteen of one of his men, he exclaimed, "Never, boys! Never will I yield an inch! I have too much Irish blood in me to give up!" A short time after this exclamation he was a corpse. Lieutenant Bragg's battery arrived about this time. He reached the street into which we had retired, but it was impossible for him to do any thing. Finding the struggle at this point hopeless, our force originally having been deemed only sufficient to carry battery No. 1, without any expectation of finding some two or three others raking us, we were ordered to retire in order, with the view of attacking the battery at a more salient point. In the mean time, Captain Backus, of the 1st Infantry, succeeded in stationing himself, with some fifty men, in a tan-yard, which was about one hundred and thirty yards in the rear of battery No. 1, and nearer the town; in this yard was a shed, facing battery No. 1: its roof was flat, encompassed by a wall about two feet high, which was an excellent breastwork for his men. About twenty yards to the southwest of the battery was a large building, with very thick

walls, used as a distillery. On the top of this building sand-bag embrasures had been constructed, and it was occupied by the enemy. The gorge of battery No. 1 was open toward the shed. Captain Backus, with his men, drove the enemy from the distillery with considerable loss. About this time he received information that we had been ordered to retire.

Our firing having ceased, he was about withdrawing, when he again heard firing in front of the battery, and at the same time all the guns of the battery opened in the direction of the fire. This was the advance of two companies of 4th Infantry, about ninety strong, upon whom the fire of the enemy's batteries were concentrated, and actually mowed them down. It was actually ninety men advancing to storm a work defended by five hundred! It was here the gallant Hoskins and Woods fell, bravely cheering their men, and the generous Graham was wounded. Backus determined to retain his position; reposted his men on the roof of the shed, and shot down the enemy at their guns, firing through the open gorge of the work.

At this time the Mississippi and Tennessee regiments, under the command of General Quitman, advanced under a very heavy fire, and gained possession of the battery, after a very severe loss. The galling fire of Backus saved many of their gallant men. The greater part of the enemy had been driven from the work before it was taken possession of by the command of General Quitman. Major-general Butler was wounded in the leg while leading, in company with General Hamer, the 1st Ohio Regiment. In retiring from the city, we were exposed to a galling fire from the citadel. A ball took a man's head off, and threw it and part of his gun high in the air.

When the division re-formed our terrible loss became apparent. In the 3d Infantry, its gallant commander, Major Lear, was severely wounded by a ball entering at his nostril and coming out at the back of his ear. Lieutenant D. S. Irwin, adjutant of the 3d Infantry, was killed by a shot in the neck. Captain G. P. Field was killed by Lancers while retiring. Lieutenant Hoskins, of the 4th Infantry, Lieutenant Woods, of the 2d (serving with the 4th), were killed, and Lieutenant Graham mortally wounded. Major Abercrombie, of the 1st Infantry, was slightly wounded; Captain La Motte was shot in the arm; Lieutenant Dillworth had a leg shot off; Lieutenant Terret was wounded and taken prisoner. The division was then ordered to the captured work to support Ridgely's battery, about being ordered into the city.

During this time the mortar and three twenty-four-pound howitzers were playing upon the city; one of them, having been taken to the captured work, was now firing into Fort Diablo. While under cover of the battery, we were ordered to enter the city immediately, and carry, if possible, a work of the enemy apparently but a few streets off. The command which went on that fearful expedition was chiefly made up from the 3d and 4th Infantry. The moment we left the cover of the work we were exposed to a galling fire of musketry, escopets [escopettes, carbines], and artillery. We pushed steadily along, taking advantage of every shelter to approach the work. Captain L. N. Morris, 3d Infantry, led the column. Crossing one street, we were exposed in full to the guns (mounted in barbette) of a *tête de pont* [bridgehead], which commanded the passage of El Puente Purissima. The fire from it was perfectly awful. We advanced through several gardens and streets, and at last worked our way to a spot where we were slightly sheltered from the shower of lead. The enemy had occupied these houses, and were driven from them by the determined advance of our men. We could not proceed any further, having arrived at an impassable stream, on the opposite side of which the enemy were in force with three pieces of artillery, from which an incessant fire was kept up on us. In fact, every street was blockaded, and every house a fortification; and on all sides our gallant officers and men were shot down. Our command did not number over one hundred and fifty, and the enemy were at least a thousand strong at the bridge. It would have been madness to storm it with a force so inadequate.

It was at this point that Captain L. N. Morris, while bravely leading his regiment, received a mortal wound; the shot passed through his body, killing him immediately. Going into action with five seniors, at this critical moment the command of the 3d Infantry devolved upon myself. Captain Bainbridge had been wounded in the hand just after leaving the captured battery. A few moments after Captain Morris fell, Lieutenant Hazlitt, of the 3d, received his death-wound.

Here it was that the undaunted courage and bravery of the American soldier showed itself. Although exposed to a deadly fire, they would advance by file, assure themselves of their aim, fire, retire and load, and again return to the spot where the balls were flying thick and fast. At one time a whole regiment, coming to re-enforce the command already at the bridge, was exposed to the fire of our men: it was very effective.

Major W. Graham was the senior officer of the 4th Infantry with this advanced command. The enemy being strongly re-enforced, our cartridges nearly exhausted, the command was ordered to retire. This was done coolly and calmly, under (if possible) an increased fire. On arriving near the captured battery the command was forced to lie down flat in the road, under cover of a very small embankment of an irrigating ditch, for more than an hour, exposed to an incessant fire of bullets, ball, and shells, until ordered to take position under cover of the captured work.

Lieutenant Ridgely, with a section of his battery, advanced to the street leading to the *"tête de pont,"* and fired several rounds, but, finding they were perfectly useless, his pieces were withdrawn. Lieutenant Bragg, with his battery, put to flight some little show of a charge of Lancers. Captain Shivers, with his company, did good service. The volunteers were all ordered to camp, excepting the 1st Kentucky, which was not in the action, having been kept as a guard over the mortar. They, with the 1st, 3d, and 4th Infantry, and Captain Shivers's company, were ordered to remain, to hold the captured work.

Just before dark an express arrived from General Worth stating that he had been successful in taking two heights, and would storm the one commanding the Bishop's Palace to-morrow at day-dawn. There was a smile of satisfaction passed over our good general's face, and when it was announced to the command we gave three cheers. A traverse was immediately thrown up, under the superintendence of Lieutenant Scarritt, Engineers, as a cover from the fire of the citadel. The 3d Infantry, with two companies of the 1st Kentucky Regiment, occupied the battery, the balance the distillery and houses in the neighborhood. The night set in cold, and, to complete our misery, it rained; the men had neither dinner nor supper, and, without even a blanket, were forced to lie down in the mud. Battery No. 1 mounted five pieces: one twelve-pounder, one nine, two sixes, and one howitzer.

While such were the operations under the immediate eye of General Taylor, General Worth, with his division, was moving for the Saltillo road. A large body of cavalry and some infantry disputed his further passage. The charge of the cavalry was met by the battalion of light troops under Captain C. F. Smith, and Captain M'Cullough's company of Rangers. The enemy charged by squadrons, and had to turn the foot of a hill before reaching our men. On they came, our men standing like rocks, and many a saddle was emptied by their unerring aim. The first squadron was completely mixed up with our advance, when on came the second.

Lieutenant Hays, of Duncan's battery, unlimbered the guns in a minute, and poured in round shot over the heads of our men. This dispersed the whole body, and the cry was, "Sauve qui peut!" In this sharp engagement, the enemy, it is presumed, lost one hundred, the colonel among the number.

As soon as the cavalry had retired, the enemy (from "Independence Hill," west of the Palace) opened upon our column a fire from a twelve-pounder. Under this fire the division marched two miles, incurring very little, if any loss. Out of range of this height, another battery of one gun opened from a hill, called "Federation" (between these heights the road to Saltillo runs), and con-

tinued the fire until the division marching on the Saltillo road were out of range. At this point General Worth decided to storm the battery on Federacion Hill. Captain C. F. Smith, 2d Artillery, was selected, with about three hundred men, half regulars, and the rest Texans, under Major Chevalier, for this service. After the departure of Captain Smith, Captain Miles, with the 7th Infantry, was ordered to march to his support. His orders required him to take a direct route to the hill, through a cornfield, which would afford him slight shelter.

The advance of Captain Miles was unobserved by the enemy until he had nearly reached the small stream (the Arroyo Topa) which runs south of the city, and courses its way along the base of the hill upon which the battery was situated. As soon as the head of the column debouched, a discharge of grape was opened upon them, without injuring a man. Before crossing the river, two more discharges of grape were received, and the Infantry stationed upon the hill commenced a plunging fire—not a man was injured. As the regiment crossed the river, it was formed under a point of rock, out of reach of the enemy. Detachments were then sent forward under Lieutenants Grant, Little, and Gardner, to keep the enemy employed, and divert their attention from the advance of Captain Smith.

About this time Colonel Smith, commanding the 2d Brigade, arrived, with the 5th Infantry, and ordered Captain Miles, with the 7th, to follow that regiment in an attack upon Fort Soldado, a temporary breast-work on an eminence to the southeast of Federacion. As the brigade moved on, it was discovered that Captain Smith, with his command, had possession of the height.

The 2d Brigade formed in line within four hundred yards of the redoubt, and rapidly advanced. It received one discharge of grape from a twelve-pounder, and not a few escopet balls; several were wounded. The advance continued rapidly until within a hundred yards, when the charge was made at double quick. The enemy fled in every direction. In this affair the left wing of the 7th entered the redoubt with that of the 5th. There were also many of Captain Blanchard's gallant company of Louisiana Volunteers and Texan Rangers well up with the advance, each and all striving for the post of honor.

Colonel Smith immediately made the following disposition of his command: Captain Smith to retain possession of the first height stormed; Captain Miles, with the 7th, to hold the last height taken; and Captain Scott, with the 5th Infantry, to move on the same ridge, further east. In this position the 2d Brigade remained during the afternoon and night of the 21st; the 7th Infantry receiving, for several hours, the fire from the Bishop's Palace, which was returned by the captured gun under charge of Lieutenant Dana, of the 7th Infantry.

Soon after dark, General Worth communicated with Colonel Smith, informing him that at daybreak the next morning he intended storming the height above the Bishop's Palace, and that Captain Miles, with three companies of the 7th, must move in the direction of the Palace, to create a diversion.

September 22d. Let us return to the eastern extremity of the city, where the command occupying battery No. 1, as soon as day dawned, were forced to lie flat down in the mud to cover themselves from the spiteful fire from Fort Diablo, which was incessantly kept up. Just at the gray dawn of day, lying on my back, I witnessed the storming of the height which commanded the Bishop's Palace. The first intimation we had of it was the discharge of musketry near the top of the hill. Each flash looked like an electric spark. The flashes and the white smoke ascended the hill side steadily, as if worked by machinery. The dark space between the apex of the height and the curling smoke of the musketry became less and less, until the whole became enveloped in smoke, and we knew it was gallantly carried. It was a glorious sight, and quite warmed up our cold and chilled bodies.

Firing commenced on us as soon as the day clearly dawned. Many shells were thrown from the citadel, none of which burst in the work,

although they fell all around us. Lieutenant Scarritt was busily employed putting the battery and distillery in a better state of defense.

Captain Bainbridge assumed command of the 3d Infantry in the morning. The 1st, 3d, and 4th Infantry, and Kentucky regiment were relieved by a command under General Quitman, of Colonel Davis's Mississippi regiment. Returning to camp, we were exposed to a cross and enfilading fire from the enemy's batteries. A corporal of the 4th Infantry was cut in two, and one man wounded. We had to scatter along to prevent being fired at in a body. The division were delighted to reach their camp, to have one night's rest.

We had hardly arrived when an express came in, stating that General Worth had carried the castle, and another, from whence, I presume, will never be known, that the enemy were coming out to meet us in the plain! We were again immediately under arms, and marched out; no enemy appearing, we returned. At sunset the regiment followed to the grave the remains of the lamented Morris.

At daylight on the 22d, as I have previously mentioned, the attack was made upon the height commanding the Bishop's Palace, by a command under Colonel Childs, composed of artillery and infantry, and some Texans under Colonel Hays. At the moment the storming party commenced the ascent, the command under Captain Miles descended toward the palace, giving three cheers to attract the attention of the enemy; in return for their cheers, they received a shower of grape. This movement held the enemy in check at the castle, and prevented him from succoring his flying forces on the hill above, which was carried with great gallantry and slight loss. Captain Gillespie fell mortally wounded, the first man to enter the breast-work. Soon after, General Worth ordered up the 5th Infantry, Captain Smith's command, and Captain Blanchard's company of Louisiana Volunteers, to re-enforce Colonel Childs. With great exertion, a howitzer was placed in position, under charge of Lieutenant Roland, which played with a plunging fire upon the castle with great precision and effect. A light corps under Captain Vinton, composed of artillery, Blanchard's company and Texans, on the left of the hill, kept up a continued fire of musketry, which was returned with spirit by the enemy.

About noon the Mexican cavalry deployed before the palace, and made an attempt to charge our skirmishers. They were repulsed, and pursued closely by Vinton's command, preventing many from again entering the castle, rushing in themselves through every opening, and driving the enemy with consternation before them. Lieutenant Ayers was the first to enter and pull down the flag of the enemy, and run up the star-spangled banner. Great credit is due to Captain Vinton for his gallantry. General Worth, after the castle was taken, moved down all his forces and ammunition train from the ranch of the Saltillo road, and so remained during the night of the 22d, directing the 5th Infantry and Blanchard's company to return to the redoubt on the hill, where the 7th was stationed.

September 23d. From our camp we had the pleasure of hearing General Worth open upon the town from the castle about 7 o'clock. A report was circulated that the enemy were attempting to escape. The whole command was immediately under arms, and marched almost within range of the enemy's guns. So many commanding points were in our possession, that we were momentarily in expectation of their capitulation. It was cheering to see Worth pouring it into them, and that, too, with their own pieces and ammunition.

The rapid discharge of small-arms at the eastern end of the city gave notice that the engagement had again commenced. The regiment of Texas cavalry under Colonel Woods had dismounted, and, with the Mississippians, under Colonel Davis, were sharply at work. The Mississippians at daybreak took possession of Fort Diablo (from which we had received such a destructive fire on the 21st and 22d), without any resistance, the enemy having abandoned it, taking with them their guns during the night. General Quitman was in command. These troops fought most gallantly, driving the enemy before them from house to house, their rifles picking them off wherever a Mexican's body or head presented itself.

Bragg's battery was ordered into the city, and the 3d Infantry was ordered to support it. When we got within range of the guns of the citadel, the battery crossed the field of fire at full gallop; not one was injured.

The 3d took a more circuitous route, and came up under cover. When we arrived the city had been cleared of the enemy on a line with, and within two squares of, the Cathedral, which is situated in the main Plaza, and in which they had been concentrated. General Quitman, General Henderson, General Lamar, Colonel Wood, and Colonel Davis all displayed distinguished gallantry; several of their men were wounded, and some few killed. Bragg's battery and the 3d Infantry dashed in among them, and shared the fight for the remainder of the day. The firing was very severe, but nothing compared to that on the 21st, except at one street running directly from the Cathedral. To cross that street you had to pass through a shower of bullets. One of Bragg's pieces played up this street with very little effect, as the weight of metal was entirely too light. Sergeant Weightman, Bragg's first sergeant, worked his piece like a hero, and was shot through the heart while aiming his gun. The Mexicans, whenever the piece was pointed at them, would fall behind their barricade, and at that time we could cross without a certainty of being shot; as soon as it was fired, their balls (as if bushels of hickory nuts, were hurled at us) swept the street. Our men crossed it in squads. "Go it, my boys," and away some would start; others would wait until the enemy had foolishly expended at space their bullets, and then they would cross.

General Taylor was in town with his staff, on foot, walking about, perfectly regardless of danger. He was very imprudent in the exposure of his person. He crossed the street in which there was such a terrible fire in a walk, and by every chance should have been shot. I ran across with some of my men, and reminded him how much he was exposing himself, to which he replied, "Take that ax and knock in that door."

When we commenced on the door the occupant signified, by putting the key in and unlocking it, if we had no objection, he would save us the trouble. It turned out to be quite an extensive apothecary-shop. The proprietor, Doctor San Juan (there are more St. Johns in this country than stones), was a very respectable-looking Esculapius, and offered us some delicious, ripe limes and cool water. I took some of the former, but declined the latter, as it was hinted it might be poisoned. One of the men, not so sensitive, made himself a governor lemonade, and told me it was "first rate," and advised me to take some. The doctor said Ampudia was in the Plaza with four thousand men, and that two thousand were in the citadel. The house on the opposite corner had been broken open. It was a grocery store; in it the men found bread and other edibles.

Bursting open another door, we came upon five rather genteel-looking women, with some children, and one or two men. They were on their knees, each with a crucifix, begging for mercy. As soon as they saw me, the cry was, "Capitano! capitano!" I reassured them by shaking hands, and, by the expression of my countenance, signified there was no danger. They appeared very grateful to find their throats were not to be cut. Although we are fiercely fighting, and the blood of our officers and men has freely flowed, yet not one act of unkindness have I heard reported as being committed by either regular or volunteer.

General Taylor, finding the field-pieces of little use, ordered us to retire to camp as soon as the volunteers had withdrawn. Their withdrawal was ordered upon the supposition that General Worth would commence throwing shells into the city in the afternoon. The mortar was sent to him yesterday. It was a difficult matter to get the volunteers out; they were having their own fun. The enemy sent in a flag of truce today, asking a cessation until the women and children could be removed. The general, of course, declined; such a degree of politeness should not have been expected at this late hour. The flag is a good symptom; their time is drawing near. I hardly think they will hold out another day.

It is reported many were leaving the heights with pack-mules this morning. Had not General Worth taken possession of the Saltillo road, I question whether many would not have been off yesterday. Thus far they have fought most bravely, and with an endurance and tenacity I did not think they possessed.

On our march back to camp, I was very much amused at a remark of an Irishman: "Faith, boys, we have had a Waterloo time of it; three days' fighting! The French fought against the combined powers of Europe; we are the combined powers of Europe and America! We have a little of all among us, and the whole can't be bate!"

Source: Henry, William Seaton. *Campaign Sketches of the War with Mexico*. New York: Harper & Brothers, 1847, pp. 193–209.

THE BATTLE OF BUENA VISTA, FEBRUARY 22–23, 1847

Account of the Battle
Brevet Major William Seaton Henry
Published 1847

After Major General Winfield Scott invaded Mexico by way of Veracruz, Zachary Taylor was ordered to assume a defensive position at Monterrey. He decided instead to leave only a small garrison there and at Saltillo, and to advance with 4,650 men to occupy Agua Nueva, 18 miles south of Saltillo. He did not know that Antonio López de Santa Anna was just 35 miles from Agua Nueva. On February 21, 1847, Taylor's scouts spotted the large Mexican army, and he withdrew to Buena Vista, just south of Saltillo, where he could mount a more effective defense. Outnumbered three to one, Taylor needed as big a defensive advantage as he could get. When, on February 22, Santa Anna demanded his surrender, Taylor refused. The Mexican commander

opened up a brief artillery barrage. This was fol-
lowed by maneuvering on both sides before the
battle began in earnest on February 23.

In the initial stage, Santa Anna drove the Ameri-
cans back, but Jefferson Davis (the future president
of the Confederate States of America) rallied his
Mississippi Rifles into a vigorous counterattack
against the Mexican cavalry just as it was position-
ing itself to flank Taylor's main formation. Under the
counterattack, the Mexicans began to fall back, until
they linked up with reinforcements. The augmented
Mexican force again turned the tide in Santa Anna's
favor—until two U.S. artillery batteries supported
Davis's Mississippians and an Indiana regiment in
yet another counterattack that caught Santa Anna
flat-footed.

In the excerpt that follows, Brevet Major Wil-
liam Seaton Henry betrays the racist attitude toward
Mexicans that was all too typical of Americans of
this period.

Before General Taylor had completed his
arrangements for the defense of the city [Buena
Vista], on the morning of the 22d he received
information of the advance of the enemy, and
immediately repaired to camp. Clouds of dust
announced the approach of the foe, who arrived
in position between 10 and 11 A.M., with
immense masses, sufficiently strong to have
brought on an immediate engagement. All
silently but firmly awaited the attack, when, true
characteristic of the Mexican, a white flag made
its appearance, and with it Surgeon-general
Lindenberger, bearing the following communication from Santa Anna:

"You are surrounded by twenty thousand
men, and can not, in any human probability, void
suffering a rout, and being cut to pieces with
your troops; but, as you deserve consideration
and particular esteem, I wish to save you from
a catastrophe, and for that purpose give you this
notice, in order that you may surrender at discretion, under the assurance that you will be treated
with the consideration belonging to the Mexican
character, to which end you will be granted an
hour's time to make up your mind, to commence

from the moment when my flag of truce arrives
in your camp.

"With this view, I assure you of my particular
consideration.

"God and Liberty. Camp at Encantada, February 22d, 1847.

"ANTONIO LOPEZ DE SANTA ANNA.

"To Gen. Z. Taylor, comm'g the forces of the
United States."

To which, without the necessity of one hour's
consideration, our brave general made the following brief but characteristic reply:

"Headquarters, Army of Occupation,
Near Buena Vista, Feb. 22, 1847.

"*Sir*,—In reply to your note of this date, sum-
moning me to surrender my force at discretion,
I beg leave to say that I decline acceding to your
request. With high respect, I am, sir,

"Your obedient servant,   Z. TAYLOR,

"Maj. Gen. U. S. Army, commanding.

"Señor Gen. D. Antonio Lopez de Santa Anna,
Commander-in-chief, La Encantada."

Hours rolled by, and no attack was made.
The rear columns of the enemy could be distinctly seen coming up. A demonstration on our
fight caused a section of Bragg's battery, supported by the 2d Kentucky foot, to be detached
to that point where they bivouacked for the
night. Toward evening the light troops of the
enemy engaged ours on the left, composed of
detachments of Arkansas and Kentucky cavalry,
dismounted, and a rifle battalion of the Indiana
Brigade, under Major Gorman, the whole commanded by Colonel Marshall. An occasional shell
was thrown by the enemy into this part of our line
with no effect. The skirmishing of the light troops
was continued until after dark, with trifling loss
on our part. Three pieces of Washington's battery, under Captain O'Brien (with whom served
Lieutenant Bryan, of the Topographical Corps,
supported by the 2d Indiana Regiment), were
detached to our left. In this position the troops
bivouacked without fires, resting on their arms.

General Taylor, with the Mississippi regiment and squadron of 2d Dragoons, repaired to
Saltillo. During the day, a large body of cavalry,

some fifteen hundred strong, under the command of General Minon, had thrown themselves into the valley by a pass through the mountains, and were visible in the rear of the city. In anticipation of victory, this strong force was thus posted to cut off and harass our retreat. The city was occupied by four companies of Illinois Volunteers, under Major Warren of the 1st Regiment; a field-work, commanding the approaches, was garrisoned by Captain Webster's company, with two twenty-four-pound howitzers. The train was defended by two companies of Mississippi Rifles, under Captain Rodgers, with one field-piece, under Captain Shover.

During the night of the 22d the enemy threw a large body of light troops on the mountain side, for the purpose of outflanking our left. At this point the action was renewed early on the morning of the 23d. Our riflemen, under Colonel Marshall, re-enforced by three companies of Illinois Volunteers, under Major Trail, handsomely maintained their position, and used their rifles with great effect. About 8 o'clock a heavy column moved up the road and threatened our center, but were driven back by the fire of Washington's battery. All attempts upon our right, from the nature of the ground, would have been time and labor thrown away. Santa Anna saw this, and determined, if possible, to gain and outflank our left, stationed on an extensive plain. For this purpose, large masses of both infantry and cavalry were collected in the ravines, under cover of the ridges. The 2d Indiana and 2d Illinois regiments formed the left of our line, the former supporting O'Brien's three pieces. Brigadier-general Lane had the immediate command at this point. To bring the artillery into more effective range, O'Brien was ordered to advance. His pieces were served with terrible effect against an overwhelming mass of the enemy. The firing at this point was very severe. The Mexican artillery poured in its grape and canister, to cover the advance of their forces. The 2d Indiana regiment broke in confusion, unable to withstand the galling fire, and left the artillery unprotected. Captain O'Brien, thus deserted, was forced to retire, leaving one of his pieces, at which every man and horse was either killed or wounded. All efforts to rally the flying regiment failed; a few, by the gallantry of Major Dix, Paymaster U. S. Army, were brought back, and with their colonel (Bowles), attached themselves to the Mississippi regiment, and did good service the remainder of the day.

The left of our line giving way, afforded the enemy an immense advantage, who, pushing forward their masses, forced our light troops on the mountain side to retire. Many of the latter were not rallied until they reached the depot at Buena Vista, where they afterward assisted in the defense of the train. The 2d Illinois regiment, to which had been attached a section of Sherman's battery, were driven before the advancing columns. The enemy continued pouring in their masses of infantry and cavalry; the base of the mountain seemed covered with men, and their bright arms glistened in the sun. Our rear was in danger; the tide of battle was decidedly against us; the fortunes of the day seemed cast upon a die, when, at this critical juncture, General Taylor arrived upon the field, and occupied a commanding position on the elevated plateau. His presence restored confidence. The Mississippi regiment, under the gallant Davis, was ordered to the left, and immediately engaged the masses which had turned our flank. They nobly sustained a fearful struggle against overwhelming odds, and added fresh laurels to those already gained. The 2d Kentucky, under Colonel M'Kee, with a section of artillery, under Captain Bragg, had been previously ordered to the support of our left. This command, with a portion of the 1st Illinois, under Colonel Hardin, were soon fiercely engaged in the fight, and partially recovered the lost ground. The batteries of Sherman and Bragg, stationed on the plateau, played with dreadful effect upon the advancing masses, and especially upon those who had gained our rear. The Mississippi regiment, fighting manfully, and sustaining, without flinching, more than their share of the fight, were re-enforced by the 3d Indiana, under Colonel Lane, and a piece of artillery under Lieutenant Kilburn. The struggle at this point was dreadful; repeated efforts were made, both by the cavalry and infantry, to force our line, but were signally repulsed with great loss. Our sheet anchor, the artillery, literally mowed down their masses; the precision and rapidity of their fire was the admiration of all.

The squadrons of regular cavalry, and Captain Pike's, of the Arkansas cavalry, were under the command of Brevet Lieutenant-colonel May. He was ordered to hold in check the masses which had gained our rear, in conjunction with the Kentucky and Arkansas cavalry, under Colonels Marshall and Yell. The enemy still, with the greatest pertinacity, continued the attack upon our left. Different sections and pieces, under Sherman, Bragg, O'Brien, Thomas, Reynolds, Kilburn, French, and Bryan, were extended along the front, and belched forth their incessant fire. The iron hail, directed with the greatest judgment and coolness, rent their ranks, staggered their masses, and the cannon's roar drowned the horrid yell of battle, and the shrieks of expiring hundreds. Short-lived was the enemy's shout of triumph at their temporary success; under our galling fire they gave way. Lieutenant Rucker, with his squadron of 1st Dragoons, was ordered to dash in among them; this he did in handsome style.

A large body of cavalry, who had gained our rear, threatened an attack upon our train at Buena Vista. Colonel May, with his command, with two pieces under Lieutenant Reynolds, was dispatched to strengthen that point. Before his arrival, the enemy had been gallantly met and repulsed by the Arkansas and Kentucky cavalry. They broke into two columns; one, sweeping by the ranch, received an effective fire from the fugitive forces, composed in part of Major Trail's and Gorman's command, who had been reorganized by the advice and exertions of Major Munroe, of the artillery; the other, gaining the base of the mountain, received a terrific fire from the pieces under Lieutenant Reynolds.

In the charge at Buena Vista, the gallant Colonel Yell fell, at the head of his regiment; and Adjutant Vaughn, of the Kentucky cavalry,

yielded up his life like a true soldier. Colonel May, with his command, and portions of the Arkansas and Indiana troops, kept in check the right of the enemy. Their masses, crowded into ravines, were played upon incessantly by our artillery; the havoc was dreadful. The position of that portion of the enemy who had gained our rear was extremely critical, and their capture appeared certain. Santa Anna saw the crisis, and, by conduct unbecoming a true soldier, which only tended to increase the dishonor and baseness of a character already conspicuous for both in history, dispatched a white flag to General Taylor, asking him "what he wanted." General Taylor immediately dispatched General Wool with a white flag to answer it, and ordered our firing to cease. The interview could not be effected, as the Mexicans continued to fire, thus adding unparalleled treachery to the other acts of barbarity for which they are celebrated. Santa Anna's object was effected; the greater portion of his cavalry regained their lines. This could have been prevented by a breach of the sanctity of the white flag; but, thank God, that blot remains alone with the enemy. A formidable force, during their retreat, received a severe fire of musketry: and Reynolds's artillery, beautifully served, dealt death and destruction among them.

During the day, the cavalry under General Miñon occupied the road between the battlefield and Saltillo, and threatened the city. They were fired upon from the redoubt in charge of Captain Webster, and moved off toward Buena Vista. Captain Shover moved forward with his piece, supported by a miscellaneous command of volunteers, fired several shots with great effect, and drove them into the ravines which led to the lower valley; they were accompanied in this pursuit by a piece of Webster's battery, under Lieutenant Donaldson, supported by Captain Wheeler, with his company of Illinois Volunteers. The enemy made one or two attempts to charge the pieces, but were driven back in confusion, and left the plain for the day.

In the mean time, the firing had nearly ceased upon the main field. It was but the prelude to the fierce and last struggle for the day—a struggle which tested the courage and firmness of our army, and rendered, if possible, more conspicuous the strength and dreadful efficiency of our artillery, and the skill and gallantry of its able commanders. Santa Anna, re-enforced by his cavalry, under cover of his artillery, with horse and foot charged our line. The shock was gallantly sustained by our small band of heroes. On they came in overwhelming masses, their reserve fresh and eager for the contest, their artillery pouring in a dreadful fire, the whole under the immediate eye of their chief. The 2d Kentucky, 1st Illinois, and O'Brien, with two pieces, stood the brunt of the attack. On they came; their deadly fire thinned our ranks; the infantry in support of O'Brien's piece were routed, and that gallant young officer was forced to retire, leaving his piece in the hands of the enemy.

Our batteries now stood conspicuous; such was the rapidity of their movements, that both officers and men seemed gifted with ubiquity; so dreadful was their fire, it could not be resisted. The enemy fell back in disorder. The gallant Hardin and M'Kee, with their regiments, charged the flying hosts with a degree of courage rarely equaled. The enemy, seeing the small force in pursuit, like magic turned upon them, and came up in myriads. For a short time the carnage was dreadful on both sides. We were a mere handful in opposition to their legions. Again our men were routed, and the day seemed lost without redemption. Brent and Whiting, of Washington's battery, covered the retreat of the remnants of these gallant regiments, who had so nobly borne the hottest of the fight.

General Taylor stood calm and unmoved upon the plateau—all eyes were turned upon him. The leaden messengers of death swept harmlessly by his person, while hundreds were passing to futurity. Bragg, with his battery, had arrived at the point of fearful struggle. Alone and unsupported was that battery and that brave old chief. Confident to the last of victory, he ordered his trusty captain to unlimber—to load with grape, and await the arrival of their masses until they nearly reached the muzzles of his pieces. On came the enemy, like legions of fiends, certain of victory. When almost within grasp of the battery, Bragg opened his fire. The first volley staggered them, the second opened streets through their ranks, and the third put them in full retreat, and saved the day. The Mississippi regiment and 3d Indiana supported the batteries on the plateau; the former arrived in time to throw in a galling fire, and add their might to the discomfiture of the enemy.

In this last conflict we sustained a great loss. Colonel Hardin, Colonel M'Kee, and Lieutenant-colonel Clay fell at the head of their regiments, sustaining a desperate conflict against an overwhelming force. Thrice during the day had our artillery turned the tide of battle; thrice had the masses of the enemy fallen before its terrible hail, and thus maintained the glory of the American arms. The battle had now raged for ten hours. No further attempt was made to force our lines, and our troops, weary and exhausted, sank on the battle-field, surrounded by the dead and dying, without a fire to cheer them and warm their benumbed limbs, to obtain that rest which was necessary to fit them for the conflict on the morrow. The wounded were removed to Saltillo, and every preparation was made to meet the enemy should the attack be renewed. Ere the sun rose they had fallen back upon Agua Nueva, leaving the field strewed with their dead and dying. Brigadier-general Marshall made a forced march from Rincanada, with a re-enforcement of Kentucky cavalry and a battery of heavy guns, under Captain Prentiss, 1st Artillery, but too late to participate in the engagement Our loss was very severe, two hundred and sixty-seven killed, four hundred and fifty-six wounded, and twenty-three missing. The enemy, at the least calculation, must have lost two thousand. Five hundred of their dead were left upon the field of battle. Twenty-eight of our officers were killed on the field, and forty-one were wounded.

Source: Henry, William Seaton. *Campaign Sketches of the War with Mexico.* New York: Harper & Brothers, 1847, pp. 311–322.

The Amphibious Assault and Siege against Veracruz, March 9–29, 1847

Account of the Landing and Siege

Ulysses S. Grant
Published 1885

On the night of March 9, 1847, Major General Winfield Scott executed the first amphibious landing in U.S. Army history, landing 10,000 troops at Veracruz, which offered little resistance. The weather—severe storms—throughout the next two weeks imperiled the continuation of the landings, particularly of artillery; all was in place before Veracruz by March 22, when Scott commenced bombardment of the city. His heavy mortars failing to bring surrender, Scott requested naval fire from Commodore Matthew C. Perry, commander of the invasion flotilla. This brought Veracruz to its knees within five days.

Characteristically of his magnificent memoir, Ulysses S. Grant provides a vivid picture of the action at Veracruz.

When General Scott assumed command of the army of invasion, I was in the division of General David Twiggs, in Taylor's command; but under the new orders my regiment was transferred to the division of General William Worth, in which I served to the close of the war. The troops withdrawn from Taylor to form part of the forces to operate against Veracruz, were assembled at the mouth of the Rio Grande preparatory to embarkation for their destination. I found General Worth a different man from any I had before served directly under. He was nervous, impatient and restless on the march, or when important or responsible duty confronted him. There was not the least reason for haste on the march, for it was known that it would take weeks to assemble shipping enough at the point of our embarkation to carry the army, but General Worth moved his division with a rapidity that would have been commendable had he been going to the relief of a beleaguered garrison. The length of the marches was regulated by the distances between places affording a supply of water for the troops, and these distances were sometimes long and sometimes short. General Worth on one occasion at least, after having made the full distance intended for the day, and after the troops were in camp and preparing their food, ordered tents struck and made the march that night which had been intended for the next day. Some commanders can move troops so as to get the maximum distance out of them without fatigue, while others can wear them out in a few days without accomplishing so much. General Worth belonged to this latter class. He enjoyed, however, a fine reputation for his fighting qualities, and thus attached his officers and men to him.

The army lay in camp upon the sand-beach in the neighborhood of the mouth of the Rio Grande for several weeks, awaiting the arrival of transports to carry it to its new field of operations. The transports were all sailing vessels. The passage was a tedious one, and many of the troops were on shipboard over thirty days from the embarkation at the mouth of the Rio Grande to the time of debarkation south of Veracruz. The trip was a comfortless one for officers and men. The transports used were built for carrying freight and possessed but limited accommodations for passengers, and the climate added to the discomfort of all.

The transports with troops were assembled in the harbor of Anton Lizardo, some sixteen miles south of Veracruz, as they arrived, and there awaited the remainder of the fleet, bringing artillery, ammunition and supplies of all kinds from the North. With the fleet there was a little steam propeller dispatch-boat—the first vessel of the kind I had ever seen, and probably the first of its kind ever seen by any one then with the army. At that day ocean steamers were

On March 9, 1847, General Scott led the amphibious landing of some 10,000 U.S. troops some three miles south of Veracruz in order to avoid the artillery fire from the city. *(Library of Congress)*

rare, and what there were were sidewheelers. This little vessel, going through the fleet so fast, so noiselessly and with its propeller under water out of view, attracted a great deal of attention. I recollect that Lieutenant Sidney Smith, of the 4th infantry, by whom I happened to be standing on the deck of a vessel when this propeller was passing, exclaimed, "Why, the thing looks as if it was propelled by the force of circumstances."

Finally on the 7th of March, 1847, the little army of ten or twelve thousand men, given Scott to invade a country with a population of seven or eight millions, a mountainous country affording the greatest possible natural advantages for defence, was all assembled and ready to commence the perilous task of landing from vessels lying in the open sea.

The debarkation took place inside of the little island of Sacrificios, some three miles south of Veracruz. The vessels could not get anywhere near shore, so that everything had to be landed in lighters or surf-boats; General Scott had provided these before leaving the North. The breakers were sometimes high, so that the landing was tedious. The men were got ashore rapidly, because they could wade when they came to shallow water; but the camp and garrison equipage, provisions, ammunition and all stores had to be protected from the salt water, and therefore their landing took several days. The Mexicans were very kind to us, however, and threw no obstacles in the way of our landing except an occasional shot from their nearest fort. During the debarkation one shot took off the head of Major Albertis. No other, I believe, reached anywhere near the same distance. On the 9th of March the troops were landed and the investment of Veracruz, from the Gulf of Mexico south of the city to the Gulf again on the north, was soon and easily effected. The landing of stores was continued until everything was got ashore.

Veracruz, at the time of which I write and up to 1880, was a walled city. The wall extended from the water's edge south of the town to the water again on the north. There were fortifications at intervals along the line and at the angles. In front of the city, and on an island half a mile out in the Gulf, stands San Juan de Ulloa, an enclosed fortification of large dimensions and great strength for that period. Against artillery of the present day the land forts and walls would prove elements of weakness rather than strength. After the invading army had established their camps out of range of the fire from the city, batteries were established, under cover of night, far to the front of the line where the troops lay. These batteries were intrenched and the approaches sufficiently protected. If a sortie had been made at any time by the Mexicans, the men serving the batteries could have been quickly reinforced without great exposure to the fire from the enemy's main line. No serious attempt was made to capture the batteries or to drive our troops away.

The siege continued with brisk firing on our side till the 27th of March, by which time a considerable breach had been made in the wall surrounding the city. Upon this General Morales, who was Governor of both the city and of San Juan de Ulloa, commenced a correspondence with General Scott looking to the surrender of the town, forts and garrison. On the 29th Veracruz and San Juan de Ulloa were occupied by Scott's army. About five thousand prisoners and four hundred pieces of artillery, besides large amounts of small arms and ammunition, fell into the hands of the victorious force. The casualties on our side during the siege amounted to sixty-four officers and men, killed and wounded.

Source: Grant, Ulysses S. *Personal Memoirs of U.S. Grant.* 1885. Reprint, New York: Da Capo Press, 1982, pp. 58–61.

THE BATTLE OF CERRO GORDO, APRIL 18, 1847

Account of the Battle
Anonymous
Published 1848

A veteran of the War of 1812, David E. Twiggs was colonel of the 2nd U.S. Dragoons at the start of the war and was promoted to brigadier general after the Battle of Resaca de la Palma. As commanding officer of the 2nd Division of Regulars, he participated in Winfield Scott's invasion. Cerro Gordo was one of the battles fought as Scott advanced on Mexico City. Twiggs was assigned to reduce the principal Mexican redoubt situated in the rocky defile that effectively blocked the national highway leading to Mexico City. The description of Twiggs's attack upon the Mexican fort that follows is from an eye-witness's account published in The Mexican War and Its Warriors *(1848).*

On the 18th, General Twiggs was ordered forward from the position he had already captured, against the fort which commanded the Sierra. Simultaneously an attack on the fortifications on the enemy's left was to be made by Generals Shields and Worth's divisions, who moved in separate columns, while General Pillow advanced against the strong forts and difficult ascents on the right of the enemy's position. The enemy, fully acquainted with General Scott's intended movement, had thrown large bodies of men into the various positions to be attacked. The most serious enterprise was that of Twiggs, who advanced against the main fort that commanded the Sierra. Nothing can be conceived more difficult than this undertaking. The steep and rough character of the ground, the constant fire of the enemy in front, and the cross fire of the forts and batteries which enfiladed our lines, made the duty assigned to General Twiggs one of surpassing difficulty.

Nothing prevented our men from being utterly destroyed but the steepness of the ascent under which they could shelter. But they sought no shelter, and onward rushed against a hailstorm of balls and musket-shot, led by the gallant Harney, whose noble bearing elicited the applause of the whole army. His conspicuous and stalwart frame at the head of his brigade, his long arm waving his men on to the charge, his sturdy voice ringing above the clash of arms and din of conflict, attracted the attention and admiration alike of the enemy and of our own men. On, on, he led the columns, whose front lines melted before the enemy's fire like snowflakes in a torrent, and stayed not their course until leaping over the rocky barriers, and bayoneting their gunners, they drove the enemy pellmell from the fort, delivering a deadly fire into their ranks, from their own guns, as they hastily retired. This was truly a gallant deed, worthy the Chevalier Bayard of our army, as the intrepid Hamey is well styled. General Scott, between whom and Colonel Harney there had existed some coolness, rode up to the colonel after this achievement, and remarked to him—"Colonel Harney, I cannot now adequately express my admiration of your gallant achievement, but at the proper time I shall take great pleasure in thanking you in proper terms." Harney, with the modesty of true valour, claimed the praise as due to his officers and men. Thus did the division of the gallant veteran, Twiggs, carry the main position of the enemy, and occupy the front which commanded the road. It was here the enemy received their heaviest loss, and their general, Vasquez, was killed. A little after, General Worth, having, by great exertions, passed the steep and craggy heights on the enemy's left, summoned a strong fort in the rear of the Sierra to surrender. This fort was manned by a large force under General Pinzon, a mulatto officer of considerable ability and courage, who, seeing the Sierra carried, thought it prudent to surrender, which he did with all his force. General Shields was not so fortunate in the battery which he attacked, and which was commanded by General La Vega. A heavy fire was opened on him, under which the fort was carried with some loss by the gallant Illi-

noisians, under Baker and Bennett, supported by the New Yorkers, under Burnett. Among those who fell under this fire was the gallant general, who received a grape-shot through his lungs, by which he was completely paralyzed, and thrown into a critical and dangerous state. On the enemy's right, General Pillow commenced the attack against the strong forts near the river. The Tennesseeans, under Haskell, led the column, and the other volunteer regiments followed. This column unexpectedly encountered a heavy fire from a masked battery, by which Haskell's regiment was nearly cut to pieces, and the other volunteer regiments were severely handled. General Pillow withdrew his men, and was preparing for another attack, when the operations at the other points having proved successful, the enemy concluded to surrender. Thus the victory was complete, and four generals, and about six thousand men, were taken prisoners by our army. One of their principal generals and a large number of other officers killed. The Mexican force on this occasion certainly exceeded our own.

According to the account of the captured officers, Santa Anna had in his lines at least eight thousand men, and without the intrenchments about six thousand, of which a third was cavalry. The army was composed of the best soldiers in Mexico. The infantry who had fought so bravely at Buena Vista, and all the regular artillerists of the republic, including several naval officers, were present. Some of the officers whom General Scott released at the capitulation of Veracruz without extorting the parole on account of their gallantry, were found among the killed and wounded. Of the latter was a gallant young officer named Halzinger, a German by birth, who excited the admiration of our army during the bombardment of Veracruz, by seizing a flag which had been cut down by our balls, and holding it in his right hand until a staff could be procured. He had been released by General Scott without a parole, and was found on the field of Cerro Gordo dangerously wounded. In addition to the loss of the enemy in killed and taken they lost about thirty pieces of brass cannon, mostly of large calibre, manufactured at the royal foundry of Seville. A large quantity of fixed ammunition, of a very superior quality, together with the private baggage and money-chest of Santa Anna, containing twenty thousand dollars, was also captured.

Source: Frost, J. *The Mexican War and Its Warriors.* New Haven, Conn., and Philadelphia: H. Mansfield, 1848, pp. 146–153.

Account of the Battle
Ulysses S. Grant
Published 1885

Grant gives a generous eyewitness account of Cerro Gordo in his memoirs.

Cerro Gordo is one of the higher spurs of the mountains some twelve to fifteen miles east of Jalapa, and Santa Anna had selected this point as the easiest to defend against an invading army. The road, said to have been built by Cortez, zigzags around the mountain-side and was defended at every turn by artillery. On either side were deep chasms or mountain walls. A direct attack along the road was an impossibility. A flank movement seemed equally impossible. After the arrival of the commanding-general upon the scene, reconnaissances were sent out to find, or to make, a road by which the rear of the enemy's works might be reached without a front attack. These reconnaissances were made under the supervision of Captain Robert E. Lee, assisted by Lieutenants P. G. T. Beauregard, Isaac I. Stevens, Z. B. Tower, G. W. Smith, George B. McClellan, and J. G. Foster, of the corps of engineers, all officers who attained rank and fame, on one side or the other, in the great conflict for the preservation of the unity of the nation. The reconnaissance was completed, and the labor of cutting out and making roads by the flank of the enemy was effected by the 17th of the month. This was accomplished without the knowledge of Santa Anna or his army, and over ground where he supposed it impossible. On the same day General Scott issued his order for the attack on the 18th.

The attack was made as ordered, and perhaps there was not a battle of the Mexican war, or of any other, where orders issued before an engagement were nearer being a correct report of what afterwards took place. Under the supervision of the engineers, roadways had been opened over chasms to the right where the walls were so steep that men could barely climb them. Animals could not. These had been opened under cover of night, without attracting the notice of the enemy. The engineers, who had directed the opening, led the way and the troops followed. Artillery was let down the steep slopes by hand, the men engaged attaching a strong rope to the rear axle and letting the guns down, a piece at a time, while the men at the ropes kept their ground on top, paying out gradually, while a few at the front directed the course of the piece. In like manner the guns were drawn by hand up the opposite slopes. In this way Scott's troops reached their assigned position in rear of most of the intrenchments of the enemy, unobserved. The attack was made, the Mexican reserves behind the works beat a hasty retreat, and those occupying them surrendered. On the left General Pillow's command made a formidable demonstration, which doubtless held a part of the enemy in his front and contributed to the victory. I am not pretending to give full details of all the battles fought, but of the portion that I saw. There were troops engaged on both sides at other points in which both sustained losses; but the battle was won as here narrated.

The surprise of the enemy was complete, the victory overwhelming; some three thousand prisoners fell into Scott's hands, also a large amount of ordnance and ordnance stores. The prisoners were paroled, the artillery parked and the small arms and ammunition destroyed. The battle of Buena Vista was probably very important to the success of General Scott at Cerro Gordo and in his entire campaign from Veracruz to the great plains reaching to the City of Mexico. The only army Santa Anna had to protect his capital and the mountain passes west of Veracruz, was the one he had with him confronting General Taylor. It is not likely that he would have gone as far north as Monterey to attack the United States troops when he knew his country was threatened with invasion further south. When Taylor moved to Saltillo and then advanced on to Buena Vista, Santa Anna crossed the desert confronting the invading army, hoping no doubt to crush it and get back in time to meet General Scott in the mountain passes west of Veracruz. His attack on Taylor was disastrous to the Mexican army, but, notwithstanding this, he marched his army to Cerro Gordo, a distance not much short of one thousand miles by the line he had to travel, in time to intrench himself well before Scott got there. If he had been successful at Buena Vista his troops would no doubt have made a more stubborn resistance at Cerro Gordo. Had the battle of Buena Vista not been fought Santa Anna would have had time to move leisurely to meet the invader further south and with an army not demoralized nor depleted by defeat.

Source: Grant, Ulysses S. *Personal Memoirs of U.S. Grant.* 1885. Reprint, New York: Da Capo Press, 1982, pp. 63–64.

THE BATTLES OF CONTRERAS AND CHURUBUSCO, AUGUST 19–20, 1847

"Dispatch communicating Scott's official report of the Battles of Contreras and Churubusco"
Major General Winfield Scott
August 28, 1847

After defeating Santa Anna at the Battle of Cerro Gordo, Winfield Scott advanced to Jalapa and then to Puebla, which surrendered without resistance on May 15, 1847. He halted here, mainly to give many

of his soldiers an opportunity to recuperate from the yellow fever that was endemic to the region. As he prepared to march out of Puebla to attack Mexico City, he learned that the State Department's Nicholas P. Trist had begun peace negotiations with Santa Anna. Scott decided to apply maximum pressure to Santa Anna by quickly capturing Mexico City and so committed his entire army to the advance, thereby leaving his long lines of communication undefended. It was a calculated gamble.

Departing Puebla on August 7, Scott's army arrived at Ayolta on August 10. The road from this village to Mexico City, 14 miles away, was well covered by fortified positions. Scott sent Robert E. Lee, his chief engineer, to find an alternate route to the Mexican capital. Lee found a way through Pedregal, a wide lava bed, to the village of Contreras. Because it was generally deemed impassable, Pedregal was undefended; however, the force Scott sent under Brevet Major General Gideon J. Pillow, while it reached Contreras, was pushed out of the village on August 19. Scott sent reinforcements, which mounted a fresh attack at dawn on August 20, routing the Mexican defenders. Seven hundred Mexicans died in the Battle of Contreras, and 800 were captured, including four generals. Scott lost 60 killed or wounded.

No sooner was this battle over than Scott led a pursuit of the retreating Mexicans, who assumed a defensive stand at Churubusco, using a stone-walled church and convent as fortification. The battle was perhaps the hottest of the war, and Scott made slow headway against the defenders. In the end, it was Mexican ammunition, not the will to fight, that brought them defeat. The Battle of Churubusco produced nearly 4,000 Mexican casualties, and Scott's losses, though much less, were nevertheless heavy: 155 killed, 876 wounded.

Scott sent this report to William L. Marcy, the secretary of war, in Washington, D.C.

Headquarters of the army,
Tacubaya, at the gates of Mexico, August 28, 1847.

Sir:—My report No. 31, commenced in the night of the 19th instant, closed the operations of the army with that day.

This lithograph depicts the Battle of Churubusco on August 20, 1847. Located three miles from Mexico City, Churubusco was a convent that the Mexicans turned into a fortress, but after a deadly battle it fell to U.S. troops. *(Library of Congress)*

The morning of the 20th opened with one of [a] series of unsurpassed achievements, all in view of the capital, and to which I shall give the general name—battle of Mexico.

In the night of the 19th, Brigadier Generals [James] Shields, P. F Smith, and [John] Cadwallader, and Colonel Riley, with their brigades, and the 15th regiment, under Colonel Morgan, detached from Brigadier General [Franklin] Pierce, found themselves in and about the important position—the village, hamlet, or hacienda, called, indifferently, Contreras, Ansalda, San Geronimo, half a mile nearer to the city than the enemy's entrenched camp, on the same road, towards the factory of Magdalena.

That camp had been, unexpectedly, our formidable point of attack the afternoon before, and we had now to take it, without the aid of cavalry or artillery, or to throw back our advanced corps upon the road from San Augus-

tin to the city, and thence force a passage through San Antonio.

Accordingly, to meet contingencies, Major General [William J.] Worth was ordered to leave, early in the morning of the 20th, one of his brigades to mask San Antonio, and to march, with the other, six miles, via San Augustin, upon Contreras. A like destination was given to Major General [John A.] Quitman and his remaining brigade in San Augustin—replacing, for the moment, the garrison of that important depot with Harney's brigade of cavalry, as horse could not pass over the intervening rocks, &c. to reach the field.

A diversion for an earlier hour (daylight) had been arranged for the night before, according to the suggestion of Brigadier General Smith, received through the engineer, Captain [Robert E.] Lee, who conveyed my orders to our troops remaining on the ground opposite the enemy's centre—the point for the diversion or a real attack, as circumstances might allow.

Guided by Captain Lee, it proved the latter, under the command of Colonel Ransom, of the 9th, having with him that regiment and some companies of three others—the 3d, 12th, and rifles.

Shields, the senior officer at the hamlet, having arrived in the night, after Smith had arranged with Cadwallader and Riley the plan of attack for the morning, delicately waived interference; but reserved to himself the double task of holding the hamlet with his two regiments (South Carolina and New York volunteers) against ten times his numbers on the side of the city, including the slopes to his left, and, in case the camp in his rear should be carried, to face about and cut off the flying enemy.

At 3 o'clock [A.M.] the great movement commenced on the rear of the enemy's camp, Riley leading, followed successively by Cadwallader's and Smith's brigades, the latter temporarily under the orders of Major Dimick, of the 1st artillery—the whole force being commanded by Smith, the senior in the general attack, and whose arrangements, skill, and gallantry always challenge the highest admiration.

The march was rendered tedious by the darkness, rain, and mud; but about sunrise, Riley, conducted by Lieut. Tower, engineer, had reached an elevation behind the enemy, whence he precipitated his columns; stormed the entrenchments; planted his several colors upon them, and carried the work—all in seventeen minutes.

Conducted by Lieut. Beauregard, engineer, and Lieutenant Brooks, of [Brigadier General David E.] Twigg's staff—both of whom, like Lieut. Tower, had in the night, twice reconnoitered the ground—Cadwallader brought up to the general assault two of his regiments—the voltigeurs and the 11th; and at the appointed time, Col. Ransom, with his temporary brigade, conducted by Captain Lee, engineer, not only made the movement to divert and distract the enemy, but, after crossing the deep ravine in his front, advanced, and poured into the works and

upon the fugitives many volleys from his destructive musketry.

In the mean time Smith's own brigade, under the temporary command of Major Dimick, following the movements of Riley and Cadwallader, discovered opposite to and outside of the works, a long line of Mexican cavalry, drawn up as a support. Dimick, having at the head of the brigade the company of sappers and miners, under Lieut. Smith, engineer, who had conducted the march, was ordered by Brigadier General Smith to form line faced to the enemy, and in a charge against a flank, routed the cavalry.

Shields too, by the wise disposition of his brigade and gallant activity, contributed much to the general results. He held masses of cavalry and infantry, supported by artillery, in check below him, and captured hundreds, with one General (Mendoza) of those who fled from above.

I doubt whether a more brilliant or decisive victory—taking into view ground, artificial defences, batteries, and the extreme disparity of numbers—without cavalry or artillery on our side—is to be found on record. Including all our corps directed against the entrenched camp, with Shield's brigade at the hamlet, we positively did not number over 4500 rank and file; and we knew by sight, and since more certainly by many captured documents and letters, that the enemy had actually engaged on the spot 7000 men, with at least 12,000 more hovering within sight and striking distance—both on the 19th and 20th. All not killed or captured, now fled with precipitation.

Thus was the great victory of Contreras achieved: one road to the capital opened; 700 of the enemy killed; 813 prisoners, including, among 88 officers, 4 generals; besides many colors and standards; 22 pieces of brass ordnance—half of large caliber; thousands of small arms and accoutrements; an immense quantity of shot, shells, powder, and cartridges, 700 pack mules, many horses, &c.—all in our hands.

It is highly gratifying to find that, by skillful arrangement and rapidity of execution, our loss in killed and wounded, did not exceed, on the spot, 60; among the former the brave Captain

Charles Hanson, of the 7th infantry—not more distinguished for gallantry than for modesty, morals, and piety. Lieut. J. P. Johnston, 1st artillery, serving with Magruder's battery, a young officer of the highest promise, was killed the evening before.

One of the most pleasing incidents of the victory is the recapture, in the works, by Captain Drum, 4th artillery, under Major Gardner, of the two brass six pounders, taken from another company of the same regiment, though without the loss of honor, at the glorious battle of Buena Vista—about which guns the whole regiment had mourned for so many long months! Coming up, a little later, I had the happiness to join in the protracted cheers of the gallant 4th on the joyous event; and, indeed, the whole army sympathizes in its just pride and exultation.

The battle being won before the advancing brigades of Worth's and Quitman's divisions were in sight, both were ordered back to their late positions—Worth to attack San Antonio in front with his whole force, a soon as approached in the rear by Pillow's and Twiggs's divisions, moving from Contreras through San Angel and Coyoacan. By carrying San Antonio we knew that we should open another—a shorter and better road to the capital for our siege and other trains.

Accordingly, the two advanced divisions and Shield's brigade marched from Contreras, under the immediate orders of Major Gen. Pillow, who was now joined by the gallant Brig. Gen. Pierce, of his division, personally thrown out of activity late in the evening before by a severe hurt received from the fall of his horse.

After giving necessary orders, on the field, in the midst of prisoners and trophies, and sending instructions to [Brigadier General William S.] Harney's brigade of cavalry, left at San Augustine to join me, I personally followed Pillow's movement.

Arriving at Contreras, two miles by a cross road, from the rear of San Antonio, I first detached Captain Lee, engineer, with [Captain Philip] Kearney's troop, (1st dragoons,) supported by the rifle regiment under Major Lor-

ing, to reconnoitre that strong point; and next despatched Major General Pillow, with one of his brigades, (Cadwallader's) to make the attack upon it, in concert with Major General Worth, on the opposite side.

At the same time, by another road to the left, Lieutenant Stevens, of the engineers, supported by Lieutenant G. W. Smith's company of sappers and miners, of the same corps, was to reconnoitre the strongly fortified church or convent of San Pablo, in the hamlet of Churubusco—one mile off.—Twiggs, with one of his brigades (Smith's—less the rifles) and Captain Taylor's field battery, were ordered to follow and to attack the convent. Major Smith, senior engineer, was despatched to concert with Twiggs the mode and means of attack, and Twiggs's other brigade (Riley's) I soon ordered up to support him.

Next (but all in ten minutes) I sent Pierce (just able to keep the saddle) with his brigade (Pillow's division) conducted by Captain Lee, engineer, by a third road, a little farther to our left, to attack the enemy's right and rear, in order to favor the movement upon the convent, and cut off the retreat towards the capital. And, finally, Shields, senior brigadier to Pierce, with the New York and South Carolina volunteers, (Quitman's division,) was ordered to follow Pierce, closely, and to take the command of our left wing. All these movements were made with the utmost alacrity by our gallant troops and commanders.

Finding myself at Coyoacan, from which so many roads conveniently branched, without escort or reserve, I had to advance, for safety, close upon Twiggs's rear. The battle now raged from the right to the left of our whole line.

Learning, on the return of Captain Lee, that Shields, in rear of Churubusco, was hard pressed, and in danger of being outflanked, if not overwhelmed, by greatly superior numbers, I immediately sent, under Major [Edwin V.] Sumner, 2d dragoons, the rifles (Twiggs' reserve) and Capt. [Henry Hopkins] Sibley's troop, 2d dragoons, then at hand, to support our left, guided by the same engineer.

About an hour earlier, Worth had, by skillful and daring movements upon the front and right, turned and forced San Antonio—its garrison, no doubt, much shaken by our decisive victory at Contreras.

His second brigade (Colonel Clarke's) conducted by Captain Mason, engineer, assisted by Lieutenant Hardcastle, topographical engineer, turned the right, and by a wide sweep came out upon the high road to the capital. At this point the heavy garrison (3,000 men) in retreat was, by Clarke, cut in the centre, one portion, the rear, driven upon Dolores, off to the right; and the other upon Churubusco, in the direct line of our operations. The first brigade, (Colonel Garland's) same division, consisting of the 2d artillery, under Major Galt, the 3d artillery, under Lieutenant Colonel Belton, and the 4th infantry, commanded by Major [Robert E.] Lee [who had been promoted from captain], with Lieutenant Colonel Duncan's field battery (temporarily) followed in pursuit through the town, taking one general prisoner, the abandoned guns, (five pieces,) much ammunition, and other public property.

The forcing of San Antonio was the second brilliant event of the day.

Worth's division being soon reunited in hot pursuit, he was joined by Maj. Gen. Pillow, who, marching from Coyoacan and discovering that San Antonio had been carried, immediately turned to the left, according to my instructions, and though much impeded by ditches and swamps, hastened to the attack of Churubusco.

The hamlet of scattered houses, bearing this name, presented, besides the fortified convent, a strong field-work (tête du pont [bridgehead]) with regular bastions and curtains, at the head of a bridge over which the road passes from San Antonio to the capital.

The whole remaining forces of Mexico—some 27,000 men—cavalry, artillery, and infantry, collected from every quarter—were now in, on the flanks or within supporting distance of, those works, and seemed resolved to make a last and desperate stand; for if beaten here, the feebler defences at the gates of the city—four miles off—could not, as was well known to both parties, delay the victors an hour.—The capital of an ancient empire, now of a great republic; or an early peace, the assailants were resolved to win. Not an American—and we had less than a third of the enemy's numbers—had a doubt as to the result.

The fortified church or convent, hotly pressed by Twiggs, had already held out about an hour, when Worth and Pillow—the latter having with him only Cadwallader's brigade—began to manoeuvre closely upon the tête du pont, with the convent at half gun-shot, to their left. Garland's brigade, (Worth's division,) to which had been added the light battalion under Lieut. Col. Smith, continued to advance in front, and under the fire of a long line of infantry, off on the left of the bridge; and Clarke, of the same division, directed his brigade along the road or close by its side. Two of Pillow's and Cadwallader's regiments, the 11th and 14th, supported and participated in this direct movement: the other (the voltigeurs) was left in reserve. Most of these corps—particularly Clarke's brigade—advancing perpendicularly, were made to suffer much by the fire of the tête du pont, and they would have suffered greatly more by flank attacks from the convent, but for the pressure of Twiggs on the other side of that work.

This well combined and daring movement at length reached the principal point of attack, and the formidable tête du pont was, at once, assaulted and carried by the bayonet. Its deep wet ditch was first gallantly crossed by the 8th and 5th infantry, commanded, respectively, by Maj. Waite and Lieut. Colonel Scott—followed closely by the 6th infantry (same brigade) which had been so much exposed in the road—the 11th regiment, under Lieut. Col. Graham, and the 14th, commanded by Col. Trousdale, both of Cadwallader's brigade, Pillow's division. About the same time, the enemy, in front of Garland, after a hot conflict of an hour and a half, gave way, in retreat towards the capital.

The immediate results of this third signal triumph of the day were: three field-pieces, 192 prisoners, much ammunition and two colors, taken in the tête du pont.

Lieut. J. F. Irons, 1st artillery, aid-de-camp to Brigadier Gen. Cadwallader, a young officer of great merit and conspicuous in battle on several previous occasions, received in front of the work, a mortal wound. (Since dead.)

As the concurrent attack upon the convent favored, physically and morally, the assault upon the tête du pont, so, reciprocally, no doubt the fall of the latter contributed to the capture of the former. The two works were only some 450 yards apart; and as soon as we were in possession of the tête du pont, a captured four-pounder was turned and fired—first by Captain Larkin Smith, and next by Lieutenant Snelling, both of the eighth infantry—several times upon the convent. In the same brief interval, Lieutenant Colonel Duncan, (also of Worth's division,) gallantly brought two of his guns to bear, at a short range, from the San Antonio road, upon the principal face of the work, and on the tower of the church, which, in the obstinate contest, had been often refilled with some of the best sharp-shooters of the enemy.

Finally, twenty minutes after the tête du pont had been carried by Worth and Pillow, and at the end of a desperate conflict of two hours and a half, the church, or convent—the citadel of the strong line of defence along the rivulet of Churubusco—yielded to Twiggs' division, and threw out, on all sides, signals of surrender. The white flags, however, were not exhibited until the moment when the 3d infantry, under Captain Alexander, had cleared the way by fire and bayonet, and had entered the work. Captain J. M. Smith and Lieutenant O. L. Shephered, both of that regiment, with their companies, had the glory of leading the assault. The former received the surrender, and Captain Alexander instantly hung out, from the balcony, the colors of the gallant 3d. Major Dimick, with a part of the 1st artillery, serving as infantry, entered nearly abreast with leading troops.

Captain Taylor's field battery, attached to Twiggs' division, opened its effective fire, at an early moment, upon the out works of the convent and the tower of its churches. Exposed to the severest fire of the enemy, the captain, his officers and men, won universal admiration; but at length much disabled, in men and horses, the battery was, by superior orders, withdrawn from the action thirty minutes before the surrender of the convent.

Those corps, excepting Taylor's battery, belonging to the brigade of Brig. Gen. Smith, who closely directed the whole attack in front, with his habitual coolness and ability; while Riley's brigade—the 2d and 7th infantry, under Capt. T. Morris and Lieut. Col. Plympton, respectively—vigorously engaged the right of the work and part of its rear. At the moment, the rifles, belonging to Smith's, were detached in support of Brig. Gen. Shields' on our extreme left; and the 4th artillery, acting as infantry, under Maj. Gardner, belonging to Riley's brigade, had been left in charge of the camp, trophies, &c., at Contreras. Twiggs' division, at Churubusco, had thus been deprived of the services of two of its most gallant and effective regiments.

The immediate results of this victory were—the capture of 7 field pieces, some ammunition; one color, three generals, and 1,261 prisoners, including other officers.

Captains E. A. Capron and M. J. Burke, and Lieut. S. Hoffman, all of the 1st artillery, and Capt. J. W. Anderson and Lieut. Thomas Easley, both of the 2d infantry—five officers of great merit—fell gallantly before this work.

The capture of the enemy's citadel was the fourth great achievement of our arms in the same day.

It has been stated that, some two hours and a half before, Pierce's, followed closely by the volunteer brigade, both under the command of Brigadier General Shields—had been detached to our left to turn the enemy's works;—to prevent the escape of the garrisons, and to oppose the extension of the enemy's numerous corps, from the rear, upon and around our left.

Considering the inferior numbers of the two brigades, the objects of the movements were difficult to accomplish. Hence the reinforcements (the rifles, &c.,) sent forward a little later.

In a winding march of a mile around to the right, this temporary division found itself on the edge of an open wet meadow, near the road from San Antonio to the capital, and in the presence of some 4,000 of the enemy's infantry, a little in rear of Churubusco, on that road. Establishing the right at a strong building, Shields extended his left, parallel to the road, to outflank the enemy towards the capital. But the enemy extending his right, supported by 3,000 cavalry, more rapidly (being favored by their ground) in the same direction, Shields concentrated the division about a hamlet, and determined to attack in front. The battle was long, hot, and varied; but, ultimately, success crowned the zeal and gallantry of our troops, ably directed by their distinguished commander, Brig. Gen. Shields. The 9th, 12th, and 15th regiments, under Col. Ransom, Captain Wood, and Col. Morgan, respectively, of Pearce's brigade, (Pillow's division,) and the New York and South Carolina volunteers, under Cols. Burnett and Butler, respectively, of Shields' own brigade, (Quitman's division,) together with the mountain howitzer battery, now under Lieut. Reno, of the ordnance corps, all shared in the glory of this action—our fifth victory in the same day.

Brigadier General Pierce, from the hurt of the evening before—under pain and exhaustion—fainted in the action. Several other changes in command occurred on this field. Thus Colonel Morgan being severely wounded, the command of the 15th infantry devolved on Lieutenant Colonel Howard; Colonel Burnett receiving a like wound, the command of the New York volunteers fell to Lieutenant Colonel Baxter; and on the fall of the lamented Colonel P. M. Butler—earlier badly wounded, but continuing to lead nobly in the hottest of the battle—the command of the South Carolina volunteers devolved—first on Lieut. Col. Dickenson, who being severely wounded, (as before the siege of Veracruz) the regiment ultimately fell under the orders of Major Gladden.

Lieuts. David Adams and W. R. Williams of the same corps; Capt. Augustus Quarles, and Lieut. J. B. Goodman of the 15th, and Lieut. E. Chandler, New York volunteers—all gallant officers, nobly fell in the same action.

Shields took 380 prisoners, including officers; and it cannot be doubted that the rage of the conflict between him and the enemy, just in the rear of the tête du pont and the convent, had some influence on the surrender of those formidable defences.

As soon as the tête du pont was carried, the greater part of Worth's and Pillow's forces passed that bridge in rapid pursuit of the flying enemy. These distinguished generals, coming up with Brigadier General Shields, now also victorious, the three continued to press upon the fugitives to within a mile and a half of the capital. Here, Col. Harney, with a small part of his brigade of cavalry, rapidly passed to the front, and charged the enemy up the nearest gate.

The cavalry charge was headed by Captain Kearney, of the 1st dragoons, having in squadron, with his own troop, that of Captain McReynolds of the 3d—making the usual escort to general headquarters; but being early in the day detached for general service, was now under Col. Harney's orders. The gallant captain not hearing the recall, that had been sounded, dashed up to the San Antonio gate, sabreing, in his way all that resisted. Of the seven officers of the squadron, Kearney lost his left arm; McReynolds and Lieut. Lorimer Graham were both severely wounded, Lieut. R. S. Ewell, who succeeded to the command of the escort, had two horses killed under him. Major F. D. Mills, of the 15th infantry, a volunteer in this charge, was killed at the gate.

So terminated the series of events which I have but feebly presented. My thanks were but freely poured out on the different fields—to the abilities and science of generals and other officers—to the gallantry and prowess of all—the rank and file included. But a reward infinitely higher—the applause of a grateful country and government—will, I cannot doubt, be accorded, in due time, to so much merit, of every sort, displayed by this glorious army, which has now overcome all difficulties—distance, climate, ground, fortifications, numbers.

It has in a single day, in many battles, as often defeated 32,000 men; made about 3,000 prisoners, including eight generals (two of them ex-presidents) and 205 other officers; killed or wounded 4,000 of all ranks—besides entire corps dispersed and dissolved; captured 37 pieces of ordnance—more than trebling our siege train and field batteries—with a large number of small arms, a full supply of ammunition of every kind, &c., &c.

These great results have overwhelmed the enemy.

Our loss amounts to 1,053—killed 139, including 16 officers: wounded, 876, with 60 officers. The greater number of the dead and disabled were of the highest worth. Those under treatment, thanks to our very able medical officers, are generally doing well.

I regret having been obliged, on the 20th, to leave Major General Quitman, an able commander, with a part of his division—the fine 2d Pennsylvania volunteers and the veteran detachment of U. States marines—at our important depot, San Augustin. It was there that I had placed our sick and wounded; the siege, supply, and baggage trains. If these had been lost, the army would have been driven almost to despair; and considering the enemy's very great excess of numbers, and the many approaches to the depot, it might well have become emphatically the post of honor.

After so many victories, we might, with but little additional loss, have occupied the capital the same evening. But Mr. Trist, commissioner, &c., as well as myself, had been admonished by the best friends of peace—intelligent neutrals and some American residents—against precipitation; lest, by wantonly driving away the government and others—dishonored—we might scatter the elements of peace, excite a spirit of national desperation, and thus, indefinitely postpone the hope of accommodation. Deeply impressed with this danger, and remembering our mission—to conquer a peace—the army very cheerfully sacrificed to patriotism—to the great wish and want of our country—the éclat that would have followed an entrance—sword in hand—into a great capital.—Willing to have something to this republic—of no immediate value to us—on which to rest her pride, and to recover temper—I halted our victorious corps at the gates of the city, (at least for a time,) and have them now cantoned in the neighboring villages, where they are still sheltered and supplied with all necessaries. . . .

I have the honor to be, sir, with high respect, your most obedient servant,

WINFIELD SCOTT.

Source: Documents of the U.S.-Mexican War. "Major-General Winfield Scott, near Mexico City, to William L. Marcy, Secretary of War, at Washington, D.C. Dispatch communicating Scott's official report of the Battles of Contreras and Churubusco." Available online. URL: http://www.dmwv.org/mexwar/documents/candc.htm. Accessed on February 5, 2010.

THE BATTLE OF CHAPULTEPEC, SEPTEMBER 13, 1847

Description of Chapultepec
Lieutenant Sutten, 15th U.S. Infantry
Published 1849

By the time he reached Chapultepec Castle, a hilltop fortress defending the approach to Mexico City, Winfield Scott had about 8,000 combat ready troops, whereas Santa Anna commanded a defensive force of at least 15,000. An aggressive officer, Scott was both determined and methodical in his campaign against Mexico City. On September 8, 1847, he seized El Molino del Rey, a cannon foundry just west of Chapultepec. He began the assault on Chapultepec on September 13 by unleashing an artillery barrage followed by a three-pronged attack over the approaches to the hilltop fortress. His men were met with heavy fire from the castle but nevertheless overran it by 9:30 in the morning.

In the following excerpt from an account published in The Mexican War by Edward D. Mansfield, one of Scott's infantry officers, a Lieutenant Sutten, describes Chapultepec.

The Castle is about ten feet high, and the whole structure, including the wings, bastions, parapets, redoubts, and batteries, is very strongly built, and of the most splendid architecture. A splendid dome decorates the top, rising in great majesty about twenty feet above the whole truly grand and magnificent pile, and near which is the front centre, supported by a stone arch, upon which is painted the coat-of-arms of the republic, where once floated the tri-colored banner, but is now decorated by the glorious stars and stripes of our own happy land. Two very strongly-built atone walls surround the whole, and at the west end, where we stormed the works, the outer walls are some ten feet apart, and twelve or fifteen feet high, over which we charged by the help of fascines. It was defended by heavy artillery, manned by the most learned and skilful gunners of their army, including some French artillerists of distinction. The infantry force consisted of the officers and students of the institution, and the national guards, and chosen men of war of the republic—the whole under the command of General Bravo, whom we made prisoner. The whole hill is spotted with forts and outposts, and stone and mud walls, which were filled with their picket or castle guard. A huge high stone-wall extends around the whole frowning craggy mount, and another along the southeast base, midway from the former and the castle. A well-paved road leads up in a triangular form to the main gate, entering the south terre-plein; and the whole works are ingeniously and beautifully ornamented with Spanish fastidiousness and skill.

Source: Mansfield, Edward D. The Mexican War: History of Its Origin and a Detailed Account of the Victo-

ries Which Terminated in the Surrender of the Capital. New York: A. S. Barnes, 1849, p. 294.

Eyewitness View of the Assault on Chapultepec
Anonymous Officer in Major General John A. Quitman's Corps
Published 1849

The following account of the assault was published in Edward D. Mansfield's The Mexican War *(1849).*

After about an hour's hard firing, the enemy's fire began to slacken, and the word was given to charge. We rushed forward, and in three minutes we carried the first battery. The rifles entered the battery with the storming party, which was commanded by one of its captains. We followed the fugitives close up to the aqueduct, and, turning to the left, clambered up the steep path to the castle. The enemy were running down in crowds, and the slaughter was tremendous in the road and orchard. Our men were infuriated by the conduct of the Mexicans at [the Battle of] Molino del Rey [September 8], and took but few prisoners. The castle was completely torn to pieces; nearly every part was riddled by our shot, while the pavements and fortifications were completely torn up by the shells. In it were crowds of prisoners of every rank and color; among whom were fifty general officers, and about a hundred cadets of the Mexican military academy. The latter were pretty little fellows, from ten to sixteen years of age. Several of them were killed fighting like demons, and indeed they showed an example of courage worthy of imitation by some of their superiors in rank.

Source: Mansfield, Edward D. *The Mexican War: History of Its Origin and a Detailed Account of the Victories Which Terminated in the Surrender of the Capital.* New York: A. S. Barnes, 1849, pp. 298–299.

THE BATTLE OF MEXICO CITY, SEPTEMBER 13–14, 1847

Account of the Battle

Ulysses S. Grant
Published 1885

The fall of Chapultepec prompted most of the Mexican army defending Mexico City from within the capital to withdraw by night, so that when the 1st and 4th Divisions, under William J. Worth and John A. Quitman, respectively, cautiously entered the city, they found it undefended. The formal honor of entering the city to accept its surrender was accorded to Quitman's Division, but it was Worth who personally hauled down the Mexican flag flying over the National Palace, then turned to a U.S. Marine, who hoisted the Stars and Stripes. The formal surrender took place at the Zócalo plaza in front of the National Palace.

There were incidents. Some Mexican soldiers shot at the American soldiers from rooftops, but the sniper fire was suppressed by the time General Scott marched into the city. Ulysses S. Grant described the action in his memoirs.

The City of Mexico is supplied with water by two aqueducts, resting on strong stone arches. One of these aqueducts draws its supply of water from a mountain stream coming into it at or near Molino del Rey, and runs north close to the west base of Chapultepec; thence along the centre of a wide road, until it reaches the road running east into the city by the Garita San Cosme; from which point the aqueduct and road both run east to the city. The second aqueduct starts from the east base of Chapultepec, where it is fed by a spring, and runs north-east to the city. This aqueduct, like the other, runs in the middle of a broad road-way, thus leaving a space on each side. The arches supporting the aqueduct afforded protection for advancing troops as well as to those engaged defensively. At points on the San Cosme road parapets were thrown across, with an embrasure for a single piece of artillery in each. At the point where both road and aqueduct turn at right angles from north to east, there was not only one of these parapets supplied by one gun and infantry supports, but the houses to the north of the San Cosme road, facing south and commanding a view of the road back to Chapultepec, were covered with infantry, protected by parapets made of sandbags. The roads leading to garitas (the gates) San Cosme and Belen, by which these aqueducts enter the city, were strongly intrenched. Deep, wide ditches, filled with water, lined the sides of both roads. Such were the defences of the City of Mexico in September, 1847, on the routes over which General Scott entered. . . .

General Quitman, a volunteer from the State of Mississippi, who stood well with the army both as a soldier and as a man, commanded the column acting against Belen. General Worth commanded the column against San Cosme. When Chapultepec fell the advance commenced along the two aqueduct roads. I was on the road to San Cosme, and witnessed most that took place on that route. When opposition was encountered our troops sheltered themselves by keeping under the arches supporting the aqueduct, advancing an arch at a time. We encountered no serious obstruction until within gun-shot of the point where the road we were on intersects that running east to the city, the point where the aqueduct turns at a right angle. I have described the defences of this position before. There were but three commissioned officers besides myself, that I can now call to mind, with the advance when the above position was reached. One of these officers was a Lieutenant Semmes, of the Marine Corps. I think Captain Gore, and Lieutenant Judah, of the 4th infantry, were the others. Our progress was stopped for the time by the single piece of artillery at the angle of the roads and the infantry occupying the house-tops back from it.

West of the road from where we were, stood a house occupying the south-west angle made by

On September 14, 1847, General Winfield Scott led his troops on a triumphal entry into Mexico City to accept the surrender of the Mexicans and raise the U.S. flag in the Zócalo, the grand plaza in the center of the city. *(Library of Congress)*

the San Cosme road and the road we were moving upon. A stone wall ran from the house along each of these roads for a considerable distance and thence back until it joined, enclosing quite a yard about the house. I watched my opportunity and skipped across the road and behind the south wall. Proceeding cautiously to the west corner of the enclosure, I peeped around and seeing nobody, continued, still cautiously, until the road running east and west was reached. I then returned to the troops, and called for volunteers. All that were close to me, or that heard me, about a dozen, offered their services. Commanding them to carry their arms at a trail, I watched our opportunity and got them across the road and under cover of the wall beyond, before the enemy had a shot at us. Our men under cover of the arches kept a close watch on the intrenchments that crossed our path and the house-tops

beyond, and whenever a head showed itself above the parapets they would fire at it. Our crossing was thus made practicable without loss.

When we reached a safe position I instructed my little command again to carry their arms at a trail, not to fire at the enemy until they were ordered, and to move very cautiously following me until the San Cosme road was reached; we would then be on the flank of the men serving the gun on the road, and with no obstruction between us and them. When we reached the south-west corner of the enclosure before described, I saw some United States troops pushing north through a shallow ditch near by, who had come up since my reconnaissance. This was the company of Captain Horace Brooks, of the artillery, acting as infantry. I explained to Brooks briefly what I had discovered and what I was about to do. He said, as I knew the ground and he did not, I might go on and he would follow. As soon as we got on the road leading to the city the troops serving the gun on the parapet retreated, and those on the house-tops near by followed; our men went after them in such close pursuit—the troops we had left under the arches joining—that a second line across the road, about half-way between the first and the garita, was carried. No reinforcements had yet come up except Brooks's company, and the position we had taken was too advanced to be held by so small a force. It was given up, but retaken later in the day, with some loss.

Worth's command gradually advanced to the front now open to it. Later in the day in reconnoitring I found a church off to the south of the road, which looked to me as if the belfry would command the ground back of the garita San Cosme. I got an officer of the voltigeurs, with a mountain howitzer and men to work it, to go with me. The road being in possession of the enemy, we had to take the field to the south to reach the church. This took us over several ditches breast deep in water and grown up with water plants. These ditches, however, were not over eight or ten feet in width. The howitzer was taken to pieces and carried by the men to its destination. When I knocked for admission a priest came to the door who, while extremely polite, declined to admit us. With the little Spanish then at my command, I explained to him that he might save property by opening the door, and he certainly would save himself from becoming a prisoner, for a time at least; and besides, I intended to go in whether he consented or not. He began to see his duty in the same light that I did, and opened the door, though he did not look as if it gave him special pleasure to do so. The gun was carried to the belfry and put together. We were not more than two or three hundred yards from San Cosme. The shots from our little gun dropped in upon the enemy and created great confusion. Why they did not send out a small party and capture us, I do not know. We had no infantry or other defences besides our one gun.

The effect of this gun upon the troops about the gate of the city was so marked that General Worth saw it from his position. He was so pleased that he sent a staff officer, Lieutenant Pemberton—later Lieutenant-General commanding the defences of Vicksburg—to bring me to him. He expressed his gratification at the services the howitzer in the church steeple was doing, saying that every shot was effective, and ordered a captain of voltigeurs to report to me with another howitzer to be placed along with the one already rendering so much service. I could not tell the General that there was not room enough in the steeple for another gun, because he probably would have looked upon such a statement as a contradiction from a second lieutenant. I took the captain with me, but did not use his gun.

The night of the 13th of September was spent by the troops under General Worth in the houses near San Cosme, and in line confronting the general line of the enemy across to Belen. The troops that I was with were in the houses north of the road leading into the city, and were engaged during the night in cutting passage-ways from one house to another towards the town. During the night Santa Anna, with his army—except the deserters—left the city. He liberated all the convicts confined in the town, hoping, no doubt, that they would inflict upon us some injury before daylight; but several hours after Santa Anna was out of the way, the city authorities sent a delegation to General Scott to ask—if not demand—an armistice, respecting church property, the rights of citizens and the supremacy of the city government in the management of municipal affairs. General Scott declined to trammel himself with conditions, but gave assurances that those who chose to remain within our lines would be protected so long as they behaved themselves properly.

General Quitman had advanced along his line very successfully on the 13th, so that at night his command occupied nearly the same position at Belen that Worth's troops did about San Cosme. After the interview above related between General Scott and the city council, orders were issued for the cautious entry of both columns in the morning. The troops under Worth were to stop at the Alameda, a park near the west end of the city. Quitman was to go directly to the Plaza, and take possession of the Palace—a mass of buildings on the east side in which Congress has its sessions, the national courts are held, the public offices are all located, the President resides, and much room is left for museums, receptions, etc. This is the building generally designated as the "Halls of the Montezumas."

Source: Grant, Ulysses S. *Personal Memoirs of U.S. Grant.* 1885. Reprint, New York: Da Capo Press, 1982, pp. 72–73, 75–80.

DAILY LIFE (AND DEATH) IN THE U.S.-MEXICAN WAR, 1846–1847

Diary Entries
Private Joshua E. Jackson
August 1846–March 1847

Joshua E. Jackson was a private in Company E, 4th Regiment, Illinois Volunteers. He embarked from New Orleans, bound for the war, on July 31, 1846, and was mortally wounded at the Battle of Cerro Gordo, April 18, 1847. These excerpts from his diary record the excitement, monotony, and misery of the Mexican campaign.

31 July 1846—This morning at 7 o'clock we loaded our baggage on board the *Sea Lion* and at 3 o'clock p.m. we left Orleans. At half past three we were at the battleground where the honorable General Jackson fought his battle, and the 3rd Reg. of Ills. volunteers was encamped there waiting for a vessel to come to take them aboard.

1 Aug 1846—We traveled all night and at 6 o'clock a.m. we arrived at the mouth of the Mississippi River to wait until the steamer *Malinda*

could tow us out into the Gulf of Mexico . . . at 10 o'clock a.m. we were towed out about ten miles in the Gulf and there let loose for Brazas Island. We saw thousands of porpoise from two to ten feet long and other fish to tedious to mention. There was no breeze worth naming. We tossed about the remainder of the day, the boys were very lively and singing "O, for the Rio Grande" and watching the beautiful bubbles and other curiosities. By this time it is night and we have to retire to bed until daylight.

. . .

9 Aug 1846—This morning at daylight we were in sight of land. The courage of the soldiers was beginning to get better, the sight of land cheered them up. At 7 o'clock we cast anchor in about four miles of land. We lay there until late in the evening, waiting for a tow to come after us. I thought it was the longest day I ever saw though I said nothing. At five o'clock p.m. the boat came after us and we all got aboard of her and at 7 p.m. we landed on land at Brazas, Santiago Island. This was joyful times for soldiers . . . The soldiers were scattered all over the island without their tents.

. . .

12 Aug 1846—This morning we had orders to strike tents for a march. The boys were all over their sea sickness and were all aken [aching] for a march. Company E was ordered to march up the Rio Grande 16 miles to clear off a camp ground. At 7 o'clock this morning we took up the line of march for the Rio Grande. The day was very warm and disagreeable, the first four miles were very sandy, the rest of the way was very muddy, bad roads. We suffered for water on the way. At 2 o'clock p.m. we reached the camp ground where we started for. This is on the Rio Grande, about 9 miles from the mouth there are about 6000 men encamped here. We rested about an hour and then went to work in a thick boddy of muskete [mesquite] to clear for an encampment.

A typical U.S. Army officer of the period, Bezaleel W. Armstrong, West Point graduate (1845), second lieutenant, Second Dragoons, served at Veracruz and Mexico City. *(National Archives)*

At night we were very tired, we just lay down on the ground, without any tents and rested very comfortable until about midnight we were bothered with ants and lizards and other insects of this country.

14 Aug 1846—This morning the soldiers were wishing themselves at home, some wishing for something to eat, while others were cursing them for such darned fools for volunteering. This morning I went to the 3rd Reg't Indiana Volunteers and found three of my cousins and got what I could eat and enjoyed myself very well for the day, and returned to camp in the evening.

Texas, found nothing worth looking at. There was no timber or grass, but plenty of weedy vines and shrubs which were all thorns. There is nothing that grows in this country that I have seen but has thorns on, and the land that I have seen is not worth describing. I returned to camp this evening very tired, this day was very warm, we have not drilled any yet, since we crossed the Gulf. . . .

18 Aug 1846—This morning we received orders to drill 6 hours a day. This is bound to be hard on us, for it is so tremendously warm. The boys were taken sick tolerable fast. . . .

. . .

24 Aug 1846—The boys are still getting sick very fast this morning. Jessa McPearson was taken very bad. There were several of the boys very low and sickness still increasing everyday. Late this evening Lieut. Benjamin Howard was taken very suddenly sick and remained so all night. . . .

27 Aug 1846—This morning some of the boys were a little better. I was no better myself. At 10 o'clock this morning Jessa McPearson died. This was the first death that we have had out of our DeWitt Company, and several of the boys were very bad homesick. Especially E. O. Hill, he took a hearty cry once every day. At 3 o'clock p.m. we buried our friend McPhearson. . . .

8 Sep 1846—This morning at 4 o'clock Isaac Richards departed this life, with a short spell of sickness. Calvin Pain and Lieut. Howard are very low yet, the rest of the boys are some better I think. We don't pretend to drill now, for there are hardly enough well ones to care for the sick. . . .

6 Nov 1846—. . . Sickness is decling [declining], there are no more than 2 or 3 deaths a days now. The sick throughout the army, as far as I hear, are getting better.

16 Nov 1846—This morning we received orders to prepare for the voyage to Tampico. This was reviving. Col. Baker was so proud that he had us parade and marched us up town and all around the city, then paraded us before a regiment of regulars, then returned to camp all tired and hungry. We thought no hardship of this for we

were proud of the news of leaving a damned hog hole. . . .

28 Nov 1846—This morning Company "E" drawed their money which was $32.50 and there was immediate order to load their baggage on the Steamer *Troy*. . . .

14 Dec 1846—. . . About 10 o'clock the 3rd Reg't accompanied the Tennessee Cavalry, marched through town on their way to Tampico. We artillerymen had to stay in town about ten days to drill, when the infantry was a going out of town 16 miles and there stay until the artillery got ready to go. . . .

19 Dec 1846—This morning there were 2 volunteers and one regular soldier found dead, that the Mexicans had killed through the night. There was a great fuss raised about it, but nothing done though a great many threats made about what would be done. . . .

21 Dec 1846—This morning at 7 o'clock we were ordered to strike tents and load up baggage for a march which we did in short order for we were anxious. . . . then marched on very lively through Chaperell thickets in first part of the day. After that through a beautiful prairie plain that was almost covered with wild horses and mules, and hundreds of wild cattle, this looked beautiful. . . .

26 Jan 1847—I went out to see the beauty of the green trees, the blossoms and wandered around in the woods about half of the day. In my walk I saw several curiosities, the first was a banion tree that was 117 steps around and 63 trunks to it, this was a great curiosity. The second was an animal in the shape of a alligator, only it finns on its back, head like a snake, legs about 6 inches long, claws like a bat and Its tail extended back from its hind legs like a lizard. This was about 3 feet and could climb a tree as quick as a squir-

rel, now I am past the camp. This morning S. P. Glenn, George Boyer, Wm. Alsup came to our camp and we all went out to look at my large tree, while we were out we found another that had 107 trunks and was 65 steps around it. We sported and played under the green shade in sight of the rich smelling roses as long as we wanted to, then returned to camp about night. We were tired enough to sleep though it was impossible to sleep sound here for the fleas and ticks bothered us so as to keep us on the move the most of the time, and when we do sleep we have to sleep with one eye open to keep the lizards from running in our mouths and ears—this is facts.

. . .

19 Feb 1847—This morning Gen. Qultman came out to see us drill and I knew that we would have a hard time of it. Shortly after Gen. Quitman landed in camp we received orders to dress in our best and prepare for drill, which we did and then marched out on the parade ground, where the sun pored down its furious heat, which was enough to kill a common man. We drilled about 3 hours and returned to camp almost melted.

. . .

27 Mar 1847—This day the Mexicans surrendered up the city [Veracruz] to Gen. Scott

. . .

28 Mar 1847—Everything seemed lively and cheerful—the boys seemed lively and singing and cutting around and talking about going home and to the city. . . .

Source: Jackson, Joshua E. "Mexican War Diary of Joshua E. Jackson." Available online. URL: http://free pages.genealogy.rootsweb.ancestry.com/~kvanchieri/ MexicanWarDiary.html. Accessed on February 5, 2010.

The Civil War

From the beginning of the American republic, the issue of slavery threatened to tear the nation apart as lawmakers repeatedly attempted to enact compromises in a doomed effort to maintain the balance of congressional representation between Southern slave states and Northern free states. Three major packages of legislation—the Missouri Compromise of 1820, the Compromise of 1850, and the Kansas-Nebraska Act of 1854—postponed outright civil war even as they intensified the underlying conflict. In the end, the election of Abraham Lincoln as president in 1860 brought the situation to a crisis that could not be postponed. Although Lincoln was not an abolitionist (an advocate of outlawing slavery), he did propose halting the extension of slavery to new states and territories. As southerners saw it, this would eventually and inevitably put a free-state majority in Congress, thereby spelling the end of slavery.

During the months following Lincoln's election, most of the slaveholding states seceded from the Union. Deeming secession an unconstitutional violation of federal sovereignty, Lincoln prepared for war, even as the seceded states formed themselves into the Confederate States of America.

The Battle of Fort Sumter and the Anaconda Plan

At 4:30 on the morning of April 12, 1861, Pierre Gustave Toutant Beauregard, one of many senior U.S. Army officers who had resigned their commissions to serve in the provisional army of the Confederate States of America, ordered an artillery barrage against Fort Sumter, in Charleston Harbor. The fort held through Saturday, April 13, when Major Robert Anderson (who had been Beauregard's artillery instructor at West Point) surrendered.

With the Civil War now begun, Lincoln turned to his senior military commander, Winfield Scott, the elderly hero of the War of 1812 and the U.S.-Mexican War, for a war plan. Hoping to buy time to organize an army large enough and sufficiently well equipped to fight the rebellion, Scott proposed using a naval blockade to cut off Southern Atlantic and Gulf ports while 60,000 land troops invaded the Confederacy and a flotilla of naval gunboats sailed down the Mississippi to take the major port of New Orleans. Scott had likened the plan to a boa constrictor strangling the rebels, and the press, both in the

North and South, derided the blockade as "Scott's Anaconda." It is true that, at the outset, the relatively few ships of the U.S. Navy were spread too thinly to enforce the blockade adequately, but as the Union built and launched more vessels, the "Anaconda" actually proved highly effective.

The First Battle of Bull Run

In July 1861, Lincoln ordered Major General Irvin McDowell to lead his army of 35,000 men, massed in Alexandria, Virginia, against some 20,000 Confederates under P. G. T. Beauregard, who were encamped at Manassas Junction, on Bull Run Creek, a position that controlled the best route to Richmond, the Confederate capital. The Union's intention was to bring the war to a quick end by capturing Richmond, and the operation began in high spirits and the expectation of easy victory. The Confederates were indeed initially forced to retreat, but a counterattack soon drove back one entire Union division, providing enough time for reinforcements to arrive at Bull Run Creek. The First Battle of Bull Run, on July 21, pitted 35,000 Union troops against about 30,000 Confederates.

McDowell managed to force the Confederates from their defensive positions, also turning the Confederate left flank. But just as the rebel line began to break, Brigadier General Thomas J. Jackson led Virginia troops in a fierce defensive stand. This prompted General Barnard Bee to point to Jackson and declare: "There's Jackson standing like a stone wall! Rally behind the Virginians!" In this way, Jackson earned the sobriquet "Stonewall," by which he became known to history, and the battle was saved for the Confederates, who, late in the day, mounted a massive counterthrust that smashed through the Union lines, sending the Federals into retreat. Union losses at the First Battle of Bull Run were 2,896 killed, wounded, and missing. Confederate casualties amounted to 1,982.

McClellan Takes Command

After the Bull Run debacle, Lincoln replaced McDowell as commander of the Army of the Potomac with George Brinton McClellan, a young commander who had won modest victories in western Virginia at Philippi (June 3, 1861) and Rich Mountain (July 11). McClellan instantly proved both popular and efficient, transforming the Army of the Potomac from an undisciplined rabble into a credible fighting force; however, his first engagement at the head of the army resulted in defeat at the Battle of Ball's Bluff (October 21, 1861), fought about 30 miles up the Potomac from Washington, and after this, he repeatedly postponed any major action while he continued to organize and train his troops.

The Western Theater

While McClellan seemed to mark time in the war's eastern theater, intense and momentous action developed farther west. In September, Kentucky ended its declared neutrality and openly sided with the Union. Immediately, the Confederate general Leonidas Polk invaded the state, occupying Columbus, on the commanding bluffs above the Mississippi River. The Union's Brigadier General Ulysses S. Grant countered by capturing Paducah, Kentucky, which controlled the mouths of the Tennessee and Cumberland Rivers; however, the Confederate general Albert Sidney Johnston (no relation to Joseph E. Johnston, the ranking Confederate officer in command at First Bull Run) reinforced Columbus, which firmed up Confederate control of the Mississippi and also built Fort Donelson on the Cumberland River and Fort Henry on the Tennessee River, thereby securing potential routes for an invasion of the North.

In November 1861, Major General Henry Wager Halleck was given command of Union forces west of the Cumberland River, and Brigadier General Don Carlos Buell was assigned command east of that river. After Union general George H. Thomas defeated the Confederates at Mill Springs, Kentucky, on January 19, 1862, Halleck sent Grant, commanding a force of 15,000 and reinforced by a squadron of iron-clad gunboats under naval Flag Officer Andrew Foote, to take Fort Henry, which fell on February 6, 1862. Grant then advanced against Fort Donelson on the Cumberland. After a three-day assault, it, too, fell to Grant on February 16, 1862. His position now untenable, Johnston evacuated Nashville, Tennessee, and abandoned the strategically critical Columbus, Kentucky.

The Battle of Shiloh

Despite these major victories, Union commanders hesitated to close in for the kill, and that lack of aggressiveness gave the Confederate generals Beauregard and Johnston a reprieve to regroup at Corinth, Mississippi. Grant made camp with some 42,000 men at Pittsburg Landing, Tennessee, on the west bank of the Tennessee River, just northeast of the Confederate position at Corinth. Establishing his headquarters tent next to a log-built Methodist meeting house called Shiloh Chapel, Grant was confident that the Confederates would remain in their Corinth encampment, and he therefore failed to defend his own camp adequately. To his stunned dismay, Albert Sidney Johnston and P. G. T. Beauregard staged a surprise attack on April 6.

For its first dozen hours, the Battle of Shiloh looked to be a lopsided Confederate triumph until one of Grant's subordinates, William Tecumseh Sherman, rallied his troops, thereby staving off a rout. Other Union commanders also resisted steadfastly, buying time for the arrival of reinforcements and the turning of the tide against the Confederates. In the fierce contest, Johnston was mortally wounded—depriving the Confederacy of one of its best generals.

On April 7, Beauregard withdrew to Corinth, and thus the battle ended. On both sides, the costs were unprecedented. Of 62,682 Union sol-diers engaged at Shiloh, 1,754 were killed; 8,408 wounded; and 2,885 went missing. Confederate losses were 1,723 killed; 8,012 wounded; and 959 missing out of 40,335 men engaged.

The Combat in Missouri

At the outbreak of the war, Missouri was torn between its Confederate-aligned governor and its predominantly pro-Union legislature. The defeat of Union forces at the Battle of Wilson's Creek on August 10, 1861, did not discourage the inept commander of the Union's newly created Western Department, Brigadier General John Charles Frémont, from unilaterally declaring martial law in Missouri on August 30, proclaiming the emancipation of the state's slaves, and confiscating the property of Confederate sympathizers. Guerrilla warfare in the state intensified, and the Confederate general Sterling Price won another victory at Lexington, Missouri, on September 13, 1861. Relieved of command, Frémont was transferred to West Virginia. But the damage had already been done; a pro-Confederate rump minority of the Missouri legislature convened in October 1861 at Neosho and voted to secede. Even though the Neosho group was not the legally constituted legislature, the Confederate president Jefferson Davis welcomed the state into the Confederacy.

The Battle of Pea Ridge

When Union reinforcements under Brigadier General Samuel R. Curtis arrived in Missouri, Price withdrew into Arkansas, intending to link up with a Confederate unit under Ben McCulloch. General Earl Van Dorn reinforced the commands of both Price and McCulloch, bringing Confederate forces in Arkansas to 17,000 men versus the 11,000 troops under Curtis. Outnumbered, Curtis took up a defensive position at Pea Ridge, on high ground overlooking Little Sugar Creek. Skirmishing broke out near Elkhorn Tavern on March 7, followed by a pitched battle on March 8, which resulted in the withdrawal of Confederate forces. This made for a Union strategic victory but, measured by casualties, a tactical defeat: Of 11,250 Federal troops engaged at Pea Ridge, 1,384 were killed, wounded, or missing, whereas 800 of 14,000 Confederates became casualties. The Union's costly victory at Pea Ridge drove the Neosho legislature out of the state but also intensified the guerrilla warfare between pro-Union "Jayhawkers" and pro-Confederate "Bushwhackers." Counting all of the guerrilla actions and skirmishes, 1,162 engagements took place in Missouri during the course of the Civil War—fully 11 percent of all Civil War battles.

The Far Western Theater

In the Southwest, the Confederate lieutenant colonel John Robert Baylor swept through the southern New Mexico Territory and proclaimed the Confederate Territory of Arizona, which included all of present-day Arizona in addition to New Mexico south of the 34th parallel. Baylor's virtually unopposed advance was followed during the winter of 1861–62 by a bigger Confederate invasion led by General Henry Hopkins Sibley, whose mission was to capture the silver mines of Colorado in an effort to help finance the cash-strapped Confederacy. Sibley advanced up the Rio Grande, intent on capturing Fort Union, headquarters of the Union commander E. R. S. Canby, and gaining control of the Santa Fe Trail. Sibley defeated Canby at Valverde, New Mexico, on February 21, 1862, took Santa Fe, then advanced to Fort Union via La Glorieta Pass through the Sangre de Cristo Mountains. There, on March 26, 1862, a force of Union regulars under Colonel John Slough and Colorado volunteers commanded by Major John M. Chivington engaged Sibley's Texas troops in a two-day battle, ending on March 28. Because Sibley withdrew back to Texas, some have dubbed this battle the "Gettysburg of the West." Indeed, it marked the turning point against the Confederates in the Southwest.

After participating at La Glorieta, Colonel James H. Carleton and his 1st California Regiment of Infantry (the "California Column") swept through New Mexico Territory. The culminating battle of this campaign was fought on April 15, 1862, at Picacho Peak, New Mexico, and constituted the westernmost action of the Civil War. It put an end to the fleeting existence of the Confederate Territory of Arizona.

As for Texas, Governor Sam Houston supported the Union during the secession crisis, but on February 2, 1861, his state seceded despite him, and Houston resigned. A U.S. Navy assault in October 1862 captured the key port of Galveston, which the Confederates retook on January 1, 1863. Nevertheless, the Union maintained a naval blockade of the port, and by late 1863, with the Mississippi River under Union control, Texas was effectively isolated from the rest of the Confederacy.

Plans for the Peninsula Campaign

President Lincoln and his administration had much to be pleased about with the course of the war in the West, but George B. McClellan, now general in chief of the Union's armies, seemed reluctant to take the offensive in the eastern theater, and on March 11, 1862, Lincoln reduced his responsibilities to command of the Army of the Potomac only. Lincoln now urged him to lead that army from Washington to Richmond. Instead, McClellan decided on an indirect approach, proposing to transport the Army of the Potomac by water to a position below the lines of the Confederate general Joseph E. Johnston, thereby outflanking him without a major battle. McClellan ferried his troops down to Fort Monroe, near Newport News and Hampton Roads, in the southeastern corner of Virginia, well south of Richmond. His intention was, after landing, to advance north toward Richmond via the peninsula separating the York from the James Rivers. That geographical feature gave the operation its name, the Peninsula (or Peninsular) Campaign, which was also a hopeful and grandiose reference to the triumphal "Peninsular Campaign" of Napoléon.

In the meantime, Major General Ambrose E. Burnside landed a Union force at Roanoke Island, North Carolina, on February 7, 1862; defeated the Confederate garrison there on the next day; then advanced to the North Carolina mainland, where he took New Bern on March 14 and Beaufort on April 26. All were minor Union victories.

The Battle of Hampton Roads: USS *Monitor* v. CSS *Virginia* (ex-USS *Merrimack*)

A pathologically cautious commander, McClellan, about to launch the Peninsula Campaign, fretted that the Confederate ironclad *Virginia* (modified from a salvaged wooden U.S. Navy ship, the *Merrimack,* also spelled *Merrimac*) menaced his water route. To oppose the *Virginia*, the U.S. Navy had hurriedly built and launched (on March 6, 1862) the USS *Monitor,* a low-profile, steam-driven, iron-hulled vessel, fitted with a truly innovative revolving turret mounting two 11-inch guns. On March 8, the *Monitor* set out for Hampton Roads, Virginia, where conventional wooden-hulled U.S. Navy warships, which blockaded the harbor, opened fire on the *Virginia*. With cannonballs bouncing harmlessly off her ironclad sides, the *Virginia* counterattacked, sinking the USS *Cumberland* and severely damaging four other Union vessels. When the *Monitor* arrived on March 9, she took up a position to protect one of the disabled ships, USS *Minnesota,* and engaged the *Virginia* in a three-hour exchange of fire. In the end, the Battle of Hampton Roads was a draw (although the *Monitor* not only saved the

Minnesota but also prevented the Confederates from breaking the blockade of Richmond), but the nature of naval battle was changed forever. The era of the "modern" battleship commenced.

The Peninsula Campaign Begins

Ninety thousand men of the Army of the Potomac finally landed in Virginia on April 4, 1862. After advancing toward Yorktown on April 5, McClellan, who erroneously believed that he was outnumbered, halted to set up a siege instead of storming the town. (As it turned out, Yorktown was defended by a mere 15,000 Confederates.) McClellan's delay gave General Johnston ample time to reinforce Richmond's defenses.

In the meantime, Robert E. Lee and the other principal Confederate military commanders counted on President Lincoln's assigning the very highest priority to defending Washington, D.C., thereby siphoning off manpower from McClellan. This, they reasoned, would allow them to offset their inferior numbers against the superior Union forces. Stonewall Jackson was sent on a sweep through Virginia's Shenandoah Valley in an operation designed to give the impression that an invasion of Washington was imminent and thereby prompt the Union to divide its forces. The first battle of Jackson's Shenandoah campaign was fought on March 23, 1862, at Kernstown, near Winchester, Virginia, and resulted in a tactical defeat for Jackson, yet, in a larger sense, a strategic victory for the Confederates. The engagement convinced Northern leaders that Washington was indeed the Confederate target, and 35,000 men were instantly detached from McClellan's forces to defend the capital. This served to exacerbate McClellan's excessive caution at Yorktown. In the end, Jackson's Shenandoah Valley campaign proved brilliant. Employing about 17,000 men, he effectively tied down more than 50,000 Union soldiers, thereby denying McClellan the massive numbers he believed necessary to mount an attack on Richmond. The Shenandoah campaign saved the Confederate capital and substantially prolonged the war.

The Capture of New Orleans

In April 1862, U.S. Navy flag officer David Glasgow Farragut sailed his fleet up the Mississippi in an assault on New Orleans. By April 24, he had neutralized the defensive forts, allowing Major General Benjamin Butler to capture the forts and take the city of New Orleans. This put the Confederacy's major Mississippi port in Union hands.

The Peninsula Campaign Continues

By the time McClellan finally attacked Yorktown, Confederate forces had withdrawn toward Richmond, and McClellan's subordinates, George Stoneman and Joseph Hooker, were dispatched to engage the rear guard of Confederate cavalry under James Ewell Brown ("Jeb") Stuart on May 4–5 at Williamsburg. McClellan claimed victory at Yorktown and Williamsburg, both minor battles.

By the end of May, the main portion of the Army of the Potomac was north of the Chickahominy River, except for a single corps under by Major General Erasmus Darwin Keyes. The Confederate general Joseph E. Johnston attacked Keyes at Fair Oaks and Seven Pines on May 31, 1862, resulting in an inconclusive but bloody battle in which 5,031 of 41,797 Union troops engaged were killed or wounded and 6,134 of 41,816 Confederates also became casualties. Johnston was so badly wounded that he had to be replaced by Robert E. Lee—up to this point a commander of little distinction.

On June 12–15, 1862, Jeb Stuart led 1,200 Confederate cavalrymen in a spectacular reconnaissance that completely circled the Union positions in Virginia. Known as "Stuart's Ride," this exploit made the Confederate cavalryman a legend and added to the humiliation of McClellan, who was shamed into finally beginning his drive to Richmond in earnest. He was intercepted on June 25, at Oak Grove, near Mechanicsville, along the Chickahominy River, but prevailed and took up a position at Oak Grove.

"The Seven Days"

Oak Grove was the first of what would be called the Seven Days, or the Seven Days Battles. Lee intended to position most of his Army of Northern Virginia, 65,000 troops, on the north bank of the Chickahominy in order to overrun the 25,000 Union troops under the Union major general Fitz-John Porter, who was isolated on the northern bank. It was a bold plan, which left only a thin line defending Richmond. Unfortunately for Lee, Stonewall Jackson failed to join the attack against Porter, which made the Battle of Mechanicsville inconclusive, allowing Porter to retreat with his army intact. However, the battle was sufficient provocation for McClellan to withdraw the Army of the Potomac away from Richmond and back toward the James River.

In sharp contrast to McClellan, Lee was vigorously aggressive. He took every possible opportunity to attack the withdrawing Union army, although McClellan's corps commanders employed brilliant rear-guard actions and short, sharp counterattacks to exact a substantial cost on Lee. At the Battle of Gaines's Mill on June 27, 1862, 34,214 Union troops were engaged, of whom 893 died; 3,107 were wounded; and 2,836 were reported missing. The Confederates lost 8,751 killed and wounded, but their aggression spurred McClellan into withdrawing even farther, all the way to the James. Lee planned a complex attack against McClellan's new position, which, in the end, proved too complex to coordinate effectively. The Battle of Savage's Station began with a vigorous Confederate assault on June 29, but it petered out inconclusively. Casualties were 1,590 Union troops killed or wounded for a loss of 626 Confederates.

Withdrawing from Savage's Station, McClellan concentrated his forces at Frayser's Farm, behind White Oak Swamp. He also deployed a line to Malvern Hill to protect the Union supply trains. Lee attacked again, and again failed to achieve a decisive result, but did push McClellan farther back. Union casualties at the Battle of Frayser's Farm on June 30 were 2,853 killed or wounded, whereas Confederate losses were greater: 3,615 killed or wounded.

McClellan's next stand was at Malvern Hill, a low rise alongside the James River. Occupying the high ground, McClellan was in a most advantageous position. Despite this, Lee attacked on July 1, hoping at last to pummel the Army of the Potomac. Yet again, Lee's subordinate commanders failed to coordinate with one another, and the Battle of Malvern Hill ended in Lee's repulse. Predictably, McClellan declined to counterattack, instead withdrawing to Harrison's Landing, farther from Richmond than where he had begun.

The Peninsula Campaign achieved little or nothing, although the Seven Days, an outright strategic failure, did gain some tactical advantage for the Union. Commanding the larger army, McClellan had sustained about 16,000 casualties, killed and wounded, whereas Lee's smaller force suffered nearly 20,000 casualties—but saved Richmond. Disgusted with McClellan, Lincoln removed him from command of the Army of the Potomac and replaced him with John Pope.

The Battle of Cedar Mountain and Raid on Catlett's Station

Jackson struck part of Pope's army at Cedar Mountain, near Culpepper, Virginia, on August 9, forcing Pope to withdraw north of the Rappahannock River. Lee took the unorthodox and risky step of dividing his army in the presence of the enemy, placing half his forces under the command of Major General James Longstreet to occupy Pope's front and sending the rest of his army, under Stonewall Jackson, to wheel around and make a surprise attack on the rear of Pope's army.

In the meantime, elements of Pope's army raided Jeb Stuart's camp, capturing his adjutant as well as Stuart's ornate plumed hat and scarlet-lined cloak. This provoked Stuart to lead a cavalry raid behind Pope's lines on August 22. Overrunning Pope's headquarters at Catlett's Station, Stuart appropriated $35,000 in payroll cash, seized Pope's personal baggage (including his dress uniform), captured 300 prisoners, and obtained battle plan documents. Four days later, Jackson also struck Pope, disrupting his supply depot at Manassas Junction, Virginia (site of the Bull Run battle), and severing his rail and telegraph communications. This moved Pope to pursue Jackson. Jackson eluded Pope until August 28, when he attacked the Union brigadier Rufus King at Groveton, a hot skirmish in which the Union's "Black Hat Brigade" (also called the "Iron Brigade") demonstrated the heroism for which it would become legendary at the Battle of Gettysburg.

The Second Battle of Bull Run

Aware now of Jackson's position, Pope formed up his army near Groveton, adjacent to the site of the Battle of Bull Run. He launched an attack on August 29, 1862, driving Jackson back and prompting Pope to declare victory—prematurely, as it turned out.

The Union commander was entirely unaware that the second half of Lee's divided army, under Longstreet, was in the wings, and on August 30, Longstreet launched five divisions against Pope's flank along a two-mile front. Pope was badly beaten: Of the 75,696 Union troops engaged against the Confederates' 48,527, Pope lost 1,724 killed; 8,372 wounded; and 5,958 missing. Confederate losses were 1,481 killed; 7,627 wounded; and 89 missing. Yet Longstreet's failure to attack on the first day of battle compromised the Confederate victory. Although defeated, Pope's forces were still very much intact—which was more than could be said of Pope's reputation. McClellan was recalled to assume command of the Army of the Potomac, and Pope was relieved.

The Battle of Antietam

Although the Confederate victory at Second Bull Run was not decisive, Lee decided to exploit it as best he could. Reasoning that the Northern public was badly demoralized, he decided to assume the offensive by invading the North, a move he hoped would push Lincoln toward negotiating an end to the war favorable to the South.

On September 5, 1862, the 55,000 men of Lee's Army of Northern Virginia crossed into Maryland, one of the Union's "border" states (slaveholding states that did not secede from the Union). As usual, McClellan grossly overestimated the size of Lee's army and therefore avoided decisive action, but merely sent Brigadier General Alfred Pleasanton to engage elements of the invasion force at South Mountain on September 14. Although this minor battle was a Union victory, it gave Lee time to set up a strong line through the western Maryland town of Sharpsburg, behind Antietam Creek. McClellan intended to attack both of Lee's flanks, then throw his reserves against Lee's center. The initial assault, on September 17, was poorly coordinated; nevertheless, Union general Joseph "Fighting Joe" Hooker pushed Stonewall Jackson's brigade so far back that Lee was forced to order up his reserves. They were engaged by midday, focusing the fight on a sunken farm road that was soon christened

"Bloody Lane," after the five hours of slaughter that took place here.

Late in the afternoon, Major General Ambrose Burnside led a Union division across a stone bridge that still bears his name. He punched through the Confederate line but was in turn devastated by a counterattack from A. P. Hill. Lee's army had taken a severe blow, but Lee rallied a countercharge that drove the Federals back. Nevertheless, it was Lee who had to do most of the withdrawing, pulling his forces back to the outskirts of Sharpsburg. This gave McClellan an opportunity to pursue, but, still laboring under the misapprehension that he was outnumbered, the Union commander allowed Lee to escape back across the Potomac and into Virginia.

Because McClellan had pushed back a Confederate invasion of the North, Antietam may be counted as a Union victory. Yet it was hardly decisive—and it was horrifically costly. In what most historians consider the single bloodiest day of the war, 2,108 Union troops were killed; 9,549 wounded; and 753 went missing out of 75,316 engaged. Of the Confederates' 51,844 men, about 2,700 were killed; 9,024 wounded; and approximately 2,000 went missing. President Lincoln was deeply disappointed by the results, but he deemed Antietam a sufficient victory to warrant his issuing a Preliminary Emancipation Proclamation on September 23, 1862, which put the South on notice that, on January 1, 1863, those slaves in the parts of the Confederacy that were not yet under the control of the Union army would be liberated.

As for McClellan, he did nothing to capitalize on the narrow victory at Antietam, whereas the "defeated" Lee sent Jeb Stuart on a lightning raid into Pennsylvania. Riding toward the Pennsylvania town of Chambersburg during October 9–12, 1862, Stuart led his cavalrymen around McClellan's idle army, an action so humiliating that Northern public opinion turned irreversibly against the Union commander. On November 7, McClellan was again relieved of command of the Army of the Potomac, and this time he was replaced by Ambrose Burnside, a popular and earnest, but ultimately inept, officer.

The Battle of Fredericksburg

Burnside deployed his forces north of the Rappahannock River at Warrenton, Virginia, 30 miles from Lee's army, which consisted of two corps commanded by Stonewall Jackson and James Longstreet. Had Burnside been a skilled tactician, he would have attacked between the separated wings of Lee's army, defeating each in detail. Determined, however, to strike a single decisive blow against the entire enemy force, he advanced on Richmond and attacked at Fredericksburg. Even having made this error, Burnside might have triumphed had he attacked immediately, for Longstreet's corps was delayed. Union general Edwin V. Sumner's division lay just across the Rappahannock on November 17. Had Burnside ordered him to cross immediately, he could have mauled Jackson's isolated corps. Instead, Burnside waited for pontoon bridges to be put in place, a delay that gave Longstreet ample time to entrench defensively in the hills south of Fredericksburg. By December 11, when the Union crossings finally began, 78,000 Confederates were very strongly positioned. As if his delay were not blunder enough, Burnside ordered an artillery barrage before he commenced the crossing. Doubtless, this was meant to neutralize Confederate snipers, but all the barrage actually accomplished was to level the town. This both enraged the Confederates and furnished an open field of fire for the defenders dug into the hills around the town.

The battle began in earnest on December 13, 1862, as Burnside made one hopeless assault after another, 14 disastrous charges in all, before he finally withdrew in defeat. Of the 106,000 Union soldiers engaged, 12,700 were killed or wounded. Confederate losses were 5,300 killed or wounded out of some 72,500 engaged. It was—and it remains—the costliest defeat in history of the U.S. Army.

After the Fredericksburg tragedy, the Army of the Potomac holed up in winter quarters until January 20, 1863, when Burnside launched a plan to envelop Lee's army via a river crossing called Banks's Ford. Unfortunately, two days of icy rain churned the battle-scarred landscape into a quagmire, bogging down the army in the so-called "Mud March" and moving President Lincoln to replace Burnside on January 26, 1863, with Joseph "Fighting Joe" Hooker.

The Battle of Chancellorsville

When Hooker took command of the Army of the Potomac, it had been reinforced to a strength of 130,000, more than double that of Lee's 60,000-man Army of Northern Virginia. Confident of victory, Hooker deployed a third of the army under Major General John Sedgwick to make a diversionary attack across the Rappahannock above Robert E. Lee's entrenchments at Fredericksburg while he personally led another third of the army up the Rappahannock to strike at Lee on his left flank and rear. With the exception of some 10,000 cavalrymen assigned to disrupt Lee's lines of communication to Richmond, the rest of Army of the Potomac would be held in reserve at Chancellorsville, to reinforce either Sedgwick's or Hooker's wings, as required.

It was a good if unimaginative plan, and by April 30, 1863, Hooker had positioned some 70,000 men in Chancellorsville and dispatched his cavalry to cut the Richmond, Fredericksburg and Potomac Railroad. Grasping Hooker's intentions, however, Lee sent his own cavalry, under Jeb Stuart, to take control of the roads in and out of Chancellorsville, thereby preventing Hooker from conducting reconnaissance. Thrown into confusion, Hooker panicked and allowed the initiative to slip from his hands. He now deployed his men defensively just outside of Chancellorsville. Thanks to Stuart's reconnaissance, Lee also understood that Hooker meant to attack him from the flank and rear, advancing through a thicket known as "the Wilderness." To foil this, Lee sent 10,000 men under Jubal Early to divert the Union troops at Fredericksburg, while he led the rest of his army against Hooker's defenses at Chancellorsville.

As he had done against Pope at the Second Battle of Bull Run, Lee divided his army. On the night of May 1, Jackson's corps stealthily advanced through the "the Wilderness," acquiring a position from which it could hit Hooker's exposed flank. This done, Lee divided his outnumbered army yet again, allotting 26,000 men to Jackson for the attack against Hooker's flank, while retaining 17,000 to strike at Hooker's front. In the meantime, Early would continue to tie down the Union troops who were at Fredericksburg. Jackson attacked just before dusk on May 2, routing a Federal corps and knocking Hooker's entire army out of its prepared defenses.

By May 4, Hooker was in full retreat. He did not stop until the Army of the Potomac was north of the Rappahannock. Having faced at the Battle of Chancellorsville an army less than half the size of his, Hooker suffered 17,000 casualties. That was a devastating 17 percent casualty rate. Yet Lee, victorious, incurred an even higher casualty rate of 25 percent—13,000 men. The worst of all Confederate losses was Thomas "Stonewall" Jackson, mortally wounded by friendly fire.

Prelude to Gettysburg

The South's Pyrrhic victory at Chancellorsville persuaded Lee that it was time to invade the North a second time in order to undermine the Union's will to continue the fight and prompt it to negotiate a favorable peace. The gamble was a desperate one, since the price of failure was quite possibly the destruction of the entire Army of Northern Virginia.

On June 3, 1863, Lee began his advance, dividing his army into three corps. The corps commanded by James Longstreet paused at Culpepper Court House, Virginia, while a corps under Richard S. Ewell attacked Union detachments that were still in the lower Shenandoah Valley. The third corps, commanded by A. P. Hill, remained where it was, at Fredericksburg, to fight Union forces there. Hooker's plan was simply to ignore these movements and advance offensively against Richmond, but Lincoln felt this exposed Washington and the rest of the North to excessive risk. He ordered Hooker to go on the defensive and track Lee. This resulted in a skirmish at Franklin's Crossing, Virginia, followed by a cavalry fight at Brandy Station on June 9. After 12 hours of battle, Union casualties were 936 killed, wounded, and captured; Confederate losses totaled 523, and Jeb Stuart remained in possession of the field. Although Brandy Station was therefore a Union defeat, the Union cavalry had performed well against the legendary Stuart and, what is more, provided Hooker with the crucial intelligence that Lee was heading north. Yet the battle also alerted Lee that Hooker was aware of his movements. Lee assumed that Hooker would now turn to advance on Richmond, and therefore, on June 10, he sent Ewell against the remaining Union garrisons in the Shenandoah Valley. This, Lee hoped, would induce Lincoln to recall the bulk of Army of the Potomac to defend the capital.

Ewell attacked at Berryville (June 13) and Martinsburg (June 14) without decisive result, but his attack on Winchester, Virginia (June 13–15), captured virtually the entire garrison there, 3,538 men. In the meantime, the Army of Northern Virginia began crossing the Potomac into Maryland on June 15. Jeb Stuart led a cavalry screen to prevent the Union cavalry from ascertaining whether Lee intended to advance against Washington or invade Pennsylvania. After fighting skirmishes in the Virginia hamlets of Aldie (June 17), Middleburg (June 19), and Upperville (June 21), Stuart headed east on what became known as the "Gettysburg Raid," which badly disrupted Hooker's supply lines.

Stuart caused much consternation, but because the Union forces were more dispersed than he had anticipated, the Gettysburg Raid took much longer than planned. Indeed, for 10 days, Stuart was out of contact with Lee, who was effectively rendered blind as he penetrated deeper into Pennsylvania. It was not until June 28 that he learned that the entire Army of the Potomac was concentrated around Frederick, Maryland, directly south of the 50-mile-long exposed flank of the Army of Northern Virginia. At this time, Lee also acquired another piece of intelligence: Joseph Hooker had been replaced as commander of the Army of the Potomac by Major General George Gordon Meade. What neither Lee nor Meade knew at this time was that the two principal opposing armies were about to meet in the crossroads Pennsylvania town of Gettysburg.

The War in Kentucky and Mississippi, August–October 1862

Throughout the Civil War, events in the eastern theater typically overshadowed those occurring farther west. On August 14, 1862, the Confederate major general Edmund Kirby Smith left Knoxville, Tennessee, to invade central Kentucky. His colleague Braxton Bragg left Chattanooga to join him two weeks later. On August 30, the Union general Don Carlos Buell ordered the pursuit of these invaders. A battle developed at Munfordville, Kentucky on September 14, 1862, and again there two days later, resulting in the surrender of the entire Union garrison of 4,133 men. Had Bragg exploited this significant victory, he could have badly crippled Buell's forces in the region. Instead, he decided to await the arrival of more troops under Kirby Smith. However, on September 19, the Union general William S. Rosecrans defeated 17,000 Confederate troops under Sterling Price at Iuka, Mississippi, forcing Price to withdraw to the south, with the Confederate general Earl Van Dorn intending to join him en route. Van Dorn paused to attack Corinth, Mississippi, on October 3, believing the town to be lightly held by a few Union troops. In fact, he was appalled to discover some 23,000 of Rosecrans's men there, and General Grant moved quickly to reinforce the position. After very heavy fighting on October 4, Van Dorn's force retreated to Holly Springs.

Van Dorn's defeat now isolated Bragg in Kentucky, cutting him off from all hope of reinforcement. General Buell attacked Bragg at Perryville, Kentucky, on October 8, bringing to bear nearly 37,000 men against Bragg's 16,000. Both Bragg and Kirby Smith were ousted from Kentucky and pushed into eastern Tennessee, but Buell chose not to pursue them to annihilation. For this evidence of complacency, Buell was relieved as commander of the Department of the Ohio and replaced by Rosecrans.

The Vicksburg Campaign, December 1862–July 1863

By the middle of October 1862, the Confederates had been driven out of Kentucky, and Ulysses S. Grant decided that the next step was to gain control of the Mississippi River. The key was the capture of Vicksburg, Mississippi, a formidable fortress town occupying a high bluff overlooking the river. In December, Grant set up an advance base at Holly Springs, Mississippi, in preparation for a planned movement of 40,000 troops down the Mississippi Central Railroad to link up with William Tecumseh Sherman and 32,000 troops, coming by steamboat. Van Dorn's Confederate cavalry raided the Holly Springs encampment on December 20, destroying a massive stockpile of supplies, then going on to raid one Union outpost after another. Simultaneously, another Confederate general, Nathan Bedford Forrest, destroyed some 60 miles of railroad. Together, these actions stopped Grant's advance, which left Sherman unsupported, so that his attempt to take Chickasaw Bluffs (a few miles north of Vicksburg) failed on December 27–29, 1862.

As best he could, Grant blockaded Vicksburg and spent months looking for a way to take the city. While the blockade was ongoing, he used corps under James B. McPherson and Sherman to take Jackson, Mississippi, on May 14, 1863, and then attacked the Confederate-held Champion's Hill on May 16. After the fall of this bastion, Grant was finally in position for a frontal attack on Vicksburg. The first assault, on May 19, was repulsed, as was a second, on May 22. Grant then decided to mount a full-scale siege, including continuous bombardment by some Union artillery. It was this pounding that finally brought the town to its knees. Surrender came on July 4, 1863, and, with it, control of the Mississippi River—a blow from which the Confederacy never recovered.

The Battle of Gettysburg

Vicksburg fell just one day after the Union victory at Gettysburg. Together, these victories represented the turning point of the Civil War, virtually ensuring that the Union would prevail.

The prelude to Gettysburg came on June 30, 1863, when a Confederate infantry brigade stumbled upon Brigadier General John Buford's Union cavalry brigade on a reconnaissance foray near the Pennsylvania town. This chance encounter became the basis of what most historians regard as the most momentous battle of the Civil War. Buford understood that the Confederate infantry unit was the advance guard of the Army of Northern Virginia, and he also instantly grasped the importance of holding the high ground called McPherson's Ridge, just west of town, until more of the Army of the Potomac could join battle. Whoever possessed the high ground in the contest to come would have a great advantage. Therefore, despite being badly outnumbered, Buford decided to fight rather than withdraw.

The Battle of Gettysburg began at 9:00 on the morning of July 1. Buford's dismounted cavalry held off the first waves of Confederate infantry as Major General John Reynolds's I Corps and Major General O. O. Howard's XI Corps arrived. Despite this reinforcement, the Confederates had by this time mustered most of their superior strength, and the situation become confused, especially after Reynolds fell to a sniper's bullet. By the end of the day, the Federals had been driven off McPherson's Ridge as well as their other positions west and north of Gettysburg. They retreated into the town itself, fighting hand-to-hand before withdrawing southeast via the Baltimore Pike.

The first day of the Battle of Gettysburg ended in a Confederate victory. Robert E. Lee instructed Ewell to press his initial gains, "if practicable." Ewell took this latitude as permission to wait, and thus gave the Army of the Potomac sufficient reprieve to establish itself on a new stretch of high ground, East Cemetery Hill, Cemetery Ridge, and Culp's Hill, running from due south to southeast of town. The Confederates had also used the lull to take up high-ground positions, at Oak Hill, northwest of town, and at Seminary Ridge, west of Gettysburg.

On July 2, Lee was anxious to finish what had been started the day before. General Longstreet, however, believed that most of the Army of the Potomac would soon arrive, and he feared that the Army of Northern Virginia would then be overrun. He advised Lee to practice what he called "strategic offense-tactical defense"—that is, to coax the enemy into attacking where and when it was most strategically advantageous to the Confederate army; then, when attacked, to respond by inflicting substantial losses on the Federals. This was essentially the tactic that had succeeded so well at the two Bull Runs, at Antietam, and at Fredericksburg. To implement it now, Longstreet proposed withdrawing to the south so as to move against Meade from the rear. Lee objected, insisting that he would not undermine the morale of his army by withdrawing it after it had won a victory. He would attack.

On this day, the Union line was deployed in what has often been described as a giant fishhook pattern. The barb end of the hook was just south of Culp's Hill, the turn of the hook was at Cemetery Hill, and the tie end of the hook's straight shaft was located at two hills south of town, called Little Round Top and Big Round Top. Lee ordered Longstreet to attack the Union left, the shaft of the fishhook running along Cemetery Ridge and terminating at the Little and Big Round Tops. Lee was positioned northwest of the fishhook, where the curve met the shaft, and Ewell, to the north and northeast, above the curve of the fishhook, was to get ready to swing down to smash into the Union's right.

George Gordon Meade, the Union commander, appreciated the fact that he was surrounded on three sides, but he was also aware that he occupied high ground commanding clear fields of observation and fire. Moreover, his strength was superior to Lee's—nearly 90,000 versus 75,000. The Union situation was both highly dangerous and very powerful.

The Union corps at the tie end of the fishhook, terminating at the Round Tops, was under the command of the impulsive Major General Daniel Sickles. Acting without orders from Meade, he advanced his III Corps to Houck's Ridge and the Peach Orchard northwest of the Round Tops, recklessly exposing the Union's left flank to Longstreet. Fortunately, Longstreet was as cautious as Sickles was impulsive, and he delayed attacking until four in the afternoon. One of Longstreet's subordinate commanders, Major General John Bell Hood, struck III Corps through an area called the Devil's Den, pushing the corps back to Little Round Top. It was just before this attack that Brigadier General Gouverneur K. Warren, Meade's chief engineer, took note that Little Round Top was undefended. Instantly realizing that Hood's division would seize the hill and thereby gain a position from which it could crush the Union's flank, Warren hurried a brigade under

Colonel Strong Vincent to occupy Little Round Top. Vincent soon fell, but another brigade, under Brigadier General Stephen Weed, also began engaging Hood. Weed's southernmost regiment, at the south end of the Federal flank, was the 20th Maine, commanded by Colonel Joshua Lawrence Chamberlain, in civilian life a professor of rhetoric at Bowdoin College. The battered regiment was at less than half strength with fewer than 500 men, including some deserters who had been put under his guard. Outnumbered though he was and short of ammunition, Chamberlain not only repulsed a charge by Alabama troops, but defeated them, thereby saving the entire Union line.

The Round Tops held, but the Confederates turned their attention next to the Union positions on Cemetery, East Cemetery, and Culp's Hills. All held, except for Culp's Hill. But, at 4:30 on the morning of July 3, the Federals counterattacked there and, after seven hours of fighting, regained the position.

At the start of day three of the battle, Lee recognized that the Union army was still in possession of the high ground, but he was confident that he had so worn down the Army of the Potomac that he could destroy it with an all-out attack. Despite Longstreet's protests, he ordered a massive charge, which history has named after George Pickett, who actually commanded just three of the nine brigades—a total of 12,500 men—committed to the attack.

Pickett's Charge began at 1:45 in the afternoon. Before it was over, 7,500 of the 12,500 engaged were killed or wounded, and the Battle of Gettysburg was over—a terrible Confederate defeat. The Union fielded 88,289 men at Gettysburg, of whom 3,155 were killed and another 14,529 were wounded, mortally wounded, or captured; 5,365 went missing. Of 75,000 Confederates engaged, 3,903 were killed; 18,735 were wounded, mortally wounded, or captured; and 5,425 were reported missing in action.

Meade had driven the Confederates out of the North, but he declined to pursue Lee's battered Army of Northern Virginia back into

Virginia. Had he done so, he might well have broken the back of the Confederate military and hastened the end of the war. Nevertheless, the Union victory at Gettysburg, coupled with Grant's capture of Vicksburg, not only heartened the war-weary North, it ended whatever hope the South still held for securing foreign support for the Confederate cause. It certainly ended any hope the South had for victory.

The Chickamauga Campaign

The siege of Vicksburg and the Battle of Gettysburg exhausted both sides, and the pace of the war slowed after these engagements, temporarily shifting from Mississippi and Pennsylvania to central Tennessee and northern Georgia. The Union's William Starke Rosecrans, commanding the Army of the Cumberland, forced the Confederate general Braxton Bragg to withdraw to Chattanooga in August, whereupon Rosecrans attacked the Western and Atlantic Railroad, Bragg's supply and communications line to Atlanta. With this link severed, Bragg was forced to evacuate Chattanooga, which Rosecrans took on August 21.

Having captured Chattanooga, the next logical step would have been for Rosecrans to concentrate his forces there and resupply them before resuming his offensive against Bragg. Anxious to maintain momentum, however, Rosecrans hardly paused, pushing his three battle-weary corps toward the Georgia border in pursuit of Bragg. The Confederates halted at La Fayette, Georgia, 25 miles south of Chattanooga, and, after taking on reinforcements, counterattacked Rosecrans on September 19 at Chickamauga Creek, on the Georgia-Tennessee line.

The fighting took place in a dense wood amid utter confusion on both sides. At the end of the first day of battle, much blood had been shed, but neither side had gained any advantage. On the night of September 19–20,

both sides dug in, and at 9:00 on September 20, the Confederates attacked. Rosecrans struggled to obtain an accurate picture of how his units were deployed. Believing there was a gap in his right flank, he ordered troops from what he also believed was his left to move right to plug the gap. In fact, there was no gap, and, even worse, Rosecrans inadvertently created a gap by moving troops out of his right flank. The Confederate general Longstreet saw the gap and attacked through it at 11:30, badly mauling divisions commanded by Major General Philip Sheridan and Brigadier General Jefferson Columbus Davis. This drove the Union's right into its left, putting the Army of the Cumberland in great peril. Believing that all had been lost, Rosecrans and two of his corps commanders, Thomas Leonidas Crittenden and Alexander McDowell McCook, fled to Chattanooga, but Major General George Henry Thomas, acting on his own initiative, stood fast and rallied sufficient units to block Longstreet on the south. Another Union general, Gordon Granger, deliberately disobeyed his orders, which were to remain in place to protect the army's flank, and reinforced Thomas with two brigades. Thanks to this, Thomas held the field, saving the army from annihilation and earning for himself the epithet of the "Rock of Chickamauga." Nevertheless, casualties were staggering: Of 58,222 Union troops engaged, 1,657 were killed; 9,756 wounded; and 4,757 went missing. Confederate losses were 2,312 killed; 14,674 wounded; and 1,468 missing out of 66,326 engaged.

The Siege of Chattanooga and the Battle of Lookout Mountain

After Chickamauga, the Army of the Cumberland withdrew to Chattanooga, where Braxton Bragg laid siege to them. Two corps under Joseph Hooker were detached from Meade's

Army of the Potomac to lift the siege. They arrived on October 2, even as Sherman led part of his Army of the Tennessee east from Memphis, and Ulysses S. Grant, now in command of all military operations west of the Alleghenies, opened up a supply route (known as the "Cracker Line") to beleaguered Chattanooga.

The designated rallying point for the Union forces sent against Bragg was Bridgeport, Alabama. Sherman arrived there on November 15, and on the 24th, Grant ordered Hooker to take Lookout Mountain, which loomed 1,100 feet over the Tennessee River just outside Chattanooga. Hooker fought uphill from eight in the morning until after midnight, soldiers from the 8th Kentucky Regiment planting the Stars and Stripes atop the mountain on the morning of November 25. Later that same day, Thomas led the Army of the Cumberland against Confederate rifle pits at the base of Missionary Ridge south of Chattanooga, east of Lookout Mountain. Not only did Thomas's troops take the rifle pits but, entirely on their own initiative, they continued on, up Missionary Ridge, sweeping all Confederate forces before them, breaking Bragg's line and setting the seal on Confederate defeat in the near West.

The Overland Campaign

Ulysses S. Grant's triumph at Vicksburg convinced President Lincoln to appoint him general in chief of the Union armies on March 9, 1864. Grant refocused Union strategy on destroying the enemy army rather than on taking and occupying territory. Grant would personally fight Lee's Army of Northern Virginia, while his most trusted subordinate, William Tecumseh Sherman, would fight the Confederates' Army of Tennessee, now under the command of Joseph E. Johnston, who had replaced Bragg. Sherman's assignment was to move down the route of the Western and Atlantic Railroad, advancing inexorably against Atlanta, in the process eating up the Army of Tennessee. As Sherman moved toward Atlanta, forcing Johnston to fight him in order to defend the city, Grant would advance on Richmond, not so much with the object of taking the Confederate capital as for the purpose of destroying the Army of Northern Virginia, which would be obliged to come to the capital's defense. In addition to the main body of the Army of the Potomac (nominally commanded by George G. Meade, but ultimately directed by Grant), Grant aimed two other armies at Richmond: the Army of the James, 33,000 men under Benjamin Butler, and a force in the Shenandoah Valley, led by Franz Sigel.

The so-called Overland Campaign began on May 4, 1864, when the 120,000-man Army of the Potomac crossed the Rapidan River to engage Lee's 66,000-man Army of Northern Virginia. Lee boldly usurped the initiative by attacking the army as it passed through the tangled and densely forested area known as the Wilderness. Lacking an open field for deployment, Grant was unable to exploit his overwhelming strength or use his artillery. The fighting in the Wilderness spanned May 5–8, and Grant was defeated with losses of 17,666 (2,246 killed; 12,073 wounded; and the rest missing) out of 101,895 actively engaged. Confederate records indicate that, of 61,025 engaged, 7,500 were killed, wounded, or missing. Two Confederate generals were killed, another was mortally wounded, and four more were wounded but recovered, including James Longstreet, hit by friendly fire.

Although defeated at the Wilderness, Grant advanced rather than withdrew, moving on to Spotsylvania Court House, at a crossroads on the way to Richmond. Knowing that he could afford to lose more men than Lee could, Grant was determined to force his opponent to fight and fight again. With each battle, regardless of outcome, the Army of Northern Virginia would inexorably waste away. The Battle of Spotsylvania Courthouse spanned May 8–21, with Grant always shifting his troops to the left, continually probing for Lee's flank in an effort to turn it. Lee, however, persisted in evading destruction.

As the armies of Grant and Lee held one another in a death grip, Philip Sheridan, commanding the Army of the Potomac's 10,000-man cavalry, launched a breakout toward Richmond intended to draw Jeb Stuart and the Confederate cavalry, about 4,500 troopers, into a fight. Stuart blocked Sheridan near an abandoned wayside inn called Yellow Tavern, just six miles north of Richmond. The two cavalry forces engaged on May 11, Sheridan withdrawing after three hours; however, Stuart was mortally wounded in the fight—a terrible blow to Lee.

On the same day as the Battle of Yellow Tavern, Grant ordered Major General Winfield Scott Hancock to attack Richard Ewell's corps, which was deployed at Spotsylvania in entrenchments shaped like an inverted U. From this, the battle drew its name: Mule Shoe. The attack commenced at 4:30 on the morning of May 12 and soon became a hand-to-hand struggle that continued well into the night before ending inconclusively. Grant advanced south to fight at the North Anna River (May 24) and then at Totopotomoy Creek (May 26–30). Each time, Lee's defenses held, but each time, his Army of Northern Virginia bled more and more.

While the principal forces of Grant and Lee battered one another in northeastern Virginia, the Union major general Franz Sigel was defeated by General John C. Breckenridge at New Market, in the Shenandoah Valley, on May 15, and Benjamin Butler's compact Army of the James was effectively bottled up on Virginia's Bermuda Hundred peninsula. This permitted Lee to draw badly needed reinforcements from that front to use against Grant.

Those reinforcements were present on the night of June 1, when Grant and Lee raced toward a crossroads called Cold Harbor, six miles northeast of Richmond. During the first two days of the Battle of Cold Harbor, June 1–2, Grant lost 5,000 men as he beat against Lee's entrenchments. On June 3, Grant hurled 60,000 troops against Lee. Some 7,000 fell in a single hour, after which Grant withdrew his army under cover of darkness and crossed the

Chickahominy. Defeated yet again, Grant yet again chose to advance.

Lee reasonably assumed that he was headed for Richmond and therefore deployed most of his troops defensively in the outskirts of the city. But Grant managed to outwit Lee, rapidly shifting to a new objective: Petersburg, a rail junction vital to the supply of Richmond and the Confederate armies. When 16,000 Union troops arrived at Petersburg on June 15, there were only 3,000 Confederates, under P. G. T. Beauregard, on hand to defend the city. Had the commander of this first Union contingent, Major General William Farrar "Baldy" Smith, acted quickly, Petersburg would have fallen—and Richmond would almost certainly have soon followed. Instead, Smith first delayed and then mishandled his assaults against Petersburg during June 15–18, which allowed Beauregard time to reinforce his position. Grant had no choice but to settle in for a long siege.

One more opportunity for quick victory presented itself, however. Henry Pleasants, a regimental colonel who had been in civilian life a coal mining engineer, proposed tunneling under the Confederate fortifications around Petersburg and blowing them up. A spectacular 500-foot-long tunnel was completed on July 27, was duly packed with four tons of black powder, and was detonated on July 30, tearing a gaping hole in the enemy entrenchments. The follow-up, however, was so tragically bungled—with Union troops crowding into the blast crater and bogging down in the ruined maze of the Confederate entrenchments—that the "Battle of the Crater" turned from a potentially war-winning Union triumph to a particularly gruesome defeat. The Petersburg siege dragged on for nine months.

The Atlanta Campaign

While Grant laid siege to Petersburg, Sherman marched out of Chattanooga, bound for Atlanta. General Johnston pulled back before him, gathering reinforcements along the way. Under the circumstances, it was a sound strategy. Outnumbered, Johnston knew he could not defeat Sherman in direct battle, but if he could delay the capture of Atlanta until after the elections of 1864, he might be able to cost Lincoln reelection, thereby bringing into office a Democratic administration that might well negotiate a favorable peace. But the Confederate president, Jefferson Davis, would not stand for a strategy of retreat and, on July 17, he replaced the prudent Johnston with the impetuous John Bell Hood, who was determined to fight it out.

Sherman saw that Atlanta was strongly defended by earthworks and so decided to attack indirectly, by severing the four rail lines into the city, a tactic that would force the Confederates either to come out for a fight or to retreat. It was a sound plan, except for one flaw—a gap left between James B. McPherson's Army of the Tennessee and John M. Schofield's Army of the Ohio on the one hand and George H. Thomas's Army of the Cumberland on the other. While Schofield and McPherson approached Atlanta from the east, Thomas crossed Peachtree Creek, north of the city. Perceiving the gap, Hood attacked it on July 20, igniting the Battle of Peachtree Creek. Thomas beat off Hood's onslaught, however, and successfully linked up with McPherson and Schofield. Undaunted, on July 22, Hood attacked McPherson's Army of the Tennessee. McPherson fell in the battle, but his men rallied and, with their superior numbers, forced Hood back into his defensive works.

Having cut the rail lines north and east of the city, Sherman brought his army down around to the southwest, to seize the Macon and Western Railroad there. On July 28, Hood once again attacked the Army of the Tennessee (which was now commanded by O. O. Howard) at Ezra Church, just west of the city. Howard repulsed Hood, inflicting heavy losses on him.

Sherman saw that Atlanta now lay within his grasp, but he also recognized that Hood's army, though battered, was still intact. If Hood could manage to hold on long enough, the Confederate general Nathan Bedford Forrest might well attack from the rear—with devastating results.

Sherman therefore took a new tack. On August 25, he suddenly called off the bombardment of Hood's entrenchments, and on the next day—apparently—he disappeared. Hood assumed that Sherman had retreated.

That, of course, is just what Sherman wanted him to assume. He had in fact only swung down far to the south, cutting the Macon and Western Railroad, the last rail connection into the city. It was September 1 before Hood grasped what Sherman had done, and to avoid being trapped in the isolated city, he evacuated. Sherman then marched into the city, unopposed, on September 2 and transformed it into a fortress. Early in October, leaving a corps in Atlanta, he set out in pursuit of Hood. At Allatoona Pass, on October 5, Hood menaced a Union supply depot commanded by Brigadier General John M. Corse. When Hood demanded his surrender, Corse refused in obedience to Sherman's famous signal, "Hold the fort."

Sherman's victory at Atlanta not only deprived the Confederacy of a major rail hub, it ensured the reelection of Lincoln, which, in turn, meant that the war would be fought to total victory rather than negotiated settlement. Because Sherman had concluded that the Confederacy was disintegrating, he proposed breaking off from the pursuit of Hood to advance instead with 60,000 of his troops southeast to Savannah in a "March to the Sea." This, Sherman argued, would cut the Confederacy in two, north and south, just as the victories along the Mississippi River had severed it east from west, and would also put Sherman in position to attack Lee's Army of Northern Virginia from the south even as Grant continued to bear down on it from the north. Grant agreed, so that, in mid November, Sherman and Hood actually turned away from each other as Sherman marched east to the sea and Hood withdrew west toward Nashville.

Hood's intention was to coordinate with Nathan Bedford Forrest in an attack on the 30,000 men under Major General George H. Thomas, who had been sent to clear the Confederates out of Tennessee. Hood believed that his attack would force Sherman to come to Thomas's rescue, not only clearing Sherman out of Atlanta but compelling him to abandon his March to the Sea. In the meantime, on November 11, Sherman ordered everything of military significance in Atlanta destroyed. The result, by November 16, was a blaze that consumed virtually all of the city.

As for General Thomas, anticipating problems from Hood and Forrest, he reinforced his strength to 50,000 men in Nashville during early November. Hood tried to force the Union general John M. Schofield to a finish fight at Spring Hill, Tennessee, on November 29, but Schofield withdrew to a position at Franklin, just south of Nashville. On November 30, the frustrated and impetuous Hood ordered a frontal assault on Schofield's well-defended position. Of the 18,000 men Hood fielded, more than 6,000 were killed or wounded at the Battle of Franklin, after which Schofield continued his march to Nashville to unite with Thomas's force. Hood was outnumbered two to one when Thomas attacked him on December 15–16 in the Battle of Nashville, decisively defeating the Confederates. An extraordinary rearguard action by Forrest staved off the outright destruction of the Confederates' Army of Tennessee, but it was effectively neutralized as a fighting force.

Now freed from any threat posed by Hood, there was nothing to prevent Sherman from continuing his march southeast from Atlanta, toward Savannah, cutting a swath of destruction as he went with the object of destroying the South's will to fight. Savannah surrendered without a fight on December 22, 1864, and Columbia, capital of South Carolina fell on February 17, 1865, amid fires that destroyed half the town. On the next day, the Confederates abandoned Fort Sumter as Union troops closed in on Charleston.

Endgame

While Sherman was taking Atlanta, then marching to the sea, and while the Union forces in Ten-

nessee were neutralizing both Hood and Forrest, the Confederates continued to look for ways to defend Richmond. One strategy was to menace Washington, which Jubal Early did in a raid out of the Shenandoah Valley during July 1864. By the 11th, Early had reached the outer forts defending the capital but was chased away the next day by the 25th New York Cavalry and the Army of the Potomac's VI Corps. Early then turned to harassing small Union units in the Shenandoah Valley, prompting Grant to send Sheridan with 48,000 men to "pacify" the Valley. He not only pursued Early but burned barns and crops and destroyed cattle throughout a region that served as the breadbasket of the Confederacy.

In truth, the war was lost for the Confederacy. At Petersburg, the defenders were starting to starve. Lee persuaded President Jefferson Davis that only a breakout from Petersburg and a retreat southeast, to unite the Army of Northern Virginia with the tattered remnants of the Army of Tennessee, could keep the fight going, possibly resulting in a negotiated peace rather than abject surrender. Leaving Petersburg would mean the fall of Richmond, but at least the army would remain intact.

Lee ordered Major General John Brown Gordon to attack a hardened Union position called Fort Stedman, which was along the Union siege lines. The attack took place in the predawn hours of March 25, 1865, but was soon countered. Of 12,000 men engaged, the Confederates lost 4,000 killed, wounded, or captured, and the idea of a breakout had to be abandoned.

As for Grant, he continued working the siege. All along he had been extending his lines westward in order to force Lee to stretch his much thinner lines until they broke. On March 31, Sheridan, returned from the Shenandoah Valley with 12,000 cavalry troopers, rode to Five Forks, a junction vital to the Confederate line of supply. Lee sent George Pickett with somewhere between 10,000 and 19,000 troops—the figure is much disputed—to hold Five Forks, but Sheridan outgeneraled him, routed his forces, and took Five Forks, along with at least 5,000 prisoners of war.

Lee's Petersburg lines finally shattered on April 2, yielding to a thrust from Grant. Lee withdrew his men to Petersburg, then retreated west toward Amelia Court House. In the meantime, Jefferson Davis ordered the Confederate government to evacuate Richmond. A provisional capital was set up in Danville, Virginia.

By this time, the proud Army of Northern Virginia consisted of fewer than 50,000 men. With them, Lee marched west, hoping to be resupplied at Amelia Court House, and hoping as well to gain access there to the Danville and Richmond Railroad, which could transport his army to join Johnston's. By April 5, most of Lee's army had reached Amelia Court House, 30 miles west of Petersburg, but Sheridan and others blocked his access to the railroad. Worse, the rations and other supplies Lee had anticipated obtaining were nowhere to be found. Lee then turned to the southwest, bound for Rice Station, another supply opportunity. Relentless, Grant ordered attacks to intercept Lee. At Little Sayler's Creek, Confederate forces under Richard S. Ewell were defeated, and one-third of what remained of the Army of Northern Virginia was captured.

The Confederate general John Brown Gordon rallied survivors of the Battle of Little Sayler's Creek and led them west to High Bridge, across the Appomattox River at Farmville. There he joined Longstreet in retreating across the bridge, but neither commander thought to burn the bridge behind them, and as a result, Union forces rapidly closed on the rear of Lee's army.

The Battles of Appomattox Station and Appomattox Court House

On April 8, what remained of Lee's army was concentrated between Appomattox Station, on the rail line, and Appomattox Court House, a few miles to the northeast. A division commanded by Brigadier General George A. Custer attacked Appomattox Station, driving off two Confederate divisions and capturing their supply train. Custer then advanced toward Appomattox Court House. There Sheridan, with the main body of Union troops, caught up with Custer and prepared to launch a major attack on the next day. But, on April 9, the Confederate generals John Brown Gordon and Fitzhugh Lee attacked first. Union cavalry and infantry closed in from the northeast and the southwest, trapping the Confederates. Lee now asked for terms, and later that day, he met Grant in the McLean farm house, where the two commanders negotiated the surrender of the Army of Northern Virginia.

Neither Grant nor Lee had the authority to end the Civil War, but the surrender of the Confederacy's principal army effectively brought the conflict to its conclusion. The rest was anticlimax. Montgomery, Alabama, fell on April 12, and Federal troops entered Mobile the same day. On April 13, Sherman occupied Raleigh, North Carolina, where, during April 17–18, he and General Johnston hammered out a broad armistice. Abraham Lincoln had been assassinated on April 14, and his successor, Andrew Johnson, repudiated the Sherman-Johnston armistice but, on April 26, approved an armistice that was identical to what Grant had offered Lee. On this date also, the Confederate cabinet met for the last time, to dissolve itself and, in so doing, to dissolve the Confederate States of America. On May 10, President Johnson declared that armed resistance was "virtually at an end," although, just three days later, at Palmito Ranch, near Brownsville, Texas, Confederate troops under Edmund Kirby Smith skirmished with Federals before surrendering on May 26. The very last Confederate commander to surrender was Stand Watie, son of a full-blooded Cherokee father and half-blooded Cherokee mother. A brigadier general in the provisional army of the Confederate States of America, he laid down arms on June 23, 1865, at Doakville, Indian Territory.

Of the 1,556,000 soldiers who served in the Union army during the Civil War, 359,528 were killed and 275,175 were wounded. Of the approximately 850,000 men of the Confederate forces, at least 258,000 died, and some 225,000 were wounded.

DOCUMENTS

THE BATTLE OF FORT SUMTER, APRIL 12–13, 1861

The First Shot of the Civil War: The Surrender of Fort Sumter
Stephen D. Lee
Published 1888

Pierre Gustave Toutant Beauregard, one of the many senior U.S. Army officers who had resigned their commissions to serve in the "provisional army" of the Confederate States of America, was in command of troops in and around Charleston, South Carolina. Pursuant to orders from the Confederate president Jefferson Davis, Beauregard demanded the surrender of Fort Sumter, in Charleston Harbor, the Federal garrison of which was commanded by Major Robert Anderson, who had been Beauregard's artillery instructor at West Point. On the afternoon of April 11, 1861, two of Beauregard's officers rowed across Charleston Harbor to Fort Sumter to deliver the surrender demand. Captain Stephen D. Lee was one of these emissaries.

At 4:30 the next morning, when Anderson refused to surrender, Beauregard unleashed an artillery barrage against the fort, which held out through Saturday, April 13. Captain Lee provided this account of the surrender of the first shot of the war to Clarence Buel and Robert U. Johnston for their 1888 Battles and Leaders of the Civil War.

This demand was delivered to Major Anderson at 3:45 P.M., by two aides of General Beauregard, James Chesnut, Jr., and myself. At 4:30 P.M. he handed us his reply, refusing to accede to the demand; but added, "Gentlemen, if you do not batter the fort to pieces about us, we shall be starved out in a few days." The reply of Major Anderson was put in General Beauregard's hands at 5:15 P.M., and he was also told of this informal remark. Anderson's reply and remark were communicated to the Confederate authorities at Montgomery. The Secretary of War, L.P. Walker, replied to Beauregard as follows: "Do not desire needlessly to bombard Fort Sumter. If Major Anderson will state the time at which, as indicated by him, he will evacuate, and agree that in the meantime he will not use his guns against us, unless ours should be employed against Fort Sumter, you are authorized thus to avoid the effusion of blood. If this, or its equivalent, be refused, reduce the fort as your judgment decides to be most practicable."

The same aides bore a second communication to Major Anderson, based on the above instructions, which was placed in, his hands at 12:45 A.M., April 12th. His reply indicated that he would evacuate the fort on the 15th, provided he did not in the meantime receive contradictory instructions from his Government, or additional supplies, but he declined to agree not to open his guns upon the Confederate troops, in the event of any hostile demonstration on their part against his flag. Major Anderson made every possible effort to retain the aides till daylight, making one excuse and then another for not replying. Finally, at 3:15 A.M., he delivered his reply. In accordance with their instructions, the aides read it and, finding it unsatisfactory, gave Major Anderson this notification:

FORT SUMTER, S.C., April 12, 1861, 3:20 A.M.—SIR: By authority of Brigadier-General Beauregard, commanding the Provisional Forces of the Confederate States, we have the honor to notify you that he will open the fire of his batteries on Fort Sumter in one hour from this time. We have the honor to be very respectfully, Your obedient servants, JAMES CHESNUT JR., Aide-de-camp. STEPHEN D. LEE, Captain C. S. Army, Aide-de-camp.

The above note was written in one of the casemates of the fort, and in the presence of Major Anderson and several of his officers. On receiving it, he was much affected. He seemed to realize the full import of the consequences, and the great responsibility of his position. Escorting us to the boat at the wharf, he cordially pressed our hands in farewell, remarking, "If we never meet in this world again, God grant that we may meet in the next."

It was then 4 A.M. Captain James at once aroused his command, and arranged to carry out the order. He was a great admirer of Roger A. Pryor, and said to him, "You are the only man to whom I would give up the honor of firing the first gun of the war"; and he offered to allow him to fire it. Pryor, on receiving the offer, was very much agitated. With a husky voice he said, "I could not fire the first gun of the war." His manner was almost similar to that of Major Anderson as we left him a few moments before on the wharf at Fort Sumter. Captain James would allow no one else but himself to fire the gun.

The boat with the aides of General Beauregard left Fort Johnson before arrangements were complete for the firing of the gun, and laid on its oars, about one-third the distance between the fort and Sumter, there to witness the firing of "the first gun of the war" between the States. It was fired from a ten-inch mortar at 4:30 A.M., April 12th, 1861. Captain James was a skillful officer, and the firing of the shell was a success. It burst immediately over the fort, apparently about one hundred feet above.

The firing of the mortar woke the echoes from every nook and corner of the harbor, and in this the dead hour of the night, before dawn, that shot was a sound of alarm that brought every soldier in the harbor to his feet, and every man, woman and child in the city of Charleston from their beds. A thrill went through the whole city.

It was felt that the Rubicon was passed. No one thought of going home; unused as their ears were to the appalling sounds, or the vivid flashes from the batteries, they stood for hours fascinated with horror.

Source: EyewitnesstoHistory.com. "The First Shot of the Civil War: The Surrender of Fort Sumter, 1861." Available online. URL: http://www.eyewitnesstohistory.com/sumter.htm. Accessed on February 8, 2010.

THE FIRST BATTLE OF BULL RUN, JULY 21, 1861

Letter to His Mother
Corporal Samuel English
Published 1888

The First Battle of Bull Run, on July 21, 1861, pitted 35,000 Union troops against about 30,000 Confederates near Manassas Creek in Virginia, a short march from Washington, D.C. Union general Irvin McDowell was expected to bring the war to a quick end by defeating the "rebels" here, then marching on to and capturing Richmond, the capital of the rebellion. Although the Confederates were soon forced to retreat, they mounted a vigorous counterattack that drove back one entire Union division, buying time for the arrival of Confederate reinforcements, which turned the battle against the Union. Union soldiers and civilians alike were shocked by the Confederate victory. Samuel J. English, a Union corporal in Company D, 2nd Rhode Island Volunteers, described the action and the "misery" that followed it in a letter to his mother written shortly after the battle but not published until 1888.

Sunday, the 21st about 2 o'clock the drums beat the assembly, and in ten minutes we were on our march for Bull Run having heard the enemy were waiting to receive us, our troops then numbering 25 or 30 thousand which were divided into three columns ours under Col Hunter taking the right through a thick woods. About eleven o'clock as our pickets were advancing through the woods a volley was poured in upon them from behind a fence thickly covered with brush; the pickets after returning the shots returned to our regiment and we advanced double quick time yelling like so many devils.

On our arrival into the open field I saw I should judge three or four thousand rebels retreating for a dense woods, firing as they retreated, while from another part of the woods a perfect hail storm of bullets, round shot and shell was poured upon us, tearing through our ranks and scattering death and confusion everywhere; but with a yell and a roar we charged upon them driving them again into the woods with fearful

loss. In the mean time our battery came up to our support and commenced hurling destruction among the rebels.

Next, orders were given for us to fall back and protect our battery as the enemy were charging upon it from another quarter, and then we saw with dismay that the second R. I. [Rhode Island] regiment were the only troops in the fight; the others having lagged so far behind that we had to stand the fight alone for 30 minutes; 1100 against 7 or 8 thousand. It was afterwards ascertained from a prisoner that the rebels thought we numbered 20 or 30 thousand from the noise made by us while making the charge. While preparing to make our final effort to keep our battery out of their hands, the 1st R.I. regiment then came filing over the fence

The battle at Bull Run, or Manassas, in Virginia, on July 21, 1861, was the first major battle of the Civil War. *(Library of Congress)*

and poured a volley out to them that drove them under cover again; they were followed by the New York 71st and the Hampshire 2nd regiments, with 2,000 regulars bringing up the rear who pitched into the "Sechers" (Secessionists) most beautifully.

Our regiments were then ordered off the field and formed a line for a support to rally on in case the rebels over powered our troops. When the line had formed again I started off for the scene of action to see how the fight was progressing. As I emerged from the woods I saw a bomb shell strike a man in the breast and literally tear him to pieces. I passed the farm house which had been appropriated for a hospital and the groans of the wounded and dying were horrible.

I then descended the hill to the woods which had been occupied by the rebels at the place where the Elsworth zouaves made their charge; the bodies of the dead and dying were actually three and four deep, while in the woods where the desperate struggle had taken place between the U.S. Marines and the Louisiana zouaves [volunteers], the trees were spattered with blood and the ground strewn with dead bodies. The shots flying pretty lively round me I thought best to join my regiment; as I gained the top of the hill I heard the shot and shell of our batteries had given out, not having but 130 shots for each gun during the whole engagement. As we had nothing but infantry to fight against their batteries, the command was given to retreat; our cavalry not being of much use, because the rebels would not come out of the woods.

The R.I. regiments, the New York 71st and the New Hampshire 2nd were drawn into a line to cover the retreat, but an officer galloped wildly into the column crying the enemy is upon us, and off they started like a flock of sheep every man for himself and the devil take the hindermost; while the rebels' shot and shell fell like rain among our exhausted troops.

As we gained the cover of the woods the stampede became even more frightful, for the baggage wagons and ambulances became entangled with the artillery and rendered the scene even more dreadful than the battle, while the plunging of the horses broke the lines of our infantry, and prevented any successful formation out of the question. The rebels being so badly cut up supposed we had gone beyond the woods to form for a fresh attack and shelled the woods for full two hours, supposing we were there, thus saving the greater part of our forces, for if they had begun an immediate attack, nothing in heaven's name could have saved us. As we neared the bridge the rebels opened a very destructive fire upon us, mowing down our men like grass, and caused even greater confusion than before. Our artillery and baggage wagons became fouled with each other, completely blocking the bridge, while the bomb shells bursting on the bridge made it "rather unhealthy" to be around. As I crossed on my hands and knees, Capt. Smith who was crossing by my side at the same time was struck by a round shot at the same time and completely cut in two. After I crossed I started up the hill as fast as my legs could carry and passed through Centreville and continued on to Fairfax where we arrived about 10 o'clock halting about 15 minutes, then kept on to Washington where we arrived about 2 o'clock Monday noon more dead than alive, having been on our feet 36 hours without a mouthful to eat, and traveled a distance of 60 miles without twenty minutes halt.

The last five miles of that march was perfect misery, none of us having scarcely strength to put one foot before the other, but I tell you the cheers we rec'd going through the streets of Washington seemed to put new life into the men for they rallied and marched to our camps and every man dropped on the ground and in one moment the greater part of them were asleep. Our loss is estimated at 1,000, but I think it greater, the rebels lost from three to five thousand.

Source: EyewitnesstoHistory.com. "The First Battle of Bull Run, 1861." Available online. URL: http://www.eyewitnesstohistory.com/bullrun.htm. Accessed on February 8, 2010.

THE BATTLE OF HAMPTON ROADS: USS *MONITOR* V. CSS *VIRGINIA*, MARCH 9, 1862

Account of the Battle
Lieutenant Samuel Dana Greene, USN
Written 1884

The celebrated March 9, 1862, duel between the all-iron USS Monitor *and the ironclad CSS* Virginia *(formerly the USS* Merrimack) *in Hampton Roads off the Virginia coast was the first naval battle between "modern" battleships. Although it ended in a tactical draw, it was a strategic victory for the Union because it defeated the Confederacy's effort to disrupt the U.S. Navy's blockade of southern ports. Lieutenant Samuel Dana Greene was executive officer of the USS* Monitor. *Here he describes what he saw from his ship's gun turret—a fully enclosed rotating turret that was itself a major innovation in naval warfare—when Captain John Warden gave the order to engage the CSS* Virginia *[ex-USS* Merrimack], *which was firing on the grounded USS* Minnesota, *a conventional wooden ship that was part of the Union blockading force. (Note that Greene uses the* Merrimack's *original name in this account, but he spells it without the final k.)*

Worden lost no time in bringing it [the *Monitor*] to test. Getting his ship under way, he steered direct for the enemy's vessels, in order to meet and engage them as far as possible from the *Minnesota*. As he approached, the wooden vessels quickly turned and left: Our captain . . . made straight for the *Merrimac*, which had already commenced firing; and when he came within short range, he changed his course so as to come alongside of her, stopped the engine, and gave the order, "Commence firing!" I triced [raised] up the [gun] port, ran out the gun, and, taking deliberate aim, pulled the lockstring. The *Mer-*

rimac was quick to reply, returning a rattling broadside (for she had ten guns to our two), and the battle fairly began. The turrets and other parts of the ship were heavily struck, but the shots did not penetrate; the tower was intact, and it continued to revolve. A look of confidence passed over the men's faces, and we believed the *Merrimac* would not repeat the work she had accomplished the day before.

The fight continued with the exchange of broadsides as fast as the guns could be served and at very short range, the distance between the vessels frequently being not more than a few yards. Worden skillfully maneuvered his quick-turning vessel, trying to find some vulnerable point in his adversary. Once he made a dash at her stern, hoping to disable her screw, which he thinks he missed by not more than two feet. Our shots ripped the iron of the *Merrimac*, while the reverberation of her shots against the tower caused anything but a pleasant sensation. While Stodder, who was stationed at the machine which controlled the revolving motion of the turret, was incautiously leaning against the side of the tower, a large shot struck in the vicinity and disabled him. He left the turret and went below, and Stimers, who had assisted him, continued to do the work. . . .

The effect upon one shut upon a revolving drum [that is, inside the *Monitor*'s turret] is perplexing, and it is not a simple matter to keep the bearings. White marks had been placed upon the stationary deck immediately below the turret to indicate the direction of the starboard and port sides, and the bow and stern; but these marks were obliterated early in the action. I would continually ask the captain, "How does the *Merrimac* bear?" He replied, "On the starboard-beam," or "On the port-quarter," as the case might be. Then the difficulty was to determine the direction of the starboard-beam, or port-quarter, or any other bearing. It finally resulted, that when a gun was ready for firing, the turret would be started on its revolving journey in search of the target, and when found it was taken "on the fly," because the turret could not be accurately controlled.

On March 9, 1862, the USS *Monitor* and the CSS *Virginia* (formerly the *Merrimack*) engaged in the first battle between two ironclad ships. It ended in a draw, and neither ship ever fought in another battle. *(Library of Congress)*

Once the *Merrimac* tried to ram us; but Worden avoided the direct impact by the skillful use of the helm, and she struck a glancing blow, which did no damage. At the instant of collision I planted a solid 180-pound shot fair and square upon the forward part of her casemate . . . but the charge, being limited to fifteen pounds, in accordance with peremptory orders to that effect from the Navy Department, the shot rebounded without doing any more damage than possibly to start some of the beams of her armor-backing.

. . . The battle continued at close quarters without apparent damage to either side. . . . Two important points were constantly kept in mind: first, to prevent the enemy's projectiles from entering the turret through the port-holes,—for the explosion of a shell inside, by disabling the men at the guns, would have ended the fight, as there was no relief gun's crew on board; second, not to fire into our own pilot-house. A careless

or impatient hand, during the confusion arising from the whirligig motion of the tower, might let slip one of our big shot against the pilot-house. For this and other reasons I fired every gun while I remained in the turret.

Soon after noon a shell from the enemy's gun, the muzzle not ten yards distant, struck the forward side of the pilot-house directly in the sight-hole, or slit, and exploded, cracking the second iron log and partly lifting the top, leaving an opening.

Worden was standing immediately behind this spot, and received in his face the force of the blow, which partly stunned him, and, filling his eyes with powder, utterly blinded him. . . . The flood of light rushing through the top of the pilot-house, now partly open, caused Worden, blind as he was, to believe that the pilot-house was seriously injured, if not destroyed; he therefore gave orders to put the helm to starboard and "sheer off." Thus the *Monitor* retired temporarily from the action, in order to ascertain the extent of the injuries she had received. At the same time Worden sent for me . . . I went forward at once, and found him standing at the foot of the ladder leading to the pilothouse.

He was a ghastly sight, with his eyes closed and the blood apparently rushing from every pore in the upper part of his face. He told me that he was seriously wounded, and directed me to take command. . . . I found that the iron log was fractured and the top partly open; but the steering gear was still intact, and the pilot-house was not totally destroyed, as had been feared. In the confusion of the moment resulting from so serious an injury to the commanding officer, the *Monitor* had been moving without direction. During this time the *Merrimac,* which was leaking badly, had started in the direction of the Elizabeth River; and, on taking my station in the pilot-house and turning the vessel's head in the direction of the *Merrimac,* I saw that she was already in retreat. A few shots were fired at the retiring vessel, and she continued on to Norfolk. . . . The fight was over.

Source: "In the *Monitor* Turret." Available online. URL: http://www.mariner.org/uss-monitor-center/eye-witness-accounts-samuel-dana-greene. Accessed on February 8, 2010.

THE FAR WESTERN THEATER: THE BATTLE OF GLORIETA PASS, MARCH 26–28, 1862

After-Action Report, Battle of Glorieta Pass
Colonel John P. Slough
March 29, 1862

The Confederate general Henry Hopkins Sibley, determined to capture the silver mines of Colorado to help finance the Southern war effort, marched up *the Rio Grande toward Fort Union, headquarters of the Union commander E. R. S. Canby. His objective was to seize control of the Santa Fe Trail, principal avenue of trade and communication in the region. After defeating the outnumbered Canby at Valverde, New Mexico, on February 21, 1862, Sibley occupied the town of Santa Fe, from which he proceeded to Fort Union via the Glorieta Pass through the Sangre de Cristo Mountains. It was at this pass, on March 26, 1862, that Union regulars under Colonel John Slough and Colorado volunteers commanded by Major John M. Chivington intercepted Sibley, fighting a two-day battle that forced Sibley's withdrawal. Although relatively small in scale, the battle has sometimes been called the "Gettysburg of the West" because it ended the string of Confederate victories in the Southwest.*

Slough sent this battle report to his commanding officer, Colonel Canby, the day after the culminating phase of the Battle of Glorieta Pass, the March 28 fight at Pigeon's Ranch.

Kozlowski's Ranch, March 29, 1862
COLONEL: Learning from our spies that the enemy, about 1000 strong, were in the Apache Canon [*sic*] and at Johnson's Ranch beyond, I concluded to reconnoiter in force, with a view of ascertaining the position of the enemy and of harassing them as much as possible; hence left this place with my command, nearly 1,300 strong, at 8 o'clock yesterday morning. To facilitate the reconnaissance I sent Maj. J. M. Chivington . . . with about 430 officers and picked men, with instructions to push forward to Johnson's. With the remainder of the command I entered the canon, and had attained but a short distance when our pickets announced that the enemy was near and had taken position in a thick grove of trees, with their line extending from mesa to mesa across the canon, and their battery, consisting of four pieces, placed in position. I at once detailed a considerable force of flankers, placed the batteries in position, and placed the cavalry—nearly all dismounted—and the remainder of the infantry in position to support the batteries.

Before the arrangement of my forces was completed the enemy opened fire upon us. The action began about 10 o'clock and continued until after 4 p.m. The character of the country was such as to make the engagement of the bushwhacking kind. Hearing of the success of Major Chivington's command, and the object of our movement being successful, we fell back in order to our camp. Our loss in killed is probably 20 . . . ; in wounded probably 50 . . . ; in missing probably over 100. In addition we took some 25 prisoners and rendered unfit for service three pieces of their artillery. We took and destroyed their train of about 60 wagons, with their contents, consisting of ammunition, subsistence, forage, clothing, officers' baggage, etc. . . . During the engagements the enemy made three attempts to take our batteries and were repelled in each with severe loss.

The strength of the enemy, as received from spies and prisoners, in the canon was altogether some 1,200 or 1,300, some 200 of whom were at or near Johnson's Ranch, and were engaged by Major Chivington's command. The officers and men behaved nobly. My thanks are due to my staff officers for the courage and ability with which they assisted me in conducting the engagement. As soon as all the details are ascertained I will send an official report of the engagement.

Source: U.S. War Department. *The War of the Rebellion: A Compilation of the Official Records of the Union and Confederate Armies*. Washington, D.C.: Government Printing Office, 1883, 9:533–534.

After-Action Report, Battle of Glorieta Pass
Lieutenant Colonel William Read Scurry
March 30, 1862

Lieutenant Colonel William Read Scurry, who commanded a portion of the Texas (Confederate) forces at the Battle of Glorieta Pass, reported to his commanding officer, Henry Hopkins Sibley, after withdrawing from the pass to Santa Fe. Scurry mistakenly believed that the battle had ended in a Confederate victory.

Santa Fe, N. Mex., March 30, 1862
GENERAL: I arrived here this morning with my command and have taken quarters for the present in this city. I will in a short time give you an official account of the battle of Glorieta, which occurred on day before yesterday, in the Canon [sic] Glorieta, about 22 miles from this city, . . . when another victory was added to the long list of Confederate triumphs.

The action commenced at about 11 o'clock and ended at 5:30, and, although every inch of the ground was well contested, we steadily drove them back until they were in full retreat our men pursuing until from sheer exhaustion we were compelled to stop.

Our loss was 33 killed and I believe, 35 wounded. . . . Major Pyron had his horse shot under him, and my own cheek was twice brushed by a Minie ball, each time drawing blood, and my clothes torn in two places. I mentioned this simply to show how hot was the fire of the enemy when all of the field officers upon the ground were either killed or touched. . . .

Our [supply] train was burned by a party who succeeded in passing undiscovered around the mountains to our rear. . . . The loss of the enemy was very severe, being over 75 killed and a large number wounded.

The loss of my supplies so crippled me that after burying my dead I was unable to follow up the victory. My men for two days went unfed and blanketless unmurmuringly. I was compelled to come here for something to eat. At last accounts the Federalists were still retiring towards Fort Union. The men at the train blew up the limberbox and spiked the 6-pounder I had left at the train, so that it was rendered useless, and the cart-burners left it.

. . . From three sources, all believed to be reliable, Canby left Craig on the 24th.
Yours in haste, W.R. SCURRY

P.S. I do not know if I write intelligently. I have not slept for three nights, and can scarcely hold my eyes open. W.R.S.

Source: U.S. War Department. *The War of the Rebellion: A Compilation of the Official Records of the Union and Confederate Armies.* Washington, D.C.: Government Printing Office, 1883, 9:541–542.

THE BATTLE OF SHILOH, APRIL 6–7, 1862

Account of the Battle
Sir Henry Morton Stanley
Published 1909

Born in Wales, Henry Morton Stanley (1841–1904) was a journalist who became most famous for his African explorations and his search for the missionary David Livingstone. Before this, however, he came to the United States in 1859, at age 18, and subsequently fought on the Confederate side in the Civil War. Taken prisoner at Shiloh, he joined the Union army, from which he deserted. His autobiography, published in 1909, includes perhaps the most vivid firsthand account of the Battle of Shiloh ever published. The battle awoke Americans, northerners and southerners alike, to the reality of just how bloody this civil war would be.

On April 2, 1862, we received orders to prepare three days' cooked rations. Through some misunderstanding, we did not set out until the 4th; and, on the morning of that day, the 6th Arkansas Regiment of Hindman's brigade, Hardee's corps, marched from Corinth to take part in one of the bloodiest battles of the West. We left our knapsacks and tents behind us. After two days of marching, and two nights of bivouacking and living on cold rations, our spirits were not so buoyant at dawn of Sunday, the 6th April, as they ought to have been for the serious task before us. Many wished, like myself, that we had not been required to undergo this discomfort before being precipitated into the midst of a great battle.

Military science, with all due respect to our generals, was not at that time what it is now. Our military leaders were well acquainted with the science of war, and, in the gross fashion prevailing, paid proper attention to the commissariat. Every soldier had his lawful allowance of raw provender dealt out to him; but, as to its uses and effects, no one seemed to be concerned. Future commanding generals will doubtless remedy this, and when they meditate staking their cause and reputation on a battle, they will, like the woodman about to do a good day's work at cutting timber, see that their instruments are in the best possible state for their purpose.

Generals Johnston and Beauregard proposed to hurl into the Tennessee River an army of nearly 50,000 rested and well-fed troops, by means of 40,000 soldiers, who, for two days, had subsisted on sodden biscuit and raw bacon, who had been exposed for two nights to rain and dew, and had marched twenty-three miles! Considering that at least a fourth of our force were lads under twenty, and that such a strenuous task was before them, it suggests itself to me that the omission to take the physical powers of those youths into their calculation had as much to do with the failure of the project as the obstinate courage of General Grant's troops. According to authority, the actual number of the forces about to be opposed to each other was 39,630 Con-

The battle at Shiloh Church in southwestern Tennessee broke out on April 6, 1862, and raged throughout the day, taking a terrible toll of casualties on both sides. *(Library of Congress)*

federates against 49,232 Federals. Our generals expected the arrival of General Van Dorn, with 20,000 troops, who failed to make their appearance; but, close at hand to Grant, was General Buell's force of 20,000, who, opportunely for Grant, arrived just at the close of the day's battle.

At four o'clock in the morning, we rose from our damp bivouac, and, after a hasty refreshment, were formed into line. We stood in rank for half an hour or so, while the military dispositions were being completed along the three-mile front. Our brigade formed the centre; Cleburne's and Gladden's brigades were on our respective flanks.

Day broke with every promise of a fine day. Next to me, on my right, was a boy of seventeen, Henry Parker. I remember it because, while we stood-at-ease, he drew my attention to some violets at his feet, and said, "It would be a good idea to put a few into my cap. Perhaps the Yanks won't shoot me if they see me wearing such flowers, for they are a sign of peace." "Capital," said I, "I will do the same." We plucked a bunch, and arranged the violets in our caps. The men in the ranks laughed at our proceedings, and had not the enemy been so near, their merry mood might have been communicated to the army.

We loaded our muskets, and arranged our cartridge-pouches ready for use. Our weapons were the obsolete flintlocks, and the ammunition was rolled in cartridge-paper, which contained powder, a round ball, and three buckshot. When we loaded we had to tear the paper with our teeth, empty a little powder into the pan, lock it, empty the rest of the powder into the barrel, press paper and ball into the muzzle, and ram home. Then the Orderly-sergeant called the roll, and we knew that the Dixie Greys were present to a man. Soon after, there was a commotion, and we dressed up smartly. A young Aide galloped along our front, gave some instructions to the Brigadier Hindman, who confided the same to his Colonels, and presently we swayed forward in line, with shouldered arms. Newton Story, big, broad, and straight, bore our company-banner of gay silk, at which the ladies of our neighbourhood had laboured.

As we tramped solemnly and silently through the thin forest, and over its grass, still in its withered and wintry hue, I noticed that the sun was not far from appearing, that our regiment was keeping its formation admirably, that the woods would have been a grand place for a picnic; and I thought it strange that a Sunday should have been chosen to disturb the holy calm of those woods.

Before we had gone five hundred paces, our serenity was disturbed by some desultory firing in front. It was then a quarter-past five. "They are at it already," we whispered to each other. "Stand by, gentlemen,"—for we were all gentlemen volunteers at this time,—said our Captain, L. G. Smith. Our steps became unconsciously brisker, and alertness was noticeable in everybody. The firing continued at intervals, deliberate and scattered, as at target-practice. We drew nearer to the firing, and soon a sharper rattling of musketry was heard. "That is the enemy waking up," we said. Within a few minutes, there was another explosive burst of musketry, the air was pierced by many missiles, which hummed and pinged sharply by our ears, pattered through the tree-tops, and brought twigs and leaves down on us. "Those are bullets," Henry whispered with awe.

At two hundred yards further, a dreadful roar of musketry broke out from a regiment adjoining ours. It was followed by another further off, and the sound had scarcely died away when regiment after regiment blazed away and made a continuous roll of sound. "We are in for it now," said Henry; but as yet we had seen nothing, though our ears were tingling under the animated volleys.

"Forward, gentlemen, make ready!" urged Captain Smith. In response, we surged forward, for the first time marring the alignment. We trampled recklessly over the grass and young sprouts. Beams of sunlight stole athwart our course. The sun was up above the horizon. Just then we came to a bit of packland, and overtook our skirmishers, who had been engaged in exploring our front. We passed beyond them. Nothing now stood between us and the enemy.

"There they are!" was no sooner uttered, than we cracked into them with levelled muskets. "Aim low, men!" commanded Captain Smith. I tried hard to see some living thing to shoot at, for it appeared absurd to be blazing away at shadows. But, still advancing, firing as we moved, I, at last, saw a row of little globes of pearly smoke streaked with crimson, breaking-out, with spurtive quickness, from a long line of bluey figures in front; and, simultaneously, there broke upon our ears an appalling crash of sound, the series of fusillades following one another with startling suddenness, which suggested to my somewhat moidered sense a mountain upheaved, with huge rocks tumbling and thundering down a slope, and the echoes rumbling and receding through space. Again and again, these loud and quick explosions were repeated, seemingly with increased violence, until they rose to the highest pitch of fury, and in unbroken continuity. All the world seemed involved in one tremendous ruin!

This was how the conflict was ushered in—as it affected me. I looked around to see the effect on others, or whether I was singular in my emotions, and was glad to notice that each was possessed with his own thoughts. All were pale, solemn, and absorbed; but, beyond that, it was impossible for me to discover what they thought of it; but, by transmission of sympathy, I felt that they would gladly prefer to be elsewhere, though the law of the inevitable kept them in line to meet their destiny. It might be mentioned, however, that at no time were we more instinctively inclined to obey the voice of command. We had no individuality at this moment, but all motions and thoughts were surrendered to the unseen influence which directed our movements. Probably few bothered their minds with self-questionings as to the issue to themselves. That properly belongs to other moments, to the night, to the interval between waking and sleeping, to the first moments of the dawn—not when every nerve is tense, and the spirit is at the highest pitch of action.

Though one's senses were preternaturally acute, and engaged with their impressions, we plied our arms, loaded, and fired, with such nervous haste as though it depended on each of us how soon this fiendish uproar would be hushed. My nerves tingled, my pulses beat double-quick, my heart throbbed loudly, and almost painfully; but, amid all the excitement, my thoughts, swift as the flash of lightning, took all sound, and sight, and self, into their purview. I listened to the battle raging far away on the flanks, to the thunder in front, to the various sounds made by the leaden storm. I was angry with my rear rank, because he made my eyes smart with the powder of his musket; and I felt like cuffing him for deafening my ears! I knew how Captain Smith and Lieutenant Mason looked, how bravely the Dixie Greys' banner ruffled over Newton Story's head, and that all hands were behaving as though they knew how long all this would last. Back to myself my thoughts came, and, with the whirring bullet, they fled to the blue-bloused ranks afront. They dwelt on their movements, and read their temper, as I should read time by a clock. Through the lurid haze the contours of their pink faces could not be seen, but their gappy, hesitating, incoherent, and sensitive line revealed their mood clearly.

We continued advancing, step by step, loading and firing as we went. To every forward step, they took a backward move, loading and firing as they slowly withdrew. Twenty thousand muskets were being fired at this stage, but, though accuracy of aim was impossible, owing to our labouring hearts, and the jarring and excitement, many bullets found their destined billets on both sides.

After a steady exchange of musketry, which lasted some time, we heard the order: "Fix Bayonets! On the double-quick!" in tones that thrilled us. There was a simultaneous bound forward, each soul doing his best for the emergency. The Federals appeared inclined to await us; but, at this juncture, our men raised a yell, thousands responded to it, and burst out into the wildest yelling it has ever been my lot to hear. It drove all sanity and order from among us. It served the double purpose of relieving pent-up feelings, and transmitting encouragement along the attacking line. I rejoiced in the shouting like the rest. It reminded me that there were about four hundred companies like the Dixie Greys, who shared our feelings. Most of us, engrossed with the musket-work, had forgotten the fact; but the wave after wave of human voices, louder than all other battle-sounds together, penetrated to every sense, and stimulated our energies to the utmost.

"They fly!" was echoed from lip to lip. It accelerated our pace, and filled us with a noble rage. Then I knew what the Berserker passion was! It deluged us with rapture, and transfigured each Southerner into an exulting victor. At such a moment, nothing could have halted us.

Those savage yells, and the sight of thousands of racing figures coming towards them, discomfited the blue-coats; and when we arrived upon the place where they had stood, they had vanished. Then we caught sight of their beautiful array of tents, before which they had made their stand, after being roused from their Sunday-morning sleep, and huddled into line, at hearing their pickets challenge our skirmishers. The half-dressed dead and wounded showed what a surprise our attack had been. We drew up in the enemy's camp, panting and breathing hard. Some precious minutes were thus lost in recovering our breaths, indulging our curiosity, and reforming our line. Signs of a hasty rouse to the battle were abundant. Military equipments, uniform-coats, half-packed knapsacks, bedding, of a new and superior quality, littered the company streets.

Meantime, a series of other camps lay behind the first array of tents. The resistance we had met, though comparatively brief, enabled the brigades in rear of the advance camp to recover from the shock of the surprise; but our delay had not been long enough to give them time to form in proper order of battle. There were wide gaps between their divisions, into which the quick-flowing tide of elated Southerners entered, and compelled them to fall back lest they should be surrounded. Prentiss's brigade, despite their most desperate efforts, were thus hemmed in on all sides, and were made prisoners.

I had a momentary impression that, with the capture of the first camp, the battle was well-nigh over; but, in fact, it was only a brief prologue of the long and exhaustive series of struggles which took place that day.

Continuing our advance, we came in view of the tops of another mass of white tents, and, almost at the same time, were met by a furious storm of bullets, poured on us from a long line of blue-coats, whose attitude of assurance proved to us that we should have tough work here. But we were so much heartened by our first success that it would have required a good deal to have halted our advance for long. Their opportunity for making a full impression on us came with terrific suddenness. The world seemed bursting into fragments. Cannon and musket, shell and bullet, lent their several intensities to the distracting uproar. If I had not a fraction of an ear, and an eye inclined towards my Captain and Company, I had been spell-bound by the energies now opposed to us. I likened the cannon, with their deep bass, to the roaring of a great herd of lions; the ripping, cracking musketry, to the incessant yapping of terriers; the windy whisk of shells, and zipping of minie bullets, to the swoop of eagles, and the buzz of angry wasps. All the opposing armies of Grey and Blue fiercely blazed at each other.

After being exposed for a few seconds to this fearful downpour, we heard the order to "Lie down, men, and continue your firing!" Before me was a prostrate tree, about fifteen inches in diameter, with a narrow strip of light between it and the ground. Behind this shelter a dozen of us flung ourselves. The security it appeared to offer restored me to my individuality. We could fight, and think, and observe, better than out in the open. But it was a terrible period! How the cannon bellowed, and their shells plunged and bounded, and flew with screeching hisses over us! Their sharp rending explosions and hurtling fragments made us shrink and cower, despite our utmost efforts to be cool and collected. I marvelled, as I heard the unintermitting patter, snip, thud, and hum of the bullets, how anyone could live under this raining death. I could hear the balls beating a merciless tattoo on the outer surface of the log, pinging vivaciously as they flew off at a tangent from it, and thudding into something or other, at the rate of a hundred a second. One, here and there, found its way under the log, and buried itself in a comrade's body. One man raised his chest, as if to yawn, and jostled me. I turned to him, and saw that a bullet had gored his whole face, and penetrated into his chest. Another ball struck a man a deadly rap on the head, and he turned on his back and showed his ghastly white face to the sky.

"It is getting too warm, boys!" cried a soldier, and he uttered a vehement curse upon keeping soldiers hugging the ground until every ounce of courage was chilled. He lifted his head a little too high, and a bullet skimmed over the top of the log and hit him fairly in the centre of his forehead, and he fell heavily on his face. But his thought had been instantaneously general; and the officers, with one voice, ordered the charge; and cries of "Forward, forward!" raised us, as with a spring, to our feet, and changed the complexion of our feelings. The pulse of action beat feverishly once more; and, though overhead was crowded with peril, we were unable to give it so much attention as when we lay stretched on the ground.

Just as we bent our bodies for the onset, a boy's voice cried out, "Oh, stop, please stop a bit, I have been hurt, and can't move!" I turned to look, and saw Henry Parker, standing on one leg, and dolefully regarding his smashed foot. In another second, we were striding impetuously towards the enemy, vigorously plying our muskets, stopping only to prime the pan and ram the load down, when, with a spring or two, we would fetch up with the front, aim, and fire.

Our progress was not so continuously rapid as we desired, for the blues were obdurate; but at this moment we were gladdened at the sight of a battery galloping to our assistance. It was time for the nerve-shaking cannon to speak. After two rounds of shell and canister, we felt the pressure on us slightly relaxed; but we were still some-

what sluggish in disposition, though the officers' voices rang out imperiously. Newton Story at this juncture strode forward rapidly with the Dixies' banner, until he was quite sixty yards ahead of the foremost. Finding himself alone, he halted; and turning to us smilingly, said, "Why don't you come on, boys? You see there is no danger!" His smile and words acted on us like magic. We raised the yell, and sprang lightly and hopefully towards him. "Let's give them hell, boys!" said one. "Plug them plum-centre, every time!"

It was all very encouraging, for the yelling and shouting were taken up by thousands. "Forward, forward; don't give them breathing time!" was cried. We instinctively obeyed, and soon came in clear view of the blue-coats, who were scornfully unconcerned at first; but, seeing the leaping tide of men coming on at a tremendous pace, their front dissolved, and they fled in double-quick retreat. Again we felt the "glorious joy of heroes." It carried us on exultantly, rejoicing in the spirit which recognises nothing but the prey. We were no longer an army of soldiers, but so many school-boys racing, in which length of legs, wind, and condition tell.

We gained the second line of camps, continued the rush through them, and clean beyond. It was now about ten o'clock. My physical powers were quite exhausted, and, to add to my discomfiture, something struck me on my belt-clasp, and tumbled me headlong to the ground.

I could not have been many minutes prostrated before I recovered from the shock of the blow and fall, to find my clasp deeply dented and cracked. My company was not in sight. I was grateful for the rest, and crawled feebly to a tree, and plunging my hand into my haversack, ate ravenously. Within half an hour, feeling renovated, I struck north in the direction which my regiment had taken, over a ground strewn with bodies and the debris of war.

The desperate character of this day's battle was now brought home to my mind in all its awful reality. While in the tumultuous advance, and occupied with a myriad of exciting incidents, it was only at brief intervals that I was conscious of wounds being given and received; but now, in the trail of pursuers and pursued, the ghastly relics appalled every sense. I felt curious as to who the fallen Greys were, and moved to one stretched straight out. It was the body of a stout English Sergeant of a neighbouring company, the members of which hailed principally from the Washita Valley. At the crossing of the Arkansas River this plump, ruddy-faced man had been conspicuous for his complexion, jovial features, and good-humour, and had been nicknamed "John Bull." He was now lifeless, and lay with his eyes wide open, regardless of the scorching sun, and the tempestuous cannonade which sounded through the forest, and the musketry that crackled incessantly along the front.

Close by him was a young Lieutenant, who, judging by the new gloss on his uniform, must have been some father's darling. A clean bullet-hole through the centre of his forehead had instantly ended his career. A little further were some twenty bodies, lying in various postures, each by its own pool of viscous blood, which emitted a peculiar scent, which was new to me, but which I have since learned is inseparable from a battle-field. Beyond these, a still larger group lay, body overlying body, knees crooked, arms erect, or wide-stretched and rigid, according as the last spasm overtook them. The company opposed to them must have shot straight.

Other details of that ghastly trail formed a mass of horrors that will always be remembered at the mention of Shiloh. I can never forget the impression those wide-open dead eyes made on me. Each seemed to be starting out of its socket, with a look similar to the fixed wondering gaze of an infant, as though the dying had viewed something appalling at the last moment. "Can it be," I asked myself, "that at the last glance they saw their own retreating souls, and wondered why their caskets were left behind, like offal?" My surprise was that the form we made so much of, and that nothing was too good for, should now be mutilated, hacked, and outraged; and that the life, hitherto guarded as a sacred thing, and protected by the Constitution, Law, Ministers of Justice, Police, should, of a sudden,—at least, before I can realise it,—be given up to death!

An object once seen, if it has affected my imagination, remains indelibly fixed in my memory; and, among many other scenes with which it is now crowded, I cannot forget that half-mile square of woodland, lighted brightly by the sun, and littered by the forms of about a thousand dead and wounded men, and by horses, and military equipments. It formed a picture that may always be reproduced with an almost absolute fidelity. For it was the first Field of Glory I had seen in my May of life, and the first time that Glory sickened me with its repulsive aspect, and made me suspect it was all a glittering lie. In my imagination, I saw more than it was my fate to see with my eyes, for, under a flag of truce, I saw the bearers pick up the dead from the field, and lay them in long rows beside a wide trench; I saw them laid, one by one, close together at the bottom,—thankless victims of a perished cause, and all their individual hopes, pride, honour, names, buried under oblivious earth.

My thoughts reverted to the time when these festering bodies were idolized objects of their mothers' passionate love, their fathers standing by, half-fearing to touch the fragile little things, and the wings of civil law out-spread to protect parents and children in their family loves, their coming and going followed with pride and praise, and the blessing of the Almighty over-shadowing all. Then, as they were nearing manhood, through some strange warp of Society, men in authority summoned them from school and shop, field and farm, to meet in the woods on a Sunday morning for mutual butchery with the deadliest instruments ever invented, Civil Law, Religion, and Morality complaisantly standing aside, while 90,000 young men, who had been preached and moralized to, for years, were let loose to engage in the carnival of slaughter.

Only yesterday, they professed to shudder at the word "Murder." To-day, by a strange twist in human nature, they lusted to kill, and were hounded on in the work of destruction by their pastors, elders, mothers, and sisters. Oh, for once, I was beginning to know the real truth! Man was born for slaughter! All the pains taken to soothe his savage heart were unavailing! Holy words and heavenly hopes had no lasting effect on his bestial nature, for, when once provoked, how swiftly he flung aside the sweet hope of Heaven, and the dread of Hell, with which he amused himself in time of ease!

As I moved, horror-stricken, through the fearful shambles, where the dead lay as thick as the sleepers in a London park on a Bank Holiday, I was unable to resist the belief that my education had been in abstract things, which had no relation to our animal existence. For, if human life is so disparaged, what has it to do with such high subjects as God, Heaven, and Immortality? And to think how devotional men and women pretended to be, on a Sunday! Oh, cunning, cruel man! He knew that the sum of all real knowledge and effort was to know how to kill and mangle his brothers, as we were doing to-day! Reflecting on my own emotions, I wondered if other youths would feel that they had been deluded like myself with man's fine polemics and names of things, which vanished with the reality.

A multitude of angry thoughts surged through me, which I cannot describe in detail, but they amounted to this, that a cruel deception had been practised on my blank ignorance, that my atom of imagination and feeling had been darkened, and that man was a portentous creature from which I recoiled with terror and pity. He was certainly terrible and hard, but he was no more to me now than a two-legged beast; he was cunning beyond finding out, but his morality was only a mask for his wolfish heart! Thus, scoffing and railing at my infatuation for moral excellence as practised by humanity, I sought to join my company and regiment.

The battle field maintained the same character of undulated woodland, being, in general, low ridges separated by broad depressions, which sunk occasionally into ravines of respectable depth. At various places, wide clearings had been made; and I came across a damp bottom or two covered with shrubs. For a defensive force there were several positions that were admirable as rallying-points, and it is perhaps owing to these, and the undoubted courage exhibited by the Federal troops, that the battle was so protracted. Though our attack had been a surprise, it was certain that they fought as though they were resolved to deny it; and, as the ground to be won from the enemy was nearly five miles in depth, and every half mile or so they stood and obstinately contested it, all the honours of the day were not to be with us.

I overtook my regiment about one o'clock, and found that it was engaged in one of these occasional spurts of fury. The enemy resolutely maintained their ground, and our side was preparing for another assault. The firing was alternately brisk and slack. We lay down, and availed ourselves of trees, logs, and hollows, and annoyed their upstanding ranks; battery pounded battery, and, meanwhile, we hugged our resting-places closely. Of a sudden, we rose and raced towards the position, and took it by sheer weight and impetuosity, as we had done before. About three o'clock, the battle grew very hot. The enemy appeared to be more concentrated, and immovably sullen. Both sides fired better as they grew more accustomed to the din; but, with assistance from the reserves, we were continually pressing them towards the river Tennessee, without ever retreating an inch.

About this time, the enemy were assisted by the gun-boats, which hurled their enormous projectiles far beyond us; but, though they made great havoc among the trees, and created terror, they did comparatively little damage to those in close touch with the enemy.

The screaming of the big shells, when they first began to sail over our heads, had the effect of reducing our fire; for they were as fascinating as they were distracting. But we became used to them, and our attention was being claimed more in front. Our officers were more urgent; and, when we saw the growing dyke of white cloud that signalled the bullet-storm, we could not be indifferent to the more immediate danger. Dead bodies, wounded men writhing in agony, and assuming every distressful attitude, were frequent sights; but what made us heart-sick was to see, now and then, the well-groomed charger of an officer, with fine saddle, and scarlet and yellow-edged cloth, and brass-tipped holsters, or a stray cavalry or artillery horse, galloping between the lines, snorting with terror, while his entrails, soiled with dust, trailed behind him.

Our officers had continued to show the same alertness and vigour throughout the day; but, as it drew near four o'clock, though they strove to encourage and urge us on, they began to abate somewhat in their energy; and it was evident that the pluckiest of the men lacked the spontaneity and springing ardour which had distinguished them earlier in the day. Several of our company lagged wearily behind, and the remainder showed, by their drawn faces, the effects of their efforts. Yet, after a short rest, they were able to make splendid spurts. As for myself, I had only one wish, and that was for repose. The long-continued excitement, the successive tautening and relaxing of the nerves, the quenchless thirst, made more intense by the fumes of sulphurous powder, and the caking grime on the lips, caused by tearing the paper cartridges, and a ravening hunger, all combined, had reduced me to a walking automaton, and I earnestly wished that night would come, and stop all further effort.

Finally, about five o'clock, we assaulted and captured a large camp; after driving the enemy well away from it, the front line was as thin as that of a skirmishing body, and we were ordered to retire to the tents. There we hungrily sought after provisions, and I was lucky in finding a supply of biscuits and a canteen of excellent molasses, which gave great comfort to myself and friends. The plunder in the camp was abundant. There were bedding, clothing, and accoutrements without stint; but people were so exhausted they could do no more than idly turn the things over. Night soon fell, and only a few stray shots could now be heard, to remind us of the thrilling and horrid din of the day, excepting the huge bombs from the gun-boats, which, as we were not far from the blue-coats, discomforted only those in

the rear. By eight o'clock, I was repeating my experiences in the region of dreams, indifferent to columbiads and mortars, and the torrential rain which, at midnight, increased the miseries of the wounded and tentless.

An hour before dawn, I awoke from a refreshing sleep; and, after a hearty replenishment of my vitals with biscuit and molasses, I conceived myself to be fresher than on Sunday morning. While awaiting day-break, I gathered from other early risers their ideas in regard to the events of yesterday. They were under the impression that we had gained a great victory, though we had not, as we had anticipated, reached the Tennessee River. Van Dorn, with his expected reinforcements for us, was not likely to make his appearance for many days yet; and, if General Buell, with his 20,000 troops, had joined the enemy during the night, we had a bad day's work before us. We were short of provisions and ammunition, General Sidney Johnston, our chief Commander, had been killed; but Beauregard was safe and unhurt, and, if Buell was absent, we would win the day.

At daylight, I fell in with my Company, but there were only about fifty of the Dixies present. Almost immediately after, symptoms of the coming battle were manifest. Regiments were hurried into line, but, even to my inexperienced eyes, the troops were in ill-condition for repeating the efforts of Sunday. However, in brief time, in consequence of our pickets being driven in on us, we were moved forward in skirmishing order. With my musket on the trail I found myself in active motion, more active than otherwise I would have been, perhaps, because Captain Smith had said, "Now, Mr. Stanley, if you please, step briskly forward!" This singling-out of me wounded my *amour-propre*, and sent me forward like a rocket. In a short time, we met our opponents in the same formation as ourselves, and advancing most resolutely. We threw ourselves behind such trees as were near us, fired, loaded, and darted forward to another shelter. Presently, I found myself in an open, grassy space, with no convenient tree or stump near; but, seeing a shallow hollow some twenty paces ahead, I made a dash for it, and plied my musket with haste. I became so absorbed with some blue figures in front of me, that I did not pay sufficient heed to my companion greys; the open space was too dangerous, perhaps, for their advance; for, had they emerged, I should have known they were pressing forward. Seeing my blues in about the same proportion, I assumed that the greys were keeping their position, and never once thought of retreat. However, as, despite our firing, the blues were coming uncomfortably near, I rose from my hollow; but, to my speechless amazement, I found myself a solitary grey, in a line of blue skirmishers! My companions had retreated! The next I heard was, "Down with that gun, Secesh, or I'll drill a hole through you! Drop it, quick!"

Half a dozen of the enemy were covering me at the same instant, and I dropped my weapon, incontinently. Two men sprang at my collar, and marched me, unresisting, into the ranks of the terrible Yankees. *I was a prisoner!*

When the senses have been concentrated upon a specific object with the intensity which a battle compels, and are forcibly and suddenly veered about by another will, the immediate result is, at first, stupefying. Before my consciousness had returned to me, I was being propelled vigorously from behind, and I was in view of a long, swaying line of soldiers, who were marching to meet us with all the precision of drill, and with such a close front that a rabbit would have found it difficult to break through. This sight restored me to all my faculties, and I remembered I was a Confederate, in misfortune, and that it behoved me to have some regard for my Uniform. I heard bursts of vituperation from several hoarse throats, which straightened my back and made me defiant.

"Where are you taking that fellow to? Drive a bayonet into the—— ——! Let him drop where he is!" they cried by the dozen, with a German accent. They grew more excited as we drew nearer, and more men joined in the opprobrious chorus. Then a few dashed from the ranks, with

levelled bayonets, to execute what appeared to be the general wish.

I looked into their faces, deformed with fear and fury, and I felt intolerable loathing for the wild-eyed brutes! Their eyes, projected and distended, appeared like spots of pale blue ink, in faces of dough! Reason had fled altogether from their features, and, to appeal for mercy to such blind, ferocious animalism would have been the height of absurdity, but I was absolutely indifferent as to what they might do with me now. Could I have multiplied myself into a thousand, such unintellectual-looking louts might have been brushed out of existence with ease—despite their numbers. They were apparently new troops, from such back-lands as were favoured by German immigrants; and, though of sturdy build, another such mass of savagery and stupidity could not have been found within the four corners of North America. How I wished I could return to the Confederates, and tell them what kind of people were opposing them!

Before their bayonets reached me, my two guards, who were ruddy-faced Ohioans, flung themselves before me, and, presenting their rifles, cried, "Here! stop that, you fellows! He is our prisoner!" A couple of officers were almost as quick as they, and flourished their swords; and, amid an expenditure of profanity, drove them quickly back into their ranks, cursing and blackguarding me in a manner truly American. A company opened its lines as we passed to the rear. Once through, I was comparatively safe from the Union troops, but not from the Confederate missiles, which were dropping about, and striking men, right and left.

Quickening our pace, we soon were beyond danger from my friends; after which, I looked about with interest at the forces that were marching to retrieve their shame of yesterday. The troops we saw belonged to Buell, who had crossed the Tennessee, and was now joined by Grant. They presented a brave, even imposing, sight; and, in their new uniforms, with glossy knapsacks, rubbers undimmed, brasses resplendent, they approached nearer to my idea of soldiers than our dingy grey troops. Much of this fine show and seeming steadiness was due to their newer equipments, and, as yet, unshaken nerves; but, though their movements were firm, they were languid, and lacked the élan, the bold confidence, of the Southerners. Given twenty-four hours' rest, and the enjoyment of cooked rations, I felt that the Confederates would have crumpled up the handsome Unionists within a brief time.

Though my eyes had abundant matter of interest within their range, my mind continually harked back to the miserable hollow which had disgraced me, and I kept wondering how it was that my fellow-skirmishers had so quickly disappeared. I was inclined to blame Captain Smith for urging me on, when, within a few minutes after, he must have withdrawn his men. But it was useless to trouble my mind with conjectures. I was a prisoner! Shameful position! What would become of my knapsack, and my little treasures,—letters, and souvenirs of my father? They were lost beyond recovery!

On the way, my guards and I had a discussion about our respective causes, and, though I could not admit it, there was much reason in what they said, and I marvelled that they could put their case so well. For, until now, I was under the impression that they were robbers who only sought to desolate the South, and steal the slaves; but, according to them, had we not been so impatient and flown to arms, the influence of Abe Lincoln and his fellow-abolitionists would not have affected the Southerners pecuniarily; for it might have been possible for Congress to compensate slave-owners, that is, by buying up all slaves, and afterwards setting them free. But when the Southerners, who were not averse to selling their slaves in the open market, refused to consider anything relating to them, and began to seize upon government property, forts, arsenals, and war-ships, and to set about establishing a separate system in the country, then the North resolved that this should not be, and that was the true reason of the war. The Northern people cared nothing for the "niggers,"—the slavery

question could have been settled in another and quieter way,—but they cared all their lives were worth for their country. . . .

Source: Stanley, Sir Henry Morton. *The Autobiography of Sir Henry Morton Stanley,* edited by Dorothy Stanley, 186–204. Boston and New York: Houghton Mifflin, 1909.

THE OCCUPATION OF NEW ORLEANS, MAY 1862–APRIL 1865

Letter to President Jefferson Davis
Alexander Walker
September 13, 1862

Major General Benjamin F. Butler occupied New Orleans beginning on May 1, 1862, and immediately introduced a harsh regime, which included the infamous Order No. 28—the so-called Woman Order. When some New Orleans women insulted Union officers, Butler responded with this order, directing that such women "be regarded and held liable to be treated as a woman of the town plying her avocation"—that is, be treated as prostitutes. Among those who protested Butler's policies was New Orleans resident and Southern journalist Alexander Walker. Butler responded to Walker's complaints by imprisoning him on Ship Island. From his cell, Walker wrote to the Confederate president Jefferson Davis, painting a vivid picture of Butler's administration. The Lincoln administration removed Butler as military governor of New Orleans on December 16, 1862.

A close prisoner on this desolate island with some fifty others of my fellow citizens, I have thought it my duty at every risk to communicate to you some, at least, of the incidents of the administration of the brutal tyrant who has been sent by the United States government to oppress, rob, assault, and trample upon our people in every manner which the most fiendish ingenuity and most wanton cruelty could devise and in gross violation of all the laws and usages of the most remorseless wars between civilized and even savage nations and tribes.

Previous to my committal to Ship Island as a close prisoner, where I was consigned with seven other respectable citizens to a small hut, fifteen feet by twenty, exposed to rain and sun, without permission to leave except for a bath in the sea once or twice a week, I had prepared an elaborate statement of the outrages perpetrated by Butler upon our people, or rather of the more flagrant ones, which I committed to Reverdy Johnson, a commissioner of the United States who had been sent out to investigate and report upon certain transactions of Butler. Mr. Johnson received this document, but stated that his mission related exclusively to certain issues which had arisen between Butler and the foreign consuls. He manifested, however, some sympathy for our wronged people and some disgust for the excesses and villainies of Butler. Shortly after Mr. Johnson's departure, I was sent to Ship Island.

A description of the causes and circumstances of the imprisonment of our citizens who are now held on this island will afford some of the mildest illustrations of Butler's brutality. There are about sixty prisoners here, all of whom are closely confined in portable houses and furnished with the most wretched and unwholesome condemned soldiers' rations. Some are kept at hard labor on the fort; several, in addition to labor, are compelled to wear a ball and chain, which is never removed. Among these is Mr. Shepherd, a respectable, elderly, and weakly citizen, who is charged with secreting certain papers belonging to the naval officer of the Confederate States, which the latter left in his charge when he departed from New Orleans. Mr. Shepherd had the proof that the officer who had deposited these documents afterward returned and took them and that they had been carried into the Confederate States. This testimony Butler would not receive and declared that, if it existed, it would make no difference in his case.

Doctor Moore, a dealer in drugs, is also at hard labor with ball and chain, on the charge of having sent a few ounces of quinine into the Confederate States. There are five prisoners condemned and employed at hard labor on the charge of intending to break their parole as prisoners of war, captured at Fort Jackson. There is also a delicate youth from the country who is subjected to the same treatment on the charge of being a guerrilla, the term which Butler applies to the partisan rangers organized under the act of congress of the Confederate States. Alderman Beggs, on the charge of denouncing those who, having taken the oath to the Confederate States, afterward swore allegiance to the United States, and Mr. Keller, a vendor of books, stationery, and scientific apparatus, on the charge of permitting a clerk to placard the word "Chickahominy" on a skeleton which was suspended in his show window for sale for the use of students of anatomy, are condemned also to close imprisonment and hard labor for two years. The others mentioned above are condemned for a longer period.

A like condemnation and punishment were imposed upon Judge John W. Andrews, a most respectable citizen, recently a member of the judiciary of the state, of the legislature, and of the City Council, and a prominent merchant. This gentleman is advanced in years and in very delicate health. There is little hope that his health can long sustain his present burdens and hardships. The circumstances of Mrs. Phillips' imprisonment are probably known to you. As, however, I desire this to be an authentic and studiously accurate statement of the facts, I will here relate them.

In the raid of the U.S. troops near Warrenton, Miss., a young officer named De Kay was mortally wounded. He died in New Orleans, and an attempt was made by Federal authorities to get up a pompous funeral ceremony and procession in honor of so "gallant and heroic a young officer" who had fallen in an expedition which had no other purpose or object but the pillage of defenseless farms and villages. The efforts to excite the sympathies of our people on this occasion proved a ridiculous failure and the funeral ceremony had no aspect of solemnity or even propriety, a long line of carriages composing the cortege designed for the Union citizens being all empty.

As this procession passed the residence of P. Phillips, Esq., Mrs. Phillips, standing on the balcony with several lady friends, was observed by some Federal officer to smile, so it was charged. She was immediately arrested and taken before Butler, who, in the most brutal and insolent manner, sought to terrify the heroic lady. In this he did not succeed. While denying that her gaiety had any reference whatever to the funeral ceremony, Mrs. Phillips refused to make any apologies or concessions to the vulgar tyrant. Thereupon, she was condemned to close imprisonment in a filthy guardroom, thence to be transported to Ship Island, where she was to be held in close confinement for two years, with no other fare but soldiers' rations; no intercourse or correspondence with any person except through General Butler. This sentence was published in the newspapers, accompanied by words of the grossest insult and most vulgar ribaldry, in which Mrs. Phillips was denounced as "not a common but an uncommon bad woman," referring to his proclamation [Order No. 28], denounced by Lord Palmerston and the whole civilized world as "so infamous," in which his soldiers are authorized to treat "as common women plying their profession" all who may manifest any contempt or discourtesy toward them.

To add further insult, in the order condemning Mr. Keller, it was made part of his sentence to permit him to hold converse and intercourse with Mrs. Phillips, to which condition this honest man was induced to protest from the belief that his fellow prisoner was a notorious courtesan of the city who bore the name of Phillips. This protest was published in the paper with Butler's order granting the request of Keller, so as to convey to the world the idea that a poor vendor of periodicals declined association with a lady of the highest respectability, the wife of a distinguished lawyer and ex-member of Congress. I can bear personal testimony to the rigorous execution of the sentence against Mrs. Phillips, having been imprisoned for weeks in a building adjoining to that which she was never allowed to leave. Such was the treatment of a delicate lady of the highest refinement, the mother of nine children.

The case of Judge Andrews presents another striking example of the brutality and dishonesty of Butler. The charge against him imputed the horrid crime of having received and exhibited, nine months before the arrival of Butler in the city, a cross which had been sent to him by a young friend in our army at Manassas and which, it was represented, was made of the bones of a Yankee soldier. No proof whatever was adduced that such exhibition had ever been made by Judge Andrews in exultation, and the cross, after being received, was destroyed before Butler arrived in the city. In his first interview with the authorities of the city, Butler had declared that he would take no cognizance of any acts committed before he occupied the city and established martial law therein. This solemn and oft-repeated pledge he has violated in a thousand instances. . . .

So much for the prisoners at Ship Island, with the facts of whose cases I am personally acquainted. I refrain from any reference to my own case, hard as my doom is, closely confined on this island with all my property appropriated by the enemy and my family placed under strict espionage and subject to many annoyances, insults, and discomforts. With all its trials and hardships the condition of the prisoners here is quite easy and endurable compared with that of those who are confined in the damp and unwholesome casemates of Forts Jackson and Saint Philip, on the Mississippi, and in Fort Pickens, on Santa Rosa Island.

Among the latter is the mayor of the city, who has been imprisoned for four months for the offense of writing a letter to Butler protesting against his order relative to the treatment of the ladies of the city and declaring his inability to maintain the peace of the city if the Federal soldiers were thus authorized to insult and outrage our women at their own pleasure and will. The secretary of the mayor, who wrote the letter signed by the mayor, was included in the same committal and imprisonment. Several members of the Council, for like or smaller offenses, suffer the same punishment.

Doctor Porter, a wealthy dentist and citizen, is imprisoned for requiring the Citizens' Bank, the pet bank and place of deposit of Butler and his agent in his vast schemes of corruption and extortion, to pay checks in the currency which Butler alone allowed the banks to pay. George C. Laurason, formerly collector of the port of New Orleans, suffers a like penalty for applying for a passport to go to Europe, where his family now is. Thomas Murray, as president of that benevolent institution known as the Free Market, which supplied the families of the soldiers with the means of subsistence; Charles Heidsieck, a French citizen, the owner of the celebrated wine manufactory in France; Mr. Dacres and other British citizens; Mr. Mire, a wealthy and highly respectable Spanish citizen, the owner of extensive sawmills in Florida and the contractor to supply the French Navy with timber, are all imprisoned at Fort Pickens for endeavoring to pass the lines without taking the oath prescribed by Butler for foreigners, which oath requires them to reveal to the United States all information they may have respecting the acts and designs of Confederate States on pain of being regarded and treated as enemies and spies. There are, too, many prisoners who are confined on the information of political and person enemies as dangerous characters for offenses alleged to have been committed by the months and years before Butler's arrival the city.

Doctor McPhevroa, an elderly and most respectable citizen, was condemned to the casemates of Fort Jackson for speaking in a circle of his friends of Butler's proclamation, No. 28, that relative to the ladies of New Orleans, as "infamous," the very epithet which Lord Palmerston in the House of Commons declared as the only appropriate one. Dr. Warren Stone,

the distinguished surgeon and philanthropist, was consigned to a like punishment for refusing to recognize an individual who had been announced as president of a Union association and, yet, who a few months before had made in public a most violent speech against the Yankees and had advised our people to cut the throats of all invaders.

Several ladies of the highest social position have been imprisoned for the expression of sympathy with the Confederates and the wearing of ribbons of certain colors. Mrs. Dubois, an elderly lady long engaged in the business of teaching our children, was imprisoned on the charge of not being able to account for certain keys and books belonging to the schools, which were never in her possession. All the members of the Finance Committee of the City Council are imprisoned for authorizing the subscription of the city to the fund for its defense; and several hundred of our citizens who subscribed to this fund have been compelled to pay 25 percent of their subscription to Butler, under threat of imprisonment at hard labor. To swell this exaction to the sum of $300,000, all the cotton factors of the city who had united in a circular address to the planters advising them not to send their cotton to New Orleans were assessed in sums of $500 and $250, which they had to pay or go to prison.

The treatment of a venerable citizen named Roberts, a farmer living a short distance from Baton Rouge, is one of peculiar atrocity. A son of Mr. Roberts, a soldier of [the] Confederate Army, having come on sick leave to see his parents, a detachment of the Twenty-first Indiana Regiment was sent to arrest him. The young man, hearing the approach of armed men, went out to meet them, when several shots were fired by the Indianians, one of which killed young Roberts. The father, seeing the danger of his son, seized a gun and fired through the door, slightly wounding Colonel McMillan, the commander of the detachment. He was then arrested and charged with having killed his own son, and was taken with the rest of his family from his house, the body of his son being brought out and laid on the ground. The building, all the outhouses, barns, and stables were burned to the ground, and his mules, horses, and cattle were driven off to the Federal camp. Old Mr. Roberts was condemned to close imprisonment for twenty years, and this imprisonment he is now undergoing at Fort Pickens. . . .

A Mr. Levy, a respectable merchant, was imprisoned for one month for stating to a Federal that he heard that Baton Rouge had been evacuated, when it really had been evacuated. Another citizen was arrested in the cars and imprisoned for saying that the distress for cotton in England would soon increase; and another for repeating what had been published in the Delta that "Richmond had fallen," such a remark being regarded as ironical after the Confederate victories in the first days of July. A great many have been imprisoned on the information of their slaves that they had concealed or destroyed arms, and the informers emancipated. Mr. Lathrop, a respectable lawyer, is now undergoing, in the parish prison, a sentence of two years' imprisonment for "kidnapping" his own slave, who had been appropriated by a Federal officer. This sentence, Butler declared, was intended as a warning to the people not to interfere with the servants of his officers, meaning the slaves of our citizens appropriated by them.

A number of our citizens, enrolled as partisan rangers or in the state militia, have been closely imprisoned and threatened with death as guerrillas or pirates. W. E. Seymour, late a captain in one of the regiments in the defense of the state and honorably paroled, is a close prisoner at Fort Saint Philip and his property all confiscated on account of an obituary notice which appeared in his own paper, the Bulletin, of his father, the late gallant Col. I. G. Seymour, of the Sixth Louisiana, who fell in the battle at Gaines' Mill. The writer of the article, Mr. Devis, an old and infirm citizen, was subjected to a like punishment and is now a prisoner at Fort Pickens. Besides these instances, there are a great many citizens who have only escaped imprisonment by the payment of large fines, and in many cases by corrupting Federal officers of influence.

To enumerate the cases of confiscation by order of Butler, and in many cases even by the order of his subordinates, would exceed the bounds I have affixed to this report. I have, however, kept a record of these cases and will communicate them at some other time. Suffice it to say that nearly all the large and commodious houses of our citizens, especially those of absentees and officers in our army and government, have been thus appropriated. Officers of no higher grade than lieutenants occupy houses which have cost our citizens $30,000, and where furniture has been removed, and, when deficient, any articles which the appropriators may deem necessary to their comfort are purchased at the expense of the owners of the property. The wives and families of our citizens are frequently ejected from their houses to make way for coarse Federal officers and the Negro women whom they appropriate as their wives and concubines. Ships have been loaded with costly articles of furniture stolen—they say confiscated—from our citizens and transmitted North to the families of Federal officers. Many a house in New England is even now resounding with the tones of pianos thus stolen from the parlors of our citizens. A vast amount of silver has been appropriated in like manner. The example set by Butler in appropriating the house of General Twiggs's minor heir and furnishing it in a most lavish and luxurious style at the expense of the estate, and in transmitting the plate and swords of the deceased veteran to Lowell; the seizure and removal to the North of the statue of Washington by Powers and of the state library from the capital at Baton Rouge, have been extensively followed by Butler's subordinates.

Nor have I here space to expose the extortions of Butler through the agency of his brother, an abandoned gambler and speculator, who has compelled our citizens by all kinds of threats to sell their property to him at rates fixed by him, who has monopolized all the shipping employed by the United States to transport the produce thus forced from our people, who has acted as broker to obtain remissions of penalties and the restoration of fugitive slaves, in many cases on condition of the payment of half their value and on pledges of half of the growing crops. In this manner have the plantations within fifty miles of New Orleans been taxed. Many of them, unable to secure even these terms, have been depopulated.

You have doubtless been made acquainted with the proceedings of Butler to compel our citizens to take the oath of allegiance to the United States—the prohibition of all trade to those who have not taken the oath and the seizure of their funds in bank. The last device will be to compel all those who do not take that oath to register themselves as enemies of the United Stat when they will be either imprisoned o driven from the city and their property confiscated. These orders, especially the oath requirement, are applicable as well to women as to men. Indeed, the malice of Butler against females is more bitter and insatiable than that against males. A placard in his office in large letters bears this inscription: "The venom of the she adder is as dangerous as that of the he adder."

And this is but a feeble and deficient present-ment of the enormities and brutalities of this cowardly and brutal monster. It is in vain that some of his subordinates remonstrate and protest against many of his acts. He will permit no one to thwart his two great objects—to bid highest for the favor of the Northern mob and to accumu-late a vast fortune by extortion and plunder. The extent to which this latter purpose is carried will surpass all similar efforts of great robbers from Verres down.

I content myself with this mere epitome [summary] of Butler's crimes. At some other more favorable occasion I will present them in greater detail and with the authentic proofs which I cannot now command. It would not be becoming in me to solicit or suggest that some steps be taken by the president and govern-ment of the Confederate States to correct and to avenge these wrongs done our people. I have full confidence that all will be done in that behalf

which can be done. I cannot but say, however, that a feeling prevails among our people that they have been forgotten or abandoned by the government for which they suffer, or an appre-hension that the true state of affairs is not known or appreciated by our government. That this may not any longer be the case I have incurred the peril of writing this memoir in a close prison on a desolate island, with a Federal sentinel at the door and the broadside of a Federal frigate frowning upon all in the bay.

Source: U.S. War Department. The War of the Rebel-lion: A Compilation of the Official Records of the Union and Confederate Armies. Washington, D.C.: U.S. Government Printing Office, 1880, 4:880–885.

THE BATTLE OF ANTIETAM, SEPTEMBER 17, 1862

Account of the Battle
Colonel Frederick Hitchcock
Published 1904

The initial Union assault at the Battle of Antietam, on September 17, was flawed in its execution, but the Union general Joseph "Fighting Joe" Hooker nevertheless managed to drive back Stonewall Jack-son's Confederate brigade, thereby forcing Robert E. Lee to order up his reserves. These forces were fully engaged by midday, when the principal fighting took place along a sunken farm road. The five-hour combat here was so brutal that the road was soon christened "Bloody Lane." Frederick Hitchcock (1837–1924), who ended the war a colonel but who was a Union lieutenant in the 132nd Pennsyl-vania Volunteers in September 1862, described his approach to the fighting at "Bloody Lane" in his book War from the Inside *(1904).*

We . . . moved, as I thought, rather leisurely for upwards of two miles, crossing Antietam Creek, which our men waded nearly waist deep,

The Battle of Antietam—the Dunker church and the dead *(Library of Congress)*

emerging, of course, soaked through, our first experience of this kind. It was a hot morning and, therefore, the only ill effect of this wading was the discomfort to the men of marching with soaked feet. It was now quite evident that a great battle was in progress. A deafening pandemonium of cannonading, with shrieking and bursting shells, filled the air beyond us, towards which we were marching. An occasional shell whizzed by or over, reminding us that we were rapidly approaching the "debatable ground."

Soon we began to hear a most ominous sound which we had never before heard, except in the far distance at South Mountain, namely, the rattle of musketry. It had none of the deafening bluster of the cannonading so terrifying to new troops, but to those who had once experienced its effects, it was infinitely more to be dreaded. These volleys of musketry we were approaching sounded in the distance like the rapid pouring of

shot upon a tinpan, or the tearing of heavy canvas, with slight pauses interspersed with single shots, or desultory shooting.

All this presaged fearful work in store for us, with what results to each personally in the future, measured probably by moments, would reveal. How does one feel under such conditions? To tell the truth, I realized the situation most keenly and felt very uncomfortable. Lest there might be some undue manifestation of this feeling on my conduct, I said to myself, this is the duty I undertook to perform for my country, and now I'll do it, and leave the results with God. My greater fear was not that I might be killed, but that I might be grievously wounded and left a victim suffering on the field. The nervous strain was plainly visible upon all of us. All moved doggedly forward in obedience to orders, in absolute silence so far as talking was concerned. The compressed lip and set teeth showed that nerve and resolution had been summoned to the discharge of duty. A few temporarily fell out, unable to endure the nervous strain.

Source: Hitchcock, Frederick. War from the Inside: The Story of the 132nd Regiment, Pennsylvania Volunteer Infantry, in the War for the Suppression of the Rebellion, 1862–1863. Philadelphia: Lippincott, 1904, pp. 56–58.

"With Burnside at Antietam"
David Thompson
Published 1884

David Thompson was a Union private in Company G, 9th New York Volunteers, a regiment of "zouaves," whose uniforms imitated the flamboyant French North African colonial style. Of the 600 men of his regiment who crossed Antietam Creek on the afternoon of the battle, 45 were killed in action and another 176 were wounded. Thompson became a prisoner of war, captured by men of the 15th Georgia Regiment. Confined in Libby Prison at Richmond, Virginia, he was soon paroled to the North.

So the morning wore away and the fighting on the right ceased entirely. That was fresh anxiety—the scales were turning perhaps, but which way? About noon the battle began afresh. This must have been Franklin's men of the Sixth Corps, for the firing was nearer, and they came up behind the center. Suddenly a stir beginning far upon the right, and running like a wave along the line, brought the regiment to its feet. A silence fell on every one at once, for each felt that the momentous "now" had come. Just as we started I saw, with a little shock, a line-officer take out his watch to note the hour, as though the affair beyond the creek were a business appointment which he was going to keep.

When we reached the brow of the hill the fringe of trees along the creek screened the fighting entire, and we were deployed as skirmishers under their cover. We sat there two hours. All that time the rest of corps had been moving over the stone bridge and going into position on the other side of the creek. Then [we] were ordered over a ford which had been found below the bridge, where the water was waist deep. One man was shot in mid-stream.

At the foot of the slope on the opposite side the line was formed and we moved up through the thin woods. Reaching the level we lay down behind a battery which seemed to have been disabled. There, if anywhere, I should have remembered that I was soaking wet from my waist down. So great was the excitement, however, that I have never been able to recall it. Here some of the men, going to the rear for water, discovered in the ashes of some hay-ricks which had been fired by our shells the charred remains of several Confederates. After long waiting it became noised along the line that we were to take a battery that was at work several yards ahead on the top of a hill. This narrowed the field and brought us to consider the work before us more attentively.

Right across our front, two hundred feet or so away, ran a country road bordered on each side by a snake fence. Beyond this road stretched a plowed field several hundred feet in length, sloping up to the battery which was hidden in a corn field. A stone fence, breast-high, inclosed the field on the left, and behind it lay a regiment of Confederates, who would be directly on our flank if we should attempt the slope. The prospect was far from encouraging, but the order came to get ready for the attempt.

Our knapsacks were left on the ground behind us. At the word a rush was made for the fences. The line was so disordered by the time the second fence was passed that we hurried forward to a shallow undulation a few feet ahead, and lay down among the furrows to re-form, doing so by crawling up into line. A hundred feet or so ahead was a similar undulation to which we ran for a second shelter. The battery, which at first had not seemed to notice us, now, apprised of its danger, opened fire upon us. We were getting ready now for the charge proper, but were still lying on our faces. Lieutenant-Colonel Kimball was ramping up and down the line. The discreet regiment behind the fence was silent. Now and then a bullet from them cut the air over our head, but generally they were reserving their fire for that better show which they knew they would get in a few minutes. The battery, however, whose shots at first went over our heads, had depressed its guns so as to shave the surface of the ground. Its fire was beginning to tell.

I remember looking behind and seeing an officer riding diagonally across the field—a most inviting target—instinctively bending his head down over his horse's neck, as though he were riding through driving rain. While my eye was on him I saw, between me and him a rolled overcoat with its traps on bound into the air and fall among the furrows. One of the enemy's grape-shot had plowed a groove in the skull of a young fellow and had cut his overcoat from his shoulders. He never stirred from his position, but lay there face downward, a dreadful spectacle. A moment after, I heard a man cursing a comrade for lying on him heavily. He was cursing a dying man.

As the range grew better, the firing became more rapid, the situation desperate and exasperating to the last degree. Human nature was on the race, and there burst forth form it the most vehement, terrible swearing I have ever heard. Certainly the joy of conflict was not ours that day. The suspense was only for a moment, however, for the order to charge came just after. Whether the regiment was thrown into disorder or not, I never knew. I only remember that as we rose, and started all the fire that had been held back so long was loosed. In a second the air was full of the hiss of bullets and the hurtle of grape-shot. The mental strain was so great that I saw at the moment he singular effect mentioned, I think, in the life of Goethe on a similar occasion—the whole landscape for an instant turned slight red.

I see again, as I saw it then in a flash, a man just in front of me drop his musket and throw up his hands, stung into vigorous swearing by a bullet behind the ear. Many men fell going up the hill, bit it seemed to be all over in a moment, and I found myself passing a hollow where a dozen wounded men lay—among them our sergeant-major who was calling me to come down. He had caught sight of the blanket rolled across my back, and called me to unroll it and help to carry from the field one of our wounded lieutenants.

Source: EyewitnesstoHistory.com. "Courage at Antietam, 1862" (originally: "With Burnside at Antietam." In *Battles and Leaders of the Civil War.* Vol. 1: *From Sumter to Shiloh,* by Robert U. Johnson and Clarence Buel. New York: The Century Company, 1888). Available online. URL: http://www.eyewitnesstohistory.com/antiet.htm. Accessed on February 8, 2010.

THE BATTLE OF GETTYSBURG, JULY 1–3, 1863

Diary Entries
Lieutenant Colonel James Fremantle
July 1–4, 1863

Lieutenant Colonel James Fremantle (Sir Arthur James Lyon Fremantle, 1835–1901), an officer in Britain's elite Coldstream Guards, was attached to Robert E. Lee's Confederate Army of Northern Virginia as an observer. His war diary covers three fateful months of the Civil War and includes reports of conversations with the likes of Robert E. Lee, Jefferson Davis, Jeb Stuart, Joseph E. Johnston, and James Longstreet, among others. Fremantle was literally at Lee's side through the Gettysburg battle. The diary, which painted an admiring picture of the southern war effort, was originally published in the South in 1864.

1st July, Wednesday.—We did not leave our camp till noon, as nearly all General Hill's corps had to pass our quarters on its march towards Gettysburg. One division of Ewell's also had to join in a little beyond Greenwood, and Longstreet's corps had to bring up the rear. During the morning I made the acquaintance of Colonel

Walton, who used to command the well-known Washington Artillery, but he is now chief of artillery to Longstreet's corps d'armée. He is a big man, ci-devant [former] auctioneer in New Orleans, and I understand he pines to return to his hammer.

Soon after starting we got into a pass in the South Mountain, a continuation, I believe, of the Blue Ridge range, which is broken by the Potomac at Harper's Ferry. The scenery through the pass is very fine. The first troops, alongside of whom we rode, belonged to Johnson's division of Ewell's corps. Among them I saw, for the first time, the celebrated "Stonewall" Brigade, formerly commanded by Jackson. In appearance the men differ little from other Confederate soldiers, except, perhaps, that the brigade contains more elderly men and fewer boys. All (except, I think, one regiment) are Virginians. As they have nearly always been

on detached duty, few of them knew General Longstreet, except by reputation. Numbers of them asked me whether the General in front was Longstreet; and when I answered in the affirmative, many would run on a hundred yards in order to take a good look at him. This I take to be an immense compliment from any soldier on a long march.

At 2 P. M. firing became distinctly audible in our front, but although it increased as we progressed, it did not seem to be very heavy.

A spy who was with us insisted upon there being "a pretty tidy bunch of blue-bellies in or near Gettysburg," and he declared that he was in their society three days ago.

After passing Johnson's division, we came up to a Florida brigade, which is now in Hill's corps; but as it had formerly served under Longstreet, the men knew him well. Some of them (after the General had passed) called out to their com-

Dead on the battlefield of Gettysburg, July 1863 (National Archives)

rades, "Look out for work now, boys, for here's the old bull dog again."

At 3 P. M. we began to meet wounded men coming to the rear, and the number of these soon increased most rapidly, some hobbling alone, others on stretchers carried by the ambulance corps, and others in the ambulance wagons. Many of the latter were stripped nearly naked, and displayed very bad wounds. This spectacle, so revolting to a person unaccustomed to such sights, produced no impression whatever upon the advancing troops, who certainly go under fire with the most perfect nonchalence. They show no enthusiasm or excitement, but the most complete indifference. This is the effect of two years' almost uninterrupted fighting.

We now began to meet Yankee prisoners coming to the rear in considerable numbers. Many of them were wounded, but they seemed already to be on excellent terms with their captors, with whom they had commenced swapping canteens, tobacco, &c. Among them was a Pennsylvanian Colonel, a miserable object from a wound in his face. In answer to a question. I heard one of them remark, with a laugh, "We're pretty nigh whipped already." We next came to a Confederate soldier carrying a Yankee color, belonging, I think, to a Pennsylvania regiment, which he told me he had just captured.

At 4.30 P. M. we came in sight of Gettysburg, and joined General Lee and General Hill, who were on the top of one of the ridges which form the peculiar feature of the country around Gettysburg. We could see the enemy retreating up one of the opposite ridges, pursued by the Confederates with loud yells. The position into which the enemy had been driven was evidently a strong one. His right appeared to rest on a cemetery, on the top of a high ridge to the right of Gettysburg, as we looked at it.

General Hill now came up and told me he had been very unwell all day, and in fact he looks very delicate. He said he had had two of his divisions engaged, and had driven the enemy four miles into his present position, capturing a great many prisoners, some cannon, and some colors. He

said, however, that the Yankees had fought with a determination unusual to them, He pointed out a railway cutting, in which they had made a good stand; also, a field in the centre of which he had seen a man plant the regimental color, round which the regiment had fought for some time with much obstinacy, and when at last it was obliged to retreat, the color-bearer retired last of all, turning round every now and then to shake his fist at the advancing rebels. General Hill said he felt quite sorry when he saw this gallant Yankee meet his doom.

General Ewell had come up at 3.30, on the enemy's right (with part of his corps), and completed his discomfiture. General Reynolds, one of the best Yankee generals, was reported killed. Whilst we were talking, a message arrived from General Ewell, requesting Hill to press the enemy in the front, whilst he performed the same operation on his right. The pressure was accordingly applied in a mild degree, but the enemy were too strongly posted, and it was too late in the evening for a regular attack. The town of Gettysburg was now occupied by Ewell, and was full of Yankee dead and wounded. I climbed up a tree in the most commanding place I could find, and could form a pretty good general idea of the enemy's position, although the tops of the ridges being covered with pine-woods, it was very difficult to see anything of the troops concealed in them. The firing ceased about dark, at which time I rode back with General Longstreet and his Staff to his headquarters at Cashtown, a little village eight miles from Gettysburg. At that time troops were pouring along the road, and were being marched towards the position they are to occupy tomorrow.

In the fight to-day nearly 6,000 prisoners had been taken, and 10 guns. About 20,000 men must have been on the field on the Confederate side. The enemy had two corps d'armée engaged. All the prisoners belong, I think, to the 1st and 11th corps. This day's work is called a "brisk little scurry," and all anticipate a "big battle" to-morrow.

I observed that the artillery-men in charge of the horses dig themselves little holes like graves, throwing up the earth at the upper end. They ensconce themselves in these holes when under fire.

At supper this evening, General Longstreet spoke of the enemy's position as being "very formidable." He also said that they would doubtless intrench themselves strongly during the night.

The Staff officers spoke of the battle as a certainty, and the universal feeling in the army was one of profound contempt for an enemy whom they have beaten so constantly, and under so many disadvantages. . . .

2d July, Thursday . . . Colonel Sorrell, the Austrian, and I arrived at 5 A. M. at the same commanding position we were on yesterday, and I climbed up a tree in company with Captain Schreibert, of the Prussian army. Just below us were seated Generals Lee, Hill, Longstreet, and Hood, in consultation—the two latter assisting their deliberations by the truly American custom of whittling sticks. General Heth was also present; he was wounded in the head yesterday, and although not allowed to command his brigade, he insists upon coming to the field.

At 7 A. M. I rode over part of the ground with General Longstreet, and saw him disposing of McLaws's division for to-day's fight. The enemy occupied a series of high ridges, the tops of which were covered with trees, but the intervening valleys between their ridges and ours were mostly open, and partly under cultivation. The cemetery was on their right, and their left appeared to rest upon a high rocky hill. The enemy's forces, which were now supposed to comprise nearly the whole Potomac army, were concentrated into a space apparently not more than a couple of miles in length. The Confederates inclosed them in a sort of semicircle, and the extreme extent of our position must have been from five to six miles at least. Ewell was on our left; his headquarters in a church (with a high cupola) at Gettysburg; Hill in the centre; and Longstreet on the right. Our ridges were also covered with pine-woods at the tops, and generally on the rear slopes. The artillery of both sides confronted each other at the edges of

these belts of trees, the troops being completely hidden. The enemy was evidently intrenched, but the Southerners had not broken ground at all. A dead silence reigned till 4.45 P. M., and no one would have imagined that such masses of men and such a powerful artillery were about to commence the work of destruction at that hour.

Only two divisions of Longstreet were present to-day—viz., McLaws's and Hood's—Pickett being still in the rear. As the whole morning was evidently to be occupied in disposing the troops for the attack, I rode to the extreme right with Colonel Manning and Major Walton, where we ate quantities of cherries, and got a feed of corn for our horses. We also bathed in a small stream, but not without some trepidation on my part, for we were almost beyond the lines, and were exposed to the enemy's cavalry.

At 1 P. M. I met a quantity of Yankee prisoners who had been picked up straggling. They told me they belonged to Sickles's corps (3d, I think), and had arrived from Emmetsburg during the night. About this time skirmishing began along part of the line, but not heavily.

At 2 P. M. General Longstreet advised me, if I wished to have a good view of the battle, to return to my tree of yesterday. I did so, and remained there with Lawley and Captain Schreibert during the rest of the afternoon. But until 4.45 P. M. all was profoundly still, and we began to doubt whether a fight was coming off to-day at all. At that time, however, Longstreet suddenly commenced a heavy cannonade on the right. Ewell immediately took it up on the left. The enemy replied with at least equal fury, and in a few moments the firing along the whole line was as heavy as it is possible to conceive. A dense smoke arose for six miles; there was little wind to drive it away, and the air seemed full of shells—each of which appeared to have a different style of going, and to make a different noise from the others. The ordnance on both sides is of a very varied description. Every now and then a caisson would blow up—if a Federal one, a Confederate yell would immediately follow. The Southern troops when charging, or to express their delight, always yell in a manner peculiar to themselves. The Yankee cheer is much more like ours; but the Confederate officers declare that the rebel yell has a particular merit, and always produces a salutary and useful effect upon their adversaries. A corps is sometimes spoken of as a "good yelling regiment."

So soon as the firing began, General Lee joined Hill just below our tree, and he remained there nearly all the time, looking through his field glass—sometimes talking to Hill and sometimes to Colonel Long of his Staff. But generally he sat quite alone on the stump of a tree. What I remarked especially was, that during the whole time the firing continued, he only sent one message, and only received one report. It is evidently his system to arrange the plan thoroughly with the three corps commanders, and then leave to them the duty of modifying and carrying it out to the best of their abilities.

When the cannonade was at its height, a Confederate band of music, between the cemetery and ourselves, began to play polkas and waltzes, which sounded very curious, accompanied by the hissing and bursting of the shells.

At 5.45 all became comparatively quiet on our left and in the cemetery; but volleys of musketry on the right told us that Longstreet's infantry were advancing, and the onward progress of the smoke showed that he was progressing favorably; but about 6.30 there seemed to be a check, and even a slight retrograde movement. Soon after 7, General Lee got a report by signal from Longstreet to say "we are doing well." A little before dark the firing dropped off in every direction, and soon ceased altogether. We then received intelligence that Longstreet had carried every thing before him for some time, capturing several batteries, and driving the enemy from his positions; but when Hill's Florida brigade and some other troops gave way, he was forced to abandon a small portion of the ground he had won, together with all the captured guns, except three. His troops, however, bivouacked during the night on ground occupied by the enemy this morning.

Every one deplores that Longstreet will expose himself in such a reckless manner. To-day he led a Georgian regiment in a charge against a battery, hat in hand, and in front of everybody. General Barksdale was killed and Semmes mortally wounded; but the most serious loss was that of General Hood, who was badly wounded in the arm early in the day. I heard that his Texans are in despair. Lawley and I rode back to the General's camp, which had been moved to within a mile of the scene of action. Longstreet, however, with most of his Staff, bivouacked on the field.

Major Fairfax arrived at about 10 P. M. in a very bad humor. He had under his charge about 1,000 to 1,500 Yankee prisoners, who had been taken to-day; among them a general, whom I heard one of his men accusing of having been "so G——d d——d drunk, that he had turned his guns upon his own men." But, on the other hand, the accuser was such a thundering blackguard, and proposed taking such a variety of oaths in order to escape from the U. S. army, that he is not worthy of much credit. A large train of horses and mules, &c., arrived to-day, sent in by General Stuart, and captured, it is understood, by his cavalry, which had penetrated to within six miles of Washington.

3d July, Friday.———At 6 A. M. I rode to the field with Colonel Manning, and went over that portion of the ground which, after a fierce contest, had been won from the enemy yesterday evening. The dead were being buried, but great numbers were still lying about; also many mortally wounded, for whom nothing could be done. Amongst the latter were a number of Yankees dressed in bad imitations of the Zouave costume. They opened their glazed eyes as I rode past in a painfully imploring manner.

We joined Generals Lee and Longstreet's Staff: they were reconnoitring and making preparations for renewing the attack. As we formed a pretty large party, we often drew upon ourselves the attention of the hostile sharpshooters, and were two or three times favored with a shell. One of these shells set a brick building on fire which was situated between the lines. This building was filled wounded, principally Yankees, who, I am afraid, must have perished miserably in the flames. Colonel Sorrell had been slightly wounded yesterday, but still did duty. Major Walton's horse was killed, but there were no other casualties amongst my particular friends.

The plan of yesterday's attack seems to have been very simple—first a heavy cannonade all along the line, followed by an advance of Longstreet's two divisions and part of Hill's corps. In consequence of the enemy's having been driven back some distance, Longstreet's corps (part of it) was in a much more forward situation than yesterday. But the range of heights to be gained was still most formidable, and evidently strongly intrenched.

The distance between the Confederate guns and the Yankee position—i. e., between the woods crowning the opposite ridges—was at least a mile—quite open, gently undulating, and exposed to artillery the whole distance. This was the ground which had to be crossed in to-day's attack. Pickett's division, which has just come up, was to bear the brunt in Longstreet's attack, together with Heth and Pettigrew in Hill's corps. Pickett's division was a weak one (under 5,000), owing to the absence of two brigades.

At noon all Longstreet's dispositions were made; his troops for attack were deployed into line, and lying down in the woods; his batteries were ready to open. The general then dismounted and went to sleep for a short time. The Austrian officer and I now rode off to get, if possible, into some commanding position from whence we could see the whole thing without being exposed to the tremendous fire which was about to commence. After riding about for half an hour without being able to discover so desirable a situation, we determined to make for the cupola near Gettysburg, Ewell's headquarters. Just before we reached the entrance of the town, the cannonade opened with a fury which surpassed even that of yesterday.

Soon after passing through the toll-gate at the entrance of Gettysburg, we found that we had got into a heavy cross-fire; shells both from Federal and Confederate passing over our heads with great frequency. At length two shrapnel shells burst quite close to us, and a ball from one of them hit the officer who was conducting us. We then turned round and changed our views with regard to the cupola—the fire of one side being bad, enough, but preferable to that of both sides. A small boy of twelve years was riding with us at the time: this urchin took a diabolical interest in the bursting of the shells, and screamed with delight when he saw them take effect. I never saw this boy again, or found out who he was.

The road at Gettysburg was lined with Yankee dead, and as they had been killed on the 1st, the poor fellows had already begun to be very offensive. We then returned to the hill I was on yesterday. But finding that to see the actual fighting, it was absolutely necessary to go into the thick of the thing, I determined to make my way to General Longstreet. It was then about 2.30. After passing General Lee and his Staff, I rode on through the woods in the direction in which I had left Longstreet. I soon began to meet many wounded men returning from the front; many of them asked in piteous tones the way to a doctor or an ambulance. The further I got, greater became the number of the wounded. At last I came to a perfect stream of them flocking through the woods in numbers as great as the crowd in Oxford-street in the middle of day. Some were walking alone on crutches composed of two rifles, others were supported by men less badly wounded than themselves, and others were carried on stretchers by the ambulance corps; but in no case did I see a sound man helping the wounded to the rear, unless he carried the red badge of the ambulance corps. They were still under a heavy fire; the shells were continually bringing down great limbs of trees, and carrying further destruction amongst this melancholy procession. I saw all this in much less time than it takes to write it, and although astonished to meet such vast numbers of wounded, I had not seen enough to give me an idea of the real extent of the mischief.

When I got close up to General Longstreet, I saw one of his regiments advancing through the woods in good order; so, thinking I was just in time to see the attack, I remarked to the General that "I wouldn't have missed this for any thing." Longstreet was seated at the top of a snake fence at the edge of the wood, and looking perfectly calm and imperturbed. He replied, laughing, "The devil you wouldn't! I would like to have missed it very much; we've attacked and been repulsed: look there!"

For the first time I then had a view of the open space between the two positions, and saw it covered with Confederates slowly and sulkily returning towards us in small broken parties, under a heavy fire of artillery. But the fire where we were was not so bad as further to the rear; for although the air seemed alive with shell, yet the greater number burst behind us.

The General told me that Pickett's division had succeeded in carrying the enemy's position and capturing his guns, but after remaining there twenty minutes, it had been forced to retire, on the retreat of Heth and Pettigrew on its left. No person could have been more calm or self-possessed than General Longstreet under these trying circumstances, aggravated as they now were by the movements of the enemy, who began to show a strong disposition to advance. I could now thoroughly appreciate the term bulldog, which I had heard applied to him by the soldiers. Difficulties seem to make no other impression upon him than to make him a little more savage.

Major Walton was the only officer with him when I came up—all the rest had been put into the charge. In a few minutes Major Latrobe arrived on foot, carrying his saddle, having just had his horse killed. Colonel Sorrell was also in the same predicament, and Captain Goree's horse was wounded in the mouth.

The General was making the best arrangements in his power to resist the threatened advance, by advancing some artillery, rallying the stragglers, &c. I remember seeing a General (Pettigrew, I think it was) come up to him, and report that "he was unable to bring his men up again." Longstreet turned upon him and replied, with some sarcasm: "Very well; never mind, then, General; just let them remain where they are: the enemy's going to advance, and it will spare you the trouble."

He asked for something to drink: I gave him some run out of my silver flask, which I begged he would keep in remembrance of the occasion; he smiled, and, to my great satisfaction, accepted the memorial. He then went off to give some orders to McLaws's division. Soon afterwards I joined General Lee, who had in the mean while come to that part of the field on becoming aware of the disaster. If Longstreet's conduct was admirable, that of General Lee was perfectly subline. He was engaged in rallying and in encouraging the broken troops, and was riding about a little in front of the wood, quite alone—the whole of his Staff being engaged in a similar manner further to the rear. His face, which is always placid and cheeful, did not show signs of the slightest disappointment, care, or annoyance; he was addressing to every soldier he met a few words of encouragement, such as, "All this will come right in the end: we'll talk it over afterwards; but, in the mean time, all good men must rally. We want all good and true men just now," &c. He spoke to all the wounded men that passed him, and the slightly wounded he exhorted "to bind up their hurts and take up a musket" in this emergency. Very few failed to answer his appeal, and I saw many badly wounded men take off their hats and cheer him. He said to me, "This has been a sad day for us, Colonel—a sad day; but we can't expect always to gain victories." He was also kind enough to advise me to get into some more sheltered position, as the shells were bursting round us with considerable frequency.

Notwithstanding the misfortune which had so suddenly befallen him, General Lee seemed to observe every thing, however trivial. When a mounted officer began licking his horse for shying at the bursting of a shell, he called out. "Don't whip him, Captain; don't whip him. I've got just such another foolish horse myself, and whipping does no good."

I happened to see a man lying flat on his face in a small ditch, and I remarked that I didn't think he seemed dead; this drew General Lee's attention to the man, who commenced groaning dismally. Finding appeals to his patriotism of no avail, General Lee had him ignominiously set on his legs by some neighboring gunners.

I saw General Wilcox (an officer who wears a short round jacket and a battered straw hat) come up to him, and explain, almost crying, the state of his brigade. General Lee immediately shook hands with him and said cheerfully, "Never mind, General, all this has been MY fault—it is I that have lost this fight, and you must help me out of it in the best way you can." In this manner I saw General Lee encourage and reanimate his somewhat dispirited troops, and magnanimously take upon his own shoulders the whole weight of the repulse. It was impossible to look at him or to listen to him without feeling the strongest admiration, and I never saw any man fail him except the man in the ditch.

It is difficult to exaggerate the critical state of affairs as they appeared about this time. If the enemy or their general had shown any enterprise, there is no saying what might have happened. General Lee and his officers were evidently fully impressed with a sense of the situation; yet there was much less noise, fuss, or confusion of orders than at an ordinary field-day; the men, as they were rallied in the wood, were brought up in detachments, and lay down quietly and coolly in the positions assigned to them.

We heard that Generals Garnett and Armistead were killed, and General Kemper mortally wounded; also, that Pickett's division had only one field-officer unhurt. Nearly all this slaughter took place in an open space about one mile square, and within one hour.

At 6 P. M. we heard a long and continuous Yankee cheer, which we at first imagined was an indication of an advance; but it turned out to be their reception of a general officer, whom we saw riding down the line, followed by about thirty horsemen. Soon afterwards I rode to the extreme front, where there were four pieces of rifled can-

non almost without any infantry support. To the nonwithdral of these guns is to be attributed the otherwise surprising inactivity of the enemy. I was immediately surrounded by a sergeant and about half-a-dozen gunners, who seemed in excellent spirits and full of confidence, in spite of their exposed situation. The sergeant expressed his ardent hope that the Yankees might have spirit enough to advance and receive the dose he had in readiness for them. They spoke in admiration of the advance of Pickett's division, and of the manner in which Pickett himself had led it. When they observed General Lee they said, "We've not lost confidence in the old man: this day's work won't do him no harm. 'Uncle Robert' will get us into Washington yet; you bet he will!" &c. Whilst we were talking, the enemy's skirmishers began to advance slowly, and several ominous sounds in quick succession told us that we were attracting their attention, and that it was necessary to break up the conclave. I therefore turned round and took leave of these cheery and plucky gunners.

At 7 P. M., General Lee received a report that Johnston's division of Ewell's corps had been successful on the left, and had gained important advantages there. Firing entirely ceased in our front about this time; but we now heard some brisk musketry on our right, which I afterwards learned proceeded from Hood's Texans, who had managed to surround some enterprising Yankee cavalry, and were slaughtering them with great satisfaction. Only eighteen out of four hundred are said to have escaped.

At 7.30, all idea of a Yankee attack being over, I rode back to Moses's tent, and found that worthy commissary in very low spirits, all sorts of exaggerated rumors having reached him. On my way I met a great many wounded men, most anxious to inquire after Longstreet, who was reported killed; when I assured them he was quite well, they seemed to forget their own pain in the evident pleasure they felt in the safety of their chief. No words that I can use will adequately express the extraordinary patience and fortitude with which the wounded Confederates bore their sufferings.

I got something to eat with the doctors at 10 P. M., the first for fifteen hours.

I gave up my horse to-day to his owner, as from death and exhaustion the staff are almost without horses.

4th July, Saturday.—I was awoke at daylight by Moses complaining that his valuable trunk, containing much public money, had been stolen from our tent whilst we slept. After a search it was found in a wood hard by, broken open and minus the money. Dr. Barksdale had been robbed in the same manner exactly. This is evidently the work of those rascally stragglers, who shirk going under fire, plunder the natives, and will hereafter swagger as the heroes of Gettysburg.

Lawley, the Austrian, and I walked up to the front about 8 o'clock, and on our way we met General Longstreet, who was in a high state of amusement and good humor. A flag of truce had just come over from the enemy, and its bearer announced among other things that "General Longstreet was wounded and a prisoner, but would be taken care of." General Longstreet sent back word that he was extremely grateful, but that, being neither wounded nor a prisoner, he was quite able to take care of himself. The iron endurance of General Longstreet is most extraordinary; he seems to require neither food nor sleep. Most of his staff now fall fast asleep directly they get off their horses, they are so exhausted from the last three days' work.

Whilst Lawley went to headquarters on business, I sat down and had a long talk with General Pendleton (the parson) chief of artillery. He told me the exact number of guns in action yesterday. He said that the universal opinion is in favor of the twelve-pounder Napoleon guns as the best and simplest sort of ordnance for field purposes.

Nearly all the artillery with this army has either been captured from the enemy or cast from old 6-pounders taken at the early part of the war.

At 10 A. M. Lawley returned from headquarters, bringing the news that the army is to commence moving in the direction of Virginia this evening. This step is imperative from want of ammunition. But it was hoped that the enemy might attack during the day, especially as this is the 4th of July, and it was calculated that there was still ammunition for one day's fighting. The ordnance train had already commenced moving back towards Cashtown, and Ewell's immense train of plunder had been proceeding towards Hagerstown by the Fairfield road ever since an early hour this morning.

Johnson's division had evacuated during the night the position it had gained yesterday. It appears that for a time it was actually in possession of the cemetery, but had been forced to retire from thence from want of support by Pender's division, which had been retarded by that officer's wound. The whole of our left was therefore thrown back considerably.

At 1 P. M. the rain began to descend in torrents, and we took refuge in the hovel of an ignorant Pennsylvania boor. The cottage was full of soldiers, none of whom had the slightest idea of the contemplated retreat, and all were talking of Washington and Baltimore with the greatest confidence.

At 2 P. M. we walked to General Longstreet's camp, which had been removed to a place three miles distant, on the Fairfield road. General Longstreet talked to me for a long time about the battle. He said the mistake they had made was in not concentrating the army more, and making the attack yesterday with 30,000 men instead of 15,000. The advance had been in three lines, and the troops of Hill's corps who gave way were young soldiers, who had never been under fire before. He thought the enemy would have attacked had the guns been withdrawn. Had they done so at that particular moment immediately after the repulse, it would have been awkward; but in that case he had given orders for the advance of Hood's division and M'Laws's on the right. I think, after all, that General Meade was right not to advance—his men would never have stood the tremendous fire of artillery they would have been exposed to.

Rather over 7,000 Yankees were captured during the three days; 3,500 took the parole;

the remainder were now being marched to Richmond, escorted by the remains of Pickett's division. It is impossible to avoid seeing that the cause of this check to the Confederates lies in the utter contempt felt for the enemy by all ranks.

Wagons, horses, mules and cattle captured in Pennsylvania, the solid advantages of this campaign, have been passing slowly along this road (Fairfield) all day; those taken by Ewell are particularly admired. So interminable was this train that it soon became evident that we should not be able to start till late at night. As soon as it became dark we all lay round a big fire, and I heard reports coming in from the different generals that the enemy was retiring, and had been doing so all day long. M'Laws reported nothing in his front but cavalry videttes. But this, of course, could make no difference to General Lee's plan; ammunition he must have—he had failed to capture it from the enemy (according to precedent;) and as his communications with Virginia were intercepted, he was compelled to fall back towards Winchester, and draw his supplies from thence. General Milroy had kindly left an ample stock at that town when he made his precipitate exit some weeks ago. The army was also encumbered with an enormous wagon train, the spoils of Pennsylvania, which it is highly desirable to get safely over the Potomac.

Shortly after 9 P. M. the rain began to descend in torrents.—Lawley and I luckily got into the doctors' covered buggy, and began to get slowly under way a little after midnight.

Source: Fremantle, Sir Arthur James Lyon. *Three Months in the Southern States: April, June, 1863.* Mobile, Ala.: S. H. Goetzel, 1864, pp. 127–139.

Letter to His Fiancée
Major General George E. Pickett
July 4, 1863

On the afternoon of July 3, over the vigorous objections of his second in command, General James Longstreet, Robert E. Lee ordered a massive infantry assault on the well-defended Union high-ground positions at Gettysburg. History has named the assault Pickett's Charge, after Major General George E. Pickett, who commanded three of the nine brigades committed to the operation. As gallant as it was futile and foolhardy, Pickett's Charge cost 7,500 Confederate casualties of the 12,500 engaged. With the failure of this operation, the Battle of Gettysburg ended in Lee's defeat. A disconsolate Pickett described the action in a heartbreaking letter written to his fiancée.

On the Fourth—far from a glorious Fourth to us or to any with love for his fellowmen—I wrote you just a line of heartbreak. The sacrifice of life on that bloodsoaked field on the fatal 3rd was too awful for the heralding of victory, even for our victorious foe, who, I think, believe as we do, that it decided the fate of our cause. No words can picture the anguish of that roll call— the breathless waits between the responses. The "Here" of those who, by God's mercy, had miraculously escaped the awful rain of shot and shell was a sob—a gasp—a knell—for the unanswered name of his comrade called before his. There was no tone of thankfulness for having been spared to answer to their names, but rather a toll and an unvoiced wish that they, too, had been among the missing.

But for the blight to your sweet young life, but for you, only you, my darling, your soldier would rather by far be out there, too, with his brave Virginians—dead. Even now I can hear them cheering as I gave the order, "Forward"! I can feel their faith and trust in me and their love for our cause. I can feel the thrill of their joyous voices as they called out all along the line, "We'll follow you, Marse George. We'll follow you, we'll follow you." Oh, how faithfully they kept their word, following me on, on to their death, and I, believing in the promised support, led them on, on, on. Oh, God!

I can't write you a love letter today, my Sallie, for, with my great love for you and my gratitude to God for sparing my life to devote to you,

The climax of the Battle of Gettysburg came on the afternoon of July 3, with the so-called Pickett's Charge, when nine Confederate brigades came charging across an open field, only to be mowed down by the Union forces. *(Library of Congress)*

comes the overpowering thought of those whose lives were sacrificed—of the brokenhearted widows and mothers and orphans. The moans of my wounded boys, the sight of the dead, upturned faces flood my soul with grief; and here am I, whom they trusted, whom they followed, leaving them on that field of carnage, leaving them to the mercy of———and guarding 4,000 prisoners across the river back to Winchester. Such a duty for men who a few hours ago covered themselves with glory eternal.

Well, my darling, I put the prisoners all on their honor and gave them equal liberties with my own soldier boys. My first command to them was to go and enjoy themselves the best they could, and they have obeyed my order. Today, a Dutchman and two of his comrades came up and told me that they were lost and besought me to help them find their commands. They had been with my men and had gotten separated from their own comrades. So I sent old Floyd off on St. Paul to found out where they belonged and deliver them.

This is too gloomy and too poor a letter for so beautiful a sweetheart, but it seems sacrilegious, almost, to say I love you, with the hearts that are stilled to love on the field of battle.

Your Soldier

Source: Pickett, George E. *The Heart of a Soldier; As Revealed in the Intimate Letters of Genl. George E. Pickett CSA.* New York: Seth Moyle, 1913, pp. 101–103.

THE OVERLAND CAMPAIGN, MAY 4–JUNE 1864

"How Men Die in Battle"
Frank Wilkeson
Published 1886

Frank Wilkeson (1848–1913), who described himself in his 1886 Civil War memoir only as a "private in the Army of the Potomac," actually attained the rank of captain. He became famous after the war as an explorer and surveyor of the Pacific Northwest and an authority on the Indians of that region. In the following narrative, he describes the violence of battle in its ultimate result: the deaths of young men. The Battle of the Wilderness, which began Ulysses S. Grant's Overland Campaign, offered many examples.

Almost every death on the battlefield is different. And the manner of the death depends on the wound and on the man, whether he is cowardly or brave, whether his vitality is large or small, whether he is a man of active imagination or is dull of intellect, whether he is of nervous or lymphatic temperament. I instance deaths and wounds that I saw in Grant's last campaign.

On the second day of the Battle of the Wilderness, where I fought as an infantry soldier, I saw more men killed and wounded than I did before or after in the same time. I knew but few of the men in the regiment in whose ranks I stood; but I learned the Christian names of some of them.

The man who stood next to me on my right was called Will. He was cool, brave, and intelligent. In the morning, when Corps II was advancing and driving Hill's soldiers slowly back, I was flurried. He noticed it and steadied my nerves by saying, kindly: "Don't fire so fast. This fight will last all day. Don't hurry. Cover your man before you pull the trigger. Take it easy, my boy, take it easy, and your cartridges will last the longer." This man fought effectively. During the day I had learned to look up to this excellent soldier and lean on him.

Toward evening, as we were being slowly driven back to the Brock Road by Longstreet's men, we made a stand. I was behind a tree firing, with my rifle barrel resting on the stub of a limb. Will was standing by my side, but in the open. He, with a groan, doubled up and dropped on the ground at my feet. He looked up at me. His face was pale. He gasped for breath a few times, and then said faintly: "That ends me. I am shot through the bowels." I said: "Crawl to the rear. We are not far from the entrenchments along the Brock Road." I saw him sit up and indistinctly saw him reach for his rifle, which had fallen from his hands as he fell. Again I spoke to him, urging him to go to the rear. He looked at me and said impatiently: "I tell you that I am as good as dead. There is no use in fooling with me. I shall stay here." Then he pitched forward dead, shot again and through the head. We fell back before Longstreet's soldiers and left Will lying in a windrow of dead men.

When we got into the Brock Road entrenchments, a man a few files to my left dropped dead, shot just above the right eye. He did not groan, or sigh, or make the slightest physical movement, except that his chest heaved a few times. The life went out of his face instantly, leaving it without a particle of expression. It was plastic and, as the facial muscles contracted, it took many shapes. When this man's body became cold and his face hardened, it was horribly distorted, as though he had suffered intensely. Any person who had not seen him killed would have said that he had endured supreme agony before death released him. A few minutes after he fell, another man, a little farther to the left, fell with apparently a precisely similar wound. He was straightened out and lived for over an hour. He did not speak, simply lay on his back, and his broad chest rose and fell, slowly at first, and then faster and faster, and more and more feebly, until he was dead. And his face hardened, and it was almost terrifying in its painful distortion. I have seen dead soldiers' faces which were wreathed in smiles and heard their comrades say that they had died happy.

Wounded soldiers rest under trees at Marye's Heights, Fredericksburg, after the Battle of Spotsylvania Courthouse, May 1864. *(National Archives)*

I do not believe that the face of a dead soldier, lying on a battlefield, ever truthfully indicates the mental or physical anguish, or peacefulness of mind, which he suffered or enjoyed before his death. The face is plastic after death, and as the facial muscles cool and contract, they draw the face into many shapes. Sometimes the dead smile, again they stare with glassy eyes, and lolling tongues, and dreadfully distorted visages at you. It goes for nothing. One death was as painless as the other.

After Longstreet's soldiers had driven Corps II into their entrenchments along the Brock Road, a battle-exhausted infantryman stood behind a large oak tree. His back rested against it. He was very tired and held his rifle loosely in his hand. The Confederates were directly in our front. This soldier was apparently in perfect safety. A solid shot from a Confederate gun struck the oak tree squarely about four feet from the ground; but it did not have sufficient force to tear through the tough wood. The soldier fell dead. There was not a scratch on him. He was killed by concussion.

While we were fighting savagely over these entrenchments, the woods in our front caught fire, and I saw many of our wounded burned to death. Must they not have suffered horribly? I am not at all sure of that. The smoke rolled heavily and slowly before the fire. It enveloped the wounded, and I think that by far the larger portion of the men who were roasted were suffocated before the flames curled round them. The spectacle was courage-sapping and pitiful, and it appealed strongly to the imagination of the spectators; but I do not believe that the wounded soldiers, who were being burned, suffered greatly, if they suffered at all.

Wounded soldiers, it mattered not how slight the wounds, generally hastened away from the battle lines. A wound entitled a man to go to the rear and to a hospital. Of course there were many exceptions to this rule, as there would necessarily be in battles where from 20,000 to 30,000 men were wounded. I frequently saw slightly wounded men who were marching with their colors. I personally saw but two men wounded who continued to fight.

During the first day's fighting in the Wilderness, I saw a youth of about twenty years skip and yell, stung by a bullet through the thigh. He turned to limp to the rear. After he had gone a few steps he stopped, then he kicked out his leg once or twice to see if it would work. Then he tore the clothing away from his leg so as to see the wound. He looked at it attentively for an instant, then kicked out his leg again, then turned and took his place in the ranks and resumed firing. There was considerable disorder in the line, and the soldiers moved to and fro—now a few feet to the right, now a few feet to the left. One of these movements brought me directly behind this wounded soldier. I could see plainly from that position, and I pushed into the gaping line and began firing. In a minute or two the wounded soldier dropped his rifle and, clasping his left arm, exclaimed: "I am hit again!" He sat down behind the battle ranks and tore off the sleeve of his shirt. The wound was very slight—not much more than skin-deep. He tied his handkerchief around it, picked up his rifle, and took position alongside of me. I said: "You are fighting in bad luck today. You had better get away from here." He turned his head to answer me. His head jerked, he staggered, then fell, then regained his feet. A tiny fountain of blood and teeth and bone and bits of tongue burst out of his mouth. He had been shot through the jaws; the lower one was broken and hung down. I looked directly into his open mouth, which was ragged and bloody

and tongueless. He cast his rifle furiously on the ground and staggered off.

The next day, just before Longstreet's soldiers made their first charge on Corps II, I heard the peculiar cry a stricken man utters as the bullet tears through his flesh. I turned my head, as I loaded my rifle, to see who was hit. I saw a bearded Irishman pull up his shirt. He had been wounded in the left side just below the floating ribs. His face was gray with fear. The wound looked as though it were mortal. He looked at it for an instant, then poked it gently with his index finger. He flushed redly and smiled with satisfaction. He tucked his shirt into his trousers and was fighting in the ranks again before I had capped my rifle. The ball had cut a groove in his skin only. The play of this Irishman's face was so expressive, his emotions changed so quickly, that I could not keep from laughing.

Near Spotsylvania I saw, as my battery was moving into action, a group of wounded men lying in the shade cast by some large oak trees. All of these men's faces were gray. They silently looked at us as we marched past them. One wounded man, a blond giant of about forty years, was smoking a short briarwood pipe. He had a firm grip on the pipestem. I asked him what he was doing. "Having my last smoke, young fellow," he replied. His dauntless blue eyes met mine, and he bravely tried to smile. I saw that he was dying fast. Another of these wounded men was trying to read a letter. He was too weak to hold it, or maybe his sight was clouded. He thrust it unread into the breast pocket of his blouse and lay back with a moan.

This group of wounded men numbered fifteen or twenty. At the time, I thought that all of them were fatally wounded and that there was no use in the surgeons wasting time on them, when men who could be saved were clamoring for their skillful attention. None of these soldiers cried aloud, none called on wife, or mother, or father. They lay on the ground, palefaced, and with set jaws, waiting for their end. They moaned and groaned as they suffered, but none of them flunked. When my battery returned from the front, five or six hours afterward, almost all of these men were dead. Long before the campaign was over I concluded that dying soldiers seldom called on those who were dearest to them, seldom conjured their Northern or Southern homes, until they became delirious. Then, when their minds wandered and fluttered at the approach of freedom, they babbled of their homes. Some were boys again and were fishing in Northern trout streams. Some were generals leading their men to victory. Some were with their wives and children. Some wandered over their family's homestead; but all, with rare exceptions, were delirious.

At the North Anna River, my battery being in action, an infantry soldier, one of our supports, who was lying face downward close behind the gun I served on, and in a place where he thought he was safe, was struck on the thighs by a large jagged piece of a shell. The wound made by this fragment of iron was as horrible as any I saw in the army. The flesh of both thighs was torn off, exposing the bones. The soldier bled to death in a few minutes, and before he died he conjured his Northern home, and murmured of his wife and children.

In the same battle, but on the south side of the river, a man who carried a rifle was passing between the guns and caissons of the battery. A solid shot, intended for us, struck him on the side. His entire bowels were torn out and slung in ribbons and shreds on the ground. He fell dead, but his arms and legs jerked convulsively a few times. It was a sickening spectacle. During this battle I saw a Union picket knocked down, probably by a rifle ball striking his head and glancing from it. He lay as though dead. Presently, he struggled to his feet, and, with blood streaming from his head, he staggered aimlessly round and round in a circle, as sheep afflicted with grubs in the brain do. Instantly, the Confederate sharpshooters opened fire on him and speedily killed him as he circled. Wounded soldiers almost always tore their clothing away from their wounds so as to see them and to judge of their character. Many of them would

smile and their faces would brighten as they realized that they were not hard hit and that they could go home for a few months. Others would give a quick glance at their wounds and then shrink back as from a blow, and turn pale as they realized the truth that they were mortally wounded. The enlisted men were exceedingly accurate judges of the probable result which would ensue from any wound they saw. They had seen hundreds of soldiers wounded, and they had noticed that certain wounds always resulted fatally. They knew when they were fatally wounded, and after the shock of discovery had passed, they generally braced themselves and died in a manly manner. It was seldom that an American or Irish volunteer flunked in the presence of death.

Source: Wilkeson, Frank. "How Men Die in Battle." In *Recollections of a Private Soldier in the Army of the Potomac.* New York: G. P. Putnam's Sons, 1886, pp. 197–207.

THE PRISONER OF WAR EXPERIENCE, 1864–1865

Entries from *Andersonville Diary*
John L. Ransom
July–August 1864

On July 22, 1862, the military authorities of the United States and the Confederacy concluded the so-called Dix-Hill Cartel, by which it was agreed that prisoners would be exchanged within 10 days of capture. The cartel never really functioned well, but the principle of releasing prisoners of war (POWs) on "parole"—their solemn promise not to fight again—prevailed until General Grant, acting on President Lincoln's orders, called a halt to all prisoner parole and exchange on April 17, 1864. From this point on, POWs on both sides were subjected to conditions that ranged from squalid to brutal. The most notorious of all POW camps was a

Confederate compound, Camp Sumter, which was better known by the name of the adjacent town: Andersonville.

Set in the sweltering heart of Georgia, Andersonville was built to accommodate 10,000 POWs. By August 1864, it held 33,000 in conditions of severe privation, starvation, exposure, and disease. Its most notorious commandant, Captain Henry Wirz, earned a reputation for deliberate and extravagant cruelty. Of 45,000 prisoners confined at Andersonville during 1864–65, 13,000 died and were buried in marked graves. Because many prisoners were dumped into unmarked mass graves, the actual death toll was almost certainly higher.

John L. Ransom (1843–1919), first sergeant, 9th Michigan Cavalry Regiment, was one of the 45,000 Union soldiers who suffered at Anderson- *ville. Quartermaster of Company A, 9th Michigan Volunteer Cavalry, he was just 20 years old when he was captured by Confederates in Tennessee in 1863. Following an unsuccessful attempt to escape from Andersonville, he received medical aid from Confederate civilians who took pity on him. Ransom wrote the diary in camp but did not publish it until 1881. It is widely considered one of the great POW documents of any war.*

July 3 [1864]. Three hundred and fifty new men from West Virginia were turned into this summer resort this morning. They brought good news as to successful termination of the war, and they also caused war after coming among us. As usual, the raiders proceeded to rob them of their valuables, and a fight occurred in which hun-

Andersonville, Georgia, was a Confederate prison camp where more than 33,000 Union prisoners of war were confined under increasingly deteriorating conditions. *(Library of Congress)*

dreds were engaged. The cutthroats came out ahead. Complaints were made to Captain Wirtz [Henry Wirz] that this thing would be tolerated no longer; that these raiders must be put down, or the men would rise in their might and break away if assistance was not given with which to preserve order.

Wirtz flew around as if he had never thought of it before, issued an order to the effect that no more food would be given us until the leaders were arrested and taken outside for trial. The greatest possible excitement—hundreds that have before been neutral and noncommital are now joining a police force; captains are appointed to take charge of the squads, which have been furnished with clubs by Wirtz. As I write, this middle of the afternoon, the battle rages. The police go right to raider headquarters, knock right and left, and make their arrests. Sometimes the police are whipped and have to retreat, but they rally their forces and again make a charge in which they are successful.

Can lay in our shade and see the trouble go on. Must be killing some by the shouting. The raiders fight for their very life and are only taken after being thoroughly whipped. The stockade is loaded with guards who are fearful of a break. I wish I could describe the scene today. A number killed. After each arrest a great cheering takes place. Night. Thirty or forty have been taken outside of the worst characters in camp, and still the good work goes on. No food today and don't want any. A big strapping fellow called "Limber Jim" heads the police. Grand old Michael Hoare is at the front and goes for a raider as quick as he would a Rebel. Patrol the camp all the time and gradually quieting down. The orderly prisoners are feeling jolly.

July 4. The men taken outside yesterday are under Rebel guard and will be punished. The men are thoroughly aroused, and now that the matter has been taken in hand, it will be followed up to the letter. Other arrests are being made today, and occasionally a big fight. Little Terry, whom they could not find yesterday, was today taken. Had been hiding in an old well, or hole in the ground. Fought like a little tiger, but had to go. "Limber Jim" is a brick and should be made a major general if he ever reaches our lines. Mike Hoare is right up in rank, and true blue. William B. Rowe also makes a good policeman, as does "Dad" Sanders. Battese says he "no time to fight, must wash." Jimmy Devers regrets that he cannot take a hand in, as he likes to fight, and especially with a club. The writer hereof does no fighting, being on the sick list. The excitement of looking on is most too much for me. Can hardly arrest the big graybacks [lice] crawling around.

Captain Moseby is one of the arrested ones. His right name is Collins and he has been in our hundred all the time since leaving Richmond. Has got a good long neck to stretch. Another man whom I have seen a good deal of, one Curtiss, is also arrested. I haven't mentioned poor little Bullock for months, seems to me. He was most dead when we first came to Andersonville, and is still alive and tottering around. Has lost his voice entirely and is nothing but a skeleton. Hardly enough of him for disease to get hold of. Would be one of the surprising things on record if he lives through it, and he seems no worse than months ago. It is said that a court will be formed of our own men to try the raiders. Anyway, so they are punished. All have killed men, and they themselves should be killed. When arrested, the police had hard work to prevent their being lynched. Police more thoroughly organizing all the time.

An extra amount of food this P.M., and police get extra rations, and three out of our mess is doing pretty well, as they are all willing to divide. They tell us all the encounters they have, and much interesting talk. Mike has some queer experiences. Rebel flags at half-mast for some of their great men. Just heard that the trial of raiders will begin tomorrow.

July 5. Court is in session outside and raiders being tried by our own men. Wirtz has done one good thing, but it's a question whether he is entitled to any credit, as he had to be threatened with a break before he would assist us. Rations again today. I am quite bad off with my diseases, but still there are so many thousands so much worse off that I do not complain much, or try not to however.

July 6. Boiling hot, camp reeking with filth, and no sanitary privileges; men dying off over 140 per day. Stockade enlarged, taking in eight or ten more acres, giving us more room, and stumps to dig up for wood to cook with. Mike Hoare is in good health; not so Jimmy Devers. Jimmy has now been a prisoner over a year and, poor boy, will probably die soon. Have more mementos than I can carry, from those who have died, to be given to their friends at home. At least a dozen have given me letters, pictures, etc., to take North. Hope I shan't have to turn them over to someone else.

July 7. The court was gotten up by our own men and from our own men; judge, jury, counsel, etc. Had a fair trial and were even defended, but to no purpose. It is reported that six have been sentenced to be hung, while a good many others are condemned to lighter punishment, such as setting in the stocks, strung up by the thumbs, thumbscrews, head hanging, etc. The court has been severe, but just. Mike goes out tomorrow to take some part in the court proceedings.

The prison seems a different place altogether; still, dread disease is here and mowing down good and true men. Would seem to me that 300 or 400 died each day, though officially but 140 odd is told. About 27,000, I believe, are here now in all. No new ones for a few days. Rebel visitors, who look at us from a distance. It is said the stench keeps all away who have no business here and can keep away. Washing business good. Am negotiating for a pair of pants. Dislike fearfully to wear dead men's clothes and haven't to any great extent.

July 8. Oh, how hot, and oh, how miserable. The news that six have been sentenced to be hanged is true, and one of them is Moseby. The camp is thoroughly under control of the police now, and it is a heavenly boon. Of course, there is some stealing and robbery, but not as before. Swan, of our mess, is sick with scurvy. I am gradually swelling up and growing weaker. But a

few more pages in my diary. Over 150 dying per day now, and 26,000 in camp. Guards shoot now very often. Boys, as guards, are the most cruel. It is said that if they kill a Yankee they are given a thirty-day furlough. Guess they need them as soldiers too much to allow of this. The swamp now is fearful, water perfectly reeking with prison offal and poison. Still men drink it and die. Rumors that the six will be hung inside. Bread today and it is so coarse as to do more hurt than good to a majority of the prisoners. The place still gets worse.

Tunneling is over with; no one engages in it now that I know of. The prison is a success as regards safety; no escape except by death, and very many take advantage of that way. A man who has preached to us (or tried to) is dead. Was a good man, I verily believe, and from Pennsylvania. It's almost impossible for me to get correct names to note down; the last-named man was called "the preacher," and I can find no other name for him. Our quartette of singers a few rods away is disbanded. One died, one nearly dead, one a policeman, and the other cannot sing alone, and so where we used to hear and enjoy good music evenings, there is nothing to attract us from the groans of the dying. Having formed a habit of going to sleep as soon as the air got cooled off and before fairly dark, I wake up at 2 or 3 o'clock and stay awake. I then take in all the horrors of the situation. Thousands are groaning, moaning, and crying, with no bustle of the daytime to drown it. Guards every half hour call out the time and post, and there is often a shot to make one shiver as if with the ague. Must arrange my sleeping hours to miss getting owly in the morning. Have taken to building air castles of late, on being exchanged. Getting loony, I guess, same as all the rest.

July 9. Battese brought me some onions, and if they ain't good, then no matter; also a sweet potato. One-half the men here would get well if they only had something in the vegetable line to eat, or acids. Scurvy is about the most loathsome disease, and when dropsy takes hold with the scurvy, it is terrible. I have both diseases but keep them in check, and it only grows worse slowly. My legs are swollen, but the cords are not contracted much, and I can still walk very well. Our mess all keep clean, in fact are obliged to or else turned adrift. We want none of the dirty sort in our mess. Sanders and Rowe enforce the rules, which is not much work, as all hands are composed of men who prefer to keep clean. I still do a little washing, but more particularly haircutting, which is easier work. You should see one of my haircuts. Nobby! Old prisoners have hair a foot long or more, and my business is to cut it off, which I do without regard to anything except get it off.

I should judge that there are 1,000 Rebel soldiers guarding us, and perhaps a few more, with the usual number of officers. A guard told me today that the Yanks were "gittin licked," and they didn't want us ex changed; just as soon as we should die here as not; a Yank asked him if he knew what exchange meant; said he knew what shootin' meant, and as he began to swing around his old shooting iron, we retreated in among the crowd. Heard that there were some new men belonging to my regiment in another part of the prison; have just returned from looking after them and am all tired out. Instead of belonging to the 9th Michigan Cavalry, they belong to the 9th Michigan Infantry. Had a good visit and quite cheered with their accounts of the war news.

Someone stole Battese's washboard and he is mad; is looking for it—may bust up the business. Think Hub Dakin will give me a board to make another one. Sanders owns the jacknife of this mess, and he don't like to lend it either; borrow it to carve on roots for pipes. Actually take solid comfort "building castles in the air [day dreaming]," a thing I have never been addicted to before. Better than getting blue and worrying myself to death. After all, we may get out of this dod-rotted hole. Always an end of some sort to such things.

July 10. Have bought of a new prisoner quite a large (thick, I mean) blank book so as to continue my diary. Although it's a tedious and tiresome task, am determined to keep it up. Don't know of another man in prison who is doing likewise. Wish I had the gift of description that I might describe this place. Know that I am not good at such things, and have more particularly kept track of the mess which was the "Astor House Mess" on Belle Isle [James River island location of a POW camp in Richmond] and is still called so here. Thought that Belle Isle was a very bad place, and used about the worst language I knew how to use in describing it, and so find myself at fault in depicting matters here as they are. At Belle Isle we had good water and plenty of it, and I believe it depends more upon water than food as regards health. We also had good pure air from up the James River. Here we have the very worst kind of water. Nothing can be worse or nastier than the stream drizzling its way through this camp. And for air to breathe, it is what arises from this foul place. On all four sides of us are high walls and tall trees, and there is apparently no wind or breeze to blow away the stench, and we are obliged to breathe and live in it. Dead bodies lay around all day in the broiling sun, by the dozen and even hundreds, and we must suffer and live in this atmosphere. It's too horrible for me to describe in fitting language.

There was once a very profane man driving a team of horses attached to a wagon in which there were forty to fifty bushels of potatoes. It was a big load and there was a long hill to go up. The very profane man got off the load of potatoes to lighten the weight, and started the team up the hill. It was hard work, but they finally reached the top and stopped to rest. The profane man looked behind him and saw that the end board of the wagon had slipped out just as he had started, and there the potatoes were, scattered all the way along up the hill. Did the man make the very air blue with profanity? No, he sat down on a log, feeling that he couldn't do the subject justice and so he remarked: "No! it's no use, I can't do it justice." While I have no reason or desire to swear, I certainly cannot do this prison justice. It's too stupendous an undertaking. Only those who are here will ever know what Andersonville is.

July 11. This morning, lumber was brought into the prison by the Rebels, and near the gate a gallows erected for the purpose of executing the six condemned Yankees. At about 10 o'clock they were brought inside by Captain Wirtz and some guards, and delivered over to the police force. Captain Wirtz then said a few words about their having been tried by our own men and for us to do as we choose with them, that he washed his hands of the whole matter, or words to that effect. I could not catch the exact language, being some little distance away. I have learned by inquiry their names, which are as follows: John Sarsfield, 144th New York; William Collins, alias Moseby, Co. D, 88th Pennsylvania; Charles Curtiss, Battery A, 5th Rhode Island Artillery; Pat Delaney, Co. E, 83d Pennsylvania; A. Munn, U.S. Navy; and W. R. Rickson of the U.S. Navy.

After Wirtz made his speech he withdrew his guards, leaving the condemned at the mercy of 28,000 enraged prisoners, who had all been more or less wronged by these men. Their hands were tied behind them, and one by one they mounted the scaffold. Curtiss, who was last, a big stout fellow, managed to get his hands loose and broke away and ran through the crowd and down toward the swamp. It was yelled out that he had a knife in his hand, and so a path was made for him. He reached the swamp and plunged in, trying to get over on the other side, presumably among his friends. It being very warm he overexerted himself, and when in the middle or thereabouts, collapsed and could go no farther. The police started after him, waded in and helped him out. He pleaded for water and it was given him. Then led back to the scaffold and helped to mount up.

All were given a chance to talk. Munn, a good-looking fellow in Marine dress, said he came into the prison four months before, perfectly honest and as innocent of crime as any fellow in it. Starvation, with evil companions, had made him what he was. He spoke of his mother and sisters in New York, that he cared nothing as far as he himself was concerned, but the news that would be carried home to his people made him want to curse God he had ever been born. Delaney said he would rather be hung than live here as the most of them lived, on their allowance of rations. If allowed to steal could get enough to eat, but as that was stopped had rather hang. Bid all good-bye. Said his name was not Delaney and that no one knew who he really was, therefore his friends would never know his fate, his Andersonville history dying with him. Curtiss said he didn't care a——, only hurry up and not be talking about it all day; making too much fuss over a very small matter. William Collins, alias Moseby, said he was innocent of murder and ought not to be hung; he had stolen blankets and rations to preserve his own life, and begged the crowd not to see him hung as he had a wife and child at home, and for their sake to let him live.

The excited crowd began to be impatient for the "show" to commence as they termed it. Sarsfield made quite a speech; he had studied for a lawyer; at the outbreak of the rebellion he had enlisted and served three years in the army, been wounded in battle, furloughed home, wound healed up, promoted to first sergeant and also commissioned; his commission as a lieutenant had arrived but had not been mustered in when he was taken prisoner; began by stealing parts of rations, gradually becoming hardened as he became familiar with the crimes practised; evil associates had helped him to go downhill, and here he was. The other did not care to say anything. While the men were talking, were interrupted by all kinds of questions and charges made by the crowd, such as "don't lay it on too thick, you villain," "get ready to jump off," "cut it short," "you was the cause of so and so's death," "less talk and more hanging," etc., etc.

At about 11 o'clock, they were all blindfolded, hands and feet tied, told to get ready, nooses adjusted, and the plank knocked from under. Moseby's rope broke and he fell to the ground, with blood spurting from his ears, mouth, and nose. As they was lifting him back to the swinging-off place, he revived and begged for his life, but no use, was soon dangling with the rest, and died very hard. Munn died easily, as also did

Delaney; all the rest died hard, and particularly Sarsfield, who drew his knees nearly to his chin and then straightened them out with a jerk, the veins in his neck swelling out as if they would burst. It was an awful sight to see, still a necessity. Moseby, although he said he had never killed anyone, and I don't believe he ever did deliberately kill a man, such as stabbing or pounding a victim to death, yet he has walked up to a poor sick prisoner on a cold night and robbed him of blanket, or perhaps his rations, and if necessary using all the force necessary to do it. These things were the same as life to the sick man, for he would invariably die. The result has been that many have died from his robbing propensities. It was right that he should hang, and he did hang most beautifully, and Andersonville is the better off for it. None of the rest denied that they had killed men, and probably some had murdered dozens. It has been a good lesson; there are still bad ones in camp, but we have the strong arm of the law to keep them in check.

All during the hanging scene the stockade was covered with Rebels, who were fearful a break would be made if the raiders should try and rescue them. Many citizens, too, were congregated on the outside in favorable positions for seeing. Artillery was pointed at us from all directions ready to blow us all into eternity in short order; Wirtz stood on a high platform in plain sight of the execution and says we are a hard crowd to kill our own men. After hanging for half an hour or so, the six bodies were taken down and carried outside. In noting down the speeches made by the condemned men, have used my own language; in substance it is the same as told by them. I occupied a near position to the hanging and saw it all from first to last, and stood there until they were taken down and carried away. Was a strange sight to see, and the first hanging I ever witnessed. The raiders had many friends who crowded around and denounced the whole affair, and, but for the police, there would have been a riot; many both for and against the execution were knocked down. Some will talk and get into trouble thereby; as long as it does no good there

is no use in loud talk and exciting arguments; is dangerous to advance any argument, men are so ready to quarrel.

Have got back to my quarters, thoroughly prostrated and worn out with fatigue and excitement, and only hope that today's lesson will right matters as regards raiding. Battese suspended washing long enough to look on and see them hang and grunted his approval. Have omitted to say that the good Catholic priest attended the condemned. Rebel Negroes came inside and began to take down the scaffold; prisoners took hold to help them and resulted in its all being carried off to different parts of the prison to be used for kindling wood, and the Rebels get none of it back and are mad. The ropes even have been gobbled up, and I suppose sometime may be exhibited at the North as mementos of today's proceedings. Mike Hoare assisted at the hanging. Some fears are entertained that those who officiated will get killed by the friends of those hanged. The person who manipulated the "drop" has been taken outside on parole of honor, as his life would be in danger in here.

Jimmy thanks God that he has lived to see justice done the raiders; he is about gone—nothing but skin and bone and can hardly move hand or foot; rest of the mess moderately well. The extra rations derived from our three messmates as policemen helps wonderfully to prolong life. Once in a while some of them gets a chance to go outside on some duty and buy onions or sweet potatoes, which is a great luxury.

July 12. Good order has prevailed since the hanging. The men have settled right down to the business of dying, with no interruption. I keep thinking our situation can get no worse, but it does get worse every day, and not less than 160 die each twenty-four hours. Probably one-fourth or one-third of these die inside the stockade, the balance in the hospital outside. All day and up to 4 o'clock P.M., the dead are being gathered up and carried to the south gate and placed in a row inside the dead line. As the bodies are stripped of their clothing, in most cases as soon as the breath leaves and in some cases before, the row of dead presents a sickening appearance. Legs drawn up and in all shapes. They are black from pitch-pine smoke and laying in the sun. Some of them lay there for twenty hours or more, and by that time are in a horrible condition.

At 4 o'clock, a four- or six-mule wagon comes up to the gate, and twenty or thirty bodies are loaded onto the wagon and they are carted off to be put in trenches, one hundred in each trench, in the cemetery, which is eighty or a hundred rods away. There must necessarily be a great many whose names are not taken. It is the orders to attach the name, company, and regiment to each body, but it is not always done. I was invited today to dig in a tunnel but had to decline. My digging days are over. Must dig now to keep out of the ground, I guess. It is with difficulty now that I can walk, and only with the help of two canes.

July 13. Can see in the distance the cars go poking along by this station, with wheezing old engines, snorting along. As soon as night comes a great many are blind, caused by sleeping in the open air, with moon shining in the face. Many holes are dug and excavations made in camp. Near our quarters is a well about five or six feet deep, and the poor blind fellows fall into this pit hole. None seriously hurt, but must be quite shaken up. Half of the prisoners have no settled place for sleeping, wander and lay down wherever they can find room.

Have two small gold rings on my finger, worn ever since I left home. Have also a small photograph album with eight photographs in. Relics of civilization. Should I get these things through to our lines they will have quite a history. When I am among the Rebels, I wind a rag around my finger to cover up the rings, or else take them and put in my pocket. Bad off as I have been, have never seen the time yet that I would part with them. Were presents to me, and the photographs have looked at about one-fourth of the time since imprisonment. One prisoner made some buttons here for his little boy at home, and gave them to me to deliver, as he was about to die. Have them sewed onto my pants for safekeeping.

July 14. We have been too busy with the raiders of late to manufacture any exchange news, and now all hands are at work trying to see who can tell the biggest yarns. The weak are feeling well tonight over the story that we are all to be sent North this month, before the 20th. Have not learned that the news came from any reliable source. Rumors of midsummer battles with Union troops victorious. It's "bite dog, bite bear" with most of us prisoners; we don't care which licks, what we want is to get out of this pen. Of course, we all care and want our side to win, but it's tough on patriotism. A court is now held every day and offenders punished principally by buck and gagging, for misdemeanors. The hanging has done worlds of goods, still there is much stealing going on yet, but in a sly way, not openly. Hold my own as regards health. The dreaded month of July is half gone, almost, and a good many over 150 die each day, but I do not know how many. Hardly anyone cares enough about it to help me any in my inquiries. It is all self with the most of them. A guard by accident shot himself. Have often said they didn't know enough to hold a gun. Bury a Rebel guard every few days within sight of the prison. Saw some women in the distance. Quite a sight. Are feeling quite jolly tonight since the sun went down.

Was visited by my new acquaintances of the 9th Michigan Infantry, who are comparatively new prisoners. Am learning them the way to live here. They are very hopeful fellows and declare the war will be over this coming fall, and tell their reasons very well for thinking so. We gird up our loins and decide that we will try to live it through. Rowe, although often given to despondency, is feeling good and cheerful. There are some noble fellows here. A man shows exactly what he is in Andersonville. No occasion to be any different from what you really are. Very often see a great big fellow in size, in reality a baby in action, actually sniveling and crying, and then again you will see some little runt, "not bigger than a pint of cider," tell the big fellow to "brace up" and be a man. Stature has nothing to do as regards nerve, still there are noble big fellows as well as noble little ones. A Sergeant Hill is judge and jury now, and dispenses justice to evildoers with impartiality. A farce is made of defending some of the arrested ones. Hill inquires all of the particulars of each case, and sometimes lets the offenders go as more sinned against than sinning. Four receiving punishment.

July 15. Blank cartridges were this morning fired over the camp by the artillery, and immediately the greatest commotion outside. It seems that the signal in case a break is made is cannon firing. And this was to show us how quick they could rally and get into shape. In less time than it takes for me to write it, all were at their posts and in condition to open up and kill nine-tenths of all here. Sweltering hot. Dying off 155 each day. There are 28,000 confined here now.

July 16. Well, who ever supposed that it could be any hotter; but today is more so than yesterday, and yesterday more than the day before. My coverlid has been rained on so much and burned in the sun, first one and then the other, that it is getting the worse for wear. It was originally a very nice one, and homemade. Sun goes right through it now, and reaches down for us. Just like a bake oven. The rabbit mules that draw in the rations look as if they didn't get much more to eat than we do. Driven with one rope line, and harness patched up with ropes, strings, etc. Fit representation of the Confederacy. Not much like U.S. Army teams. A joke on the Rebel adjutant has happened. Someone broke into the shanty and tied the two or three sleeping there, and carried off all the goods. Tennessee Bill (a fellow captured with me) had charge of the affair and is in disgrace with the adjutant on account of it. Everyone is glad of the robbery. Probably there was not $10 worth of things in there, but they asked outrageous prices for everything. Adjutant very mad, but no good. Is a small, sputtering sort of fellow.

July 17. Cords contracting in my legs and very difficult for me to walk—after going a little ways have to stop and rest and am faint. Am urged by some to go to the hospital but don't like to do it; mess say had better stay where I am, and Bat-

tese says shall not go, and that settles it. Jimmy Devers anxious to be taken to the hospital but is persuaded to give it up. Tom McGill, another Irish friend, is past all recovery; is in another part of the prison. Many old prisoners are dropping off now this fearful hot weather; knew that July and August would thin us out; cannot keep track of them in my disabled condition. A fellow named Hubbard, with whom I have conversed a good deal, is dead; a few days ago was in very good health, and it's only a question of a few days now with any of us.

Succeeded in getting four small onions about as large as hickory nuts, tops and all, for two dollars Confederate money. Battese furnished the money but won't eat an onion; ask him if he is afraid it will make his breath smell? It is said that two or three onions or a sweet potato eaten raw daily will cure the scurvy. What a shame that such things are denied us, being so plenty the world over. Never appreciated such things before but shall hereafter. Am talking as if I expected to get home again. I do.

July 18. Time slowly dragging itself along. Cut some wretch's hair most every day. Have a sign out "Haircutting," as well as "Washing"; and, by the way, Battese has a new washboard made from a piece of the scaffold lumber. About half the time do the work for nothing, in fact not more than one in three or four pays anything—expenses not much though, don't have to pay any rent. All the mess keeps their hair cut short, which is a very good advertisement. My eyes getting weak with other troubles. Can just hobble around. Death rate more than ever, reported 165 per day; said by some to be more than that, but 165 is about the figure. Bad enough without making any worse than it really is. Jimmy Devers most dead and begs us to take him to the hospital and guess will have to. Every morning the sick are carried to the gate in blankets and on stretchers, and the worst cases admitted to the hospital. Probably out of 500 or 600, half are admitted. Do not think any lives after being taken there; are past all human aid. Four out of every five prefer to stay inside and die with their friends rather than go to the hospital. Hard stories reach us of the treatment of the sick out there, and I am sorry to say the cruelty emanates from our own men who act as nurses. These deadbeats and bummer nurses are the same bounty jumpers the U.S. authorities have had so much trouble with. Do not mean to say that all the nurses are of that class, but a great many of them are.

July 19. There is no such thing as delicacy here. Nine out of ten would as soon eat with a corpse for a table as any other way. In the middle of last night I was awakened by being kicked by a dying man. He was soon dead. In his struggles he had floundered clear into our bed. Got up and moved the body off a few feet, and again went to sleep to dream of the hideous sights. I can never get used to it as some do. Often wake most scared to death, and shuddering from head to foot. Almost dread to go to sleep on this account. I am getting worse and worse, and prison ditto.

July 20. Am troubled with poor sight, together with scurvy and dropsy. My teeth are all loose and it is with difficulty I can eat. Jimmy Devers was taken out to die today. I hear that McGill is also dead. John McGuire died last night; both were Jackson men and old acquaintances. Mike Hoare is still policeman and is sorry for me. Does what he can. And so we have seen the last of Jimmy. A prisoner of war one year and eighteen days. Struggled hard to live through it, if ever anyone did. Ever since I can remember have known him. John Maguire, also, I have always known. Everybody in Jackson, Michigan, will remember him, as living on the east side of the river near the wintergreen patch, and his father before him. They were one of the first families who settled that country. His people are well-to-do, with much property. Leaves a wife and one boy. Tom McGill is also a Jackson boy and a member of my own company. Thus you will see that three of my acquaintances died the same day, for Jimmy cannot live until night, I don't think. Not a person in the world but would have thought either one of them would kill me a dozen times enduring hardships. Pretty hard to tell about such things. Small

squad of poor deluded Yanks turned inside with us, captured at Petersburg. It is said they talk of winning recent battles. Battese has traded for an old watch and Mike will try to procure vegetables for it from the guard. That is what will save us, if anything.

July 21. And Rebels are still fortifying. Battese has his hands full. Takes care of me like a father. Hear that Kilpatrick is making a raid for this place. Troops (Rebel) are arriving here by every train to defend it. Nothing but cornbread issued now, and I cannot eat it any more.

July 22. A petition is gotten up signed by all the sergeants in the prison, to be sent to Washington, D.C., begging to be released. Captain Wirtz has consented to let three representatives go for that purpose. Rough that it should be necessary for us to beg to be protected by our government.

July 23. Reports of an exchange in August. Can't stand it till that time. Will soon go up the spout.

July 24. Have been trying to get into the hospital, but Battese won't let me go. George W. Hutchins, brother of Charlie Hutchins of Jackson, Michigan, died today—from our mess. Jimmy Devers is dead.

July 25. Rowe getting very bad. Sanders ditto. Am myself much worse, and cannot walk, and with difficulty stand up. Legs drawn up like a triangle, mouth in terrible shape, and dropsy worse than all. A few more days. At my earnest solicitation was carried to the gate this morning to be admitted to the hospital. Lay in the sun for some hours to be examined, and finally my turn came, and I tried to stand up, but was so excited I fainted away. When I came to myself I lay along with the row of dead on the outside. Raised up and asked a Rebel for a drink of water, and he said: "Here, you Yank, if you ain't dead, get inside there!" And with his help was put inside again. Told a man to go to our mess and tell them to come to the gate, and pretty soon Battese and Sanders came and carried me back to our quarters; and here I am, completely played out. Battese flying around to buy me something good to eat. Can't write much more. Exchange rumors.

July 26. Ain't dead yet. Actually laugh when I think of the Rebel who thought if I wasn't dead I had better get inside. Can't walk a step now. Shall try for the hospital no more. Had an onion.

July 27. Sweltering hot. No worse than yesterday. Said that 200 die now each day. Rowe very bad and Sanders getting so. Swan dead, Gordon dead, Jack Withers dead, Scotty dead, a large Irishman who has been near us a long time is dead. These and scores of others died yesterday and day before. Hub Dakin came to see me and brought an onion. He is just able to crawl around himself.

July 28. Taken a step forward toward the trenches since yesterday and am worse. Had a wash all over this morning. Battese took me to the creek; carries me without any trouble.

July 29. Alive and kicking. Drank some soured water made from meal and water.

July 30. Hang on well, and no worse.

Aug. 1. Just about the same. My Indian friend says: "We all get away."

Aug. 2. Two hundred and twenty die each day. No more news of exchange. . . .

Aug. 13. A nice spring of cold water has broken out in camp, enough to furnish nearly all here with drinking water. God has not forgotten us. Battese brings it to me to drink. . . .

Aug. 20. Some say 300 now die each day. No more new men coming. . . .

Aug. 26. Still am writing. The letter from my brother has done good and cheered me up. Eyesight very poor and writing tires me. Battese sticks by; such disinterested friendship is rare. Prison at its worst.

Aug. 27. Have now written nearly through three large books, and still at it. The diary, am confident, will reach my people if I don't. There are many here who are interested and will see that it goes North. . . .

Sept. 6. Hurrah! Hurrah!! Hurrah!!! Can't holler except on paper. Good news. Seven detachments ordered to be ready to go at a moment's notice.

Later. All who cannot walk must stay behind. If left behind, shall die in twenty-four hours. Battese says I shall go.

Later. Seven detachments are going out of the gate; all the sick are left behind. Ours is the tenth detachment and will go tomorrow, so said. The greatest excitement; men wild with joy. Am worried fearful that I cannot go, but Battese says I shall.

Sept. 7. Anxiously waiting the expected summons. Rebels say as soon as transportation comes, and so a car whistle is music to our ears. Hope is a good medicine and am sitting up and have been trying to stand up but can't do it; legs too crooked and with every attempt get faint. Men laugh at the idea of my going, as the Rebels are very particular not to let any sick go, still Battese says I am going.

Most Dark. Rebels say we go during the night when transportation comes. Battese grinned when this news come and can't get his face straightened out again.

Marine Hospital, Savannah, Ga., Sept. 15, 1864. A great change has taken place since I last wrote in my diary. Am in heaven now compared with the past. At about midnight, September 7, our detachment was ordered outside at Andersonville, and Battese picked me up and carried me to the gate. The men were being let outside in ranks of four, and counted as they went out. They were very strict about letting none go but the well ones, or those who could walk. The Rebel adjutant stood upon a box by the gate, watching very close. Pitch-pine knots were burning in the near vicinity to give light. As it came our turn to go, Battese got me in the middle of the rank, stood me up as well as I could stand, and, with himself on one side and Sergeant Rowe on the other, began pushing our way through the gate. Could not help myself a particle, and was so faint that I hardly knew what was going on. As we were going through the gate the adjutant yells out: "Here, here! hold on there, that man can't go, hold on there!" and Battese crowding right along outside. The adjutant struck over the heads of the men and tried to stop us, but my noble Indian friend kept straight ahead, halloo-ing: "He all right, he well, he go!" And so I got outside, and adjutant having too much to look after to follow me. After we were outside, I was carried to the railroad in the same coverlid which I fooled the Rebel out of when captured, and which I presume has saved my life a dozen times. We were crowded very thick into boxcars. I was nearly dead and hardly knew where we were or what was going on.

We were two days in getting to Savannah. Arrived early in the morning. The railroads here run in the middle of very wide, handsome streets. We were unloaded, I should judge, near the mid-dle of the city. The men, as they were unloaded, fell into line and were marched away. Battese got me out of the car and laid me on the pavement. They then obliged him to go with the rest, leav-ing me; would not let him take me. I lay there until noon with four or five others, without any guard. Three or four times, Negro servants came to us from houses nearby and gave us water, milk, and food. With much difficulty I could set up but was completely helpless. A little after noon a wagon came and toted us to a temporary hospital in the outskirts of the city, and near a prison pen they had just built for the well ones. Where I was taken it was merely an open piece of ground, having wall tents erected and a line of guards around it. I was put into a tent and lay on the coverlid. That night some gruel was given to me, and a nurse whom I had seen in Andersonville looked in, and my name was taken.

The next morning, September 10, I woke up and went to move my hands, and could not do it; could not move either limb so much as an inch. Could move my head with difficulty. Seemed to be paralyzed, but in no pain whatever. After a few hours a physician came to my tent, examined and gave me medicine, also left medicine, and one of the nurses fed me some soup or gruel. By night I could move my hands. Lay awake considerable through the night thinking. Was happy as a clam in high tide. Seemed so nice to be under a nice clean tent, and there was such cool, pure air. The surroundings were so much better that I thought now would be a good time to die, and I didn't care one way or the other.

Next morning the doctor came, and with him Sergeant Winn. Sergeant Winn I had had a little acquaintance with at Andersonville. Doctor said I was terribly reduced, but he thought I would improve. Told them to wash me. A nurse came and washed me, and Winn brought me a white cotton shirt and an old but clean pair of pants; my old clothing, which was in rags, was taken away. Two or three times during the day I had gruel of some kind, I don't know what. Medicine was given me by the nurses. By night I could move my feet and legs a little. The cords in my feet and legs were contracted so, of course, that I couldn't straighten myself out. Kept thinking to myself, "Am I really away from that place Ander-sonville?" It seemed too good to be true.

Source: Ransom, John L. *Andersonville Diary.* Philadel-phia: Douglas Brothers, 1883, pp. 75–95.

The Atlanta Campaign, May 7–September 2, 1864; and Sherman's March to the Sea, November 15–December 22, 1864

Letter to His Wife
Major Thomas T. Taylor
July 26, 1864

The Atlanta Campaign consisted of major bat-tles, including those at Kennesaw Mountain and Peachtree Creek, but it was also marked by many smaller actions, including exchanges between lines of skirmishers. Union major Thomas T. Taylor (1836–1908) of Georgetown, Ohio, commanded 15 skirmisher companies in the 47th Ohio Infantry Reg-

iment during the Atlanta Campaign. He described the action he led during July 22, 1864, in a letter to his wife, Netta Taylor, written four days later.

In the morning as usual at daylight I went down to the skirmish line to learn the condition of things. Soon Gen'l Morgan L. Smith sent an order to move forward my line and feel the enemy. I pushed forward and soon began driving his [the enemy's skirmish] line. At his skirmish pits I redressed it [Taylor's own line] and advanced on his main works and soon drove his skirmishers in, but without giving them time to form I hurried forward with a shout and a volley which set the rebels skedaddling and a regiment of reserves in full and rapid retreat. In the main [out-lying] works I again dressed the line and pursued them, capturing a few prisoners and two lines of skirmish pits and drove them square into their [main] works and occupied with my line a portion of the corporation of Atlanta, not more than 600 yards from their forts. Here they served us with 'minnies' [minié balls—standard-issue rifle musket ammunition], case and solid shot and shells. I soon discovered where their skirmish pits were and made my line crawl forward in some places within 20 yards of them and build rail barricades. I found one set [of his own skirmishers] timid and awkward and I had to crawl up to a point where I wished a post, show them the bearings and range and help them build it. . . .

Their skirmishers were kept so close that I had only two wounded by musket balls. One solid shot knocked down a rail pile and buried the men under it. A Captain thought destruction had come and wished to retire but I make it a point never to give up my ground if my flanks are protected [and] so they rebuilt it. I sent back for shovels to dig good pits but our Division General was not at liberty to send them to us. Our men in authority appeared to think the enemy were evacuating Atlanta because they were moving columns to the left. About 9 or 10 a.m. Logan's Senior Aide came out and I showed him how earnestly they [the Confederates] were working in town upon their fortifications and

asked if it looked like an evacuation. He said no. I then asked him for tools, but they came not. Our Commanders appeared infatuated with the thought of evacuation of Atlanta.

After a time two regiments of infantry and a section of artillery were sent out as a second reserve. I laid down and got a good nap and awoke about 12 1/2 m. Just after I got up Lieut. [Adolph] Ahlers [of the 47th Ohio] and two men were wounded near me and I was struck with dirt, bark or something and Ahlers reported me wounded. My negro went to the rear with the horses, but came back. About 1 p.m. I moved to a high point in the line and sat down. Firing soon commenced and became very heavy on the extreme left and in the rear . . .

Oh! how anxiously I listened and waited, how anxious for the cheers! The enemy cheered before [his] charges, our men cheered after repulsing [them]. For two hours they appeared to drive our line back until it was at almost right angles with my [the XV Corps'] line. Can you imagine how my heart throbbed, every pulsation grew more rapid. There I sat under a big oak tree . . . only 600 yards from the main line of [enemy] works, from which solid shot was being thrown and case & shells, too, with fearful rapidity at and over us. I was anxious not from fear, but dread that we might lose our advantage, the ground we had gained and again be compelled to retake it by charges. At three o'clock the tide of war seemed rolling back. I could not mistake those cheers and that firing—the enemy at last were checked and being driven oh, how rapidly. At 4 p.m. we had regained our old lines and the fighting on the left had subsided like a fierce rain & wind storm, [and] only gusts and sobs sounded in the ear.

My attention was called from this by a Captain saying; 'Look, Major, look!' What a grand sight—I was almost entranced by it. The enemy's [Major General Thomas C.] Hindman's Division of 25 regiments [commanded by Maj. Gen. John C. Brown] were moving out of the works and deploying in line of battle. How well they moved, how perfectly and how grandly did the first line advance with the beautiful 'battle flags' waving in the breeze [and] not an unsteady step nor a waver was perceptible in it. Anon they moved by the right flank, then halted and fronted and a second line was formed. I saw them complete it and an Officer rode a short distance from us to advance their skirmish line & [I] ordered several of the men to shoot him but they failed. I then saw the 4th Div [skirmish] line [to the left] break and run, called my line to attention and remained until I saw their line of battle approach within 250 yards of us.

By the retreat of the 4th Div. [skirmishers], my left was exposed and I marched back to my first reserve. Here I shall tell you that as soon as I saw the 2nd [Confederate battle] line form and the advance toward us begin, I sent back word. At the reserve we halted and again opened [fire] on the enemy, drove in his skirmishers and, when the line flanked us on the left and was within about fifty yards [I] rallied on the 2nd reserve. Here we made a fine little fight and broke their [skirmish] lines but being outflanked we were compelled to fall back. In making this distance part of the time I moved leisurely and part lively—picked up a canteen of coffee and moved for the [Union] works when some miserable [Southern] traitor with murder stamped on his countenance deliberately shot at me. But I was a little too far away & his bullet almost spent struck me a glancing blow in the muscles of my left thigh as I was lifting my leg to run. I knew if I was hurt it would bleed in my boot so I went on as rapidly as I could as other bullets were dropping too close to make it at all pleasant.

The rebels reformed and advanced upon our main line in three columns. Two columns moved up on our right . . . and were both after a heavy fire severely repulsed and took refuge behind some outbuildings and a large house where they reformed. About twenty yards from our works on the left of the rail and wagon roads is a ravine which at the railroad was so thick [with] undergrowth as to completely screen as well as protect an advancing column. The railway through our lines is built in a cut about 15 feet deep. On the left of the railway was a section of artillery occupying three rods [about 50 feet]. [The] width of

cut at top [is] 3 rods [and] between cut & wagon road on right of railroad is a space four rods wide [65 feet], protected by a log earthwork terminating a few feet from the railway. The wagon road is almost two rods [33 feet] wide and on the right of this road was a section of artillery [two cannons] occupying about three rods more and all of this space of 15 rods had only one company in position [and only] one platoon [of] 16 men . . . was between the [artillery] section in the space between the wagon and rail roads. The cut was open and clear, nowhere was it occupied by troops nor blockaded, the wagon road was likewise open and unoccupied by works or troops. When Col. [Wells S.] Jones, 53rd Ohio, came for the reserve, he suggested to Genl's Smith & [Brigadier General John] Lightburn the propriety of burning said outbuildings & placing his regiment in rear of this artillery to support it and shut the gaps, yet they disdained the proffer and they were not filled.

Concealed by the dense smoke of the artillery the first we saw of the third [enemy] column it was rushing in the gap in the wagon road around the low works between the rail & wagon roads and over the parapet at the guns. Every one was surprised but none thought of moving, the platoon between the guns fired and fought with bayonets & butts of their muskets, the other platoon lying down in the rear of it could not fire without killing their comrades and artillerists in their front. Some of the men [in the platoon] were bleeding at the ears and nose from the concussion, yet fought until all were killed, wounded and captured except four.

I started across the road to move the other platoon to make it effective when I happened to look at the upper end of the cut and saw a column of rebels deploying from it. This 2nd [Union] platoon was shut in by a line of fire on every side and to avoid capture retired. Simultaneously the whole line began to fall back. Gen'l Smith moved over to the right & Lightburn went off on a run. I heard no order given and after vainly trying to rally the men dashed into the woods, where on a small ridge I halted a few men and again tried to form [a line]. Then, hearing someone shouting halt, I went to the road supposing it was one of our officers trying to form the line. I came within five feet of a rebel officer on a white horse with a flag in his hand and a revolver in the other. I took this in at a glance, he said 'Halt! we'll treat you like men.' I said, 'Hell, stranger, this is no place for me to halt!' and went for the bushes. I told a man at my elbow to shoot him. When I got out of his reach I went slow and got some men of the 47th to go down and run off two caissons which the artillery had abandoned. I then went down to the works. Lt. Col. Wallace & Capt. [Hananiah D.] Pugh [of the 47th Ohio] while striving vainly to form a line were captured, [Capt. Charles] Haltentof wounded and Adjt. [John W.] Duecherman wounded. Only four officers [of the 47th Ohio] were left.

I was relieved as Div. Picket Officer to take command of the regiment and reformed it very quickly and then was ordered forward and marched up the road some distance by the flank. . . . I [then] was ordered into line [and] to fix bayonets and to retake the works [with] one small company and [some men] from other regiments [who] joined me. . . . I advanced on the 'double quick' and got within a few feet of the works, when such was the hail storm of fire and bullets which swept over us that both flag staffs were shot off, the regiment's standard was torn from the staff by the fragment of a shell, one color bearer killed, and a color corporal wounded, [and] others as a matter of course fell. Finding I was completely flanked [I] withdrew to avoid capture.

On account of an entanglement and the dense undergrowth in my rear, the command became separated. Meeting a line upon a ridge in the rear advancing I halted and with them made a second assault. A portion of the regiment under Capt. [Joseph L.] Pinkerton went to the right of the railroad. I kept on the left, we reached the point I reached in the first assault but were again compelled to fall back. This time we went to an open field when reforming as best we could, [then] again advanced. Upon reaching the crest of the first ridge the men halted and laid down to avoid the sheet of bullets which swept over. . . . I pushed

through the line, dashed ahead, shouting, cheering and exhorting [but] only one man followed. I went fifty yards in this manner and finally halted and gave three lusty cheers, [then] without waiting I pushed on and in a moment had the pleasure to see that the line was hurrying [forward]. I soon struck another line [of Federal troops] on the left which had halted. I sent Capt. Pinkerton & Lieut. [William] Brachman with a portion of the regiment again on the right, while I with the rest of it and the remainder of [the men from other regiments] pushed up immediately on the left, pouring a continuous and deadly fire upon the enemy, driving them from their works and recapturing a section of artillery upon the left of the railway which the [Rebels] had turned upon us. . . .

Lightburn said we had disgraced ourselves. I told him 'that was enough of that! I would show him whether we had.' I had no idea that I had such determination, such stubbornness or strength. I was almost frantic, yet perfectly sane—directed the entire line. All the officers obeyed me and ran to me for advice and directions. I saw men perform prodigies, display the most unparalleled valor. One man, Joseph Bedol [Bedall] of Co. 'D', was surrounded and knocked by rebels, he came to, jumped up & wounded them and knocked a fourth down with his fist and escaped.

Dear, I would not write this to any other one as it seems egotistical, but is nevertheless true. The men of the Division give me credit for much more.

Source: HistoryNet.com. "Eyewitness to the Battle of Atlanta." Available online. URL: http://www.historynet.com/eyewitness-to-the-battle-of-atlanta.htm. Accessed on February 5, 2010.

Letter to James M. Calhoun, Mayor, City of Atlanta
Lieutenant General William T. Sherman
September 12, 1864

After the Confederate general John Bell Hood withdrew from Atlanta, William Tecumseh Sherman set up a Union occupation of the city and then ordered a complete evacuation. The mayor and two representatives of the city council appealed the order, claiming that it worked an unbearable hardship on the citizens. Sherman's reply was at once blunt and uncompromising yet sympathetic. Above all, it remains an eloquent statement on the nature of civil war and "total war"—war waged against the enemy civilian population as well as the enemy army.

HEADQUARTERS MILITARY DIVISION of the MISSISSIPPI in the FIELD

Atlanta, Georgia,
James M. Calhoun, Mayor,
E.E. Rawson and S.C. Wells, representing City
Council of Atlanta.

Gentleman: I have your letter of the 11th, in the nature of a petition to revoke my orders removing all the inhabitants from Atlanta. I have read it carefully, and give full credit to your statements of distress that will be occasioned, and yet shall not revoke my orders, because they were not designed to meet the humanities of the cause, but to prepare for the future struggles in which millions of good people outside of Atlanta have a deep interest. We must have peace, not only at Atlanta, but in all America. To secure this, we must stop the war that now desolates our once happy and favored country. To stop war, we must defeat the rebel armies which are arrayed against the laws and Constitution that all must respect and obey. To defeat those armies, we must prepare the way to reach them in their recesses, provided with the arms and instruments which enable us to accomplish our purpose. Now, I know the vindictive nature of our enemy, that we may have many years of military operations from this quarter; and, therefore, deem it wise and prudent to prepare in time. The use of Atlanta for warlike purposes is inconsistent with its character as a home for families. There will be no manufacturers, commerce, or agriculture here,

General William Tecumseh Sherman *(National Archives)*

for the maintenance of families, and sooner or later want will compel the inhabitants to go. Why not go now, when all the arrangements are completed for the transfer, instead of waiting till the plunging shot of contending armies will renew the scenes of the past month? Of course, I do not apprehend any such things at this moment, but you do not suppose this army will be here until the war is over. I cannot discuss this subject with you fairly, because I cannot impart to you what we propose to do, but I assert that our military plans make it necessary for the inhabitants to go away, and I can only renew my offer of services to make their exodus in any direction as easy and comfortable as possible.

You cannot qualify war in harsher terms than I will. War is cruelty, and you cannot refine it; and those who brought war into our country deserve all the curses and maledictions a people can pour out. I know I had no hand in making this war, and I know I will make more sacrifices to-day than any of you to secure peace. But you cannot have peace and a division of our country. If the United States submits to a division now, it will not stop, but will go on until we reap the fate of Mexico, which is eternal war. The United States does and must assert its authority, wherever it once had power; for, if it relaxes one bit to pressure, it is gone, and I believe that such is the national feeling. This feeling assumes various shapes, but always comes back to that of Union. Once admit the Union, once more acknowledge the authority of the national Government, and, instead of devoting your houses and streets and roads to the dread uses of war, I and this army become at once your protectors and supporters, shielding you from danger, let it come from what quarter it may. I know that a few individuals cannot resist a torrent of error and passion, such as swept the South into rebellion, but you can point out, so that we may know those who desire a government, and those who insist on war and its desolation.

You might as well appeal against the thunderstorm as against these terrible hardships of war. They are inevitable, and the only way the people of Atlanta can hope once more to live in peace and quiet at home, is to stop the war, which can only be done by admitting that it began in error and is perpetuated in pride.

We don't want your Negroes, or your horses, or your lands, or any thing you have, but we do want and will have a just obedience to the laws of the United States. That we will have, and if it involved the destruction of your improvements, we cannot help it.

You have heretofore read public sentiment in your newspapers, that live by falsehood and excitement; and the quicker you seek for truth in other quarters, the better. I repeat then that, but the original compact of government, the United States had certain rights in Georgia, which have never been relinquished and never will be; that the South began the war by seizing forts, arsenals, mints, custom-houses, etc., etc., long before Mr. Lincoln was installed, and before the South had one jot or title of provocation. I myself have seen in Missouri, Kentucky, Tennessee, and Mississippi, hundreds and thousands of women and children fleeing from your armies and desperadoes, hungry and with bleeding feet. In Memphis, Vicksburg, and Mississippi, we fed thousands and thousands of the families of rebel soldiers left on our hands, and whom we could not see starve. Now that war comes to you, you feel very different. You deprecate its horrors, but did not feel them when you sent car-loads of soldiers and ammunition, and moulded shells and shot, to carry war into Kentucky and Tennessee, to desolate the homes of hundreds and thousands of good people who only asked to live in peace at their old homes, and under the Government of their inheritance. But these comparisons are idle. I want peace, and believe it can only be reached through union and war, and I will ever conduct war with a view to perfect an early success.

But, my dear sirs, when peace does come, you may call on me for any thing. Then will I share with you the last cracker, and watch with you to shield your homes and families against danger from every quarter.

Now you must go, and take with you the old and feeble, feed and nurse them, and build for them, in more quiet places, proper habitations to shield them against the weather until the mad passions of men cool down, and allow the Union and peace once more to settle over your old homes in Atlanta. Yours in haste,

W.T. Sherman, Major-General commanding

Source: "General William Tecumseh Sherman to the Mayor and Councilmen of Atlanta." Available online. URL: http://www.rjgeib.com/thoughts/sherman/sherman-to-burn-atlanta.html. Accessed on February 5, 2010.

Diary Entries: Account of Sherman's March to the Sea
Dolly Sumner Lunt
January–December 1864

Born in Maine in 1817, Dolly Sumner Lunt moved to Georgia when she was a young woman to live with her married sister. Lunt taught school in Covington, Georgia, where she married Thomas Burge. His death in 1858 left Dolly to manage their plantation and slaves on her own. By this time she had been writing her diary for 10 years, and it became an increasing source of comfort to her during her years of widowhood (she remarried in 1865) and the Civil War. Though primarily a personal journal that offers insight into southern life at the time, the diary also provides riveting descriptions of the war in the South, in particular Sherman's March to the Sea, from a civilian's point of view. (The bracketed comments were included in the original 1918 edition of her diary.)

JANUARY 1, 1864. A new year is ushered in, but peace comes not with it. Scarcely a family but has given some of its members to the bloody war that is still decimating our nation. Oh, that its ravages may soon be stopped! Will another year find us among carnage and bloodshed? Shall we be a nation or shall we be annihilated? . . . The prices of everything are very high. Corn seven dollars a bushel, calico ten dollars a yard, salt, sixty dollars a hundred, cotton from sixty to eighty cents a pound, everything in like ratio.

JULY 22, 1864. [The day of the Battle of Atlanta] We have heard the loud booming of cannon all day. Mr. Ward [the overseer] went over to the burial of Thomas Harwell, whose death I witnessed yesterday. They had but just gone when the Rev. A. Turner, wife, and daughter drove up with their wagons, desiring to rest awhile. They went into the ell [a large back room] and lay down, I following them, wishing to enjoy their company. Suddenly I saw the servants running to the palings, and I walked to the door, when I saw such a stampede as I never witnessed before. The road was full of carriages, wagons, men on horseback, all riding at full speed. Judge Floyd stopped, saying: "Mrs. Burge, the Yankees are coming. They have got my family, and here is all I have upon earth. Hide your mules and carriages and whatever valuables you have."

Sadai [Mrs. Burge's nine-year-old daughter] said:

"Oh, Mama, what shall we do?"

"Never mind, Sadai," I said. "They won't hurt you, and you must help me hide my things."

I went to the smoke-house, divided out the meat to the servants, and bid them hide it. Julia [a slave] took a jar of lard and buried it. In the meantime Sadai was taking down and picking up our clothes, which she was giving to the servants to hide in their cabins; silk dresses, challis, muslins, and merinos, linens, and hosiery, all found their way into the chests of the women and under their beds; china and silver were buried underground, and Sadai bid Mary [a slave] hide a bit of soap under some bricks, that mama might have a little left. Then she came to me with a part of a loaf of bread, asking if she had not better put it in her pocket, that we might have something to eat that night. And, verily, we had cause to fear that we might be homeless, for on every side we could see smoke arising from burning buildings and bridges.

Major Ansley, who was wounded in the hip in the battle of Missionary Ridge, and has not recovered, came with his wife, sister, two little ones, and servants. He was traveling in a bed in a small wagon. They had thought to get to Eatonton, but he was so wearied that they stopped with me for the night. I am glad to have them. I shall sleep none to-night. The woods are full of refugees.

JULY 23, 1864. I have been left in my home all day with no one but Sadai. Have seen nothing of the raiders, though this morning they burned the buildings around the depot at the Circle [Social Circle, a nearby town]. I have sat here in the porch nearly all day, and hailed every one that passed for news. Just as the sun set here Major Ansley and family came back. They heard of the enemy all about and concluded they were as safe here as anywhere. Just before bedtime John, our boy, came from Covington with word that the Yankees had left. Wheeler's men were in Covington and going in pursuit. We slept sweetly and felt safe.

SUNDAY, JULY 24, 1864. No church. Our preacher's horse stolen by the Yankees. This raid is headed by Guerrard and is for the purpose of destroying our railroads. They cruelly shot a

George Daniel and a Mr. Jones of Covington, destroyed a great deal of private property, and took many citizens prisoners.

JULY 27, 1864. Major Ansley and family have remained. We are feeling more settled and have begun to bring to light some of the things which we had put away.

JULY 28, 1864. I rose early and had the boys plow the turnip-patch. We were just rising from breakfast when Ben Glass rode up with the cry: "The Yankees are coming. Mrs. Burge, hide your mules!"

How we were startled and how we hurried the Major to his room! [The Yankees did not come that day, but it was thought best to send Major Ansley away. He left at 2 A.M.]

JULY 29, 1864. Sleepless nights. The report is that the Yankees have left Covington for Macon, headed by [General] Stoneman, to release prisoners held there. They robbed every house on the road of its provisions, sometimes taking every piece of meat, blankets and wearing apparel, silver and arms of every description. They would take silk dresses and put them under their saddles, and many other things for which they had no use. Is this the way to make us love them and their Union? Let the poor people answer whom they have deprived of every mouthful of meat and of their livestock to make any! Our mills, too, they have burned, destroying an immense amount of property.

AUGUST 2, 1864. Just as I got out of bed this morning Aunt Julia [a slave] called me to look down the road and see the soldiers. I peeped through the blinds, and there they were, sure enough, the Yankees—the blue coats!

I was not dressed. The servant women came running in. "Mistress, they are coming! They are coming! They are riding into the lot! There are two coming up the steps!"

I bade Rachel [a slave] fasten my room door and go to the front door and ask them what they wanted. They did not wait for that, but came in and asked why my door was fastened. She told them that the white folks were not up. They said they wanted breakfast, and that quick, too.

"Thug" [short for "Sugar," the nickname of a little girl, Minnie Minerva Glass, now Mrs. Joe Carey Murphy of Charlotte, North Carolina, who had come to pass the night with Sadai] and Sadai, as well as myself, were greatly alarmed. As soon as I could get on my clothing I hastened to the kitchen to hurry up breakfast. Six of them were there talking with my women. They asked about our soldiers and, passing themselves off as Wheeler's men, said:

"Have you seen any of our men go by?"

"Several of Wheeler's men passed last evening. Who are you?" said I.

"We are a portion of Wheeler's men," said one.

"You look like Yankees," said I.

"Yes," said one, stepping up to me; "we are Yankees. Did you ever see one before?"

"Not for a long time," I replied, "and none such as you." [These men, Mrs. Burge says further, were raiders, Illinois and Kentucky men of German origin. They left after breakfast, taking three of her best mules, but doing no further injury.]

To-night Captain Smith of an Alabama regiment, and a squad of twenty men, are camped opposite in the field. They have all supped with me, and I shall breakfast with them. We have spent a pleasant evening with music and talk. They have a prisoner along. I can't help feeling sorry for him.

AUGUST 5, 1864. Mr. Ward has been robbed by the Yankees of his watch, pencil, and shirt.

NOVEMBER 8, 1864. To-day will probably decide the fate of the Confederacy. If Lincoln is reelected I think our fate is a hard one, but we are in the hands of a merciful God, and if He sees that we are in the wrong, I trust that He will show it unto us. I have never felt that slavery was altogether right, for it is abused by men, and I have often heard Mr. Burge say that if he could see that it was sinful for him to own slaves, if he felt that it was wrong, he would take them where he could free them. He would not sin for his right hand. The purest and holiest men have owned them, and I can see nothing in the scriptures which forbids it. I have never bought or sold slaves and I have tried to make life easy and pleasant to those that have been bequeathed me by the dead. I have never ceased to work. Many a Northern housekeeper has a much easier time than a Southern matron with her hundred negroes.

NOVEMBER 12, 1864. Warped and put in dresses for the loom. Oh, this blockade gives us work to do for all hands!

NOVEMBER 15, 1864. Went up to Covington to-day to pay the Confederate tax. Did not find the commissioners. Mid [a slave] drove me with Beck and the buggy. Got home about three o'clock. How very different is Covington from what it used to be! And how little did they who tore down the old flag and raised the new realize the results that have ensued!

NOVEMBER 16, 1864. As I could not obtain in Covington what I went for in the way of dye stuffs, etc., I concluded this morning, in accordance with Mrs. Ward's wish, to go to the Circle. We took Old Dutch and had a pleasant ride as it was a delightful day, but how dreary looks the town! Where formerly all was bustle and business, now naked chimneys and bare walls, for the depot and surroundings were all burned by last summer's raiders. Engaged to sell some bacon and potatoes. Obtained my dye stuffs. Paid seven dollars [Confederate money] a pound for coffee, six dollars an ounce for indigo, twenty dollars for a quire of paper, five dollars for ten cents' worth of flax thread, six dollars for pins, and forty dollars for a bunch of factory thread.

On our way home we met Brother Evans accompanied by John Hinton, who inquired if we had heard that the Yankees were coming. He said that a large force was at Stockbridge, that the Home Guard was called out, and that it was reported that the Yankees were on their way to Savannah. We rode home chatting about it and finally settled it in our minds that it could not be so. Probably a foraging party.

Just before night I walked up to Joe Perry's to know if they had heard anything of the report. He was just starting off to join the company [the Home Guard], being one of them.

NOVEMBER 17, 1864. Have been uneasy all day. At night some of the neighbors who had been to town called. They said it was a large force moving very slowly. What shall I do? Where go?

NOVEMBER 18, 1864. Slept very little last night. Went out doors several times and could see large fires like burning buildings. Am I not in the hands of a merciful God who has promised to take care of the widow and orphan?

Sent off two of my mules in the night. Mr. Ward and Frank [a slave] took them away and hid them. In the morning took a barrel of salt, which had cost me two hundred dollars, into one of the black women's gardens, put a paper over it, and then on the top of that leached ashes. Fixed it on a board as a leach tub, daubing it with ashes [the old-fashioned way of making lye for soap]. Had some few pieces of meat taken from my smoke-house carried to the Old Place [a distant part of the plantation] and hidden under some fodder. Bid them hide the wagon and gear and then go on plowing. Went to packing up mine and Sadai's clothes.

I fear that we shall be homeless.

The boys came back and wished to hide their mules. They say that the Yankees camped at Mr Gibson's last night and are taking all the stock in the county. Seeing them so eager, I told them to do as they pleased. They took them off, and Elbert [the black coachman] took his forty fattening hogs to the Old Place Swamp and turned them in.

We have done nothing all day—that is, my people have not. I made a pair of pants for Jack [a slave]. Sent Nute [a slave] up to Mrs. Perry's on an errand. On his way back, he said, two Yankees met him and begged him to go with them. They asked if we had livestock, and came up the road as far as Mrs. Laura Perry's. I sat for an hour expecting them, but they must have gone back. Oh, how I trust I am safe! Mr. Ward is very much alarmed.

NOVEMBER 19, 1864. Slept in my clothes last night, as I heard that the Yankees went to neighbor Montgomery's on Thursday night at one o'clock, searched his house, drank his wine, and took his money and valuables. As we were not disturbed, I walked after breakfast, with Sadai, up to Mr. Joe Perry's, my nearest neighbor, where the Yankees were yesterday. Saw Mrs. Laura [Perry] in the road surrounded by her children, seeming to be looking for some one. She said she was looking for her husband, that old Mrs. Perry had just sent her word that the Yankees went to James Perry's the night before, plundered his house, and drove off all his stock, and that she must drive hers into the old fields. Before we were done talking, up came Joe and Jim Perry from their hiding-place. Jim was very much excited. Happening to turn and look behind, as we stood there, I saw some blue-coats coming down the hill. Jim immediately raised his gun, swearing he would kill them anyhow.

"No, don't!" said I, and ran home as fast as I could, with Sadai.

I could hear them cry, "Halt! Halt!" and their guns went off in quick succession. Oh God, the time of trial has come!

A man passed on his way to Covington. I hallooed to him, asking him if he did not know the Yankees were coming.

"No—are they?"

"Yes," said I; "they are not three hundred yards from here."

"Sure enough," said he. "Well, I'll not go. I don't want them to get my horse." And although

within hearing of their guns, he would stop and look for them. Blissful ignorance! Not knowing, not hearing, he has not suffered the suspense, the fear, that I have for the past forty-eight hours. I walked to the gate. There they came filing up.

I hastened back to my frightened servants and told them that they had better hide, and then went back to the gate to claim protection and a guard. But like demons they rush in! My yards are full. To my smoke-house, my dairy, pantry, kitchen, and cellar, like famished wolves they come, breaking locks and whatever is in their way. The thousand pounds of meat in my smoke-house is gone in a twinkling, my flour, my meat, my lard, butter, eggs, pickles of various kinds—both in vinegar and brine—wine, jars, and jugs are all gone. My eighteen fat turkeys, my hens, chickens, and fowls, my young pigs, are shot down in my yard and hunted as if they were rebels themselves. Utterly powerless I ran out and appealed to the guard.

"I cannot help you, Madam; it is orders."

As I stood there, from my lot I saw driven, first, old Dutch, my dear old buggy horse, who has carried my beloved husband so many miles, and who would so quietly wait at the block for him to mount and dismount, and who at last drew him to his grave; then came old Mary, my brood mare, who for years had been too old and stiff for work, with her three-year-old colt, my two-year-old mule, and her last little baby colt. There they go! There go my mules, my sheep, and, worse than all, my boys [slaves]!

Alas! little did I think while trying to save my house from plunder and fire that they were forcing my boys from home at the point of the bayonet. One, Newton, jumped into bed in his cabin, and declared himself sick. Another crawled under the floor,—a lame boy he was,—but they pulled him out, placed him on a horse, and drove him off. Mid, poor Mid! The last I saw of him, a man had him going around the garden, looking, as I thought, for my sheep, as he was my shepherd. Jack came crying to me, the big tears coursing down his cheeks, saying they were making him go. I said:

"Stay in my room."

But a man followed in, cursing him and threatening to shoot him if he did not go; so poor Jack had to yield. James Arnold, in trying to escape from a back window, was captured and marched off. Henry, too, was taken; I know not how or when, but probably when he and Bob went after the mules. I had not believed they would force from their homes the poor, doomed negroes, but such has been the fact here, cursing them and saying that "Jeff Davis wanted to put them in his army, but that they should not fight for him, but for the Union." No! Indeed no! They are not friends to the slave. We have never made the poor, cowardly negro fight, and it is strange, passing strange, that the all-powerful Yankee nation with the whole world to back them, their ports open, their armies filled with soldiers from all nations, should at last take the poor negro to help them out against this little Confederacy which was to have been brought back into the Union in sixty days' time!

My poor boys! My poor boys! What unknown trials are before you! How you have clung to your mistress and assisted her in every way you knew.

Never have I corrected them; a word was sufficient. Never have they known want of any kind. Their parents are with me, and how sadly they lament the loss of their boys. Their cabins are rifled of every valuable, the soldiers swearing that their Sunday clothes were the white people's, and that they never had money to get such things as they had. Poor Frank's chest was broken open, his money and tobacco taken. He has always been a money-making and saving boy; not infrequently has his crop brought him five hundred dollars and more. All of his clothes and Rachel's clothes, which dear Lou gave before her death and which she had packed away, were stolen from her. Ovens, skillets, coffee-mills, of which we had three, coffee-pots—not one have I left. Sifters all gone!

Seeing that the soldiers could not be restrained, the guard offered me to have their [of the negroes] remaining possessions brought into my house, which I did, and they all, poor things, huddled together in my room, fearing every movement that the house would be burned.

A Captain Webber from Illinois came into my house. Of him I claimed protection from the vandals who were forcing themselves into my room. He said that he knew my brother Orrington [the late Orrington Lunt, a well known early settler of Chicago]. At that name I could not restrain my feelings, but, bursting into tears, implored him to see my brother and let him know my destitution. I saw nothing before me but starvation. He promised to do this, and comforted me with the assurance that my dwelling-house would not be burned, though my out-buildings might. Poor little Sadai went crying to him as to a friend and told him that they had taken her doll, Nancy. He begged her to come and see him, and he would give her a fine waxen one. [The doll was found later in the yard of a neighbor, where a soldier had thrown it, and was returned to the little girl. Her children later played with it, and it is now the plaything of her granddaughter.]

He felt for me, and I give him and several others the character of gentlemen. I don't believe they would have molested women and children had they had their own way. He seemed surprised that I had not laid away in my house, flour and other provisions. I did not suppose I could secure them there, more than where I usually kept them, for in last summer's raid houses were thoroughly searched. In parting with him; I parted as with a friend.

Sherman himself and a greater portion of his army passed my house that day. All day, as the sad moments rolled on, were they passing not only in front of my house, but from behind; they tore down my garden palings, made a road through my back-yard and lot field, driving their stock and riding through, tearing down my fences and desolating my home—wantonly doing it when there was no necessity for it.

Such a day, if I live to the age of Methuselah, may God spare me from ever seeing again!

As night drew its sable curtains around us, the heavens from every point were lit up with flames from burning buildings. Dinnerless and supperless as we were, it was nothing in comparison with the fear of being driven out homeless to the dreary woods. Nothing to eat! I could give my guard no supper, so he left us. I appealed to another, asking him if he had wife, mother, or sister, and how he should feel were they in my situation. A colonel from Vermont left me two men, but they were Dutch, and I could not understand one word they said.

My Heavenly Father alone saved me from the destructive fire. My carriage-house had in it eight bales of cotton, with my carriage, buggy, and harness. On top of the cotton were some carded cotton rolls, a hundred pounds or more. These were thrown out of the blanket in which they were, and a large twist of the rolls taken and set on fire, and thrown into the boat of my carriage, which was close up to the cotton bales. Thanks to my God, the cotton only burned over, and then went out. Shall I ever forget the deliverance?

To-night, when the greater part of the army had passed, it came up very windy and cold. My room was full, nearly, with the negroes and their bedding. They were afraid to go out, for my women could not step out of the door without an insult from the Yankee soldiers. They lay down on the floor; Sadai got down and under the same cover with Sally, while I sat up all night, watching every moment for the flames to burst out from some of my buildings. The two guards came into my room and laid themselves by my fire for the night. I could not close my eyes, but kept walking to and fro, watching the fires in the distance and dreading the approaching day, which, I feared, as they had not all passed, would be but a continuation of horrors.

NOVEMBER 20, 1864. This is the blessed Sabbath, the day upon which He who came to bring peace and good will upon earth rose from His tomb and ascended to intercede for us poor fallen creatures. But how unlike this day to any that have preceded it in my once quiet home. I had watched all night, and the dawn found me watching for the moving of the soldiery that was encamped about us. Oh, how I dreaded those that were to pass, as I supposed they would straggle and complete the ruin that the others had commenced, for I had been repeatedly told that they would burn everything as they passed.

Some of my women had gathered up a chicken that the soldiers shot yesterday, and they cooked it with some yams for our breakfast, the guard complaining that we gave them no supper. They gave us some coffee, which I had to make in a tea-kettle, as every coffeepot is taken off. The rear-guard was commanded by Colonel Carlow, who changed our guard, leaving us one soldier while they were passing. They marched directly on, scarcely breaking ranks. Once a bucket of water was called for, but they drank without coming in.

About ten o'clock they had all passed save one, who came in and wanted coffee made, which was done, and he, too, went on. A few minutes elapsed, and two couriers riding rapidly passed back. Then, presently, more soldiers came by, and this ended the passing of Sherman's army by my place, leaving me poorer by thirty thousand dollars than I was yesterday morning. And a much stronger Rebel!

After the excitement was a little over, I went up to Mrs. Laura's to sympathize with her, for I had no doubt but that her husband was hanged. She thought so, and we could see no way for his escape. We all took a good cry together. While there, I saw smoke looming up in the direction of my home, and thought surely the fiends had done their work ere they left. I ran as fast as I could, but soon saw that the fire was below my home. It proved to be the gin house [cotton gin] belonging to Colonel Pitts.

My boys have not come home. I fear they cannot get away from the soldiers. Two of my cows came up this morning, but were driven off again by the Yankees.

I feel so thankful that I have not been burned out that I have tried to spend the remainder of the day as the Sabbath ought to be spent. Ate dinner out of the oven in Julia's [the cook's] house, some stew, no bread. She is boiling some corn. My poor servants feel so badly at losing what they have worked for; meat, the hog meat that they love better than anything else, is all gone.

NOVEMBER 21, 1864. We had the table laid this morning, but no bread or butter or milk. What a prospect for delicacies! My house is a perfect fright. I had brought in Saturday night some thirty bushels of potatoes and ten or fifteen bushels of wheat poured down on the carpet in the ell. Then the few gallons of syrup saved was daubed all about. The backbone of a hog that I had killed on Friday, and which the Yankees did not take when they cleaned out my smokehouse, I found and hid under my bed, and this is all the meat I have.

Major Lee came down this evening, having heard that I was burned out, to proffer me a home. Mr. Dorsett was with him. The army lost some of their beeves in passing. I sent to-day and had some driven into my lot, and then sent to Judge Glass to come over and get some. Had two killed. Some of Wheeler's men came in, and I asked them to shoot the cattle, which they did.

About ten o'clock this morning Mr. Joe Perry [Mrs. Laura's husband] called. I was so glad to see him that I could scarcely forbear embracing him. I could not keep from crying, for I was sure the Yankees had executed him, and I felt so much for his poor wife. The soldiers told me repeatedly Saturday that they had hung him and his brother James and George Guise. They had a narrow escape, however, and only got away by knowing the country so much better than the soldiers did. They lay out until this morning. How rejoiced I am for his family! All of his negroes are gone, save one man that had a wife here at my plantation. They are very strong Secesh [Secessionists]. When the army first came along they offered a guard for the house, but Mrs. Laura told them she was guarded by a Higher Power, and did not thank them to do it. She says that she could think of nothing else all day when the army was passing

but of the devil and his hosts. She had, however, to call for a guard before night or the soldiers would have taken everything she had.

NOVEMBER 22, 1864. After breakfast this morning I went over to my grave-yard to see what had befallen that. To my joy, I found it had not been disturbed. As I stood by my dead, I felt rejoiced that they were at rest. Never have I felt so perfectly reconciled to the death of my husband as I do to-day, while looking upon the ruin of his lifelong labor. How it would have grieved him to see such destruction! Yes, theirs is the lot to be envied. At rest, rest from care, rest from heartaches, from trouble. . . .

Found one of my large hogs killed just outside the grave-yard.

Walked down to the swamp, looking for the wagon and gear that Henry hid before he was taken off. Found some of my sheep; came home very much wearied, having walked over four miles.

Mr. and Mrs. Rockmore called. Major Lee came down again after some cattle, and while he was here the alarm was given that more Yankees were coming. I was terribly alarmed and packed my trunks with clothing, feeling assured that we should be burned out now. Major Lee swore that he would shoot, which frightened me, for he was intoxicated enough to make him ambitious. He rode off in the direction whence it was said they were coming, Soon after, however, he returned, saying it was a false alarm, that it was some of our own men. Oh, dear! Are we to be always living in fear and dread! Oh, the horrors, the horrors of war!

NOVEMBER 26, 1864. A very cold morning. Elbert [the negro coachman] has to go to mill this morning, and I shall go with him, fearing that, if he is alone, my mule may be taken from him, for there are still many straggling soldiers about. Mounted in the little wagon, I went, carrying wheat not only for myself, but for my neighbors. Never did I think I would have to go to mill! Such are the changes that come to us!

History tells us of some illustrious examples of this kind. Got home just at night.

Mr. Kennedy stopped all night with us. He has been refugeeing on his way home. Every one we meet gives us painful accounts of the desolation caused by the enemy. Each one has to tell his or her own experience, and fellow-suffering makes us all equal and makes us all feel interested in one another.

DECEMBER 22, 1864. Tuesday, the nineteenth of the month, I attended Floyd Glass's wedding. She was married in the morning to Lieutenant Doroughty. She expected to have been married the week after the Yankees came, but her groom was not able to get here. Some of the Yankees found out in some way that she was to have been married, and annoyed her considerably by telling her that they had taken her sweetheart prisoner; that when he got off the train at the Circle they took him and, some said, shot him.

The Yankees found Mrs. Glass's china and glassware that she had buried in a box, broke it all up, and then sent her word that she would set no more fine tables. They also got Mrs. Perry's silver.

DECEMBER 23, 1864. Just before night Mrs. Robert Rakestraw and Miss Mary drove up to spend the night with me. They had started down into Jasper County, hoping to get back their buggy, having heard that several buggies were left at Mr. Whitfield's by the Yankees.

Nothing new! It is confidently believed that Savannah has been evacuated. I hear nothing from my boys. Poor fellows, how I miss them!

DECEMBER 24, 1864. This has usually been a very busy day with me, preparing for Christmas not only for my own tables, but for gifts for my servants. Now how changed! No confectionery, cakes, or pies can I have. We are all sad; no loud, jovial laugh from our boys is heard. Christmas Eve, which has ever been gaily celebrated here, which has witnessed the popping of fire-crackers [the Southern custom of celebrating Christmas with fireworks] and the hanging up of stockings, is an occasion now of sadness and gloom. I have nothing even to put in Sadai's stocking, which hangs so invitingly for Santa Claus. How disappointed she will be in the morning, though I have explained to her why he cannot come. Poor children! Why must the innocent suffer with the guilty?

DECEMBER 25, 1864. Sadai jumped out of bed very early this morning to feel in her stocking. She could not believe but that there would be something in it. Finding nothing, she crept back into bed, pulled the cover over her face, and I soon heard her sobbing. The little negroes all came in: "Christmas gift, mist'ess! Christmas gift, mist'ess!"

I pulled the cover over my face and was soon mingling my tears with Sadai's. . . .

Source: Lunt, Dolly Sumner (Mrs. Thomas Burge). *A Woman's Wartime Journal; An Account of the Passage over a Georgia Plantation of Sherman's Army on the March to the Sea, as Recorded in the Diary of Dolly Sumner Lunt (Mrs. Thomas Burge).* New York: Century Company, 1918, pp. 3–45.

THE PETERSBURG SIEGE: THE BATTLE OF THE CRATER, JULY 30, 1864

"Brilliant Page in History of War: Eye Witness Describes Bloody Battle of the Crater"
Captain John C. Featherston
Published 1908

A captain in the 9th Alabama Regiment, John C. Featherston was among the defenders of the Petersburg fortifications when Union soldiers under Major General Ambrose Burnside detonated a mine under the Confederate lines and then made an ill-fated charge into those lines in an effort to bring the siege to a rapid conclusion. Featherston's account of the Battle of the Crater is the most vivid and complete extant, and it provides a rare Confederate perspective on the engagement.

On the night of the 29th of July, 1864, Wilcox's old brigade of Alabamians, at that time commanded by Gen. J. C. C. Saunders, which was one of the five brigades composing Mahone's (formerly Anderson's), division, was occupying the breastworks to the right of Petersburg, at a point known as the Wilcox farm. The division consisted at the time of Wilcox's "old brigade" of Alabamians, Wright's Georgia brigade, Harris' Mississippi brigade, Mahone's Virginia brigade, and Perry's Florida brigade (by whom commanded at the time I fail to remember). All was quiet in our immediate front, but an incessant and rapid fire was going on to our left and immediately in front of Petersburg, where the main lines of the hostile armies were within eighty yards of each other. There was a rumor that the Federals were attempting to undermine our works, and were keeping up this continuous fire to shield their operations. The Confederate army had dug counter mines in front of our works at several points, but failed to sink them sufficiently deep to intercept the enemy and thwart their efforts, as was subsequently proven.

During the night of the 29th (I think about 2 o'clock), we received orders to get our men under arms and ready for action at a moment's notice, which convinced us that General Lee had important information. We remained thus until between daybreak and sunrise of the 30th of July, when suddenly the quiet and suspense was broken by a terrific explosion on our left. The news soon reached our lines that the enemy had exploded a mine under a fort then known as "Elliott's Salient," subsequently named the "Crater," from its resemblance in shape to the crater of a volcano, and during the terrible struggle one in active operation, caused by the smoke and dust which ascended therefrom. Mahone's was the "supporting division" of the army while in front of Petersburg, and consequently' whenever the enemy was making serious attacks this command, or a part of it, was sent to reinforce the point assailed. Hence it was in many hard-fought battles while the army was in front of Petersburg.

Was a Bloody Fight.

Of the many battles in which this command engaged, however, none will equal or even approximate in bloody and stubborn fighting the battle of the "Crater," where the loss on the Federal side was five thousand and on the Confederate side one thousand eight hundred, out of the small number engaged, and all on about two acres of land. For quite awhile after the explosion all was quiet; but then commenced a severe cannonade by the Yankees, which was promptly replied to by the Confederate artillery.

Soon orders were received for two of our brigades to move to the point of attack. The Virginia and Georgia brigades, being on the right of the division, were withdrawn from the works in such a manner as not to be seen by the enemy, who were entrenched in strong force immediately in our front, and dispatched as directed. This occurred about 8 or 9 o'clock. About 10 o'clock an order came, delivered by that gallant officer, R. R. Henry, of Mahone's staff, for the Alabama (Wilcox's old) brigade. We were quietly withdrawn from the works, leaving the space which the three brigades had covered unoccupied except by a few skirmishers—one man every twenty paces—commanded by Maj. J. M. Crow, a brave officer of the Ninth Alabama regiment.

By a circuitous route we arrived at Blandford cemetery, and then entered a "zigzag," or circuitous, covered way, through which we had to pass in single file in order to shield ourselves from the fire of the enemy. We soon came out of the covered way into a slight ravine which ran .parallel with the enemy's line of fortifications and also our own, in which was the fort, now famous as the "Crater," and then occupied by the enemy.

Situation Explained.

As we came out of the covered way we were met by General Mahone, himself on foot, who called the officers to him, explained the situation, and gave us orders for the fight. He informed us that the brigades of Virginians and Georgians had successfully charged and taken the works on the left of the fort, but that the fort was still in the possession of the enemy; as was also a part of the works on the right of it, and we of the Alabama brigade were expected to storm and capture the fort, as we were the last of the reserves, it being necessary to retain our other two brigades in the main trenches. He directed us to move up the ravine as far as we could walk unseen by the enemy, and then to get down and crawl still farther up until we were immediately in front of the fort, then to lie down on the ground until our artillery, in the rear, could draw the fire of the enemy's artillery, which was posted on a ridge beyond their main line and covering the fort. When this was accomplished our artillery would cease firing, and then we should rise up and move forward in a stooping posture at "trail arms," with bayonets fixed, and should not yell or fire a gun until we drew the fire of the infantry in the fort and the enemy's main lines, and then we should charge at a "double-quick," so as to get under the walls of the fort before the enemy could fire their park of some fifty pieces of artillery stationed on the hill beyond their works. He further informed us that he had ordered our men, who then occupied the works on either side of the fort, to fire at the enemy when they should show themselves above the top of the fort or along their main line, so as to shield us as much as possible from their fire.

As we were leaving him he said: "General Lee is watching the result of your charge."

Brigade Moves Forward.

The officers then returned to their places in line and ordered the men to load and fix bayonets. Immediately the brigade moved up the ravine as ordered. As we started a soldier, worse disfigured by dirt, powder and smoke than any I had before seen, came up to my side and said: "Captain, can I go in this charge with you?" I replied: "Yes. Who are you?" He said: "I am———(I have forgotten his name), and I belong to———South Carolina regiment. I was blown up in that fort, and I want to even up with them. Please take my name, and if I get killed inform my officers of it." I said: "I have no time now for writing. How high up did they blow you?" He said: "I don't know; but as I was going up I met the company commissary coming down, and he said: 'I will try to have breakfast ready by the time you get back.'"

I have often since wished that even under those desperate circumstances, I had taken his name and regiment, for he was truly a "rough diamond," a brave fellow. He went in the charge with us, but I do not know whether he survived it or not. I never saw him again; but if he is alive and this page should ever meet his eye, I trust he will write to me.

Wilcox's old brigade, then commanded and led by the gallant and intrepid brigadier general, J. C. C. Saunders, as above stated, with Capt. George Clark, another brave office, assistant adjutant general, was composed of the following regiments: Eighth Alabama, Capt. M. W. Mordecai commanding; Ninth Alabama, Col. J. H. King commanding; Tenth Alabama, Capt. W. L. Brewster commanding; Eleventh Alabama, Lieut. Col. George P. Tayloe commanding; Fourteenth Alabama, Capt. Elias Folk commanding.

Ninth Alabama in Front.

The Ninth Alabama, being on the right of the brigade, was in front as we ascended the ravine, or depression, to form line of battle. I copy from the Petersburg Express the names of the officers who commanded the companies of this regiment, and would include a similar list of the officers of the other regiments but for the unfortunate fact that their names were not given. They are as follows: Company A, Captain Hayes commanding; Company C, Sergt. T. Simmons commanding; Company D. Capt, J. W. Cannon commanding; Company E, Lieut. M. H. Todd commanding; Company F, Capt. John C. Featherston commanding; Company H, Lieut. R. Fuller commanding; Company I, Lieut. B. T. Taylor commanding; Company K, Lieut. T. B. Baugh commanding.

By the report of Capt. George Clark, assistant adjutant general, this brigade of five regiments carried into the battle of the "Crater" 628 men, and of this number it lost eighty-nine. The brigade early in the war had numbered about five thousand. It will be observed that such had been our losses in former battles that regiments were commanded by captains and companies by sergeants, some of the companies having been so depleted that they had been merged into other companies.

After we had crawled up in front of the fort and about two hundred yards therefrom, we lay down flat on the ground, and our batteries, in the rear, opened fire on the enemy's artillery in order to draw their fire. This was done that we might charge without being subjected to their artillery fire, in addition to that of the fort and the main line, which latter was only eighty yards beyond the fort. But the enemy appeared to understand our object, and declined to reply. Our guns soon ceased firing, and we at once arose and moved forward, as directed, in quick time at a trail arms, with bayonets fixed.

Cruel Spectacle Presented.

In a short distance we came in view of the enemy, both infantry and artillery, and then was presented one of the most awfully grand and cruel spectacles of that terrible war. One brigade of six hundred and twenty-eight men was charging a fort in an open field, filled with the enemy to the number of over five thousand, supported by a park of artillery said to number fifty pieces. The line of advance was in full view of the two armies and in range of the guns of fully twenty thousand men, including both sides. When we came within range we saw the flash of the sun-

light on the enemy's guns as they were leveled above the walls of that wrecked fort. Then came a stream of fire and the awful roar of battle. This volley seemed to awaken the demons of hell, and appeared to be the signal for everybody within range of the fort to commence firing. We raised a yell and made a dash in order to get under the walls of the fort before their artillery could open upon us, but in this we were unsuccessful. The heavy guns joined in the awful din, and the air seemed literally filled with missiles.

The Virginians, Georgians and South Carolinians commenced firing from the flanks at the fort and at the enemy's main line, as did our artillery, and the enemy's infantry and artillery from all sides opened upon us.

On we went, as it seemed to us, literally "into the mouth of hell." When we got to the walls of the fort we dropped down on the ground to get the men in order and let them get their breath. While waiting we could hear the Yankee officers in the fort trying to encourage their men, telling them, among other things, to "remember Fort Pillow." (In that fort Forrest's men had found negroes and whites together, and history tells what they did for them.)

Novel Methods of Fighting.

Then commenced a novel method of fighting. There were quite a number of abandoned muskets with bayonets on them lying on the ground around the fort. Our men began pitching them over the embankment, bayonet foremost, trying to harpoon the men inside, and both sides threw over cannon balls and fragments of shells and earth, which by the impact of the explosion had been pressed as hard as brick. Everybody seemed to be shooting at the fort, and doubtless many were killed by their friends. I know some of the Yankees were undoubtedly so killed.

In almost less time than I can tell it we were in condition to go in. Col. H. H. King ordered the men near him to put their hats on their bayonets and quickly raise them above the fort, which was done, and, as he anticipated, they were riddled with bullets. Then he ordered us over the embankment, and over we went, and were soon engaged in a hand-to-hand struggle of life and death. The enemy shrank back, and the death grapple continued until most of the Yankees found in there were killed. This slaughter would not have been so great had not our men found negro soldiers in the fort with the whites. This was the first time we had met negro troops, and the men were enraged at them for being there and at the whites for having them there.

The explosion had divided the pit into two compartments. As soon as we had possession of the larger one, the Yankees in the smaller one cried out that they would surrender. We told them to come over the embankment. Two of them started over with their guns in their hands, but, their intentions being mistaken, they were shot and fell back. We heard those remaining cry: "They are showing us no quarter; let us sell our lives as dearly as possible." We then told them to come over without their guns, which they did, and all the remainder, about thirty in number, surrendered and were ordered to the rear.

Yankees Kill Yankees.

In the confusion and in their eagerness to get from that point they went across the open field, along the same route over which we had charged. Their artillery, seeing them going to the rear, as we were told, under a subsequent flag of truce, thought that they were our men repulsed and retreating, so they at once opened fire on them, killing and wounding quite a number of their own men. One poor fellow had his arm shot off just as he started to the rear, and returning said: "I could bear it better if my own had not done it."

This practically ended the fight inside the fort; but the armies outside continued firing at this common center, and it seemed to us that the shot, shell and musket balls came from every point of the compass and the mortar shells rained down from above. They had previously attacked from below. So this unfortunate fort was one of the few points in that war, or any other the his-

tory of which I have read, which had the unique distinction of having been assailed from literally every quarter.

The slaughter was fearful. The dead were piled on each other. In one part of the fort I counted eight bodies deep. There were but few wounded compared with the killed. There was an incident which occurred in the captured fort that made quite an impression on me. Among the wounded was the Yankee general, Bartlett. He was lying down and could not rise. Assistance was offered him, but he informed those who were assisting him that his leg was broken; and so it was, but it proved to be an artificial leg made of cork. One of our officers ordered a couple of negroes to move him, but he protested, and I believe he was given white assistance. The general, afterwards, so I have been informed, became an honored citizen of Virginia, though at that time, I must say, I never would have believed such a thing possible. One of our soldiers seeing the cork leg and springs knocked to pieces, waggishly said: "General, you are a fraud. I thought that was a good leg when I shot it."

As the dust and smoke cleared away the firing seemed to lull, but there was no entire cessation of firing that evening. Indeed, by the sharpshooters it was continued for months.

Fort Reconstructed.

After dark tools were brought in with which we reconstructed the wrecked fort. In doing this we buried the dead down in the fort by covering them with earth, as the fire of the enemy was entirely too severe to carry them out. We were therefore forced to stand on them and defend our position while we remained in the fort, which was until the following Monday night.

As we went over the embankment into the fort one of my sergeants, Andrew McWilliams, a brave fellow, was shot in the mouth, and the ball did not cut his lips. It came out of the top of his head. He was evidently yelling with his mouth wide open. He fell on top of the embankment with his head hanging in the fort. We pulled him down in the fort, and that night carried him out and buried him.

During the night, in strengthening the wrecked fort, we unearthed numbers of Confederate soldiers who were killed and buried by the explosion. I remember in one place there were eight poor fellows lying side by side with their coats under their heads. They seemed never to have moved after the explosion. We buried them in the fort, in the excavation, "Crater," made by the explosion, fifty-four negroes and seventy-eight Yankees, exclusive of those buried in the trenches.

That night after the work was done we slept in the fort over those who slept "the sleep that knows no waking" and with those who slept that sleep caused by exhaustion. The morning came as clear and the day as hot and dry as the preceding one. The sharpshooters were exceeding alert, firing every moment, each side momentarily expecting active hostilities to be renewed. While the wounded in the fort and our trenches had been removed during the night and were being cared for, the ground between the main lines of the two armies was literally covered by wounded and dead Federals, who fell in advancing and retreating. We could hear them crying for relief, but the firing was so severe that none dared to go to them either by day or night.

Flag of Truce Raised.

About noon or a little later there went up a flag of truce immediately in our front. The flag was a white piece of cloth about a yard square on a new staff. General Saunders ordered the sharpshooters to cease firing. Then a Yankee soldier, with a clean white shirt and blue pants jumped on top of their works, holding the flag, and was promptly followed by two elegantly uniformed officers. General Saunders asked those of us near him if we had a white handkerchief. All replied: "No." A private soldier near by said to the men around him: "Boys, some of you take off your shirt and hand it to the general," to which another replied: "Never do that; they will think we have hoisted the black flag."

The general finally got a handkerchief, which answered the purpose, though not altogether suitable for a drawing room. He and Capt. George Clark, assistant adjutant general, tied it to the ramrod of a musket, and Captain Clark, with one man carrying the improvised flag, went forward to meet the Yankee flag. (I have frequently thought that the "get up" of these flags of truce graphically illustrated the condition of the two armies.) They met half way, about forty yards from each line. After a few minutes' interview, the Yankee officer handed to Captain Clark a paper. They then withdrew to their respective sides. In handing this communication to General Saunders, Captain Clark said: "They are asking for a truce to bury their dead and remove their wounded."

Terms Agreed On.

The communication was forwarded to the proper authorities, and proved to be from General Burnside, who commanded the Federal troops in front; but, not being in accordance with the usages and civilities of war, it was promptly returned, with the information that whenever a like request came from the general commanding the Army of Northern Virginia, it would be entertained. Within a few hours the Federals sent another flag of truce, conveying a communication, which was properly signed and addressed, and the terms of the truce were agreed on. These terms were that they could remove their wounded and bury their dead in a ditch, or grave, to be dug just half way between the two lines. They brought in their details, including many negroes, and the work was commenced and continued for about four hours. In that ditch, about one hundred feet in length, were buried seven hundred white and negro Federal soldiers. The dead were thrown in indiscriminately, three bodies deep. When this work was commenced I witnessed one of the grandest sights I ever saw. Where not a man could be seen a few minutes before, the two armies arose up out of the ground, and the face of the earth was peopled with men. It seemed an illustration of Cadmus sowing the dragon's teeth. Both sides came over their works, and, meeting in the center, mingled, chatted, and exchanged courtesies, as though they had not sought in desperate effort to take each other's lives but an hour before.

During the truce I met Gen. R. B. Potter, who commanded, as he informed me, a Michigan division in Burnside's corps. He was extremely polite and affable, and extended to me his canteen with an invitation to sample its contents, which I did, and found it containing nothing objectionable. He then handed me a good cigar and for a time we smoked the "pipe of peace."

General Ferrerro [Ferrero] Pointed Out

In reply to a question from me as to their loss in the battle on Saturday, he replied that they had lost five thousand men. While we were talking a remarkably handsome Yankee general in the crowd came near us. I asked General Potter who he was, and was informed that he was [Brigadier] General [Edward] Ferrero [Ferrero], who commanded the negro troops. I said: "I have some of his papers which I captured in the fort," and showed them to General Potter. He then said: "Let me call him up and introduce him, and we will show him the papers and guy him." I replied, however, that we down south were not in the habit of recognizing as our social equals those who associated with negroes. He then asked me to give him some of Ferrerro papers. He wanted them for a purpose. I did so. The others I kept, and they are lying before me as I write. He also asked me to point out to him some of our generals, several of whom were then standing on the embankment of the wrecked fort. (I noticed that none of our generals except Saunders of the Alabama brigade, who had harge of affairs, came over and mingled with the crowd.) I pointed out to him Generals Harris, of Mississippi, and A. P. Hill, and finally pointed out General Mahone, who was dressed in a suit made of tent cloth,

with a roundabout jacket. Be it remembered that General Mahone was quite small, and did not weigh much, if any, over one hundred and twenty-five pounds. Potter laughingly said: "Not much man, but a big general."

When the dead were buried each side returned to its entrenchments, and soon the sharpshooters were firing at each other when and wherever seen. True "war is hell." Saunders' Alabama brigade continued to occupy the "Crater," which they had captured on Saturday about 2 o'clock, until Monday night, August 1, when under cover of darkness, we were relieved by another brigade, as was also the gallant Virginia brigade, which had, by a charge, captured the intrenchments on the left of the "Crater." The two brigades returned to their former positions at the Wilcox farm. I do not remember when the Georgia brigade was relieved.

History in Letters.

I am not writing this alone from memory, but in addition thereto from letters contemporaneously written to my wife, whom I had but a short time before married, which letters, as well as extracts from Richmond papers of that date, as contemporary records, will probably prove of sufficient interest to publish herewith.

The Petersburg correspondent of the *Richmond Dispatch* of July 30, 1864, after describing the charge made by the Virginia and Georgia brigades, says:

> About this time General Mahone, having ordered up Saunders' Alabama brigade, sent it forward to recapture the rest of the works. Led by their gallant brigadier, they moved forward in splendid style, making one of the grandest charges of the war, and recapturing every vestige of our lost grand and other lost guns and capturing thirty-five commissioned officers, including Brigadier General Bartlett, commanding first brigade, first division, ninth corps, three hundred and twenty-four white

and one hundred and fifty negro privates, and two stands of colors.

Under date of Sunday, 31, the Richmond Dispatch reports:

All quiet today. Our wounded are being cared for, and the dead on both sides in our lines are being buried.

   Still they come. Saunders of the Alabama brigade has just sent in another battle flag, thrown away by the enemy yesterday and picked up by General Saunders's men this morning.

   General Saunders reports that he has buried in the mine alone fifty-four negroes and seventy-eight Yankees, exclusive of the men buried in the trenches.

The following extract is from the *Dispatch* of August 3, 1864:

For five hours the work of burying the dead went vigorously forward. The Yankees brought details of negroes, and we carried their negro prisoners out under guard to help them in their work. Over seven hundred Yankees, whites and negroes, were buried. A. P. Hill was there with long gauntlets, a slouch hat and round jacket. Mahone, dressed in little boy fashion out of clothes made from old Yankee tent cloth, was beside himself. The gallant Harris of the Mississippi brigade, and the gallant intrepid Saunders, who but forty-eight hours before had so successfully retaken those works, the best looking and best dressed Confederate officer present, was sauntering leisurely about, having a general superintendence over the whole affair.

Soldiers Fraternize.

"Whilst the truce lasted the Yankees and the "Johnny Rebs" in countless numbers flocked to the neutral grounds, and spent the time in chatting and sight-seeing. The stench,

however, was quite strong, and it required a good nose and a better stomach to carry one through the ordeal. About 9 o'clock, the burial being completed, the officers sent the men back to the trenches on each side. The officers bade each other adieu and returned to their respective lines." . . .

Source: Featherston, John C. "Brilliant Page in History of War: Eye Witness Describes Bloody Battle of the Crater—The Losses Were Heavy." *Southern Historical Society Papers* 36 (1908): 161–173.

ROBERT E. LEE SURRENDERS THE ARMY OF NORTHERN VIRGINIA, APRIL 9, 1865

Account of Robert E. Lee's Surrender at Appomattox
Ulysses S. Grant
Published 1885

Grant's Personal Memoirs of U.S. Grant *is one of the most valuable and eloquent records of the Civil War and a masterpiece of American literature. His recollection of the surrender of Robert E. Lee and his Army of Northern Virginia, a force broken but unbowed, is profoundly moving for all its quiet dignity and detail. The narrative paints a dual portrait of the character of the two most important commanders of the Civil War.*

On the 8th I had followed the Army of the Potomac in rear of Lee. I was suffering very severely with a sick headache, and stopped at a farmhouse on the road some distance in rear of the main body of the army. I spent the night in bathing my feet in hot water and mustard, and putting mustard plasters on my wrists and the back part of my neck, hoping to be cured by morning. During the night I received Lee's answer to my letter of the 8th, inviting an interview between the lines on the following morning. But it was for a different purpose from that of surrendering his army, and I answered him as follows:

HEADQUARTERS ARMIES OF THE U. S.,
April 9, 1865.

GENERAL R. E. LEE,
Commanding C. S. A.

Your note of yesterday is received. As I have no authority to treat on the subject of peace, the meeting proposed for ten A.M. to-day could lead to no good. I will state, however, General, that I am equally anxious for peace with yourself, and the whole North entertains the same feeling. The terms upon which peace can be had are well understood. By the South laying down their arms they will hasten that most desirable event, save thousands of human lives and hundreds of millions of property not yet destroyed. Sincerely hoping that all our difficulties may be settled without the loss of another life, I subscribe myself, etc.,

U. S. GRANT,
Lieutenant-General.

I proceeded at an early hour in the morning, still suffering with the headache, to get to the head of the column. I was not more than two or three miles from Appomattox Court House at the time, but to go direct I would have to pass through Lee's army, or a portion of it. I had therefore to move south in order to get upon a road coming up from another direction.

When the white flag was put out by Lee, as already described, I was in this way moving towards Appomattox Court House, and consequently could not be communicated with immediately, and be informed of what Lee had done. Lee, therefore, sent a flag to the rear to advise Meade and one to the front to Sheridan, saying that he had sent a message to me for the purpose

This 1865 Currier and Ives lithograph, which depicts Generals Lee and Grant at the signing of the surrender in the farmhouse at Appomattox Court House, provided many Americans with their first image of this epochal event. *(Library of Congress)*

of having a meeting to consult about the surrender of his army, and asked for a suspension of hostilities until I could be communicated with. As they had heard nothing of this until the fighting had got to be severe and all going against Lee, both of these commanders hesitated very considerably about suspending hostilities at all. They were afraid it was not in good faith, and we had the Army of Northern Virginia where it could not escape except by some deception. They, however, finally consented to a suspension of hostilities for two hours to give an opportunity of communicating with me in that time, if possible. It was found that, from the route I had taken, they would probably not be able to communicate with me and get an answer back within the time fixed unless the messenger should pass through the rebel lines.

Lee, therefore, sent an escort with the officer bearing this message through his lines to me.

> April 9, 1865.
> GENERAL: I received your note of this morning on the picket-line whither I had come to meet you and ascertain definitely what terms were embraced in your proposal of yesterday with reference to the surrender of this army. I now request an interview in accordance with the offer contained in your letter of yesterday for that purpose.
> R. E. LEE, General.
> LIEUTENANT-GENERAL U. S. GRANT,
> Commanding U. S. Armies.

When the officer reached me I was still suffering with the sick headache, but the instant I saw the contents of the note I was cured. I wrote the following note in reply and hastened on:

> April 9, 1865.
> GENERAL R. E. LEE,
> Commanding C. S. Armies.
> Your note of this date is but this moment (11.50 A.M.) received, in consequence of my having passed from the Richmond and Lynchburg road to the Farmville and Lynchburg road. I am at this writing about four miles west of Walker's Church and will push forward to the front for the purpose of meeting you. Notice sent to me on this road where you wish the interview to take place will meet me.
> U. S. GRANT,
> Lieutenant-General.

I was conducted at once to where Sheridan was located with his troops drawn up in line of battle facing the Confederate army near by. They were very much excited, and expressed their view that this was all a ruse employed to enable the Confederates to get away. They said they believed that Johnston was marching up from North Carolina now, and Lee was moving to join him; and they would whip the rebels where they now were in five minutes if I would only let them go in. But I had no doubt about the good faith of Lee, and pretty soon was conducted to where he was. I found him at the house of a Mr. McLean, at Appomattox Court House, with Colonel Marshall, one of his staff officers, awaiting my arrival. The head of his column was occupying a hill, on a portion of which was an apple orchard, beyond a little valley which separated it from that on the crest of which Sheridan's forces were drawn up in line of battle to the south.

Before stating what took place between General Lee and myself, I will give all there is of the story of the famous apple tree.

Wars produce many stories of fiction, some of which are told until they are believed to be true. The war of the rebellion was no exception to this rule, and the story of the apple tree is one of those fictions based on a slight foundation of fact. As I have said, there was an apple orchard on the side of the hill occupied by the Confederate forces. Running diagonally up the hill was a wagon road, which, at one point, ran very near one of the trees, so that the wheels of vehicles had, on that side, cut off the roots of this tree, leaving a little embankment. General Babcock, of my staff, reported to me that when he first met General Lee he was sitting upon this embankment with his feet in the road below and his back resting against the tree. The story had no other foundation than that. Like many other stories, it would be very good if it was only true.

I had known General Lee in the old army, and had served with him in the Mexican War; but did not suppose, owing to the difference in our age and rank, that he would remember me, while I would more naturally remember him distinctly, because he was the chief of staff of General Scott in the Mexican War.

When I had left camp that morning I had not expected so soon the result that was then taking place, and consequently was in rough garb. I was without a sword, as I usually was when on horseback on the field, and wore a soldier's blouse for a coat, with the shoulder straps of my rank to indicate to the army who I was. When I went into the house I found General Lee. We greeted each other, and after shaking hands took our seats. I had my staff with me, a good portion of whom were in the room during the whole of the interview.

What General Lee's feelings were I do not know. As he was a man of much dignity, with an impassible face, it was impossible to say whether he felt inwardly glad that the end had finally come, or felt sad over the result, and was too manly to show it. Whatever his feelings, they were entirely concealed from my observation; but my own feelings, which had been quite jubilant on the receipt of his letter, were sad and depressed. I felt like anything rather than rejoicing at the downfall of a foe who had fought so long and valiantly, and had suffered so much for a cause, though that cause was, I believe, one of the worst for which a people ever fought, and one for which there was the least excuse. I do not question, however, the sincerity of the great mass of those who were opposed to us.

General Lee was dressed in a full uniform which was entirely new, and was wearing a sword of considerable value, very likely the sword which had been presented by the State of Virginia; at all events, it was an entirely different sword from the one that would ordinarily be worn in the field. In my rough traveling suit, the uniform of a private with the straps of a lieutenant-general, I must have contrasted very strangely with a man so handsomely dressed, six feet high and of faultless form. But this was not a matter that I thought of until afterwards.

We soon fell into a conversation about old army times. He remarked that he remembered me very well in the old army; and I told him that as a matter of course I remembered him perfectly, but from the difference in our rank and years (there being about sixteen years' difference in our ages), I had thought it very likely that I had not attracted his attention sufficiently to be remembered by him after such a long interval. Our conversation grew so pleasant that I almost forgot the object of our meeting. After the conversation had run on in this style for some time, General Lee called my attention to the object of our meeting, and said that he had asked for this interview for the purpose of getting from me the terms I proposed to give his army. I said that I meant merely that his army should lay down their arms, not to take them up again during the continuance of the war unless duly and properly exchanged. He said that he had so understood my letter.

Then we gradually fell off again into conversation about matters foreign to the subject which had brought us together. This continued for some little time, when General Lee again interrupted the course of the conversation by suggesting that the terms I proposed to give his army ought to be written out. I called to General Parker, secretary on my staff, for writing materials, and commenced writing out the following terms:

APPOMATTOX C. H., VA.,
Apl 19th, 1865.

GEN. R. E. LEE,
Comd'g C. S. A.
GEN: In accordance with the substance of my letter to you of the 8th inst., I propose to receive the surrender of the Army of N. Va. on the following terms, to wit: Rolls of all the officers and men to be made in duplicate. One copy to be given to an officer designated by me, the other to be retained by such officer or officers as you may designate. The officers to give their individual paroles not to take up arms against the Government of the United States until properly exchanged, and each company or regimental commander sign a like parole for the men of their commands. The arms, artillery and public property to be parked and stacked, and turned over to the officer appointed by me to receive them. This will not embrace the side-arms of the officers, nor their private horses or baggage. This done, each officer and man will be allowed to return to their homes, not to be disturbed by United States authority so long as they observe their paroles and the laws in force where they may reside.

Very respectfully,
U. S. GRANT,
Lt. Gen.

When I put my pen to the paper I did not know the first word that I should make use of in writing the terms. I only knew what was in my mind, and I wished to express it clearly, so that there could be no mistaking it. As I wrote on, the thought occurred to me that the officers had their own private horses and effects, which were important to them, but of no value to us; also that it would be an unnecessary humiliation to call upon them to deliver their side arms.

No conversation, not one word, passed between General Lee and myself, either about private property, side arms, or kindred subjects. He appeared to have no objections to the terms first proposed; or if he had a point to make against them he wished to wait until they were in writing to make it. When he read over that part of the terms about side arms, horses and private property of the officers, he remarked, with some feeling, I thought, that this would have a happy effect upon his army.

When, after a little further conversation, General Lee remarked to me again that their army was organized a little differently from the army of the United States (still maintaining by implication that we were two countries); that in their army the cavalrymen and artillerists owned their own horses; and he asked if he was to understand that the men who so owned their horses were to be permitted to retain them. I told him that as the terms were written they would not; that only the officers were permitted to take their private property. He then, after reading over the terms a second time, remarked that that was clear.

I then said to him that I thought this would be about the last battle of the war—I sincerely hoped so; and I said further I took it that most of the men in the ranks were small farmers. The whole country had been so raided by the two armies that it was doubtful whether they would be able to put in a crop to carry themselves and their families through the next winter without the aid of the horses they were then riding. The United States did not want them and I would, therefore, instruct the officers I left behind to receive the paroles of

his troops to let every man of the Confederate army who claimed to own a horse or mule take the animal to his home. Lee remarked again that this would have a happy effect.

He then sat down and wrote out the following letter:

> HEADQUARTERS ARMY OF
> NORTHERN VIRGINIA,
> April 9, 1865.
> GENERAL:—I received your letter of this date containing the terms of the surrender of the Army of Northern Virginia as proposed by you. As they are substantially the same as those expressed in your letter of the 8th inst., they are accepted. I will proceed to designate the proper officers to carry the stipulations into effect.
>
> R. E. LEE, General.
> LIEUT.-GENERAL U. S. GRANT.

While duplicates of the two letters were being made, the Union generals present were severally present to General Lee.

The much talked of surrendering of Lee's sword and my handing it back, this and much more that has been said about it is the purest romance. The word *sword* or *side arms* was not mentioned by either of us until I wrote it in the terms. There was no premeditation, and it did not occur to me until the moment I wrote it down. If I had happened to omit it, and General Lee had called my attention to it, I should have put it in the terms precisely as I acceded to the provision about the soldiers retaining their horses.

General Lee, after all was completed and before taking his leave, remarked that his army was in a very bad condition for want of food, and that they were without forage; that his men had been living for some days on parched corn exclusively, and that he would have to ask me for rations and forage. I told him "certainly," and asked for how many men he wanted rations. His answer was "about twenty-five thousand;" and I authorized him to send his own commissary and quartermaster to Appomattox Station, two or three miles away, where he could have, out of the trains we had stopped, all the provisions wanted. As for forage, we had ourselves depended almost entirely upon the country for that.

Generals Gibbon, Griffin and Merritt were designated by me to carry into effect the paroling of Lee's troops before they should start for their homes—General Lee leaving Generals Longstreet, Gordon and Pendleton for them to confer with in order to facilitate this work. Lee and I then separated as cordially as we had met, he returning to his own lines, and all went into bivouac for the night at Appomattox.

Soon after Lee's departure I telegraphed to Washington as follows:

HEADQUARTERS APPOMATTOX
C. H., VA.,
April 9th, 1865, 4.30 P.M.

HON. E. M. STANTON,
Secretary of War, Washington.
General Lee surrendered the Army of Northern Virginia this afternoon on terms proposed by myself. The accompanying additional correspondence will show the conditions fully.

U. S. GRANT,
Lieut.-General.

When news of the surrender first reached our lines our men commenced firing a salute of a hundred guns in honor of the victory. I at once sent word, however, to have it stopped. The Confederates were now our prisoners, and we did not want to exult over their downfall.

I determined to return to Washington at once, with a view to putting a stop to the purchase of supplies, and what I now deemed other useless outlay of money. Before leaving, however, I thought I would like to see General Lee again; so next morning I rode out beyond our lines towards his headquarters, preceded by a bugler and a staff-officer carrying a white flag.

Lee soon mounted his horse, seeing who it was, and met me. We had there between the lines, sitting on horseback, a very pleasant conversation of over half an hour, in the course of which Lee said to me that the South was a big country and that we might have to march over it three or four times before the war entirely ended, but that we would now be able to do it as they could no longer resist us. He expressed it as his earnest hope, however, that we would not be called upon to cause more loss and sacrifice of life; but he could not foretell the result. I then suggested to General Lee that there was not a man in the Confederacy whose influence with the soldiery and the whole people was as great as his, and that if he would now advise the surrender of all the armies I had no doubt his advice would be followed with alacrity. But Lee said, that he could not do that without consulting the President first. I knew there was no use to urge him to do anything against his ideas of what was right.

I was accompanied by my staff and other officers, some of whom seemed to have a great desire to go inside the Confederate lines. They finally asked permission of Lee to do so for the purpose of seeing some of their old army friends, and the permission was granted. They went over, had a very pleasant time with their old friends, and brought some of them back with them when they returned.

When Lee and I separated he went back to his lines and I returned to the house of Mr. McLean. Here the officers of both armies came in great numbers, and seemed to enjoy the meeting as much as though they had been friends separated for a long time while fighting battles under the same flag. For the time being it looked very much as if all thought of the war had escaped their minds. After an hour pleasantly passed in this way I set out on horseback, accompanied by my staff and a small escort, for Burkesville Junction, up to which point the railroad had by this time been repaired.

Source: Grant, Ulysses S. *Personal Memoirs of U.S. Grant.* 1885. Reprint, New York: Da Capo Press, 1982, pp. 552–560.

INDEX